The GROWTH *of*
AMERICAN
DEMOCRACY

STREET

SCHOOL

WEEKLY CLARION

TAVERN

MECHANIC ST.

THE GROWTH OF
AMERICAN DEMOCRACY

Social : Economic : Political

*One of the people! Born to be
Their curious epitome.*

R. H. Stoddard

THE CENTURY HISTORICAL SERIES
WILLIAM E. LINGELBACH, EDITOR

THE GROWTH
OF
AMERICAN DEMOCRACY

Social : Economic : Political

BY

JEANNETTE P. NICHOLS
Sometime Professor of History
Wesleyan College

AND

ROY F. NICHOLS
Professor of History
University of Pennsylvania

D. APPLETON-CENTURY COMPANY
INCORPORATED

NEW YORK   LONDON

Sole among nationalities, these States have assumed the task to put in forms of lasting power and practicality ... the democratic republican principle, and the theory of development and perfection by voluntary standards, and self reliance. WALT WHITMAN, *Democratic Vistas*.

PREFACE

The experiment of creating and maintaining a unique republic has been the predominating interest of the people of the United States. Their creation has evolved in an isolated area, discovered and peopled by a much older civilization, under circumstances which left the pioneers and their descendants relatively free and unhampered by direct foreign influence. The character of this American society has been variously described by succeeding generations, but the increasing tendency has been to denominate it a Democracy. In fact today there is no phrase more frequently spoken or more carelessly defined, than the term "American Democracy." The classic statements most generally revered by Americans have described the experiment as unique because it was dedicated to the equality of men.

This concept of democracy has never included the idea that all men should be maintained at an equal level. Rather, it implies that each shall be given an equal opportunity to reach the level to which his abilities entitle him, unhampered by the control or hindrance of any form of human behavior by a privileged group. Politically, all are supposed to be equal before the law and may vote and hold office. Economically, all should have the right to earn a decent living, to accumulate savings if they so desire, and to raise the level of their standard of living if they are capable. Socially and culturally, all should enjoy liberty of behavior and the pursuit of their ambitions and their interests so long as a reasonable degree of social responsibility governs this liberty. The history of this democracy must embrace therefore a synthesis of American endeavor to establish the ideal socially, economically, and politically.

The course of this experiment has been conditioned by a conflict between two trends produced by the peculiar circumstances of its setting. These trends are the struggle for wealth and power, so generously stimulated by the great resources of the hemisphere, and the desire for a larger measure of freedom and happiness for the individual than has ever been afforded by older civilizations. These conflicting trends have developed simultaneously and often coöperatively. For many years they seemed compatible and correlating. But of late there has been questioning. Can the liberties possible in an age of unused resources and unsettled acres be maintained in a society hemmed in by

vii

urban living and dominated by mechanical processes? Can America maintain her individuality across a plane-spanned ocean? The success or failure of American Democracy may well be determined by the ability of this versatile society to continue to harmonize changing conditions to fit the cherished spirit of equality.

ACKNOWLEDGMENTS

In unravelling the tangled skein of recent American history generous coöperation has been extended at Washington, where so much of that history has been made:—at the Department of Agriculture by Mr. Everett E. Edwards; at the Department of Commerce by Mr. Amos E. Taylor; at the Department of Labor by Miss Mary Anderson, the late Miss Estelle M. Stewart, Mr. Hugh Hanna and Mr. Witt Bowden; at the Library of Congress by Miss Margaret W. Stewart and the Staffs of the Reading Room and Reference services; at the National Emergency Council by Miss Harriet Root; at the Treasury Department by Mr. Arthur V. Sullivan. For critical reading of various portions the authors are also indebted to Professor Edward P. Cheyney, Miss Fola M. LaFollette, Professor F. Cyril James, Professor William E. Lingelbach and Professor Arthur P. Whitaker. The work of preparing illustrations was facilitated by Mr. Julian P. Boyd, librarian, at the Historical Society of Pennsylvania. Particular thanks are due Dr. John C. Fitzpatrick of Washington for his skilful collaboration on the end papers.

TABLE OF CONTENTS

CREATING A SOCIETY
1575—1763

ESTABLISHING INDEPENDENCE
1763—1819

xi

THE IMPACT OF LARGE SCALE ORGANIZATION
1878—1900

THE PROGRESSIVE ERA
1900—1914

THE UNITED STATES IN A WORLD AT WAR

1914—1918

WHAT PRICE PROSPERITY

1918—1933

THE NEW DEAL

1933—

ILLUSTRATIONS

---

[1] The cartoons for the early period are from contemporary prints; those for 1860 to 1890 are from *Harper's Weekly* and *Frank Leslie's;* the recent cartoons are from newspapers noted under each illustration.

MAPS, GRAPHS AND CHARTS

CREATING A SOCIETY
1575–1763

CHAPTER I

THE ENGLISH MIGRATION TO AMERICA

On the third of February 1575 the directors of the Muscovy Company voted to open a new chapter in the history of mankind, albeit reluctantly and in ignorance. For then it was that these London merchants licensed Martin Frobisher, a confirmed rover of the seas, to seek a passage to far-off Cathay by sailing northwestward around the "island" of America.

English Reluctance to Venture Westward

Full three-quarters of a century England had known of America, for as long ago as 1497 John Cabot in the pay of Bristol merchants had sailed for Asia and had happened upon Newfoundland. Yet none had followed him thither save the fishermen who annually made their catch off the bleak shores of the strange new coast. Scarce a soul dreamed of any other form of American venture.

There were weighty reasons for English reluctance to turn westward. The British Isles were off in a corner of Europe and English interests were confined primarily to the islands and to the neighboring shores of the Continent. Such narrow horizons limited the vision of Englishmen and they did not readily conceive of distant projects. And even if there had been the imagination, there was not the means. Expeditions across the Atlantic were likely to be extremely expensive and hazardous and England had little surplus capital; none could be spared for so uncertain a venture. The economy of the nation was still largely feudal. Land was the principal form of wealth and it could not be used for mercantile pursuits. There were one or two ancient companies of merchants such as the Merchant Adventurers and the Staplers but their dealings were almost entirely confined to trade in cloth and wool with the nearby Low Countries. Few people made much money and the English had relatively little to spend and less to invest.

Other circumstances were even more discouraging to far-flung enterprise. The English merchant marine was handicapped. It was poor in ships. Westward sailing was made difficult and tedious by the ill favor of the winds which generally blew in the wrong direction. Then, England had powerful enemies, particularly the Spanish, who controlled so much of the New World. The Spanish navy dominated the sea-lanes leading to the attractive regions of America and their sea strength was such that if English mariners did set out for the shadowy lands, they must sail far to the north in dangerous waters to avoid their foes. Thus only the forbidding northern shores of America were conveniently accessible and they offered slight inducement for the risk.

But despite these difficulties, English enterprise was at length to turn to the western continents. For in western Europe the Modern Age was evolving out of Medievalism. This new spirit was awakening the English people who were about to achieve great heights in many forms of endeavor. The great epoch of Elizabeth was moving towards its zenith, and it was an age in which a marvelous creative talent, all unsuspected, was to make England a leader in shaping modern civilization.

The mightiest force in the creation of this new spirit was a social change of great significance. A new class was taking a prominent place in English life. The old feudal order of privileged and bound was giving way before the enterprise of a number of industrious and intelligent individuals who were to produce a middle class. Various obscure people were industriously laboring to increase England's wealth and prosperity. Many of the feudal domains were turned into sheep pastures. Quantities of fine woolen cloth were manufactured and carried far abroad by English traders who sold it for gold and silver. A number of Englishmen were growing rich; and though they had little fame, their strong boxes were filling with gold coin. They found that money gave them power and influence which they sought to use to their own advantage and the variety of their investments and interests increased. Also there had been a redistribution of property which freed more wealth for active enterprise. When the Church had been separated from Rome in the reign of Henry VIII, the Crown confiscated much of the large property of the monasteries and a great deal of this wealth passed into the hands of those more adroit in its use; a new fund of capital was at the disposal of business. England was leaving her feudal economy and preparing to take the lead in the rise of modern capitalism which was to dominate the western world.

The power and influence of the middle class were courted by those "progressive" monarchs, the Tudors. They encouraged the business men who valued peace and needed prosperity and who were willing to back with their money, a monarch who could keep order and promote their interests outside of England. The Tudors and their advisers saw the need of an adequate merchant marine and lent their help to the new merchant interest in building up a shipping worthy of the new age. Henry VIII had given much attention to the navy and nautical science and patronized experts in maritime affairs. One of his protegés, Fletcher of Rye, in 1539 developed the art of tacking, whereby ships were rigged and maneuvered to sail against the wind. Thereafter, the voyage to the westward, was much less difficult a venture. New and larger ships, too, began to fly the English flag and Englishmen of adventurous tastes sought the seas in increasing numbers.

Finally England emerged as a European power. The Tudors saw the value to the kingdom and to themselves of foreign influence and sought to promote it by shrewd participation in the crafty intrigues which marked the diplomacy of the day. English diplomats, true servants of their Tudor masters, thrust themselves into the affairs of continental Europe and Henry VIII crossed swords with Francis I of France, Charles V of Spain and Germany, and in a certain sense, with the Pope himself. For family and religious reasons, the rivalry was keenest with Catholic Spain, a land which was creating a huge empire in America. These new forces were combining to produce an expansive England. The stage was set for the new enterprise of the Elizabethan era.

The organization of large-scale business ventures at the mid point of the sixteenth century paved the way for a real interest in America. England was heavily in debt and had to gather large sums of money to export to foreign creditors. The government just then under the regents of Edward VI was unable to act efficiently. Agricultural production was disorganized due to the shift from tilling the soil to raising sheep. Unemployment was widespread, for thousands of tenants had been cast adrift when their fields were turned into sheep pastures. Foreign trade was falling off; in fact, the things England needed cost too much. Cheaper ways of obtaining imports must be found. Such conditions caused the more progressive London merchants much anxious thought as they discussed the matter among themselves in the year 1552. It became apparent to them that new methods were necessary.

Spain and Portugal were increasing their wealth by new ventures in unknown fields, and by sailing to the west and to the southeast had found riches. Might not England gain what was needed by similar voyages? Capitalists including members of the Merchant Adventurers began to plan a new organization for larger operations. Old Sebastian Cabot, now living in London on a crown pension, was called in to give counsel. Clearly there were but two possible roads to the riches of the east, to the northwest or to the northeast; along other routes the Spanish or the Portuguese blocked the way. During 1553-1555 the enterprising London merchants sent out explorers to the northeast, established relations with Russia and formed a new company, the Muscovy or Russian Adventurers; Cathay or China was yet to be found. For the next generation at Muscovy House there congregated the most active and progressive merchants of the kingdom.

The public, too, began to extend its imagination into these fields. Richard Eden translated *A Treatyse of the Newe India* (1553) and Peter Martyr's *Decades of the Newe Worlde* (1555). Englishmen could now read about these shadowy continents. Difficulties with France and Spain, especially the latter, were multiplying and the rivalry with that power focussed attention upon the steady supply of wealth which came to Spain from America, to England's disadvantage. In the meantime, Elizabeth had ascended the throne and new signs of vigorous policies were not slow in appearing. She would use any means at hand to curb Spanish pretensions. As early as 1563 the Queen backed Thomas Stukely, a boisterous international adventurer, in an expedition to Florida to curb Spanish expansion, and sought to procure for this enterprise the experience and aid of Jean Ribaut who had recently led a French venture to that same region and who was then a refugee in England. Ribaut did not go and Stukely turned the expedition into a pirate cruise but Florida began to grow attractive and when two years later John Hawkins came back from his famous voyage to America he brought detailed information. He described the gold, the silver, the copper, the pearls with no meagre vocabulary; Florida became a fad, the name was on many tongues and often did the adventurous or impecunious dream of easy-found wealth in this pleasant land. America had attracted public attention.

In the meantime, the Muscovy proprietors had not reached Cathay by the northeastern route and the idea of trying the northwest began to circulate. Something must be done to cut down the charges of the too numerous foreign middlemen who taxed English trade. Martin Frobisher had been venturing along the Guinea coast and began to vision more profitable exploits in searching for a northwest passage. His acquaintance, Sir Humphrey Gilbert, a member of the Muscovy Company, had striven since 1566 to gain the Queen's assent to a search for a northwest passage. Sir Humphrey wrote a "Discourse" to prove the possibility of a northwest passage and the desirability of seeking it. He realized the difficulty of "selling" a new idea in such troubled times and sought to find cogent arguments for his project. Among other reasons he gave the current economic difficulties, England's need of direct trade routes, new markets for her cloth, and a greater fund of ready money. Most significantly, in view of later developments, he stressed the condition of unemployment. The countries yet to be discovered might be settled by the unemployed, which then so troubled England because through want they were "enforced to commit outrageous offences whereby they are dayly consumed with the gallows."

In spite of the efforts of Frobisher and Gilbert and their influential friends, the Muscovy Company refused to approve. Twice Elizabeth's ministers urged the Company to license Frobisher without avail. Finally, they converted Michael Lock, the principal director of the Company, and on the famous 3 February 1575 the license was issued.

After tedious delay, Frobisher's expedition set sail 15 June 1576.

He reached North America and entered the strait which bears his name. This was not Cathay, but as he brought back a stone which was claimed to contain gold, he became famous over night. The Queen now contributed a charter and £1000 which enabled him to go back in 1577 to open mines and if feasible to leave a colony there through the winter. He returned to England that fall from his second expedition with two hundred tons of ore for assayers to quarrel about and Michael Lock was encouraged to plan a permanent settlement. In 1578 a fleet of fifteen ships with their crews and one hundred colonists set out under Frobisher only to meet failure. The climate was too rigorous; they found no gold. They came back that same year and the first attempt by Englishmen at American settlement was a failure.

In the meantime, Sir Humphrey Gilbert was busy with his own plans of settlement and with a scheme for harrying the Spanish power. Elizabeth granted Gilbert letters patent for planting a colony in America whereby he was to rule and own such territories as he should find, reserving to the Crown one fifth part of the profits. His first expedition was a failure and for a while his colonization scheme seemed as dead as Frobisher's mining town. But the English imagination was awakening. Drake and the other freebooters were daring rash exploits against the Spanish king's treasure and his gold was paying off the English debt. Gilbert took advantage of this enthusiasm to raise capital. He sold large tracts of American land to prominent people. He negotiated with wealthy Catholics and sold them a million acres, so that they might find a refuge in America. He enlisted the support of his half-brother, Walter Raleigh. The geographer, Richard Hakluyt, managed the publicity and published a little book, *Divers Voyages* which recounted all he could learn of American exploration.

On the fifth anniversary of the grant of his charter, 11 June 1583, Gilbert set sail with five ships and 260 men of all ranks and occupations. On 5 August, he landed and took possession of Newfoundland. Then began the usual folly. All hands turned to seeking gold that was not to be found, sickness broke out, his expedition became mutinous and Gilbert must perforce turn back. However, he was not to suffer the indignity of reporting failure; his ship was lost in a storm and he took his place in the legends of early America.

His spirit lived on in Sir Walter Raleigh. He received a charter in 1584 and in 1585 and 1587 planted and replanted a colony on the coast of North Carolina. It was a failure and this venture on the island of Roanoke disheartened as well as impoverished him, for he had spent the equivalent of a million dollars without return. In 1589 he sold his charter rights to the coast area, which he had named Virginia in honor of Elizabeth, the Virgin Queen, to some London merchants. They in turn planned an expedition but failed to carry it out because open war with Spain had now begun and too much was to be gained easily by privateering and pillaging Spanish merchant and treasure ships. The "lusty rogues and sturdy beggars," whose numbers caused many to think that England was overpopulated, could be used in the wars and in privateering. The attention of English businessmen had been turned to America, it is true, but as yet their imagination had not proceeded much beyond the establishment of mines and trading posts and the spoiling of Spain. Nevertheless, Gilbert and Raleigh, the epic writer Hakluyt, and a few others had caught the vision of an English empire beyond the sea.

Commercial Enterprise Leads the Way

In spite of the disasters attending the ventures of Frobisher, Gilbert and Raleigh the idea of American settlement could not die. Their exploits and those of Drake and the freebooters served as advertising while the silent forces of economic, social and religious change constantly pressed toward colonization.

The last years of Elizabeth's reign, after the failure of Raleigh's enterprise, were years of commercial stagnation deepened by the long drawn-out war with Spain. Periods of business depression are apt to reveal very clearly any existing economic weaknesses and this recession was no exception. In the first place, England's lack of self-sufficiency was proven once again, for the war kept the kingdom in constant danger of being cut off from some vital source of supply. In the second place, the cost of living had increased so that fixed incomes in many cases had become inadequate. As estates were handed down intact from father to eldest son, this shrinkage of the purchasing power of income meant that no savings, in many cases, could be put aside for younger sons. Consequently, many of the gentry who otherwise would have been content to remain at home were thrown upon their own resources. It was not easy to find lucrative employment in England but America might offer a field of endeavor. Finally, the close of the Spanish war called for the demobilization of much of the armed force and many an adventurous soldier found himself footloose and fancy free in the midst of a depression; more than ever did England seem overpopulated. All of these conditions acted as direct stimuli toward adventuring in this fabulous and baffling America.

The revival of interest in America that followed upon these conditions was at first largely advanced by the merchants. England found herself in a new position commercially, no longer was she off in a corner. The development of trans-Atlantic navigation by the Spanish had widened and readjusted trading routes and had brought the British Isles much nearer the center of commercial activity. Also, British merchants had learned that individuals were not best fitted to exploit America;

corporations must be formed. The East India Company had been organized recently for the exploitation of the far east and capitalists began to plan for like organizations to operate in what might have been termed at that time, the far west.

Between 1602 and 1605 at least four voyages were made to America and in the latter year certain Catholics under Lord Zouche started another plan for a refuge for those of their faith who found conditions in England so oppressive. This group advanced to the point of sending over a vessel to look for a suitable place. Lord Zouche's proposal roused a protest in the Privy Council itself and caused the assignees of Walter Raleigh to bestir themselves to protect their interests. A counter-proposal was made by a powerful Protestant group of merchants, soldiers and government officials who contended that, as private colonies had ever been a failure, an undertaking should now be tried by a syndicate under governmental patronage. King James I approved the latter project and two groups of soldiers and merchants were organized under royal patents, issued 10 April 1606, in the business centers of London and Plymouth. Important in these groups were Sir Thomas Smythe, one of the most adventurous business men of the day, Richard Hakluyt, the publicity expert, and military men like Sir Thomas Gates.

The London Company acted most effectively and got together a hundred and five men in three small ships which set sail 20 December 1606 to establish what proved to be the first permanent English settlement in America. Jamestown was the result and commercial enterprise had started what it was hoped would be a profitable venture.

If it were to succeed, the proposed trading post must attract settlers and the London Company sought to advertise the new location. Their efforts were successful in attracting the interest of people from various classes. In the first three years there migrated some 400, mostly of humble origin; only 30% could be classed as gentlemen. Their early hardships were intense and most of them died but Captain John Smith provided the courageous leadership necessary to prevent utter extinction and in the meantime newcomers arrived in sufficient numbers to maintain the colony. After 1609 Sir Thomas Smythe took over active control in London. He reorganized the staff, issued more attractive advertising literature and introduced better managerial methods. Under his more effective direction a hardier type of immigrant including more farmers was secured.

Under these improved conditions about 1400 men and women went to Virginia during the next decade; but the company earned no dividends, so in 1618 another reorganization took place. Sir Edwin Sandys became the new manager and his ideas were advanced for his time. Liberal offers of land and self-government were his prescription to stimulate migration and in one year 1200 people went out. By 1625, when

King James took over all the London Company's charters and other possessions, in order to confound his enemies among its stockholders, 5649 persons had at various times come to the colony. Though scarce 2000 of these were still in Virginia, the colony was on a permanent foundation and an outpost of empire had been established. More important, the idea of America was becoming more attractive in England. The survival of the colony and the advertising of the London and Plymouth Companies were doing their work. America might prove more than a field for trade; it might also be a place for happier and freer living.

The Quest for Liberty

Had English interest been confined to the adventurous and speculative, England's American empire might never have been more than a series of trading posts and company projects for producing raw materials. But the character of the American nation was to be formed by forces much stronger than love of adventure or desire for wealth. The rise of the middle class and the development of the religious reformation were to be particularly potent in turning English attention to America, not as a source of possible gain, but as an experiment station in the creation of a reformed social order.

The emergence of the middle class was accompanied by many social readjustments and as society resists change, there were many conflicts and much unhappiness. One of the most fertile fields for struggle was religious. As the middle class sought liberty to live their own lives, they were desirous particularly of religious freedom because the old religion was dominated by the hierarchy and priesthood. During the reign of Elizabeth this conflict was accentuated by the appearance of a strong reform group known as Puritans. They wished to change the manner of worship in the Church of England, to make it more matter of fact and less symbolic, to develop discipline and moral standards of personal conduct, and to lay more emphasis upon the chief reformation tenet that man's relations with God were direct and personal and not conducted through the ministrations of a priesthood.

Most of the Puritans were willing to remain within the established church and work for its reform in the meantime minimizing the use of the prayer book, simplifying the service and church decoration and placing the emphasis upon preaching. In the matter of church government there were those who sought to reintroduce the practice of appointing elders or chief laymen; their ideal was a presbyterian form in which presbyteries or synods, meetings of the preachers and elders, instead of bishops, would determine matters of church policy. The main body of the Puritans as much as possible put their ideas into practice without actually leaving the Church of England. Naturally, their policies produced a lack of uniformity; in some parishes the conduct of religion varied little from that utilized when the church was loyal to the Pope, while in others, especially in the southeast of England, the pastor and people worshipped in a fashion hardly recognizable to those faithful to the church as established by law.

The conflict of opinion and practice had a wider significance than its effect upon religious observance. The government controlled the church, Elizabeth appointed the bishops and was herself the "supreme governor." The sixteenth century was not a period in which governments willingly tolerated views opposing those officially held; and when Elizabeth displayed impatience with people who sought to modify ritual and government the matter took on a political aspect. Various statutes were passed and orders issued which showed clearly that Elizabeth discountenanced this lack of uniformity; but her displeasure was exhibited only sporadically and the magnitude of her other problems prevented a consistent policy. Nevertheless the Queen's attitude was perfectly apparent and her opponents were often recruited among those whose religious ideas she attempted to modify. Liberty of conscience and freedom of religious observance began to be issues which many who disliked the Queen's policies, her arbitrary rule, her "pomp and vain glory," or her governmental program could use in formulating protest among a large group of sober and industrious people.

As a result, the conflict took on a social as well as a political aspect. The nobles and the tenantry, the country squires and the yeomen, the visible remnants of the old feudal order, were generally content with little religious change, now that the monasteries had been broken up and their lands re-distributed. But the new ideas were very attractive to the townsmen and to the rising merchant class who felt the need of honesty and sobriety in business dealings and knew the wealth-producing possibilities of hard work and who also took a more decided interest in management. To a director in a corporation the idea of a "session" or committee of elders to manage a church was a logical thing. Besides the small townsmen were no longer feudal in their outlook. As their mercantile horizon widened, and their profits grew, their feeling of importance strengthened; but they were in a society that was still organized along feudal lines and in a church dominated by a hierarchy. They were independent in spirit and fond of their own opinions and did not relish the insignificant place allotted them in the episcopal church organization.

In spite of these general conditions the line must not be too clearly drawn according to region or class. People from all walks of life, even from the nobility and country gentry became Puritan and many a *nouveau riche* middle class citizen revered the Church of England as a mark of his own social rise. But neighbor did contend with neighbor, families divided and high churchman and Puritan often refused to remain on speaking terms one with another.

The religious, political and social cleavage became most apparent in the case of a small group who began to appear more prominently in the latter years of Elizabeth's reign. The members of this group were convinced that there must be a return to the early Christian custom of independent, self-governing congregations. For them, they felt, there was no virtue in the Church of England, and conscience demanded that they come out and be separate, worshipping in independent congregations according to their own interpretation of the Scriptures. Though these "Separatists," as they were called, were neither many nor important in wealth or social standing, still they were intense and persistent and were bound to spread. Worse still, from the point of view of the government, they were a bad example. The Church of England was the state church and the medieval idea of uniformity was still too strong to brook the notion of more than one organization. Separatists were not only schismatic but unpatriotic and as the Queen sought to subdue those who opposed her rule, she was also determined to destroy those who opposed her church.

As these Separatists grew in numbers and as the Puritans increased their wealth and power, Elizabeth's position changed. While Mary Queen of Scots was alive and while Philip of Spain threatened, Elizabeth could not afford too many enemies at home and she frequently ignored the Puritan tendencies away from the rule of the bishops. But Mary was at length executed and Philip's grand armada dispersed. Elizabeth's power was safe and she could turn upon this stiff-necked generation who sought to reform conduct and worship according to ideas with which she did not sympathize. The result was the act passed in 1593 designed to curb Puritans as well as Separatists by inflicting punishments of death or banishment upon those who persisted in their faith. Two of their leaders, Barrowe and Greenwood were hanged at Tyburn. Others were arrested and some few abjured the realm that same year, fleeing to Holland where they established a church in Amsterdam.

From these years onward under Elizabeth and James, the lot of Puritan and more especially Separatist was less and less pleasant and many thought of emigrating. Some time in these years the idea dawned upon these serious-minded folk that in America where a number of them had made investments, all too profitless as yet, there ought to be a haven of refuge where they with God's help might establish His Holy Commonwealth. Theirs too was a vision, not of empire, but of liberty.

About the time the London and Plymouth companies were formed, a small group of these serious-minded people in the Nottinghamshire village of Scrooby had banded together in a Separatist congregation which, contrary to law, met each Sabbath for independent worship. Many of their neighbors ridiculed them and scoffed at their peculiar ideas; some even went so far as to lodge a complaint. Though local authorities were not disposed to deal severely with them, it became apparent that King James was going to make war upon non-conformity in general. The possibility of serious persecution began to prey upon their minds, already harassed by the torture of the gossip and ridicule of neighbors. Since they were liable to imprisonment, loss of property and banishment, the Scrooby congregation began to talk of a migration to Holland such as had been undertaken a decade previous by the church now at Amsterdam. To leave in a body with their possessions would be no easy matter for it would call attention to their non-conformity and invite the confiscation of their small property under the law of 1593. They must go secretly; and only after great difficulty and much frustration did they in any measure succeed. Less than a hundred finally congregated in Amsterdam in 1607 and 1608 and moved thence to Leyden.

In the decade following their number increased to some two hundred but the peace and prosperity they had anticipated did not come in generous measure. To be sure they were free to worship as they chose but they were aliens in a strange land and not very prosperous aliens at that. They began to long for an English community where their children might grow up as Englishmen, for more profitable ways of earning a living, and for that comfort and independence which might come to them in an American community of their own founding.

After much discussion they decided to move to America. In 1619 they obtained permission from the London Company to make a settlement, and received assurance that the King would not interfere with their religious customs. The great problem remaining was funds. They were thrifty and reliable and both Dutch and English promoters were anxious to have them undertake colonization in their territories. Thomas Weston, a London merchant, came to Holland to talk over possibilities and John Carver and Robert Cushman went back to confer in London. Finally an agreement was reached although its actual details satisfied no one. Weston and some London associates agreed to supply money for the journey and the emigrants were to repay their backers from the fruit of their labors in America.

With these difficult negotiations at length concluded, obstacles were by no means overcome. When the final test came only thirty-five of the Leyden congregation were able and willing to go. Recruits were necessary and sixty-seven were found with difficulty in London who were willing to join the company, for motives which were scarcely religious. With these "Pilgrims" the Mayflower at length set sail from Plymouth 6 September 1620. The voyage was long and dangerous, and the ship was driven out of its course so that when the emigrants finally arrived in America they found themselves entirely outside of the London Company's territory. There was nothing to do, however, but to make the best of it and on 21 December 1620, they landed at Plymouth and under the leadership of John Carver and William Brewster, ably assisted by one of the recruits, Miles Standish, they began settlement.

The land upon which the Pilgrims had inadvertently stumbled was situated in the domain of the Plymouth Company. This corporation had not been a successful venture. To be sure it had sent out an expedition before the London Company but that voyage had been a failure and the lone colony which on the second voyage it had attempted to plant, barely survived a terrible winter on the Maine coast (1607-8) and returned to discourage further such attempts. One of the principal men in this company, Sir Ferdinando Gorges, in the years 1614-1618 had attempted to put some life into it by hiring Captain John Smith to manage it and to make voyages. The sum of Smith's success, however, was his book published in 1616 entitled *A Description of New England* which had a wide distribution and proved an able second to Hakluyt's works. Just about the time the Pilgrims set sail, the Plymouth company had been reorganized in 1620 under the title of the Council for New England. One of its first acts was to grant a patent to the leaders of the Pilgrim colony at Plymouth permitting them to remain within their dominion.

The reorganized company attempted no more colonizing on its own account but contented itself with granting permits to others for settling on its vast estate. Two of its leading stockholders, the aforesaid Gorges and Captain John Mason, secured such grants and in 1622 began ventures on their own account. Mason's activity resulted in scattering settlements which formed the nucleus of New Hampshire and Gorges' plans laid the foundation for Maine. Many lesser grants were made in the area to be known as Massachusetts and by 1630 some 2100 people were scattered over the territories of the old Plymouth Company. Meanwhile Virginia's population had grown to 3000 and some 4000 people were in the English West Indies. Growth was slow but events were shaping themselves to accelerate it; the great migration was about to begin.

A combination of factors, social, political, religious and economic was forming to produce a veritable exodus from England in the years succeeding 1629. Conditions for many were becoming intolerable because Charles I was proceeding to rule without Parliament by resorting to arbitrary taxation and ignoring the personal rights of his subjects hallowed by custom. His chief ecclesiastic, Archbishop Laud, attempted to enforce religious uniformity by similar high-handed methods. Economic conditions, too, were bad in southeastern England, where the strongest Puritan communities were located. Their industries were in a decline and in the towns wages were low, while food prices remained high. From 1620 to 1635 there were "hard times" in England which discouraged many. The staid and sober Puritan country gentlemen were also disturbed by new social conditions. Their quiet precincts were being invaded by *nouveaux riches* traders from London who wished to become landed gentry. These parvenus bought landed estates and introduced extravagant expenditures and ungodly ways of life. The Puritan squires were not rich enough to compete with this style, had they thought it desirable, and their moral sense was horrified by the new laxity in society. The lot of the Puritan, set about by these political, religious, economic and social attacks upon his standards, was not happy.

In 1623 a group of such men in the vicinity of Dorchester in Dorsetshire had sought to increase their fortunes by backing a trading post and fishing station in New England. Little had come of it save a small settlement at Salem; nevertheless, the south country investors persisted in their efforts, organized and reorganized, and sent out a few more ships and settlers. In 1629 their enterprise assumed final shape as the "Governor and Company of Massachusetts Bay in New England," a stock company similar in many respects to the London Company. The stockholders decided to take their charter and migrate in a body. In the spring of 1630 therefore, sixteen vessels and 1000 colonists were assembled and sailed to America, where in the vicinity of Boston harbor the colony of Massachusetts Bay was planted.

The migration of the Massachusetts Bay Company was closely followed by another project undertaken from somewhat similar motives. Following the death of Queen Mary in 1558, the Catholics in England had suffered sporadic persecution. Legally they could not be said to exist, as they had no recognized rights. Nevertheless, many still remained, though politically and socially without the pale. At all stages in American enterprise, some of their faith had been interested in establishing a refuge there. Now the realization of such a hope was at hand. Sir George Calvert, a politician of influence under the Stuarts, had been converted to the Catholic faith and he had been considering a plan for a colony. He wished to promote his fortunes at the same time that he organized a place where Catholics might have freedom.

He died before he could carry out his plan, but in 1634 his son, the second Lord Baltimore, succeeded. Under a charter procured two years previously whereby Charles I granted the Baltimores the proprietorship of certain land north of Virginia, to be known as Maryland, a little group of twenty gentlemen, four priests and two hundred laborers founded St. Mary's. However, Calvert's hope was realized only in small part as Catholics migrated less freely than he desired. To make the colony more prosperous, the proprietor therefore invited Protestant immigrants who soon outnumbered their Catholic associates. Religious toleration was maintained, sometimes with difficulty, and the Baltimore family continued their ownership of this slow-growing community.

Shortly after the Maryland settlers began their work, New England became the scene of further planting. In 1636 Massachusetts Bay began to get rid of certain radicals who did not agree with the Puritan order of government. Roger Williams was banished first. He gathered to him others who built Providence and shortly thereafter various free spirits organized Portsmouth, Newport and Warwick. These four towns Roger Williams succeeded in uniting as the colony of Providence Plantations and obtained a patent of self-government from commissioners of the Long Parliament in 1643. Here any "otherwise minded" people were welcome.

Less radical but no less independent were the Puritans who left Massachusetts Bay to settle along the Connecticut River. Rev. Thomas Hooker, pastor of the church at Newtown in Massachusetts, was moved to lead his people into the Connecticut Valley to establish Hartford. He was not contentious like Williams, but there he could obtain freedom from the Massachusetts Bay leaders who controlled matters pretty much according to their own will. Besides the valley of the great river was much more fertile. So a peaceful secession took place. Around Dutch trading posts already established some settled Hartford and Weathersfield in 1635 while others went higher up the river to found Windsor. In the meantime the Puritan noblemen Lord Brooke and Lord Saye and Sele had secured a grant of land at the mouth of the Connecticut and there in the same year planted a colony at Saybrook. Two years later came a group from old England led by John Davenport and Theophilus Eaton, strictest of Puritans. Their company had suffered under the persecution of Archbishop Laud and had come to the New World to establish a Biblical Commonwealth. Their immediate destination was Boston but one winter there convinced them that they could be happier by themselves; so in 1638 they sailed to the site of New Haven and there builded the theocracy which they called by that name. Strictest of all the new communities, their colony marked the high point of the Puritan migration.

By 1640 more than 65,000 Englishmen were in America scattered somewhat as follows:

Massachusetts	14,000
Connecticut	2,000
Rhode Island	300
New Hampshire and Maine	1,500
Maryland	1,500
Virginia	8,000
West Indies	40,000

Figures are faulty and inadequate and our knowledge of human motives is always incomplete; nevertheless, it can be said that the dominating force in colonization in the twenty years, 1620-1640, had been exerted by those who thought more of religious freedom and liberty of action than they did of dividends or the accumulation of wealth. The Puritans might not numerically be able to count a great or overwhelming majority; but in New England, where at that time had settled most of the English who came to the continental area, their ideas of social ordering dominated.

The score of years marked by the Puritan revolution and Commonwealth did not check the tide of migration from England although it somewhat changed its character. The Puritans as a group were no longer so much interested in America, their energies were required at home to carry through their political experiment. Civil war and governmental change, however, were not without effect. Some royalist sympathizers sought refuge, especially after the King was beheaded, in Virginia where loyalty to the Crown was still popular; their number probably has been over-rated. Also a number of peace-loving people, especially of the mercantile class, sought a less troubled field of operations in America, where there was none of this civil war, so hard upon business.

A third group directly stimulated by the war was one of the most important in the colonial migration, indentured servants. Wages were low in England during the first half of the seventeenth century and the labor market was glutted. Many wished to get to the new world, but the fare was high. Few laborers, had they been able to save their wages for a life time, could have become possessed of the six to ten pounds necessary to procure passage. In the new world, especially in Virginia and Maryland, labor was scarce and the profits from tobacco tempting. As a result hundreds began to take advantage of a form of migration which met both needs. Numerous men and some women began to make agreements whereby in return for transportation to the colonies they would work for a term of years, usually five, as indentured servants to some colonist willing to pay their passage. At the conclusion of this term of service, freedom and some land or money came to the erstwhile servant and he thereby became a property holder. Such an arrangement was bound to be attractive.

When the civil war broke out many prisoners were sent over as indentured servants by whichever side was in control, and during the period of the Commonwealth, many who were captured in the Irish and Scotch wars were disposed of likewise. Paupers were gathered from the poorhouses and the streets of London. Condemned felons also were occasionally sent over under indenture, not only to relieve the crowded jails, but likewise as an experiment in criminal reformation. So well did this idea work that the great number who came for this purpose settled down to a respectable and industrious life. The wilderness where there was plenty of land, little to steal and few of the temptations of more

advanced civilization proved an excellent destroyer of criminal proclivities. Under such conditions either by force or by their own free
will, some 2000 indentured servants arrived annually in Virginia alone.
Migration therefore in the years 1640-1660 was steady but uneventful;
no new projects were undertaken but the shiploads of emigrants continued to distribute themselves among the colonies scattered along the
Atlantic shore.

The Projects of the Restoration

A new phase of the English migration of the 17th century began with
the restoration of the Stuarts in 1660. During the Civil War and the
era of the Commonwealth, many a loyal friend of the King had suffered
in fortune. Estates had been confiscated, property dispersed. With the
return of the monarchy came the question of rewarding loyalty. The
treasury was by no means overflowing but there were the American
possessions where fortunes might be made. To the easy-going Charles II,
the granting of large slices of these distant possessions was a cheap way
of paying debts and rewarding loyal followers. Besides, under Puritan
rule, England had become definitely converted to big business. The
politicians who surrounded the throne had many modern ideas about
the relation between business prosperity and governmental policy. The
Commonwealth had issued a series of navigation laws which aimed to
secure all profits from colonial enterprise to English merchants and
had sought to increase colonial possessions by conquest. These policies
Charles' government continued.

One of the first fruits of restoration interest in America, therefore,
was a new colonization project. Some friends of Charles became interested in planting a colony south of Virginia. Conditions in Barbados
were not happy because of quarrels over land grants and a number of
the planters were ready to leave. One of the most influential, Col. John
Colleton, came to England for the purpose of obtaining means to secure
lands south of Virginia whither the Barbadians who were discontented
might migrate and establish profitable trade relations with the islands.
Incidentally, they might secure the southern area against the pretensions
of the Spanish. Colleton interested Anthony Ashley Cooper and they
associated with them six staunch friends of the King, Clarendon, Albemarle, Lord John Berkeley, Carteret, Craven, and Sir William Berkeley,
governor of Virginia. Toward such a group of friends, Charles could
hardly be ungenerous, so he granted them an indefinite tract of land
south of Virginia to be known as Carolina, and later threw in the
Bahama islands as a safeguard to the passage between the proposed
colony and Barbados. The charter passed the seals in 1663.

Plans for settling this region had been undertaken as early as 1629 and a few settlers had attempted unsuccessfully to locate in the Cape Fear region of what became North Carolina. In fact when the charter was granted some Virginians had actually settled in the Albemarle Sound region. These planters were not disturbed by the new proprietors and were given a government and land privileges similar to those existing in Virginia. The real interest of the promoters, however, was in a colony which they intended to plant themselves. They authorized John Locke to prepare an elaborate plan, offered inducements to settlers, and in 1669 sent off an expedition. After much hardship, then almost inevitable, the company of one hundred augmented by three score others taken on at Barbados, landed at Charleston harbor in 1670. Here a settlement was established which suffered and struggled under indifferent leadership. Emigrants came to both North and South Carolina in the years following and as the location of Charleston proved highly suitable, that portion of the Carolinas prospered.

While the Carolina project was taking shape, the governing group in England undertook a second and more predatory venture. For forty years the New England colonies had been separated from the southern settlements, not only by the boundaries of the grants to the old London and Plymouth Companies, but also by the intrusion of settlements of other nationalities. The Dutch had come adventuring over the seas even as the English had done. After an English navigator in their employ, Henry Hudson, had discovered the Hudson River country in 1609, traders from Holland had come to frequent that region in search of furs and had established trading posts. After the organization of the Dutch West India Company in 1621, such activity became more sustained and in 1623 New Amsterdam was given a permanent place, followed in the years succeeding by settlements on Long Island and Staten Island and along the Hudson as far north as Fort Orange (Albany).

Sweden also had developed colonial ambitions and after the forming of the Swedish West India Company, an expedition was sent to the Delaware Valley in 1638 where a colony was planted within the next few years. Scattering settlements followed along the banks of that river in what are now Delaware, Pennsylvania and New Jersey. The Dutch on the Hudson could not view with complacency these projects, weak though they were, and in 1655 conquered them. By 1660 the Dutch and Swedish colonists on the Hudson and the Delaware numbered some 10,000 souls rather discontented with the arbitrary Dutch rule.

During the Commonwealth Dutch and English rivalry had led to hostility which the Restoration government was nothing loath to encourage. War was inevitable. Charles and his associates were egged on by American complaints. The Dutch had settled on land claimed by the Council for New England under whose authority settlers had located on Long Island. These resisted Dutch pretensions. Finally activities on the Connecticut River had brought the Dutch into conflict with the English Puritans. All told, the Dutch were a nuisance and a menace to English profits—besides, they were reported as almost defenceless. In 1664, therefore, Charles granted to his brother James, Duke of York, the land between the Connecticut and the Delaware as well as Long Island and northeastern Maine. The Duke of York immediately sent an expedition under Col. Richard Nicolls to seize his new domain. It was no difficult task and thus the English dominions were consolidated from the St. Lawrence to the undetermined southern boundary of the Carolinas. That portion of the newly acquired territory along the Hudson was renamed New York and the Dutch settlers were permitted to retain their property.

Meanwhile, even before Nicolls had demanded the surrender of the Dutch, the Duke of York had given away a portion of his new estate. Two of his close friends Lord Berkeley and Sir George Carteret had requested a grant and had received the lower portion, between the Delaware and the Hudson, which they named New Jersey. Some few Dutch and Swedish settlers were already there and Nicolls granted lands to people from Long Island and New England. These established the town of Elizabeth in 1664. The new proprietors set out on an ambitious scheme to promote their possessions. They made liberal concessions and advertised them so effectively, especially in New England, that many came into the new development. In one instance in 1666 a town moved in a body from Connecticut and laid out Newark. The destruction of the Dutch power had cleared the way for new projects.

The last phase of the English migration in the seventeenth century found its motive power in another struggle for freedom of conscience. Religious and social difficulties had by no means been abolished by the Restoration. Dissenters were as numerous as ever and they were burdened by oppressive laws. The Catholics, too, were becoming more prominent and no less a man than the Duke of York, the heir apparent, was of their faith. Attempts were made to prevent his accession to the throne and the last years of Charles' reign were disturbed by the Popish plot and like intrigues. But the new migration was not to be particularly Catholic, rather it was to be marked by an ambitious social experiment which was to be the climax of seventeenth century American enterprise.

England had scarcely been conscious of the emergence of a new Christian sect. But under the leadership of George Fox, a small group of vigorous individualists who to that day seemed strangely radical was beginning to attract attention. These men and women, known to themselves as the Society of Friends and to others as Quakers, sought extreme simplicity in their relations with God and man. They believed in direct communion with God by means of the illumination of the "inner light" and the equality of all. Thus they saw no need of priests and paid scant respect to privilege of any sort. They strove for a democratic, individualistic order of society and worship where all were alike followers of the dictates of conscience. Furthermore, they practiced non-resistance; they refused to fight against their enemies, to enter the army or to pay for military support, and declined to take oaths. These two latter practices naturally brought them into conflict with the civil power and as they were very free in speech and in

A

Further Account

Of the Province of

PENNSYLVANIA

AND ITS

IMPROVEMENTS.

For the Satisfaction of those that are Adventurers, and enclined to be so.

IT has, I know, been much expected from me, that I should give some farther Narrative of those parts of *America*, where I am chiefly interested, and have lately been; having continued there above a Year after my *former Relation*, and receiving since my return, the freshest and fullest Advices of its *Progress* and *Improvement*. But as the reason of my coming back, was a *Difference* between the *Lord Baltamore* and my self, about the *Lands of Delaware*, in consequence, reputed of mighty moment to us, so I wav'd publishing any thing that might look in favour of the Country or inviting to it, whilst it lay under the Discouragement and Disreputation of that Lord's claim and pretences.

But since they are, after many fair and full hearings before the *Lords* of the *Committee* for *Plantations* justly and happily *Dismist*, and the things agreed; and that the *Letters* which daily press me from all Parts, on the subject of *America*

A   *rica*

Pennsylvania Publicity
(Circulated to attract emigrants)

proclaiming their views they were considered dangerous to the peace and safety of the realm. Even during the Commonwealth some of them had been imprisoned and after 1660 more were persecuted.

As so many others before them, they too began to think of the New World as a refuge and in 1673 two of their number, John Fenwick and Edward Byllynge, purchased Lord Berkeley's share of New Jersey for a thousand pounds. Settlers began to enter the western part of New Jersey, especially along the Delaware, while the proprietors with difficulty attempted to maintain their rights against the agents of the Duke of York and the Carterets. During the course of their troubles, a recent convert came to be interested in their project. William Penn, son of Admiral Sir William Penn, courtier and creditor of the King and friend of the Duke of York, had become a Quaker in 1667 or 1668 and had had business dealings with Fenwick and Byllynge, arbitrating a dispute between them and acting as a trustee for the latter's creditors. When the Duke of York's agent, Sir Edmond Andros, interfered with the Quaker settlements, Penn pleaded the cause of the Friends before the Duke and secured a new arrangement whereby William Penn and eleven Quaker associates bought out Carteret's heirs and Fenwick's claims, in 1681 and 1682. New Jersey now belonged entirely to the Friends.

In the meantime, William Penn had devised a larger plan. He wished to try the "Holy Experiment" of a Quaker colony dominated by their own ideas of government and social order. New Jersey had already been settled by many other elements and was hardly suitable. As the King owed him a good deal of money he petitioned Charles in 1680 to pay this debt by granting him land on the west shore of the Delaware. Charles agreed readily enough and on 4 March 1681 signed a charter for the colony of Pennsylvania. The Duke of York contributed his rights to the land around Delaware Bay. By these acts, in spite of the protests and long drawn out opposition of the proprietors of Maryland, Penn and his heirs maintained possession of the territory on the western shore of the Delaware which became the colonies of Pennsylvania and Delaware. In 1682 Philadelphia was laid out and the Holy Experiment was on its road to becoming a reality. More tolerant than any other foundation except Rhode Island, it invited all who would to come. People from many countries arrived and its growth marked a new and more cosmopolitan phase in the development of the British empire in America.

In this fashion between 1607 and 1682 a series of settlements was planted from Carolina to Maine. In them, by 1690, dwelt some 200,000 people, still predominantly English, all owing allegiance to the British Crown. These seventy-five years of migration had called forth much of endurance and ingenuity and the manner in which the settlers overcame the wilderness and builded communities was to be the first demonstration of a way of life and order of society to be known as American.

CHAPTER II

COLONY BUILDING

The thousands who came to America in the first century of migration faced the task of living a strange new life. The wilderness of seashore, river valley and forest peopled by the so-called "Indians" held many curious and often tragic surprises in store for them. Under the strain of these unforeseen and bewildering hardships, many perished or weakened. Those who followed immediately the first expeditions often found but feeble remnants of the bands who had set out with such high hopes. The newcomers therefore had to contend not only with the original perils, but with the contagion of the pervading despair. Somehow, enough survived to keep alive the greater number of the settlements and to provide a welcome and a place of sojourn for the continuing arrivals who were to labor with them to complete the solution of the difficult problems of colony building.

Reorientation

The material equipment transported by the pioneers to conquer the wilderness was slight. The tiny ships in which they came, often of scarce a hundred tons burden, could carry little besides their human freight. But the colonists, though their possessions were few, had a varied equipment of habits, customs and skills and a mighty arsenal of ideas and purposes.

Most of the venturers were obscure and simple folk who came from small towns and farming districts in England where life had been going on for centuries without much change. Their habits and customs were old-fashioned and even archaic as compared to the new ways emerging in the populous centers of the changing England even then becoming "modern." These people so unaccustomed to change must now make radical adjustments and learn new ways of living, many of them at an age when such reorientation is difficult.

Some few came by force; a great many came to find more comfortable means and a more satisfactory social position. But most dynamic was the notable number who came to form a new community based upon principles of liberty for the individual in religion, in government and in shaping a way of life. Most of the emigrants were convinced that in some way their American experiment would mean greater freedom and more happiness. The importance of this psychological equipment cannot be over-estimated. The series of commonwealths which was to become the United States was founded on hope and was the manifestation of a great optimism.

Thus equipped the colonists were thrust into the task of adjusting themselves to wilderness conditions or perishing. The climate was varied and uncertain, and generally different from the English weather to which they were accustomed. There were dangers from exposure and starvation which cost the lives of many. Even more difficult was the problem of relations with the aboriginal inhabitants. Scattered over the scene of English settlements in small clearings where they carried on primitive agriculture, roaming through the forest, or fishing by stream and seashore, a sparse semi-nomadic "Indian" population lived in a Stone Age culture. They were loosely organized in tribes and those whom the English colonists first met were generally either the Algonquian or Iroquoian stock. At first the Indians considered the white men as gods but soon were taught a different story and though they seemed inclined in some localities to be friendly, they soon learned by experience that many of the newcomers were grasping and ruthless, and war and massacre resulted.

The two civilizations were to prove incompatible because of the inability of the Indians to grasp the idea of private property in land. They lived a wandering life, even those who engaged in agriculture stayed in a clearing only a short while. For it soon became overgrown with weeds and it seemed easier to move to a new clearing than root out the new growth. Also they hunted over wide ranges and the white man's proclivity for cutting down forests and building walls and fences cut off their food supply. The whites often went through the form of land purchase with the Indians, but the latter never understood the principal of perpetual alienation of land, especially when the rum which they received in return was so soon consumed, the cloth worn out, or the trinkets lost. Enraged by the loss of hunting grounds, fired by the white man's alcohol, and stimulated in later days by England's enemies, a treacherous and barbarous warfare became intermittent. The conflict brought out the worst in both races and cost many lives. The colonists gained from the Indians useful agricultural knowledge and skill in woodcraft, but beyond that the natives contributed little to mark the new civilization then in the process of creation.

No less exacting was the need for food. Each colony planned to bring sufficient supply to feed the settlers until a planting and harvest could be completed. The trading post colonies even expected to continue dependence upon Europe for most of their food, while they bent their energies to mining, lumbering and even manufacturing. However, their ships were too small and the voyages were longer than was expected.

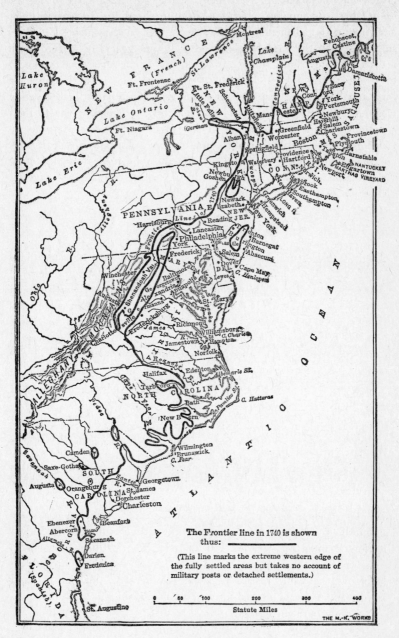

The Frontier line in 1740 is shown
thus: ▬▬▬

(This line marks the extreme western edge of
the fully settled areas but takes no account of
military posts or detached settlements.)

0   50   100   200   300   400
Statute Miles

THE M.-N. WORKS

Colonial Frontiers in 1740

Also, English merchants were not used to gathering large quantities of suitable food supplies which could be purchased for such expeditions and frequently adequate provisions were just not available. The result was that the first boatloads of colonists generally arrived with rations running short. Furthermore, many of the first-comers sought too energetically for gold which they never found, as in Virginia, or came too late in the season to plant crops, as in Plymouth. Starvation was too frequent a reality. Had not some of the Indians come to their aid, there would have been few if any survivors in some of the early ventures. These initial hardships and the great distance from Europe taught a much needed lesson. Provision must be made for cultivating the soil and for raising food. Agriculture became the almost universal occupation of the seventeenth century colonists.

Agricultural Economy

English agricultural habits had to be supplanted by a new technique adapted to the wilderness. In this task the Indian, though despised and feared, was of great assistance. He raised two plants which should be represented on the American coat-of-arms, so important were they in the founding of the nation. Maize, or Indian corn, could be grown in almost any portion of the thirteen colonies, it could be eaten in a pleasing variety of ways and it became the great food staple of the Atlantic Coast settlements. Tobacco, on the other hand, though it could be widely cultivated only in the southern colonies, was a great money maker and when in 1612 John Rolfe, Pocahontas' husband, raised the first crop in Virginia, it began its career as the dominant agricultural concern of that region. Under Indian tutelage the colonists learned to cultivate these two crops.

The first task was to cope with the great forests. Following Indian custom the colonists girdled the trees, planted seed corn in the spaces between and left the trunks to be removed later. The stumps could and did frequently remain indefinitely while crop after crop was sown and gathered in these uneven fields. The colonists following Indian directions planted the corn in hills with fish for fertilizer. Lessons in woodcraft from their strange and treacherous neighbors proved invaluable as the white man learned the Indian ways of hunting and trapping. Turkey and deer meat became staples of diet and furs provided clothing and income.

European ways of farming were by no means altogether abandoned. English food crops were attempted immediately. The first settlers in both Virginia and New England sought to raise grains of European origin. With oats, rye, barley and hay, they were successful, especially in New England, but with the great staple, wheat, there was trouble.

The soil of Virginia proved too rich and it grew rank, producing little grain. In New England, a successful crop proved very uncertain, the summers were too short and the soil thin and rocky. In fact, after the blight of 1644 and successive years its production declined. Corn was too easy and too useful a rival to invite further expensive experiment. The colonists not only made use of the peas, beans, pumpkins, squash, sweet potatoes and melons which the Indians cultivated, but introduced good English vegetables such as turnips, onions, carrots and cucumbers. The Pilgrims ordered seed for white potatoes from England as early as 1629, but the cultivation of this staple does not seem to have been common until after the Scotch-Irish immigration about 1700. Wild cherries, plums, grapes and various berries were brought under cultivation. Apple trees were imported from Europe and bore fruit at Boston as early as 1639. The possibilities of hard cider production soon made the apple the most popular colonial fruit and orchards a frequent feature of the landscape.

Live-stock was brought from Europe immediately. Cows, horses, sheep and hogs were sent to Virginia in 1609 and the New England settlers were not long in bringing over farm animals and poultry. In New England the long winters and lack of fodder made their care difficult and little attention was paid to maintaining good breeds. The condition of the cattle was generally miserable and the disease and mortality among them became dangerous to the profits and health of the colonists. Under such conditions, the dairying of this early period could not be very important, but hogs flourished on acorns, making salt pork an easy trading staple.

The acquisition of New York and the development of the middle colonies brought a more prosperous agricultural area under English control. This region had a soil much better adapted to diversified farming than New England and the farmers in it never became wedded to one crop as the Virginians and Marylanders had in the case of tobacco. The fertile limestone soil of the river valleys and hospitable climatic conditions favored the cultivation of wheat, which soon became the most important crop, averaging more bushels per acre than in England. Other grains, vegetables and fruits also flourished and were extensively cultivated while the good pastures made livestock raising more practical. Such fertility was a constant invitation to agriculture and many left their rocky New England farmsteads to profit thereby.

Intimately connected with the spread of agriculture was the distribution of land. Here two conflicting principles were immediately apparent representing the great social change that marked the times, i.e., the feudal and the individualistic. Various experiments in both were tried but wilderness conditions favored the latter and it finally triumphed. In both Virginia and Plymouth the land at first was considered the property of the company or association and the settlers as employees. Plots were assigned to each and the crop was supposed to be turned over to the authorities and in turn distributed to each according to his needs.

Agricultural production under such circumstances did not flourish; so in 1614 in Virginia and in 1623 in Plymouth it was abandoned and individuals were granted lands for their unrestricted use, at first as tenants, but before long as owners of the soil. When the Massachusetts Bay Company established itself at Boston and vicinity, land was apportioned to each settler, and when new towns or villages were established the colony granted land in fee simple to the new community. The townsmen apportioned some of their acres among themselves, in the meantime holding a reserve both as common pasturage or as provision for future comers. In these towns the inhabitants generally owned a small plot about their houses and a larger one away from the center where they cultivated their major crops. Under such a system each man's holdings were relatively small, rarely exceeding one hundred acres and therefore agricultural labor was less of a problem. A man and his sons could generally work a farm.

In the South likewise various methods of land distribution were tried. After the initial experiment of feudal control, Virginia granted land generously, offering it as an inducement to settlers. Those who came themselves received land and those who brought others with them obtained in addition for each man a so-called "head right" of fifty or one hundred acres, paying a small annual rent to the King generally in tobacco. In this way, large estates were made possible at least to a small number. In Maryland, the proprietor made grants in similar manner to stimulate migration; in so doing he maintained nominal ownership of the land, requiring a very small rental to be paid to him. As agricultural labor was a problem in Virginia and Maryland, these colonies were anxious to induce as many as would to come over as indentured servants. So it was provided that at the conclusion of his term, the servant became a landholder, receiving in Maryland a land grant automatically. In such manner in the seventeenth century, Virginia and Maryland became provinces where moderate sized farms were the order of the day; five hundred acres was an average holding in Virginia. Some large plantations there were and a few Negro slaves, but the day of that economy was not yet.

The middle colonies had a different system. When the English government captured the Dutch settlements they found the ownership of land vested in patroons, or proprietors of great estates, with many of the inhabitants in the Hudson Valley in a state of tenantry. Such a manorial system was continued by the English in New York, and the proprietors in New Jersey and later in Pennsylvania adopted the practice of seeking revenues from quit-rents, though there was little uniformity. Farms under this system were larger than in New England, and tenants more frequent. Tenantry, however, did not suit Americans and landlords were not happy. In practice much of the so-called rented land was freehold and the quit-rent was placed so low as to be a negligible charge. Nevertheless, even that was begrudged and oftentimes could not be collected. Landlords were European institutions not relished in free America and individual ownership became ever more extensive as the colonies grew. Feudal customs could not long survive in the new world.

Thus thousands of farms large and small were scattered over the colonial countryside. More than 90% of the colonials were farmers and their mode of life bred in them an intense individualism. These farmers of the seventeenth century, meanly equipped with spades, hoes, scythes, sickles, flails and only occasionally a plough, carried on their work in wasteful fashion. In the southern and middle colonies land was plentiful and there was no incentive to spare the soil. There was little or no fertilization or rotation of crops; tobacco was raised until the soil became exhausted, then a new field was started. New England agriculture was less haphazard. The rocky hillsides needed more care and then too the common ownership of reserve lands by the towns made them more economical. Some attempt was ventured at conservation by allowing the fields occasionally to lie fallow and to serve as pasture. All told it was a frontier agriculture, crude and wasteful, largely managed by struggling small farmers. The day of scientific agriculture or large scale management was still afar off.

The colonists had a minimum of social organization and lacked the services of distribution, cooperation, protection, and culture which today are taken for granted. The individual had to depend upon himself almost entirely. His few neighbors were cooperative and each aided the other as much as possible but the resources of all were limited. From their backers in England hardly anything could be expected. Therefore the colonists had to become self-reliant and equal to all emergencies or else perish. They must supply their own food, protection, clothing, entertainment and medical care. These primitive communities could provide none of those necessities. Unless a man maintained himself as a woodsman and trapper, there was but one really effective way to meet all those needs and that was to establish a home and a family.

A sturdily built house could serve as a fortification. A wife and children would provide the comfort, care and labor necessary to make the home a self-sustaining and measurably happy unit. The needs of colonial economy placed a premium upon large families. Early mar-

412

riages and many children were the rule and small boys and girls were trained to help in the manifold tasks which crude agricultural methods and the lack of labor-saving devices made necessary. The high birth rate, however, was somewhat offset by the heavy toll of disease and infant mortality, for childbearing was too frequent, there was no knowledge of child hygiene and midwifery was ignorant and superstitious. Nevertheless longevity records were made for the advantages of plain living, hard work in the open air and simple diet made the chances of those who survived their twenties favorable to a hearty old age, especially among the men. The family was the great institution of the colonists and all life centered around the fire-side.

The homes themselves in the seventeenth century gradually improved. In the early days the relative mildness of the southern climate had permitted Virginia settlers to content themselves with tents, bough shelters or rude board houses of no particular style. But brick was brought over as ballast as early as 1611 and became a construction staple. In New England, on the other hand, the winters were hard and more substantial building was necessary. English habits proved tenacious, and thatch for roofs which had been used in England where wood was scarce, continued to be used in America where wood was plentiful. Around Massachusetts Bay conical huts of tree limbs and sod, or thatched cottages, were the first dwellings; and the rough-hewn board houses of the Pilgrims persisted for many years. However crude and comfortless these primitive homes may seem today, it must be remembered that the average Englishman at that time was not much better off. In England, glass, chimneys, pewter and silverware and even beds and pillows, instead of straw pallets, had but recently come into use. In America, fuel and building material were plentiful.

By the close of the seventeenth century houses were usually very plain rectangular structures with a large chimney or two. In the northern colonies it was customary to construct steep roofs to shed the snow, and to provide cellars for winter storage, while in the planting areas the houses were built less sturdily and entirely above ground. At first, the windows were without glass and were closed by wooden shutters but as the communities prospered glass was imported or manufactured locally and hinged windows with diamond or oblong panes became more common. Thatched roofs and half-timbered houses filled in with brick or clay gave way to shingles and clapboards, while brick construction proved itself more attractive. As the colonists prospered they added rooms to their houses and built new dwellings and the old one or two room cabins were either enlarged by ells and wings or else relegated to more humble uses as barns or slave quarters.

These homes were very plainly furnished. The colonists brought with them some of the heavy ornate furniture common in England, carved cupboards, four post bedsteads and the like, but space was scarce on the crowded emigrant ships and a chest was often the only possession of the new arrival which could aid in furnishing a frontier home. Furniture was made at home or by the local carpenter. It was plain, solid and hard for there was little time which could be spent on ornamentation and fine work, and no money with which to support skilled cabinet makers. Tableware too was of the simplest, china almost unknown, glassware scarce. Wooden trenchers and bowls, pewter plates and mugs, or perhaps only gourds, knives, crude spoons and forks in a few instances; such was the dinner service of the colonists.

Each home thus equipped was a center of industry as well as an abode. The farmer and his wife had to make many things. He could very conveniently be a carpenter, blacksmith, shoemaker, tanner, brewer, weaver and cabinet maker. She was a spinner of thread, tailoress, nurse and even a doctor, as well as cook, baker, laundress, dressmaker and maid of all work. Each household tried to be self-sustaining, but certain things which could not be made in the home had to be procured.

Implements, weapons, better utensils and furniture, as well as many luxuries must be provided either by local ingenuity or by trade. Industry in the colonies had another stimulus: the hope of profit entertained by English backers, as well as the immediate needs of the colonists. The idea that the colonies were to prove a source of revenue to English stockholders died hard and before it perished a number of experiments in industry were hazarded. England was getting short of wood and there was hope of transferring the smelting and glass making works to the new world where fuel was plentiful. Ships' stores and potash for the woolen industry were also sought from the forests.

As a result of these hopes, artisans were transported to Virginia as early as 1608 to establish rude factories and that same year the colony sent back a cargo of iron ore, soap, ashes, lumber, pitch and tar. By 1620 three ironworks had been established and ships' stores, wainscoting, clapboards and potash had been sent back to England at intervals. The profits from tobacco were too tempting, however, and Virginia became a planting rather than an industrial colony. Manufacturing did not cease altogether but it was confined to a few artisans in the infrequent towns or to the plantations. Some planters maintained a number of workers who spun thread and wove cloth, tanned leather and made shoes, brewed and distilled. A well-equipped plantation might also have a carpenter, a glazier, a weaver, a blacksmith, a brickmaker and a cooper. In general it may be said that each farmer knew something of many trades and depended upon Europe when he wanted what he could not make or repair himself.

In New England and later in the middle colonies the same handicraft system prevailed, with the colonial farmer a jack of all trades.

But in this northern region towns were more frequent and artisans could make a living plying their trades. Many of the towns held out special inducements to shoemakers, carpenters, blacksmiths and the like to settle among them and Boston soon supported even a goldsmith, in fact, several of them. Besides agriculture was so difficult that New England was forced to manufacture in order to have something to trade for the European goods they needed. Lumbering and ship building were almost immediately undertaken, a saw mill was built in what was to be New Hampshire perhaps as early as 1623 and ship yards were established in the best seaports. Mills for grinding corn being indispensable windmills succeeded the crude mortar and pestle and then by 1633 a water power mill was built at Dorchester. Salt was manufactured by various processes. A tannery was built in Lynn and John Winthrop of that place worked out an ambitious scheme for establishing an iron furnace, which by 1648 was producing eight tons a week.

Cloth making was also started immediately. Flax was introduced in Massachusetts and linen was manufactured therefrom. However, it was a difficult process and woolen cloth was found to be easier to make. Farmers began to keep sheep and make homespun. In 1643 some fullers came over from Yorkshire and established a fulling mill at Rowley; by 1675 New England was exporting woolen cloth. There were few things which the New Englanders did not try and Yankee ingenuity became a byword.

Trade developed hand in hand with industry. The colonies needed implements, arms and ammunition, clothes, leather, glass and in the early years even food. Regular importations from the mother country therefore commenced at once. As they became better established, trade in food, clothes and leather was not so necessary but the importation of luxuries and foreign wares became more important. The southern colonies depended on tobacco to pay their European balances after the first few years. The elaborate machinery whereby the planters exported their crop to London agents, who credited them with the proceeds and then filled their orders for European goods, necessarily left them in debt to their agents and much dissatisfied with British merchants. These debts were a continual source of grievance.

In New England trading was bound to supersede all other economic activity in profit making possibilities. There was so little that Europe wanted that concentration on fish, fur and lumber was necessary to provide sufficient purchasing power in England. Plymouth started it by exporting a cargo of beaver skins and clapboards and exports steadily grew. The waters off the New England coast abounded in fish and a race of fishermen rapidly congregated and provided cargoes for export to the Azores and the Catholic countries of southern Europe. Fish and lumber, in the form of barrel or pipe staves, freighted many a trading vessel which went to those ports and came back laden with wine. Furs were also a profitable item and New England trappers sought the beaver and other fur-bearing animals so that the merchants might send their pelts to Europe.

Intercolonial trade, in course of time, became a source of profit. At first the New England people had disposed of their small surplus at home to the constant stream of new-comers who needed to purchase supplies and labor upon arrival. But by 1640 that stream had diminished in size, prices fell and there was an economic crisis, perhaps the first in British America, during 1641-2. The enterprising now sought to restore their prosperity by turning to intercolonial trade. New England had more to offer her neighbors especially in the West Indies than she had to sell to England. Corn, salt pork, pickled beef, flour, butter, lumber and horses were sent down in exchange for sugar, indigo, cotton, dyewood, hides, cocoa and Spanish iron. The southern colonies, too, could join in the traffic offering tobacco and provisions. Merchants prospered in this trade and moderate wealth became a dream possible of fulfillment. The lure of profit which had been destroyed by early hardship was revived.

Learning Self-Government

The great American achievement of the seventeenth century was not to be the result of economic prowess. The peculiar genius of the American colonists was demonstrated far more significantly by their success in organizing communities. The talent that these colonists possessed for creating "bodies politick" which could survive and grow into stronger and more effective states was the dominating factor in the evolution of the American nation.

The propensity for community building developed even before the emigrants left England. In fact, the promoters of the experiments gave more thought to the organization and control of their projects than to the physical well-being of their colonists. England was in the throes of a century of political planning and changing and the colonial schemes reflected this creative activity. Each enterprise went through a preliminary stage of paper planning in England and came to America with various preconceived schedules. True they seldom proved immediately practical and sometimes hindered more than they helped; the wilderness rather than the English imagination dictated the character of these social structures.

The original plans for some of the colonies provided for extensive control to be exercised from London by proprietors or promoters who knew little or nothing about American conditions. Their instructions left slight discretion to those who were to lead the expeditions. Obviously such plans were not practical, the American shores were too far away and communication was too uncertain and too slow; a letter, if conditions were right, might receive an answer in six months. A wilderness outpost could not be administered in such fashion and self-government was inevitable, though it was not achieved without some experiments in the contrary method.

The Virginia colony was the first to obtain political responsibility. In the first plan, the King had intended to supervise the London Company through a council sitting in London. This council was to appoint a council in Virginia which was to rule strictly according to instructions received periodically from the capital. Those who were to make up the bulk of the population were considered as hired servants of the company without political privileges. Such a system did not work very well. In order to stimulate migration and to produce a better spirit in the colony itself, a measure of self-government was established in 1619, whereby representatives of the colonists were permitted to participate in legislation. The colonists entered into their new governmental responsibilities vigorously and even though in 1625 King James took over the colony and made it Crown property, he and his successors made no change in the representative system. The King's governor frequently sought to limit the functions of the assembly and tried to govern for long periods without it, but the institution remained. In Maryland, too, a legislature developed shortly after the founding which was allowed by Lord Baltimore, for he soon learned that self-government in local affairs at least was necessary to attract settlers.

In New England, self-government flourished from the beginning. The Pilgrims were a religious congregation used to some self-government and on the voyage to America they formed a "civil body politick" with a formal covenant in which the power to enact just and equal laws was definitely set forth. The Massachusetts Bay colony was a corporation with a charter and government by stockholders. As outsiders came to the colony they demanded a share in the government and within four years the Company was forced to organize a legislature composed in part of the representatives of the growing number of towns. Connecticut, New Haven and Rhode Island set up their own governments and like the Massachusetts colonies elected their own officials. In these arrangements the English Crown must perforce acquiesce for there was trouble enough at home to bar any interference. Thus a fashion was set which all the later colonies followed.

Progress toward self-government was not marked solely by the creation of colonial assemblies. There were other laboratories more numerous and more fruitful which made extensive contributions to American political experiment, these were the local units within the various colonies. In 1634 Virginia established a county and parish system of local organization. Under this system which was also used in Maryland and the Carolinas, English customs were taken over bodily. Local control was vested in the hands of the more influential landowners, who as justices of the peace and vestrymen, gave direction to affairs much as the local squires did at home.

In New England, conditions were different, here the colonists had invented the local unit known as the town. The colonists in this region were mostly townsmen and also many of them had migrated in congregations. Therefore, this town church organization was naturally followed in the new world. The same people often composed town and church and they assumed to govern themselves without any particular authorization. The Massachusetts Bay Company charter had no provision for local government or the creation of towns but even as the chartered company immediately transformed itself into a self-governing colony so the local communities likewise assumed political functions. The center of the scheme was the congregational meeting which became known as the town meeting. Here all might come and speak but on most matters voting was confined to the freemen who in general must be church members. The town meeting managed town affairs, especially the common land, elected representatives to the legislature and chose local officials in large numbers. The town was also the unit in New Hampshire, Connecticut and Rhode Island.

When New Netherland was captured and Pennsylvania and New Jersey organized, a mixture of local institutions evolved. Community functions were divided between towns or villages and counties, but in these instances, too, localities either were granted or assumed a generous measure of authority. In such wise self-government through representative assembly and town meetings or county supervisors became a reality; but these colonies were still too near Europe to be really democratic, church membership or property-holding were among the qualifications for voting and universal manhood suffrage existed nowhere. The communities were generally controlled by small groups of those who were well-to-do. The aristocratic ideas so well recognized in England were not forgotten. Nevertheless, the germ of democracy was there.

Having gained self-government, the colonists experimented with it actively. Especially in New England, there was a strong desire to order the community along exalted spiritual lines by means of government; a holy commonwealth was to be established according to Biblical precept. Not only in the New England colonies where the professed ideal of a holy commonwealth would lead one to expect a stern measure of control, but in the southern colonies as well, the statute books provided evidence of strict ideals of human conduct. When the first Virginia legislature met in 1619 it enacted laws against Sabbath breaking, gambling, idleness and intoxication and aimed to curb extravagance in personal attire by assessing local taxes according to the clothes which a single man or a married couple possessed. Massachusetts and Connecticut were even stricter. However, no locality regulates its conduct so much by statute law as by community habit. Consequently, in the southern colonies statutes of this nature largely fell into disuse because the temper of the people was altogether contrary to the spirit of these early laws. In New England, however, such legislation fitted in more exactly with popular habit and thus social approval lent force to the laws.

Compared with the legal system of England, the laws dealing with crime were humane. The death penalty was little used. Men were too scarce to be slaughtered for minor crimes, besides there was not much to steal. Death was reserved for murder, treason and rebellion though in New England it was prescribed for heresy and witchcraft. A few examples of burning at the stake are recorded and in 1659-60, four Quakers were hanged at Boston after they refused to be banished. Massachusetts Bay Colony had come to America to enjoy a society of its own ordering and those who disagreed with this order were not welcome, witness Roger Williams and Mrs. Hutchinson. Sometimes mutilation, such as cutting off ears or tongues, or branding were inflicted, but quite generally, ridicule was looked upon as a valuable punishing agency. Many a culprit was condemned to sit in the stocks or stand in the pillory to enjoy the jibes of his fellow citizens and an occasional application of mud, soft fruit, stale eggs or even stones. Prisons were rare, crime was scarce, and the criminal legislation was largely designed to keep the indentured servants in hand.

Laws regulating economic enterprise were designed to protect the consumer by maintaining standard goods and just prices. Poverty and lack of surplus goods made colonial lawmakers seek to ensure if possible an adequate supply of staples. Embargoes were frequently laid upon the export of necessities and bounties and monopolies were granted to encourage production or manufacture. The rampant individualism and laissez-faire of a later date were foreign to seventeenth century colonial legislation; the consumer and the needs of the community were not thought to be helped by such theories.

The colonists must needs use their self-governing powers to protect their communities from external danger. In the South there were some difficulties with Spanish neighbors, but in general the Indians were the chief menace. In the early days, Virginia suffered a good deal but after 1645 there was comparative peace. In New England conditions were reversed. After early success, misunderstandings and bloodshed developed. In 1637 the Pequot war broke out and in 1675-6, a larger conflict, known as King Philip's War. These dangers and fear of trouble, with Dutch and French on the borders, caused an interesting experiment in colonial cooperation. After the Pequot War and a boundary dispute between Massachusetts and Plymouth, the latter two colonies with Connecticut and New Haven joined in 1643 to organize the United Colonies of New England. It was a loose federation with a decided guarantee of the independence of each unit; but some matters of mutual concern, especially defence, were placed under the control of joint commissioners. The organization was not very effective, the members did not easily agree, and after King Philip's defeat, it became inactive. Nevertheless, it had inaugurated a precedent for inter-colonial union.

Self-government flourished. Massachusetts absorbed New Hampshire (1641-1643) and Maine (1652-1658) and was practically independent; so were Plymouth, Connecticut, New Haven and Providence Plantations (Rhode Island). In the proprietary and royal colonies, the settlers were ever ready to assume new powers and to quarrel with authority. In Virginia resentment against the arbitrary rule of royal government produced Bacon's rebellion in 1676 when a group of back country planters, discouraged by a depression sought to lighten the exactions of an oppressive governor.

The Stuarts could do little to curb this spirit. The most ambitious effort was made by King James II in 1686 when he combined Massachusetts, New Hampshire, Plymouth, Connecticut and Rhode Island under one governor. Two years later, he joined New York and New Jersey to this group under a newly organized Dominion of New England. This scheme was cut short the same year when James was deposed. Ominous of future difficulty was the beginning of parliamentary interest in the colonies. To protect English merchants against Dutch rivalry Parliament had begun to experiment with navigation laws, greatly restricting the freedom of colonial trade by requiring that it be largely confined to the British empire and cut off from lucrative foreign dealings. This interference with colonial merchants in the next century was to bear unexpected fruit. In the meantime, the colonies continued their lessons in self-government. Quite unconsciously these scattered settlements were developing a self-sufficient attitude which might some day prove incompatible with British exactions upon their loyalty.

Cultural Lag

While the tasks of finding food and shelter and organizing effective government may have seemed all preoccupying to the colonists, they were doing much besides which was of greatest importance in constituting a new society. They were caring for many other of the universal needs of mankind by creating American social customs.

In organization as in environment, the new society was to be fundamentally different from anything European for the English customs which were least adapted for transplanting were those of ranks and orders. To be sure some attempts were made to establish social distinctions; in the Carolinas an attempt was even made to create a colonial nobility, but in general, few who had English titles or social privileges migrated. Some who were gentlemen bore the title "master." Skilled workmen and freeholders were known as "goodmen." Such ranking persisted for a while, especially in New England, and certain regulations were instituted to make these distinctions more apparent, by limiting the finery of those of the lesser ranks and permitting the gentlemen and their families more privileges of adornment. Penalties were sometimes enacted for transgressions by reducing men from one estate to another. Such a system could not long survive, however, in a country where land was so easily obtainable; and the democracy of widely and generally distributed property ownership gradually replaced the old European scheme.

Pleasant social customs were relieving the monotony of hard work and danger, especially in the South. Here there were few towns and people lived widely scattered. But they made opportunities for society. Guests were pleasant diversions and southern hospitality became famous; visiting, dancing and card playing were much enjoyed pastimes. Court days when the planters gathered at the county seats, race meets, and hunts, all provided occasions for hilarious recreation.

In the North, the need for recreation was met in a different way. In New York there was the jolly town life which the Dutch had inaugurated but in the remainder of the colonies the atmosphere was decidedly that which the Puritan founders of New England had created. The center of community life outside the home was the church. Each town was not so much a "body politick" as it was a congregation. The founders had come to their new and difficult environment to carry out a serious purpose—to perform the will of God as revealed to them through the Bible and by the manifestation of God's Holy Spirit to them personally.

Life to many of these serious minded people was a continual searching for a knowledge of the will of God. Their belief that each was foredestined either for salvation or damnation gave much cause for introspection; only by the searchings of the heart and the detection of signs of grace could one be sure of salvation. Consequently, many sought continually for sure signs of their regeneration. The little time they could spend away from work, they wished to use in study of the Scriptures, inward searching and meeting together to hear from their minister his words of admonition, advice and revelation. It was not so much that they disliked pleasure, harmless and otherwise, but they felt it to be a waste of time and a distraction from this all-absorbing quest for the knowledge of their souls' salvation. This vital interest in religion combined with their belief that society should be God's holy commonwealth, made pleasure of a frivolous and care-free sort undesirable in the early days of most New England communities. The church was the place where they met each other frequently and in a very sober and decorous sense it was the social as well as the religious center.

In such communities north and south, preoccupied as they were with the difficulties of colonial life there was little chance for the development of cultural interests. Life must be maintained and man's creative abilities were too fully engrossed in conquering the frontier to have time or energy for art, music or literature. Such encouragement as there was for culture came largely from religion.

In the South there was little or no attempt to develop literary tastes. Some few had brought English books but there was not even an effective religious interest to stimulate the expression of ideas. The attempted establishment of the church in Virginia and Maryland was not very successful. The parishes were too large, the people too poor to provide either adequate congregations or adequate support for the clergy. The result was a few churches inadequately served by men often ill-qualified for the ministry. During the seventeenth century all attempts at ecclesiastical reform or cultural improvement were blocked by the unfavorable economic and social conditions produced by the straggling plantation system.

In New England, on the other hand, a definite cultural foundation was laid. The Puritan had an idea, a definite and strongly held purpose governed his enterprise. His coming was urged by a creative impulse. After much thought and study, the leaders had created a concept of an ideal community and they were possessed of a distinct and active, though rather narrow, literary and intellectual interest. They talked and listened to others talk, many of their leaders were of the clergy. So pronounced were they in their views that there was quite naturally constant disagreement from the start of their enterprise and the production of a copious literature of religious controversy.

The ministers of the churches were the leaders in thought and the writers of the day. They were not very familiar with current English literature, seemingly knowing little of Shakespeare, Ben Jonson or the later day Milton; but they did know the Bible and Puritan literature. Their calling provided them the opportunity for speaking extensively and frequently and as the audiences they faced were intelligent and able to criticize, careful preparation was desirable. Much sermon writing was the result and after the introduction of the first printing press at Cambridge in 1639 many a disquisition was printed. Before long, differences of opinion led to much controversy and John Cotton,

Roger Williams and Thomas Hooker wrote and wrote again, disputing over doctrinal points and more fundamental questions such as freedom of worship.

But the clergymen and the Puritan lay leaders were statesmen as well as church members. Their primary purpose had been the establishment of a religious utopia. So, much of the planning had to be recorded and then of course there was more controversy, as advocates of theocracy and democracy matched their wits in pamphlet wars. The clerical penmen also must justify their religious and political independence to the English authorities and the same men that were attempting to stamp out dangerous heresies in the colonies must themselves disprove the charge of too great liberalism and independence made from England.

A more general literary tendency by no means confined to New England arose out of the novelty of the colonial adventure and the desire for publicity. Colonization brought with it a flood of new experiences and quite a number, whether John Smith in Virginia or William Bradford in Plymouth, were moved to set down their impressions. Descriptions were sent back to England and published; others like Bradford's never saw the light of day until centuries later.

Of light literature there was none except in the form of some scattering verse. Nathaniel Ward, Michael Wigglesworth and Anne Bradstreet sought to cultivate inspiration and some of Mistress Bradstreet's poetry is pure delight. Wilderness conquest and state building, however, left little opportunity for *belles lettres* and the Puritan's seriousness of purpose and dislike of symbolism gave him little appreciation of, or sympathy for, art. Newspapers and periodicals did not exist.

The greatest cultural achievement of the seventeenth century was the establishment of a lasting interest in public education. In the South settlement was too scattered for much community schooling. The children were generally taught at home or in small private school houses, maintained very informally by the families in the vicinity, and conducted sometimes by a tutor, sometimes by the parish clergyman or lay reader, sometimes by one of the mothers. In the North, town conditions and Puritan ideals made a more elaborate system possible and desirable.

The Puritans were very much interested in an intelligent and literate community. Their religious authority was based upon Biblical precepts and their community ideal was a group of people able to read, write and debate. Children therefore must be taught to read and write, and for good business ciphering was also necessary. Many of the Puritans were English university men, clergy and layity, and in the early years they provided the schools. By 1647 the Massachusetts Bay colony was ready to make common schools mandatory and passed a law requiring each town to provide one. The law was not always obeyed and within twenty years after its passage enthusiasm for education at public expense had somewhat waned; but the ideal had been established and was later to flourish mightily.

More ambitious even were some in the Bay Colony who saw the need for higher education. So in 1636 at Cambridge a college was established, soon called Harvard after its first benefactor, which after some initial hardships and under the enlightened leadership of Henry Dunster graduated its first class in 1642. A respectable number of the New England colonists were university men, mostly from Cambridge, and they cherished this new Cambridge experiment and watched its growth, little dreaming of the elaborate structure of university education which was to develop from it.

There could be little achievement in science in a region so far away from scientific interest. Nevertheless, the new world did lead to some elementary contribution because the strange flora and fauna so interested educated observers, like the Reverend John Banister and his clerical brother, John Clayton, both of Virginia, that they made reports which were published in the transactions of the Royal Society in England. In New England the desire to convert and Christianize the natives led to another scientific enterprise. John Eliot and his colaborers in this vineyard studied the Indian language intensively and accomplished the tremendous task of reducing it to written form and translating the Bible into this strange speech.

Medical science remained very defective despite the great amount of need. Epidemics such as yellow fever and bubonic plague, climatic diseases such as malaria and the results of hardship and exposure found the colonists with little means to resist them. Doctors were few and such that were in the colonies were often nothing more than quacks. Medical knowledge, even the best in Europe, seems today to have been grossly inadequate and ridden with superstitions and horrid dosings. The colonial doctor resorted to vile concoctions which often made the patient much sicker than had he been left alone or else resorted to blood-letting and thus weakened him at a time when he needed his strength most. Worst of all was the prevalent belief in witchcraft which convinced many a sick person that he was bewitched and made him resort to charms and hocus-pocus, even to Indian witch doctors or their practices. The best treatment devised was probably the simple rules and herb remedies which one house-owner handed on to another and while they may not have helped much, still did not have the decidedly harmful effects which the crude medical practice of the day produced.

In the arts as well there was little room for interest. Boston was able to support several goldsmiths, notably John Hull, who made silver cups, bowls, tankards and other utensils in a manner which gave them the distinction of being the first craftsmen of taste in the new society. Also, there was a small number of portrait painters. Scattering examples of their work have come down to us among the few artistic survivals of the time. Such indulgence was possible only by the most prosperous and had their taste been better it would not have availed them. Artists were few and they of the sign painter variety who seldom produced anything of merit. They are the American "primitives" however, and as such are cherished. Only by death was any sculptural tendency stimulated and the curious gravestones of the period with skulls, cherubs and willow trees adorning the biographical mementoes of the dead, are our first contributions to the art of Phidias and Michael Angelo.

Thus, the close of the seventeenth century saw the foundations of American society firmly laid. Europeans, mostly English, equipped with the settled habits of an old society, had come to a wilderness. They had adjusted their habits sufficiently to sustain life and to begin the accumulation of wealth. They had created a series of self-governing communities wherein might be found approximations to democracy. It was a great achievement, but it had not been accomplished without great cost. Not only had many lives and much capital been lost, but culturally there had been a great sacrifice. The conquest of the wilderness had meant the abandonment of many European habits, customs and skills, of which succeeding generations knew less and less as they adopted new ways more fitted to their environment. Most important was the destruction of folk-art. Thus, because of this cultural lag, the colonists were much worse off from the standpoint of skill in the arts at the end of the first century than at the beginning. The frontier was a destroying agent and fostered a materialistic and practical viewpoint which was to become a predominant characteristic of the American people.

Socially life in small and isolated communities or on scattered farms was the chief characteristic of the seventeenth century existence. Individuals lived in practically self-sustaining social units, three thousand miles across the ocean from England. The small settlements themselves had little to do with one another, roads were few and poor, bridges generally non-existent. For slow horseback and boat travel, distances were great and there was little journeying or communication among the colonists. The whole persuasion of seventeenth century life was to urge the settlers to stay within a very circumscribed circle. It was still the day of small things and local interests, of preoccupation with the all absorbing problems of simple existence. But the beginning of a new and experimental society had been made, a society in which bulked large the rights and responsibilities of the individual, as a shareholder in a common enterprise.

CHAPTER III

AMERICAN FOLKWAYS

By the beginning of the eighteenth century it was apparent that the English colonial experiment was unique, presenting a marked contrast to those of the Spanish and French. While the colonies of these latter powers were prone to depend upon Europe, the English were becoming in large measure independent. There were numerous reasons for this. Not only was there an initial racial and cultural difference between the settlers, but the English had not intermarried with the Indians as had the Spanish and French. More important was the fact that the English mother country neglected the American settlements and forced them to shift for themselves. Under these conditions the pioneers of the first century had laid the foundation for an independent society. Their work, however, was but the beginning.

Creating an American Culture

In the years from 1690 to 1763 many changes were to be wrought. Now that the colonies were stronger and less preoccupied with the first hard problems of wilderness life, the American imagination was freed. By the end of the first century, many of the colonists were of the second or third generation of those born in the new world and were possessed of native familiarity with American conditions. They were no longer so cumbered with European training and habits as their elders had been. They were ready to assume social characteristics which marked them as American rather than British. This tendency was accelerated by the fact that the coming of many more non-English was creating a decidedly cosmopolitan atmosphere.

Conditions in Europe were encouraging a new series of migrations to America. Louis XIV of France had inaugurated policies which were to increase the population of the English colonies decidedly. First he determined to drive Protestantism out of his realm in 1685 and shortly thereafter he invaded Germany and ravished the Rhine Valley. These policies caused French and Germans in large numbers to flee to America. French Huguenots sought to preserve their religion in the new world and became useful citizens in several of the colonies. The Germans fleeing from their ruined homes came first to New York but as they were badly treated there they soon heeded the persuasion of William

Penn's agent. Extensive settlements of Pennsylvania Germans were made near Philadelphia. Others went into the Shenandoah Valley and other regions of the southern back country.

About 1700 another group appeared. The Scotch colonists, settled in the north of Ireland at the beginning of the sixteen-hundreds, had prospered economically to such an extent that their industries, especially textiles, had become a menace to English manufactures. Parliament listened to the complaints of home capitalists and placed numerous restrictions upon the Scotch-Irish trade. The loss of livelihood thereupon persuaded many to look to migration to America as a solution of their difficulties.

Other strains, Welsh, Irish, Scotsmen, Hebrews and Swiss came in less pronounced numbers and mingled their enterprise and varied experiences with those of other groups. The population increased rapidly. In 1690 there had been 200,000, by 1710, 350,000 and in 1760 it is estimated that there were 1,500,000 in the thirteen colonies. The size of the influx of non-English meant that the new American society was not to be formed entirely according to an English pattern but was to be a cosmopolitan fusion, a product of the melting pot.

This new American society was marked by more varied interests and endeavors. There was now time to give some thought and energy to culture which had been sadly neglected in the press of wilderness conquest. The various colonies were more experienced in the settled ways of long established society and there was to be found a more apparent difference than formerly between rich and poor. Not that this difference was hard and fast, for there was ample opportunity for many a poor man to become rich, but at least in the older regions the former levelling of frontier poverty had passed away. The great mass of the people lived lives which were simple and lacking in unusual features. A larger proportion than in the first century were artisans, small tradesmen and laborers in the towns, who dwelt in plain houses, simply furnished, with church or tavern as social centers. Humble as was their lot most of them lived as independent householders and heads of families. They suffered from no "inferiority complexes."

The great majority of the provincials, however, were farmers and lived the drab, hardworking lives of those who till the soil. Farmhouses, whether north or south, were still much as they had been in the preceding century, perhaps a little larger and more sturdily built. Out on the frontier a new type of dwelling was becoming the fashion, for the log cabin was coming into its own. In all of these homes furniture was scanty and plain, and there was little attempt at ornamentation. Only in weaving the table and bed coverings did the colonial housewives strive for artistic effect; and the patterns and designs worked out in their farm kitchens have become prized heirlooms. Clothes were made

HOMES OF AVERAGE AMERICANS IN THE EIGHTEENTH CENTURY

Guilford, Conn.; Piscataway, N. J.; Yorktown, Va.

to wear as long as possible and to keep out the weather. A good suit
or a best dress would last two frugal generations, and a watch and a
ring or two might be the only jewelry owned by an entire family.
There was not much variety in life and in some communities existence
was already embittered by a sense of unjust treatment at the hands
of the more favored aristocracy of wealth.

In the more populous centers there had emerged a substantial class
of wealthy and educated people who took the lead in their communities
and formed a provincial "society." Their wealth and position led them
to seek greater display and comfort and in seeking them they established
standards of taste which were to be the first cultural achievements of
the American colonists. They demanded better quality and were able to
pay for it. Their desire for elegant homes and fine furniture brought
about the return of the skill in architecture, cabinet work and decoration which the frontier had for a time almost obliterated.

Pride in building vigorously asserted itself. In the towns fine square
houses of wood, brick and stone in the Georgian style pleased the eye;
and on the great estates north and south manor and plantation houses
became show places. No pains were spared in their decoration; all sorts
of fine woodwork and plaster ornamentation were created by workmen
who had their own sense of beauty and plenty of time in which to
utilize it. The decorated mantels of wood or marble, the carved wainscoting, the graceful stairways which these architects and artisans created
have stood the test of time and are widely copied in modern construction. Public edifices too, were created with the same taste and skill.
Churches were rebuilt in the new style of Christopher Wren and their
picturesque spires and beautiful porches decorated many a village green.
Each colony must have its government buildings and their capitols frequently were evidence of the talents of budding architects who understood the "colonial" style. The interiors of fine buildings, public as
well as private, were equipped with furniture made according to the
graceful designs of the English cabinet makers of the day, copied and
often improved by American artisans. It was an age of simple beauty
and dignity.

Art was given the patronage of the wealthy. There was a proud
demand for portraiture. No longer was the featuring of the dignitaries,
divine and secular, entrusted to the local sign painter. A number of
commonplace painters with not enough talent to become distinguished
in their European homes, but sufficiently trained to make an impression
upon the colonials, migrated to America and prospered. Charles Bridges
came from England to Virginia where he travelled between 1730 and
1750 from mansion to mansion and painted wealthy planters like Col.
Byrd and their families, in the style of Sir Peter Lely. Gustavus Hes-
selius, of Swedish origin, meanwhile painted in Maryland and Pennsyl-

vania, going outside the realm of portraiture at least once with a "Last Supper" to decorate a Maryland parish church. Jeremiah Theüs, a Swiss, spent most of his American sojourn in South Carolina. The best trained of these migrants was John Smibert, a Scotsman who had studied in London and Italy. He settled in Boston and not only worked on portraits but reproduced old masters and conveyed artistic enthusiasm to at least one young American.

The creative spirit of the colonies was working to produce its own talent. A few American youths felt the urge to artistic expression and were allowed to follow their bent. Robert Feke born in 1705 on Long Island, found support in Boston and Philadelphia and though self-trained, produced some excellent portraits. More important were John Singleton Copley and Benjamin West. The former was the young Bostonian influenced by Smibert and Feke. He developed into a brilliant portrait artist and when the Revolution threatened, loyalist that he was, he removed to London where he became famous. Benjamin West was born at the same time near Philadelphia. He had the opportunity to study in Italy and then settled in London where, like Copley, he found fame. Some of his large historical canvasses came back to the United States and a number of young Americans went to London to study under him; some of them were to win renown. Patronage from the rich was encouraging the development of artistic creation. America had at length become able to support and train a few youths in other than practical occupations.

Not only the decoration of homes, but of the person demonstrated the quality of American taste. The dress of the wealthy elaborately copied the fashions of Georgian England. Silk, lace, fine linen and embroidery were the style for both men and women; and the ornate fashion of men's attire, in those days of knee-breeches and silk stockings, embroidered waistcoats and silver shoe buckles, is quite beyond the imagination of our modern day. Hair dressing too was an art and the expensive powdered coiffures of the women and the curled wigs of the men made an imposing showing. Much penetrating perfume was an evident substitute for bathing.

The diet of the wealthy was as elaborate as their fashions. A great deal of heavy food to eat and much to drink weighted down the menus of the day. A profusion of dishes loaded every fashionable table and the sideboards groaned with the variety of decanters, bottles and queer shaped flasks which were spread forth to promote good fellowship and aid overworked digestions.

In New England, society was more staid, with less amusement and more talk, but in New York and Charleston gay social functions marked the governor's court, regular "seasons" were danced through, games of chance were popular, and race meets were centers of social attraction.

EIGHTEENTH CENTURY MANSIONS

Stratford, Conn.; Germantown, Pa.; on the James River, Va.

In the plantation districts there was much visiting and many a gay house party would seem quite modern to youth of the present day.

The increasing wealth and leisure produced a demand for more varied amusements and the colonials caught their first glimpses of the American stage. The Puritan atmosphere and the crudeness of the frontier did not permit the theatre an easy start or a flourishing career. But despite the prejudice, the opposition of powerful groups in the various important communities, and the lack of theatrical traditions, wandering troupes of players left faint traces of their labors in the annals of the early eighteenth century. The first theatre seems to have been located at Williamsburg, Virginia, as early as 1716, and playhouses were advertised in New York and Philadelphia in 1732 and 1742. Most of the actors and the plays came from abroad but in 1767 the first American play, Thomas Godfrey's *Prince of Parthia,* made its appearance upon Philadelphia boards. These ventures, however, did not mean that interest in the drama was widespread or that the theatre was popular. Only in the larger seaboard cities was there any attempt at play production and that was sporadic, generally hampered by legal restrictions and social disapproval. To large numbers of people theatre-going was sinful and socially undesirable.

Changes in taste and in the standards of living could not fail to have their effect upon such an important colonial interest as religion. While Anglican and Congregational churches still were legally the state churches in several of the colonies, their sway was less potent. Tendencies were at work in the direction of diversity and toleration. The heretical sects of the first century which had been persecuted in New England were now firmly organized in the middle region. The Quakers had a colony of their own, where they welcomed all faiths; and in Pennsylvania, New Jersey, New York and Rhode Island, the home of religious toleration, the Baptists were flourishing. French Protestant churches were organized by the Huguenots; Jewish synagogues were established. The German Protestants flocked to America in a great variety of sects, Moravian, Lutheran, Dunkard, Mennonite and others. Anglicanism, too, spread into the northern colonies.

During the eighteenth century a number who were indifferent to or dissatisfied with Calvinism, but who were interested in religion, discovered the Church of England and entered its membership. The spread of Anglicanism in the North was aided materially by the work of an organization established by the English church known as the Society for the Propagation of the Gospel in Foreign Parts, commonly called the S.P.G., which sent missionaries to America to preach and build up parishes. Their work was effective, especially in the middle colonies, and grew so that agitation started for the appointment of an American bishop, to have charge of colonial religious matters. Naturally the Congregational clergy were suspicious of this move, as an attempt to establish Anglicanism in New England, and warned their membership against it. The bishop was never appointed but fear of such a step was a factor in stimulating colonial discontent.

The multiplication of faiths did much to make religious toleration an institution even in the Puritan colonies. No longer were Anglicans, Baptists and Quakers in Massachusetts and Connecticut taxed to support the established churches, which left them less sufficiently supplied and private contributions had to be encouraged. Nevertheless, Sunday attendance at some church still remained obligatory and in Connecticut "outsiders" were still denied the vote.

More dangerous to religion than schism and sectarianism was the tendency toward unbelief. In Europe it was the "Age of Reason" and rationalism attracted growing numbers. "Natural Rights," and "man's understanding," as described by Locke and Hobbes and other of the prophets of the then "new psychology" and political science, seemed more convincing as an explanation and a guide than the laws of God as interpreted by the clergy. Science, too, as vitalized by the physical laws formulated by Newton, seemed so authentic that God's guidance was no longer necessary. Common sense as developed by Benjamin Franklin, with shrewd wit in pithy sayings, took the place with some of the more exacting Old Testament ethics. Natural law displaced Calvinism in the beliefs of those who either were attracted by the apparent clarity of the new ideas or were tired of the older and sterner discipline.

Prosperity, religious diversity and unbelief were undermining the strength of religion in a manner which could not be ignored. Devout clergy and laymen began to take thought and search for a means of revival. They did not seek in vain for the people, especially in New England, though they may have fallen away through prosperity and indifference, for the most part had been rigorously trained and needed only a quickening appeal to restore them to their former loyalty. Besides the Germans, Scotch-Irish and French Huguenots brought a great contribution of evangelical zeal which made their example potent. The anxieties and uncertainties of the French wars and the economic depression of the early years of the eighteenth century also contributed their influence to cause a renewed searching of hearts.

The country was in a frame of mind ready for a great revival and when in 1734 Jonathan Edwards began preaching a return to personal faith and sinless life, his pleas fell upon willing ears. Up and down the country the thrill of revival spread. Not only did Edwards exhort effectively and vitally in New England, but in the middle colonies Presbyterian, Baptist and Dutch Reformed clergymen were preaching fervent evangelical sermons. George Whitefield, a forerunner of a new group later to be known as Methodists, was travelling through the colonies drawing crowds to hear his sermons; and just at the end of the period (1766) the Methodist church was organized in New York. Into the southern soil, especially in North Carolina where the established church was moribund, and in the back country of Virginia, evangelical religion spread and rooted itself firmly. This "Great Awakening," as it is called, stirred people to violent emotional outbursts and shook many from the mental lethargy which the prosperity, succeeding the hard pioneer struggles, had produced. It was a sort of mental housecleaning, preparing the colonists for the strange and unexpected happenings and the dangerous experiments of the years encircling 1776. It has been called the "way-shower" of the Revolution.

Education was still closely allied with religion and reflected its condition. The diversity of sects was especially influential in directing the progress of higher education. The various denominations were much interested in the proper instruction of their young people in their beliefs and felt it desirable to establish independent colleges. The multiplication of religions very directly affected education because as the sects prospered they became more interested in proper instruction. The more orthodox Congregationalists feared that Harvard was becoming too liberal; so in 1701 Yale was founded. Anglicans established William and Mary in Virginia in 1693, and Kings (later Columbia) in New York in 1754. Presbyterians founded Princeton in 1746; the Baptists, Rhode Island College (later Brown) in 1764; the Dutch Reformed, Queens (later Rutgers) in 1766. Interest in Indian education accounts for the establishment of Wheelock's Indian School (1754) at Hanover, New Hampshire, which became Dartmouth in 1769. Indirectly, religion also was responsible for the only non-sectarian establishment of the period; for Whitefield's preaching promoted in 1740 a scheme for a charity school in Philadelphia, which developed into an academy which in turn became the College of Philadelphia and the University of Pennsylvania.

In most of these colleges, the instruction was formalized; students were expected to recite accurately the lessons assigned for memorizing. The classics, Latin, Greek and now and then Hebrew were emphasized. There was some drill in grammar, rhetoric and declamation, with instruction in logic to aid the formation of rational thought processes, so dear to the learned of that day. Most college boys were taught divinity and ethics. For mathematics there was some arithmetic and geometry, and science was touched lightly in a little astronomy and physics. But the mathematical and scientific concerns might easily be omitted. When Franklin came to plan for his academy (the future University of Pennsylvania) he was enthusiastic over a more realistic curriculum. Under his influence more emphasis was placed on science. Modern languages pushed in beside the ancient tongues and courses in history, government and international law gave the student some slight sense of social science. Instruction in agriculture and trade was urged by Franklin in a spirit of modern vocational guidance.

Unfortunately, the expanding interest in higher education did not mean a corresponding improvement in elementary training. The Massachusetts law of 1647 prescribing common schools had not been obeyed. The plans of William Penn, who thought education a responsibility of the state, and the laws in Maryland and South Carolina designed to establish school systems, all failed to produce the desired results. The decline in the old religious interest and the multiplication of new sects with their own private schools further reduced the urge for an expensive tax-supported system. Besides, the growing wealthy classes north and south preferred to educate their children at their own expense by employing private tutors or by sending them to private academies. They felt that the increase of population made public schools too expensive to the tax-payers. Illiteracy was common, even successful men of affairs and most women had to use their "marks" when executing documents. Nevertheless, the ideal of free schools, though somewhat eclipsed, was not dead and was destined for a revival at a later time.

All signs pointed to the fact that the colonial mental horizon was extending and pre-occupation with problems of mere existence was ceasing to be so all-absorbing. More people were reading. More books were imported, respectable private libraries were in the process of collection and there were a few lending libraries in both northern and southern colonies. Most important was a rather prosaic change, which was to have an incalculable effect upon the reading habits of the people, a veritable revolution in light and heat. The introduction of stoves and lamps in the homes of the more well-to-do to replace fireplaces and candles made possible warm rooms in which to sit and a good light by which to read. When the day's work was done, and quite frequently it was no longer such a hard day's work as in the early years, one could now sit down comfortably and without eyestrain enjoy the pleasures of reading.

Under such auspices, some literary experiments were initiated. Two magazines, *The American Magazine and Historical Chronicle* (Boston, 1743) and Benjamin Franklin's *General Magazine and Historical Chronicle* (Philadelphia, 1741) made their appearance; but more significant was the beginning of American newspaper history. In 1704 the *Boston News-Letter* made its bow and Benjamin Franklin issued the first number of the *Pennsylvania Gazette* in 1729. These journalistic attempts were followed by others until by 1756 newspapers had been established in all the colonies except New Jersey, Delaware and Georgia. As papers they were generally not very revealing, their four pages had numerous advertisements, much belated European news, and a few literary gems of uncertain water. Local items were not numerous because all in the locality knew what was going on. Benjamin Franklin's journalistic venture and the pungent aphorisms of his *Poor Richard's Almanac* made him the foremost writer of his day. Journalists were beginning to figure in public affairs and to influence public opinion. So much so that the authorities in 1735 sought to muzzle John Peter Zenger, a New York editor. He was arrested and tried for libel because of certain articles appearing in his paper attacking the governor. Andrew Hamilton, a prominent Philadelphia lawyer, was called to his defense and despite contrary instructions by the judge, the jury refused to convict him. A great victory for the freedom of the press had been won which was to figure significantly as one of the precedents for freedom of expression, so vital to any true democracy.

The distribution of periodicals and the practice of writing letters was encouraged by the organization of a postal service and such missives as well as the newpapers now had a means of circulation. In 1691 mail began to be carried regularly from Massachusetts to Pennsylvania by way of New York at rather high rates. By 1732 the service had been extended south to Virginia and in 1753 when Benjamin Franklin and William Hunter were appointed deputy postmasters-general, the service was further enlarged and improved. The inter-change of news and opinions was much facilitated by the innovation and too much cannot be said of its importance in promoting closer relationship among the various communities.

Most revealing were the evidences that general intellectual interest was stirring—that Americans were beginning to think in broader and more comprehensive terms. Scientific and philosophic advance could be noted. The wretched practice of medicine was mitigated. Youthful aspirants for medical knowledge began to go to foreign universities and hospitals. New devices, like inoculation against smallpox, were introduced in the face of great popular distrust. A medical school destined to be part of the University of Pennsylvania was established in Philadelphia in 1765 on the eve of the Revolution. A number of scientists appeared who were experimentally minded. James Logan and John Bartram of Philadelphia and Cadwallader Colden of New York were earnest botanists who corresponded with the great Linnæus. They collected specimens and made experiments while Bartram established a botanical garden in Philadelphia whither he transplanted many new varieties gathered in his extensive explorations. A number of southerners had similar interests, notably William Byrd whose observations gained him election as a fellow of the Royal Society.

The greatest of them all was the far-famed Dr. Franklin whose interests were wide enough to embrace all realms of knowledge and all fields of human behavior. Not only was he a printer, compiler of almanacs, author of proverbs, journalist and postmaster, but he was an educator and scientist. He conducted notable experiments in electricity and worked on a variety of problems. He labored to spread intellectual interest by organization. Not only did he lay plans for the Academy and College of Philadelphia, but he organized the Library Company of Philadelphia, one of a flock of lending libraries which sprang up in that vicinity. The most ambitious of his achievements as an organizer grew out of his Junto or club, formed in 1727 for discussion of scientific problems; it became an academy, was again reorganized in 1769 and thereafter was known as the American Philosophical Society. Here a variety of papers of scientific interest were presented and the society was conducted on the plan of contemporary French philosophical groups. Its transactions showed the extent of the American interest and the meetings made Philadelphia the intellectual center of the colonies. Such were the beginnings of American culture.

Economic Expansion

While these cultural interests were struggling for expression, the colonists discovered some new paths to wealth. Through industrious effort, they had accumulated sufficient capital to enable them to branch out into more ambitious projects. Commerce became more elaborate and profitable. New facilities had to be provided. When cargoes had been small, boats of light draft could ply from inlet to inlet and up and down the rivers and creeks; but trade could no longer be carried on so simply. Larger population, greater crops and more extensive needs called for bigger ships, capital, wharves, warehouses, insurance, and reliable news; such facilities could only be supplied in well-equipped seaports. Also new regulations of the home government requiring goods to be taxed at regular ports of entry, emphasized the importance of commercial centers. Boston, Philadelphia, New York, Charleston and later Baltimore and Savannah became bustling shipping depots.

Great Britain tried to keep the colonial trade strictly within the empire, but British markets were too limited and the large profits of trade with other countries were too attractive. Colonial ships sailed into many strange waters. One of the most lucrative of these far flung enterprises took colonial sea captains up the gold coast of Africa. The trade involved a triple exchange of molasses, rum and slaves. Yankee skippers purchased molasses in the West Indies and carried it to New England distilleries to be made into rum. Casks of this stimulant were shipped to Africa to be traded for Negro slaves who in turn were carried back to the West Indies to be exchanged for molasses. The profits from this traffic were large and it expanded as increasing funds were needed to meet the bills for colonial imports from Europe. The

COLONIAL TRADE ROUTES

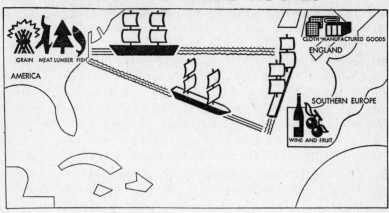

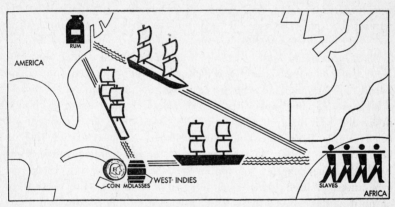

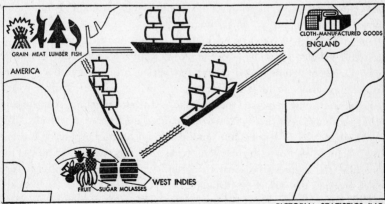

From Hacker, Modley, Taylor, *The United States:*
A Graphic History, Modern Age Books, Inc.

PICTORIAL STATISTICS, INC.

frequent wars of the period made great demands for food and raw materials, and they made privateering against England's enemies a profitable profession. The strong boxes of the merchants grew heavier and their risks more daring with each new success.

The growing traffic called for ships and the colonies had extraordinary facilities for supplying them. Ship-building in the eighteenth century became extremely profitable to many colonials. Tidal streams which flowed from the New England hills to the sea through excellent harbors, provided ideal locations for shipyards. Right at hand were the gnarled white oak and smooth white pine for keels, elbows, planks and tall straight masts. Tar, pitch and turpentine, too, were easily obtainable and long practice bred a race of skillful shipwrights. New England seaports resounded with the noise of builders at work on hundreds of ships. The yards on the Piscataqua in New Hampshire could turn out 200 ships a year; 72 vessels were on the ways at one time at Newburyport, Massachusetts. So cheaply could vessels be built that they were ordered from abroad. Spain, Portugal and particularly England purchased eagerly and at the close of the French and Indian wars 30% of English commercial vessels were of American origin.

An ally of ocean born commerce was the profitable fishing industry. New England vessels bore fishermen who swept the deep from Long Island to Newfoundland where the "banks" supplied some of the richest fishing grounds in the world. Codfish, mackerel and bass were brought in by the boat load to coast stations, where they were cleaned and dried on great flakes extending over many acres. Gloucester and Marblehead were the centers for this traffic in the eighteenth century. New England alone exported 10 million pounds of fish in 1700 and the generations of hardy fishermen increased the catch as the years went on until at the close of the colonial period 665 fishing boats from New England bore 4405 men to catch codfish and brought home hauls annually worth a million and a quarter.

Yankee seamen were called far afloat by another rich treasure of the deep, for whales abounded off the New England coast and sperm oil and whalebone commanded a ready market. These giant creatures proved dangerous to hunt and prodigious to handle, but Yankee pluck and endurance were equal to the task. At first, whaling was largely an off-shore affair; when whales were sighted off the coast of Nantucket or elsewhere, the fishermen put out in small boats to harpoon them and drag them to shore to be cut up, tried out for oil and stripped for bone. By the eighteenth century regular whaling vessels were in use which scoured the seas eager for the cry: "Thar she blows!" Nantucket was the great center, New Bedford, also in Massachusetts, was developing and Sag Harbor on Long Island was busy. By the outbreak of the Revolution there was a colonial whaling fleet of 360 vessels which

LIVING IN COMFORT

Drawing-room, Almodington, Somerset County, Maryland; *Bedroom,* Duncan House, Haverhill, Mass.; *Kitchen,* Van Cortlandt Mansion, N. Y. City

sailed from the Arctic circle to the Falklands and even to the shores of Africa. Truly New Englanders lived by scent of salt air and gained great profit from going down to the sea in ships.

Commerce was not confined to ships and the sea, there was money in a great inland traffic which lured much colonial and European enterprise and capital. This was the fur trade. In northern forests, particularly, the animals grew heavy pelts which could protect many a European noble or wealthy commoner from the penetrating cold of northern Europe. As European supplies were limited and giving out, there was great demand for the American furs. Beaver, mink, fox, otter, raccoon and bear were plentiful and healthy in America, so the hunt was on. As supplies along the coast were soon exhausted hunters and trappers had to find their way through the great forests beyond settlement and then beyond the Appalachians. So far flung was this trade through the northern woods that large capital and extensive operations were necessary. In the eighteenth century colonial merchants had the capital or could get it from England to organize a great traffic extending from the Great Lakes through the southern Appalachians.

There were three divisions of this trade. The English had taken over the old Dutch traffic and Albany prospered as a depot. Here English trappers and hunters started out to rival the French woodsmen in tapping the great western sources. They enlisted the Iroquois as middlemen and established a series of stations to which these allies brought skins they obtained from the Indians of the Lake regions. Philadelphia was the headquarters for a trade extending via Lancaster into the Susquehanna Valley and westward under venturesome traders like George Croghan into the Ohio Valley. Charleston via Augusta was the depot for a southern trade which penetrated into the Mississippi Valley but was not operated by stations. Fur bearing animals were much scarcer in this region, much of the traffic was really a leather trade in deerskins and individual trappers travelled literally thousands of miles gathering in the scattered peltries.

This traffic called for a heavy investment and a large organization. Extensive supplies of "trucking" goods, like trinkets, bright cloth, hatchets, guns, and particularly hard liquor had to be assembled and distributed to agents and trappers. They scattered over thousands of miles of trail and trackless forest. They dealt with the Indians, oftentimes at great meetings where the redmen gathered with their packs. Frequently these trading periods were prolonged debauches at which the Indians were made drunk and cheated outrageously. The pelts thus traded would be loaded into boats or packed on animals and brought to the headquarters. The returns were large but so extensive a capital was needed to carry on the traffic that it was controlled by relatively few rich merchants.

The fur trade was much more significant than a mere series of commercial transactions. It proved to have noteworthy social and political consequences. Its influence upon the Indians and their relations with the settlers was pernicious. Not only were the aborigines corrupted by the white men's liquor, but they were outraged by the flagrant cheating. These grievances spurred them on to revengeful raids and massacres. Also this trade placed guns, powder and iron weapons into their hands, and made them that much more dangerous. Furthermore, fur trading stirred up rivalry and conflict between the English and their neighbors, the French and Spanish. It did much to make the colonial experience hazardous and bloody.

Even more important was the influence of this traffic in opening up the vast interior. Trappers and hunters wandering ever farther into the interior were continually blazing new trails, discovering new regions and bringing back new reports of fertile acres, convenient rivers and future homesites. The trails they blazed and the knowledge they retailed were continual invitations for settlers to follow them and enjoy the wealth they described. The fur-trader was an advance agent of the onward march of settlement.

The growth of commerce reminded the merchants of the need for more colonial manufacturing. Household handicrafts were, of course, very widespread. The farmer and his family fed and clothed themselves, made and repaired tools, built their homes and outbuildings, carts and boats, manufactured furniture, tableware, candles, soap and bed linen, boxes and barrels, thread and cloth, even broadcloth. Some of these processes, such as the making of woolen and linen cloth, were complicated. All told, almost every home was a factory. Also artisans had shops in the towns and hats, shoes, pottery, rope, paper and glass were made by master journeymen and apprentices. The quantity of woolen, linen and cotton cloth began to worry English manufacturers; and as American hats, stockings, shoes and other leather goods, pottery, rope, paper and glass began to make their appearance, English producers persuaded Parliament to restrict this new competition. Ship building, and distilling, which had become the principal industries of New England, prospered, though in the case of the latter, British sugar duties threatened ruin.

Some colonial merchants were now ready to make more manufacturing advances notably in the iron industry. In the eighteenth century the superior resources of Pennsylvania were tapped and furnaces, bloomeries, slitting mills and forges were located in the Delaware and Susquehanna valleys. Steel also was produced and scythes, axes and other edged tools were put out in quantities not yet sufficient to satisfy the colonial need. The progress of this industry brought parliamentary restriction; the colonists must learn that their function was to consume not produce manufactures. Parliament, however, might just as well have tried to build a bridge over the Atlantic; duties and prohibitions on manufactures were alike ignored by the independent Americans.

While much of colonial industry was still domestic and while most commerce was carried on by individual merchants, both industry and commerce needed larger capital. Companies arose, especially in the iron industry where it was convenient for local merchants to unite in organizing shareholders to invest their money in a forge or bloomery. Likewise ships were often fitted out and loaded by a group of traders who shared proportionately in the profits and risks. Fur-trading and land speculating companies such as the Hudson's Bay Company in the far north and the Susquehanna and Ohio Companies began operations. There was even a monopoly; the United Company of Spermaceti Candlers (Newport, R. I., 1702) was an inter-colonial concern which controlled the industry in a manner prophetic of the future.

The growing business of the colonies was much hampered by an insufficient supply of currency. There were limited quantities of European coins, English, Spanish, French, Dutch and the like, which were used largely to settle European balances. Even for this purpose the amount was hardly adequate; but where domestic business was concerned, the circulation was so limited as to make necessary a resort to substitutes. Wampum, tobacco, and skins served as money and much colonial trade was carried on by barter. Massachusetts attempted a local mint but it was not sufficiently productive to help the situation. In preparing to meet the expenses caused by her participation in the first French and Indian War (1689-1697), Massachusetts began the printing of paper money. This practice was carried on so consistently and the paper depreciated so greatly that the little hard money in the colony was withdrawn from circulation and hoarded. Other colonies also made many such issues legal tender.

As in commerce and in manufacturing, so in the issue of paper the colonists experienced British interference. British merchants, and proprietors with creditor interests in the colonies, found their dues and their rents threatened by this debauchery of the medium of exchange. Colonial governors, upon instructions from the Crown or the proprietors, vetoed the acts of the colonial assemblies authorizing paper money and in 1751 an act of Parliament prohibited the use of this currency in the New England provinces except in time of war or emergency. The use of paper currency, however, had been learned and the delights of cheap money had been tasted; a practice had been initiated which was to be revived repeatedly especially in times of war or economic stress. From that time until the present, no long stretch of years has been allowed to elapse without some yielding to the temptation to issue inferior money, in spite of bitter opposition from creditor interests.

The financial needs of American business called for credit as well as currency, but facilities for it were indeed slight. English merchants accepted much colonial business on a credit basis, especially with southern planters whose accounts were carried from generation to generation; but the charges made for this service by English firms were very heavy. The colonies themselves were not equipped to mobilize their capital and to extend credit because funds were scattered and inadequate. The most notable attempt at banking was the Massachusetts Land Bank chartered in 1741, which issued a currency based upon land as security. This institution was suppressed by Parliament; but in the meantime, a quantity of notes had been issued to the ruin of many who had invested in it. Not until the Revolution did a permanent banking institution emerge. Marine insurance, however, began to be written in Philadelphia as early as 1721, at a great saving from the heavy charges of British firms. Fire insurance was undertaken in the same city in 1752 by the Philadelphia Contributionship for the Insurance of Houses from Loss by Fire.

In the South similar tendencies toward larger operations were noticeable. The plantation system was coming into its own and was the all engrossing enterprise of those with initiative and business ability. Tobacco planting flourished but its cultivation quickly exhausted the soil. Farsighted planters realized that they must have large landholdings if they were to continue to plant, otherwise their impoverished acres could have no rest and there would be no new fields to open up in place of the old. The appearance of a new labor supply removed the greatest hindrance to large operation, for the Negro slave made large plantations possible and profitable. Negroes had been imported as early as 1619 but the supply had been limited and planters had preferred indentured servants. After British capitalists organized the Royal African Company in 1672, the traffic began to grow. When the privilege of the *asiento,* wrested from Spain in 1713, gave British traders the contract to supply Spanish America with Negroes, a regular service was assured. Under these conditions the trade became organized and the supply abundant. The growth of both slavery and the plantation system was further encouraged by a new commodity. In the 1690's Madagascar rice was planted in the marshy coastal district of the Carolinas and since the work in the malarial rice fields was not such as white labor could stand, slaves were imported in large numbers. By 1715 more than half the population of South Carolina was of the African race.

Thus enterprise and the desire to do big things had their way in the South and large tobacco and rice plantations multiplied in Virginia and South Carolina. The planter became the dominating figure in these communities. His crops were sold to English merchants who maintained agents in the few cities and towns in the South, and he bought his supplies from the firms to whom he consigned his goods. These London firms carried the planters' accounts for years with increasingly unfavorable balances against the colonists. During the eighteenth century, in many instances, the plantation owner's tastes became more expensive

THE COLONIAL ECONOMY

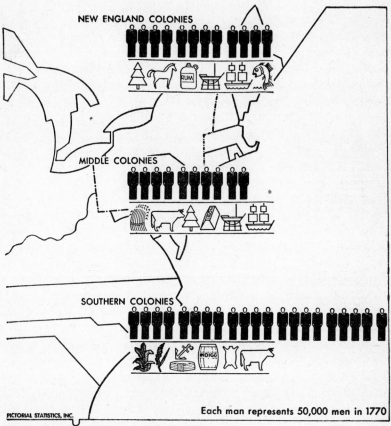

From Hacker, Modley, Taylor, *The United States:*
   A Graphic History, Modern Age Books, Inc.

and exceeded his income. Many a luxurious plantation home could not fail to remind its owner that it was a luxury which represented a growing debt, the payment of which was becoming more remote every year.

Important as were the plantation lords, they were not numerous. Many a small planter who was not successful enough to acquire a large holding, either became a tenant, or more likely moved west to the back country. Besides, a great many of the new European emigrants were going directly to the western counties, either renting or purchasing their land from the great landlords. They operated small farms and had no part in the plantation scheme except perhaps a hope of acquiring sufficient wealth some day to enter the ranks of the barons. At least 60% of the farmers in the southern colonies had small holdings which could be worked without slaves or indentured labor.

This preoccupation with agriculture coupled with the new interest in big projects launched numerous real estate booms. The swelling tide of immigrants and the expansion of settlement brought into play the talents of the real estate speculator. Individuals and groups sought to anticipate or influence the tide of migration and secured land in large grants which they planned to subdivide profitably. To do so they had to attract the new-comers. In New England speculative "proprietors" secured whole townships from the legislatures and then proceeded to induce settlers to go to these outlying districts, thereby contributing to the wealth of the "absentee landlords." In New York, the governors made lavish grants and enormous manors were peopled with tenants whose lot was not always happy because of the exactions of the landlords. In the southern colonies many a planter was a land speculator as well. Grants were easy to obtain and men like William Byrd and Lord Fairfax had princely possessions and formed companies to develop them. The Ohio Company with interests located beyond the Alleghanies was to play an historic role in the onward march of the nation. The disposal of land called for much of the "science" of modern real estate salesmanship, with the sale rather than the future comfort of the buyer, the main thought in the mind of the speculator.

In these various expansive projects many a venturer prospered and the earnest pursuit of wealth had been given an encouraging start. The vast treasure house of America was being explored and exploited. Vested interests in land and trade were maintained by substantial men of wealth who were gaining social and political privileges and becoming jealous of any attempts to control or curtail profits. Even to those who did not succeed there remained the ever present hope that fortune would smile on the next venture. The service of mammon was not the least of the interests of the new American society.

The Incubation of Independence

While the colonists were creating American folkways and increasing their wealth, they were learning more fully the arts of independent self-government. The colonial legislatures were assuming greater responsibilities and gaining a stronger sense of their rights and privileges which they were ever more determined should not be interfered with by the home government. To this growing spirit of independence, the home government unwittingly contributed.

After years of experimenting with committees of parliament and the privy council, a board of trade was established in 1696 to oversee colonial affairs and to advise the King and his ministers upon all matters colonial. They possessed only powers of investigation and advice, but their industry was prodigious and their influence generally potent. The duties of the board were enlarged from time to time by the gradual extension of Crown control over the proprietary colonies. The owners of New Jersey (1702), the Carolinas (1729) and Georgia (1752) [1] found their tasks too difficult and surrendered their titles to the King. By mid-century royal governors ruled eight of the thirteen colonies and the Penns [2] and the Baltimores had to submit the names of their appointees to the government for approval. In no case, however, was the colonial assembly abolished and the privileges of partial self-government enjoyed under the proprietors were continued under the Crown.

One of the chief concerns of the English government in the eighteenth century was proper regulation of imperial trade. Following the prevailing theories of mercantilism navigation laws were extended during the reign of Charles II to make certain that the profits of colonial trade were kept within the empire and concentrated as much as possible in the hands of English merchants. New restrictions were laid upon colonial freedom of trade and a band of customs officials established in the colonial ports to enforce the laws. They reported a woeful lack of respect and obedience on the part of colonists so another statute was passed in 1696 to tighten the regulations. Courts of admiralty were organized in the colonies to handle revenue cases according to the accepted practices of admiralty law, which, unlike the English common law, made no use of juries in its procedure. To carry out these restrictions the Board of Trade gave the governors minute instructions which were supposed to be carried out to the letter in spite of the fact that they frequently harmonized neither with colonial conditions nor colonial preferences.

Despite these efforts at control, the reality of the situation was that the mother country attempted very little and left the colonists much to themselves. These were the years marked by "salutary neglect" and the Americans profited thereby. The thirteen colonial governments functioned effectively and lawyers, merchants, journalists and politicians developed an ever increasing independence. Political practice had not been limited exclusively to isolated colonial capitals. The years following 1689 were marked by a series of wars with the French and Indians which called forth successive intercolonial cooperative projects. Legisla-

[1] Georgia had been established in 1732 under the direction of General James Oglethorpe as an experiment in social reform. He hoped that it might be a community which would rehabilitate the criminal and otherwise unfortunate.

[2] Delaware was recognized by Penn as a colony in 1703, to a degree independent of Pennsylvania although under the same governor.

tures and politicians of the various colonies were called upon to contribute to the support and management of joint operations and therein they gained experience which was to prove invaluable in the coming revolution, then hardly dreamed of.

The penetration of the French into the Mississippi and Ohio valleys and their proximity to the New England and New York border settlements had been a constant annoyance to the colonists; and French influence with the Indians made them a menace. Real estate speculation in western lands and the fur trade were hampered and endangered, and there was fear that the French might attempt conquest. In Europe the ambitions of Louis XIV to extend French control aroused general apprehension among the various powers; and England became especially concerned when he espoused the cause of the exiled Stuarts and sought to invade the island kingdoms. War broke out in 1689, 1701, 1744 and 1756; and in 1740 and 1754 warlike measures were undertaken in the colonies prior to the declaration of actual warfare in Europe. The colonial wars were reflections of European rivalries; but they were also, in a very real sense, struggles for self-defence and trade advantage, and the legislatures were called upon to arrange very active participation.

Colonial troops saw service in all of these wars. Twice they conquered French Acadia (Nova Scotia) and at length reduced the great fortress of Louisbourg on Cape Breton Island. Some of their commanders such as Sir William Phips, William Pepperrell, and George Washington rendered valiant account of themselves. Quite significantly these wars revived the idea of intercolonial cooperation. During the first of them, an intercolonial congress met in New York in May 1690 to plan for defence; while in the last, the Board of Trade in London ordered a convention of colonial representatives to meet with delegates from Indian tribes at Albany in June 1754. Not only did the latter conference place Indian affairs upon the agenda but it also took up the question of united action. Several plans were discussed; and finally a scheme of Benjamin Franklin's to be known as the Albany Plan of Union, was adopted. Had this been carried out, it would have provided for a federal system under a British governor-general and an intercolonial parliament but it was too radical a change to gain the approval of the British government or of the colonies.

These wars came to a successful conclusion and by the final treaty signed in Paris in 1763, Great Britain acquired Canada and the eastern half of the Mississippi Valley from France, and Florida from France's ally, Spain. In return for the latter posession, Great Britain caused New Orleans and the western Mississippi valley to be transferred to Spain, which now controlled a vast empire from the straits of Magellan to the headwaters of the Mississippi. The victory left the provincials with a distinct sense of achievement. They had organized successful armies and by cooperating among themselves they had demonstrated their own superiority over the best armies of Europe. But they also had a distinct sense of grievance.

British officers had seemed unable to recognize the merit of the militia commanders. Time and time again leading colonial soldiers, like the Virginia colonel, George Washington, had been slighted and humiliated by English officers of inferior rank. In fact, any regular officer ranked above any holder of a militia commission and even in the last campaign, which brought about the surrender of Canada, the colonial troops received what to them seemed to be studied insults. Many a colonial militia officer had unpleasant memories of slights and indignities at the hands of arrogant and stubborn English martinets.

The American colonists now well established and becoming more conscious of their own independent existence were dwelling in thirteen colonies. But climate and topography were producing other and equally significant divisions. These thirteen colonies were divided into three sections, and in turn each of these sections was cut into two parts. New England and the southern colonies presented themselves as two areas with pronounced differences; between them were the middle colonies, unlike the other two but with characteristics less picturesque or distinguished. Each of these sections had two divisions, the older settlements along the seaboard, and the back country where a frontier was being marked out by the expansion of westward settlement. In these various localities, people had different habits and customs and lived different lives; their unlikeness produced consequences of great future significance.

In this second century of colonial growth, a truly American society had evolved. It was no longer so English, but cosmopolitan. Its ways of life had become settled, its standard of living higher and there were signs of a cultural interest not possible in the former period. Economic life had expanded and enterprise had developed modern methods. A large and influential group of wealthy and aristocratic merchants and land owners had found in America a place of great opportunity. More than ever these colonies had been called upon to manage their own affairs and even to engage actively in affairs of international moment. They had reached the stage when they could advance their own frontiers and create new communities where the democratic spirit might flourish to offset the growing dominance of the masters of colonial wealth. This American society was prepared to undertake an even more independent rôle in the world if the occasion should arise. Though they were still, in their own opinion, loyal British subjects, circumstances had conspired to make them independent and resourceful Americans.

ESTABLISHING INDEPENDENCE

1763–1819

CHAPTER IV

THE DECLARATION OF INDEPENDENCE

The wars of the eighteenth century had completed the education of the colonies for independence. They now had extensive knowledge of the indifference, the inefficiency and the short-sightedness of the home government and at the same time had discovered that they could shift for themselves. Peace brought neither relaxation nor opportunity to forget these lessons. Rather new demands were made upon the Americans to protect their interests.

New Problems of Empire

Great Britain was in difficulties and the colonies shared in the general concern. There was a general post-war depression and debts presented an appalling burden. The colonies themselves owed three-quarters of a million pounds. Presumably, had the mother country returned to her former indifference and neglect, the Americans would have set themselves to improving their financial position and their very real loyalty to the Crown would have suffered no particular strain. However, the British government was beset by difficulties which prevented such a return to old conditions.

During the prolonged period of war, Great Britain had increased the national debt to the staggering sum of £130,000,000. Also much new territory had been acquired and this entailed new expense. Plans for funding this debt and meeting the new costs had to be made when London capitalists were struggling with the universal financial depression. They would inevitably attempt to persuade the government to shift as much of the pressing financial burden as possible upon the colonials. It was evident therefore that these financial questions were bound to produce a conflict of interest which would strain to dangerous limits the loyalty of the colonies.

The colonial capitalists, merchants, planters, land speculators and fur traders were likewise in difficulties. They needed freedom and generous policy so that they might quickly expand and regain lost ground. On the other hand, such freedom would bring them into direct competition with the London interests who wanted them to pay their debts and buy British goods rather than develop greater economic independence. In the post-war readjustments, whose interests would be regarded, those of British capital or of American enterprise? One would have to be sacrificed to the other.

The condition of the British government was such that fumbling and blundering were inevitable, for party politics was in a low state. Factions, rather than parties, squabbled among themselves, each faction out for the possession of offices and power. None of them had any policy except to stay in office as long as possible by whatever means lay nearest at hand. Statesmanship was notoriously lacking at a time when insistent problems and an economic depression called for talent of a high order.

The financial problem was handled in a fashion peculiarly political. The ministry had to raise money in some manner that might not alienate the support of the wealthy landed and mercantile groups who could wield much political power. Under such circumstances it was inevitable that a scheme to tax the colonies should be considered. Hitherto they had escaped levies because they had supported themselves; but now that the ministry had decided to station 10,000 troops in the colonies to guard them, and to keep watchful eye upon the new French, Spanish and Indian subjects, it seemed obvious that the colonies ought to bear part of the burden of their support. Furthermore, the colonial customs service cost the Crown four times as much as the revenue it collected; and in time of economic depression, both English merchants and West Indian planters were objecting to the callous disregard with which the seaboard colonists treated the navigation laws (p. 61). Evidently it was time to reorganize the enforcement of the trade laws, to make them as effective and productive of revenue as possible. This decision was made just when the colonists were suffering from post-war economic depression, and were facing the task of paying their own debts by increasing local taxation.

Under such circumstances the government inaugurated a policy of increasing taxes and trade regulations. A new general customs act, passed in 1764, was the first step. Special pains were taken to make effective a tax which proved particularly obnoxious to the colonists, namely that on sugar and molasses. The tax of six pence per gallon on molasses established in 1733 had been so high that the law had been universally disregarded; under the act of 1764 the duty was reduced to three pence and specific regulations provided for its collection. Such a tax would materially reduce the profits of colonial merchants.

In addition the policy hitherto followed of permitting the colonists a drawback, or partial return of import duties paid, on goods which they imported from foreign countries via England was abandoned. Taxes also were increased upon a number of commodities such as wine from Madeira and the Azores which the colonists imported in large quantities. To enforce the collection of these taxes, heavy bonds and elaborate certificates were required of the ship masters in order to make certain that their ships carried only goods loaded in England or the colonies. The navy was ordered to enforce these acts by patrols. Colonial governors were ordered to be more strict in supervising the customs service. Penalties for violation of the law were made heavier and certain inducements were offered to encourage prosecutions for violation.

The duties under this revenue act were calculated to produce but one-seventh of the sum needed to support the colonial guard; consequently, a second scheme was devised, namely a stamp tax. This device had proved both productive of revenue and easy to collect in Great Britain and was now imposed upon the colonists by the law of 1765. Newspapers and pamphlets, dice, playing cards and all legal documents and certificates including college diplomas were to be stamped. To complete the provision for the troops a quartering act, passed in the same year, ordered the colonies to supply barracks and part of the food and equipment of the soldiers. Another act (1764) in the series forbade the issue of legal tender paper money in all the colonies. This measure was passed at the same time that the revenue and stamp acts required the payment of the proceeds of duties and taxes into the Exchequer in London. Such a plan the colonies took wrongly to mean that most of their small supply of gold and silver would have to be sent to England. In reality the government had no such immediate intention, as the money was actually left in the colonies to be spent there.

The second problem, hardly of less importance, was administrative. The new territory, with its alien population, obtained from the French and Spanish had to be governed and a new Indian menace guarded against. The French had been dislodged from Canada and the Mississippi Valley, and the Spanish from Florida. Great Britain's new territories literally surrounded the thirteen colonies on three sides; French, Spanish and Indians were now British subjects and the manner in which the new imperial population was to be treated could not but concern the Atlantic seaboard colonists. Hardly had the new area been acquired than it presented difficulties. An Ottawa chief, Pontiac, at the head of a federation of tribes, started a revolt in 1763; and though the uprising was put down within a year it furnished food for thought.

Even before this revolt the British government had sought to deal more effectively with the Indians by appointing in 1761, two Indian superintendents—one for the northern and the other for the southern Indians. By 1763 the Board of Trade had come to the conclusion that until the Indians were more settled and more accustomed to the new order it would be better to segregate them and forbid fur traders, land speculators or settlers to aggravate them. To this end the Proclamation of 1763 announced the organization of three new provinces,

Canada, and East and West Florida. The land between Florida and the Great Lakes, between the Mississippi and the Appalachians, was to be set off as an Indian reservation from which white men, other than government agents, were to be barred. The prohibition of communication between Indians and whites was planned to be but temporary, though that feature was not known in the colonies. Such a policy immediately stirred up resentment for to the Americans it destroyed a great potential source of wealth. It denied their claims to lands beyond the mountains, cut off valuable trading grounds and ruined plans for great real estate speculation.

Grievance and Protest

As the news of these various proposals, financial and administrative, gradually spread through the colonies, resentment accumulated. It was evident that the British mercantile interests were to be protected at the expense of the Americans. For every one of these policies would cost the colonists money, advantage and prospect of immediate profit. Protest soon took definite form. A number of colonial merchant-capitalists were highly incensed and local political leaders, trained in the colonial legislatures, were ready to make common cause with them. They set about to organize those who were disgruntled to make effective protest. Written petitions to the home government were prepared and in some of the New England colonies agreements were made to purchase no English goods if the obnoxious taxes and regulations were persisted in. In their petitions they argued that the new revenue act would effectually ruin their already declining trade; and as a protest against the stamp tax they developed a new theory, the theory of unconstitutionality. Drawing upon their knowledge of British law and custom, they made a distinction on the one hand between external or commercial taxes, which they had accepted previously in theory at least, and on the other hand, internal or direct taxes such as the contemplated stamp tax. The latter levy they declared was a violation of the time-honored dogma that no Englishman could be taxed directly without being represented in the legislative body which laid the tax. Such petitions were received in London before the stamp law was enacted but Parliament refused to consider them.

When the news of the actual passage of the Stamp Act reached America, there was general indignation. Stamps would have to be affixed to printed matter and to legal documents of all sorts; and collectors had been appointed in each of the colonies to sell them. Lawyers, clergymen, editors, business men were to have daily evidence before them of British authority; and no one could read a newspaper, make a will, pay a bill or play a game of cards without being reminded that the Crown was taxing them. Merchants who had been disturbed by new customs regulations were further exasperated by the bother and expense of affixing stamps to the great variety of their papers. Planters as well as merchants were indignant. They were always short of cash and in debt. Where would they get the money to pay the impost? George Washington feared that there was not enough actual money in the provinces to pay these new taxes. Artisans and laborers in the towns, many of whom were out of work and suffering from the depression, saw only harder times ahead.

Colonial wrath exploded. Merchants organized in local associations. Committees were formed to correspond with leaders in neighboring colonies. Local clubs which included many in poor circumstances with a few who were better off were formed or revived, for such groups had been a feature of colonial politics. Known as the Sons of Liberty, they could be easily roused to direct action. When the names of the stamp agents were announced, mobs formed and in some cases destroyed property. Committees, too, were active and whether persuaded by mob or local committee advice, the agents generally saw the light. When the Stamp Act went into effect in November, none of the stamp agents nor any one else could be found to handle the unpopular levy.

More formal action was also taken. The Virginia Assembly passed resolutions of protest and the Massachusetts legislature invited an intercolonial conference to meet in New York, October 1765. This body gathered at the appointed time with delegates present from nine colonies and addressed a dignified protest to the Crown, making a plea against taxation without representation. New York set an example when merchants and the public agreed not to buy British goods; and in the various colonies organizations were formed to discourage the purchase of British commodities, sometimes by force. Business was more than ever stagnant.

In England circumstances joined with the colonial petitions in urging repeal of the Stamp Tax. The wheel of politics had turned, another crowd of office holders had succeeded the Grenville ministry which proposed the impost. London merchants began a drive for relief so that American orders might come in once more. The new ministry seemed nothing loathe to overturn the unpopular work of their predecessors and in 1766 the Stamp Act was repealed, though the politicians were careful to pass a declaratory act reasserting parliamentary authority to tax the colonies.

The colonists' victory, however, was short-lived for the budget was still unbalanced; and yet a third ministry was compelled to seek a second way to secure revenue. They could think of nothing more original than new duties to be levied on paper, glass, paint and tea, in 1767, and another attempt to make the customs service more effective.

By sticking to external taxation they hoped to soothe colonial feeling. But many new English officials were sent to America to prosecute violators of the revenue laws in the admiralty courts, where no jury trials were possible. The revised system of port regulation imposed fees and burdensome formalities to such an extent that colonial merchants suffered still more losses. Colonial governors and judges were now to be paid from the customs revenue and thus be freed from the colonial legislatures. From the British standpoint, on the other hand, affairs were more satisfactory, annual revenue from the colonies increased from £2,000 to £30,000 and in the seven years from 1764 to 1771 the colonials paid some £200,000 in taxes.

The British government did not confine itself to laying new duties and enforcing its customs laws; it went further and interfered with the self-governing privileges of the colonists. In 1767 the New York legislature had been disbanded because it would not bear its share in supporting troops within the borders of the colony. Next the Massachusetts legislature was threatened. Early in 1768 that body had addressed a famous circular letter to the other colonies suggesting cooperation in protest and argument. This letter angered the ministry, especially its newest member, Lord Hillsborough. The office of secretary of state for the colonies had just been created and its first occupant lost no time in ordering the Massachusetts legislature to recall this letter or be dissolved. The legislators chose to suffer the latter and were dispersed by the royal governor. Rumors also became current that the local courts were to be disregarded and colonists accused of crime were to be sent to England for trial. The hard-won privileges of self-government seemed about to be lost.

The new taxes, the renewed attempts at enforcement and the interference with colonial self-government aroused the resentment of large groups of the colonists just as the stamp tax had done. The merchants, especially in Boston, began to revive the non-importation agreements and the Sons of Liberty became restive again. So active were the patriotic organizations in Boston that the customs officials felt their authority in danger, and asked for troops to protect them and their work. Two regiments were dispatched to the New England port, and Massachusetts was required to contribute to their support. The presence of these troops was a constant source of irritation to the Boston townspeople and the less peaceable of them did what they could to make life unpleasant for the red-coats. The climax came on 5 March 1770, when a few of the soldiers, much provoked by some Boston tormentors, fired on them and killed four colonists. News of this bloodshed spread throughout the colonies like wild fire and became known as the "Boston Massacre." Life as well as rights was now in danger.

Despite the increased bitterness which it produced, the violence seemed to clear the air for a time. The troops were withdrawn from the streets of Boston and by a fortunate coincidence reassuring news came from England. Before report of the massacre had reached London, still another ministry had come into power and had withdrawn all the taxes save that on tea. Peace returned and trade revived, the hard times succeeding the war were over, and as the non-importation agreements had been effective, the colonists had the balance of trade in their favor. People were more prosperous and less discontented and for a time it seemed as though the trouble would blow over.

The provincials, however, in the course of this experience had become better acquainted with ideas of rights—their rights—and of liberty. They had been schooled in the defence of self-government

Lord North Forcing the Tea down the Throat of America

and to many the defiance offered to overbearing British officials had been stimulating. The populace had shaken themselves free of certain restraints of conduct and had asserted themselves. Their leaders, like Samuel Adams in Boston, had tasted the fruits of power. These lessons could not be unlearned nor these experiences forgotten. Isolated incidents of resistance to authority occurred in the years 1771-1773; and only another attempt by the British government to assert some prerogative hateful to the colonies would be needed in bring out open resistance again. The British ministry was not long in supplying the occasion.

One of the greatest of the English corporations, the East India Company, was in financial difficulties and faced bankruptcy. To aid it the ministry decided in 1773 to grant the company the privilege of selling its tea directly to the colonies free of all taxes, which heretofore had been collected in England; the commodity was to be subject only to the tea duty levied in America. This tax exemption meant that since the tea could be purchased by the colonials at a price lower than any one else paid, the tea would be even cheaper than smuggled tea—then a common drink. But such a privilege meant that the tea would be sold directly to the colonists and the colonial merchants would not handle it or make money from it. This was an ominous precedent, for if such a privilege were granted to one English corporation, a similar privilege of direct sale might be given to British dealers in other commodities and thus further harm the business of the colonials. Furthermore, it was just another example of British interference.

Had this occurred in 1763, rather than in 1773, perhaps little more than grumbling would have resulted; but much had happened in the decade and the colonists had learned the power of their protests. So the tea, it was generally agreed, would not be purchased; and in Boston some of the local enthusiasts for colonial rights disguised themselves as Indians and on 16 December 1773 threw the tea, then stored on shipboard into the harbor. Elsewhere the sale of the tea was stopped by various methods. Such defiance could not be brooked. British ministerial patience, never very abundant, was exhausted. In 1774, a series of acts was passed depriving Massachusetts of self-government and closing the port of Boston to trade.

Armed Resistance

Politicians and merchants now had common cause and the people at large knew another flagrant example of the precarious state of their rights and liberties. Something must be done to protect themselves from further tyranny. Massachusetts needed help and the necessity for renewed intercolonial cooperation advanced nationalism another step. Throughout the colonies, local committees of correspondence had been writing to one another and creating machinery for joint action. The Stamp Act congress had proved a useful precedent; and the cooperation of merchants of the various colonies in non-importation agreements had met success. The time had now come for another move toward cooperation, one that was to provide permanent machinery.

Virginia took the lead; not only was she sympathetic to Boston but she had a new grievance. The so-called Quebec Act recently passed, and certain ministerial regulations had placed under the jurisdiction of the province of Quebec much western land which Virginia claimed. To make matters worse a British company seemed about to receive grants there, which would prevent Virginia's title from ever being revived, deprive her of future taxable assets and ruin choice speculative possibilities. In spite of the fact that the royal governor had dissolved the Virginia legislature for officially expressing sympathy with Massachusetts, its members reconvened. They passed a resolution suggesting that an annual congress of delegates from the various colonies be instituted.

The response was immediate, and at the suggestion of Massachusetts, delegates from all colonies except Georgia met in Philadelphia, 5 September 1774, in what is known as the First Continental Congress. This body remained in session seven weeks and laid the basis for organized union. Besides issuing a Declaration of Rights and Grievances and petitioning the King for redress, the Congress adopted the Articles of Association, whereby they agreed not to trade with Great Britain and to abandon altogether the slave trade. Furthermore, committees to see that this agreement was enforced were to be appointed in each town and county; the committees of correspondence were charged to be even more active.

In the meantime, the people of Massachusetts were preparing to protect themselves against the British coercive measures. The legislature in spite of royal orders continued to function, the militia was newly equipped and stores and munitions collected. At various times the British commander in Boston sought to wipe out these stores by sending detachments to search for them and destroy them. On 19 April 1775 the colonists resisted an expedition of this character at Lexington and Concord, and although they lost a goodly quantity of stores, they inflicted severe punishment upon the British force. But far more significant, the King's troops had killed colonial militia and blood had been spilled. These "embattled farmers" had "fired the shot heard round the world."

Militia detachments immediately thronged the roads leading to Boston. They were marching to aid Massachusetts. Others undertook independent action, notably Ethan Allen's men when they captured Fort Ticonderoga. When the Second Continental Congress met in May 1775 it immediately was faced with the fact of fighting. Still professing to be composed of loyal subjects who were only resisting oppression, the Congress issued an address explaining why it was necessary to fight. Then it proceeded to create an army. The Massachusetts militia and the regiments from the middle and southern colonies which had joined them were made into a "Continental" army to be commanded by George Washington of Virginia. In the midst of these vigorous preparations, Congress took time to send one more petition to England. Far from heeding it, the King issued a proclamation denouncing the colonists as rebels, and Parliament passed an act prohibiting trade with them. The ministry began to gather an army to coerce the Americans, and finding the British force insufficient, hired Hessian soldiers to make up the necessary enrollment.

It was evidently to be war. Before Washington could take command of the new army the British had driven some of its detachments away from their fortifications on Bunker Hill, 17 June 1775. This second bloodshed accompanied by heroism on the part of the patriots further charged the war-like spirit. More militia arrived at Cambridge where Washington made his headquarters. He promptly invested Boston and besieged it with such effect that the British evacuated it in March 1776.

The fact of war, in spite of protestations of loyalty, raised a new question. Why should the colonists remain part of the British empire? Liberty and freedom were much more attractive than subjection to the far away British. Independence ought to be the goal. Their protestations of loyalty seemed rather hollow when they were arming to resist the soldiers of the Crown. At least so thought Thomas Paine and he set out to argue for independence. Paine was a young English ne'er-do-well who had tried his hand at many things from preaching to tax collecting. Franklin had met him in England and sent him to Philadelphia where he made his living by writing. Well equipped to conduct independence propaganda, his vigorous and appealing pamphlet "Common Sense" reached a wide audience to whom a move for independence seemed to be "common sense." North Carolina started official action in the spring of 1776 by instructing her delegates in the Continental Congress to vote for independence. Virginia soon followed and in June, one of her delegates, Richard Henry Lee, introduced a resolution "that these united colonies are, and of right out to be, free and independent States." Thomas Jefferson of the same colony was made chairman of a committee to draft the famous Declaration of Independence and did most of the writing of the great document which was adopted July 4. The bell in the tower of Independence Hall now in truth could vigorously "proclaim liberty." The British colonies were resolved to be a nation.

The Declaration of Independence was an announcement that had to be enforced by five more years of active war. Great Britain was not going to part with her colonies without a struggle, and continued to send troops to beat them into submission. All told, about 100,000 red coats and Hessians were mustered in American camps besides perhaps fifty thousand Tories and an indeterminate number of Indians. It was no small task for the inexperienced and ill-equipped colonials to organize a force sufficient to repel seasoned veterans. There was much enthusiasm to make up for scanty equipment and the glow of patriotic emotion was an asset of greatest value.

Most important, a real leader was at hand for the difficult task.

George Washington, born of a planter family in Virginia, had been used to responsibility. His father died young and his elder brother was sickly, so from his boyhood he had been engaged in plantation management on an increasing scale. The combination of many acres, poor soil and slave labor had taught him to manage difficult enterprises with patience, diligence and infinite labor. As surveyor and militia officer in the French and Indian war he had learned the frontier and the devious arts of warfare and his experiences had been sharpened by defeat, misunderstanding and rebuff from English military men. It was just the education needed for the struggle ahead of him. He overcame treachery, cowardice, deceit and neglect and transmitted his own courage and strength to his ragged armies. Few men could have had the

Britannia Dismembered
(A contemporary cartoon)

combination of qualities necessary to triumph in such an uncertain venture.

His first recruits were the colonial militia organizations and out of these he made a militia army at Cambridge, Massachusetts, in the months after Bunker Hill. Not until January 1777 did Congress establish a national army into which recruits were directly received who were not connected with any of the state militia organizations. The latter, however, continued to be a large proportion of the force under arms. At no time does the armed strength of the colonials seem to have been more than 80,000; 22,000 was the largest force assembled at any one place and many times the armies in the field were less than 10,000 strong. Enlistments were frequently for short periods, and during the winter, when there was no fighting and only cold and hunger to be endured, the Continental army dwindled to pitiful remnants. Such was the force with which the new American republic sought to cope with the British regulars.

An adequate navy was yet more difficult to develop. War vessels were expensive to build and required large sums for maintenance. Early in the conflict New England seamen, like those at Marblehead, formed themselves into a naval militia and occasionally made forays upon British supply ships. 2000 privateers at one time or another were commissioned to prey upon British commerce. Their exploits were of the utmost value as contributions to independence. Insurance rates on British shipping went up tremendously; and the consternation which continual losses created among British merchants led them to give only lukewarm support to the war and in later years to urge its conclusion. However, in but one outstanding instance did the Americans muster a fleet, and that was in 1779 when through the aid of the French the American commander, John Paul Jones, with a flag ship and four smaller vessels, gave battle to the British and won a victory off the English coast. This action between the *Bonhomme Richard* and the *Serapis* and their consorts was the spectacular naval event of the war. But the privateers remained the successful maritime force. Only in such wise could the colonists hope to make their small power felt by the greatest navy of the time.

The main effort was concentrated on military campaigns. Washington and his army had seen service before the signing of the Declaration of Independence. In March 1776 the British had been forced to evacuate Boston and the American commander had moved his force to New York to await a threatened British attack. For British re-enforcements had been sent to Halifax and an expedition was preparing for an elaborate attempt to destroy rebellion. The British under Sir William Howe sought to capture New York and thus drive an entering wedge through the center of the colonies. In this they were all too successful. In August 1776, they captured New York City and later drove Washington through New Jersey into Pennsylvania. The patriot general, however, turned suddenly and by a brilliant counter-stroke defeated a large Hessian contingent at Trenton, on Christmas night. A few days later he won another victory at Princeton. These successes caused the British to retire to the vicinity of New York where they spent the winter while Washington encamped at Morristown.

General Howe did not campaign vigorously and seemed interested rather in seeking to conciliate and to negotiate a peace. He also enjoyed himself in comfortable colonial cities. He was furthermore confronted with difficult obstacles and his home government gave him none too generous support; the fact that he was of the opposition party in English politics perhaps contributed to his lack of energy. All these preferences and prejudices did not make him a very active general. In the spring of 1777 the war office produced a plan of conquest. An expedition was to be sent from Canada down the Hudson, which Howe was supposed to meet by moving up that stream and to perfect thereby the separation of the New England colonies from the rest. Howe meanwhile had concluded that the best way to bring peace was to capture Philadelphia, the capital of the United States, and disperse Congress. The war office was inefficient in communicating its scheme to Howe and he went off on his own campaign.

After much delay, he took the army by sea from New York around into the Chesapeake where he landed at the head of the bay. Washington sought to oppose him at Brandywine Creek, 11 September 1777; and when he failed to prevent the British general from entering Philadelphia, he made a second unsuccessful attempt to defeat him at Germantown, 4 October 1777. After these disasters, Washington could do nothing but keep troubled watch from the bleak hills of Valley Forge, while Howe made merry in Philadelphia, and Congress helplessly debated at York, Pa. This winter of 1777-1778 was the darkest hour of the patriot cause but there was one bright spot. The expedition from Canada under Burgoyne did not penetrate very far into northern New York before it was defeated at Saratoga by Gen. Horatio Gates and forced to surrender en masse 14 October 1777. Events proved that this victory was to turn the tide.

Great Britain had numerous enemies in Europe, notably France and Spain, who naturally were not averse to seeing the British power curtailed. The leaders in the Continental Congress counted on this fact and even before the adoption of the Declaration of Independence had sent agents abroad (March 1776). France, it was hoped, would be most likely to lend aid, and the hope was realized; Vergennes, the Minister of Foreign Affairs, proved favorable. Through his influence, the American agents, Silas Deane and Arthur Lee, were able to make arrangements whereby the French and Spanish governments furnished capital to a dummy trading company which in turn supplied arms, ammunition and other equipment to the colonies. In this way over 90% of the powder used by the Continental army during the first two years of the war was obtained. When the news of the surrender of Burgoyne had been received by Congress, they decided to capitalize it. Benjamin Franklin now at Paris was encouraged to seek recognition with renewed ardor. Success crowned his efforts and on 6 February 1778 a treaty of alliance was signed.[1] The news of this great event came to Washington just as the long and dreary winter at Valley Forge was giving way to spring.

The report of the French alliance was most unwelcome to the British and spurred them to renewed activity. General Howe's resig-

---

[1] Spain and the Netherlands did not join the colonies in alliance but they not only loaned money and gave commercial privileges but finally went to war with Great Britain and effectively diverted her attention even if they won no spectacular victories.

nation was accepted and Sir Henry Clinton made his successor. The troops were ordered to withdraw from Philadelphia, because it was feared that a French fleet might blockade the Delaware and bottle up the British forces. The presence of too many privateers in the waters of the lower Delaware and off the capes, caused the British forces to be marched overland. Washington sought to meet them and strike a decisive blow. He almost succeeded at Monmouth Court House, New Jersey, 28 June 1778, but lost most of the hoped for advantage by the stupidity of General Charles Lee. After this lost opportunity he could only march to the Hudson above New York City and await the coming of the French forces. But the united victory which Washington hoped for and which Great Britain feared did not materialize. The French fleet did not attack New York or capture Newport and the rest of 1778 and 1779 went by with neither side strong enough to attack the other.

Away to the west, while the armies were watching each other in the east, an empire was being won. George Rogers Clark, a major in the Virginia militia, came to Gov. Patrick Henry with a plan to conquer the territory north of the Ohio and east of the Mississippi. With the small force that Henry could spare him, he made a well nigh impossible march into that country, in the winter of 1778-1779, and was completely successful. The great area known thereafter as the North-west Territory was captured from the British and the United States now had possession of the long coveted lands beyond the mountains.

In the meantime, the British were somewhat relieved of their apprehensions by the ineffectiveness of French aid and decided to transfer the field of activity to the southern colonies. They had enjoyed an initial success when Savannah was captured, 29 December 1778, and there was promise of much Tory support. The result was the capture of a second city, Charleston, in May 1780. Washington was able to do little but he sent first Gates and then Gen. Nathanael Greene to oppose British advance under Lord Cornwallis as best they might. Their efforts were balked by several defeats; nevertheless, Cornwallis found his task difficult. While he might capture seaports and win victories he could not maintain his power very far from the coast. His troops were not sufficient to guard his conquests; and, after the watchful Greene had superseded the rather ineffective Gates, he had a foe who followed him continually and constantly annoyed and endangered him. He made a long march through North Carolina where he found little resistance and less glory. Finally Cornwallis established a base on the York River at Yorktown, Virginia, upon orders of his commander, Sir Henry Clinton, still in New York.

Washington in the meanwhile hoped that the French force, now much enlarged, would join him and capture New York; but the French decided that Cornwallis at Yorktown would be a more desirable prize. They took naval control of the Chesapeake and Washington marched to join them. This joint siege of Yorktown, successfully terminated 19 October 1781, when the British commander surrendered. The loss of this second army was the last straw to England; reconquest was evidently impossible. The British debt had mounted up, expenses were increasing and income declining. American privateers had thrown English commerce into a sad state of demoralization which was not decreased by the attacks of French, Spanish and Dutch war vessels. There was but one thing to do and that was to make peace.

Benjamin Franklin, John Adams and John Jay undertook peace negotiations in 1782 at Paris. In the treaty which was finally signed, Great Britain acknowledged the independence of the United States and recognized the Mississippi as the western boundary. The Floridas were returned to Spain and Canada remained British; but in neither case were definite, undisputed boundaries fixed, and the seed was thus planted for later dispute and trouble. The American fishermen were to be permitted to make their catches in Canadian waters and to dry their fish on the Canadian and Newfoundland shores, while on the other hand the British were conceded free navigation of the Mississippi.

A question which caused much trouble in the conference was the status of the Loyalists. The English sought vigorously to have their civil rights and their confiscated property restored. At length, the American commissioners agreed that there should be no further confiscation of Tory property or persecution of Tory persons. They promised, further, that Congress should recommend that the states restore the confiscated property and repeal the laws which deprived Loyalists of their civil rights. Concerning the various debts owed British merchants, amounting to more than £5,000,000, the United States agreed that they should be met, while England on her part agreed to pay for slaves freed and property destroyed in her coastal raids during the war. As far as the promises of the Americans went, they were no more than gestures because Congress had no authority in these matters; and time was to show how small was the regard which the states had for the provisions of this treaty. Nevertheless, on the basis of this agreement peace was proclaimed in Paris 20 February 1783 and the last British troops left New York 25 November. The military victory was complete.

Changes Wrought by the War

The successful resort to arms was but one phase of the revolutionary movement. The struggle profoundly affected all of colonial life. New governments had to be created, the armies fed, clothed, armed and financed, new business ventures undertaken and radical changes made in the erstwhile provincial social order.

The struggle for independence made necessary many political changes. Local government, as far as towns and counties were concerned, was not much affected; but the provincial political organization had to be revised and new machinery created to meet the needs of independence. Before the Declaration the Continental Congress advised the colonies to form independent state governments, and between 1776 and 1783 this advice was followed. In Rhode Island and Connecticut, where the colonial charters had provided for independent self-government, the legislatures went no further than to re-enact their charters as constitutions with but a change in title. In the other eleven colonies, however, more radical adjustments were imperative. Royal and proprietary governors could no longer be permitted to function and so an executive branch and a new judiciary had to be created.

Distrust of the executive, acquired during the colonial days when the governors represented Crown or proprietor and quarreled with the assemblies, influenced constitution makers to allow the newly created executives relatively little power. Their right of veto was sharply curbed and in some instances, generally in New England, a council was provided to share the executive responsibility with the governor. Pennsylvania in fact for a while did without one. The legislatures representing the people were to be the great repositories of power. They were composed of two houses, except in Pennsylvania, and were subject to few limitations, other than those detailed in the bills of individual rights which were to be found in most of the new constitutions.

Yet they were not altogether democratic. Some property or tax paying qualification was required for office holding and the suffrage and thus many men were denied the vote; also the legislatures were not truly representative in many states, for the older tidewater settlements had more than their share of lawmakers and the new regions of the back country were left with much cause to complain of their lack of representation. Furthermore, religious qualifications still persisted in many of the states; and those other than trinitarian Protestants frequently found themselves disqualified, at least from office holding. In general, the makers of the new constitutions agreed that the judiciary should be somewhat more independent than had been the case in the colonies; and provision was made for the appointment of judges, either by legislature or executive, for life or during good behavior. Religious freedom was guaranteed and in some instances the emancipation of slaves begun.

The greatest problem was not, however, the reorganization of state governments, but the creation of a national government. It is extremely significant that at no time does there seem to have been any intention on the part of any of the individual states to remain separate from the rest. Independence had been declared and won in federation and plans for formal confederation were concluded in the months immediately after the Declaration of Independence. On 15 November 1777 a constitution known as the Articles of Confederation was submitted to the states for ratification and in March, 1781, the scheme went into effect. This plan provided for a "perpetual union" of the states in a confederation, to be governed by a congress similar to the Continental Congress, consisting of one house composed of delegates from each state. In legislating each state had one vote and the agreement of nine states was necessary to pass a bill. The states jealously guarded their control of commerce and the taxing power and the Congress of the Confederation could only ask the states for what it needed. Furthermore, its functions were limited almost exclusively to the conduct of foreign affairs, and the administration of the common territory west of the Alleghanies.

Neither federal executive nor judiciary was provided, nor could an amendment be made except by unanimous consent of the states. However, the basis of national citizenship was laid down by the guarantee to citizens of one state going into another, of the privilege of citizenship in the latter. Furthermore, it was stipulated that the records and judicial proceedings of any state should be recognized in all the others and extradition of fugitives was provided for. Most of the power was retained by the states themselves and a very little was sparingly allotted to the federation. The important fact, however, was that the formal federation existed.

The Revolution left its mark upon economic life. In the regions where the armies were operating there was great demand for food, not only for the Continental troops but also for the British and French armies. In these regions agriculture was stimulated by high prices and by the gold which both British and French paid for their supplies. Also as the new state governments confiscated much land from those loyal to the Crown and then sold it, the time was opportune for farmers to enlarge their acreage. As there was not much capital, a number of farmers borrowed money to pay for these lands with the expectation that the high prices would last long enough to enable them to pay off their debts. However, as the fighting was restricted and transportation was bad, the great mass of farmers were slightly affected by the conflict.

Industry was greatly stimulated. All British restrictions were now without effect. Clothes, arms, munitions, equipment of all sorts, and salt were much needed. There were no established manufactures capable of producing sufficient quantities of any of this equipment. Clothing

had been largely imported or manufactured in the homes. Shoes had
been made to fill individual orders by local cobblers, or had been crudely
put together at home. The small forges and foundries were wholly
incapable of providing enough cannon and shot; facilities for making
muskets and manufacturing gunpowder 'were likewise very limited.
Manufacturing responded to the stimulus of war needs in spite of
the fact that payments in Continental paper were not the best encouragement. Numerous small concerns started operations though most of
them were little more than home industries. In the iron business larger
forges and foundries were built to manufacture artillery.

Business was brisk during the war period. Commerce was free now
from British navigation laws; and when France allied herself to the
new nation and Spain went to war with Great Britain, most of the
important seaports except the English were open to American ships.
Patriot privateers, too, swelled trade by their captures and the goods
and money which they brought home. The warehouses of the American
merchants were well stocked with European goods. Naturally, as the
fortunes of the new country were in a very uncertain state, and as the
currency was debauched by a flood of paper money, business profiteers
were not absent; gamblers schemed to gain by the falling price of the
paper money; and clandestine sales to the British, though they brought
in gold, added to the uncertainty because of the risk often involved.

Many prospered during the war but unfortunately this prosperity
was never shared by the Continental treasury. The finances of the
governments were generally in a hopeless condition for the states could
not contribute much and the patriots had little to lend. The available
coin always had been insufficient to meet the growing needs of the
colonists; and for war demands, it was totally inadequate. The Continental Congress tried to borrow at home and abroad, with only
moderate success. It fell back upon large issues of paper money which
depreciated so rapidly that sale of produce in return for this currency
amounted practically to a gift.[1] Robert Morris, the treasury's chief
support was often unable to find funds for the smallest expenses. In
spite of his handicaps he made some progress toward establishing sound
finance; he used a part of the gold borrowed from France to help
establish the first bank, the Bank of North America, which was opened
in Philadelphia in 1781.

The most significant of the changes wrought by the Revolution
were social, for in the organization of society there was a revolution
indeed. Neighborhoods were no longer the same, for many familiar

---

[1] $8,000,000 in specie was borrowed from abroad. Congress borrowed $67,000,-
000 at home and with the states issued $450,000,000 in paper money. The vari-
ous states contributed $1,500,000 in specie and $54,000,000 in paper. The total
cost of the war is estimated as $104,000,000 in gold values.

figures were absent from the streets. Not only did the war take its toll of casualties (at least 10,000 were killed and wounded) but an important element who opposed independence was banished or in flight. There is no way of knowing how extensive that opposition was for it varied from year to year and intensified and diminished according to the patriot success. John Adams estimated that at least one-third of the colonists were opposed to the war and that numerous others were indifferent. Such conditions left active Patriots in the minority. Worse, when the army seemed in danger of destruction, that minority of patriots seemed smaller than it really was.

The Loyalists, or Tories, were men of all ranks and conditions who believed that there was no justification for this treasonable rebellion against the Crown. Most important among them were large numbers of comfortable, conservative and prosperous men, who not only were loyal to the Crown, but who feared certain tendencies displayed by the more radical of the Patriots. Though there were a number of wealthy men who were heart and soul in the patriot cause, the move in the northern colonies took on the guise of a popular uprising against a ruling class. Small tradesmen and farmers openly advocated confiscation of the land of the Tories. Many of the most influential colonial families, leaders in the provincial society which gathered around the governor and British officials, despised and feared the "rebels" and gave services and money for suppressing the rebellion. Loyalist regiments were mustered into the Brtish army and many a Tory farmer sold supplies to the royal commissaries.

In the South, the conflict took on more of the aspect of a civil war than of a popular uprising. Many of the plantation owners had much the same point of view that the English country gentlemen possessed and were as loyal to the Crown as ever the cavaliers had been in the previous century. Others, just as conservative in economic and social views, felt that the politicians in the mother country were trying to gouge them and poach upon their rights; they joined the Patriots. So it was plantation-owner against his neighbor; small farmer against small farmer. The strength of the Tories in the South grew during the latter part of the war when the British were actively campaigning in the region. But neither loyalty to the Crown nor the desire for independence was confined to any section or class.

Many communities in both sections were divided into bitter factions and old antagonisms and jealousies found their vent in quarrels under the guise of serving one cause or the other. In country districts neighbors often engaged in clandestine and marauding civil war, in which life and property were frequently lost and much of anxiety and hazard added to the struggle. Many a Patriot felt he must remain at home to protect his family against Tory pillagers, and the army suffered in consequence. Patriot farmers found themselves at a disadvantage, too, when their neighbors indifferent or hostile to the patriot cause, sold their produce to British quartermasters for gold while the reward of patriotism was only depreciated paper. Such division of opinion and recompense had been more of a handicap than lack of equipment or even defeat in battle.

Naturally the Patriots sought to punish their opponents and the Tories cherished their loyalty at extreme cost to themselves. State legislatures confiscated their property and caused their imprisonment. Frequently their neighbors made it so unpleasant for them that they were forced to leave their homes, while in extreme cases tar and feathers hastened their exit. Some simply retreated to towns within the British lines, others went to England or the West Indies, and a third group settled in Canada; the latter two groups numbered somewhere between sixty and one hundred thousand persons. The property which was abandoned or confiscated, valued at £9,000,000, was kept by the state or sold to new owners. In this way some great estates were broken up, others became public land.

With the departure of the wealthy Tories, there disappeared an aristocratic ruling element in political and social circles, and in their place came a new leadership. Ambitious and energetic Patriots, adherents of republican principles, often quite humble in fortune, gained prominence through their services to the cause of liberty. They settled in the seats of the mighty. They dominated the legislatures and abolished quit rents and primogeniture, which had done so much to maintain landed estates. Furthermore, they did what they could to encourage small holdings in fee simple, for one of the ideals of the Revolution was economic independence for the common man. This break up of large holdings did much to make the distribution of property more democratic and to give point to the Revolutionary ideal of equality.

The cause of equality and human freedom was further advanced during the Revolution by the legislators in the states under the leadership of men like Jefferson. Religious freedom was forwarded by statutes or constitutional provisions abandoning established churches and taxation therefor. Shortly after the cessation of conflict three well-organized and independent church groups were established. The Anglican or Episcopal church broke away from English ties and secured an American bishop, Samuel Seabury, to direct its affairs. A Roman Catholic bishop, the patriotic John Carroll of Baltimore, was appointed to nourish an American church. At the same time, new Methodist congregations united in an organization and shortly adopted the episcopal system; the most notable organizer among them was Bishop Francis Asbury. These organizers had much to do for there had been a falling away under the rationalist spirit of the Revolutionary thought and many of the religious ties had weakened. Freedom for Negro slaves was written into certain of the northern constitutions. Criminal law was made more humane. Furthermore, there was some slight evidence that a few of the leaders were thinking of education as a public responsibility. Though these were only signs, the new leadership and the new ideals, however, were facts.

In this fashion a republic had been created, based upon widely distributed property and the political rights of the individual. The old order which smacked of aristocracy, had been swept away and a new and more responsive leadership had arisen, not from any British ruling class but from the ranks of the colonists themselves. The Patriots had achieved this in cooperation and while the states felt themselves to be independent sovereigns they had accomplished their important task in concert, in union. Often they spoke of themselves as "Americans" and alluded to "national" projects. In the years between 1763 and 1783, political independence had been won by thirteen sovereign and united states; but something more vital had been achieved, a group of three million people were beginning to learn that they were in fact a nation.

CHAPTER V

CREATING THE REPUBLIC

The treaty of peace and the withdrawal of the British troops relaxed the strain of unnatural activity, intense effort and anxiety under which the people of the United States had been living for nearly a decade. The reaction brought a feeling of carelessness, a loss of unity and national feeling and an attempt to return to the petty concerns of everyday life where there was much to divert them. All was not well in the new republic but for the time being the new problems called forth no constructive handling, rather they invited further confusion.

Post-war Difficulties

Economic depression had settled down upon the business life of the nation. The expansion of agriculture and manufacturing induced by the war was no longer needed. Agricultural prices dropped but the mortgages remained to be paid. The new manufacturers were faced with a failing demand and foreign competition; only hard times and perhaps ruin seemed ahead of them. The merchants, too, were badly off with high-priced stocks of goods bought during the war-time inflation and with ships now dumping at American ports; British surplus had accumulated while the war cut off trade. Now the British manufacturers were eager to sell their accumulations at prices with which the American merchants, with their expensive war-time stocks, could not compete. Able neither to sell their goods nor pay their debts, many faced ruin. Stirred by the danger of debtors' prisons, businessmen began to look for remedies.

The condition of the currency contributed heavily to the unstable situation. The vast quantity of paper money, Continental and state, was almost worthless and most of the small amount of specie which the country possessed was exported to pay for the flood of foreign bargains. The general government was without funds and could pay neither the principal nor interest of its large indebtedness; many who had invested their substance patriotically in government obligations were in dire straits. Besides the states were heavily in debt and some of the more thrifty were setting heavy taxes to pay their obligations; property owners were quick to groan under these burdens. Most apparent of all the ills was the prevalence of unemployment. Many a soldier, even more sailors, especially privateersmen, and some laborers were unable to find work and were on the precarious edge of starvation.

As always, the uncertainties of the economic disorganization affected the poor most directly. In spite of the destruction of the "Tory" power in society, class divisions survived, for in many cases war profiteers sought to assume the pretensions of the exiles. Most apparent was a sharp division between debtor and creditor. So many were in debt and there was so little opportunity of earning the money to satisfy creditors or to pay taxes. The holders of mortgages and notes and tax collectors went to law and there were frequent foreclosures, especially on farms bought at wartime prices. Much land was in process of changing hands and many an independent farmer must become a tenant or migrate to the westward and make a new start.

The frequent foreclosures and dispossess actions, as well as the general hardships of the depression, told upon the nerves. People were frightened and began fumbling for a remedy. Then, as many times later, they turned to government, politicians made promises and popular agitations for new laws were set on foot. In seven of the thirteen states "radical" groups were formed to secure drastic legislation in behalf of the debtor. Their chief demand was more paper money; cheap money would be easy to get and when made legal tender would enable the debtors to free themselves from their obligations. Laws were also demanded to prevent foreclosures or court actions to collect debts. Such "stay" laws would provide a virtual moratorium until times became better.

Legislation of this character so distasteful to men of substance was very attractive to the mass; it seemed to promise security and freedom from debt. Wherever they could, political leaders of popular parties forced such laws through state legislatures. They succeeded in New York, Pennsylvania, New Jersey, Rhode Island, North Carolina, South Carolina and Georgia, where paper money was issued in larger quantities and made legal tender. Woe betide any merchant in these states who tried to refuse this rag money. The mobs which had learned violence in the preliminaries of the Revolution came forth again to threaten merchants and even the courts and their officers. Court houses were attacked, courts disbanded and in Massachusetts such an attack upon the Northampton county court led by Daniel Shays in 1786 was so threatening that 4400 militia were called out to put down this "rebellion." Many a lover of law and order and substantial property holder became fearful of anarchy, for if the state governments "went radical," no power, certainly not the feeble Congress, existed to protect the rights of those who wished to enforce the law of contracts.

Economic disorganization induced frequent quarrels among the states. Certain of the larger commonwealths like Pennsylvania, where new industries were struggling, were trying to protect themselves from foreign competition by means of high tariffs. But other states, chiefly agricultural, were interested only in obtaining what they needed as cheaply as possible; no tariffs of theirs contained protective features. Foreign goods, therefore, flowed freely into the latter states and were easily smuggled into the protected states to the further discomfort of the hard-pressed manufacturers. As Congress had no authority over interstate or foreign commerce, no power existed which could enforce uniformity in commercial regulations. But how could the weakness of Congress be overcome?

Discontent and disorganization were almost universal and spread even beyond the Alleghanies where settlers in what were to become Kentucky and Tennessee struggled to set up local government in spite of neglect by the central government. During the Revolution, restless

Beyond the Appalachians

spirits had gone beyond the mountains. In 1769 Daniel Boone had begun to explore the Kentucky region and in the same year settlers crossed into western North Carolina to the Watauga Valley where under the leadership of James Robertson and John Sevier, an independent community was organized as the Watauga Association (1772-1778). In 1774 James Harrod made the first settlement in Kentucky at Harrodsburg and in 1775 Daniel Boone, acting for Judge Richard Henderson, cut a trail up from the Cumberland Gap and established Boonesboro, Kentucky, with hardy Watauga settlers. Henderson tried to organize his Kentucky settlements as the state of Transylvania in 1775 but Virginia objected. Thereafter his agent, Robertson, in 1779 led more Wataugans into the present state of Tennessee where they established Nashville; they tried to organize the Cumberland settlements into a separate state but at length had to yield to North Carolina. After the latter state gave up her frontier lands to the federal government in 1784, John Sevier sought to organize these western settlements into the commonwealth of Franklin and Virginia consented that Kentucky become a state. But Congress failed to act; North Carolina repealed its act of cession and resumed jurisdiction over the Tennessee region.

These western settlers felt keenly the neglect of the Congress, because of their dangerous situation. The southwestern Indians, the Cherokees, Chickasaws, Choctaws and Creeks were not pleasant neighbors, especially when urged by the Spanish to be otherwise. Congress worried about these conditions but the national army could hardly be said to exist and besides the southern states claimed this trans-Appalachian region as theirs and were jealous of even the weak interference of Congress. The southerners were further disgruntled because of Spanish restrictions on trade through the port of New Orleans. Here again Congress was powerless to help; American diplomats with no force of arms behind them could gain no concessions from the contemptuous Spanish government. So the western settlers, like their poor brethren in the East, were restive and talked of establishing their own governments, independent of the far away and powerless East. Eastern leaders, Washington among them, feared that the West might be lost to the nation.

International troubles were not the least which beset the new republic. The federation was independent and so recognized by treaty but that did not mean that it was treated with much consideration or accorded much influence. This lack of prestige damaged American trade. Before the Revolution colonial ships had been permitted British registry and under that flag were received in the ports of the world, enjoying the privileges accorded to that symbol of power. Such protection had been destroyed by independence and the Stars and Stripes meant little to European port officers. The terms of the French alliance included commercial concessions and open ports, but even the French placed some restrictions on West Indian trade and Great Britain and Spain prohibited it altogether, thereby depriving American merchants of most important prospects. Great Britain crippled the whaling industry by high tariffs and refused to make any treaty or even send over a representative. Spain, on the other hand, dispatched Gardoqui to Philadelphia and consented to a treaty which permitted commerce with her European ports; but she barred access to her American colonies and kept the mouth of the Mississippi tightly closed. The Jay-Gardoqui treaty therefore became so unpopular in the Southwest that it failed of ratification. There seemed no way to enforce diplomatic pretensions. How could a nation which didn't pay its debts, or even the interest, and whose citizens refused to pay their bills, expect any concessions from Europe?

The people were restless, the states were quarrelling, westerners talked secession, foreign nations slighted the government, business was bad, and state governments had "gone radical." Congress was helpless, without power, without funds, without adequate armed force, worst of all, without prestige. The politicians who now made up its membership could not deal effectively with such perplexities. In vain, Congress requested funds from the states. The latter were having too hard a time, raising money for their own immediate needs, to permit heavier taxes for federal requisitions. Little money was sent to Philadelphia and so empty did the national treasury become that Congress in 1783 felt it wise to flee to Princeton lest they be attacked by a band of unpaid soldiers who were demanding money.

Twice Congress sought power to levy funds. They sent to the states in 1781 a proposal to permit Congress to collect an import duty of 5% but it was defeated by the refusal of one state, Rhode Island, to consent. A proposition of 1783 which would have permitted duties on specified articles for twenty-five years also failed. Only one other resource seemed left to Congress, namely, the sale of the public lands.

Jefferson in 1784 prepared a plan of government for the vast territory north of the Ohio and west of Pennsylvania which had been ceded to the Confederation by Virginia, New York, Massachusetts and Connecticut. Congress adopted this plan and in the next year ordered the region surveyed. The land was to be laid out in townships, six miles square, made up of thirty-six sections of 640 acres each in a township. Portions were set aside for satisfying the claims of Revolutionary soldiers and one-third of any minerals found were reserved for the Confederation. There was no thought in those days of any need for conservation of natural resources.

The bulk of the land was to be sold at auction in minimum lots of 640 acres at a minimum price of one dollar per acre. The sales were to be held in the various thirteen states. Four sections in the center of each township were to be withheld to be sold later when land values had appreciated. The money received for the sale of one section in each township was to be turned over to the support of education, a provision of great future significance for it was the basis of the elaborate systems of free education for which these states became noted. But few purchased and within three years only 73,000 acres had been sold to individuals in spite of inducements offered in the way of credit facilities. Congress therefore turned to a new policy, selling large blocks to companies and individuals at reduced prices. The most famous of these sales was made to the Ohio Company composed principally of New England veterans who purchased 5,000,000 acres for $500,000 in 1787.

Stable government was offered as further inducement for purchase in the form of the Ordinance of 1787 which provided for an immediate, temporary government for the whole territory. A governor, three judges and a secretary were to be appointed by Congress to adapt laws to the

The State Department in 1783

HOMES OF FIRST GOVERNMENT IN PHILADELPHIA

Independence Hall on Election Day

territory and to govern it. Plans were provided for future self-government and the admission of portions as states as soon as the population was sufficient to warrant these advances. The bill of rights which this ordinance contained, for the benefit of any settlers who might seek homes in this new area, was a noteworthy statement of American ideals of social organization. Freedom of religion, of speech and of the press as well as the usual rights of individuals to be tried by jury, to petition, and to bear arms were all stipulated. Support for public education was guaranteed and slavery was forbidden in all this area. In spite of all these liberal provisions, the land did not sell and the national treasury, still empty, only emphasized the weakness of the government.

While things seemed to be at their worst, events were shaping a more auspicious future. There were signs, more apparent today than perhaps they were then, that the depression was lifting. Trade was expanding. Commercial treaties had been made with Holland, Prussia and Sweden and trading under the American flag increased in the Baltic. The British West India trade grew extensive again, in spite of English prohibitions, and importers were once more in funds. Manufacturers became more prosperous. States granted subsidies, bounties and lottery privileges. Societies were organized to promote better methods of manufacturing. These societies began to study the new machines which England was using in her industrial centers. Industry revived and emphasized a new prosperity although the old handicraft methods were still used. The enterprising manufacturers were hampered by a lack of capital with which to try new methods. Moreover, labor was scarce because of the attractions of land owning and farming.

Plans for westward development and improved transportation facilities which might bind the sections more closely together were also signs of a new optimism and the rebirth of creative impulses. George Washington led in these plans. He had extensive holdings in western lands and was anxious to promote the building of a canal which would make the Potomac and James Rivers paths of commerce and communication. He also had a project for a canal through the dismal swamp to make access to North Carolina easier. Development companies like the Ohio Company interested in western lands, were attempting to open up town sites beyond the Alleghanies. American enterprise was reawakening.

Adopting the Constitution

The beginnings of prosperity sharpened the consciousness of the need of a stronger central government. The Confederation was too weak for practical men of affairs. National prestige and credit, property interests, means of livelihood and the very liberty which had cost such a struggle were in jeopardy. As need of change became more widely recognized the first steps toward effecting it were being taken. In 1785 a committee representing Virginia and Maryland met at Mt. Vernon with George Washington to discuss the question of regulating navigation on the Potomac River and Chesapeake Bay. During their deliberations they talked of the general disordered state of commercial regulation and concluded that a larger conference should be held to which representatives of the other states should be invited. Virginia called such a meeting to convene at Annapolis, Maryland, in 1786 and when delegates from only five states came those present decided to report to the states and to Congress the need for a general convention. Congress accepted the report and authorized a convention to meet in Philadelphia in May, 1787. In response to this summons, delegates from all states except Rhode Island convened to consider amendments which might make the Articles of Confederation a workable document.

A remarkable group of fifty-five of the best-known Americans made up the assemblage. George Washington was its president, James Madison kept careful and voluminous notes of its proceedings. The revered Dr. Franklin, in spite of his fourscore years, was in active attendance when his health permitted. Robert Morris, Gouverneur Morris, John Dickinson, Charles Cotesworth Pinckney, Charles Pinckney, James Wilson and Alexander Hamilton were some of the others who made the convention so able a body. Only a few of the great names were absent. Some, like Patrick Henry, Samuel Adams and John Hancock, who were secure in power and influence in their own states, were suspicious of any strong central power; Rhode Island for that reason sent no delegates. Thomas Jefferson was abroad as minister to France. Practically all of the members were substantial men who believed in law and order and in the security of property, and who were opposed to the radicals who had been jeopardizing wealth in the past few years. They were agreed that the central government must be strengthened.

Though this body was commissioned only to amend the Articles of Confederation, its members boldly determined to make a new government. About most of its details they were in general agreement but there were certain differences which were to try the patience and ingenuity of the leaders in those hot summer days of 1787.

No simple government would suffice. A system had to be created which would reconcile two different powers, the powers of local control now exercised by semi-independent states and the power of a newly created central government. Members of the convention like Madison had made an intensive study of the history of governments in general and of federal governments in particular. They were well read in James Harrington, John Locke and the Baron de Montesquieu. They were prepared to create a complicated and nicely adjusted federal system which would permit the harmonious functioning of these two sets of powers and which at the same time would prevent any one interest from ever gaining control of the central government. They divided powers between the state and federal governments, attempting a rather careful definition of those of the latter. Then the mechanism of the central government was carefully constructed.

Here colonial experience and Montesquieu's idealized conception of the British government were the models. There should be three separate and distinct branches of government, each equal and coordinate with the others. The legislative branch like the colonial legislatures and the British Parliament was to consist of two houses. This fact made it easier to settle the fundamental quarrel between the large and small states over representation in Congress. The compromise finally adopted gave small states equal representation with large in the Senate or upper house, which was to represent the states as such. Each state legislature was to choose two senators serving for six years each. In the lower house, however, the large states secured representation by population, a principle which was to be used also in apportioning direct taxes among the states. The representatives were to serve for but two years and were to be chosen by such persons as each state permitted to vote for members of the lower house of its own legislature.

This compromise between the interests of the large and small states also involved a compromise between North and South. What status was to be accorded to Negro slaves? Were they part of the population and were southern states to have much larger representation and taxes because of their slaves? It was finally agreed to count three-fifths of the Negroes for both representation and taxes. Not until the questions as to the make up of Congress were settled was anyone confident that a new order could be achieved.

The creation of an executive was not so difficult. A president was to be chosen for a term of four years, not by the people but by electors. Some feared popular elections, but the electoral system was chosen for practical reasons. The scattered nature of the population would make concentration on any one candidate impossible and the resultant number of choices would produce only a confusion in which no one would ever get anything like the majority of the votes necessary to elect. Therefore each state was to choose as many electors as it had senators and representatives and they were to meet in their respective state capitals where each was to vote for two men. When their votes were assembled in the national Congress and counted, the man who received the largest number of votes was to be President and the next highest Vice-President. The President was armed with real power. He was to be commander-in-chief of the army and navy, he could veto bills passed by Congress, his was the initiative in foreign affairs, and his powers of appointment were large.

The third branch of the new government was a federal judiciary, to be composed of a supreme court and such inferior courts as Congress might create; the Constitution left large power to Congress in organizing the judiciary. The judges for these courts were to be appointed by the President, by and with the advice and consent of the Senate, to hold office during good behavior, in default of which they might be impeached and removed only by Congress. These courts were given a judicial power which should extend to all cases, in law and equity, arising under the Constitution, the laws of the United States or treaties. They were to have jurisdiction in disputes arising between any of the United States and the federal government or in quarrels between the states or their citizens. Much depended on how the proposed federal judiciary might construe their powers.

So three branches of government were created each independent and coordinate but still checked by the others. Congressional laws had to be approved by the executive who in turn had to submit his appointments and his treaties to the Senate and who himself might be impeached and removed by Congress. The judiciary was to hear all cases arising under the laws of Congress and the Constitution and must therefore interpret them but they were appointed by the President and confirmed by the Senate; they too might be impeached by Congress. All of these branches were protected from direct influence by the public will except the lower house of Congress. Furthermore, they were chosen for a wide variety of terms and it would be impossible to effect any complete change in personnel except by revolution. Qualifications for voting for the lower house were left to the states and were thus generally hedged about by some property qualifications. The country was not yet ready for full suffrage.

These careful statesmen made certain that the central government would be strong enough to maintain social order and protect property. By five positive powers, one of which was sweeping, and by two prohibitions upon the states they forged a powerful weapon for this purpose. The power to tax granted to Congress insured the means to pay the debts so long overdue, to restore credit and to raise money for the "general welfare." Congress also was to have sole power to regulate interstate and foreign commerce, a concession which was wrung from the southern agricultural states only in return for the prohibition of export taxes and a guarantee of the continuance of the slave trade at least until 1808. This commercial power would insure uniformity of regulation and prevent quarrels between the states. The Congress furthermore had control of the public lands and the Indians and might admit new states into the union. This vast power meant control of the growth of the nation. To provide against foreign attack and domestic disturbance, the federal government possessed of tax money could organize and equip an adequate military and naval force, a bulwark of security. On the other hand, the states were forbidden to issue paper money or in any way to impair the obligation of contract. There would be no more legislation of too radical a character. Most important was the clause most famous of all whereby the federal government was granted all powers "necessary and proper" to carry out the provisions of the Constitution. What did the words "necessary and proper" mean? If they were loosely construed what might the new government not do?

In the fall of 1787 the document was signed by the members of the convention, headed by George Washington, its president, and transmitted to Congress. This body compliantly sent it to the states although it was not the series of amendments to the "Articles" which the convention had been authorized to prepare but an entire new document proposing a revolutionary change in the structure of the government. The "Articles of Confederation" forbade amendment without unanimous consent of the states but this startling document declared itself in effect if accepted by nine of the thirteen states.

The fight for ratification began and a fight it proved to be. Each state was to choose a convention to consider the proposal, to accept it or reject it. In the contests which marked the choice of these conventions, the friends and foes of the change marshalled their arguments and influence. It was new and proposed a major operation. Many who disliked innovation or who made up their minds slowly voted against it. Another group of opponents was composed of local politicians who were in positions of great influence in their states and mistrusted the effect of the new government upon their prestige. It was better to be first in a little Iberian village than second in Rome, so thought George Clinton of New York and Patrick Henry of Virginia and many others. They, fought vigorously against the new instrument as centralizing authority and destroying the sovereignty of the states. Large numbers, particularly in the country districts, thought the new plan a device of the rich to improve their fortunes and to place the burden of taxation for the support of the new government upon the farmers' lands. Others protested that nowhere in the proposed constitution were there any provisions to safeguard the rights of individuals, no guarantees for individual liberty. The whole scheme was the plan of aristocrats to set up a strong and probably tyrannical government situated so far away from most of the people that it could safely disregard the rights of the common man.

To combat this formidable opposition the friends of the document were strategically well placed. Most important was the fact that some of the best known men of the country were favorable, Washington's prestige was invaluable. Then there were skillful debaters among them, Madison, Hamilton and Jay wrote a series of masterly essays describing and explaining the new scheme and its expected benefits. These writings, known as the "Federalist" papers, were given thoughtful reading by influential people. The chaotic conditions prevalent in the preceding years were also a powerful argument and influenced many to support the new order. The conflict caused a renewal of party organization and as in the Revolution lines were drawn and labels became the fashion. The advocates of the adoption of the new plan called themselves "Federalists" thus emphasizing the idea of union rather than centralization and their opponents were generally known as "Anti-Federalists."

In Delaware, Connecticut, Georgia, New Jersey, South Carolina, Pennsylvania and Maryland, the struggle was not so intense but in Virginia, New Hampshire and Massachusetts the vote was close. In Virginia prominent politicians like Patrick Henry opposed this central government as dangerous to liberty, while in Massachusetts the farmers were afraid of the power which commercial interests might wield in the new government. New York's opposition was exceptionally bitter and perhaps the deciding factor in the final acceptance was the knowledge that ten other states had ratified and that the new organization would be perfected without New York. As a condition of ratification some of the states had received a promise from the friends of the Constitution that amendments would be added providing for a bill of rights and when this promise was in process of fulfillment, North Carolina gave her consent in 1789. Rhode Island, however, was not brought in until the next year and then only when threatened with commercial isolation.

In such manner the Constitution was ratified. No popular vote was taken upon it, and the statistics which have survived as to votes cast for members of the ratifying conventions are fragmentary. The conflict was very bitter, the means used to overcome it sometimes savored much of modern political practice. It can be ventured that only a minority actually favored its adoption but all agreed to acquiesce and to give the new scheme a trial. The states surrendered essential parts of their sovereignty with the hope that thereby they might form a "more perfect union."

Putting the New Government into Operation

When New Hampshire and Virginia ratified the Constitution almost simultaneously in June 1788, preparations could be made to put it into effect. The expiring Continental Congress duly notified the states of the completion of ratification and made provision for the election of a new Congress under the Constitution and the choice of electors who were to select the President and Vice-President. That fall representatives were elected without much campaigning or popular interest. The state legislatures chose senators and either appointed the presidential electors themselves or ordered them to be chosen by the voters on the first Wednesday of January 1789. Men who had been favorable to the adoption of the Constitution generally were selected to fill these new positions for most opponents of it remained aloof and indifferent, waiting for the scheme to fail. The electors were unanimous in their presidential choice; George Washington who had led the country to independence was surely the one to lead it to stability. With much less unanimity John Adams was chosen to be Vice-President.

On 4 March 1789, the day appointed for the new government to begin its functioning, a quorum of the houses of Congress had not arrived in New York, the temporary capital. However, by April sufficient numbers had put in an appearance and on the thirtieth Washington was duly inaugurated. By fall Congress had provided revenue, had created the necessary governmental departments, and had established the federal courts. Washington carefully selected friends of the Constitution to fill the numerous offices and put the executive machinery in complete operation. To assist him in his task, he chose Alexander Hamilton to fill the most responsible of all the new positions, Secretary of the Treasury. One old friend, General Henry Knox, was to be Secretary of War; another, Edmund Randolph, Attorney-general. John Jay was appointed Chief Justice of the Supreme Court, and meanwhile he was to continue in charge of foreign affairs until the arrival of the new secretary, Thomas Jefferson, who had been recalled from the French mission, to head the newly created Department of State. It was an able group who assumed responsibility for the success of the experiment.

Of the many difficult problems which confronted these men, by far the most important, complex and pressing was the question of financing the federal government. Congress had taken preliminary steps before the treasury was organized. It enacted a tariff on imports mainly for revenue purposes. A protective measure was demanded by Pennsylvania congressmen, then as ever after in the forefront of that movement. Although they failed to obtain a protective measure as such, the American merchant marine was fostered by a system of tonnage duties which excluded foreign ships from coastwise trade. Congress contented itself with these preliminaries and left the main burden of money-raising and fiscal policy to the new secretary.

Alexander Hamilton was a financial genius who applied himself enthusiastically to his huge task. He was well acquainted with British methods of finance and took a broad view of his problem, endeavoring to encompass in his plans devices not only for raising funds and restoring credit, but also for aiding business and stimulating general prosperity. His prophetic vision discerned the enormous potential wealth of the nation and he believed that its speedy exploitation was the key to a solvent treasury and to power in world affairs. Under this inspiration he went to work.

Hamilton's first concern was to bring order out of the confused mass of indebtedness which confronted him and to create credit. In principal and interest the United States owed about 12 millions abroad and 42 millions at home. This was a tremendous sum to raise in those days but Hamilton was by no means appalled. Far from it; his imagination leaped to assume an even greater burden. The individual states owed about 25 millions on their own account and the secretary conceived the audacious scheme of having the federal treasury assume that burden also. Good arguments supported him. The federal government had deprived the states of the right to levy tariffs and thus had cut off an important source of revenue. Furthermore, the states had borrowed this money to promote a common cause, the American Revolution; it was but fair for the new government to pay their debts. More particularly, it was his belief that this would bind the states in respect and loyalty to the Constitution.

To these ends, therefore, Hamilton in 1790 presented to Congress a plan to fund a debt of 80 millions by transforming all the variety of certificates of indebtedness into obligations of the new government. As these securities matured, the holders would be paid in full and in the meantime interest would be discharged at regular intervals. To meet the heavy interest and sinking fund charges, a large revenue would be required and Hamilton proposed to augment the funds obtained from the tariff by levying an excise on liquor. Such a tax would not further burden real estate or business and would rest lightly on most people.

The secretary's proposals called forth heated discussion in and out of Congress. All agreed that the foreign debt should be paid in full but that was as far as the agreement went. First of all there was objection to the full payment of the domestic debt of the Congress. Much of it had long since passed from the hands of those who had loaned to the government and had been sold for a pittance to speculators. Should such speculators reap handsome profits while the patriots who had made the sacrifice and had been forced to part with the unpaid obligations went empty handed? There was much force to this argument, but Hamilton's plan for the domestic debt was carried.

A second, greater struggle arose over the assumption of state debts. Thrifty states like New York and Virginia were unwilling to be taxed to pay the debts of their less provident neighbors. Such an assumption would too thoroughly centralize all authority and financial power in the hands of the federal government. When test votes showed that

the proposal was not likely to carry, Hamilton enlisted Jefferson's aid
in political bargaining. As a result the new federal capital was located
in the South, on the Potomac, and enough southern votes were won
to carry the assumption bill. One further struggle ensued though it
proved less difficult to combat. The liquor excise was fought by representatives of the back country, where whiskey was the chief commodity
and the currency of the poverty-stricken farmers on the frontier. But
on this question as on the others, Hamilton's plan triumphed.

While these plans were being put into successful operation, the secretary turned his attention to a more elaborate and original idea, namely
the founding of a Bank of the United States, to function in some
respects as did the Bank of England. The country had but three banks,
the Bank of North America in Philadelphia, and one each in New
York and Boston; their capital was not large nor their influence
important. Hamilton realized that government finances could benefit
very greatly through a credit institution in close association with the
treasury. The capital and deposits would provide funds for government
borrowing. The note issue would provide a reliable, uniform currency
such as the country sadly needed. It would have branches in the various cities where government taxes could be deposited, and bills could be
paid by draughts, thus reducing the strain on the currency supply and
making currency transportation less necessary. The institution would
also promote business expansion by assembling capital for loan to reliable
businessmen. Much hoarded money would be brought into use if there
was this sound institution in which to deposit it. For these reasons,
Hamilton recommended the establishment of a bank capitalized at 10
millions; the government was to subscribe one-fifth of the capital, the
rest was to be supplied by the public who might subscribe government
stock (the current term for bonds) up to three-fourths of the required
amount; the charter was to run for twenty years.

Once more the opposition to Hamilton came forward. Representatives
of agricultural constituencies, especially in the South, could see little
good in this plan. They said it was but a scheme of city capitalists to
increase their wealth; it would do nothing for country people. Their
strongest argument was that the Constitution contained no provision for
a government-established bank; such a proposal was clearly unconstitutional. Hamilton defended his plan with trenchant logic. Did not the
Constitution give the federal government all power "necessary and
proper" to carry out its provisions? Such a bank was both necessary
and proper to carry out the financial responsibilities placed upon the
central government by the document. The secretary overbore congressional opposition by a narrow margin.

But Washington himself hesitated. His Secretary of State, Thomas
Jefferson, was now in open opposition to Hamilton, and argued strongly

for a strict construction of the Constitution and a veto of the bank bill. Only after Hamilton had given Washington a brilliant, written justification of the founding of the bank did the President sign the bill. There was no hesitation among the moneyed people, who eagerly subscribed to the stock. On 12 December 1791 the institution opened its doors in Philadelphia which had been made a temporary capital until the new city of Washington, then building on the banks of the Potomac, should be ready for occupancy.

Hamilton's work was almost finished. He planned the establishment of a mint in Philadelphia to coin gold and silver money. The United States was to have a decimal system of bimetallic coinage with the unit a dollar of one hundred cents. A gold dollar was to weigh 24.75 grains and silver dollars were to be fifteen times as heavy. One further aid to government finance and business Hamilton advocated; in a report to Congress he proposed a protective tariff. This last was the only one of his suggestions which failed of immediate adoption but his arguments were to live after him. In the meantime, he had secured an adequate revenue and sound credit for a government which had possessed neither.

Creating a Foreign Policy

The second great test of the new government's mettle was foreign relations. Could it secure a decent respect from European powers? Several trying questions had been unsettled for nearly a decade and were a menace to the peace, prosperity and even stability of the new nation. First of all were border difficulties with Great Britain on the north and Spain on the west and south. Britain had refused to vacate the posts in the northwest area, still dominated the Great Lakes region and kept in close contact with the Indians. To the south Spain continued to close New Orleans and the Mississippi to American trade while she occupied portions of the southwest territory. Furthermore, not only did she intrigue with the Indians but she egged on discontented Tennesseans and Kentuckians when they talked of secession, and kept a number of American officers on her payroll. At first all efforts of Washington and Jefferson to change these conditions were vain. A European convulsion, however, came to American aid.

In 1789 a revolution had begun in France which was to shake the political world. The success of republicanism in that once absolute monarchy filled European politicians with dismay. Steps which Austria and Prussia took to aid Louis XVI finally caused France to declare war upon those two nations and upon Spain and Britain as well. By 1793 there was a general European war of which the United States could be by no means unconscious. The superior naval force of the British soon crippled the commerce of France who turned to the American republic as the only convenient neutral with shipping adequate to carry on her necessary trade with her West Indies. England sought to throttle this new American commerce by applying the rule of 1756. In that year, England had announced that no neutral should enjoy in war time a trade which was forbidden in time of peace. In enforcing this rule, formulated before the United States was thought of, the British fleet captured many an American ship and seaman, for Great Britain's navy needed men and that government ordered search to be made of neutral vessels for "British citizens," to be impressed back into her service. British and American seamen looked and acted much alike, mistakes were easy and frequent and the British navy was being recruited forcibly from the ranks of American seamen.

France in the meantime sought aid from her American ally on the basis of the treaty of 1778. She sent to obtain this aid a bumptious minister, Citizen Genêt, whose chief qualifications were enthusiasm and poor judgment. He arrived in Charleston and immediately treated America as if it were a French ally, fitting out privateers in southern ports and making enthusiastic speeches. The United States, however, was in no position to go to war; with little money, a small army and no navy such a step was preposterous. Besides there was the argument that the treaty of alliance had been made with the French Monarchy. That no longer existed, so the United States could no longer be bound. Much to M. Genêt's disgust, Washington and even Jefferson received him coldly and in April 1793 issued a proclamation of neutrality. This was a hard blow for France.

Great Britain meanwhile continued depredations on American commerce and popular antagonism increased to such a pitch that even the British became aware of it and feared the United States might aid France. Great Britain therefore receded a little and consented in 1794 to make a treaty. In this agreement, negotiated by John Jay, Britain promised to relinquish the fur posts. All matters of monetary claims were referred to special commissions, and thereby the United States and Britain adopted that vital principle of arbitration which they were to use so often in years to come. But Jay failed utterly to obtain satisfactory commercial privileges in the West Indies, thus arousing a wave of popular antagonism to the treaty. Unsatisfactory though it was, Washington submitted it to the Senate which ratified it by a very close vote. Thus a second war with Great Britain was avoided, for the time being at least.

Spain meanwhile viewed with alarm this friendliness with Great Britain at a time when war was about to break out between the two powers. America might easily join Britain to seize Spanish American possessions. So, to placate the United States, Spain made the treaty of 1795 which not only gave trading privileges in Europe but also opened the mouth of the Mississippi to American shipping and fixed the southern boundary favorably to American claims. From the calamities of Europe the insignificant republic gained its first advance toward international security. The United States had avoided entangling alliances; boundaries had been more definitely settled; commercial relations had been improved. Washington had laid the foundation of a foreign policy which was to become traditional in the terms of his Farewell Address delivered in 1796. "Why, by interweaving our destiny with that of any part of Europe, entangle our peace and prosperity in the toils of European ambition, rivalship, interest, humour or caprice?"

The Political Test

But the new order had still to face another test. Partisan dissension was becoming bitter. Could the constitutional structure stand the strain of politics? For a time after the adoption of the Constitution the partisanship developed in the ratification struggle had subsided. It was only a matter of time before parties would form again, however, for the English two-party tradition was a strong inheritance. Washington had entered office with no discernible opposition but the policies of his administration roused bitter antagonism, especially in Congress where Hamilton's schemes had able opponents. In Washington's own official family, there developed a deplorable lack of harmony. Jefferson and Hamilton were personally incompatible and it was not very long before the former became convinced that his rival's influence was turning Washington to aristocracy and even toward monarchy. Jefferson was a staunch republican and in his political philosophy individual rights and the interests of the common man played a large part. He thought elaborate schemes for the benefit of the rich were dangerous. Such views made him the spokesman of the people, especially those in the country districts who were suspicious of the aristocratic tone of Washington's social life and of the capitalistic character of Hamilton's plans. The French Revolution as it progressed brought the final element needed to crystallize the growing partisanship.

When France first embraced republican ideas, much enthusiasm was felt for this great event in the United States. But when the more violent phase of the Revolution advanced and the leaders not only shed blood but also proved pronouncedly anti-religious, many of the more conservative Americans lost their enthusiasm and became hostile. Such a group applauded Washington's refusal to join France in the general European war. On the other hand, many, especially followers of Jefferson, loyal to the revolutionary principles of equality, felt that Washington and more particularly Hamilton were pro-British and had been persuaded for that reason to abandon their French ally in her time of need. The coming of Genêt caused the Francophiles to burst out in enthusiastic support. A number of societies, after the fashion of the Jacobin club of Paris, were formed and at their meetings there was extravagant praise of the glorious principles of the Revolution. In these Democratic societies, as they were called, there was much opposition to Washington and more to his associates.

Two events fed the flames. The tax on whiskey became more and more unpopular in the backcountry and in Pennsylvania open resistance was offered to federal collectors. Washington felt that the prestige of the new government was at stake and determined on a vigorous show of force. In 1794 an army of 15,000 militia led by Washington himself was marched against the mutineers. Such a demonstration had the desired effect of proving the ability of the government to maintain authority, but it also gave greater strength to the popular opposition to the administration. Further, when Washington accepted the unsatisfactory Jay treaty, opposition became riotous. Jefferson had resigned from the State Department in the beginning of 1794 and he was busy building up a party, called the Democratic-Republicans, to fight for republicanism and strict construction of the Constitution. Washington and his supporters adopted the name Federalists.

At first partisanship was confined to debate and congressional contests; not until 1796 did it appear in a presidential election. In 1792 Washington had been unanimously re-elected but in spite of the importunities of his friends, he refused to consider a third term. Who was to be his successor? The Democratic-Republicans of 1796 hoped for the choice of Thomas Jefferson while the Federalists turned to the Vice-President, John Adams. The electors were pretty evenly divided but chose Adams by three votes and Jefferson had to be satisfied with the vice-presidency. This narrow margin of defeat stimulated the Democratic-Republicans to further effort and organization and Jefferson was not too occupied with presiding over the Senate to forget his ambitions for the chief magistracy. Events played into his hands.

France was still involved in a general European war and had never forgiven the refusal of the Americans and their acceptance of the Jay treaty with the British. Such policies, the French politicians declared, were all to Britain's advantage and their own attitude became more and more unpleasant. During Adams' administration, their government first of all refused to receive American diplomats and then suggested that only after the payment of a bribe could any business be transacted. This latter indignity was reported to Congress as the XYZ affair (from the unannounced names of those to be bribed) and the Federalists proclaimed it a war-provoking insult.

Hostility developed so strongly between the two nations that in 1798 naval battles actually occurred and formal war was narrowly averted.

During this furore much abuse, stimulated somewhat by opposition politicians, was heaped upon Adams and the Federalist party; to combat it Congress passed some ill-advised laws. Among them were the Alien and Sedition Acts which gave the President and the courts arbitrary powers to punish critics of the administration policy. Nothing neater could have been provided for use by Democratic-Republican politicians; they made the most of these autocratic laws denying "free speech" and "personal rights." The legislatures of Virginia and Kentucky passed vigorous resolutions denouncing centralism and upholding the rights of individuals and of the states, even suggesting that the states acting as the original sovereigns who had made the Constitution, had the right to nullify federal laws. Using this as a platform and exploiting popular discontent, long simmering against this aristocratic Federalist regime, the Democratic-Republicans were able to defeat Adams in the election of 1800.

This election had a broader significance than the fact that the Jeffersonians won. It provided a third test of the stability of the structure erected under the Constitution. During twelve years of political dominance by the Federalists, a strong opposition party had developed and had captured the government by orderly and constitutional means without disorder or bloodshed. On 4 March 1801 the Federalists quietly, even if ungraciously, yielded to the popular mandate and gave way to Jefferson and his partisans. Administratively, diplomatically and politically the new governmental system had proved itself a practical and satisfactory set of institutions.

CHAPTER VI

THE CONTINUING STRUGGLE FOR INDEPENDENCE

The United States might be a free and independent nation politically but there were many obvious signs that independence remained incomplete. Economically the new nation was in many respects still a colony of Europe. In the realm of taste, culture and artistic creation it was also distressingly crude, incoherent and imitative. But of creative energy and resources there was an abundance available for the tremendous effort required to attain both an independent economic organization and a true American culture.

Speculative Aspects of Economic Dependence

The United States was still largely dependent economically upon Great Britain. As colonists, the Americans had raised raw materials and "bought British," while the mother country supplied most of the other economic services and enjoyed the profits. Because of the post-Revolutionary depression American business had been in no position to attempt independence. Furthermore, it was hampered by being discriminated against in foreign markets, by a disordered currency and, most of all, by a lack of capital. An independent America needed manufactures, better transportation, real estate development and wider trade, for it was plain that the new republic was a great storehouse of wealth in resources. If these resources could be developed and the various services provided, necessary to round out an American system, the republic would not only be independent economically but also internationally influential because of its mobilized wealth. But this took money and money always had been scarce in America. For the nonce American business must remain in humiliating dependence upon Britain. British manufacturers, bankers, insurance companies, importers—all these took their toll and were none too considerate of American interests in taking it.

Government financing under the new Constitution gave a most effective impulse, for Hamilton performed his services in such a way as to promote business activity and strengthen the entire nation. While he was providing adequate revenue, sound credit for the government and a stable currency, he had greatly augmented the supply of capital available for business purposes. When he undertook his task the currency was well-nigh worthless, government securities were selling at from five to eight shillings in the pound and there was practically no capital available for investment. Within three years eighty millions of liquid capital in government obligations and bank stock were at the disposal of American enterprise. They could serve business as money, could be bought and sold at prices above their face value, and they supplied their holders with a steady income in interest which in turn could be invested in land, commerce or industry. Besides there was a sound bank, with branches in the various centers, which would proceed to mobilize more capital in the form of deposits and loans. With these great subsidies, American business could begin to realize its dreams. The vast undeveloped region was a tempting prospect.

Americans, like most colonials in new areas, were not without practice in speculation; it was a habit of long standing and even before Hamilton's achievements it had been stimulating. Since 1785 certain far-sighted individuals had been buying up the various certificates of indebtedness, issued by the Continental Congress and the states, at rates as low as five cents on the dollar, and the ratification of the Constitution had not raised the price beyond twenty-five cents. Shrewd speculators sent agents into the country districts with coin; and with this almost unknown medium they enticed hundreds of farmers, who almost despaired of ever obtaining even a part of the face value of their certificates, to part with these long-hoarded papers. When the new treasury plans were adopted, government securities went to par and above, whereupon the profiteers reaped a huge reward. Such success could have but one result; the speculators' appetites were whetted, their ranks were recruited, and the growing horde of hopefuls turned to new schemes.

Their leaders were the first of a long line to follow and founded a business technique which was to be one of the spectacular features of American development. Robert Morris, financier of the Revolution, William Duer, Hamilton's assistant in the Treasury, Alexander Macomb, Henry Knox, Secretary of War, were the largest operators and all were in close association with Alexander Hamilton, who somehow kept himself free from their schemes. The vivid imagination of these men turned to exploiting the great potentialities of the nation and they entered into operations which have become national habits. Americans were beginning to learn the magic of stock. Paper which was purchased one day might be sold after an interval for more than had been paid. In a period of rising prices, like this one, what could seem more likely? In the meantime this mystic paper brought in dividends or interest. It was all very tempting.

United States certificates of indebtedness and the stock of the United States Bank set the pace and changed hands at continually rising prices. A number of local banks, too, were organized and by 1800 twenty-eight were doing business with a total capital of 21 millions. Moreover, stock companies of all sorts began to be incorporated and although little of their stock passed out of the locality of their operations they made more general the notion of stock ownership. Because of the great store of land which the country possessed, the possibility of real estate speculation was very evident. A number of American promoters, either as individuals or by means of land companies, purchased gigantic tracts of land to be developed and sold in subdivisions. The transactions of Morris, Knox and Duer included millions of acres in the undeveloped portions of most of the states from Georgia to Massachusetts. They also had interests in the northwest similar to those of the Ohio Company, the Scioto Company and John Clive Symmes. Interested European capitalists sought shares in these undertakings, sent over agents to watch them and supported American stocks sold on continental exchanges. Expectation was widespread among the American plungers that European capital and European immigrants would increase and bring the development which alone could make these ambitious projects succeed.

Land companies obviously invited the formation of transportation companies. New roads must be built and old ones made passable; bridges must be erected and canals must be dug. These arteries would lead to new communities and the growing population would push thence to new Edens. Numerous turnpike, bridge and canal companies were organized to furnish these improvements and to charge toll of those who used them; dividends to the stockholders would follow, at least so the directors prophesied. In Pennsylvania a veritable transportation revolution was foreshadowed when in 1787 John Fitch successfully applied steam power to water transportation. For a while in 1790 the company which backed him was able to make regular trips on the Delaware. Two decades of intermittent experiment made the steamboat an accepted mode of water travel. When Robert Fulton's *Clermont* steamed up the Hudson from New York City to Albany in 1807, the era of steam transportation really began.

Less popular or well developed was the idea of organizing an **adequate** manufacturing industry. The industrial revolution caused by the introduction of machinery run by water power and steam had occurred in England in the decades following 1750 and the idea of utilizing the new inventions was entertained in America. England, however, forbade the exportation of them or of any models or plans which would enable any one to construct them. In the years after peace various attempts were made to circumvent these restrictions. Philadelphia capital was anxious to get these new machines and the Massachusetts legislature granted subsidies. Some units were built by mechanics brought from

England for the purpose, but the first attempts to use this method were expensive and unsatisfactory. Finally in 1790 Samuel Slater, a mechanic in the cotton industry, came over to Philadelphia in response to an advertisement but was diverted by the firm of Almy and Brown of Providence, Rhode Island, to undertake a similar prospect for them. They provided him with a machine shop and the necessary material so that he was able to construct from memory a successful set of cotton spinning machines. In 1793 the Scholfield brothers emigrated from Yorkshire and with the aid of Massachusetts capitalists erected a wool-spinning factory at Byfield. These early machines were operated by the abundant water power; not until 1803 when it was applied to a saw mill was steam used as power.

A step significant for the future was the discovery of coal in the Lehigh valley and the organization of a mining company to produce it; hereafter coal was to be gradually accepted as fuel, first by the house owner and then by the factory operator. A patent act of 1790 offered protection to inventors who might try to promote the advance of machines.

Secretary Hamilton had more ambitious plans. He urged upon Congress a program of protective tariff legislation, which failed of enactment, and he sought to organize industry. With a group of associates organized as the "Society for Establishing Useful Manufactures," he planned a great industrial center at the falls of the Passaic river in New Jersey; that dream was to become reality at Paterson but not until long after Hamilton was dead. In fact companies in general were none too prosperous or too numerous. It was still the day of individual enterprise and land and commerce produced too easy profits to permit much diversion of funds from these projects, especially to industry. Hamilton's "protective" tariff proposals, however, were to prove immortal.

The general spirit of speculation and the increase in quantity of stocks, both government and corporate, made necessary a technique for buying and selling them. At first merchants acted as brokers but more frequently the auctioneers served to dispose of such stock as might be offered. Such a market, however, was determined largely by the desire to sell, and auction sales were often uncertain as to price and generally unsatisfactory to those who wished to dispose of stock; a buyer who might pay a good price frequently was not at the sale. Therefore in 1792 a group of New York brokers who used to frequent Tontine's coffee house devised a scheme of regular exchange. They agreed to cooperate informally in handling stocks, so that buyers and sellers might each have the advantage of more regular prices and uniform commissions, thus eliminating the auctioneers. This was the beginning of the idea of a stock exchange and the first formal exchange was finally established in Philadelphia in 1800. Even before the 1792 agreement,

When Cloth Was Made in the Home

TEXTILES OLD AND NEW

Spinning Rayon by Machine

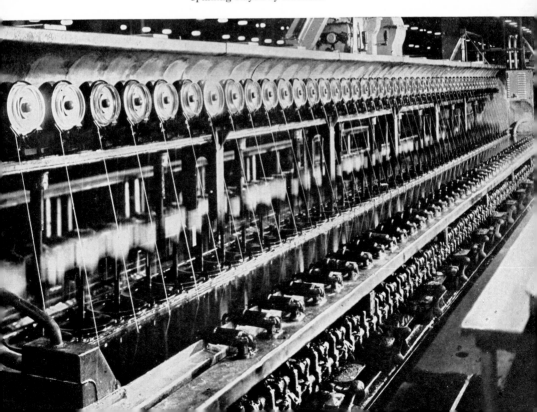

stock prices current were listed in the daily press and a certain amount of "watching the market" was indulged in by an increasing number of individuals.

Lotteries added their mite to the speculative mania. Tickets were sold in quantities and the profits after the prizes had been drawn were large. If a school or a church were to be built, if a college established, if a county wanted a new court house or even if it was planned to build a road, a canal, a bridge, or a dock, quite frequently lottery tickets were sold and the proceeds applied to the improvement. The cause of education owes much to lotteries.

Despite the optimism of the period, the expected great tide of development did not sweep over the new republic. The flood of immigrants did not come and European capital soon became otherwise interested. In 1793 the general European war broke out and fully occupied foreign money and population. The speculative enthusiasm had in fact spread too far and too fast, a reaction was inevitable. The new nation was learning about business cycles.

This initial crisis arose out of one of the many speculations of Duer and Macomb. When the market developed a tendency to keep on rising after the successful launching of Hamilton's plans, Duer and Macomb got a number of people to let them have money to operate in the bull market with a "blind pool." This was known as the "Six Per Cent Club" (U.S. 6%s were to be the chief operating tool) and with the funds subscribed Duer was going to bull the market on all sorts of shares. In the midst of his operations he failed and the "pool" crashed with him. His ruin caused a shortage in the summer of 1792 but without reversing the tide of speculation.

The recovery from Duer's fall proved temporary. Soon a new peril was at hand. Morris, Knox and William Bingham of Philadelphia, all heavily involved in land, did not obtain the expected immigrants. Morris' North America Land Company with its immense holdings in the South, and Knox's Maine empire proved unproductive. The climax was the failure of Morris' great scheme of developing the new city of Washington where many lots had been surveyed and plotted but too few came to buy. In fact too much money had become frozen in these vast real estate purchases. Foreign trade opportunities were beginning to open up in Europe, induced by the war, which also was absorbing European capital that had been counted on for bulling the American market. By the fall of 1796 the great speculators had difficulty in meeting even small obligations; in the next spring business reached a standstill. Prices fell, real estate was unsaleable and by 1798 Morris and his associates were in debtors' prison. The bubble of the first speculative mania had burst. Capital so manipulated could not be put in the permanent investments necessary for economic independence.

The Dominance of Agriculture and Commerce

An even greater obstacle in the way of economic independence was the overwhelming interest of the population in agriculture. The greater part of American vigor was still expended upon farming, since preoccupation with the land was the price exacted by the new continent for its surrender. Significant changes in agricultural method and crops were impending, which were to absorb more capital and energy and to make it even more difficult to gather the strength necessary for economic independence.

The most important of these changes was the introduction of a new crop, which not only was to dominate the economic life and social outlook of an entire section, but besides was to produce results with a vital effect upon the evolution of the nation. Cotton was about to become the staple crop of the South. In the colonial period this plant was little cultivated. Only a short-fiber variety was grown, the seeds of which were so numerous and clinging that the labor cost of separation from the fiber was almost prohibitive. Another variety less cumbered was the long-fiber grown in the Orient and successfully transplanted to the West Indies after the Revolution. Its success there induced experiments on the coast of South Carolina and Georgia. Success likewise crowned these efforts, but only over the limited area of land within thirty miles of the sea; here alone was the correct combination of soil and moisture. Long-staple cotton, as this variety was called, had an especially lengthy, silky and strong fiber which made it superior to the shorter and coarser type. European demand for it was continuous and large profits were realized. Numerous plantations were laid out on the sea islands along the coast where the absence of fresh water streams made the land unsuitable for rice cultivation. Successive crops became continuously larger until by 1805 the annual export reached nearly 9 million pounds. But the cost of preparing the fiber for market was still high and the area fit for cultivation so restricted, because of the need for seashore conditions, that this high grade lint did not become the great product of the South.

In 1793 an epoch making invention stimulated the cultivation of short-staple cotton; in that year the problem of separating economically the seeds from the short fiber was solved. Eli Whitney, a Yale graduate who was employed as a tutor on a southern plantation, invented a machine, the cotton gin, which made the marketing of large amounts of cotton possible at a low cost. The use of the gin spread rapidly and the planting of the short staple became increasingly widespread. Climatic conditions were much less of a hindrance than in the case of the long staple. Cotton growing advanced into the upland back country or Piedmont regions, especially in Georgia and South Carolina. The belt spread over southern North Carolina, South Carolina and central Georgia, where agricultural endeavor began to be turned more and more exclusively to cotton production.

The new industry extended the plantation system. Many of the farmers were small holders with five slaves or less; but the possibility of great profits from extensive cultivation placed a premium on large units. Slaves were purchaseable abroad until 1808 and in the years immediately preceding that date importations were large. In South Carolina slaves which had made up one-fifth of the population in 1790 became one-third of it by 1810. By 1806, 80,000,000 pounds of short-staple cotton were raised annually. The cotton kingdom was in the making.

The Early Cotton Gin

Agricultural advance was not confined to the South; in the East farming improvements tended to increase efficiency. New methods were being developed in Europe, scientific farming was emerging from the stage of experiment. To promote the knowledge and more general use of improved methods societies were formed, beginning in 1785 with the Philadelphia Society for Promoting Agriculture. These groups met and discussed the innovations, issued propaganda and offered prizes for improved results. State legislatures by grants of money sometimes subsidized experiment or rewarded achievement. In Massachusetts in 1807 was inaugurated Elkanah Watson's Berkshire plan whereby farmers in various localities organized and sponsored fairs, at which exhibits were held and prizes awarded. From this practice grew the county fair, through one hundred years a significant factor in the lives of country people.

The new science which the progressive farmers sought to spread emphasized restoration and conservation of soil fertility, rotation of crops, use of fertilizers and new tools and improvement of breeds of cattle, sheep and hogs. In regard to tools a great advance came when Charles Newbold in 1797 brought out a cast-iron plow; it proved much more effective than the ancient wooden models which were older than recorded history. Grain cradles began to be used instead of the sickle; and cast-steel shovels, forks and hoes took the place of iron ones.

Notable improvements in cattle breeding came as early as 1783 when the Patton family imported English high grade cattle into Maryland; the idea was gradually diffused to the great advantage of the meat and dairy industries. Hogs were penned to fatten, rather than allowed to run wild and the enormous Poland China took the place of the smaller, tougher razor-back; thus succulent and tender pork was bred.

The most spectacular advance, however, was in the breeding of sheep. Use of machinery had increased the demand for wool and a finer grade than could be sheared from American sheep was sought. The Spanish royal herds of Merino sheep produced the best wool known but their export was strictly prohibited At length in 1802 the American minister, David L. Humphreys, succeeded in sending a few home and in 1808 when Napoleon invaded Spain the ban was lifted. Possession of Merino sheep became almost a craze, fabulous prices were paid for them and otherwise normal people could not be content until they became the proud possessors of a pair of these sheep. Thousands were imported to the great improvement of the breed and the great increase in the supply of wool. Yet despite this last unusual example, progress in agriculture was slow, for farmers proved to be the most conservative of individuals, frequently disliking and distrusting change.

The greatest handicap to domestic economic development came from the fact that energies were again diverted, and with more than usual force, to Europe. During the long period of wars on the continent, opportunities appeared which could not be neglected. Ocean commerce was an American habit acquired in the colonial days and though the Revolution had badly crippled it, the taste and aptitude for it remained. In spite of the loss of privileges in the West Indian ports controlled by Great Britain and the disadvantages which secession from the British empire had caused elsewhere, the need could not be denied and the love of the sea was in American blood. Therefore if old markets were not open, the world was large and new ones could be found. Thus spurred on, America discovered the East.

Asia and Polynesia were as legendary almost as they had been in Europe in the days of Marco Polo, but American skippers cared little for that. Merchants began to turn their attention eastward and shortly after the conclusion of peace a New York vessel, the *Empress of*

EARLY AMERICAN SHIPPING

China, set out for the Orient and in 1784 reached the Celestial Empire. New England sails soon followed and in 1786 the first consul was appointed to that region and an American commercial house established at Canton. Robert Gray's exploit of sailing round the world, 1787-1790, also added to American interest and plans for regular trade from Boston, Salem and other ports began to develop.

In establishing the China trade it was necessary to provide goods which the Chinese wanted. New England or the United States in general had little to offer, as traders early discovered. Out of this need developed the practice of stopping on the west coast of North America to trade with the Indians for furs to take to China, where they were exchanged for tea, silk, fine cloth, china, lacquered ware and other oriental treasures. In the course of this three-cornered trade Captain Robert Gray in 1792 discovered the Columbia River and thus gave the United States the basis of a claim to Oregon. Also American vessels began to stop at the Hawaiian Islands and to trade in the great variety of ports which the East Indies offered. Many vessels, instead of going around Cape Horn to China and the East, went around Cape of Good Hope and engaged in trade in India, the isles of the East Indies and Australia, before reaching China. John Jacob Astor of New York, Stephen Girard of Philadelphia, the Derbys of Salem and other merchant princes were swelling their fortunes and making the American flag a well known sight on all the seven seas.

Enterprising as these new ventures were and great as were their profits, they were now to be overshadowed, as far as commercial importance was concerned, by a sudden change in world trade. New conditions were to bring clashes and finally involve the United States in war. The outbreak of the European war in 1793 had thrown the trade of the warring nations into confusion. England with her superior naval force played havoc with the French merchant marine and France feared lest she be cut off from her colonies and deprived of their products. Therefore, she threw her West Indian ports wide open to the American carriers. The tempting sea profits blinded American capitalists to less attractive domestic openings essential to national development; they returned to their first love, commerce.

The Republican Ideal Expressed

While American investment thus expanded and shifted, and the far-sighted sought the means of economic independence, a budding intelligentsia was busy asserting a new cultural independence. In the realm of the cultivation of taste and artistic ability the tone of American society was still somewhat crude and incoherent. Progress in taste, expression and scientific interest inevitably continued to lag behind more pressing concerns. Culture and science were not insistent; and besides the new nation had the great disadvantage of being able to draw freely on European achievement. Most people spoke English and if they desired to read, there was the whole of English literature at their command. If they wished better architecture or interior decoration, European ideas and objects could be imported. Nevertheless, there were forces at work to stimulate an independent culture which might truly be called American.

In the first place, the American Republic was an idea, an intellectual creation very stimulating to thought. The political problems finally solved by the Constitution had been very puzzling and drew upon the intellectual resources of American leaders rather heavily. Many ideas had to be expressed, exchanged, compared, debated, revised and finally agreed upon by a multitude of persons. Much of this had to be done in writing, and letters and pamphlets had been industriously produced, not for the purpose of copying the old formulae and rephrasing time-worn notions of polite letters but in order to make, circulate and "sell" new ideas. At length, the Constitution had been adopted and the new government put into effect, year after year proving itself a successful project. A growing sense of pride demanded that this success be advertised and preached to the rest of the world.

To proclaim a mission came very naturally to Americans. The tradition of the colonies had been one of a search for freedom, religious, political, or economic. The notion of religious purpose had been very strong and it was an easy transition from the idea of the organization of a better and more enlightened social order to that of aiding a benighted world by the power of American example. That example was described frequently, often in terms none too modest.

A second group of influences upon the American creative impulse was exerted by Europe. The French Revolution had upset the intellectual balance of the monarchical world. The events of that strenuous period fired Americans with a renewed belief in the potency of their ideals. France like the colonies had overthrown a royal power and had created a republic dedicated to social and political freedom. Jefferson and many others maintained a vigorous interest in French ideas and the organization of numerous "Democratic Societies," in emulation of the republican clubs of Paris, served a cultural as well as a political purpose. When Napoleon threw the established order of Europe into chaos, it seemed that to republicans anything was possible. The ideas of the Revolutionary age were combined, confused and disseminated with those of America. With them were jumbled other ideas, philosophic, religious and scientific, from other European centers. These influences from within and without stimulated the beginning of the American struggle for intellectual independence.

The republican ideal was potent enough to command many forms of expression. Journalists were vigorous in its propagation, poets were inspired by it, playwrights sought to make it live, musicians sang of it, novelists and historians, artists and architects made it their theme. Philadelphia, the capital city, became the center of this "Republican Expressionism." Politics in these early days were acrimonious for the followers of Jefferson feared for the ideals of republicanism with the aristocratic Federalists in power. They set about a vigorous defence propaganda.

Jefferson called upon Philip Freneau, "the poet of the Revolution" to edit a newspaper, the *National Gazette* which was to preach republicanism and attack the centralizing and aristocratic tendencies of the Federalists. Verse, too, was utilized, lyrics and doggerel, some polished, some crude; Freneau naturally set the standard of taste in this medium. Joseph Hopkinson wrote a popular song "Hail Columbia" in the same vein and music added enthusiasm to the republican spirit. These were freedom's "hearts of oak," to use Freneau's phrase, who vigorously rhymed their belief in the glory of republicanism and the rights of man. This enthusiasm was not permitted to flame unchallenged. The aristocratic Federalists demanded a hearing in condemnation of the "pollutions" of democracy. Most notable were the Hartford Wits, embracing such conservative minds as John Trumbull and Timothy Dwight, who sought by argument and ridicule to quell the "mob."

There were others who had greater literary ambitions than editorial writing and rhyme. In Philadelphia, also, labored the first American novelist, Charles Brockden Brown, who like his contemporaries in column and verse was didactic and preachy. To the westward the Pittsburgh lawyer, Hugh Henry Brackenridge, compensated himself for political defeat at the hands of the Republicans by satirizing the new society in a never ending series of volumes entitled *Modern Chivalry*. Others there were who wanted to achieve real literature, albeit possessed of more enthusiasm than talent. Their efforts at self-expression brought forth a great variety of periodicals filled with a strange miscellany, the story of experiments, rather than successes. Their importance lies in the fact that they provided a medium and stimulus for expression. Most of these "magazines" had brief and sad careers. One only survived, the *North American Review* established in 1815 still appears.

History and biography naturally were willing servants of national pride. Knowledge of the heroes of the Revolution and of their deeds could be best cherished and spread abroad if they were set down on the pages of books. Lives of Washington by such divergent writers as Parson Weems and John Marshall found ready market, and the admirers of Franklin, Jefferson, and the others were not disappointed.

Projects for publishing the records, such as the writings of the leaders, the revolutionary proceedings and the state papers of the early republican years took shape and found favor; government money was provided in some cases for their completion. Posterity must be enriched with the glorious record.

By no means least of the modes of expressing Republican exuberance was the use of the stage. In these years, legal prejudice against theatres was finally broken down, no longer did dramatic productions have to masquerade as "moral" lectures. In New York, the Park Theatre and in Philadelphia the Chestnut Street playhouse were becoming respectable and prosperous. Early American playwrights marshalled material and inspiration as had their brethren, from the democratic experiment; Republican virtues marked the heroes, aristocratic vices, the villains. Royall Tyler and William Dunlap wrote in such vein; honest republicans by their sterling virtues, nourished on democratic simplicity, frequently placed aristocratic Europeans at a disadvantage. Tyler was a literary amateur but Dunlap has the distinction of being the first American professional playwright. In the intervals allowed by his duties as manager of a New York theatre he wrote some twenty-five plays and translated as many more from French or German.

The fine arts had a limited appeal in the growing nation and in them republicanism and patriotism were predominating traits. The new society wanted its portraits painted and was particularly desirous of having likenesses of its great men. Charles Wilson Peale, Rembrandt Peale, and Gilbert Stuart made themselves famous by their pictures of Washington while engravers were kept busy making reproductions of the portraits of national heroes. Historic scenes, too, were painted and engraved so that the glory of battle and heroic deeds might be preserved. Architects felt the inspiration of the new republic for public buildings had to be provided; not only state capitols and county court houses, which took on new dignity, but a national capitol had to be designed and a series of buildings provided to house the federal government. So Major L'Enfant drew up an elaborate plan for the city and architects such as William Thornton, James Hoban and Benjamin H. Latrobe worked on the Washington buildings. Throughout the country architects such as Charles Bulfinch and many lesser lights were planning state capitols to house fittingly the new political units.

Republican Morality

Domestic republicanism and patriotism, however, were by no means the only ideas to intrigue Americans. The new philosophic concepts moving abroad definitely affected American thought. Europe's theories of natural rights and republicanism fitted in very conveniently with American independence and political interest, while other trends, notably in religion, were equally influential. Rationalism had produced a blighting effect upon religion in Europe and in America the churches could not fail to be influenced. The orthodox watched with dismay the spread of a religious attitude which had been introduced before the Revolution. This was Deism, so-called because its adherents accepted God as creator of the universe. However, their theology stopped there for they maintained that He had created it to develop according to certain fixed laws, similar to the formulated laws of physics, and that having finished the creation He no longer interfered by miracles or other forms of divine interposition. Men like Jefferson and Franklin were prominent Deists who were cold to the usual forms of religion and it was noted by many with disapproval that the Constitution made no mention of God and referred to religion only in the amendment which provided for freedom of worship. The new state had been created under auspices decidedly secular.

Orthodox New England Puritanism did not suffer so much from this doctrine as it did from the revival of an old heresy. From the early days of the Christian church there had been opposition to the dogma of the Trinity and those who did not believe in the deity of Christ appeared at various times, and were known by different names. As the rationalizing tendencies of the age began to work, a number of people raised this doubt once more and associations of these Unitarians, as they were called, were established in New York and Philadelphia. In Boston one of the religious bodies originally trinitarian changed to the unitarian form in the last years of the eighteenth century. By the beginning of the nineteenth century, the movement was strong enough to cause many of the New England churches to embrace the new order and under the leadership of William Ellery Channing of Boston these reorganized congregations began to enter into theological controversy with their Calvinistic brethren. They captured Harvard and became a religious power mightily to be reckoned with.

Unitarianism represented another tendency of the age, namely, a growing prosperity and an increasing interest in humanity. Calvinism had suited well the hard conditions of the frontier when nature was harsh and God might well be a stern judge. But now life was less austere and religion could not fail to reflect the new ease. Nature, now, it could be seen, was beautiful. God was not so apt to be thought of as a fearsome magistrate but more as a loving father. America was certainly the favored commonwealth destined by an all-wise Providence for unheard of blessings. So, when a new doctrine came across the seas to teach the possibility of progress and improvement of mankind, Americans were in many instances ready to embrace it and throw aside the

Calvinistic dogmas of predestination and the fallen state of man. Unitarianism flourished under such conditions and began to attract limited numbers outside of New England.

The progress of rationalizing religion was bound to meet opposition; a counter-reformation was inevitable and came with the new century. Many good people were much disturbed over the irreligious character of the years closing the eighteenth century. Some of them like the Methodist Bishop Asbury would not stand by and be content to watch, so they went forth along the highways and over the trails, riding the circuit and preaching a revival of religion, calling men and women back to God. The response to their fervid preaching was gratifying; many churches entered into a new phase of enthusiasm.

In 1797 an intense period of revival began and in the next twenty years a missionary spirit flourished. There was a new frontier beyond the Alleghanies, where new communities needed religion. The more evangelical of the sects such as Methodists, Baptists and Presbyterians found that they were eager to receive their gospel. Conditions were difficult and work hard. The emotionalism of evangelical preaching warmed the frontier settlements and the circuit riders founded churches as they travelled among their scattered charges. The heathen in India, China and Africa also attracted attention and organizations for home and foreign missionary work were established in the first decade of the nineteenth century. With this revival and its multiplication of churches passed the last vestige of union between church and state; even in New England this tie was broken.

The Educational Dream

As religion became less united and in many instances more rational, the secular outlook of many, especially among the well educated, became more realistic and experimental. European scientists had been revolutionizing their knowledge of the physical universe and progressing in chemistry. Research workers were continuing Franklin's experiments in electricity and other branches of physics; the laws of Newton were the bases of considerable experimentation and calculation. Much of this new knowledge was gathered together and made available in the French Encyclopedia. But more important, as far as America was concerned, was the development of machine invention, such as the Arkwright and Watts achievements in machinery and steam power. The cotton gin of Eli Whitney and the steamboats of John Fitch and Robert Fulton are justly the most famous of the inventions of the period; but it is equally important to bear in mind that a great variety of other experiments was being attempted. Machinery and labor-saving devices appealed emphatically to a people who needed so much and had so much to work with, at the same time that they were able to command but a limited supply of labor. "Yankee" inventiveness became a by-word and gadgets of all sorts were the product of this ingenuity. It was in the realm of the practical application of scientific principles rather than in theoretical interest in science that American contributions were to be made even in later years.

The series of experiments and accomplishments which marked the early years of the United States also witnessed various expressions of faith in and desire for education. The founders of the new government had dreams of a national university which should stand as the center of the nation's intellectual life; and when Washington was supervising the planning of the capital city beside the Potomac a site was designated for this purpose.

While no such national institution was established, collegiate education expanded, at least in so far as the number of institutions was concerned. From the end of the Revolution to the election of Jefferson, 21 new colleges were established and almost another score were added in the next twenty years. There was little advance in curriculum making in spite of this activity. The ancient languages dominated, taught in peculiar fashion. The classes were assigned passages from the writers and were required to parse each word although they were seldom asked to reproduce the passages in connected English. The syntax of words rather than the beauty and spirit of the classics was the objective which would ensure mental discipline. Logic, ethics and evidences of Christianity, sometimes called moral philosophy, were also learned verbatim from the textbooks of the day. For the rest it was still rhetoric and mathematics with some attention to natural philosophy, as science was usually called. Of social science there was little and hardly more modern language though in some few colleges French might be substituted for Greek. The professors were usually clergymen and there was a distinct theological air pervading the class rooms. Certain reforms were in the mind of Jefferson which moved in the direction of a more practical and secular education with some freedom of choice to be given to the students. The day of such change, however, was still far distant.

Some advance was attempted in improving professional education. The medical profession was still recruited largely by apprenticeship. An aspiring youth would become general helper and pill-boy to a physician and watch his methods. The prevalence of disease and the devastating epidemics such as yellow fever which ravished the principal cities along the seaboard were constant reminders of the inadequacy of the profession. There was woeful lack of knowledge, too, of elementary hygiene. Personal uncleanliness, lack of proper ventilation and sanitation in most dwellings, and a badly proportioned, poorly-cooked diet caused much discomfort and death. The need of better medical care called for hospitals, dispensaries and medical schools. Only Philadelphia and New York were able to support hospitals but by the end of the first quarter of the century, ten medical schools were annually sending forth graduates.

The law likewise was seeking new training methods. Law professorships began to appear more frequently in college catalogues and private law schools came into being. These latter were generally one-man institutions. Some famous jurist like Judge Tappan Reeve at Litchfield, Connecticut would receive young men as students and lecture to them. Also he would give them practice in drawing papers and preparing cases which were presented in moot courts set up in the class room. Bar associations were founded in this period which sought to standardize preparation and a few legal periodicals came and went in these years. New textbooks were written and their principles were tried out in the numerous American courts, federal and state. The legal profession was advancing to a dignity which it hitherto had failed to enjoy.

These advances in higher education were accompanied by some progress in primary instruction. The founders of the republic had much faith in popular education as was seen notably in the provisions of the Northwest Ordinances for land donations for schools in every township of the great territory. Those who were indoctrinated with the new ideal of progress felt that it was to come largely by means of educating the masses. Universal education, however, is expensive and in a land where money was scarce, the leaders might talk of education for all but the debt-burdened farmers were not going to vote the money. Consequently, the ideal could be effected only in a very limited fashion even in the Northwest Territory. In various cities and towns a cheap plan devised by an Englishman named Lancaster, whereby older students acted as monitors and heard the lessons of the younger children, was put into effect and made possible more rote learning at least. General education, however, was still in the hands of private masters and was only for those who could pay for it or were willing to accept it as recognized charity to the poor.

The great intellectual achievement which was implicit in much of the foregoing was the increasing consciousness of their own identity which the inhabitants of the new republic were acquiring. The word American had come to mean something. People now understood much more clearly that they were different from their ancestors and from their distant European cousins. They were apart from the rest of the world, they had ideas and institutions different and, as many thought, better than those of the older continent. The most noted of their various accomplishments, they thought, was their political achievement—

the republic under the Constitution. They pointed besides to the vast economic possibilities, more potential than actual; anyone must sense the great size of the national domain and imagine its possibilities for wealth production.

Culturally, too, the Americans were bound to achieve and had made a significant start. They realized with varying degrees of understanding that all this had been created by common and united effort, by cooperation in a national union. Individuals might be citizens of a variety of federated states but they were also citizens of the republic. In other words the United States of America was beginning to be a singular rather than a plural, a nation rather than a mere federation of independent states. Many did not recognize it and clung to their state loyalties but others caught a glimpse of a new order. This much sense of nationality was not the least of American achievements in these early years. The ability to formulate it accurately or readily, however, had not yet been discovered.

As a British writer in the *Edinburgh Review* commented, with more truth than kindness, "[the Americans] have done nothing for the sciences, for the arts, for literature ... In the four quarters of the globe, who reads an American book? or goes to an American play? or looks at an American picture or statue? What does the world yet owe to American physicians or surgeons? What new substances have their chemists discovered, or what old ones have they analyzed?" Long before this gibe was published in 1820, there were those at work who were trying to remove the basis for it.

CHAPTER VII

INDEPENDENCE AT LAST

This young republic in its continued search for complete independence and in its exuberant self-expression soon ran afoul of the powers of the world. Enterprising merchants and sea captains, busily extending American trade against heavy odds, were sure to conflict with vested interests abroad.

Commercial and Territorial Expansion

Those engaged in the new trade made possible by the war in Europe struggled against Britain's special determination to cut off the French from American supplies. Britain invoked the rule of 1756 and seized, as prizes for violation of it, numerous carriers bound from the West Indies to Europe. France, much incensed, accused the United States of submitting tamely to Great Britain; and her allegations added to the popular enmity toward the United States inaugurated by the neutrality proclamation and the Jay treaty. To retaliate, France declared she would treat American vessels as the United States "allowed" Great Britain to treat them and she began a similar policy of taking prizes. In less than a year 316 American vessels had been captured by the French and when in 1796 Spain entered the war as an ally of France, the privateers of that nation did the same thing; furthermore Spanish West India officials were sympathetic to French spoilation in their ports and waters. Galling as was this policy, its results, as far as profits were concerned were the opposite of discouraging. The increased hazards made the charges heavier and as relatively few vessels were captured, the many successful voyages reaped large rewards. The volume increased steadily as these figures show:

VALUE OF FOREIGN COMMERCE OF THE UNITED STATES, BOTH EXPORT AND IMPORT

1790	$43,000,000
1793	57,000,000
1795	117,000,000
1801	205,000,000
1803	120,000,000 (a brief interval of peace)
1807	246,000,000

Between 20 and 25% of the trade in the peak years was re-export business developed to avoid the rule of 1756; goods from the West Indies were brought to some port in the United States and there theoretically reshipped. That is, the bills of lading were redrawn and the cargo went as from a port of the United States to one in Europe; against such traffic the rule of 1756 did not apply. Such an enormous business with its easy wealth attracted many dollars which otherwise might have been risked in new ventures such as industries essential to economic independence. However, valuable experience and augmented capital were being accumulated, and as long as Great Britain accepted the situation profits proved satisfactory. A temporary truce between England and France, 1802 to 1803, delayed a showdown.

But agricultural as well as commercial expansion was driving the United States into conflict with European powers. The British, French and Spanish controlled her land borders and were bound ultimately to resist the press of westward-moving population. American farmers wanted new lands and a southwestern trade outlet at New Orleans.

When Spain attempted to close the port of New Orleans in 1802 conditions became intolerable and President Jefferson, although the chances seemed against it, directed James Monroe and Robert R. Livingston to broach the purchase of the city. After an initial rebuff, however, conditions became more favorable. Napoleon had been forging ahead in Europe and his plans had embraced America as well. He conceived the idea of an American empire, with a treasure house of tropical wealth in the West Indies fed from the great granary of Louisiana. He would subdue Haiti and force Spain to cede him Louisiana. The latter was easily accomplished but the former proved impossible. His inability to hold this rich island ruined his plans, and he turned instead to Europe for the conquest of England.

His new scheme invited a British attack upon Louisiana, which he could not well defend; so, when Jefferson's ministers presented again in 1803 his offer to purchase New Orleans, they were not ignored. Instead, an astounding proposition was made; would the United States buy all of Louisiana? Hardly able to believe their ears the ministers agreed to buy the vast tract for 80,000,000 francs. When he heard of it Jefferson was disturbed by lack of express authority in the Constitution; but so much did he feel that the peace, prosperity and especially the future of the nation depended upon the purchase, that he dared to abandon consistency. Jefferson's purpose was not accomplished without opposition. New England's politicians resented the addition of this great agricultural region which they foresaw would grow into states with opposing interests and unite with their southern neighbors to further curb the power of northeastern representatives in Congress.

Louisiana was nearly a hundred years old, but its great area harbored only a small population of less than fifty thousand, clustered near the mouth of the Mississippi at New Orleans. There were a few scattered settlements northward along the river with the most important at the mouth of the Missouri, St. Louis, a town destined to become a great city. The new territory gave another industry to American economy, sugar planting. Refugees from Haiti who had fled to the mainland in the previous decade had brought a valuable knowledge of this form of agriculture and had put it to good use. Jefferson had added greatly to the national wealth and had doubled the size of the American domain.

Hardships of a Weak Neutral

The purchase of Louisiana brought the United States a step nearer the European conflict. The contest between Great Britain and Napoleon broke out again the same year and brought American shipping increasing difficulties. In 1805 Napoleon seemed on the verge of invading England and perhaps of conquering the island. Everything must be done to hamper French power; and the English government determined to take all steps possible to prevent trade between France and her colonies. So, the British fleets were ordered to bar all territorial products from French ports, no matter whether they came technically or in reality direct from the United States to France. Direct trade, Great Britain had hitherto allowed, but now, backed by a court decision that it was contrary to the Rule of 1756, the government more aggressively seized and confiscated American ships and their French West Indian cargoes. Impressment of seamen too became more exasperating than ever.

During the next year, American shipping was caught between two fires. The British blockaded the European coast fom Brest to the Elbe principally to close France to Danish and Dutch commerce. This blockade in itself was not so harmful but France sought to retaliate by declaring the British Isles blockaded. As the French navy had been crippled at Trafalgar such a blockade could not be effective: but it enabled French privateers and port officials, wherever Napoleon exercised control, to seize American ships suspected of trading with England.

Naturally, Great Britain retaliated in turn. In 1807 orders in council issued from London, and a further decree from Napoleon together made it impossible for an American ship to touch at a British or a continental port without being liable to seizure by either France or England. As far as financial returns went, these restrictions did not affect the total of American profit. Shippers on account of the risk raised their prices to such a point that if one cargo out of three arrived

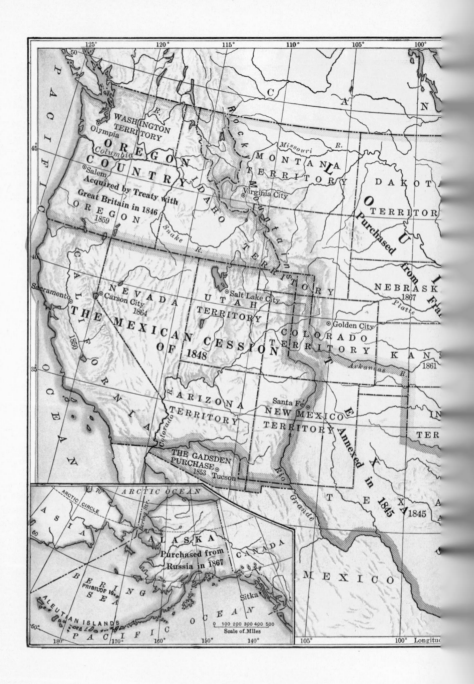

TERRITORIAL ACQUISITIONS

1776-1867

The acquisitions made by the United States from
1776 to 1867 are shown by different colors.

The boundaries of the States and Territories at the close
of 1867 are outlined by solid green lines:

The Capitals of the States and Territories
in 1867 are shown on map by:

0   100   200   400   600

Scale of Miles

safely they made money. The commercial interests nevertheless were wroth and in 1807 talked of war.

The position of the United States as a despised neutral, was an unenviable one. Were American shipping left alone, it could make fabulous profits, but the restrictions and insulting treatment cut the rewards and also hurt American pride. What was to be done to make European powers respect American neutrality? The republic was not prepared for war, and besides Jefferson had his own ideas of the proper method. During the years leading up to the Revolution, non-importation had been an effective weapon against Great Britain; might it not prove so again? In 1806, therefore, an act forbidding importation of English and French goods had been passed; but it was not put into effect, for Jefferson wanted to hold it as a reserve weapon to force Great Britain to come to some diplomatic agreement regarding impressment and neutral rights. His strategy proved unavailing and in the meantime the country was mortified and angered by a raid upon one of its war vessels by an English frigate, during which seamen were impressed from her very deck. The *Chesapeake* and *Leopard* affair, as it was called, brought war nearer. Jefferson, however, was still hopeful about peaceful coercion; and in December 1807 Congress passed an Embargo Act, at the same time putting the non-importation act into effect. Under the first no vessels could leave American ports for any foreign countries, and under the second, no goods could be brought in from England and France.

Trade stopped, ships were tied to their wharves, sailors were out of work; only those merchants whose shelves were well-stocked carried on much business. The British and French, on the other hand, gave no indication of better treatment as a result of economic coercion. To many Americans it seemed that the punishing of Europe was not worth its cost. The cost was indeed heavy. In Massachusetts alone the fleet had been earning more than 15 millions annually in freight rates not counting profits in trade. All this was stopped and the ships idled seemingly to no effect, except to cause Napoleon to issue a ludicrous decree April 1808 seizing all American ships within French reach, on the grounds that they were violating our embargo law. There seemed no limit to European insults.

Strong opposition to Jefferson's policy naturally developed in New England. A large smuggling trade sprang up in Maine and Georgia and along the northern border; ships ostensibly in the coastwise trade often found themselves helplessly driven, by contrary winds of course, into Canadian or West Indian ports, where they disposed of their cargoes. Jefferson's port officials, tried their best to compel obedience by removing sails and rigging from ships and by keeping vigilant watch. Besides, hundreds of shipowners loyally accepted the law. The result was that exports, which in 1807 had amounted to 108 millions dwindled to 22 millions in 1808.

In New England, where Federalism had been defeated of late, the old leaders seized upon this issue and condemned Jefferson for a policy so ruinous to trade and so little evocative of results. In the election of 1808 James Madison, Jefferson's chosen successor, was elected without much difficulty but he lost all the New England states except Vermont. Pressure was so strong and European results so meagre that in March 1809 Jefferson consented to the repeal of the general features of the Embargo Act on the ground that it was more expensive than war. All trade with Great Britain and France, however, remained forbidden.

Though trade improved with the repeal of the embargo, the American diplomatic position did not. England's attitude was especially trying. First, in May 1809 she refused to ratify a treaty which her minister had negotiated agreeing to withdraw the trade restrictions of her orders in council; this was particularly embarrassing as Madison had resumed trade on the strength of the negotiation before it was ratified. He retaliated by cancelling the resumption, only to be further affronted. Erskine's successor, Jackson, who was sent over in July 1809 proved as unpleasant as an English minister to America in those days could be, which is saying a good deal. He added insult to injury by intriguing with Madison's political opponents; by November the President refused to deal further with him.

The regulation forbidding trade with Great Britain and France was no more popular than the embargo had been, and opposition to it became so pronounced that in May 1810 all such bans were lifted. Of Jefferson's peaceable coercion measures, none remained on the statute books except the so-called Macon Bill #2, an ill-advised offer, addressed to England and France, that in case either would withdraw its restrictions against American commerce, the United States would refuse to trade with the other. This opened the way for another diplomatic insult. In August 1810 Napoleon declared that he had accepted this offer; so Madison forbade by proclamation any trade with Great Britain; within a few months it became apparent that Napoleon had deceived him and was still enforcing his restrictions upon American shipping. At the same time Madison's minister to England left London in disgust; England would make no concessions. Thus diplomatic relations were practically severed for a time.

For six years there had been a continuous series of indignities and losses. It was apparent that the American international position was neither dignified nor potent; seemingly the rights and interests of the republic had no diplomatic weapons of protection. National pride had been wounded frequently and the futile efforts of Jefferson and

Madison to gain redress peaceably had only placed the nation in positions more embarrassing. Both England and France seemed equally callous to American rights, though England was apt to be blunt and downright in her offensiveness while Napoleon was apt to profess friendship, at the same time deceiving and despoiling. New England was, of course, antagonistic to Jefferson and Madison, and captiously critical. But in general, that section was in no mood for war as far as the Federalists were concerned. American exports in 1810 had recovered to the value of 66 millions. Commerce on the whole flourished.

Rather the pressure for more vigorous resistance to the affronts of Europe came from the younger members of the party in power. Their strength was demonstrated in the congressional elections of 1810 and 1811 and when Congress met in November 1811 a large group of young men entered the House, Henry Clay, John C. Calhoun, Peter B. Porter, Langdon Cheves and others representing recklessness; and Madison in the White House and Monroe in the State Department began to feel their enthusiasm. These young men, many from the South and West, felt the urge of national pride which brooked no insults; then too, they had the land hunger of their sections and looked upon Florida and Canada with longing eyes; finally they lacked the caution of age and all unprepared had no hesitation in plunging the country into war.

Various feats of valour helped to stir the martial spirit. In 1810 Madison valiantly marched into West Florida and occupied it in the vicinity of Mobile, a desirable port, alleging that Spain was unable to maintain sovereignty and that the lawless character of the settlements made them a refuge for criminals and fugitive slaves and a menace to Mississippi Territory. In May 1811 an American frigate had a brush with a British war vessel, attempting to prevent trade with France, in which the *President* worsted the *Little Belt;* this in a sense atoned for the disgrace of the *Chesapeake* by the *Leopard.* Finally, later in the same year, an Indian war broke out and at the battle of Tippecanoe, William Henry Harrison defeated the redskins and incidentally confirmed the suspicion that British encouragement had had something to do with the uprising.

Such martial events were a fitting prelude to the climax. Great Britain continued her disdainful course. Though she condescended to send another minister late in 1811, her government not only refused to revoke her orders in council but also in May 1812 scolded Madison soundly for submitting to Napoleon's deception. Thereupon Madison and Monroe lost patience; Congress eagerly acceded to the President's request for a declaration of war against Great Britain, 18 June 1812.

But why war against Britain and not France? French liberties with American dignity and disregard of American interest had been equally if not more high-handed. The answer is to be found presumably in revolutionary experience. Great Britain was the traditional enemy; France had been a friend. Also, Napoleon had been more polite and was a heroic and compelling figure appealing to the American imagination. England was the same old tyrant she always had been. Finally, England was at the border and a tempting possibility, especially to the statesmen of the agricultural empire. So it was to be war again with England. By an irony of fate, England's financial interests, knowing the depleted state of the treasury, influenced the ministry to withdraw the orders in council at the moment when Congress was declaring war. Had there been a cable, the news might have reached Washington in time to prevent strife, though a similar state of affairs in 1898 failed to deter the McKinley administration.

The War of 1812

No preparations had been made for the conflict. The treasury was empty and unequal to the task of financing war. Due to partisan quarreling and the jealousy of New York interests toward Philadelphia Congress had refused in 1811 to recharter the Bank of the United States. The two or three hundred private banks lacked the means to provide the government with funds or credit and there was no banking system as such. A widespread dread of taxes hindered revenue collection.

The weapon indispensable for success—namely an adequate navy—was not provided; the navy of about twelve effective war vessels and 5,000 sailors had far more officers than ships. The War Department, with no practice or tradition of war management, was headed by Secretary Eustis, a Boston physician; the staff consisted of aged veterans incapable of prosecuting ambitious campaigns; the ranks numbered less than 7000. No roads adequate for transport and no services adequate for supplies, existed. Here was one of several paradoxes. The United States set forth to win what must be a naval war, with an army emphasis. President and Congress were interested in arming the militia and bolstering the army, which were to negotiate the border expansion so dear to the war hawks.

This paradox was twin to another. This war, supposedly for free trade and sailors' rights, was most enthusiastically supported by the interior districts and most vigorously opposed by the mercantile interests of the seacoast. The latter preferred their large, though uncertain, profits to high taxes and wholesale destruction of shipping certain in a war. The British navy would blockade their ports and the unprepared country could scarcely break the cordon. So vigorous was their opposition to the war that a combination of Federalists and disgruntled

Republicans supporting De Witt Clinton of New York nearly defeated Madison when he came up for re-election shortly after war was declared. Under such unfavorable auspices, was this war with Britain begun and, by another paradox as will be seen, was won.

Clay and other ardent "war hawks" felt that Canada was so easily to be captured that its acquisition was mainly a matter of marching. Great Britain was in the midst of vigorous war-making in Europe. She could spare little aid to her Canadian forces which were not nearly as large as those the United States was supposed to be able to bring against them, though numbers and paper armies are deceiving. With great difficulty and much confusion, militia and regular army

A Bitter Dose for Britain
(A contemporary cartoon boasting of Perry's victory)

contingents were headed up into three expeditions to conquer Canada. They all failed during the summer of 1812. The first under Hull surrendered at Detroit. The second under several generals attempted to cross the Niagara at Queenstown, but as most of the New York militia suddenly developed scruples against serving out of the state, that attempt failed. The third under old General Dearborn, which was expected to march on Montreal, never got started. Had it not been that vessels like the *Constitution* won several victories of a surprising character on the sea the year of 1812 would have passed with only ignominious defeat upon its pages.

In 1813 more realistic plans developed; Americans aimed to make military operations practicable by gaining naval control of the Great Lakes. Chauncey on Lake Ontario and Perry on Lake Erie set to work to build fleets superior to those the English could muster. Perry succeeded completely and his brilliant victory on Lake Erie is one of the few bright spots in the dreary story of the Canadian campaigns. Harrison followed up this victory by securing Detroit. Chauncey on Lake Ontario was not successful in producing anything more than a deadlock and the less said about the exploits of Wilkinson, who attempted land operations, the better. The only success in that neighborhood was the capture of York (Toronto) by Dearborn and Pike. The end of the year found little actual advance made into Canada and the small American navy was in the process of being captured or blockaded by British fleets.

By 1814 Great Britain had temporarily eliminated Napoleon and despatched a number of veterans to America to take the offensive. The Canadian forces, augmented by these tried troops, stopped the last American offensive under the younger and more effective generals, Brown and Scott. However, these new troops failed in their effort to enter the United States by Lake Champlain when Capt. Macdonough defeated the British fleet on that water. While these operations were proceeding, another fresh expedition appeared in the Chesapeake and easily captured the city of Washington. After burning the public buildings, the British attempted to capture Baltimore, but Fort McHenry blocked the way and the British expedition left the Atlantic coast to participate in an attack on New Orleans. In this year the British blockade, which heretofore had not been applied to New England because of the opposition of that section to the war, was now extended northward and American commerce was effectually strangled.

The final operation of the war was in the Southwest. There Andrew Jackson had been conducting a vigorous campaign against the Creek Indians who under English stimulus had been actively hostile. His operations were very successful and now he was called upon to meet a force of ten thousand veterans fresh from victorious European battle fields. To Jackson, however, British were British and 8 January 1815, he fought a vigorous battle before New Orleans and completely defeated the enemy. He did not know that his victory had been won after the war was over, for 24 December 1814 a peace treaty had been signed at Ghent.

So the war was fought. On land it had not been glorious. The army never numbered more than 30,000 effectives, 4000 was the maximum in any battle and only 1500 were killed in the land operations; disease proved to be more dangerous than bullets. The navy, though neglected, fared better, but beyond winning a few spectacular victories the vessels available could make little impression upon the large British navy; more effective were the 500 and more privateers which harried British commerce.

Financially too, the war had not been glorious, unpopular as it was in the section which had the most money. Of the 41 millions of bonds

which the government issued to 1 January 1815, New England subscribed for less than 3 millions. Various loans were floated at rates
more and more favorable to capitalists with the result that obligations
of 80 millions netted the treasury but 34 millions in coin value. Some
of this was paper money used for the first time since the continental
currency, of which 36 millions were issued. Most of these bills were
of large denominations and none of them were legal tender with
the result that not many of them got into general circulation. Their
value remained constantly at par during the first two years of the war.
During the first sessions of Congress in the war period, the members
showed the usual politicians' fear of voting taxes, and well they might,
so unpopular was the war. But after a year's struggle, they had to
succumb to the inevitable, and in 1813 voted internal excises and
levied a direct tax upon the states. These measures proved inadequate
and larger taxes of the same kind were voted. All told these forms
of revenue brought in very slowly a total of 25 millions.

At no time was the banking system adequate to provide the money
necessary and the federal treasury was frequently exhausted. When in
August 1814 the banks outside of New England suspended specie
payment, the treasury was helpless and the value of treasury notes
dropped below par. In November the government defaulted on interest
payments and acknowledged itself practically bankrupt. Only the coming of peace saved the nation from financial disaster. All told the war
cost about 200 millions, increasing the national debt by about 80
millions, though making a per capita indebtedness less than that of
1791.

Difficult as was the maintenance of an adequate military and naval
organization, and discouraging as was the lack of money, even more
dangerous and trying was the popular discontent which almost amounted
to treason. The war resentment and anger at British insults burned
most hotly in the followers of Jefferson and Madison. More staid
and conservative groups, especially the mercantile classes of New England, generally Federalists, could not see why there was need for fighting; the country was prosperous and developing fast, why fight? These
considered the war another example of southern domination, such as
forced the Louisiana purchase. In 1812 the governors of Massachusetts,
Connecticut and Rhode Island refused to furnish militia for the army
and these states voted solidly against Madison in the election of that
year. Their vessels went on trading and gathering in profits during
1813 and the early part of 1814, since the British sought to encourage
their resistance to the war by refraining from blockading the New
England ports. Consequently, New England made more profits while
their capitalists refused to loan these same profits to the government.
Meanwhile the rest of the country was forced to buy there and this trade

generally drew the country's specie into New England, to the bitter resentment of other sections.

Times were hard enough, money was scarce, prices were high, many were out of work, business in the other sections was at a standstill, farmers were in difficulties because they could not export their crops and taxes were heavy. To retaliate against New England an embargo act was passed in December 1813 forbidding any vessels to leave American ports. Worse still, in 1814 the English extended their blockade to New England and exports fell in value to less than 7 millions although a large illegal trade was carried on unrecorded. New England, in her turn, was more embittered and resentful.

The failure of the army, the burning of Washington, the seizure of part of Maine by the British and finally the adoption of a conscription act by Congress, moved these states to take positive action. Vermont had already set an example in 1813 by recalling her militia from the army to the defence of the state and in 1814 Massachusetts and Connecticut formed state armies to defend themselves, declaring the federal government incompetent. Even New York, Maryland, Virginia, South Carolina and Kentucky followed a similar policy for defence and other states were in process when the war ended. Was the Union in danger of falling apart?

The climax of opposition and insubordination was initiated by Massachusetts. When British troops succeeded in capturing a large part of Maine, a special session of the Massachusetts legislature was called. The federal government would not aid with troops or pay the Massachusetts militia because of the state's failure to participate in the Canadian invasion, so said the leaders. They were utterly abandoned by the federal authority, they claimed; and in October 1814 they issued a call to the New England states to meet in convention at Hartford. In the meantime at the congressional elections in New England the Federalists elected 30 and the Republicans 2. The so-called Hartford convention met with delegates from all the New England states. Their purpose was to plan to gain concessions from the federal government, in the guise of amendments to the Constitution; and it was common knowledge that some of them talked of secession if these requirements were not met. Their principal demands were that acquisition of new territory must wait upon an affirmative vote in each house; presidential tenure must be limited to one term; no two Presidents in succession might come from the same state; taxes and representation must be apportioned according to the free population.

Thus New England strove to break southern agricultural control of the government, acting on a theory of sectional independence which was to survive forty years longer. However, before they had concluded their deliberations the Ghent treaty had been signed. When their representatives came to Washington with the proposed amendments, they were met with the news of peace.

Post-War Adjustments

Peace negotiations, in fact, had been considered almost since the beginning of the war. In 1812 the Czar had offered his services as mediator and American commissioners had been appointed to proceed abroad. England refused, however, until the first defeat of Napoleon in October 1813. Thereupon she offered to negotiate directly and commissioners met in Ghent, in the summer of 1814. Great Britain refused to make any concessions and had ambitious notions of controlling the Great Lakes and taking part of Maine. However, difficulties in Europe and the failure of Wellington's veterans to do much in Canada or at Baltimore led finally to an agreement to restore everything to the status which existed at the beginning of the war.

Thus circumstances, rather than England or the United States, won the war and defined the treaty of 24 December 1814. The United States had not conquered Canada but had fastened its hold on West Florida. The coming of peace meant there would be no immediate disregard for neutral rights or the impressment of seamen, but England officially had made no concessions. Jackson's victory at New Orleans was accepted by the people of the United States as a proper climax and, taking their cue from Madison, the public gloried in a sense of victory. The triumphant Republicans laughed to scorn New England and the Federalists. Small matter was it to them that future historians were to find little that was glorious in this unfortunate war. To the young nation it was another laurel upon its military standards; Great Britain had been taught a second lesson.

This war left a train of diplomatic adjustments to follow the inconclusive treaty of peace, for it brought the United States into a new international position. Most important were those matters at issue with Great Britain left unsettled by the peace conference, such as impressment, trade privileges and the Canadian boundary. Upon the first two, Britain would make no concessions, but upon the latter she showed a willingness to yield. By the Rush-Bagot agreement of 1817, the boundary between the United States and Canada was disarmed and from then until now that three thousand mile stretch of lake, river and line has remained innocent of fortification, enjoying unbroken peace. The 49th parallel was declared by the treaty of 1818 to be the boundary between the United States and Canada from the Lake of the Woods to the Rockies and the difficult question of the possession of Oregon was postponed by the temporary expedient of arranging for joint occupation for ten years, later (1827) renewed indefinitely. No progress was made in solving the puzzle of the Maine boundary and American fishing rights in Newfoundland waters were redefined in 1818 so carelessly as to provoke a century-long dispute. Yet, in spite of a few shocks and much bellicose speech, a peace with Great Britain was inaugurated which has remained unbroken.

Spanish difficulties, too, were partly adjusted, though with little satisfaction. Spain had regained jurisdiction over Florida in 1783 but was not sufficiently strong or enterprising to do more than send a governor and a few soldiers to the several small posts which had been established. Seminole Indians and fugitive slaves roamed at will and traded with British adventurers. The acquisition of Florida had become a dream of Jefferson's when he bought Louisiana; and in 1810 and 1813 the western portion of the province was occupied. After the war of 1812 the Seminoles interfered with settlers in the Southwest and Andrew Jackson was ordered to take his Tennessee militia and punish them. He marched in vigorously, drove the Spanish out of Pensacola and St. Marks, and hanged two British whom he found aiding the Indians against him. This invasion of 1818 waked up the Spanish government and it decided it would be better to sell Florida to the United States before the latter made the formality of a sale unnecessary. In 1819 Spain agreed to transfer Florida in return for a payment of $5,000,000, to satisfy all of Spain's American creditors, and the United States agreed to the undisputed possession of Texas by the Spanish, thus abandoning a claim arising out of the indefinite provisions of the Louisiana cession treaty.

Having thus liquidated some of the questions left unsettled by the Revolution, the United States was ready for its first positive step in diplomacy. When the general peace of 1815 was finally concluded the rulers of Austria, Prussia, Russia and Great Britain signed an agreement to protect Europe from another outbreak of revolution, particularly in France. This concert of powers interfered to stamp out signs of republicanism elsewhere in Europe. In the meantime Great Britain withdrew and in 1822 France joined the three remaining powers. After suppressing a republican revolt in Spain, this alliance took up the question of America. The Spanish American provinces had been in revolt for ten years and the home government evidently was unable to bring them back to allegiance. The European foes of democracy considered the possibility at least, of sending an armed force across the seas. Great Britain objected; she was more interested in promoting trade with Latin America and opposed to the added power which might come to France if the latter took the lead as she seemed about to do. So Great Britain astonished America with a request that the United States join in a protest against invasion. In 1812 there had been war; in 1823 came an invitation to joint action!

President Monroe and his Secretary of State, John Quincy Adams, were not unmindful of the danger which might be hovering over republicanism in America. They had watched the struggles of the Spanish provinces with sympathy but with a reluctance to extend aid, primarily because they feared that the negotiation and ratification of the Florida treaty might be prevented thereby. After the ratified treaty was finally proclaimed (in February 1821) Monroe and Adams could be more sympathetic, and in 1822 they recognized some of the struggling states. Their natural opposition to intervention by Europe was sharpened by evidence that Russia had been seeking to extend her power down from Alaska along the Pacific Coast. Attempts to spread monarchical principles and power seemed to come from across both oceans. Assuredly Europe must be warned off—but not in Great Britain's company; that would be unpopular. There was perhaps a bolder attitude to take.

Monroe advised with Jefferson and Madison, as well as with Adams and the cabinet, and the die was cast. In his annual message of 1823 the President formulated his famous doctrine. He declared that except for existing colonies, America was dedicated to republicanism and no longer open to European colonization; furthermore, the United States would consider any attempt on the part of monarchies to extend their system to America as "dangerous to our peace and safety." To quiet European fears of official republican propaganda or interference in continental revolutionary wars, Monroe declared that the United States had "never taken any part" and did not intend to. The line between republicanism and monarchy was laid down somewhere in the midst of the Atlantic. This pronouncement showed the United States still on the defensive; but in years to come the Monroe Doctrine would be amenable to many uses. Europe in 1823 was not in a position to intervene; and so the United States had the satisfaction of defying (without risk) the crowned heads of Europe.

The close of the war also showed the final collapse of the old partisan rivalry. The Federalists had had the misfortune to oppose a war which ended in seeming victory for American arms; the futility of their opposition turned ridicule upon them. The exigencies of the months following the war would lead the Republicans to appropriate the boasted principles of the Federalists. They would reestablish Hamilton's bank and do many things by the loosest kind of interpretation of the Constitution. Apparently there was little left for the Federalists to cherish as their own, except a certain aristocratic aloofness which could hardly be expected to attract the votes of an increasingly democratic electorate. The Federalists' demise was undeniably indicated by the election of 1816. Their candidate, Rufus King, carried only Massachusetts, Connecticut and Delaware; while James Monroe, choice of Madison and his friends, won the presidency almost through appointment by the outgoing administration. Four years later Monroe's reelection met no formal opposition; but one electoral vote was cast against him.

In spite of these seemingly conclusive indications it must not be understood that the conservative and aristocratic temper of the Federalists had disappeared from American life. In many respects it was still strong but the Federalists, themselves inept at politics and political organization, had to bide their time till a new generation more versed in the arts of popular appeal could come forward and strive to make palatable to the populace the cherished ideals of Washington and Hamilton. As yet, however, the younger generation were neither sufficiently self-confident nor wise enough to break with the older generation; and more important, there were no groups or interests of sufficient strength or in need dire enough to supply the energy and the backing so essential to a new partisan effort. When North and South again became conscious of their differences, and when economic interests began again to plan for government aid and subsidy, then a new partisanship would arise.

The Approach of Economic Independence

The most difficult of the post-war readjustments was economic. The conflict had borne most heavily upon the incomplete and unstable business system which had been unduly stimulated by the abnormal world conditions existing between 1793 and 1813. It had been jarred rudely by the hostilities and the hope that peace would restore normal conditions proved ill-founded.

American carriers, importing agents, manufacturers and merchants suffered immediately. Foreign trade had been shattered. The British naval strength had driven American freighters from the seas and shipowners could not recoup when war ceased, because neutral carriers no longer were needed. Europe could take care of trade with American ports in its own ships, no longer menaced by privateers. Almost with official word of ratification of peace terms came British vessels well laden with her wares. Her industries had piled up great surpluses during the long war period and were desperate for markets. Price was no object. So eager were British agents to sell that they abandoned the usual forms of trade. Ignoring American importers as agents of distribution, British supercargoes sold their merchandise on the docks at auction for whatever they would bring. These masses of cheap goods crowded American products out of trade, stranding manufacturers and merchants with unsold stocks. Under these circumstances it became apparent to the manufacturers at least that if they did not receive aid they would have to go out of business. When members of Congress met in December 1815 petitions for relief in the form of protective tariff duties were pressed upon their attention.

Economic organization was further disturbed by the precarious condition of the financial system. Since the closing of the first bank of the United States in 1811, there had been no centralized, controlling banking institution of any sort. The lack gave free rein to state banks which increased in number most notably. In 1811 there had been 88, in 1813 there were 208, each one of them issuing paper money. As there were few state laws regulating the conduct of these institutions they could print money and circulate it freely, often quite beyond the range of safe banking. During the war financial difficulties had multiplied, culminating in the suspension by all banks of any attempt to redeem in coin their large emissions of paper money. The conclusion of the war therefore found business entirely dependent, for a medium of exchange, upon a depreciated paper currency with practically no hard money in the country. As business advanced after the peace it needed an expanding, reliable currency but found none. As the months succeeded one another, there seemed to be no disposition to resume specie payment, and counterfeiting and notes of defunct banks added to the uncertainty. In this instance as in the difficulties of the manufacturers, the hope of government interference and aid grew strong and Congress found awaiting it petitions for relief from the evils of demoralized finance.

Discussion centered upon tax revision and establishment of another central bank. After prolonged debate two measures of major importance were enacted. The first of these placed the revenue upon a peacetime basis and incidentally heeded a few of the plaints of the manufacturers. Cotton cloth was to be taxed 25% of its value and no cotton cloth was to be valued at less than 25¢ a yard. Such a scheme of minimum valuation was not so important at this time as the real value of coarse cloth was about that figure; but later as the price fell, it was to prove more protective. Less fortunate were the woolen manufacturers, because raw wool as well as woolen goods was taxed, the one partly offsetting the benefits derived from the other. The iron industrialists too were not favored particularly by the duty levied on rolled or hammered iron. Whether this tariff of 1816 may properly be called protective is still a matter of debate.

Secondly, the banking question was settled by providing for another bank quite similar to that promoted by Hamilton. This institution was chartered for twenty-one years and capitalized at 35 millions, three-quarters of which was to be in government obligations and one-fourth in cash. The government was to hold one-fifth of the stock and name one-fifth of the directors; the bank might establish branches. Details of organization were completed by 1 January 1817 and the government thus once more had the advantages of a place of deposit and a financial agent. Immediately the bank announced it would do business only with specie-paying banks, thus causing by 20 February a general quick return to specie payments, unfortunately temporary. As far as policy was concerned therefore, the spirit of Hamilton had triumphed.

As a final help to American carriers, Congress passed in 1817 a navigation act imposing upon foreign vessels the restrictions which the foreign country in question imposed upon American ships. So fortified with government aid and regulation, economic conditions, it was hoped, would improve; but unfortunately such a result did not follow.

Inflation intervened. Flocks of banks were established and by 1818 there were 392, almost double the number operating in 1813. Speculation was rife, especially in the western and middle states where a multitude of real estate operators welcomed banks that would loan on easy terms; it was in this section that most of the mushroom banks sprouted. Public land sales boomed as credit terms under the land act of 1800 were liberal and as the high price of farm products, especially cotton, drove up land values in northwest and southwest. At such a time, the policy of the United States bank should have been cautious, but it was the contrary. It joined in the policy of easy loans; its western branches sinned most outrageously for some of their managers proved irresponsible and ignorant of sound banking. The central organization neither watched its own branches nor, after its first move toward specie, attempted any sort of control over the state banks. Under such weak leadership only disaster could be expected.

As early as the winter of 1816 and 1817 there were hard times; soup kitchens had to be set up and charitable organizations sought to look after those out of work. By 1818 this distress had become widespread and in 1819 there was a panic. Banks again suspended payment, ships rotted at their wharves and factories closed their doors. Even the Bank of the United States was embarrassed and barely missed suspension.

Recovery from the panic was gradual. Little help came from the government, for Congress refused to pass a new tariff bill urged to protect the manufacturers. Only by a land law enacted in 1820, reducing the price to $1.25 an acre and the minimum purchase to eighty acres and requiring full cash payment, did Congress move to ease the stringency. The destruction of the credit system had put a temporary damper upon speculation in land.

Many weak banks were eliminated. The Bank of the United States itself was reorganized and the new management undertook to operate along very conservative lines. Industry twice purged, once by the influx of foreign goods and again by the financial panic, was re-erected upon a new, firmer basis. None but the soundest and best managed firms had been able to survive and they now were in a position to weather any crisis. The real beginning of American industrial strength is found in these panic years.

At last economic independence had been in large part achieved. America no longer was a mere appendage of Europe, dependent on imports for the main indispensables of daily living.[1] The new nation could look forward to continuous advance along the way of self-sufficiency. The prolonged struggle for real independence had been won.

[1] Economic independence was of course not complete. The trade-balance was for years to be against the United States due to dependence upon Europe for loans of capital to finance new enterprise.

MULTIPLYING AND DIVIDING

1819-1865

CHAPTER VIII

THE GREAT DISPERSION

So long as Europe persisted in warfare, the dependent economy of the United States kept attention chained to the activities of the fighting powers. The coming of peace and the new degree of independence which the nation had attained freed American interest and made possible a release of energy. From the close of the war of 1812 to the middle 'fifties the creative power and enthusiasm of the people of the United States were free to make what they would of a tremendous opportunity. Here was a vast expanse of territory rich in a variety of natural resources. The possibilities opened in this treasure house were enormous. A great dispersion of the people into all parts of this huge estate was inevitable.

Settlement of the West

Eighty per cent of the land belonging to the United States was vacant and waiting for men and women to occupy it and enjoy its fertility and wealth. This fact dominated the era.

Such an abundance of unused land could not fail to act as a lodestone and stimulate a restless desire to seize the resources. In this great and unknown western country fortune surely was to be found. Ever since the Revolutionary epoch and even before there had been signs of a great restlessness and many faces had turned westward. Wherever any one felt that he was not doing as well as he wished, there was the hope of better luck elsewhere. To many "elsewhere" meant the land beyond the Appalachians. This hope was felt not only in the older portion of the United States. When war ceased and reactionary statesmen sought to stifle the liberal thought stimulated by the French Revolution, thousands began to migrate from Europe to enjoy the prospect of democracy and economic opportunity. To the majority of these newcomers, the West was also the destination.

The so-called West which they sought is not easy to define, for it was less a locality than a kind of living, namely, life on the frontier, and such a mode of existence in that period cannot be given a continuous boundary. Frontier conditions were still common in central New York, western Pennsylvania and Virginia where even in 1820 large areas still had less than seven inhabitants to the square mile. In the eastern Mississippi valley such conditions were still the rule in large measure, even after the admission of Ohio, Kentucky and Tennessee as states. Across the great river in the Louisiana Purchase there were few inhabitants except at the mouth in the state of Louisiana, and at St. Louis. Settlers ventured into this frontier region particularly in times of economic distress or war. The successive crises in the East sent waves of migration beyond the mountains just as similar conditions had encouraged periodic migrations from Europe in the colonial period.

The decline in the fertility of New England soil led thousands to leave that region for the Northwest Territory. Original attempts to develop these lands in gross by companies had failed; myriad individuals were to accomplish this great task. The terms of the Northwest Ordinance were put into effect. The territory of Ohio emerged into a condition of partial self-government with a territorial legislature, and it was divided in 1800 when the land west of the present state of Ohio was made into the territory of Indiana. This was again subdivided as more people came in, by the establishment of Michigan territory in 1805 and Illinois territory in 1809. In 1802 Ohio had been made the first state carved from the Northwest Territory.

The process of statehood had already begun below the Ohio. The settlers from Virginia and North Carolina who had followed in the footsteps of Boone, Sevier and Henderson, had at length received their due; in 1792 Kentucky and in 1796 Tennessee had been admitted into the fellowship. And still the stream flowed on. The rich lands extending back from the Gulf between the Appalachians and the Mississippi were particularly attractive as cotton came into its own, and thither the hopeful went. To feed the gins new lands must be opened up, and the march into the southwest began. Government was needed and the territory of Mississippi was established in 1798 with its capital at Natchez. Here a New England governor ruled over a motley throng of French, Spanish and Americans. After the Louisiana Purchase, that great region was divided into two territories, and in 1812 the lower portion was made into the state of Louisiana.

In general the home-seekers moved into the new regions in parallel lines. Those from New England and the Middle States passed through the central New York river valley and the Great Lakes, or through western Pennsylvania and down the Ohio River. From the lakes or from the Ohio they could scatter into Ohio, Indiana, Michigan and Illinois. Those from the upper South went through mountain passes, like the Cumberland Gap, which were gateways into Kentucky, Tennessee, Mississippi and Louisiana, and into southern Ohio, Indiana and Illinois as well. This parallel march was to have a distinct influence upon the newly settled localities, as it projected eastern and southern social habits into the corresponding regions directly west. Thus transplanted, differences were somewhat modified, but not sufficiently to avoid the direful consequences of their existence.

These western settlers poured into the new regions in ever increasing numbers, practically doubling in each decade.[1] They re-enacted many of the experiences of the colonial pioneers. Once again many a man and his family cut themselves loose from home ties and long settled associations and ventured forth into a strange country. Once again was hardship the lot of a migratory people; not so much in these days from Indians, wild animals or starvation as from exposure and disease, bad roads, dangerous

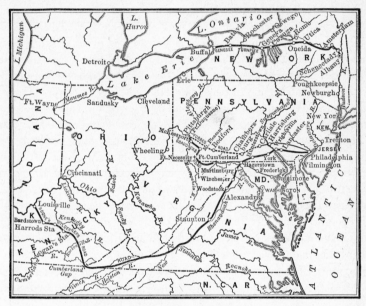

Highways to the West

streams unbridged and the weary miles of journeying by those unused to its rigors.

The large proportion of the travellers packed up their few belongings in a wagon, and driving their livestock with them, nightly pitched their tents a few miles nearer the far-away goal. Sometimes they joined with other travellers and made a cavalcade but in the main it was a family affair with much of the adventure of the road. Many transferred to flatboat at Pittsburgh and floated down the Ohio, others shipped on vessels plying the Great Lakes and upon landing either settled near some lake or river port or else once more took to the road. Many just tramped with a pack, lonely wanderers with eye ever alert for an overlooked patch of fertile land.

[1] Western population by decades:

1790— 250,000 (estimate)	1810—1,078,315	1830—3,672,569
1800— 386,413	1820—2,217,474	1840—6,376,972

In the South farmers and planters frequently went to the new regions to prospect and buy land. Then they returned to bring their families, slaves and goods in caravans which sometimes included a hundred or so persons. Such expeditions camped along the way like a military company. Some of these purchasers secured land from the government but most had to pay toll to the speculators who had picked out the best lands for profit-taking. In some fashion the newcomers got what they so eagerly sought, the land became theirs.

Life on the Frontier

Homesteads were built in the meadow patches or in clearings hewn from the forest. The prairies were avoided until later time because they lacked fuel and building material and their matted soil was too difficult for the plows of the day. Log houses and ruder out-buildings faced the trails and newly made cart-paths that were to be the future thoroughfares.

The pioneer drama was acted and re-enacted in many regions. The settler cut boughs and logs to make a shelter and then built an oblong log house of one room. The logs were made weather-tight by clay or mud stuffed into the crevices. Windows were covered by rude shutters or greased paper and floors were of dirt or of rough wooden blocks called puncheons. A great fireplace made of clay and stones served as a place to cook and as a source of heat and light. The furnishings of these cabins were sparse and rude; sometimes a few pieces brought from the old home, more often a table, a few chairs and a rude bed were contrived on the spot. A gun, a spinning wheel, an iron crane for the fireplace and a few pots and pans, had been transported. Clothes were as simple as the furniture. Men often wore deerskin shirt and breeches with moccasins and a skin cap to complete the costume. Women wore dresses of homespun with little in the way of adornment. The children were just as nondescript and even worse-fitted than their elders.

Food was very simple. Meat and game from the forest, fish from the streams, cereals and vegetables from the fields, wild fruit and berries made up the bulk of the diet. Chickens, pigs and cattle afforded variety. Grain was ground by hand or taken to some near-by mill so that bread and johnny-cake could be prepared. Corn could be easily distilled into whiskey and fruit might become apple-jack or brandy. The frontier was not lacking in potent liquid.

The clearings were centers of ceaseless activity. All worked in the fields and by the fireside. Crops were planted, tended and harvested. The food was prepared, clothes made and the chores performed near the hearthstone. Wood was cut by the cord for the yawning fireplaces.

Early Illinois Cabin,
Reproduced at
New Salem, Ill.

CIVILIZATION

Michigan Farmhouse
near Schoolcraft

MOVES WESTWARD

Sod-house on
North Dakota Plains

After the day's toil the whole family slept together in a bed which was often only a pile of straw covered with skins.

There was much danger in this rude life. There was scant protection from the winter's cold. Summer's heat, too, brought disease, particularly as water and food often were contaminated and the lack of proper drainage invited epidemics. Swampland fevers, Indian forays, forest animals and fires were constant perils to life and happiness. Hard work oftentimes induced rheumatism, sprains and ruptures. Salt pork and whiskey ruined the digestion. Children's diseases and child birth took heavy toll. Home remedies, herbs and simples, administered by the pioneer women comprised the medical aid at hand for there were few doctors on the frontier. Such was the life of the hardiest who went on ahead to tame the forest. Conditions of this sort were common on all frontiers, particularly in the Ohio valley. In the southern region when slave gangs were moved, conditions were less crude, the equipment less inadequate.

Despite these hardships, or perhaps because of them, the frontier produced a number of men and women who were well equipped to lead in the task of nation building. This severe discipline gave to many who survived it, unusual qualities of enterprise and leadership. Abraham Lincoln represents them, though he was destined to achieve a position of unique preëminence. Born in surroundings which to present-day standards seem squalid, and with slight encouragement to seek to rise above this environment, he found there the training needed to enable him to fulfill his ambitions. To natural strength of body, he added strength of mind. Having few teachers, he set his own discipline and learned to think and to express himself in terms which attracted followers. Courage, understanding of human nature, and simple but scrupulously observed standards of ethics combined with his physical and mental strength to make him a great leader. Likewise the frontier produced a superior type of womanhood which could endure and meet emergencies. Their lot was even harder than that of their colonial forbears because of the greater prevalence of fevers in the river valleys beyond the Appalachians. Few could think of themselves apart from their function as home-makers, and without recognition or much fame guided the growth of the new society. From this environment emerged many a man and woman who assumed a part in the leadership necessary to meet the great demands of the frontier upon those who sought to transform it into a fit abode for civilization.

Life of this sort was of course uncertain. These early settlers either prospered or moved on. If they prospered they cleared more land, built better houses, bought more conveniences. The forest disappeared, roads took the place of trails; fenced fields covered the traces of the old stump-studded clearings. On the other hand if these pioneers became discouraged or failed to succeed they moved on to find another frontier in which to reenact the drama; some few went back to their old homes in the East. Their places were filled by those who took advantage of what they did without experiencing the hardships. This second group prospered more easily.

In this way large areas were brought under cultivation ranging from the eighty acre farmsteads gradually hewn from the forest an acre at a time to the great southwestern plantations of hundreds of acres. Tools and methods were little different from those of colonial days though crops were more varied. In the Northwest, corn and wheat, cattle, sheep and hogs were the chief sources of livelihood. The meat, wool and wheat were sold to the East and South, while the corn either was fed to the hogs or made into whiskey, which was used as a medium of exchange. In the Kentucky region hemp and tobacco were the staples.

The Southwest was devoted to sugar and cotton. In the Louisiana country the French creoles had developed sugar planting. They had occupied the best sugar lands and as they were a clannish people, the Americans did not find it easy to mix with them. Therefore the new-comers avoided the lower farming districts and settled in the region of Baton Rogue and the Red River. In some instances they cultivated sugar but in general they turned to cotton planting. The pioneers in the Alabama and Mississippi region did likewise. In fact the increase in the cotton crop was phenomenal. In 1811 the Gulf territory had raised 5,000,000 pounds of cotton; by 1826 it produced 150,000,000 pounds and was far in advance of the old South. This great cotton district devoted itself with increasing exclusiveness to its one crop and depended upon the Northwest for much of its food—ultimately an unfortunate reliance.

In the Northwest new towns and villages began to dot the map in the midst of the farming country. Where two trails crossed, or at a convenient river or lakeside landing place, a cluster of huts was built, with a store, a blacksmith shop, a mill, sometimes an inn, such as it was, and the houses of those who supplied by trade or craft the wants of the nearby farmers. Trade flourished and a few "cities" even appeared, a portentous sign of a far off day. Cincinnati and Louisville joined New Orleans and St. Louis; Pittsburgh flourished and certain outposts for trade were located in such strategic positions as to promise a growth unprecedented; such communities bore the now familiar names of Buffalo, Detroit, Cleveland and Milwaukee.

These centers were established not only to supply the needs of the surrounding farm country, but also to gather in the scattered profits of the far western trade. While roads were few and bad and canals even more scarce, there could be no economical, direct exchange between East and West. For the supply of the farming regions a triangular system grew up. The Northwest drew from the East its manufactured goods and sent most of its agricultural surplus into the South and Southwest, which in return supplied the Northwest with the money (obtained from cotton sales abroad) to settle the balance it owed the East. The Mississippi, the Ohio and the Great Lakes were ready-made highways for this traffic.

Frontier folkways developed in these communities. Society soon found itself in the rude cooperative combinations of mutual aid and hilarity. Barn raisings, corn huskings and quilting bees, as well as weddings and holiday gatherings brought the people together for boisterous relaxation. Religion too had its social as well as spiritual mission. The denominational organizations of the East, Protestant and Catholic, were concerned with the religious needs of the frontier. Circuit riders and itinerant priests served the scattered communities. Chapels began to appear in the cross roads hamlets and as these communities grew into towns, settled clergymen became leaders of the people. Seasonal religious gatherings in the form of camp meetings were common and strenuous revivals, conducted by hardy evangelists, encouraged their listeners to receive the spirit of religion with violent manifestations of emotional frenzy.

Each community had political almost as soon as economic and religious organization; one of the first common interests in any locality was the establishment of a place of record, so that the all-important land titles might be securely registered and a form of local government established, township or county or both. When population warranted and Congress authorized it, territorial legislatures came into being; and periodically representatives of the various isolated settlements could come together and aid in forming that community consciousness which would some day, and that very shortly, make a state. In this process of political evolution crude but effective notions of justice often prevailed. Horse thieves would be most summarily dealt with by local vigilance committees because of the importance of horses in frontier economy. Other thievery and manslaughter sometimes received more lenient treatment.

Significant signs of elementary culture were soon apparent. With the growth of political interest came some wandering printer or would-be journalist, ready to establish a crude page of news, editorials, local or borrowed literary effort and advertisements, to serve as the voice of the people and to reflect and guide their opinions and politics. The first of these western newspapers was the *Kentucky Gazette* founded at Lexington in 1787. By 1824 there were 98 papers in Kentucky, Tennessee and the old Northwest. A few literary, religious and even scientific periodicals were supported and by 1840 there were 385 printing establishments in the trans-Appalachian region. Even in this early day literary ambition was stimulating writers. A variety of poets and fiction writers whose names are hardly remembered were putting their ideas in print. Theatres were built as early as 1801 and local companies, some of which travelled, brought a primitive notion of drama to none-too-particular audiences.

Education was slow in becoming established in spite of the land gifts specified by the Northwest Ordinances. The land grants were mismanaged and poverty was too prevalent to warrant rapid creation of school systems. But log schoolhouses gradually made their appearance. Teachers often were European immigrants who had known better days or college students earning a little money during vacation, and all wondered whether they could "lick" the older boys in the course of discipline. Naturally such education did not go far beyond the three "R's." The ambitious plans for complete state systems, however, were not lost sight of and, after bitter fights over the expense, were put into effect. Some of the universities were state-controlled like that of Michigan, while a few private institutions, notably Transylvania University in Kentucky, shed a cultural radiance in the rather formidable darkness.

Cultural institutions of other types began to appear. Libraries, mostly connected with the struggling universities and colleges, began to mobilize respectable collections of books. An embryo interest in the process of local growth was manifest in the historical societies which were organized in most of the states. A few men could devote themselves to scholarship and scientific investigation, usually of the surrounding environment, and called "Natural History."

In this fashion the new frontiers grew into settled communities. Their citizens were self-reliant and individualistic. They believed implicitly in the equalitarian doctrines of the nation's founders, resented control and hated special privilege. Most of them could tell tales of hardship, deprivation and danger, which the coming of prosperity and settled life did not cause them to forget. In spite of their individualism, they knew the need of cooperation, for only by it had their survival been possible. They could work together in a common cause and the community spirit of these new societies was of strong growth and exercised lasting influence. It was often to present a contrast with conditions East and South.

Out beyond this place of swarming was a vast stretch of territory known as the great American desert. Though it was a prevalent belief that it was uninhabitable the unknown region was a constant lure to the curious. Exploring became an active career for a number of adventurous spirits who liked to go beyond the haunts of men. The first notable expeditions were the product of Thomas Jefferson's wide interest. Even before he purchased Louisiana he wanted to make contacts with the Indians and promote fur trading in the trans-Mississippi region. Early in 1803 he sent his secretary Meriwether Lewis and George Rogers Clark's brother William in command of an extensive exploration which took them from St. Louis overland to the mouth of the Columbia. Later he sent explorers to the Southwest, notably Captain Zebulon Pike who went through Colorado, New Mexico and Texas in 1806 and 1807.

Shortly thereafter the profit from the fur trade began to lure trappers and traders. Agents of eastern and Mississippi valley traders began intensive operations. John Jacob Astor's American Fur Company scattered posts over the Michigan and Wisconsin regions and at the time of the War of 1812 had a post in Oregon. A competing enterprise, The Rocky Mountain Fur Company, in the 'twenties sent explorers into the area between the Missouri and the Rockies. One of these, Jedediah S. Smith, travelled extensively and made notable discoveries. He and his associates reached the Great Salt Lake and penetrated the mountains, finding a way to California by way of the South Pass. Also they made their way by land from San Francisco to the Columbia. Famous scouts of the period were employed by this company and the prowess of Jim Bridger and Kit Carson became almost mythological.

The War Department encouraged exploration. Major Stephen H. Long in 1823 made extensive journeys in the region between the Mississippi and the Missouri. General Henry Atkinson in 1825 went down into the Arkansas region. The protection of the Santa Fé trail, over which traders went to New Mexico for silver and leather, became an object of concern to the government and military posts were established. American traders and settlers were penetrating into California in the 'thirties while settlers and missionaries located in the Oregon country south of the Columbia River. The interest of important politicians, notably Senator Thomas Hart Benton of Missouri was enlisted and his son-in-law, Captain John C. Frémont, was sent out by the government to explore again the trails to California and Oregon. Much information, real and fanciful, began to penetrate back into the East. However the profits from the fur trade were of greater interest. By the late 'thirties, these were declining, as the animals were becoming scarce and at the same time fashions of dress were changing. As yet no real migration into the region beyond the hundredth meridian was undertaken but there it was, a mysterious reservoir of possible advantage.

Demands of the West

The swelling tide of western migration brought forward questions in which the government was involved. The Indians occupied lands which the settlers coveted, the new settlers wanted cheaper land from the government and help in providing transportation. New territories and states also needed to be organized. Such propositions had been considered and adjusted to fit the needs of the preceding generation with some dispute and political jockeying but the debates had not reached the intensity which was to mark those of the period to come. The projection westward of eastern and southern institutions and habits of thought were to add a sectional element to the controversies which were to arise over such matters as Indians, lands, transportation and government.

The consideration of these questions involved the intensified discussion of the two broader issues which had appeared before, namely, the extent of the powers of the federal government under the Constitution, and more important, the conflicting interests and relative strength of the sections. The latter question was further complicated by the fact that there were now three rather than two sections, for the West was to be reckoned with increasingly in the future. A tier of eight states, Ohio, Illinois, Indiana, Kentucky, Tennessee, Missouri, Alabama and Mississippi was completed by 1821 and they had great concern in the questions outlined above, interests which were separate and distinct from those of eastern and southern groups.

Their demand for the opening of more public land for settlement at lower prices was insistent and precipitated a struggle over policy in which two conflicting ideas developed. The government at first had looked upon the lands as salable property, from which revenue could be obtained. After the grants of the Confederation period, no land was offered at public sales until 1796 when Congress at length re-enacted the Land Ordinance of 1785 with some modifications. Land must be purchased at auction at a minimum of $2.00 an acre in 640 acre tracts with only a year in which to complete payment. The minimum purchase unfortunately was too large in size and price, therefore little land changed hands, in fact but 50,000 acres in four years. In 1800 a more liberal policy was enacted. 320 acre plots might be purchased on easier credit, one quarter of the $2.00 price to be paid on account and the remainder within four years. This arrangement was likewise unproductive and in 1804 the minimum purchase was further reduced to 160 acres. In spite of these concessions more land was bought by speculators to hold for a rise, than was taken by actual settlers, and little money was paid in.

By 1820 the government was owed more than $24,000,000, a sum so large that it seemed hardly likely to be collected. Distress due to the panic of 1819 was general and Congress decided to revise the land system. A new theory was taking shape, namely, that the government should turn the lands over to the public free or at a nominal price, so that they might develop them quickly and effectively, thereby advancing the interests of the nation and depriving the speculator of opportunities to make large profits.

The law of 1820 provided that hereafter land could be purchased in lots as small as eighty acres at the reduced price of one dollar and a quarter an acre cash. Having killed the credit system, Congress next provided (1821) for clearing off the debts that had accumulated under the old system, by permitting the debtors to take that proportion of their

purchases which they had paid for, and to relinquish the remainder to
the government. Under these new conditions during the decade 1820-
1830 land sales averaged in the neighborhood of 1,000,000 acres annually. In the meantime western senators and representatives reflected
a general desire on the part of their constituents for various schemes of
more liberal terms, and more and more emphasis was placed upon the
idea of free distribution of land to actual settlers. Both eastern and southern opinion in general was opposed to such generosity, for population
was leaving these regions and the possibility of many more western states
and the loss of power by the East still haunted the imagination of politicians and mill owners, or any one else who employed labor and wanted
it cheap. In the South also there was a fear, especially after the struggle
over the admission of Missouri in 1820, that the bulk of the western
states would be "free" and would hold opinions antagonistic to southern
interests. So the land question continued as a source of dispute and sectional disagreement; within it were the germs of future plagues, for
whosoever controlled the distribution of the land, controlled the destiny
of the nation.

The Indian problem was less controversial; there was general agreement among all save the Indians themselves that they should be moved.
Their animosity was a constant menace. The first crisis occurred when
Governor St. Clair of the Northwest Territory was badly defeated in
1791. "Mad Anthony" Wayne, however, had avenged this disaster at the
battle of Fallen Timbers in 1794 and the next year had exacted from the
Indians the treaty of Greenville. By this instrument, they agreed to relinquish most of Ohio, if the whites would respect their territory to the
north and west. Congress tried to live up to this treaty by legislating
to keep citizens away from the Indian lands, but to no avail. Adventurous whites seldom inquired whether their cupidity was leading them
to violate Indian treaties.

The part the Indians played during the War of 1812 made them
more than ever objects of hatred. Their northwest possessions lay
directly in the path of western settlement. They occupied large areas in
Ohio, Indiana, Illinois and practically all of Michigan and a great part
of the vast Louisiana purchase, save the state of Louisiana and the
Missouri and Arkansas regions. In the old Southwest too, much of
Mississippi and Alabama and even Georgia and Tennessee were in the
hands of various tribes. When Florida was acquired, the Seminoles were
added to the national burden and the Seminole war which began to
flare up intermittently in 1817 was a constant reminder of the bitter
conflict between the red men and the white.

Directly after the close of the War of 1812, the government sought
to remove the Indians from the paths of expansion. During the years
1815-1837, beginning with the council at Detroit in the former year,

agents held many conferences with the Indian tribes and by persuasion, bribery and occasional sharp practice negotiated a great number of treaties which pushed the Indians beyond the Mississippi River. This policy of removal was not accomplished without friction and violence.

Before Indian removals were complete extended negotiations had to be undertaken with the Creeks and the Cherokees, a disastrous war dragged on in Florida against the Seminoles (1835-1842) and Sac and Fox Indians of Illinois fought the Black Hawk War of 1832. The object, in time, was accomplished, the red men were pushed beyond the great river and their land opened to the whites. In 1834 Congress created an Indian territory in the Southwest—where Oklahoma now is—in a region into which it was hoped they could be moved and where it was presumed white men would not penetrate. The law makers of those days were not gifted with foresight into 1889.

The third problem pressed upon the attention of federal and state governments by the westward drive was adequate transportation. Roads were poor, waterways inconvenient, people were clamorous for better ways of travel and rival cities and localities wished their communications with sources of supply and trade as complete and effective as possible. The invention of steamboats had made waterways even more desirable and the introduction of these vessels on western waters was to open a new chapter in transportation. The backers of Fulton's *Clermont* through their agent, Nicholas J. Roosevelt, launched the *New Orleans* at Pittsburgh in 1811 and the next year it made a voyage to its name city. However, its engines were not forceful enough to drive it upstream and it was not until 1816 that Henry M. Shreve designed a boat that would ply the river in both directions. The Father of Waters was ready for a new commercial and passenger-carrying era, and river steamboats built like palaces became the wonder of the western country. Steamboats were also launched on the Great Lakes. Great commercial possibilities were open if roads and canals could be built to connect rivers and lakes.

Three agencies might provide roads or canals, namely, private capital, state legislatures, or Congress. The expense involved had demonstrated the difficulty of making adequate provision by private capital so it was natural that promoters should turn to government for aid. As the most needed improvements passed state boundaries the national government seemed the logical agency to undertake new lines of travel. During Jefferson's administration Albert Gallatin had made an extensive canal plan, but Congress provided only a small beginning by appropriating money in 1806 to start a great National Road, eventually to extend from Cumberland, Maryland, to St. Louis. Appropriations were continued in a small way and in 1818, when the road reached the Ohio, 130 miles had been built.

The new demands of the Northwest called for a more elaborate plan;

and the dust was shaken off Gallatin's proposals. President Madison reminded Congress of the need for an adequate system of transportation in order to draw "more closely together every part of our country, by promoting intercourse and improvements and by increasing the share of every part in the common stock of national prosperity." A bill for such a scheme passed Congress early in 1817, whereby the bonus paid by the new national bank, and the dividends to be received later from the stock owned by the government, were to be used as a fund to aid development of a transportation system. President Madison, however, was overcome by constitutional scruples in spite of his previous plea and vetoed the bill; a constitutional amendment, he felt, was necessary to give Congress the power. His successor, Monroe, was equally sensitive, making the veto of a small item the occasion for a lengthy explanation of his disapproval of government operation of such improvements. On the contrary, President John Quincy Adams was an ardent advocate of improvements and during his rule over two million dollars was spent in aiding canals by purchasing their stock; public land was granted to Illinois, Ohio and Alabama as a subsidy. Andrew Jackson, however, finally killed the idea by his veto of the Maysville Road bill in 1830 which indicated that he would approve no internal improvement legislation.

Presidential disapproval must not be thought to be the only reason for this failure. Many in New England and in the South did not want these improvements pushed ahead so fast for fear of draining off their population and raising a group of powerful western states too quickly, reasoning similar to that which urged these same groups to oppose liberal land cessions. Consequently, the government of the United States, while it gave some grants of land or purchased some stock in various improvements, never undertook any of its own except to continue the National Road to Zanesville, Ohio, and authorize a report upon its extension to the Mississippi.[1] Later events were to destroy entirely so narrow a vision.

Disappointed in their hope of federal aid, promoters of roads and canals turned to state legislatures for subsidy. Their chief success was a great artery of commerce across New York State, the Erie Canal, completed in 1825 which extended from Albany to Buffalo and made possible an all-water connection between the Great Lakes and the Atlantic. This project of the Empire State made New York the leading commercial city of the United States. Philadelphia, Boston and Baltimore were not to fall behind without a struggle. The merchants of Baltimore urged the extension of the National Road further west while the Commonwealth of Pennsylvania launched an ambitious plan of its own to

---

[1] Appropriations for the National Road were continued and it was built slowly, reaching its final stage in Vandalia, Illinois, in 1852.

offset New York's advantage. The legislature appropriated money to build a combination rail and canal route called the Portage Railroad to connect Philadelphia and Pittsburgh. By 1834 the improvement was completed at the cost of a huge debt, but all in vain. New York had become the permanent commercial capital of the nation.

Maryland and Virginia also turned to such projects and in 1828 began to extend a canal which was to run from the falls of the Potomac to the Ohio. This plan, originally promoted by George Washington, was to connect the Chesapeake and the Ohio. The United States gov-

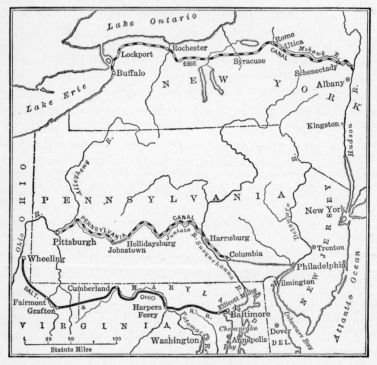

Canals and Railroads

ernment bought stock in this canal and high hopes were held out for it; but it never got beyond Cumberland, Maryland, and by its failure to cross the mountain never realized the full possibility of its usefulness. Virginia, however, built the James River and Kanawha Canal across the mountains. In New Jersey two cross-state canals were constructed, one in the northern region—the Morris and Essex Canal, which connected the Delaware with New York Bay, and which opened a route from the Pennsylvania coal regions to the sea. The other, the Delaware and Raritan, crossed the state in the central section and made it possible to carry goods in smooth water from Philadelphia to New York. In

Ohio, two great canals were projected, one from Cleveland to the Ohio and the other from Toledo to Cincinnati. Indiana and Illinois likewise built canals of convenience connecting lakes and rivers and making continuous waterways. By 1830, state, municipal and private promotion had practically completed 3908 miles of canal and had 6833 additional miles in contemplation. Given more time, a canal system of permanent national value might have been established. Baltimore, however, had discovered another way and the Baltimore and Ohio Railroad Company was undertaking a new type of transportation which was to revolutionize communication and kill the canal prospects.

Political Complications

The last problem produced by the movement of people into the western country was to prove the most difficult of them all; the question of organizing these new communities into territories and more especially into states was to provoke a quarrel which was to end at length in the tragedy of the Civil War. Prior to 1818, the question of state organization had not troubled Congress much, except slightly in the case of Louisiana; seven states had been added to the original thirteen and two more were about to be admitted to the Union. It had so happened that of these twenty-two states, eleven permitted Negro slavery while the others had abolished it either at once or gradually. Politically, however, the influence of the slave and free sections had not been equal. The Democratic tenets of Jefferson's faith and his skillful organizing talents had left the aristocratic and less resourceful Federalists at a disadvantage which their opposition to the Louisiana Purchase and the War of 1812 had not removed. Jefferson, Madison and Monroe, Virginia planters representing the great mass of the agricultural and democratic Americans, seemed firmly in the saddle. The old Federalist ideal of a strong government eager to aid business enterprise and hasten development seemed dead. Then came a fire-bell in the night.

Missouri applied for statehood, with slavery legalized, in 1818 and at the same time Arkansas desired to be given territorial status. If these areas were so organized while the Northwest seemed less attractive, the southern planter group would remain indefinitely in control, Crawford of Georgia would succeed Monroe and where would northeastern interests be? Left to languish under the indifferent policy of a laissez-faire government? Besides, there was a growing prejudice against permitting Negro slavery to spread into the new territory. Appealing to this growing prejudice, James Tallmadge of New York, a junior associate of the old Federalist, Rufus King, proposed to exclude slavery from Missouri. As the population of the northern states was by this time larger than that of the southern group, northern congressmen, if they voted together, could control the House of Representatives. Opposition to slavery was an excellent issue upon which to unite them against the South. Their power was apparent and southern members began to be concerned. Some adopted New England tactics and threatened secession if Missouri were denied entrance into the Union as she wished to enter, namely, as a slave state. The more practical looked for a solution of the problem in compromise.

After a year and a half of political maneuvering the way was found. A part of Massachusetts wanted to enter the Union as the state of Maine; to admit Maine with Missouri, one free, the other slave, would serve the purpose of keeping the balance even, twelve slave and twelve free states. But what of the future, what of Arkansas that would soon be coming forward? The answer to that question was found in establishing an arbitrary line, 36° 30', dividing the remainder of the Louisiana Purchase territory so that all states entering from the area north of the line must be free, those coming in from the South might be slave. The Congressional battle of 1819-1820-1821 over this arrangement was bitter, the North trying to assert its numerical superiority, the South endeavoring to hold a balance. Secession was threatened by the South; the changes were rung on "states rights" and the right of Missouri to have her own constitution; the North was bitter in condemning the sin of slavery and the crime of the southerners in owning slaves. Both sides were relieved when the so-called Missouri Compromise was enacted. It was hoped that no such struggle would ever again occur. The question drifted off into obscurity, no more states were destined to be made for fifteen years. But ominous arguments had been formulated and dangerous threats uttered.

So westward a motley throng of people was moving, establishing new homesteads and communities, and steadily multiplying their numbers. These pioneers were to develop the western country, increase the production of raw materials and stimulate commerce; more important, they were to form a new social grouping in these large United States. Hereafter the term "West" was to bear a separate and distinct meaning such as New England and the South already bore.

In many ways the people in these lands beyond the mountains were drawn together. They all had the pioneering instinct, sought new openings and welcomed new experiences, seemingly the more eagerly if risk and hardship were involved. The common interest in agriculture, too, was a bond which was strong, especially if eastern capitalists seemed to be exacting undue toll or obtaining undesirable advantages at the expense of the pioneers in the great valley. Furthermore there was a mutual dependence between the upper and lower regions. The southern locality with its preoccupation with cotton did not feed itself but depended for sustenance upon the northern fields always offering a surplus;

the Ohio and the Mississippi rivers made an easy channel whereby food could be transported cheaply to the South. At the same time the mouth of the great river was the natural place of export and import for the people of the upper valley; as the other alternative, transportation over the mountains to the eastern seaboard, was too costly. So, annually, more flatbottomed boats floated down the great river; and with the launching of the steamboat on its waters in 1812, the possibilities of river transport were revolutionized. The foundations seemed to have been laid for a united though enormous, inland empire dedicated to the cultivation of the soil and destined to gain fabulous wealth from its generous increase.

The empire, nevertheless, did not become homogeneous, for in it were being evolved two ways of life. The Northwest became a land of moderate-sized farms devoted to the production of food and operated by the land owners and their sons. Land was cheap, labor was scarce, each man easily became a proprietor and the new states were laid out like checker-boards in one hundred and sixty acre farms. In the South-west, on the other hand, cotton, sugar and tobacco production was most profitable when undertaken by slave labor on large plantations. So, estates worked by gangs of Negroes were the ambitious hope if not the actual realization of a large portion of these farmers. Thus, while the Northwest was dedicating itself to individualism and equality, which might easily be translated into intense love of freedom, the Southwest was following the older South in building up a social order more resem-bling feudalism. The day was to come when the basic incompatibility would become apparent for this great westward movement was in the end to demonstrate the inherent weakness of the United States. The far-sighted could see that there was danger. The nation was so large and its aggregation of communities so diverse that bitter inter-sectional rivalry might bring conflict and even dissolution. As yet however, the great mass of enterprising Americans were interested only in advance and growth, and were too preoccupied with subduing the continent to anticipate disaster.

CHAPTER IX

CONCENTRATION OF POPULATION

The great dispersion of Americans into the western country was the most significant social force of this epoch. But there was a second tendency to migrate which, though less characteristic of the time, was to be even more significant in years to come. People were beginning to gravitate toward towns and cities and the process of metropolitan growth was vigorously stimulated by expanding American enterprise. New business activity was hastening the concentration of population in urban communities.

New Business Conditions

The shift by the management of capital to new interests was highly significant. The old preoccupation with commerce had been much weakened by conditions in the war period which had caused large amounts of capital to be transferred to the rising industries. Nevertheless, the wharves hummed with activity, for from 1815 until 1837 foreign trade increased in value and its very size made necessary its concentration in certain seaports which became great centers of prosperity and wealth. Foreign trade, which in the decade 1790-1800 averaged 100 millions in value annually, rose to very little short of 225 millions each year of the decade 1830-1840. The balance of this trade favored Europe generally for as yet the United States had to buy much more than it could sell.

American trade embraced the entire world. The main imports were cloth, iron and other manufactured goods from Europe. But tea from China, coffee from Brazil, sugar from Cuba, cocoa from Central America, fruit from the tropics, spices from the South Sea Islands, and wine from Madeira, and the Canaries, called the ships of American merchants to all ports on the seven seas. They went out laden with domestic food stuffs, lumber and naval stores, tobacco and most particularly cotton for Europe and the rest of the world. In this traffic American merchants made millions.

In the early days of foreign trade a number of seaports located in all the maritime states had shared importance; but conditions had changed. The superior facilities and conveniences supplied by New York City had tended to concentrate the bulk of the import trade at that great depot. Philadelphia had to yield primacy, falling to third place. Boston still second, fell short of former glory, except as the center for far-eastern trade. The other New England ports, notably Salem, Marble-head and Newburyport, became the home of memories of maritime adventure. In the South, as tobacco fell in importance and the center of cotton culture moved to the Gulf region, New Orleans and Mobile became the great export markets. Savannah, Charleston and even Bal-timore fell in importance. In vain did southern cities hope for European import trade; the ships which sailed away loaded to the rails with cotton, brought their great return cargoes back via New York. Gotham on Manhattan island and Boston were to be the centers of commerce.

Here the merchants directed the great fleets which proudly bore the national ensign. The lumber, masts and other naval stores so generously supplied by the forests still gave American ship builders a splendid advantage in an age of wooden vessels. Ship building yards continued to be scattered along the coast, notably in New England. Regular schedules of sailing to and from Europe were organized by ship "lines." The Black Ball Line, for instance, built a fleet of "packets" which sailed regularly between New York and Liverpool. In spite of new styles of building faster ships, passages could not be brought much under two weeks and a half. A beginning had been made in the use of steam for ocean travel when an American vessel, the *Savannah,* crossed in 1819 partly under steam power. Americans were not much interested in this new possibility, however, and the harbors of New York and Boston were more alive than ever with the great canvas wings of packet boats, schooners, brigs and sloops. Boston and Gloucester were busy fishing centers where fleets of boats annually brought great catches of codfish and mackerel. New Bedford, Massachusetts, rose to great prominence as a whaling center. This adventurous chase reached its peak in 1850 when 680 whalers scoured the seas in search of sperm oil and whalebone.

Sailing ships of all kinds brought wealth to their backers and con-centrated capital in their home ports. Cities assumed a new importance as financial centers where the capitalists had their headquarters. John Jacob Astor of New York and Stephen Girard of Philadelphia were founding a new dynasty of magnates. The needs of capital meant that a great variety of services would be located in these centers, importing firms, brokers, insurance companies, middlemen of all sorts, transporta-tion directors and bankers.

This increase in business activity naturally reflected itself in the expan-sion of banking. New York and Boston were the headquarters of power-ful and long-established private banks, the Bank of the Manhattan Com-pany and the Suffolk Bank. In Philadelphia, however, in the years 1817-1833, was located the nerve center of American finance, the Second Bank of the United States. After its early disastrous career, 1817-1820, it was saved by the strict and cautious policies of its second president, Langdon Cheves and under its third executive, Nicholas Biddle, it became strong and prosperous. Biddle succeeded in becoming a financial power who could deal with the rare American millionaires, Girard and Astor. The Second Bank of the United States, with the advantage of government deposits and treasury cooperation, dominated the financial centers growing up in the newly important cities.

The development of strong business centers was not wholly confined to the East. Increasing trade with the western region and the building of transportation lines caused towns and cities to spring up in the trans-Appalachian country. Frontier trading posts and small riverside hamlets became bustling metropolises. New roads and canals produced junction points on the Great Lakes, the Ohio and the Mississippi which soon became cities. In 1840, Cincinnati had 46,000 inhabitants, Pittsburgh 21,000 and St. Louis 16,000 at a time when only five seaboard cities had more than 90,000 population. (New York, Philadelphia, Baltimore, New Orleans and Boston.) At such points, the West's business activities concentrated; there goods were shipped for distribution among the inhabitants and there the produce of the region was collected to be transported east or south to the ports for Europe.

The Industrial Revolution

Most significant of all the factors which were enlarging cities was the revolution which was bringing American industry nearer to the point of meeting the needs of the growing people. American industrialists had emerged from the panic of 1819 in improved condition. The hardships following the war of 1812 culminating in the panic had driven all but the strongest and soundest industrial organizations out of business and those remaining were in a position to launch new ventures. The industries which transformed themselves most notably were the textile manufacturers and among them the principal advances took place in the cotton group. First of all was the introduction of the power loom. Hitherto power had been used largely for spinning thread while the finished product had been woven on hand looms very largely in the homes of people in the vicinity of the spinning machinery. This was all changed in the years after 1815, when spinning and weaving by power-run machinery were first combined in one factory at Waltham. Another technical change in the cotton industry between 1820 and 1830 was the manufacture of print cotton goods. Hitherto American cotton factories had confined themselves largely to the production of coarse sheetings; finer goods with patterns and colors had been either woven by hand or imported. But improved machinery made possible the weaving of finer cotton cloth so it could be sold reasonably and the use of engraved cylinders run by power enabled manufacturers to produce goods with striking and attractive colored patterns, which gave a much finer appearance than the rather uneven pattern of home woven goods. Favorable tariff rates helped to set the stage, in New England at least, for a very significant industrial advance.

With the introduction of these technical improvements the profits possible from large scale production became apparent. To realize these gains it was necessary to purchase and house numerous expensive machines and to accomplish this corporations had to be formed and factories builded. Prior to this period most American industry had been carried on by individuals or partnerships in small mills. The new ways produced the industrial revolution and a new social phenomenon in the United States, the factory town inhabited in large part by paid workers employed by a corporation and directed by a manager, also an employee of the corporation. This was a new human relationship in American life. Heretofore, most people had been either independent farmers, artisans or merchants, or if they were employees they were in immediate and frequent contact with their employer who was a master workman or a proprietor, not a corporation. It is significant that as the developing democracy was giving the individual greater economic and political freedom in the West, the factory system of labor should be sponsoring in the East a contrary trend away from economic freedom.

This new system evolved almost exclusively in New England, although it advanced somewhat in the upper Hudson and Mohawk valleys. In New England was the water power at the falls of the rivers and there too was capital. In the years following the war of 1812 the relative percentage of capital invested in foreign commerce decreased, although the absolute total grew. So the adventurous turned their hope of profit toward the new manufacturing possibilities. The "Merrimack Manufacturing Company" was organized in 1822, capitalized at $600,000 and in 1824 their first factory opened. They had acquired the land at the falls and began to sell water power rights. The labor needed in their own and other Merrimac River factories developed the town of Lowell, and Lawrence, Massachusetts, Manchester, New Hampshire and numerous other factory towns grew up at the falls of the New England rivers. However, these corporation projects were only a part, and not a major part, of the growth of the cotton industry in the decade 1820-1830. Most of the cotton was still spun and woven in small mills managed by proprietors. Outside of northern New England the factory system developed slowly, although cotton spinning and weaving multiplied rapidly; between 1820 and 1831 the number of spindles increased four times and the number of factory looms ten times.

A slower but similar evolution can be traced in the woolen industry, on a smaller scale. The supply of raw material, unlike cotton, was never very plentiful, the process of manufacture was more complicated, the machines were more difficult to invent and required more skilled labor to operate. The household system continued and even in 1830, in New York state at least, more woolen cloth was manufactured at home than in factories. Not until 1830 when the Middlesex Company was organized at Lowell was the day of large production in woolen goods begun and then it proved a slow growth. The industry continued in a variety of small establishments, each carrying on one or two of its many complicated processes.

In the other important branch of American manufacturing, the metal industry, there was a steady growth closely related to the advance of mechanical civilization. It was not so much that new processes or consolidated organization were developed; the stimulus came rather from the increased demands for iron products. Stoves, steam engines and machines, water and gas pipes, rafters for larger buildings, all made of metal, were coming into more and general use. The market therefore called for more pig iron and its production area was enlarged. Discoveries of ore were made in the West and furnaces were established in Missouri, in Kentucky near the Ohio River and in Ohio northward to the Hocking valley. The use of anthracite coal for smelting stimulated the industry greatly in the Pennsylvania river valleys, the Delaware, the Schuylkill and the Lehigh. The amount of pig iron produced had trebled in twenty years before 1831 and had reached 191,536 tons.

Foundries for turning the pig iron into cast iron and steel, engine works and machine shops flourished, not only in New York, New Jersey and Pennsylvania but in the West as well where stationary engine builders were located in Steubenville and Cincinnati, Ohio, and in Louisville, Kentucky, as early as 1820. The center of the Pennsylvania rolling mill district was at Pittsburgh while in New England machine shops concentrated near the mills themselves. Some of the larger textile manufactures maintained their own machine shops but numerous ingenious individuals either invented machines themselves or bought the patents of others and ran small shops of their own. This great variety of metal manufacture was remarkable more for its increase of production than for any such industrial reorganization or social change as was characteristic of the textile group.

Factory Towns

The social readjustments made inevitable by the advances in the textile industries were epoch-making. Labor was necessary to run the machines and laborers had to live near the factories. This, therefore, brought a concentration of population absolutely foreign to the usual American mode of living. Previously the people, whether in country or

Ruins of Furnace at Pine Grove, Pa.

CONTRAST IN IRON AND STEEL

7500-ton Steel Press

town, had been able to command space. Even the poor were not very crowded; though their houses were small, they generally sheltered but one family and possessed a little open ground in front or rear. The ambition and reasonable expectation of a man was to become a house-holder, even if only a tenant. Factory building, however, was not matched by individual house building. Workers attracted to the factories did not find there a house for each family. Life became congested, families lived in a room or two instead of a house, tenements were built closer together in rows, with two or more stories and less open space; adequate sewage was lacking. In this early day there were un-mistakable signs of the approach of slum conditions, but the process was gradual.

These unfortunate environments were in part due to the fact that industrial change had appeared suddenly in old towns not pre-pared for the coming of factories and their operatives. In the New England area, how-ever, a number of communities were built to order at the falls of the rivers and in them some of the difficulties were avoided for a time. Here the tall, brick factory would be built at the river; nearby were constructed rows of small houses on regularly laid out streets which were rented to workers with families. As the mill owners were anxious to attract women operatives who had been ex-pert in spinning and weaving at home and

Culture in the Factory

who would work cheaply, dormitories were provided for them with house-mothers, libraries and programs of entertainment. A church and meeting hall was sometimes furnished by the company where religious and social interests might be fostered. Also the employers operated the stores which supplied the workers and reaped profits by carefully con-trolling prices.

The conveniences of these new towns were strong inducements for young people to come in from the hard labor of the farms where social opportunities were few and money scarce. Cash wages, plenty of com-pany, and even libraries, classes and lectures were eagerly sought. In fact going to a factory town to work was considered by country girls as an educational experience and an introduction to life. Travellers who visited these towns marvelled at them and wrote enthusiastically about the happy, healthful and moral life led by the workers. But it was hardly a free existence, the employer dominated even though his paternalism may have seemed very benevolent.

These halcyon conditions were but temporary. The panic of 1837, the increasing competition, and the coming of cheap labor from abroad, all worked together to reduce the standard of living among laborers. The New England country girls no longer came to the looms and spindles as to an educational institution. Long hours and low wages became the rule in the new factory towns as well as in the older communities. Meanwhile the industrial changes pushed forward with steady acceleration. Production increased, the factory worked its social transformation and new sources of wealth were exploited.

The concentration of population in cities produced problems of poverty hitherto unknown and prophetic of greater evils to come. But in the cities there were many evidences of a higher standard of living. As part of the population became more wealthy, it also wanted to become more comfortable and more efficient. Money and the inventive capacity of man made this possible.

Certain improvements affected the lives of the more well-to-do city dwellers. Public attention in the large cities such as Philadelphia and New York was drawn to the pumps and wells which furnished a supply of water easily contaminated or exhausted. A few cities built water works. New York celebrated a great advance in 1842 when it introduced Croton water brought by an aqueduct. Water was also introduced into some city houses, where it was piped to kitchen sink, to wash stand and to bathrooms. Gas was brought into use in city streets and well-to-do homes. Furthermore, heating arrangements were made more elaborate and effective for the rich. By 1850 furnaces could be installed in cellars, heat carried by pipes all through the house and introduced into the various rooms through "registers." In these homes, household tasks were somewhat lightened by the epoch-making introduction of the sewing machine, patented by Elias Howe in 1846. Women were freed from some of their traditional drudgery.

These inventions not only provided more comfort but also did their part in improving public health. The introduction of water and plumbing was followed somewhat tardily by attention to public sewage and street cleaning. Public opinion was gradually stirred to demand cleanliness but it was a slow process made difficult by the growing slums. Treatment of disease was made more effective by the discovery of anesthesia. Heretofore, operations had been dangerous or altogether impossible because of the terrible pain connected with them. But in the 1840's several physicians and scientists made epoch-making discoveries. In 1842 Dr. Crawford N. Long of Georgia used ether to quiet patients during operations but his practice was not published until 1849. In 1844 a Hartford dentist, Horace Wells, used nitrous oxide gas to aid in pulling teeth. Two years later in Boston a doctor and a chemist, Dr. W. T. G. Morton and C. T. Jackson used ether successfully in operations. Surgery was thereby revolutionized.

Public safety as well as public health was necessarily of greater concern with the development of slums. Crime and disorder increased and city government was often put to it to preserve order. Day police were practically unknown and the few night watchmen were more for the purpose of detecting fires than arresting crime. The fire forces were volunteer companies who were socially and politically active but who had none too great concern for public safety. When fires were discovered, they rushed their hand-drawn engines to the scene and quite occasionally were more interested in fighting rival companies than in putting out fires. In the late 1840's New York finally organized a uniformed police force on duty day and night. Boston and Cincinnati introduced paid fire departments. In 1852 the former city established an electric fire alarm system and the latter metropolis in the next year began the use of steam fire engines. Urban life was reaching a new stage in the improvement of the standard of living.

American Renaissance

Coincidental with the growth of urban communities came the first fine flowering of American culture. Even as the great Renaissance had flourished in Italian cities so in American metropolitan regions was to burst forth a new renaissance. This was not entirely coincidence for the activity in a prospering and expanding city has often been a powerful stimulant to cultural advance. The expenditure of so much energy, the fertility of enterprise, the wide horizons of the adventurous, the accumulation of wealth and the air of accomplishment seem to galvanize literary and artistic productivity. These cities had fine homes which needed adornment, and there lived people with leisure and means to read and to cultivate the arts. Here literary societies, lyceums, academies, museums, libraries, schools and colleges found interest and support. Here newspapers and magazines were edited, here books were published. Here was a convenient place for the meeting of minds and American cities of the early nineteenth century, throbbing with the vitality of this new day, were to be the seed beds of the American Renaissance.

The strenuous contest with the wilderness had been won. The republic had been created by the careful statesmen dominated by classical modes of thought. Now there was opportunity for a new generation who would roam more widely in the realms of thought and beauty. Adventurous intellect, aesthetic impulse could turn to more varied interests, could revel in and reveal to others the glories of an achievement which was becoming an epic tradition, of a grandly-conceived natural setting, and of a forward-looking society dedicated to progress. So inspired, a number of young men cast aside thoughts of ordinary business or professional careers to devote themselves to expressing their dreams and imaginings.

The new urban society was ready to tolerate and even to encourage them. Wealth had increased and there was money for books, works of art, and fine homes. There was leisure too in which to indulge these new tastes and a growing understanding of the sons and daughters who wished to cultivate artistic impulses. Authors and artists could depend upon a livelihood from their calling. Most of the novices came from the families of successful business men or from homes where the robust intellectual inheritance of Puritan clergymen dominated. Some few were sports of the mass who burst forth into power unheralded by any ancestral portents. All of them were born after the close of the Revolution, most of them were brought up in the electric atmosphere of republic making. When that great task had passed its initial uncertainties, some of them were already at work, others were on the threshold of their careers.

A literary renaissance flourished in three cities. The beginnings had been made at Philadelphia in the previous period, but it early yielded place. For a time the new enthusiasm seemed to be concentrating in New York, but it was in New England that the rare combination of Puritan intellect and Yankee enterprise made Boston and its surrounding towns the Florence of the American Renaissance. The Gothamite leaders were born between 1783 and 1794; Washington Irving was of a mercantile family, James Fenimore Cooper, heir of large landholders and William Cullen Bryant, emigrant from New England, son of a country doctor with a Puritan inheritance. The New England galaxy were younger. Between 1800 and 1820 were born a number who were to carry American literature and thought to heights which won the respect and admiration of the intellectual world. Emerson and Lowell were sons of clergymen and heirs of the New England ethical and intellectual interest. Longfellow and Holmes sprang from prosperous mercantile antecedents. Whittier and Hawthorne were of old colonial families, farming and seafaring, which had not enjoyed much prosperity, but which were rich in tradition. Thoreau's family was of more recent migration but shared a similar poverty. Edgar Allan Poe was the child of members of a travelling troupe of players who happened to be born in Boston but who spent most of his creative years in Philadelphia and New York. The last great figure of the period was Walt Whitman, the son of a Long Island Quaker farmer whose advent was a portent of the coming return of intellectual supremacy to New York. In their various walks of life, these men and their fellows found a common inspiration in the spirit of this new republic.

Like their immediate literary predecessors, they were filled with a sense of American potentiality. But unlike their predecessors, they were not content with boastful preachment, their skill was greater and their taste surer. In prose and verse they presented the American achievement historically and by the telling of the story they created an impression of the greatness of the task more effectively than had their didactic forbears.

Irving, Cooper and Hawthorne in prose, and Longfellow, Whittier, Lowell and Holmes in poetry were creating an American tradition which was to color the imagination of successive generations of youth. They wrote of the heroic and romantic activities of their colonial and revolutionary forefathers in a vivid fashion that was to produce an epic story much more influential than the strenuous fact-finding labors of the first professional historians, George Bancroft, William H. Prescott and Francis Parkman, then in the midst of their active careers. National achievement was a constant well-spring of inspiration.

A second enthusiasm of the new generation was the American scene. Nature had given the new society a beautiful and in some localities a majestic environment and these glories of nature inspired those who were beginning to contemplate them. They were still so near the frontier that there were many evidences of unspoiled nature, more lavish than old world poets could find. In the simple round of the seasons, the quiet beauty of the landscape, they found themes and Bryant and the New England school wrote of the forest and the field, of flowers and birds, of the majesty of the storm and the soothing peace of quiet midsummer with dignity and delicate grace, effectually capturing the freshness and the unspoiled naturalness of the countryside. In many of their poems there is a religious note, an acknowledgment of the design of a creator which rose from the Puritan background of their minds.

To the inspiration of things American was added new foreign influence, the great romantic movement which was gaining strength in England and Germany. Enthusiastic New England students were going to Europe and returning with new ideas. George Ticknor, Edward Everett and George Bancroft came home with a new sense of scholarship and of the fine quality of European literature. Among the intellectuals of New England there appeared a devotion to belles lettres. Harvard encouraged the study of European writing, and there Longfellow and Lowell, both professors, translated and interpreted the beauty, technique and taste of foreign literature. Lowell was particularly active in defining standards by critical essays and reviews in the columns of the *North American Review* and was later influential in creating the *Atlantic Monthly*. In much more unique and unusual manner Poe was devoting himself to an intense quest for beauty of expression and turned the strength of his genius to work through a vivid and weird imagination for the "rhythmical creation of beauty." He endeavored to preach his doctrines of poetical and prose forms in critical essays which appeared in New York and Philadelphia periodicals.

Passion for perfectionism was the noblest aspiration of this renaissance; it was an enthusiasm shared with numerous almost forgotten Calvinistic ancestors. Reform and social improvement were fervently preached. The anti-slavery crusade was armed by the effective weapons of the verse of Whittier and Lowell. Educational reform was the preoccupation of Bronson Alcott, Emerson's "tedious archangel." Utopia was the hope of George Ripley, Margaret Fuller and Nathaniel Hawthorne when they with numerous associates entered a cooperative community at Brook Farm in 1841. Here they labored to set an example in plain living and high thinking which might hasten the advent of a more perfect social order. Longing for greater freedom of the human spirit led Thoreau to withdraw from civil society by refusing to pay taxes and to suffer a brief jail sentence as a consequence. In this great striving for perfectionism and spiritual freedom, New England winged its farthest flight. Many a youth saw visions and became starry-eyed with zeal for a millennium not far off.

Many drew inspiration from Emerson. His interest embraced not only all phases of literary activity, but most important set him forth upon an intellectual quest. He sought the fundamental explanation of man and nature and founded a school of philosophy. The Calvinism of his Puritan ancestors was no longer either compelling or satisfying so he wandered far afield, he walked in Plato's grove, he pondered Kant's difficult thinking and learned from Wordsworth and Coleridge. These influences settled in the American environment of Emerson's life and mind and precipitated a native philosophy, American Transcendentalism. To Emerson the world of the senses, the world of matter and motion was but part of the life of man. Man was so constituted that he could apprehend another world, one which transcended or was beyond and above the world of sense. Not by the five senses, nor by intellect could this transcendental world be known, but by intuition, by man's power to grasp that shadowy world which surrounds the limited world of sense. "The best part of truth is certainly that which hovers in gleams and suggestions unpossessed before man."

With truth so defined, Emerson taught that the universe was unity held together by the spirit of God who was in all things. Mankind was a brotherhood capable of infinite comprehension of the truth and thereby of infinite improvement. So Emerson preached in terms often obscure and ambiguous but many tried to follow him; even if most of them got lost in the tortuous mazes of the philosophy still they had much joy and a feeling of emancipation in the search for this greatest of all optimism. Emerson wrote and talked and in his day was an oracle who had the respect and loyalty if not always the understanding of many a follower. Transcendentalism was America's contribution to the solution of the difficult problem of the reason for things and the nature and meaning of this human life.

Around him clustered a group of like-minded friends who were sometimes called the Transcendental Club. Margaret Fuller, Bronson Alcott, George Ripley, Theodore Parker and a few other choice spirits assembled occasionally at Emerson's home to discuss the American Genius, the True, the Good, the Beautiful and to define the Highest Aim. They supported a periodical *The Dial,* which appeared for four years, 1840-1844, edited first by Margaret Fuller and then by Emerson. They filled its pages with a variety of sense, inspiration and somewhat amusing ephemera. For most people, their thoughts were hardly clear and their influence was small and emotional, rather than intellectual. Nevertheless, they were notable in that however hazy and muddy their thoughts may have been, they were devoted to liberty, progress and that moral and intellectual strength which are essentials of democracy.

Just at the close of the period in another environment a new star appeared on the horizon, devoted to the teachings of Emerson. Walt Whitman was possessed by a love of life and a curiosity about its mysteries which led him to even bolder experiments in thought and expression. He chose to grapple realistically with the most difficult mysteries of the origin and purpose of life and personality, to develop a real understanding and love of democracy, to declare his faith in a sort of democratic millennium and to express these ideas in a new and unusual verse form. He was always a source of stimulus and a center of controversy from the day he published *Leaves of Grass,* "I celebrate myself." He more than anyone else seemed able to sense the meaning of American Democracy, though his attempts to interpret it in his peculiar verse forms baffled many and antagonized a great body of the readers of the day. He essayed to be the great interpreter of Democracy, the American Literatus, and his work is the climax of the period, the truest and most understanding interpretation of the spirit of his time.

Most significant was the fact that this interest in culture was by no means confined to the literary circles of Boston, Concord and Cambridge and their educated following. The yearning for self-improvement was rising from the mass, not trickling down from the intelligentsia. In Boston workingmen would fill lecture halls to hear grave lectures on the structure of the earth and the nature of organic life. They were equally intent upon listening to those who would interpret the masters of English literature. In the factory towns the women workers were reading and discussing not only the work of the American writers of the day, but even those of foreign authors. Some formed German classes and upon the tables in their dormitory libraries might be found foreign reviews. Some of the girls even wrote themselves and in the mill towns occasionally a magazine was published containing their work. Throughout much of New England there were regular "lyceum" programs of lectures upon which appeared most of the leading writers and orators of the day. Workers also were interested in lending libraries and read as well as listened. In New England the roots of culture reached down deep into the soil.

Cultural interest in other regions was less marked. Outside of New England and the environs of New York and Philadelphia, literature did not seem to flourish. Even in the South where the plantation aristocracy was cultured and interested in the literature and the arts no local talent appeared except a few men like the novelist, William Gilmore Simms, and he was poorly supported by even his own people. In general, it may be surmised that while the names at least of the great leaders were common property, the great mass of the population had never read a line of their writing. The common taste was keyed to melodramatic thriller and saccharine romance; for this demand a regiment of ephemeral writers produced a mass of trash which has followed them to oblivion. The American people were not addicted to reading but when they wanted to read they could not be intrigued by beauty or by the subtlety of transcendentalism. Transitory as was the product made to their order, its mass was prodigious and needs therefore to be remembered simply for its bulk. Fortunately, publishers made money by it and thus some of this capital could be invested in printing less profitable but more permanent literature.

Nearer the mass was journalism, and the renaissance marked a new epoch in that field. Improvements in printing made a penny press possible, and a penny press brought newspapers within the reach of even the poorest. So the influence of newspapers began to spread. Horace Greeley became the editor of the great New York *Tribune*. He was fully indoctrinated with certain of the humanitarian and economic novelties of the day, he preached reform, protective tariff and above all anti-slavery doctrines. His paper had wide circulation, especially the weekly edition in the rural sections of New York and nearby states, and no one will ever be able to measure accurately its mighty influence —especially in developing the growing antagonism which the North felt toward the South. James Gordon Bennett on the other hand developed modern news getting ideas and his New York *Herald* specialized in all the news fit to print and much that wasn't, but it was always news and always up to the minute. Many other lesser lights flourished and each paper had a personality behind it; it was the heyday of personal journalism now almost passed from memory.

Urban living stimulated the arts as well as literature. Portraits were much in demand but Thomas Sully and George P. A. Healy were hardly the equals of Stuart and the Peales. National pride, too, had its effect upon painting and John Trumbull did enormous canvasses of "The Surrender of Cornwallis," "The Signing of the Declaration of Independence" and "Washington Resigning his Commission," which were to adorn the rotunda of the capitol at Washington. Emanuel Leutze painted a soul stirring though rather too heroic "Washington Crossing the Delaware" and other artists filled canvasses large and small with representations of the heroic past. Nature too, generally of a stiff and formal character, attracted painters and Cole and his Hudson River school flourished.

American artistic impulse expressed itself in sculpture. Hiram Powers, Horatio Greenough and Thomas Crawford studied the works of ancient Greece and Rome and were inspired to imitate. Powers went in for nudes in a very proper age and his "Greek Slave" in some places had to be draped in muslin before it could be exhibited. Greenough sculptured a much more than life-size George Washington clad in the undress costume of a Roman senator and for years this curious statue faced the capitol, adorned as it was by the even more curious representation of Columbus on one side and on the other a frontiersman decorously struggling with a rather mild looking Indian. Crawford capped the climax by a monster figure of liberty which was to be placed on the peak of the new dome of the renovated capitol. Needless to say this work of the sculptors was but an attempt to translate the frontier into marble according to classic models.

Architecturally, too, America went to Europe for inspiration and when government buildings, state capitols and courthouses began to be erected or rebuilt the colonial styles were often cast aside and Greek temples substituted. The patent office in Washington, the second bank of the United States in Philadelphia, the sub-treasury in New York City are a few of many copies of the Parthenon or other Greek structures where western laws were now made, justice administered and business conducted. There was little of America in these buildings; it was the era of the "Classic Revival."

Music took its place beside the arts as a budding cultural interest. Community participation in musical enjoyment was stimulated by various organizations. The Musical Fund Society in Philadelphia (1820), the Handel and Haydn Society in Boston (1815) and later various German societies, were devoted to singing. Orchestras appeared in Boston and New York and by 1842, the New York Philharmonic just founded and the Boston orchestra were playing Beethoven. French and Italian opera had been sung in New Orleans since 1791, but it was not until 1825 that New York heard its first grand opera, Weber's Der Freischütz. Various companies of foreign origin came to the United States and in 1833 New York could boast an opera house. When this structure was burned six years later, it was succeeded by the famous opera house on Astor Place which was a social as well as a musical center. "Society" early adopted grand opera. A number of foreign artists came on concert tours and by the 1850's such famous luminaries as Jenny Lind, Ole Bull and Adelina Patti were received with enthusiasm. Musical training, too, began to gain attention. The Boston Academy of Music was established in 1833 and five years later instruction in music was introduced into the public schools of that city. American musicians, however, did not produce much original work. Lowell Mason wrote hymns, Stephen C. Foster composed folk songs of permanent popularity and William H. Fry wrote two operas, the first of which, "Leonore," was sung in English and Italian.

The stage was becoming more respectable though the theatre was still hardly the place for ladies. Theatres were well established now even in Boston. Edmund Kean, Junius Brutus Booth, the famous Macready and Fanny Kemble inspired romantic impulses in many an admirer. Most of these actors were of foreign birth and their popularity hindered the development of native talent. Edwin Forrest, however, a great tragedian and James H. Hackett, master of dialect and comedy were native sons and Forrest at least entered into a rivalry with Macready that led to riots in Philadelphia and New York (1848-1849) fomented by their partisans and stimulated by anti-foreign prejudices then powerful. American playwrights were busy with scripts for the players. Richard P. Smith was a private playwright for Forrest and prepared his super-dramatic roles. Robert Montgomery Bird and George Henry Boker of Philadelphia essayed romantic drama while an Irishman, Dion Boucicault, wrote melodrama for the popular taste. The actors of the day had to compete with shows of prodigies, monstrosities, minstrels, acrobats, living models and panoramas. The stage was set for Phineas T. Barnum whose shrewd showmanship grasped the essential fact of cheap entertainment, namely, "There is a new one born every minute."

Thus writers, artists, musicians, actors had learned technique and acquired taste. Their work was winning recognition but it was hardly mature. There was a crude use of newly discovered imagination, sometimes naïve, often too highly colored,—but it was the romantic age even in Europe. Taste was still selective rather than inclusive and the canons of selection were romantic and idealistic. The "facts of life" were avoided in polite literature then and for some time to come until an age of greater realism should arrive.

Winds of Controversy

The intellectual advance of the nation was stimulated by vigorous activity in another city—a city which had a purely political origin and purpose. Washington had been created to be the seat of the federal government. Here annually representatives from all parts of the nation, from all walks of life, came to plan and enact the measures thought necessary to promote the general welfare. Here grave differences of opinion representing the varied interests of the scattered population had to be resolved into positive agreement or cancel each other in stalemate.

These differences were in large part arising from the fact that the United States was in the grip of two great and divergent forces. As we have seen the population was dispersing into the great frontier regions, but it was also concentrating in urban centers. These two movements bred opposing interests, contrary demands upon government which constantly renewed a continuing political debate. Much thinking, writing and speaking engaged the energy of a variety of politically-minded citizens. Their thoughts were generally phrased in terms of a definition of the powers of government. Those who wanted aid from the national treasury used the persuasive logic of broad federal power created by Hamilton. Those in opposition spoke in the terms of strict construction of the Constitution and the reserved rights of the states formulated by Jefferson.

The diversity of interest was brought out in clear light shortly after the War of 1812 by a discussion of tariff policy. Not only was this an economic question, but it was even more political. The debate was precipitated in the midst of the panic of 1819 when certain rising urban interests began organized attempts to impress Congress with the need of subsidy for the budding industries. Representatives of the industrialists as well as the factory owners themselves came to Washington to present the case for higher tariffs. Their efforts soon bore fruit and in 1820 a tariff bill was prepared providing increased duties for manufactured cotton and woolen goods, iron, hemp and many other commodities. It soon appeared that Congress was nearly equally divided in both houses. In the areas where plantation and commercial interests were influential, congressmen and senators generally agreed that increased duties would raise the price of commodities so high that the farming population would suffer great hardship from increased expenses and that these same increases would so discourage foreign trade as to diminish if not destroy shipping. To swell the profits of a few, the many would have to bear the burden of increased expense and a group of rich men would be placed in a position of influence quite undemocratic. So the argument ran and most southern and half of the New England congressmen voted "no."

On the other hand, those directly interested in protection had allies among farming groups in the middle and western states and among the general public. The farmers believed that a thriving group of industries would provide them with a "home market" for their produce—a contrast to their later attitude. Factories needed raw materials and factory operatives had no time to raise food, consequently their needs would give the farmer ready sale for his crops. Finally many believed that the prosperity and security resulting from the economic self-sufficiency produced by protected industries would be a national blessing. Therefore the middle and western states through their representatives voted almost unanimously for the new bill, supported by the other half of the New England contingent and a few from the southwest, mostly from Kentucky. This alliance, however, was not sufficient to insure the passage of the bill through the Senate and it failed. Attempts in the next three years were no more successful; but meanwhile the industries and their allies kept up a campaign of education.

The approach of the Presidential year of 1824 brought the question more sharply before Congress because of the hope that it might be used as an issue to aid one of the candidates, Henry Clay. The bill that was introduced at this time placed heavy duties on the principal raw materials as well as upon the manufactured products. By these "compensating" rates the greater protection which woolen cloth gained was in large measure offset by the higher duty on the raw wool that had to be imported for its manufacture. The tariff of 1824 therefore was not satisfactory to the industry supposed to benefit the most. A period of prosperity, however, killed the sense of disappointment and woolen manufacture expanded nevertheless.

A business crisis in England caused the British government to reduce the duty on raw wool so much that English manufacturers would easily undersell American woolen cloth makers. The English hastened to take advantage of this opportunity to the immediate disturbance of their American competitors, who again sought congressional aid and began a more widespread organization for propaganda and influence. In 1826 those in New England met in Boston and petitioned Congress. The Massachusetts legislature did likewise and in 1827 a bill for their relief passed the House of Representatives only to be defeated in the Senate by the vote of Vice President Calhoun of South Carolina. The center of protection propaganda now shifted to Pennsylvania and at the invitation of the Pennsylvania Society for the Promotion of Manufactures a national convention of woolen manufacturers and politicians came together at Harrisburg in 1827 to discuss the economic and political advantages of a protective program for other industries as well as woolen; one hundred delegates appeared from thirteen states. When Congress met in December 1827 the protectionists were mobilized and the politicians sought to manipulate the tariff issue for their own purposes.

The opponents of President John Quincy Adams were less opposed to protection than they were to him and sought to provide a tariff ostensibly protective but so distasteful to New England (by reason of high rates on raw materials) that Adams' chief supporters would join with the South in defeating it. Certain of its defeat, the northern opponents of Adams thought they could safely vote for the bills and thereby prove that they rather than Adams and his friends were the true supporters of protection. The schemers therefore wrote a high manufactures schedule which, however, only partially satisfied the woolen people chiefly interested and offset these advances by high rates on raw material and by the abolition of certain favors which New England interests had been enjoying. Then an amendment partially satisfying the woolen manufacturers caused enough New England representatives and senators to vote for the bill and it was passed in 1828, unsatisfactory as it was, to the confusion of the political schemers. Thus "the Tariff of Abominations" which satisfied no one, nevertheless became law.

During the course of this decade of intermittent tariff debate most of the leading political minds had applied themselves to its intricacies. Henry Clay had presented a classic statement for protection while Calhoun had become the leading opponent. Laymen too had been studying the situation and Matthew Carey of Philadelphia had been writing in defense of the protective doctrines. The arguments were well established but the issue was to be a constant source of political controversy highly stimulating to thought and more so to emotion.

The conflicting interests not only showed themselves in the political activity of the time but they had a decided influence upon the developing legal institutions of the republic. They made their appearance in the courts and were fought out in spectacular battles. The growth of business brought a stream of cases before the Supreme Court which gave that body numerous opportunities to define the extent of federal power. They strove mightily with the fundamental question of the relation of government and business.

In these days of the germination of big business when corporations concerned with banking, transportation and manufacturing were emerging, legislatures were occasionally moved by debtor constituents during hard times to void the fulfillment of obligations, by passing stay laws and providing easy bankruptcies. Property holders often felt themselves endangered by local laws. Under the Constitution, no state could impair the obligation of contract, or emit bills of credit. Congress had control over interstate commerce, and under the "elastic" clause had created an institution, the Bank, to stabilize finance, and had added greatly to the wealth of the nation by purchasing territory. But many states had passed laws revising charters and easing obligations which seemed to impair contracts, they had interfered with interstate com-

merce and they had also sought to destroy or greatly hamper the operations of the Bank of the United States, by taxing its branches or attempting legal restrictions. A great many citizens were convinced that Congress had over-reached its powers under the "necessary and proper"
clause.

What views would the federal judiciary take? Would they seek to
protect contracts and federal institutions even to the extent of assuming
to review the work of state legislatures and the decisions of state courts?
Would they uphold the broad exercise of power by Congress or would
they seek to confine it to the narrow bonds of strict construction? If wide
prerogative were allowed the federal government, the influence of the
populous cities would be greater; whereas if the bulk of power were
conceded to rest with the states, the rural districts would dominate.

The course of Marshall and the majority of his associates on the
supreme bench left no doubt whatever in the minds of observers. In a
series of decisions Marshall extended the functions of the federal judiciary to the limit, and beyond the express words of the Constitution.
Any question embracing the constitutionality of any law, congressional
or state, or any decision of a state court dealing with interpretation
of the federal Constitution might be reviewed and approved or annulled by the federal judiciary. Under Chief Justice Marshall between
1809 and 1824 fourteen acts of the legislatures of eleven states were
declared void, generally because they impaired the obligation of contract.
Also decisions of the highest state courts, to the consternation of many
states rights advocates, were reviewed and reversed. The Chief Justice
ruled in favor of loose construction and sustained the broad assumption
of power by Congress. As a result of these decisions, business men and
capitalists felt that in the federal courts there was recourse from the
vagaries of popularly elected state legislatures swayed by bursts of
radical opinion. They further saw in the large policies of government
aid possible under a Constitution loosely construed, hope of accelerated
advance and prosperity. It is of no small significance that, in a time of
uncertainty as to the permanence of the Union when the agricultural
demand for states rights and laissez faire was strong, growing business
was learning the increasing advantage of powerful federal government
and the benefits of federal legislation and federal judicial interpretation.

Marshall's decisions were the subject of continuous controversy and
the rural regions anticipated with apprehension the possibility of urban
domination. They appealed vigorously to ancient pride in locality, to
states rights and sought to keep the idea of state sovereignty in vigorous
circulation. But a new sense of unity was ever growing more potent.
Not only was it emotionally appealing but it had a very practical source
of strength. American nationality, the Union, was a valuable and
effective instrument for the welfare, power, and wealth of the United

States. As Daniel Webster phrased it in his reply to Calhoun's colleague, Hayne:

It is to that Union we owe our safety at home and our consideration and dignity abroad. It is to that Union that we are chiefly indebted for whatever makes us most proud of our country. That Union we reached only by the discipline of our virtue in the severe school of adversity. It had its origin in the necessities of disordered finance, prostrate commerce, and ruined credit. Under its benign influence these great interests immediately awoke as from the dead, and sprang forth with newness of life. Every year of its duration has teemed with fresh proofs of its utility and its blessings, and although our territory has stretched out wider and wider, and our population spread farther and farther, they have not outrun its protection or its benefits. It has been to us all a copious fountain of national, social and personal happiness.... Liberty and Union, now and forever, one and inseparable.

A sense of nationality, of Union, was in the process of evolving but it was to be of slow growth. Its perfection was to be hindered and even its existence threatened by the conflict of interests arising from the contrary forces of dispersion and concentration.

CHAPTER X

THE ADVANCE OF DEMOCRACY

The great movements of population, expanding westward and concentrating in cities, were pointing the way to the achievement of political democracy. From the early days of colonial experience some form of self-government had been seemingly inevitable. Two hundred years and more of experiment were necessary, however, before its precise character was to take shape. By successive steps it had advanced in the direction of political democracy. First each locality had undertaken to manage its own concerns and to send representatives to participate in governing the colony. Then the colonies had undertaken to band together for independence and had organized a federal system. Throughout this evolution, the question of whether these self-governing communities were to be politically democratic, that is, whether all men were to be considered equally entitled to vote and to hold office, was left unanswered. Vestiges of old ideas of property and religious qualifications remained on into the nineteenth century. But social change directed the onward march toward a fuller realization of the implications of a Democratic experiment.

The Spread of Manhood Suffrage

As people went westward and formed new states, they made new constitutions. In the western country there were few great differences in wealth, most of the pioneers were in much the same state of poverty and hope. Naturally under such conditions there was no place for political distinction, all were equally capable of bearing the responsibility of voting or governing. The new states of the days after the War of 1812, Indiana, Illinois, Alabama and Missouri, provided white manhood suffrage though Mississippi clung to a tax provision. The tide of Democracy was beginning to swell.

In the East, as well, changing conditions especially in the growing cities, were adding their influence to the progress of political democracy. As more people flocked together in towns and cities, property became increasingly unsatisfactory as a qualification for suffrage. The large number disfranchised in the cities began to demand the vote and politicians, quick to see the advantage to them if these people were made voters, added their voice; city political leaders wanted large followings with which to defeat the rural vote. The example set by the West also was encouraging; the contest with aristocracy was on.

In 1818 conservative Connecticut made her suffrage qualifications more liberal, and two years later Massachusetts did the same, although neither went to the extent of giving the franchise to all men. The climax came when in 1821 New York state capitulated and granted universal manhood suffrage, even free Negroes were permitted to vote if they possessed property. Other states followed and male political democracy came into actual practice. No longer could aristocratic land-holders and merchants retain their former influence. For all there was liberty and equality if not fraternity. During these years the popular vote increased enormously. In round numbers a vote that had been 1,150,000 in the Presidential election of 1828 had become 2,400,000 in 1840, though not all of this increase was caused by the broadening franchise, for the population itself was enlarging rapidly and swelling the number of voters.

Elections too became more important and interesting. When the first state constitutions were made the country was suspicious of executives, the experience with royal governors was still fresh. Consequently, most power was placed in the hands of the legislature and governors were often permitted powers purely nominal and were chosen by the legislature rather than by direct vote; to the representatives also was given the selection of the judiciary as well. The onrush of democracy, however, changed this procedure, legislatures, too, had been found to be fickle and unstable. As a result, there was a strengthening of the executive as a curb on the legislature and the people were entrusted with more electoral power. Not only did they choose legislators and congressmen, they now began to elect state officers and even the judiciary. With the growing interest in elections and the increasing number of voters, political machinery had to be devised to meet the more complex conditions entering politics.

The old-fashioned personal politics was no longer possible. Communities were growing too large, candidates could no longer be known to everyone and judged on the basis of personal impression and community gossip. State-wide campaigns for gubernatorial and other offices made new machinery necessary. First of all the choice of candidates had to be systematized. The informal method of announcing a candidacy by public notice would not suffice; state and local conventions of delegates from political subdivisions such as wards, towns or counties met together to choose candidates. Pennsylvania and Massachusetts had early developed this method and by 1835 it was in general use, usually superseding informal meetings of citizens or legislators known as caucuses. These conventions designated committees to do the work of promoting the interests of the candidates whom they had designated and elaborate organizations of ward, town, county, and state committees came into being. This tendency to committee and convention organization was hastened by a rebirth of partisanship.

New Partisanship

The old Federalist and Democratic-Republican parties could hardly be called parties in the light of modern practice. They were too informal in their organization, and their methods were suited only to small communities and a sparse electorate. Also they had lost any true spirit of rivalry. The Federalists scarcely functioned after the War of 1812 but differences of opinion had not been abolished, nor was ambition dead. A new generation was arising which rather impatiently awaited the retirement of the fathers who had made the government. When James Monroe's term expired there was bound to be a struggle for the succession. New parties were not to be established immediately but these rivalries were to fit in with the changing conditions of society in shaping a new political order.

The campaign of 1824 was largely personal and the voters made their choices on the grounds of the popular appeal or the place of residence of the candidate. Five men were the principal contenders, John Quincy Adams, Monroe's Secretary of State, Wm. H. Crawford, his Secretary of the Treasury, John C. Calhoun, his Secretary of War, Henry Clay, Speaker of the House and Andrew Jackson, the nation's most popular soldier and Indian fighter, the hero of New Orleans. A group of the older politicians favored Crawford and attempted to give him the congressional caucus endorsement which had put forward Madison and Monroe. That plan failed and it was evident that all five were to be active candidates. Calhoun, however, was content to be Vice-President and the electors gave him that office whereupon the other four rather evenly divided the electoral vote for the chief place although Jackson received a plurality. As no one had a majority, the election was thrown into the House of Representatives. Only the three highest could be balloted for by that body, so Clay who was fourth, was eliminated. As Speaker his influence in the House was predominant and the vote of his friends for Adams made the Massachusetts man President. When he appointed Clay, Secretary of State, the supporters of Jackson who were very much embittered by his defeat charged that a bargain had been made, a corrupt bargain between a puritan (Adams) and a blackleg (Clay). The Jacksonians were determined to elect their candidate in 1828 and to do it they had to organize.

The four years of Adams' administration therefore witnessed a number of political maneuvers. In Congress the foes of the President were able to use innocent questions like participation in a Pan-American congress as a means to rally and consolidate a hostile congressional bloc led by Martin Van Buren and other friends of Jackson. The tariff too was put to political uses as described in the previous chapter. Adams himself realized what his foes were doing but he could not bring himself to use his executive powers to build up a machine of his own. Consequently in 1828, after a bitter campaign in which there were few issues and many personalities, often scurrilous, Jackson was elected by a handsome majority. His victorious partisans could scarcely wait until his inauguration to introduce political customs since·become traditional.

The election of 1828 had created a new party, a Jacksonian party. Officially it was still the old Democratic-Republican party of Jefferson but actually it was something new. Hereafter it was to be spoken of more and more frequently as the Democratic party. It was the party of manhood suffrage, of the people, many of them newly enfranchised. Its leaders realized that they had much greater numbers of voters to appeal to and they soon learned the value of organization. The civil service was turned into a political weapon. Public office was to be a reward for party service, and only loyal Jacksonians should draw government pay. Many an old clerk in the departments had to go, thousands of postmasters and customs officials were replaced by followers of Jackson. "To the victors," said one of them, "belong the spoils."

These popular leaders were also to recognize the value of popular issues, of preaching democracy. The common man and his interests were exalted and the enemies of Jackson were denominated friends of privilege and of wealth, exploiting the people. As a matter of fact, Jackson himslf was not particularly liberal on social and economic questions, but he had a personal feud with the managers of the Bank of the United States which led him to attack that institution. His followers could therefore fervently proclaim this institution as a privileged monopoly which should be destroyed in the people's interest. As its charter was soon to expire, this question was to become a burning issue.

Andrew Jackson as Indian fighter, conqueror of the British, man of action and people's champion, naturally was a figure with tremendous popular appeal, an asset of untold value to this new Democratic party. How could Jackson's rivals make headway against so formidable an organization? Clearly it must be done by building up an opposition party. Clay was the most prominent of those who were to undertake this task. He was joined by Daniel Webster and many other supporters of John Quincy Adams. Clay and Webster took advantage of Jackson's opposition to the Bank of the United States to enlist the support of its president, Nicholas Biddle, and also of those, particularly strong in the East, who believed in "sound" finance. When Jackson vetoed an internal improvement bill (May 1830) his opponents tried to make capital of this fact among western supporters of government aid.

Jackson's temper and penchant for personal difficulties further played into the hands of his opponents. A social war shook Washington. The Secretary of War, Eaton, had married the daughter of a local inn-keeper, a woman of doubtful reputation. The other administration ladies headed by Mrs. Calhoun, refused to recognize Mrs. Eaton socially. Jackson was furious, malicious gossip had done much to sadden the last years of his own wife, lately deceased, and he was certain that malice alone was behind the gossip regarding Mrs. Eaton's reputation. He straightway espoused her cause and was encouraged by his Secretary of State, Martin Van Buren, who was also a widower and consequently free to show Mrs. Eaton much attention. Calhoun, on the other hand, because of Mrs. Calhoun's attitude, lost something of Jackson's regard. Opponents of Calhoun's pretensions now stepped forward to tell Jackson that the Vice-President had advocated censuring Jackson for his arbitrary actions in Florida while Monroe was President. Jackson never took kindly to personal criticism and in spite of the long time that had elapsed since the events in question, he demanded an explanation from Calhoun. Some correspondence which followed closed with a disruption of personal relations. Van Buren more than ever was popular with Jackson. Thus, in the spring of 1830, Calhoun was in opposition and Van Buren had completely supplanted him as heir-apparent. Calhoun was to be driven finally from the Democrats and into the party of Clay and Webster by the result of tariff politics.

The national debt had been paid off almost entirely and a large surplus was in the process of piling up to an undesirable amount unless the tariff were revised. Protectionists were anxious particularly as the planters increased their demands that the duties be lowered and placed on a revenue basis. Clay was now openly a candidate for the presidency for he had been formally nominated by a national convention of his friends who called themselves "National Republicans" to distinguish their organization from the Jacksonians who still bore the ancient title of Jefferson's party, "Democratic-Republicans." This nominating convention which met in December 1831 inaugurated a method of designating candidates for the presidency which has since been regularly followed. Clay's friends in Congress also set about to revise the tariff in such fashion as to maintain protection and give Clay further claim to be called champion of this doctrine. At the same time, the opponents of Jackson decided it was good strategy to force the bank issue before the election. The bank did not need recharter for four years and Jackson was somewhat less belligerent toward it; nevertheless, Clay's friends forced the issue and in July 1832 sent two bills to the President, a protective tariff and the re-charter of the bank. Jackson signed the tariff and vetoed the re-charter. He was now committed on all three issues, internal improvements, bank and tariff, and the National Republicans rejoiced.

On the face of things, Jackson did seem to be in a difficult position. Eastern financial interests wished his defeat because of his antagonism to the bank. Western promoters of internal improvements resented his opposition to their schemes. The planter interest in the South was stirred by his acceptance of the protective tariff. Nevertheless, Jackson and Van Buren, who had displaced Calhoun as candidate for Vice-President, were elected by a great majority. The people enthusiastically

The Bank Race
(An Anti-Jackson Cartoon)

had voted for Jackson despite the opposition of the "interests." The National Republicans disappeared as a party but opposition to Jackson was by no means dead. Hardly had his re-election been achieved than a new political move was made.

The falling price of cotton in the years since 1815 had placed the southern planters in an increasingly unhappy frame of mind and in South Carolina in particular much complaint was heard against the tariff. Protection aided only northern manufacturers while on the other hand it caused southern planters to pay high prices for their manufactured goods, especially clothes for the slaves, and consequently diminished their profits. When the tariff of 1828 had been passed a number of South Carolina leaders had urged resistance and the legislature had considered a report, written by Calhoun, known as the "South Carolina Exposition" which vigorously presented the case for state sovereignty and the right of a state to protect itself against such a law by nullifying it. Now in 1832 another tariff, likewise protective, had been enacted into law, the price of cotton was still low and in South Carolina there was general indignation while in Georgia, Virginia and Mississippi there had been gestures of protest. South Carolina, therefore, thought that the time was ripe for action. Consequently, her legislature called a convention to meet in November 1832. This convention passed a Nullification ordinance which proclaimed South Carolina's refusal to obey the law. The legislature was then reconvened and measures were passed protecting the citizens of the state from any penalties which the federal government might seek to impose for disobedience of federal law. The legislators likewise strengthened the military force.

What course would Jackson pursue? He was a soldier and used to command, never had he permitted his authority to be questioned. Now a state was attempting wholesale disobedience to a law which it was his duty to enforce, moreover the leader in the nullification was Calhoun, whom he thoroughly disliked. Less than a month therefore after the South Carolina convention the President issued a proclamation to the effect that "Disunion by armed force is treason" and in the meantime sent soldiers and warships to Charleston. Thereupon he asked Congress for a "force act" to give him adequate powers. While rebellion and armed conflict were thus threatening, the politicians, notably Clay, Calhoun and Webster, were working to restore harmony by compromise.

South Carolina had found little sympathy in the other southern states rather to her chagrin and was in a position too uncomfortable to be maintained. Seemingly, therefore, all groups welcomed a dignified way out and the result was the enactment of a law reducing the tariff by slow stages over a period of ten years at the same time that the force act was passed. This Compromise Tariff of 1833 provided that by 1842 duties should be on a 20% basis; every two years beginning with 1834 10% of all duties in excess of 20% should be removed; 1 January 1842 half of the remaining excess should be dropped and on 1 July 1842 the 20% level should become general. Jackson had acted vigorously and had confounded his enemies once more. The advocates of the American system, the defenders of states rights and Jackson's personal foes, however, were not through fighting and neither was Jackson. The Bank again became the object of the President's wrath.

Jackson's veto of the bill re-chartering the Bank and the failure of Congress to override that veto plainly informed all men that after 1836 the institution would cease to exist. Jackson, however, was not content to permit it to wind up its affairs in its own way. He became convinced that it was a wise policy to take from it all government money. The loss of this sum—about nine millions, could not but cause the Bank to restrict its operations. Jackson decided therefore to cease depositing money in the Bank and gradually check out the government funds already there as the treasury needed to spend the money. His Secretary of the Treasury, Roger B. Taney, therefore made the order 26 September 1833, and the Bank suffered the consequences. Jackson's dominating qualities had again been demonstrated.

The politicians hopeful of Old Hickory's downfall were now ready for another attempt at organizing the rather incongruous opposition. Clay's scheme of appealing to national economic interests by organizing the National Republican party on the platform of the American system had not proved successful. Many who were in opposition to Jackson did not like the system, especially the states rights advocates in the South who, like Calhoun, were vigorously opposed to a tariff for protection. Some broader appeal, some more general organization, must be effected. A new issue with a more alluring appeal than benefits to the rich must be found if the popular imagination was to be weaned away from the people's idol. In various localities, therefore, notably in New York, in preparing for the spring elections of 1834 the opponents of Jackson made a vigorous attack upon his methods of ruling, upon his arbitrary and peculiarly Jacksonian tactics. Such policies, declared his enemies, were tyrannical, just as tyrannical as those of George III. As protest and even revolution had been necessary in 1776 to protect American rights from monarchical oppression, so now in 1834 the arbitrary rule of King Andrew I should be checked. In 1776 those who had risen to protect American liberties were called Whigs; now in 1834 a new group of Whigs must appear for the same purpose. In this manner a new party had its origin but it was not sufficiently united to form a national group until 1839. Meanwhile, it contented itself with various local victories and Jackson reigned undisturbed.

So powerful was the President that the question of his successor in office lay largely in his hands. Calhoun who had once aspired to this honor was now with his opponents and the clever Van Buren had been enjoying the increasing regard of the executive. He, Jackson decided, should succeed him. A national convention of the Democratic party met and ratified Jackson's will. Only one important concession did Jackson make to public opinion. One of the Mexican states, largely inhabited by emigrants from the United States, had revolted in 1836 and sought admission to the Union. Texas, however, permitted Negro slavery and the possible prejudice of northern voters against admitting more slave territory caused Jackson to abandon his purpose of receiving the state lest it alienate votes from Van Buren. The Whigs could not unite on any one candidate though various favorite sons like William Henry Harrison, Daniel Webster and Hugh L. White of Tennessee made campaigns against Van Buren in their own localities. The Democrats triumphed with little difficulty and Jackson turned over to his chosen successor the honors and duties of the Presidential office.

These contests of the so-called Jacksonian era of political partisan-ship and democracy had come to full flower in a fashion prophetic of future American political experience. The populace had the votes and appeals varying from sound argument to crude emotionalism augmented sometimes by mob coercion, bribery and the rule of bosses all appeared in this epoch, and the desirable and undesirable features of the new era flourished side by side.

The Spirit of Reform

There was more to the quality of American democracy than the machinery of universal male political participation. The Americans wished to make their democracy an instrument for social betterment. Prone as Americans were to consider their institutions superior to those of the rest of the world, they were nevertheless keen to seek their improvement. Many realized that in spite of democratic progress there were many weaknesses and inequalities which could urge the altruistic to more vigorous thinking. Such thought, indeed, had become a custom; it was a colonial inheritance. Now it was intensified to a degree that was to have momentous consequences.

The strength of religious interest had much to do with these striv-ings for social improvement. Though the rationalism which marked the revolutionary period had somewhat undermined the strength of religion inherited from colonial days, the turn of the century brought a reaction and a quickening of religious faith. The revivals of those years follow-ing 1800 were heralds of the new interest and similar manifestations marked the period, 1825-1850.

One of the most striking signs of this increasing popular interest was the frequency with which religious differences showed themselves, by controversy or schisms or both. In New England Unitarianism flourished and spread. The Presbyterians engaged in a doctrinal dispute which caused a secession called the New School. The Society of Friends divided when a number of meetings turned to unitarian or Hicksite views. It was in this period that Alexander Campbell preached a return to the simplicity of primitive Christianity and organized the Camp-bellites. Also, William Miller became convinced that the end of the world was close at hand and persuaded many to become adventists or Millerites as they were generally known. Joseph Smith organized the Mormons and gradually moved westward till Brigham Young finally established the Mormon Zion near the Great Salt Lake. Many sects less well known came from schisms even more obscure. Individuals by thousands were studying the Scriptures and continually finding new meanings which called for expression. The expression frequently led to controversy and not seldom to the establishment of a new organization,

People were alive with religious zeal. From 1800 to 1850 church membership grew from 365,900 to 3,530,000, a ten-fold multiplication while population increased only five times.

Like zeal was manifest in missionary activity and in the formation of churches in new communities. The vigorous expansion of the population and its westward march made it necessary for the settled churches in the older portions of the country to take thought for the organization and support of missions in the new areas. As early as 1801 the Congregationalists and the Presbyterians began joint work and in 1826 united with the Reformed Church in organizing the American Home Missionary Society. Other churches followed more or less formally. Societies like the American Bible Society established in 1816 did much to help by contributing Bibles and supporting agents to distribute them. Up and down the frontier these home missionaries labored travelling from place to place to preach to the scattered settlers. Their methods were most vigorous and effective for their preaching was emotional and fervid, they mingled freely with the pioneers under the crude conditions of frontier life and their days were filled with hardship and vivid experience. Many like Marcus Whitman who in 1835-1836 penetrated as far west as Oregon, acted as pathfinders and organizers of settlements and as such were among the most valuable of the pioneer builders. They laid the foundation for an ever increasing number of churches of the many denominations and gave an evangelical enthusiasm to their organizations which survived in the period when the hardships of the frontier had softened.

Quickened religious zeal strengthened the authority of the churches on matters of religion and personal conduct and clergymen regained some of their ebbing influence. In New England, especially, ministers both Unitarian and Congregational spoke with authority in political and social as well as in theological matters. In the eastern states and in Maryland the influx of immigrants gave the Roman Catholic Church its first real strength. In the South, the Presbyterian and Episcopalian churches attracted most of the wealthy while the southern yeomen quite generally were Methodist or Baptist. Clergymen in this section likewise had political and social interests and when controversies over the righteousness of slavery arose they undertook to be its apologists. Indeed feeling over this question became so bitter that the Methodists and the Baptists in North and South could no longer fellowship together and in 1845 the Methodist Church, South and the Southern Baptist Convention completed organizations independent of their northern brethren.

The religious enthusiasm of the day found many ways not primarily ecclesiastical to express itself and the church took active part in preaching progress and improvement. It was becoming very apparent that in this land of equality and unlimited opportunity there were too many people who were unfortunate and underprivileged. After the War of 1812 there had been several years of depression and public attention had been called to help widespread poverty especially in the cities by establishing organized charitable relief. The conditions of this time also focussed attention on the prevalent custom of imprisonment for debt. Thousands were annually placed in jail because they failed to pay their bills; a situation which resulted in no good for anyone. In fact such practice was harmful to society for the jails in the 'twenties and early 'thirties were too commonly miserable places, filthy and disease-ridden where criminals and offenders of all sorts and degrees were herded together often in the most indecent fashion. The institutions which were designed to punish and repress crime and to stimulate thrift were in reality often schools for criminals and beggars. Even the insane were housed in the common prisons for no other provision was made for them by the state. The families of the insane were supposed to look after them but if they became too violent, jail seemed to be the only place of restraint available to those who had no money to pay for care. Little public provision was made for the sick in the way of free hospitals or medical care. Drunkenness was flagrant and habitual and Negro slavery was a perpetual reminder to many of barbarism. All told, the situation was one which cried for a variety of reforms.

In view of these conditions, the increase of religious interest was accompanied by a vigorous reforming crusade. Charitable organizations flourished and increased in numbers while associations to promote various reforms sprang up nearly everywhere. Prison reform agitation succeeded in causing changes; in New York at Auburn a system of workshops was introduced and the prisoners set to work at various trades while in Pennsylvania a prison was built to house prisoners in small cells, in solitary confinement at hard labor. Punishment, too, was reformed. After 1835 imprisonment for debt was abolished in most of the states and the use of the death penalty restricted. This penalty had never been abused as it had been in England and now pleas were heard for its complete abandonment. This latter proposal was not heeded generally; the penalty was still reserved for the punishment of murder and treason. Hospitals for the sick and for the insane came to be provided at public expense. Due to the vigorous efforts of Miss Dorothea L. Dix and others of the enlightened who travelled thousands of miles and made many speeches advocating humane care of these unfortunates, public opinion was aroused and most states established insane asylums.

Most spectacular of all the reform movements was that which had as its object the abolition of slavery. The inconsistency between this institution and the principles of democracy had long been apparent and social disapproval had been manifest throughout the country in the first years of independence. However, the move for its abandonment was arrested by the increasing importance of cotton growing after the invention of the cotton gin; thereafter it was prized more highly and its use extended. With the advent of the reforming spirit in the 'twenties and 'thirties the attention of many quickened consciences was fixed upon slavery as an evil to be eradicated.

The year 1831 was marked by the appearance of anti-slavery agitation in a very active fashion. In January of that year William Lloyd Garrison began a violent propaganda for abolition in a newspaper which he published in Boston entitled the *Liberator*. In the columns of this paper he printed vitriolic arguments, attacks and denunciations of slavery as an inhuman and barbarous institution and illustrated his arguments with incidents gathered from various parts of the South. His methods were much resented by slave owners, especially sensitive at that time because of a second episode of that same year. In August, a Negro, Nat Turner, attempted to organize a slave insurrection in Virginia. No worse calamity than such an uprising could southern plantation owners picture. They knew too well what had happened under similar circumstances in the island of Haiti in the 1790's and they were fearful of a duplication of such frightful scenes of fire, murder and worse. Nat Turner's attempt failed utterly, but it awoke southern apprehensions and in conjunction with the rumors of Garrison's violent abolition propaganda caused southerners to fear that if Garrison's ideas were heard and understood by the slaves they might anticipate more serious attempts at rebellion.

Encouraged by British activity toward abolition in the West Indies, American abolitionists like Lewis and Arthur Tappan in New York, planned a national society which Garrison soon dominated. This body, The American Anti-Slavery Society, was organized in 1833. It issued pamphlets and books, aided periodicals, deluged Congress with petitions and for a time grew in numbers. The ranks of these zealots were divided between the militant Garrisonians and those who wished to advance with less violent propaganda, for extreme statement was inciting bitter resentment. Abolitionists were subject to vigorous counter-attacks. They were charged with disturbing the peace, inciting to riot and promoting Negro uprisings. Their fanaticism was branded as socially dangerous and in various places even in the North conservative members of society attempted to put them down by force. In Boston in 1835 Garrison was attacked by a mob and barely escaped. In 1836, at Alton, Illinois, an abolitionist editor, Lovejoy, was murdered in a riot against his printing office. Even women were subject to indignity, for in 1833 Miss Prudence Crandall, who was trying to keep a school for Negroes at Canterbury, Connecticut, was put in prison.

Such tactics on both sides were bound to rouse resentment and divide communities. Wealthy men like Gerrit Smith and the Tappan brothers, lawyers and orators like Wendell Phillips, literary men like James Russell Lowell and John Greenleaf Whittier and politicians like Salmon P. Chase and John P. Hale began activity to espouse anti-slavery propaganda. In the South educators like T. R. Dew and William Harper, politicians like Calhoun and Jefferson Davis and even clergymen, began to defend vigorously the institution as a benevolent and paternal order which brought happiness and Christian salvation to the slave, prosperity to the South, and leisure to its intelligent class to ponder the great problems of democracy and culture.

Such extremes were dangerous, however, and a third group active in business and politics strove to keep the peace. Business men like Amos Lawrence and his associates were anxious to keep the matter out of politics, and politicians like Clay and Webster were ever ready to promote compromises when flames of controversy over slavery burned too fiercely. Though the South was united in defense of its institution, the North was by no means so uniform in its sentiment of opposition. Relatively few were actual abolitionists in the sense of demanding immediate and unconditional eradication of the hated institution. Many more, however, were opposed to slavery and vigorously denounced any attempt to extend the system. On the other hand, the great mass was generally indifferent and the South had many friends who resented these bitter attacks and defended their countrymen from the charges of inhumanity. The question was constantly agitated from pulpit, press and platform during the 1830's. The northern conscience was being goaded into action.

Another reform which called forth much propaganda was the temperance question. American communities were noted for their consumption of a variety of intoxicants and intemperance was all too frequent and often disgusting. With the revival of interest in religion and morals which came after the War of 1812, propaganda against intemperance waxed militant and evangelical. The American Society for the Promotion of Temperance was established in 1826 and vigorous efforts made to persuade individuals to sign pledges of total abstinence. By 1834 there were about one million members of this organization enrolled.

This move also had a social phase. A number of reformed drunkards realized how difficult it was to keep a pledge once made and how almost impossible to compete with the social lure of the saloon. In order to provide mutual aid and sociability a group at Baltimore established a society in 1840 known as the Washingtonians to establish club rooms, to listen to temperance lectures and in general to combat the drink evil. Soon Washington societies and lodges of the Sons of

Temperance were established in many communities and by 1850 there were about 250,000 members.

Naturally the question entered politics when proposals for legislation were brought forward. Some advocated high license fees to reduce the number of saloons. Others favored sale only in packages which must be taken elsewhere, thus eliminating the saloon. A third group urged local option whereby towns, villages, or counties could vote and determine whether the sale of drinks would be permitted. Most drastic of all were the proposals for state-wide prohibition, a remedy first tried by Maine when in 1851 such a law was enacted. Many professed to discern the handwriting of a message of doom on the wall of the saloon.

While these agitations for social reforms were being prosecuted so vigorously two groups were anxious to assume a larger share of social responsibility and to make their positions more privileged and secure. The first of these was feminine. Woman in America did not enjoy the legal or political rights which are now taken for granted. If she were married, she could not legally hold or control property apart from her husband, nor in any event could she vote or hold office. Now began the agitation for property rights at least, for interest in political privileges was not so vigorously expressed. Women sought to participate more in public affairs. Frances Wright, much to the disgust of many, actually delivered public lectures and advocated schemes of social reorganization along lines of greater justice. Foremost of all the campaigners for women's rights were Elizabeth Cady Stanton and Lucretia Mott who promoted flourishing organizations of their sex. In the 'thirties and 'forties several states granted women property rights and in 1848 a large Women's Rights convention was held at which a Declaration of Independence was enthusiastically adopted. Women knew their influence, why not have it openly recognized?

The second group to seek greater security and freedom was the body of wage earners. Under the English common law such workers were presumed to make individual contracts with their employers and if they banded together to demand collective bargaining they were guilty of conspiracy as such combinations in restraint of trade were illegal. Such legal disabilities had discouraged labor organization for mutual protection. There had been some local societies formed largely for recreation and sick and death benefit funds, among the first being the Philadelphia shoemakers (1792) and the Baltimore tailors (1795). Attempts by these groups to engineer a few strikes, 1795-1809, had been frustrated by court decisions so that such action had not been found practicable. Times changed, however, with the coming of the factory. In 1827 was organized a Mechanics Union of Trade Associations in

Philadelphia and similar groups came into being in other cities. A paper, the *Mechanics Free Press,* was established in 1828 and in the next two years in New York, political action was decided upon and a workers' party organized which in the election of 1829 in that city polled 6000 out of the 20,000 votes cast. The strike began to be used as a weapon and the courts were inclined to be more lenient although conspiracy charges were sometimes successfully brought against unions in the late 'thirties. The demands of labor were for the reduction of hours to ten per day at an increased wage (frequently $1.50 a day for a skilled workman). Numerous demands were made for security for wages by allowing a mechanic's lien upon products which had been made by workers in case their employers failed to pay them. Protests were made against imprisonment for debt, militia service, and the exploitation of women and children in industry. Much stress was laid upon the need for educational opportunities for the children. The climax of this first period of the trade union movement came with the organization of a National Trades Union in 1834, an attempt at federating the various city trades unions with a membership of 26,000, by no means all of organized labor.

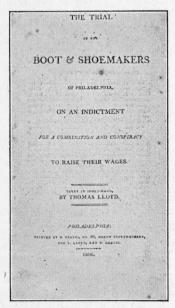

THE TRIAL

OF THE

BOOT & SHOEMAKERS

OF PHILADELPHIA,

ON AN INDICTMENT

FOR A COMBINATION AND CONSPIRACY

TO RAISE THEIR WAGES.

TAKEN IN SHORT-HAND,
BY THOMAS LLOYD.

PHILADELPHIA:
PRINTED BY B. GRAVES, NO. 40, NORTH FOURTH-STREET,
FOR T. LLOYD, AND B. GRAVES.
1806.

Labor's Legal Handicap

The panic of 1837 proved a hard blow to the unions because of the general unemployment and the oversupply of labor which accompanied this depression. During the 'forties there developed a philanthropic interest in the welfare of labor quite in keeping with the spirit of the times. Employers began to be more conscientious and devoted some of their profits to improving the lot of their workmen. Politicians began to urge a ten hour day and President Van Buren in 1840 prescribed such hours for government laborers; New Hampshire (1847) and Pennsylvania (1848) passed ten hour laws. Cooperative schemes were worked out whereby a few groups of laborers controlled or shared in control of industry and cooperative stores were established as in England whereby the workers supplied themselves with food and eliminated the middlemen's profit. Women too began to organize for collective bargaining. However, the labor union movement did not recover from the shock of the panic until the boom years just before the next depression when labor became scarcer and could once again exert collective strength. Conditions had improved because of the general philanthropic interest rather than through the coercion of collective bargaining.

Still a third phase of American interest in social improvements dealt with elaborate plans for world betterment and social reorganization. As early as 1828 an American Peace Society was established which worked for the organization of a congress of nations and a court of arbitration. American delegates attended the World Peace Congress held at London in 1843 and five years later the American proposals for an international league and arbitration were adopted by another conference at Brussels. A few Americans like Elihu Burritt took more than an academic interest in the abolition of war but their hopes were somewhat dampened by strife in Mexico and the Crimea.

Even more ambitious were schemes of social reorganization. Utopias were the order of the day. Most notable were the experiments advocated by the Scotsman Robert Owen and the Frenchman Charles Fourier. Owen planned an ideal community where life would be dedicated not only to survival but also to mutual improvement. Work would be economically apportioned and a goodly part of each day set aside for education and recreation. Life was to be intelligently supervised. A community planned along these lines was sponsored by Owen in New Harmony, Indiana, in 1826, but it proved impracticable as its members became too fond of amusement and idleness and neglected work and improvement of the mind. A more elaborate and widespread series of experiments were those developed by followers of Fourier who advocated communal life in specially ordered groups of relatively equal size. Each of these was called a phalanx and followed a carefully organized program. A number were established in various parts of the country and one or two survived quite a long period of time. The idea proved merely a fad but it indicated a belief in drastic social reorganization quite in the spirit of the times.

Popular Education—The Hope of Democracy

The most fitting instrument to promote this confidence in future improvement was wider and better education. If the United States were to prove the hope of the world, the largest possible number of intelligent and educated citizens was the great goal. Universal education of at least a primary grade became a real possibility. Gradually the idea that free education was charity fit only for the poverty-stricken was dispelled and property owners converted to the idea of being taxed to pay for teaching other people's children. The New England states had been forerunners in this move and all but Rhode Island had some form of free education carried over from the colonial period or established shortly after independence. The new western states followed New England.

Free education was less developed in the middle states and least of all in the South. The scattered character of the agricultural population in the latter section made district organization for free education impossible at that time so the real battle for increase in public schools was fought in the middle states. In the populous centers of these states, the growth of cities, the demands of labor and the increase in the number of voters, combined to increase the strength of the advocates. In Pennsylvania a law was at length achieved in 1834 although it exempted from its provisions those communities who by popular vote refused consent. In New York, where for some time localities had been permitted to tax themselves for free schools, a general law was enacted in 1849 after a favorable referendum only to be repealed after the voters withdrew their consent the next year. The struggle had to be continued and on a wider front for the laws in the New England and western states were not always carried out. In spite of the reverse in New York, by 1850 the idea of public schools was gaining strength and in the latter year 80% of the population was forced to have some sort of primary education. Though there were between 50,000 and 60,000 primary schools in session anywhere from six weeks to eight months each year, still there were at least 1,000,000 illiterates. The United States had achieved an "educational consciousness."

Next to the growth of the free school idea the increase in facilities for collegiate education was the most noticeable advance. In the first place the idea of state educational systems was being imported from Europe especially from Prussia and men like Horace Mann and Calvin E. Stowe were advocating the adaptation of such models. So in the new western commonwealths there developed the idea of statewide organization headed by a state university. Though they were aided by the grants of government land, many difficulties stood in the way. Nevertheless, some of the states notably Michigan and Wisconsin achieved their ambitions. Elsewhere the idea was not wholly absent.

North Carolina had made a beginning in 1795 which did not take the definite form of a state-controlled university until 1821. Virginia under Jefferson's leadership organized the University of Virginia in 1819. In New York a shadowy university was projected with a board of regents which should supervise such education as the state might provide; the board of regents became a reality but the university was never further organized.

The religious zeal of the period was reflected in the development of collegiate education. As the number of denominations multiplied there came a corresponding growth of colleges. Each sect wished a college where its own ideas would be nurtured and imparted to succeeding generations of youth. Various motives both secular and religious by 1850 swelled the number of institutions of collegiate or university grade to 135.

Women and professional men came in for their share of the educational enthusiasm. Heretofore women had not been considered fit subjects for much more than the mere rudiments. However, as the move for women's rights developed it was accompanied by a demand for more educational privileges. Some success attended these efforts and in 1837 Mt. Holyoke College was established while in 1834 Oberlin inaugurated co-education. A number of young ladies' seminaries too, were founded, and more girls became ambitious for books and schools. Professional education was improved. Law and medical schools were still generally proprietary establishments, conducted for profit by two or three "lecturers." Greater advance was made in technical engineering training, especially as railroad building brought a need for accurate construction knowledge. Heretofore West Point had provided practically the only formal training of this type and this ostensibly only for army officers although many men resigned from the army and went into civil life with their professional knowledge. As early as 1824 Rensselaer Polytechnic Institute in Brooklyn had been established and in the 'forties Yale and Harvard were presented with Sheffield and Lawrence Scientific Schools to care for education in engineering. Even where no definite technical school was founded the strength of the move was shown by revisions of curricula and the introduction of a broader offering of courses. The first inroads upon strictly classical training were having effect.

With the extension of primary and the broadening of collegiate education there was less progress in the extension of facilities for secondary schooling and college preparatory work. Private academies, private tutors or interested ministers and lawyers still generally supplied the need and necessarily such opportunities were not open to the poor. The increasing belief in the democracy of education stimulated the spread of free secondary or high schools. As early as 1821 such a free school had been established in Massachusetts and in 1827 that state passed a law requiring a tax-supported high school in every town of five hundred families or more. However, the idea did not flourish for by 1850 there were only seventeen throughout the United States.

With the growth of the number of schools came an increasing interest in securing more and better teachers and improved methods of instruction. Most of the teaching was done by college students earning their education or by professionals whose chief qualifications often were physical strength and ability to keep order. Such instruction was in charge of local school boards with no knowledge of education and anything like effective supervision was unknown. Massachusetts took the lead in inaugurating new methods. Horace Mann was given charge of organizing education in that commonwealth in 1837 and supervising the enforcement of uniform requirements. Two years later a normal school was established for the purpose of providing trained teachers to work under state supervision. The beginning of teacher training and supervision had been achieved. The foundation had been marked out for the elaborate structure of American education.

In such a variety of ways the consuming desire for a better America was demonstrated. The zeal for perfectionism that had its root in colonial religion was a continually compelling urge. Many times since those years of enthusiasm for a better society, new forces have interposed to deflect attention from improvement but to date this zeal for the greater good has managed to reassert itself periodically. It has been the most valuable directing force in shaping the American social order, it has colored political life and given a moral tone to American democracy. Throughout national history, no stronger issues have absorbed popular attention than pleas for reform.

CHAPTER XI

PANIC AND RECOVERY

The decade of democratic zeal for reform was marked by a major economic disaster. Financial panics have been periodic episodes in American history. Rarely have two decades passed without witnessing an economic depression and so widespread and disturbing have these catastrophes proven that they mark definite pauses in national development. The nation seemingly in these periods stops for readjustment and reconsideration, vagaries of panic psychology appear in various localities and altogether for a time at least people are strained and uneasy, reacting abnormally to conditions of life. Strange things happen in periods of panic.

Heedless Economic Expansion

The people of the United States enjoyed a consciousness of unlimited wealth, not yet in a form to be utilized. The great unsettled acreages, the possibility of their settlement, the raw material they could supply, the manufactured goods needed by a growing population, the easy profits from shrewd promotion, these attractive possibilities tempted the speculative and optimistic imagination of numerous men and women.

Agriculture and manufacturing both offered money-making opportunities. Especially in the South was agricultural expansion notable because the planters concentrated on one crop, cotton, and this had a ready sale abroad. Food production, too, advanced but not so spectacularly or with such profit. The increasing use of machines stimulated the manufacture of goods and very effectively increased those industries which were engaged in the production of machines themselves. These ventures, though feverishly developing, did not, however, contribute so much to the uncertain character of the business life of this period as did the other forms which more easily invited speculation, namely, real estate, transportation and banking.

The growing population was demanding more and more land. Land being so desirable it was easily salable and those who could manipulate the price could make money quickly and easily. The ingenious and the shrewd therefore sought to anticipate the movement of population, to acquire the soon-to-be-settled areas at low prices and then to charge the newcomers as much as they could get. Lots outside of cities especially near New York were exploited and boomed, more often to the benefit of real estate dealers than to the ultimate purchasers. Word was deviously spread abroad that Maine timber was becoming scarce and many hurried to buy some of the "small" remaining area at skyrocketing prices. Plantation lands in the southwestern states were no less attractive and land companies with glittering advertisements, literature, and high-powered salesmen painted in glowing colors the value of their holdings. Finally western townships were laid out and maps prepared showing the up-to-date arrangement and handsome improvement of future cities and towns, surely destined to be centers of wealthy and powerful states; these, too, had their promoters, generally active in eastern cities. Such appeals were not in vain and towns like Chicago might almost be said to have been sold and re-sold in New York City to persons who never saw a square foot of the land by which they hoped so greatly to profit. In spite of the fact that many an unwary purchaser found his Eden site under water when he at length reached it, many a city did thrive, many a farming area was planted and many a fortunate speculator became wealthy. The land sales taking into consideration only the public lands of the United States increased from 1,018,000 acres sold in 1828 to 20,074,000 acres sold in 1836.

No less attractive to speculators was transportation. The new regions needed easy communication with the other parts of the country and the possibilities of successful real estate speculation were often closely connected with transportation facilities. Many canal projects were launched and their stock became as much a matter of speculative interest as real estate. Many states hoping to make their localities more attractive to businessmen and settlers began to engage heavily in these schemes, pledging their state credit to raise the money and mortgaging the future taxes many years ahead. All was hope and confidence and adventurous legislators spent millions more than their state treasuries could afford.

To carry on these speculations, real estate operators and transportation managers depended upon credit supplied by banks. After 1832 it became apparent that the United States Bank was going out of existence and that the government was planning to deposit the public money in private banks. This change of banking organization and the great demand for loans proved attractive to businessmen, many of whom were without banking experience, and new banks began to spring up plentifully. There was little or no supervision of these institutions, each could issue notes up to the limit of public credulity and their loan policies were, to say the least, liberal, if not fantastic. Money could easily be borrowed and banks could easily print more. So long as nobody doubted this currency and nobody called the loans, credit was buoyant and few considered whether the bubble could be inflated indefinitely. Between 1830 and 1837, 347 new banks were established and between 1832 and 1836 bank circulation increased from 59 millions to 140 millions.

A further stimulating source of encouragement to American business was the interest which foreign capital took in its development. Not only did Americans buy much more than they sold in Europe (the balance against them in the year 1836 was 61 millions) thus insuring active and intimate business relations with European powers, but in borrowing money for speculation the United States paid high rates of interest. So for goods and for loans American businessmen were heavily in debt especially in England. If Europe did not need her money and in hope of high interest returns was willing to lend more, all would be well. Evidently, however, the whole financial structure was resting too exclusively upon a foundation of very insecure credit. Any slight accident might start a panic. Premonitory warnings had come in 1833-1834 when money became scarce partly because of the restriction of loans by the United States Bank as it was preparing to surrender its national charter. In spite of a number of failures and much uncertainty conditions righted themselves temporarily. The worst was yet to come.

In the two years before 1837 affairs had not been going very well in the business world not only in America but also in Europe. A bad harvest due to the devastations of the Hessian fly in 1836 had caused a scarcity of food in the United States and an increased purchasing from Europe, making the trade balance even more heavily against America. A fire in 1835 had burned a large part of New York City and had destroyed much property and many business records and had produced shortage and uncertainty. Besides the financial plans of the Jacksonian administration were uncertain.

Jackson's ideas in regard to finance were not very extensive nor his knowledge profound. He decided that the way to provide sound money was to destroy the Bank and to encourage the use of coin instead of uncertain paper. So he killed the Bank and placed government funds in a great variety of state banks. A law was enacted ineffectively designed to bring gold coins into circulation and Jackson also issued an order, known as the specie circular, requiring that all payments for the public lands be made in coin. In addition to this program Congress passed a bill distributing the surplus in the treasury among the states in four installments. The specie circular and the distribution act meant that a good deal of money had to be shipped into the West as 1837 advanced and left too little money in the seaboard banking centers. All these disasters and acts of the government made the unstable credit system all the more uncertain; none of them alone or even all of them together presumably could have caused the severe crisis that was to follow.

Panic

1837 saw a world-wide crash. European banks became frightened, they made demands upon England. Panic ensued. English banks needed money to meet these calls and began to demand money from those who had borrowed from them. Naturally various firms sought to collect their bills to settle their accounts at the banks or to sell their securities. Many business houses in England had much money tied up in America. The trade balance, so heavily against the United States now became a subject for British calls, British merchants had to have their money and besides could no longer buy cotton. American banks had to send large shipments of gold to England. The banks and foreign trading houses could not get the money, the price of cotton tumbled, American securities were sent home in large quantities from England to be sold for what they would bring. Like a house of cards the American structure fell. The price of flour due to the shortage of wheat was so high that in February the poor rioted in the streets of New York, demanding bread. In March three important cotton firms in New Orleans which could sell no cotton in England failed and three New York firms likewise suspended, the latter involved to the extent of nine millions. Then an avalanche of failures followed; by 11 April 128 firms had failed in New York City, thousands were out of work, business ceased. Continual runs on the banks could not be met and by 11 May most banks of the country had suspended specie payment. Neither people nor government had any money and depression was world-wide.

The finely blown and expanded bubble had broken, possessors of money had their faith in easy profits shattered and scrutinized most carefully the possibilities of any proposed purchase or investment. In the East business ceased, banks failed, imports dropped off, and manufacturing concerns either stopped work or reduced their output. Many were thrown out of work and extreme poverty and distress were all too prevalent. In the South many planters failed and their lands and slaves came upon the market at ruinously low prices. Cotton was not purchased in the great quantity needed before the panic and the price fell. The West was last to experience the panic and the longest to suffer from it. Not until the demand for crops at harvest time proved to be small did the people of this section feel the full force of the crash. There was little money and no demand for the large crops. Farmers could not sell their produce nor could they pay their taxes or their debts. Even barter was resorted to because the paper of many of the banks was practically worthless. Now the ambitious schemes of state finance and public improvement seemed like great burdens, reduced tax receipts could meet neither interest nor principal charges and defaulting seemed the only way out. General business and financial stagnation had taken the place

of the vigorous optimism that had previously made every risk seem to
be a good one.

After a period of uncertainty lasting over a year, confidence was sufficiently restored to cause the better banks to seek an agreement for the
general return to specie payments. By summer of 1838 they succeeded
and there occurred a renewed outbreak of reckless speculation. Land
sales doubled in a year and foreign credit, or at least buying abroad,
spurted ahead. The hard times in England had so reduced the price of
goods there as to attract American buyers. A shortage in the cotton crop
also permitted its owners to force the price up and they hoped to profit
much thereby. However, England was in such financial condition that
her manufacturers would not pay the high price and much cotton lay
in British warehouses unsold. In the meantime in England there had
been bad harvests in 1838 and she had been compelled to buy much food
from continental Europe and needed gold with which to pay for it.
English business thereupon instead of taking cotton in exchange for large
American purchases, refused the cotton and demanded specie. As much
as 30 millions in gold had to be exported and the banks became so
straightened in 1839 that by October most banks had again suspended
specie payment. Business was once more in a state of collapse and
financial conditions became so bad that in the next few years at least
eight states defaulted on interest payments and Mississippi repudiated
a bond issue on the ground that it was illegal. A temporary return to
specie payment was attempted by the banks in 1841 but it was hardly
undertaken before most of the institutions had to stop once more. In
1842 the sounder banks tried resumption, some under compulsion of
state law, but it was not until 1844 that credit was easy and banks
could deal confidently.

In the meantime while these deplorable conditions were causing much
distress, there were many demands for government interference and the
political leaders of state and nation were called upon to satisfy them.
Inability to meet such importunities was disastrous to many a politician.
The state legislatures hastened in some instances to pass stay laws and
exemption laws and other measures which would make it unnecessary
for debtors to pay their obligations immediately. Bankrupt laws were
enacted to make it possible for those hopelessly involved to be relieved
of their debts and in the western states where the state debts were so
tremendous there was frequent demand for repudiation. Also laws were
passed regulating banking more strictly and compelling banks which
could not pay specie to go out of business. When specie payment had
been so long deferred, especially in 1841-1842, a number of laws were
passed to make banks resume or stop functioning. In at least one case
banks were deprived of the note-issuing privilege. Finally demands were
made upon the government to assume the state debts, to recommence dis-

tributing the surplus revenue and to pass a general bankruptcy law. Whig politicians began another agitation for a re-charter of the national bank. Such demands focussed attention upon Congress and national politics.

The panic put the Democrats at a disadvantage, for a party in power during a financial stringency is always blamed for it. Besides the Whigs claimed that the destruction of the Bank and Jackson's mistaken financial policy had caused the trouble. The Democrats were not well equipped to meet popular demands at this crisis. Their principles tended to promote as little government aid as possible and the call for such interference was general. The Whigs came forward immediately with the proposal to recharter the bank. Van Buren, now unhappily President, and his advisers realized that the deposit of government money in various state banks had been a mistake. Few if any of them could now pay specie and the government lost millions. All government connections with financial institutions they concluded were disastrous so Congress was called in special session in September 1837 to provide for the immediate needs of the government and to establish a permanent policy.

Congress was asked to provide for borrowing money, to postpone indefinitely the distribution of the surplus (now non-existent) and to establish a new system of government finance. Henceforth the Democrats were determined that no banks should use government money, the treasury should be independent and should keep all money paid in until it was needed for expenditures. To this end sub-treasuries were to be established in various parts of the country to keep all government funds until paid out. The first two laws passed easily but those desiring a recharter of the United States Bank and those interested in state banks were strenuously opposed to the "divorce" of government from business and fought the passage of the sub-treasury act until July 1840 when after three defeats it was finally enacted into law. Naturally these measures could do little to aid the continuing distress and as the election of 1840 approached, the Whigs sought to take advantage of the situation.

To begin with, they took a leaf out of the Democratic book and sought a military hero. William Henry Harrison was no Jackson but he had enjoyed a somewhat varied and glamorous career, so he was presented to the people with no platform. Much clever publicity work was planned, catchy songs were written, much liquid refreshment was provided to stimulate enthusiasm. As the hero of Tippecanoe he was pictured as a dweller in a log cabin who drank hard cider. An ex-Democrat, John Tyler, who it was hoped would attract southern votes was nominated for vice-president. Times had been hard, many had been burdened with worry, popular amusements were relatively scarce, so this joyous, rollicking campaign came as a welcome release. The panic-troubled voters joined the chorus and Harrison was literally sung into office. With him came a Whig Congress eager to tackle the depression.

When Harrison was inaugurated he immediately called a special session and Clay as the principal Whig expected to dominate it and dictate a plan. But Harrison died before it convened and his successor John Tyler was not in sympathy with Clay. The general Whig plan had been to repeal the sub-treasury law, to resume distributing the proceeds of the sales of the public lands, to enact a protective tariff and to recharter the Bank. The first was easily accomplished but the second was permitted only so long as the tariff did not go above 20%. The increase in the tariff was postponed for a while and the chief center of attention was the Bank. Congress passed a re-chartering bill twice but each time it was vetoed by Tyler who had been a Democrat and who still believed in a Jeffersonian minimum of government interference. Clay had to be content therefore with a protective tariff passed in 1842 when the Compromise Tariff of 1833 had at length reduced the rates to 20%. Even the victory had a flaw because thereby the distribution of the land revenue was automatically stopped before it began.

In fact the Whigs had shown themselves hopelessly divided and unable to agree upon a program. They were defeated in 1844 on issues connected with foreign affairs which we shall treat later and when the Democrats came back into power they finally settled the question of government aid to business. They re-enacted the independent treasury bill and displaced the protective tariff of 1842 by the Walker Act of 1846 which established tariff duties on a revenue basis. It had become apparent early in the period after the rollicking campaign of 1840 that government aid was of little permanent value and that recovery from the panic was then to be accomplished by time, incurable optimism, the abundant natural resources of the nation, and the various new tools which ingenuity could press into service.

New Enterprise Aids Recovery

Since government action could do little to aid in the quest for recovery, the natural force of the people and the boundless resources at their command were to overcome the effects of the disaster. A new mode of transportation gave opportunity for profit and surplus labor. As early as 1815 there had been a scheme for the use of rails invented by John Stevens in New Jersey but not until 1822 did Pennsylvania grant a railroad charter and not until 1830 was a railroad actually put into operation when the Baltimore and Ohio and the Charleston and Hamburg began the use of locomotives on their track. The development of this form of transit was slow and by 1837 only 1500 miles had been built.

In the years following the panic, however, this mode of transportation became more popular as its utility was demonstrated and by 1850, 9000 miles had been constructed. The freight-hauling possibilities now developed by this new means, both in respect to quantity and speed were in the course of revolutionizing internal business. The paths of commerce need no longer follow water courses or be subject to the slow monotony

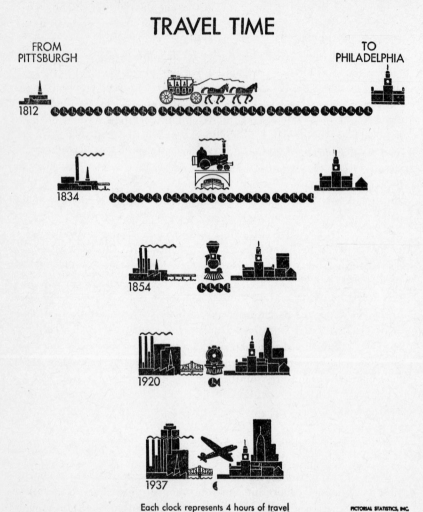

TRAVEL TIME

FROM
PITTSBURGH

TO
PHILADELPHIA

1812

1834

1854

1920

1937

Each clock represents 4 hours of travel   PICTORIAL STATISTICS, INC.

From Hacker, Modley, Taylor, *The United States:
A Graphic History*, Modern Age Books, Inc.

of canal progress—rails could be laid almost anywhere and paths directed arbitrarily to suit the needs or whims of man. So a new interest entered business and as its initial demands were heavy, a new mobilization of capital was called for. A new habit had to be learned by Americans, namely, rail travel, and they did not learn it easily. Early railroads were dangerous, uncomfortable and uncertain. Their early construction and equipment were often faulty and badly managed so that accidents were all too frequent. However, the railroad had come to stay and its possibilities stimulated anew the vision of American business. When the telegraph was perfected in 1844 the annihilation of space and time can be fairly said to have begun.

The expansion of the iron industry was closely connected with railroading in stimulating business recovery. New processes made possible a greater and better output. Hot blasts, the use of coal for fuel, refining processes such as puddling and rolling were revolutionizing the technique. The use of stoves, furnaces, gas light and plumbing continued to increase. New machines were constantly being invented, most important were those to expedite the manufacture of clothing and shoes, such as the sewing machine and pegging machines. The railroads needed locomotives and miles and miles of iron for the ever-lengthening lines of tracks. Finally, the tariff of 1842 proved a psychological stimulus and the quickening of industry which the promise of protection gave was of perhaps more value than the actual protection itself, for when the tariff of 1842 was replaced by the revenue measure of 1846, the momentum gained in the four years carried on in spite of the lowered duties.

At the same time a step was taken significant in the light of future developments, the corporation was more widely used. In spite of the unpopularity which this type of management had suffered during the war upon the Bank of the United States, the need for larger amounts of capital and more stable organization was urgent. Internal improvements, railroads and factories with expensive machinery were beyond the powers of individual capitalists while the corporation could mobilize the necessary funds. So in spite of much popular distrust, demand for incorporation became more insistent and legislatures, constitutional conventions and courts struggled with the problem of laws and regulations which would protect the public interest and the stockholder and at the same time authorize the mobilization of capital. The corporation, however, was only a small factor in business, individuals and partnerships were still the promoters.

A new spurt in commerce did its part. American interest in the Far East had been growing where diplomats had been sparring for advantage in the closed realms of the Orient. In 1833 a treaty had been made with Siam. Missionary zeal and interest in sugar planting had led a goodly number of Americans to settle in the Hawaiian Islands. Even the mysterious empires of China and Japan slowly yielded. Americans followed in British footsteps after the Opium War of 1842 when the English forced China to receive their trade advances. In 1844 an American minister, Caleb Cushing, made a treaty with China which granted trading privileges never hitherto enjoyed. But it was not until ten years later that Japan yielded slightly when Commodore Perry's squadron appeared in her waters and it was 1858 before she yielded real trading privileges.

To take advantage of these expanding interests and growing privileges, American ship builders won another triumph. Donald McKay built the clipper ships, vessels specially designed for swiftness. They would race across the seas at unheard-of speeds and outdistanced British rivals in the race for the China trade. *The Flying Cloud, Lightning, The Sovereign of the Seas* were some of the aptly descriptive names they bore as they made the Stars and Stripes the symbol of speed and navigating skill.

Changing conditions in England brought American commerce further advantage. The growing power of manufacturers in the British Isles was working for freer trade so that food and raw materials could be procured cheaply, thus cutting labor and manufacturing costs and providing freer exchange for British manufacturers. This influence finally persuaded Parliament to repeal the old British tariff, or Corn Laws, in 1846 and to withdraw the navigation restrictions against foreign vessels. American ships could now go into all parts of the British empire and American wheat and raw materials were purchased in even greater quantity. In fact, there was but one bad sign on the commercial horizon and that few noticed. Great Britain was turning to iron steamships while the Americans in the pride of their fast clippers failed to see the possibilities of the grimy vessels, nor to realize that they would take the carrying trade from the graceful sailing ships in the long run. In spite of seeming preeminence, American shipping was really in a decline.

But greatest of all of the aids to recovery was the great national estate and the unquenchable zeal for expansion of the population. The western thoroughfares were crowded. There were increasing demands for cheaper land which the government met in part only by the pre-emption law of 1841. Settlers could now go ahead of the surveyors, preempt and improve land, secure in the knowledge that they thereby gained the right of ultimate purchase and ownership.

The West was filling up and the ambition of the nation urged the government to gain new room for growth. There had been a lull in state-making after 1821 but in 1836 and 1837 the process began once more when Arkansas and Michigan were admitted. By 1845 Florida was ready and Iowa and Wisconsin joined the Union in quick succession (1846 and 1848). All the Northwest Territory except a small portion in the far distant Minnesota region was now divided into states and in the old Louisiana Purchase four commonwealths were flourishing.

Population was continually moving and in the westward area had more than doubled between 1830 and 1840 while the census of 1850 was to show a rate of increase only slightly below that of the preceding

decade. Foreign immigration too was increasing vigorously and swelling
the westward tide. Prior to 1820 but 200,000 had come from Europe
to the new United States. From 1820 to 1845 a million came in
increasing numbers each year while in but five years from 1846 to 1850
another million landed on the American shores. The Irish famine of
1846 and the European revolutions of 1848 especially in Germany, had
induced these multitudes to seek this land of opportunity where many
believed the streets to be paved with gold.

Diplomatic Rivalry and War

Such restlessness contributed much to the hunger for great possessions
which was so openly manifest in the America of the 'forties. In all
directions American eyes were turned toward the borders which might
prove elastic and there they found much to fix attention. To the northeast and the northwest was the British power and unsettled boundaries.
Where did Maine end and Canada begin? After fifty years of controversy neither government could agree; nor could they in far off Oregon
where both countries had unarbitrated claims. With the traditional
hostility toward England so strong, these disputes might foster worse
disasters than diplomatic quarrels and crises. Indeed, bloodshed in the
Maine region was only averted by something approaching a miracle.

In 1838 Canadian lumbermen entered forests claimed by Maine and
imprisoned an agent of that state sent to drive them out. Maine retaliated by arresting an official of New Brunswick. Militia were mobilized
by the state and Congress voted additional help while the War Department sent General Scott to take command. War seemed imminent and
the feeling of hostility was not decreased by events on the New York-
Canadian frontier where trouble had been rife in the winter of 1837-
1838. A brief uprising in Canada in favor of popular government had
enlisted the sympathies of the communities along the New York side
of the border and their feelings had been anything but neutral. Consequently when Canadian militia crossed over into the United States,
burned an American vessel, the *Caroline,* which was used by the rebels,
and killed an American citizen, there was much angry talk of retaliation.
Fortunately, no further hostile acts were committed and the border
settled down to suspicious waiting.

As has usually been the case, however, when the tension approached
the point of warlike demonstrations between the United States and
Great Britain, both sides expressed a willingness to negotiate. When
the Whigs, less bellicose than the Democrats, came into power in 1841,
Webster took charge of foreign relations. He was acquainted with a
number of British leaders and it seemed a good omen when one of them,
Lord Ashburton, was despatched to negotiate over the variety of matters

so long in dispute. Their friendly conferences produced the Webster-Ashburton treaty of 1842. The Maine border area was divided so as to give New Brunswick a connecting road to Quebec; for this surrender of territory, Maine was to be compensated by the federal government and Maine's citizens were accorded trade privileges in New Brunswick. A joint agreement for the suppression of the African slave trade was included but no arrangement of the Oregon limits was perfected.

American pioneers were more expeditious than the diplomats in tackling this last problem. As early as 1829 it became apparent to a few at least that the best way to secure Oregon was to settle it with Americans. Several colonization schemes were proposed but the missionaries to the Indians accomplished the most. The Methodist and the Presbyterian churches sent out Jason and Daniel Lee, Samuel Parker and Marcus Whitman and their work among the aborigines was supplemented by that of a government agent sent there in 1837. In the meantime, Senator Linn of Missouri began a long campaign to persuade Congress to take action to save this territory to the nation.

The failure of the Webster-Ashburton negotiations to include Oregon only served to quicken American interest. 1843 was the time for numerous public meetings, some quantities of resolutions and more emigrants. John C. Frémont came home with a vivid account of his explorations in that region which was published. The Oregon trail became a reality to a new generation of pioneers. But Oregon to the British was Hudson's Bay Company territory and American settlers found that the company's agent, Dr. John McLaughlin, was in command of the region at his post at the junction of the Columbia and Willamette rivers. The factor was an able officer, gifted with tact and a friendly disposition, therefore trouble was avoided but it was quite apparent to the emigrants from the United States that he considered the company's position permanent. Because of his location, hardly any Americans went beyond the Columbia river. In the meantime, Great Britain made conciliatory moves. The Oregon question might be settled amicably though there was much bellicose talk of "protecting" American rights.

The Columbia and Willamette valleys by no means absorbed the expansive energies of the United States for at the same time there was pressure toward the southwest as well. Even before Oregon attracted popular attention, there was talk of Texas. Men with vision in the Southwest looked covetously upon the fertile soil of the river valleys in the Texan plain. After the panic of 1819 had destroyed his business, Moses Austin, then of St. Louis, sought a way to restore his wealth by settling in this portion of the Spanish Empire. Because of political friends, Spain yielded to his request and made the grant. Before he could carry out his scheme, he died, but his son Stephen took up the venture and when the Spanish government was overthrown and Mexico became independent in 1821, he obtained confirmation of the grant from the new government which wanted the help of American settlers in maintaining its newly acquired independence. Austin therefore became the first of a number of "empresarios" as they were called. These men contracted to bring settlers who were to become Mexican and Catholic and who were to receive grants of land for their livelihood. From 1821 onward then a stream of emigrants went from the United States into Mexican Texas. Most failed to become Catholic and none seemed to lose their American identity. Inevitably as they became stronger and more numerous, and showed more independence, Mexico began to be fearful.

In 1830 when the Mexican government inaugurated a series of restrictions, political and economic, trouble was fast on its way. New tariff regulations were put into effect which were aimed to force Texans to buy in Mexico rather than over the border in Louisiana. Then Texas, in common with the other Mexican states, was stripped of power by Santa Anna when he converted the Republic into a military despotism and Stephen Austin himself was imprisoned. Conditions were too much like those preceding 1776. These sons of the American Revolution followed the example of their fathers. In 1836 the Texans defeated Mexican armed forces and became independent. Almost immediately they sought annexation to the United States but without success. Texas was a slaveholding area and that fact caused many in the North to oppose the acquisition of such a large addition to the southern system, so no action was taken in regard to Texas except to recognize the Lone Star republic as an independent nation. For some five years little American attention was vouchsafed the new neighbor.

In these roaring 'forties anti-British prejudices arose once more in all their venom. Just as the Webster-Ashburton treaty was concluded with its disappointing omission of the Oregon settlement, Great Britain recognized the independence of Texas and sent a commercial agent to California. News of these actions immediately awakened American suspicions which were further aroused when it became apparent that Great Britain was interested in Texas cotton and so was trying to arrange with Mexico to recognize Texas and to cease the intermittent warfare which was characteristic of the border. This latter move was especially unpalatable to the South because it was understood that Great Britain was urging Texas to abolish slavery in return for Mexican recognition. President John Tyler and his Secretary of State, John C. Calhoun, both ardent southerners, pro-slavery and anti-British, finally decided to accept a renewed proffer of annexation and signed a treaty to that effect with Texas, just as the presidential nominations were being made in 1844. Enough northern senators voted against the treaty to defeat its ratification but sentiment in various quarters for annexation had been aroused and was not to be denied.

In the maneuvering preliminary to the nominating conventions, the two most prominent candidates, Martin Van Buren, Democrat, and Henry Clay, Whig, had announced publicly their opposition to annexation. The friends of Texas, especially those in the Democratic party, consequently began to work for the defeat of Van Buren and united the question of Oregon with the Texas issue. British designs on the Columbia valley must be defeated, the United States must have all of Oregon. The campaign efforts of these expansionists succeeded and James K. Polk, not Martin Van Buren, became the Democratic nominee. "Reoccupation (of Oregon) and Reannexation" (of Texas) became the slogan occasionally enlivened by the more bellicose "54-40 or fight" which indicated a determination to own all of Oregon. A vigorous campaign elected Polk over Clay by a very narrow margin and when Congress came together in December 1844 it hastened to annex Texas by joint resolution which required the approval of only a majority in Congress rather than the two-thirds vote of the Senate necessary for the ratification of a treaty. In 1845 therefore, Texas became a state. Such a result infuriated the Mexican government and its disposition became warlike. But what of Oregon?

One of the chief arguments used against annexing Texas was that such action would precipitate war with Mexico. Such prophecy seemed about to be fulfilled but in the meantime, the Democratic party had promised to fight Great Britain unless all of Oregon was obtained. Even the jingoists of that fervent decade, however, must think twice before undertaking two wars at once. The outbreak of a war with Mexico seemed impossible to avert so Polk decided to accept a compromise dividing Oregon with Great Britain. The latter government had previously offered to surrender all territory south of the 49th parallel and now Polk agreed accepting a treaty to that effect signed 15 June 1846 at Washington. In the meantime war with Mexico had begun.

No sooner had Texas been annexed than Mexico severed diplomatic relations with the United States, continued in her refusal to pay debts which she had agreed were lawfully due, and refused to receive an envoy whom Polk sent to Mexico to treat with her. Meanwhile, the President had sent a small army to the Rio Grande to repel a threatened Mexican attack upon Texas. He felt when Mexico had rudely rejected an effort to negotiate the matters in dispute that he could not longer avoid the most effective "defensive" measures possible and became convinced that war was inevitable. He was about to ask Congress to declare war when a Mexican detachment crossed the Rio Grande and in a skirmish American blood was spilled on American soil. This news was all Polk needed to arouse Congress and on 13 May 1846 war was declared.

The Mexican War, as far as military operations were concerned, lasted some sixteen months and was a complete success, every battle being an American victory. Not only did Taylor march south from the Rio Grande but Winfield Scott captured Vera Cruz on the sea coast and penetrated the country until he finally seized Mexico City itself. At home, however, there was much opposition to the war, especially on the part of the Whigs and many others in the northern states. The uniform success of the armies however gave the opposition little opportunity for effective protest. Victories are always popular.

The most important phases of the war were not the fighting of Taylor or Scott or the politics at home, but that part of the martial activity which was dictated by the insatiable spirit of expansion so typical of these years. A third military campaign was directed westward toward Spanish California. One of the strong motives which led the Polk Administration to desire a settlement with Mexico had been the fear of English influence. News that a British agent had been established in California was not quieting and one of the compelling urges of Polk and his advisers was the desire to block any attempt of Britain to gain a new foothold. So California early entered the picture. Polk had heard that there was agitation for Californian independence so he sent a personal representative there soon after his inauguration for the purpose of doing what he could to create a desire for annexation to the United States rather than for protection by Great Britain. In the President's futile attempt at negotiation with Mexico before the outbreak of the war, he had included a plan for the purchase of California. Meanwhile, before the Californians knew that war had begun they had declared themselves independent and organized a republic. A few days later, an expedition was set on foot by the United States army and a naval force began the capture of the seaports. By December 1846 the Mexican provinces of California and New Mexico were in the hands of United States forces and the California republic gave place to military rule. When peace was made early in 1848, Mexico, completely vanquished, surrendered these two immense areas and received $15,000,000 in return. In this fashion the ambition of Pacific possessions was realized.

In spite of this tremendous success, there was some disappointment. Even Polk himself thought that the United States was acting with great restraint when it did not acquire all of Mexico. Longing eyes too were cast on Cuba and Polk in the enthusiasm of acquisition offered Spain 100 millions for the island, all to no purpose. Of more immediate importance was a foothold in Central America. The new Pacific possessions must be placed within as quick communication as possible. Journeys across continent and around the Horn were interminable so the most direct route was by sea to some isthmian point in Central America, and then across the narrow strip and a final sea voyage to California or Oregon. There were three possible isthmian routes, Panama, Nicaragua and Tehuantepec, the latter in Mexico. As Polk had not pushed the acquisition of the last named when peace was made, the other two were most before the public. A treaty with Colombia, made in 1846, when that republic had feared British aggression, was now ratified by the Senate. This agreement gave the United States a right of way over the isthmus in return for a guarantee of its neutrality and American capital shortly began the construction of a trans-isthmian railroad which was completed in 1855.

The other possibility, Nicaragua, attracted American attention, because Great Britain from her colony in British Honduras seemed to be moving to gain control of much of Central America, including the Nicaraguan route. Polk and his successors sent diplomatic agents to gain Central American good will and American politicians had another excuse to inveigh against Great Britain. Also the idea of building a canal became more popular. As usual before the situation got too critical the two powers made an agreement in 1850, known as the Clayton-Bulwer treaty. This document provided that neither nation should obtain exclusive control of trans-isthmian territory nor extend its interests further in Central America; any canal building could only be undertaken as a joint enterprise. Thus the difficulties were adjusted and trans-isthmian relations worked out, but the day of a canal was still far away. Instead, American capital established a combination stage and steamboat route across Nicaragua.

The final step in rounding out American possessions came in 1853 when Mexico was persuaded to sell the Gadsden Purchase, a strip of territory which would provide the land necessary to complete a railroad route connecting the Mississippi with California. This was the last successful expansive gesture before the Civil War but there were further efforts to gain Cuba, the Hawaiian Islands, a naval station in Santo Domingo, a strip across Panama for the protection of the railroad and much of northern Mexico, all to no avail.

These mid-century advances had brought much territory to the growing nation but unfortunately they had raised dangerous problems as well, for assimilation was to prove a much more difficult task than acquisition. In the meantime, the depressing effects of the panic of 1837 were forgotten and the enterprise of the nation was again riding high.

CHAPTER XII

SECTIONALISM *VERSUS* PROSPERITY

The acquisition of the new domain accelerated the tendency of population to disperse into western regions and it reawakened ancient sectional rivalries. The renewed conflict was destined to be more intense because its causes were more complex. The contests over the acquisition of Louisiana and the admission of Missouri which in their day had seemed to Jefferson, in the latter case at least, as terrifying as the clang of a fire-bell in the night, were to appear tame in comparison to the struggles about to break out.

The Revival of Sectionalism

The most important factor in the impending rivalry was the steadily increasing sense of insecurity which was making southern leaders apprehensive. Change had been rapid in the decade since the tariff battle of 1832-1833 and these changes had intensified southern feeling. The South in these years had definitely committed itself to one type of livelihood based upon the intensive cultivation by slave labor of a single crop, cotton. Socially, too, the South was very much of a unit, in that most of the population was loyal to the system which had become pervading, a system which was both feudal and democratic in spite of the seeming contradiction in terms.

The feudal character of southern society arose from its primary interest in land, cotton and slaves. Wealth was measured almost exclusively by the size of the plantation and slave property. But such property was not widely distributed. On the eve of the Civil War there were about 8,000,000 white people in the section and of these less than 25% were directly connected with slavery. Less than 200,000 owned as many as ten slaves and the large slave plantations were in the hands of 2600 owners. 2600 men and their families therefore controlled the bulk of southern wealth.

This slaveholding class created a distinctive way of living upon plantations which influenced the entire section. Each plantation was a community in itself and presented problems of ordering and management which were no small tax upon the owner or his overseer. The center of the plantation was the mansion house. These residences varied from classic structures with temple-like porticos to simple farmhouses only notable because they were generally larger than those required by free-labor farmers. As the weather in the cotton belt was marked by long hot summers and short mild winters, these houses were built for coolness. Wide verandahs well shaded, high-ceilinged rooms, broad halls through which any chance breeze might circulate were designed to mitigate the torrid heat of summer. Often they were but one story above a high ground-level basement. Their furnishings varied from imported French furniture, portraits in oils, fine glass, silver and china and rich carpets and draperies to plain articles of domestic manufacture.

These dwellings were generally placed far from the road and were approached through a long tree-lined avenue. Gardens were often tastefully laid out and decorated with ornamental flower urns and even statues. Behind the house were small buildings containing kitchens, stores, a spring house and other offices. Some distance away was apt to be a little village of slave quarters. Each slave family had a cabin and in the more elaborate plantations there were sometimes a church and an infirmary. A comfortable cottage housed the overseer and there was a collection of barns, storehouses and shops. The well organized plantation had slaves who were carpenters, blacksmiths, wheelwrights and skilled workers in other trades and their equipment was sometimes extensive.

The slaves were divided into two groups, the house servants and the field hands, with sometimes a third consisting of mechanics. The Negroes were organized and directed almost continuously. The Negro butler, the cook and the coachman were the aristocrats of the menage. They had a retinue of footmen, chambermaids, scullery maids, grooms and stable boys who cared for the wants of the great house. The field hands were divided into gangs under Negro foremen and the omnipotent overseer. Besides there were generally a midwife and a nurse, a number of slaves too old to work and a flock of children too young yet to be useful. Often they played with the master's children and might grow up to be maids and valets of the younger set.

The routine of the year's industry was dominated by the exactions of cotton making. From seed time until the cotton was through the gin and baled the cultivation of this white treasure was the main concern. In the short winters the place must be kept up, repairs made and perhaps new fields opened, for the methods were crude and wasteful and land often gave out. This exhaustion encouraged planters to extend their holdings and to buy new plantations in the Southwest. Often a planter owned several in different regions which he managed through overseers.

Both the planter and his wife if they were at all concerned in their extensive affairs were continually busy for there was a vast amount of detail involved. The master must oversee his overseers, keep track of the affairs of several plantations, serve as judge, doctor and disciplinarian to hundreds of irresponsible human beings who were in absolute dependence upon him. Slaves were often lazy, sometimes insubordinate, then too there was always the vague fear of slave insurrection. The mistress of the plantation had the housekeeping oversight over a household that set an elaborate table, entertained much company and was serviced by a swarm of slave girls who quite frequently were as trying as they were helpful. Her children were generally cared for by nurses but they in turn often needed to be watched. Then too the health of the plantation was her concern; she kept stocks of medicines and often spent days and nights in nursing the sick. If an epidemic broke out it could hardly be kept from the big house. Showy and luxurious as was the life in these fine houses it was burdened by much responsibility and certain fears which could never be quite banished from the mind.

The mass of the population were not large planters but small farmers who were divided into three classes. There were the yeomen or small farmers who owned no slaves but who frequently hoped by hard work and good fortune to advance into the slaveholding group. The second group was the so-called "poor white" class which gained a precarious existence generally from marginal lands in the Piedmont. The last group lived in the isolated mountain regions and are spoken of as the "mountain whites." Socially and, to a lesser extent, politically the small aristocracy of large planters dominated these groups which were numerically so much larger, with an easy and graceful domination. The bulk of these small farmers admired and respected the planter aristocracy and loyally supported the ruling class whenever southern institutions were under attack.

One reason for this solidarity was the democratic character of the feudal system. There was nothing static about the groupings described above. The wealthy group was by no means closed or exclusively hereditary. Quite frequently new estates were created by small farmers who had been thrifty and competent. Outsiders from the North or from the border states brought in capital and entered plantation production. This was particularly true in the newer gulf region of Alabama, Mississippi and Louisiana. There was a very real sense of opportunity open for all and a species of democratic feeling arising from such a realization.

A second reason for the solidarity of the South was the presence of some three million Negro slaves. In important sections of the South there were more Negroes than whites. Some of the poorer whites had only the consciousness of their Caucasian blood to mark them as better off than the Negro slaves. If the Negroes were freed or the South abolitionized, certain regions would probably be Africanized. Therefore if white supremacy were to be maintained, Negro slavery must be supported and preserved.

Furthermore, the South was consolidated in its sentiment by outside attacks. During the period since 1830, the South had been subjected to a bombardment of continually increasing intensity. There had been abolitionist orators, politicians, preachers, literary people and journalists who had joined together in accusing the southerners of fostering a barbarous institution and in demanding various remedies ranging all the way from complete abolition to the prevention of the further spread of the institution. The development of this propaganda had caused a reaction and had produced a decided defense complex in the minds of the people of the South. As an antidote to the preachments of the abolitionists there was formulated the pro-slavery argument. Slavery was justified upon religious grounds from the Bible. The institution was a positive good from the spiritual and social point of view because it lifted the slave from the jungle and gave him civilization and Christianity. It was an economic necessity in that it was the only means of gaining profit from the southern plantation system. Finally it must be maintained because its destruction would overthrow civilization and thrust parts of the South into a state of barbarism. All these factors were working to produce an unusual harmony of ideas, most of which were defensive, among an extensive section of the population which in 1850 numbered 40% of the total.

This self-consciousness on the part of the South was rendered most ominous by changes of an entirely different character which were taking place in the North. In the non-slaveholding states there was no such social or economic unity. Instead of uniformity there was diversity and confusion of interest. In the eastern states, population was tending to congregate in cities where there were all sorts and kinds of business, and where no one type dominated. While the South was interested in one form of wealth, the East was engaged in the many forms of capitalism. The entrepreneurs of this region were adept in the use of money and were anxious to move forward, to try new things and to gain the satisfactions which could be obtained from increasing their wealth and power. But there was more to it than materialism. There was an idealistic desire to make a better republic by reform and "progress" in the ways of democracy.

Naturally the focus of both East and South was the emerging West. This was the most fluid and least stable region in the national aggregation. So undeveloped was it that it was a continual invitation to come and participate in the realization of its potentialities and thither hoards of people were flocking. The West had so many needs that spelled profit to eastern capitalists. Roads, canals and railroads if built would bring greater population and trade, and if the public lands were sold cheaply or given away, new communities and large dividends to investors of capital would be the natural results. To the East, the West was a great place of opportunity if there could be proper cooperation between American enterprise and governmental power. The West should be straightway developed, new states created, new sources of wealth tapped, and a greater United States speedily achieved. Many influences in the East, therefore, joined with the western promoters in working for all sorts and kinds of government subsidies.

The South on the other hand viewed the West with a different interest. The South was not interested in the speedy development of the new section particularly as geographic conditions were dictating that it would be a free labor region which would not be in sympathy with the institution of slavery or the southern economic and social system. Therefore if the West were quickly developed, the South realized that new free states would be created which would speedily outvote the older region and relegate it to a position of political inferiority. Consequently, when the question of organizing the new territory was brought before Congress there was bound to be a conflict. The South would be aroused to protect its interests and the question was whether it could prevent a combination of eastern and western votes from admitting the new states which would eventually deprive the South of its political power. A bitter political contest seemed inevitable and dangerous.

The first guns of this sectional conflict had really been fired at the time of the war for Texan independence when John Quincy Adams led a protest which prevented Jackson from pushing annexation in 1836-1837. The real conflict, however, did not break out until the project of annexation was revived in 1842. John Quincy Adams again appeared as the leader of a small group who attacked the addition of this great slave territory both as an extension of the sin of slavery and as a tremendous increase in the political power of the South. The Democratic party, however, welcomed the Texas issue and in 1844 was returned to power on a wave of expansionist enthusiasm. But the opponents of slavery extension were not discouraged.

When the Mexican War broke out, it was apparent that the United States would obtain some territory in the Southwest which would be convenient for slave expansion. Northern politicians opposed such acquisition from the beginning by offering the Wilmot proviso forbidding the introduction of slavery into any territory acquired from Mexico. This measure failed to pass Congress but the Democratic party split into two factions when the followers of Martin Van Buren were defeated in an attempt to make the Proviso the official platform of the party. In 1848 Martin Van Buren ran as a Free Soil candidate for President and deprived Lewis Cass, the regular Democratic nominee, of enough votes to elect the Whig candidate, General Zachary Taylor of Mexican War fame.

Northern public opinion further showed its hostility to slavery by encouraging the escape of slaves to the North. A regular system of aiding fugitives was established, called the underground railroad. This was neither a railroad nor an underground affair but it was a series of arrangements along convenient routes from the South to Canada whereby sympathetic householders would hide escaping slaves during

Trails Beyond the Mississippi

the day and then in the dead of night transport them to the next "station." Many sympathetic northerners contributed money, time and energy to hurrying fugitive slaves to freedom. When at rare intervals such helpers were discovered, northern governors refused to honor requests for extradition to southern states for trial and in many ways the South was given evidence that the North was ignoring the constitutional provision requiring the return of "fugitives from labor." The climax came when the Supreme Court decided in 1842 in the Prigg Case that the return of fugitives was purely a matter for the federal government and that the states were not bound to assist in any way.

In the next few years, various northern states took advantage of this decision by passing so-called "Personal Liberty" laws which forbade their citizens to aid the return of fugitives, generally providing a fine or jail sentence as the penalty of such aid. Such evidences of hostility on the part of northern citizens served to increase the sense of injustice which was embittering the South.

These signs all pointed to a bitter fight in Congress at the slightest excuse. The struggle came when the question of governing the territory acquired from Mexico was introduced into Congress. Had the normal process of migration into this far distant region been taking its slow course the matter might not have been so fraught with peril, but an unforseen rush of circumstances intervened. In the fall of 1848 the East finally awoke to the fact that gold had really been discovered in California. By the spring of 1849 many of the adventurous and hopeful had determined to go westward to find fortunes in this far away Eldorado. During that year at least 100,000 people entered California and overwhelmed that sleepy society of some 20,000 Spaniards and Indians with a curious motley of unorganized gold seekers. Prior to this influx of population the question of the proper government of the newly acquired territory had troubled few and the little government existing was administered according to the old Mexican local customs by the unenterprising inhabitants with occasional exercise of authority by the small American military force.

The Compromise of 1850

So large and so tumultuous a population pouring as it did into California brought a serious social problem. There was an almost complete absence of law and order. Anarchy was imminent, life and property, especially in the vicinity of the gold fields, was subject to the caprice of individual strength or cunning. The situation was pressing and the inhabitants took the matter of government into their own hands. Among the newcomers were many politicians well versed in the forms of state government. With the approval of President Taylor a number of these new Californians organized a constitutional convention and a state government, while duly chosen senators and representatives were on their way to Washington to petition Congress for the admission of California as a state. The constitution which they carried with them prohibited slavery within the bounds of California.

There was no doubt that action must be taken in regard to California by Congress in 1850. California had decided she wanted to be a free state. This decision, quite in keeping with southern ideas of the rights of a state, complicated the question of admission because her entrance into the Union would destroy the balance between free and slave states which had been maintained in the Senate since the Missouri Compromise. The census returns showed that the North was growing much faster than the South and if the South were to be denied expansion room in the West, her inferiority and loss of power were inevitable. The great tides of industrialism and foreign migration were passing by the South and pouring wealth and population into the northern states at a much swifter rate than the South could produce them. Finally the price of cotton had fallen off and the planters felt poor and dissatisfied. With these circumstances oppressing them, southern leaders were bound to fight against any further loss of power.

The Congressional battle raged for months during 1850 and finally after many despaired a formula of compromise was found. California, the new territories, their government and boundaries, the return of fugitive slaves, the status of slavery in the District of Columbia, were to be disposed of so that all issues might be quieted. Southern leaders surrendered their hope of a division of the new territory by a line to the Pacific and received a stringent fugitive law to be enforced by a specially created group of federal officials independent of state aid. California was to be free as she wished and New Mexico and Utah were to have the same opportunity to choose their own way of organization. The people of the territories, not Congress, would thereafter decide the slavery issue; southern and northern sympathizers could ballot against each other at the territorial polls. New Mexico's area was left intact in spite of Texan demands for half her territory and the Lone Star State had its debts incurred during its years of independence paid by Congress as compensation. Finally, slaves could still be held in the District of Columbia but no longer could they be bought and sold there.

Thus, by compromise all questions were laid aside and with secret heart burnings the prominent in both sections generally promised to abide by the result. Moves to secede which had been launched in the South suddenly subsided and, though there was much muttering about being cheated in the bargain, the southerners generally acquiesced. Ominous of the future, however, was a widely held determination phrased in resolutions passed by the Georgia legislature, to the effect that the South had made her last concessions. In the North "Union saving" meetings rejoicing in the outcome were held in many a city and town. But here again there were disquieting incidents pointing to future danger; in spite of the new fugitive slave law, the northern people were no more ready to return fugitive slaves and a series of rescues and riots led many a southern observer to believe that the law was not worth much and that the North could not be trusted.

The excitement died down as quickly as it had flared up. Like a wave of hysteria it had passed over the political consciousness of the country. Comparing it with the situation at the time of the Missouri Compromise it shows a marked and significant change. In 1820 when Missouri sought entrance as a slave state, the New England and Middle States were afraid. To them it seemed as though the southern strength was destined to be permanent, because of its hold on the Senate and the Presidency. These northern states felt the sting of a consciousness of political inferiority, they demanded and wrested a compromise from the South. Now, however, it was the South which feared that the North had forged ahead and with the threat of the Wilmot proviso seemed about to deprive the South of its legislative veto sealed to it by its equality in the Senate. The South now demanded and received the compromise. Would it be as practicable for its purpose as the Missouri Compromise, still in effect in the Louisiana Purchase, had proved itself to be? Would the natural adaptability of American democracy still prove effective?

A Bonanza Epoch

To those not involved in the complex emotions of politics it seemed plain that everything was to be gained by adjourning sectional disputes. For the early 'fifties were years marked by a great spurt of material prosperity. There was so much wealth for all, that time spent in sectional quarreling seemed such a wasted opportunity. The energy used in conflict if directed to wealth seeking would gain such an easy reward. Would the eagerness for wealth and national power be strong enough to overcome the passions of sectional rivalry?

For the time being it seemed that this might be possible for the early years of the decade, 1850-1860 witnessed some of the greatest steps in economic advance yet recorded and for a time at least, interest in the great project of producing wealth seemed effectively to have quieted sectional animosity. In these years the national wealth was more than doubled for in 1850 the nation was worth slightly more than 7 billions while in 1860 the figure was computed as beyond 16 billions, a per capita distribution of $513.93. Such an enormous increase in mobilized resources was due to a concentration of interest which engrossed the attention of the great mass of the population. The most favorable of circumstances were cooperating to create this great preoccupation. Improved means of production and distribution were at work upon the enormous resources, still so largely unused in spite of the efforts of the preceding generation.

The tone of the economic progress of the period was taken from the gold rush of '49; it was a bonanza period. At least four unusual circumstances contributed to the great acceleration. The Mexican cession provided an enormous new area for development. The discovery of gold provided a great supply of money to be used as new capital for many an enterprise. New supplies of labor too were at hand, for the migration from Europe stimulated by the Irish famine of 1846 and the failure of most of the revolutions of 1848 caused thousands of people to seek work in America. Finally, many new tools and machines were being introduced and improvements constantly invented. The reaper in agriculture, the sewing machine and thousands of others in industry, the railroad and telegraph in transportation and communication, all these made possible a rate of increase heretofore undreamed of.

There was an abundance of everything necessary for increased production: land, labor, raw materials, machines, capital and credit. Also the facilities for distribution were much improved, railroads were penetrating into the far away places and bringing the scattered portions of the republic into convenient compass. Business too, merchandising and selling were expanding, awakening an even greater genius for promotion as well as greater foresight and optimism which too often degenerated into speculating mania. Above all, there was more of that ability to organize, to invent, to vision big enterprises and to carry them through.

Land was plenty; but half of the great estate of the United States was occupied and people were eager to buy, deterred not at all by the government's nominal charge of $1.25 per acre. The drive of population westward was steady. During the decade prior to the Civil War, the Land Office disposed of 48 million acres. To peasants from the other side of the Atlantic, the ease of acquiring land was almost miraculous.

Many improvements made agriculture much more productive. The inventiveness which had come to the aid of industry was turned to farming and a number of labor saving devices was perfected. Planting was aided by the invention of drills and seeders which did away with the old method of sowing seed broadcast by hand. Improved harrows and cultivators lessened the labor of tending the growing plants. Hay-rakes, tedders, mowers and balers made hay making a much easier task. The greatest advances were in harvesting for a truly revolutionary invention was put on the market. Cyrus H. McCormick and Obed Hussey each invented horse-drawn mechanical reapers. This invention McCormick capitalized, built a reaper factory and by 1850 had sold about 4500 of these machines. Now acres of grain could be cut in less time than it had taken to reap square rods by hand. Nearly as important as the reaper was the thresher. John B. Pitts of Albany began making these in the late 'thirties and his machines now separated the wheat from the chaff in a way far quicker and more satisfactory than the ancient process of flailing by hand. Both of these machines were great labor savers and permitted a farmer to plant many more acres than when he had to depend upon scarce farm hands.

Hardly less important was the invention of the prairie plow which solved the problem of breaking the matted soil. In 1837 a steel plow sufficiently strong to do this work was brought out by John Deere and within ten years this implement was being effectively marketed. It came at a psychological moment. The onward march of settlement had about reached the limit of the wooded regions and stood at the prairies' edge. Now these immense level stretches need no longer be avoided because of the difficulty of breaking their soil. Furthermore railroads were built to a point where they could bring fuel and building material into these treeless areas. The man on horseback armed with the newly invented Colt revolver was beginning the conquest of the plains beyond the 98th meridian. Cattle and horses flourished on these grassy prairies and on the Texas plains a great cattle industry was in its infancy. Agricultural production increased between 75 and 100% in these years.[1] The profits were unusually high. More people wanted to become farmers and the petitions for cheap land multiplied. Increased pressure was put upon Congress to give away the public lands to homesteaders. The paths of settlement were pushing into Iowa, Wisconsin, Minnesota, Nebraska and Kansas. Prairie schooners followed the dusty trails to far away Utah, Oregon and California.

Industry boomed for American genius had learned how to multiply machines. The new urban industrial centers were flourishing. Literally thousands of forgotten inventors supplied devices great and small. The more common use of coal and steam power divorced industry from waterpower sites and made factories possible in any place which had or could transport fuel. New habits of life contributed to manufacturing: gas lighting and plumbing, stoves and furnaces, and sewing machines made profits for new casting works, rolling mills and assembling plants; so did the locomotives and rails of the new transportation. Larger scale production naturally demanded more stock companies and corporations displaced many individual mill owners. In 1860 one billion was invested in industry, twice the amount of capital so used in 1850. The use of labor-saving devices and corporation control were to limit the multiplication of factories and workers at the same time as production increased. In the great industries the rate of increase of product hovered around 75% during the decade, but the number of factories multiplied only 13% and the number of laborers 36%.

In spite of this great increase in investment and profits in industry, there were certain signs that the gains were not the most substantial.

[1] The trend of agriculture (in thousands):

Year	Number of Farms	Value of Farm Property	Cotton Bales Produced	Bushels Corn Produced	Bushels Wheat Produced
1850	1,440	$3,967,340	2,140	592,070	104,800
1860	2,040	$7,980,490	3,840	838,790	173,100

In cotton textiles, the mills were producing more than the market could absorb while in the iron industry organization was poor and failure frequent. A second ominous sign was the sectional character of industry's location. While manufacturing was found in some form or other in all parts of the country, there was a growing tendency to concentrate in eastern states. Cotton and woolen manufacturing in the Ohio valley actually declined during this period because of the keenness of eastern competition. Advance in the South too was slow. Cotton spinning factories were established in the southern river valleys where waterpower was favorable but in spite of the wealth of raw material only about 6% of the total product came from southern factories. Metal industry displayed the same characteristics. Only in Richmond, Virginia was there any notable production of iron; south of that point there were but six rolling mills in the entire section.

Meanwhile expansion went merrily on, invested capital doubled and the value of the products almost kept pace. The billion dollars invested in industry in 1860 produced goods valued at a billion eight hundred million. In 1860 the products of factory, mill and mine for the first time exceeded in value those of the farm. Figures were getting beyond the range of the ordinary imagination.

Such large production in field and factory was very intimately connected with an increasingly far-flung and effective distribution system which was developed in this star decade. Transportation and exchange, whether in the form of foreign trade or domestic wholesale and retail business, forged ahead and the product of farm and industry could be shipped and placed at the disposal of the ultimate consumer in a fashion and with a facility never before dreamed of. Most notable in this improvement of distribution facilities was the advance of rail service. 1850-1860 was the great railroad decade. Most spectacular was the spurt in mileage, the 9000 miles which existed in 1850, by 1860 had become 30,000. In all parts of the country there was building though the South and West with the greatest needs gained the greatest mileage. Railroads reached Chicago and the Mississippi and penetrated to the Missouri. Lines were built from the Great Lakes to the Ohio and the Alleghanies were crossed. In the South, Atlanta and Chattanooga were becoming railway centers and a scheme was pushed through for a line from New Orleans to Chicago. However, these roads were generally short, from one principal town to another, whence another railroad went further on. In fact, one hundred miles was a long road and the comparatively short lines of travel made through traffic impossible; many changes were the lot of passengers or freight bound for any distance. Such conditions could not be long endured and steps began to be undertaken to remedy them.

One of the greatest transportation achievements in the United States was to be the organization of large railroad systems eventually making possible through traffic between the most distant points. The decade of 1850-1860 witnessed the beginning of these organizations. The New York Central was created by the consolidation of ten railroad lines from Albany to Buffalo in 1853. The Erie extended from the Hudson to Lake Erie, the fabulous distance of four hundred miles. The Baltimore and Ohio reached Wheeling on the Ohio and made connections there for Cincinnati and the Pennsylvania connected Philadelphia with Pittsburgh beyond the Alleghanies. In this fashion was laid the basis for the great consolidation of the future.

Technical improvements were accompanying the more effective organization. Early difficulties in rail, coach and locomotive construction were remedied. Iron rails of the pattern now common replaced various wooden and strap iron experiments. The early type of car resembling the stage coach was superseded by the long car with an aisle in the middle and seats each side. Locomotives, too, had departed from the old mode of a standing boiler; the horizontal boiler with a tender for fuel, the funnel shaped smokestack and the engineer's cab, generally marked the engine of the time. Still many improvements were necessary. Road beds were badly ballasted, signals were lacking and, as the roads were generally single track, collisions were too frequent. On the trains themselves, brakes were clumsy and ineffective, cars were of wooden construction, heated by stoves and lighted by oil lamps which in case of accident often caught fire and caused loss of life by trapping the passengers. The locomotives burned wood which meant frequent stops to replenish the fuel but also spread smoke and burning cinders in too generous profusion. Seats were hard, the dirty cars jolted and railroad travel was anything but pleasant. Toward the end of the decade, crude sleeping cars were introduced and though poorly furnished and uncomfortable made night travel a little more bearable. Railroad trips were still uncertain and hazardous but popular faith was growing and capital was readily invested, for when a road was really successful the returns were great.

The building of railroads and their improvement and consolidation required capital in large amounts. Generous as was local subscription and freely as foreign loans were made, the supply seldom seemed sufficient to keep pace with the promoters' imagination. As in the days of the canal furor the question of government aid was brought forward. The scruples of the strict constructionist school were still apparent but a way had been found to offset their objections. The government might not give subsidy directly to railroads but there was nothing to hinder the assignment to individual states of portions of the public land which they in turn might grant to railroad companies. Such schemes found some favor and after Senator Douglas had succeeded in piloting a land grant for Illinois through Congress in 1850 other states received like grants until by 1860 some 30 million acres had been transferred to the states which they in turn had apportioned to raillines. In such fashion a railroad from New Orleans to Chicago had been made possible.

In the meantime, the acquisition of California and the gold rush focussed the attention of enterprise upon the possibilities of a railroad to the Pacific. Such an undertaking seemed entirely too great to be considered without government aid. There was no population for hundreds of miles of plateau and mountain region, construction difficulties were tremendous and the dangers from Indians not to be discounted. Government aid, however, was not to be granted without a struggle. In 1853 appropriations were made by Congress for surveys to determine the best route and the Pierce administration made tentative favorable pronouncements. Indian titles standing in the way in the Kansas region were extinguished and the Kansas and Nebraska territories were organized. Surveys showed four practicable routes and railroad promoters had many visions of a line of rails crossing the continent, not one line alone but perhaps all four routes might be used. However, the sectional difficulties becoming so formidable in congressional politics prevented the necessary legislation and in the meanwhile railroad investments mounted to a billion dollars, half of which were supplied by European capitalists and small investors.

Communication was made more effective by other improvements. The telegraph invented in the previous decade was promoted by the Western Union Co. The wires spread a network over the continent until the final triumph when a line was completed to the Pacific and opened 26 October 1861. Experiments in an Atlantic cable across the ocean seemed successful when Cyrus Field laid one in 1858 over which messages to and from Europe were sent and received for a few weeks. But it broke before long and it was abandoned for a decade. Overland mail and freight routes were established and a line of pony express was opened in 1860 which carried messages from the Pacific coast to St. Joseph, Missouri, in ten days. Also the reduction of letter postage from 5¢ to 3¢ in 1851 aided more general correspondence.

Business could not fail to be affected by the growth of railroads and communication, for the speedy enlargement of the selling and distributing systems depended on the perfection of arteries of commerce. With the growth of population and production business had been advancing into the West and wholesale and retail organization had to be enlarged and improved continually. As cities and towns expanded in the East these services became more elaborate.

In the wholesale trade a veritable revolution was invoked by the new conditions. The early western communities had been dependent upon rivers or roads and trails for their supplies and markets. The Ohio and the Mississippi were the natural routes for the marketing of grain, other farm produce and lumber. Supplies, manufactured goods, European imports had to come from the East and were expensive because of the difficulty of overland and mountain hauling. When better roads and the great canals like the Erie and the Pennsylvania system were constructed, the new lines of travel made western hauling cheaper and thus reduced the cost of goods but they did not provide rates sufficiently attractive to compete very seriously with the old river shipping lines. Consequently there had developed a three cornered trade whereby the West shipped to the South, exported through New Orleans and bought in the East using bills drawn upon New Orleans agents to pay for the goods purchased. The East bought some foodstuffs and lumber from the West but the bulk of the surplus was shipped south by the great river.

During the decades between 1840 and 1860 three new factors entered the situation. The growing industrial population needed more food, European demand especially in England increased after 1846 when British grain tariffs were repealed and finally the railroads provided attractive freight rates and, more important, speed of delivery. The bulk of western produce now began to seek Eastern markets. The Erie canal handled most of the lumber and grain freight while the railroads had two-thirds of the traffic in flour and the greater part of that in merchandise and livestock. No longer were economic ties with the South as binding and the Mississippi while it held its own absolutely, was relatively of less importance. When the uncertain days of 1860-1 approached this change of western economic interest was to prove very significant.

Retail trade as well was expanding. As the western communities grew in number and size, they needed more places to trade. Wandering peddlers could not long suffice and as farms stretched out, country stores with their miscellaneous stock appeared at the cross roads. Here much of the business was done by barter; farm produce was exchanged for goods, which the storekeeper had gotten through some jobber or other middleman in Chicago, Cincinnati or Cleveland. As the crossroads grew into towns, the country stores were no longer adequate and specialized services developed, dry goods stores, hardware stores, groceries, bakeries, butcher shops, furniture stores, drug stores, all these appeared in greater or less profusion according to the size of the town. Taverns became saloons and the retail liquor business generally throve. In one or two great cities a third step in retailing produced the first department stores, when a variety of lines of goods were mobilized under one roof to lure the taste and satisfy the needs of the "shopper." In most places, however, the storekeeper specializing in one particular kind of goods, met the needs of the individual buyer. He bought his goods from jobbers on "time" and tried to do a cash business. He generally went to the cities on buying trips or ordered by mail; the travelling salesman was hardly an institution. Business so organized depended largely upon the shrewdness and individual initiative of the small merchant and there was great diversity of methods of merchandising; prices too, varied and bargaining over the counter was the common way, the day of fixed price had hardly dawned. During this period, the influx of gold and the general monetary inflation caused by unregulated bank issues of paper money meant a continual rise in prices and in the cost of living.

The greater volume of domestic business was accompanied by a more prosperous foreign trade reaching to the far corners of the earth. Great Britain had thrown down her tariff walls; European industry needed more raw material; California and Australia had provided the world with a new money supply; and American diplomacy had opened trade opportunities with China and Japan. All these factors made buying and selling abroad a great enterprise and the figures for 1850-1860 showed two facts, first that American exports were increasing in quantity and value much faster than imports and second, that the balance of trade had at length turned in favor of the United States; by 1860 the nation sold more than it bought. Between 1850 and 1857 imports and exports trebled until each amounted to over one-third of a billion. Two-thirds of this business was with Europe; but Latin American and Asiatic trade was important and Canadian commerce after 1854 profited by a reciprocity agreement arranged that year. More than half of the imports were European manufactures. American exports were largely cotton, foodstuffs and lumber; those of manufactures doubled in value in the decade but still represented less than 10% of the total. The greatest export was cotton for American factories could use only about 20% of the crop, the bulk of it went to England and the bills on the British importing houses for the cotton proceeds helped to pay for the great mass of European imports. The great commercial advance sharply increased both the total tonnage engaged in ocean traffic and the number of American ships. By the outbreak of the Civil War, American tonnage was greater than it ever had been before or was to be again. Three-quarters of American trade was carried by American ships.

Passenger service by steamship, however, was a matter of some interest to American capitalists and in a few cases the government granted subsidies. George Law and W. H. Aspinwall organized services to Panama and the West Indies on the Atlantic and from Panama to California on the Pacific. More noticed was the attempt to compete with the British Cunard Line in the trans-Atlantic traffic. The mails and subsidies of money were granted by the government to the Ocean Steam Navigation Co. of New York, which established services to Bremen and Havre, and to Edward K. Collins who was in vigorous competition with the Cunarders between New York and Liverpool. Collins was very enterprising and for a few years persuaded Congress to grant him an annual sum of $858,000 for the carrying of mail. With this subsidy he maintained an imposing fleet of swift steamers which raced the Cunard boats with such effort as to cut down the time of trans-Atlantic crossing to less than ten days, the time still taken by some steamers. However, President Pierce who was opposed to subsidies, forced its refusal and the British regained the field. Freight after all was more profitable than passengers and the clippers carried our flag to the farthest ports in Australia and the Orient.

Weakness

The weak spot in this great series of enterprises was the system of banking and credit. It was before the days of the financier who gave his principal attention to credit and the organization of banking. Enterprisers were more interested in active management of some business or construction of some improvement and not so interested in the management of capital. The businessmen preferred to run factories or to build and manage railroads, to buy and sell rather than to dole out money and collect profits from others. Besides, due to the educational campaigns of Jefferson and Jackson, people distrusted banks, especially large ones, and banking was not a popular occupation. Early plans for sound general banking with government connections developed by Hamilton, Dallas and Biddle had been destroyed by political opposition, leaving banking to grow up haphazardly without system or regulation. Banks were numerous and becoming more so. Their numbers had increased from 824 in 1850 to 1562 in 1860, loans, deposits and note issues had all increased in about the same ratio and the capital of 217 millions in 1850 had grown to 421 millions ten years later. Two-thirds of the banking capital was concentrated in the East and in 1860 New York City alone was the home of 130 millions and the banks of that city did a business of 7 billions annually. In the South and West banking was either restricted in amount or conducted on a speculative basis without sufficient capital. The South deposited most of its surplus and did its banking business largely in New York and the West was overrun with the "wild cat" banking practices of former years.

The numerous banks functioned mainly as their directors saw fit because there was no federal and very little state regulation. If a bank chose to issue paper money far in excess of its specie reserve, there was little to hinder. The government issued no paper money and its gold and silver coinage was inadequate for the needs of business, consequently the people were dependent upon bank notes for their currency. As there was no uniformity in the soundness of the paper of the various banks, this confusion and uncertainty added to the speculative character of business.

With no organization or regulation each bank was a law unto itself and at the first sign of stringency the strong banks began to take measures to protect themselves and the many weak and speculative institutions had nowhere to look for help. Bank failures were common and the well-organized weakness of the credit facilities of the country increased the nervousness and apprehension characterizing the period of reaction and made panics more intense. Also, these conditions stimulated speculation in land, especially when credit was stretched to the limit and millions of dollars of paper money were issued on the uncertain security of fluctuating land values.

These vigorous years also revealed other signs of danger and weakness, not only in the economic structure but also in the political organization of the country as it was affected by the progress of economic development. It was not uniform throughout the country. The great strides were made in the East and West where a diversified series of projects found eager investors and promoters. In the South, however, there was concentration on cotton growing with only mild interest in railroad construction to vary it. Agricultural enterprise of this character called for large investments in land and slaves and a relatively moderate return in profits while the great variety of enterprises in the North proved much more remunerative. The South was receiving only about 5% annually on its investment while the East enjoyed a return of about 25%. The East, with a capital of but four-fifths that of the South, had an income three times greater.

Such a marked difference in turnover and capital productivity could not fail to be noted, especially in the South, and when it was considered in the light of the census returns, which showed that the population of the East and West was increasing much faster than that of the South, there could only be apprehension and uncertainty. Therefore, when the manufacturers began to seek a revival of protective tariffs, when railroad promoters and land speculators began to urge a generous distribution of public land grants to corporations and individuals, it is no wonder that southern leaders protested. For they reasoned that tariffs and subsidies would merely increase their taxes and expenses, not only without benefit to them but worse, to their permanent injury. Such improvements would tend to develop the East and West even more quickly and make possible new states in the Northwest. These states would naturally be opposed to the South, would destroy the veto power it held by reason of its equality in the Senate, and might even devastate the wealth of the South by abolishing property in slaves. Thus, this great economic advance, this display of productive power in America, which was proving so profitable seemed to brand sectional quarreling in the face of this prosperity as suicidal. Nevertheless in spite of its great promise of untold wealth in times of peace, the very bonanza tended to stimulate, on the one hand the great force driving the population to disperse into the vast West, and on the other hand the magnetic strength of the urban communities ever collecting a greater mass of people. The pull of these opposing forces tightened the tension which was aggravating bitterness and hurrying impending disaster.

CHAPTER XIII

THE IMPENDING CRISIS

The onward march of the nation was to be halted in the midst of this great period of prosperity and power. Not even national pride or love of profit and glory could protect the United States from the disasters implicit in the tightening tension. The 'fifties were to witness a series of crises pointing to the possibility of the destruction of the democratic experiment. Could democracy survive in so large a region where such conflicting forces were at work?

The Fight for Kansas

The first crisis was political. Events forced a reorganization of parties which was to put a severe strain upon the self-governing capacity of the United States. This political realignment was caused by the constant migration of population into the frontier region. Settlers called for more new land and for the opening up of new territories. The question of organizing new regions in the West was constantly before Congress. The five territories, Minnesota, Oregon, Utah, New Mexico and Washington did not satisfy the land hungry. Between the Pacific tier and latest midwestern communities was a vast plain, the balance of the Louisiana Purchase. Here were only roving bands of Indians and no white men, save Indian agents, might legally enter therein. But much of the land was fertile and through it lay the path to the Pacific. It was a constant attraction to the westward-looking populace.

The discovery of gold in California had aroused a demand for overland transportation and plans for a transcontinental railroad were in the making. Furthermore, an irregular advance guard had gravitated toward this huge no-man's land, to calculate its possibilities and to pick out fertile spots which they hoped some day to possess. More and more of this type appeared at the borders, crossed over and wandered around; in Missouri and Iowa the pressure for the opening of these areas grew greater each year. Politicians of national reputation like Thomas Hart Benton of Missouri and Senator Stephen A. Douglas of Illinois began to urge the organization of the Nebraska region into a territory. Without such organization no transcontinental railroad could be built, for railroads cannot go where there are neither settlers nor property rights. The organization of a new territory was therefore a normal and

236

necessary stage in the westward march but it was nevertheless to present a most difficult question.

This problem must be solved in the committee rooms and on the floors of Congress and Congress was in a new mood. Partisan politics were no longer very marked, there was little difference between Whig and Democrat. Instead the spirit of sectional rivalry and jealousy was the most decisive factor in the legislative halls, and the members cast aside party allegiance to follow local or personal interest.

Western representatives were anxious to get a number of promotion measures through Congress. Without adequate capital to do big things, the West wanted the government to help. The possibility of securing river improvements to make streams more navigable, to obtain public buildings and army posts, to have roads built, to secure grants of land for local railroads, all these were the hope of western congressmen. Political contests were fought out on these lines and success or failure in re-election often depended upon the representative's ability to bring home the fulfillment of his pre-election promises in local improvement appropriations. Also the drive for a more liberal distribution of the public land was a cherished western objective. On the other hand, the tariff was a matter of eastern interest, the protective cry needed only a slight measure of financial depression to force its renewed utterances. But southern representatives feared the speedy advance of the West and they hated high tariffs. How could they be persuaded to vote for these policies so assiduously advocated? The answer was that they could not be so persuaded without some drastic concessions to their own peculiar interests.

The southern attitude was apparent frequently and their representatives blocked many bills. Therefore when the question of organizing Nebraska arose their prejudices must be reckoned with. The territory lay above the Missouri Compromise line and was therefore free. Why should the South vote to organize free territories, eventually to become free states? The slaveholders in Missouri did not relish having a free territory so near as a convenient refuge for their runaway slaves. Their particular spokesman was Senator D. R. Atchison and he persuaded his southern colleagues to join him in a demand that if the territory were to be organized the Missouri Compromise should be repealed. Then, southern slaveholders might have a chance to go in and organize a territory where slavery would be permitted. Eventually, the new region might even become a slave state. The principal argument in favor of repeal was the claim that the northern members in refusing to extend the line 36° 30' through the Mexican cession to the Pacific had in effect repudiated the idea of division.

Furthermore, the principle of leaving the matter of slavery to the people of the territories if desirable for the Mexican cession must be

equally desirable for Nebraska. Senator Douglas who was promoting the
bill for the new territory cared nothing for slavery but he cared much
for western development and speculative enterprise both in railroads
and real estate. When the southern senators made their demand he
realized his bill could not pass unless he yielded, for they had the
votes. Consequently he agreed to the repeal and convinced President
Pierce that as the revised bill applied the principle of the Compromise
of 1850 (popular sovereignty) it was quite in keeping with the Democratic platform,[1] and necessary for party harmony. The result of all
this politics was the sponsoring of a bill by the Democrats to organize
two territories, Kansas and Nebraska, instead of one, to repeal the
Missouri Compromise, and to leave the question of slavery to the
inhabitants of the territories themselves. This bill became a law 30
May 1854, but it was enacted only after a bitter struggle; in fact
it was the signal for a renewal of political agitation of the sectional
issue which ended at length in civil war.

A New Party

The time was ripe for a new political outbreak. American politics,
like American business, experiences periodic cycles, each of which runs
through the life of a generation. Every score or so of years a new
generation arises which seemingly must have its political enthusiasm
and work out its political destiny by some new organization. Since
the years of the Whig ascent to power (1834-1840) there had been
a decreasing amount of enthusiasm. The Whig and Democratic labels
no longer meant very much and the former name was especially lacking
in attractiveness. There was little that was distinctive about the Whig
party, except that it was the more conservative of the two orders and
more responsive to demands of wealth and business; now it seemed even
to have lost the will to fight. Both the Democrats and the Whigs were
dominated by elder statesmen and the young and ambitious were kept
in long apprenticeship. The new generation was eager to go ahead and
it had at its disposal a variety of enthusiasms which it might use for
party reorganization.

Today we can easily point out that the free-soil anti-slavery enthusiasm
was the most significant, but it was not clear at the time that this was
so. There were two other current ideas that were also potent and
which appealed to the popular imagination, the one was liquor control
and the other, prejudice against foreigners and Catholics. These

[1] The campaign of 1852 had been a lifeless affair. Both Democrats and
Whigs had endorsed the Compromise of 1850 as "final." The Democratic
candidate Franklin Pierce defeated Gen. Winfield Scott who carried only four
states.

three causes fitted very well the typical American frame of mind. In the background of American national life were the old traditional English complexes. The religious interests of the Puritans deeply influenced succeeding generations and a hatred of such sins as slavery and intemperance as well as a dislike of Catholics which dated from the days of the Reformation were natural to many Americans. The Puritans also bequeathed to the nation a zeal for reform and a blunt mode of expressing antipathies which naturally made such questions matters of public notice and discussion. Consequently these enthusiasms found their way into politics because politicians knew the value of stressing ideas or prejudices which could attract popular interest or rouse popular excitement. These three issues had long been in and out of the central focus of political attention.

Reference has already been made to the agitation for various types of liquor legislation. The success of the movement in Maine to enact a prohibition law in 1851 stimulated the drys to more active effort in other states and for the first six years of the 'fifties the issue was fought out in many a political campaign. The Democratic party was usually "wet," so its opponents saw the value of espousing the "dry" cause which was gaining such popularity. In some states "wet" and "dry" tickets were run, in others candidates of the regular parties declared or dodged about the issue and received support or failed to get votes according to the predominant sentiment in the region. Between 1851 and 1856 all the New England states, New York, Delaware, Iowa, Illinois and Nebraska went dry, although Illinois almost immediately reversed itself. Favorable votes by Wisconsin and Indiana were nullified in one way or another. Missouri, Texas, Louisiana, Mississippi and Illinois adopted local option and Ohio by various statutes was almost entirely dry. In other words, the "drys" were in the ascendant and were a political power to be reckoned with especially as this issue appealed to the same type as were opposed to slavery. Most significant was the fact that their struggle was undermining the Democratic power in a variety of states.

The second issue which was attracting voters to organize was the "Nativist" prejudice. Ever since reformation times there had been a prejudice in the English tradition against Catholics and when in the preceding twenty years an increasing number of Catholics had migrated from Ireland that prejudice became active. These immigrants were very conspicuous especially in eastern cities because they grouped themselves together in clannish settlements giving loyal adherence to the Catholic Church and to certain political leaders in the Democratic party. Furthermore they would do laborers' work for less money than native Americans and consequently cornered the unskilled labor market. Their political power caused a counter organization and in several places, notably New York, Pennsylvania and New Jersey, "Nativist" parties appeared which though they seldom attracted many votes outside of municipal elections were a constantly perplexing factor.

The nativist movement revived at this time. Since 1846 a great wave of Irish immigration had been heading for America, augmented after 1848 by a German contingent. Their very numbers were a constant reminder of the old antipathy and events crowded upon one another. A representative of the Pope visited the United States in 1853-1854 to investigate an ecclesiastical dispute which had no political significance. Rumor began to fly around that this cardinal had come to promote a scheme of the Catholics to get control of the government. The fact that it was not true had no particular weight and secret societies began to operate in politics. The elections of 1854 especially in the East and South witnessed the appearance of a new force quite frequently spoken of as the "Know Nothings" which worked in secret and attracted large numbers of super-patriotic Americans to vote for "Nativist" tickets. They carried a number of states, notably Massachusetts, and elected a score or more congressmen. It immediately appeared to politicians that if this group could be united to those opposed to the Nebraska bill the Democrats might be universally defeated throughout the North. Events were working in that direction.

In the meantime the most significant of these three political issues also enjoyed a revival. In 1840 a few voters had supported a Liberty Party candidate for President and in 1844 this party had attracted sufficient voters from the Whigs in New York to gain for itself the credit of defeating Henry Clay. In 1848 the Free Soil party undoubtedly caused the defeat of Lewis Cass. Thus in the 'forties they had been a potent force but the Compromise of 1850 had destroyed their issue and in 1852 the party had cut no figure though still running a ticket. However, they had a shrewd group of senators and congressmen, small in number but fertile in resource. Salmon P. Chase and Joshua Giddings of Ohio, Charles Sumner of Massachusetts and Gerrit Smith of New York were alert for an opportunity to revive their waning fortunes while ever zealous in their chosen cause of arresting the spread of slavery. Therefore as soon as the idea of repealing the Missouri Compromise was advanced they launched what proved to be a thunderbolt, "An Appeal to the Independent Democrats." The press and the pulpit took up their cry and 1854 saw a variety of combinations, coalitions and alliances formed. Many northern Whigs and Democrats were attracted and joined in protest. In the same year that the Know Nothings were showing power in the East and South, there appeared a new combination, at first more potent in the West.

Enemies of the South, westerners who resented the refusal of the Democratic majority in Congress to pass promotion legislation, disgruntled politicians, old Whigs who saw a new hope in the rising power, Democrats who could not defend to northern constituencies the southern predominance in national party councils, the fighting "drys" who liked crusading against sin, and finally those who yearned for political adventure, all such heard the appeal and prepared to rally. Coalitions such as had been made occasionally since 1846 now became very popular. After earlier experiments in the spring came the notable coalition achieved at Jackson, Michigan, 4 July 1854. Here a state ticket was nominated composed of Whigs, Free Soilers and Democrats who had as their rallying cry "Restore the Missouri Compromise!" Such coalitions, sometimes called "Republican," figured successfully in the election of 1854.

When the roll of congressmen-elect was finally made up, there was one thing certain, the Democrats were in a decided minority. But the majority was so various as to defy classification; some were Republicans, some were anti-Nebraska Democrats, some were Know Nothings, some were Whigs. If these elements could be united there would emerge a powerful party capable of controlling the government. It was quite evident that no southern men would mount the free soil platform, but northern men might support Know Nothing doctrine. The new party might be an American (Know Nothing) or Nativist party, so strong was that prejudice in 1854-5. It would have the great virtue of avoiding sectional quarrelling and keeping politics on "national" ground. However, the events in Kansas pointed in another direction.

The results of the Kansas-Nebraska bill provided excellent ammunition for Republican political spell-binders and press writers. As soon as the territories were opened, settlers passed in. Nothing of note occurred in Nebraska but Kansas, just west of Missouri, became the stage of an exciting drama. The Missourians had expected to settle the territory, leaving Nebraska to the northern migrants, but this was not to be. Many who resented the repeal of the Missouri Compromise were determined to make Kansas free. An organization was established in New England to aid prospective settlers by getting them cut rates on the railroads and by selling them supplies reasonably. Their existence was unduly advertised and when northerners began to appear in Kansas in the summer and fall of 1854, many in Missouri were convinced of a plot. Northern money, they said, was being used to pay people to come and vote Kansas free. The Missouri planters would not submit to this "steal" without a struggle; so when the first territorial legislature was to be elected in March 1855 a horde of Missourians went over to vote, sometimes violently. The legislature thus chosen was overwhelmingly pro-slavery. The northern settlers in turn declared they would not submit to such robbery and an incipient civil war broke out when the free state people repudiated the territorial government and established one of their own. Some blood was shed, though less than generally advertised, conditions were very much unsettled and the Republican editors and orators made the most of it. Kansas was held up as a horrible example of the results of the repeal of the time-honored Missouri Compromise.

The Republicans saw a great chance to win in 1856 and bent every effort to gaining allies. Fortunately for them, the Kansas furor caused the Know Nothing party to split on the slavery issue and the great mass of the northern wing joined the Republicans. By this move, the great northern party feared by the South was organized in the spring of 1856. To combat this new force, the Democrats assumed a conservative rôle and chose James Buchanan, politician of long experience and "safe" views to be their leader. Their campaign was made on the issue that the conservatives must rally to save the Union from the destruction which would come if a sectional party like the Republicans should win —for then the South would surely secede. The remnant of the Whigs and the southern Know-Nothings joined to nominate ex-President Fillmore but their strength was sufficient to carry only one state, Maryland.

The Republicans entered the lists under the lead of a showy well-advertised figure, John C. Frémont, rather romantically called the "Pathfinder" because of his western explorations. He was not burdened with past political experience or known views; his platform called for free soil and a Pacific Railroad, there were to be no new slave states under Republican rule. With such a platform no southern votes could be expected, nor were they received. Frémont captured all the northern states but six and received 114 electoral votes. Had he been able to carry Pennsylvania and either Illinois or Indiana he would have been elected. In 1852 the Republican party had never been heard of, in 1856 it was within thirty-five votes of victory. The Republicans could look forward to 1860 with high hope.

Such a political uprising taking place in the short space of two years was of the utmost significance. For the first time the growing sectional antagonism had found expression in a formidable party. The Republicans made a frank sectional appeal, they were anti-southern, pledged to stop southern advance and to decrease southern power. Many southerners now thought they saw the handwriting on the wall, gone was the old nationalism based on compromise between the sections. The North was in a numerical majority and was growing fast, northern politicians were seeking to gain the power that comes to the majority and seemed careless if not antagonistic to the rights of the minority South. Could the South afford to stay in the Union if the Republicans should win? For the time being the northern party had been defeated, perhaps it might be permanently checked. Southern leaders were going to continue the fight.

The Panic of 1857

The threat of secession voiced by southern leaders during the campaign of 1856 was ominous of the troubled character of the years which were immediately to follow for the sense of relief which the fearsome enjoyed after the election was to be short-lived comfort. An economic crisis was at hand. The great bonanza was about to give out. For a decade wealth had been increasing faster and faster, more and more speculative ventures had been tried and had proved successful; apparently there was no end to the possibilities of American miracles. But the business cycle was about to complete another revolution. In 1854 certain signs appeared as warnings. A money stringency developed, the price of stocks, especially rails, fell, banks and business houses failed, industry slowed down with a noticeable unemployment resulting. This warning was brief and disregarded and 1855 and 1856 were marked by the same feverish advance; in the latter year alone, nearly 4000 miles of railroad were built.

During these flush years Americans had bought much abroad. The nation's exports were not large enough to pay these bills, but fortunately, so it seemed, European investors bought a great many American securities, notably railroad bonds and stocks. These purchases enabled American buyers to settle their balances on European exchanges without exporting specie to any large extent. In the spring of 1857, however, economic conditions were not prosperous in Europe, and consumers and investors stopped buying; worse, they began selling American securities and demanding cash. Such a policy not only cut heavily into American exporting business but it called for extensive shipments of coin to Europe.

In the United States, prices were high and stocks of goods were large, a great deal of money was tied up in land and in railroads and was not earning any immediate return. Therefore when heavy demands for coin were made from abroad, banks in the eastern cities were hard put to get it and began to call upon their western correspondents for loans when due. These correspondents tried to meet the calls by selling railroad securities and foreclosing mortgages with the result that the market for stocks and lands began to sag dangerously. Western banks were in danger for some months while heavy exports of gold were worrying the bankers of the seaboard but the crash was not precipitated until 24 August when a large credit organization failed. This was the Ohio Life Insurance and Trust Company which did an extensive business in the West and had many connections in the East as well. The large number of connections which this company had, made its failure a matter of concern to a widely scattered variety of business. Inside of a week eighteen firms failed in New York City and the number increased until the climax came in October when the refusal of the New York banks to honor their notes with specie meant that specie payment had ceased throughout the country. Not only banks and railroads, but industries as well suffered and many failed. The panic, however, was not of long duration, harvests were plentiful that year and in December New York banks resumed specie payments. Business was slow for two years but by 1860 economic enterprise had largely recovered its confidence.

The shock of the disaster caused the northern industrialists to take thought about the nature of their weaknesses. The fact of foreign competition was the most easy to grasp and the remedy right at hand. If there were a protective tariff a recurrence of these conditions would be less likely. During 1858 an organized demand for protection began to be promoted by certain manufacturing interests. In 1857, several months before the panic, Congress had passed a tariff bill designed to reduce the revenue which was piling up a surplus. Advocates of protection now pointed to this reduction as a major cause of the panic, which of course it was not and demanded higher duties. Naturally such agitation aroused the southern fear of the tariff, and did so at a time when southern leaders were led by the circumstances of the panic to be particularly arrogant on economic matters.

All sections had not suffered alike. Western land speculators and railroad promoters and eastern manufacturers and bankers had felt the full force of the shock but in the South the planters had continued relatively undisturbed. Cotton grew and Europe bought it; the money which the planters deposited or spent tended to bolster up northern banks and businesses. As a result, the southern leaders became obsessed with the idea that their section alone was stable and secure. Northern and western economic organization was weak and unreliable and without southern help from cotton, profits could not exist. The South therefore was indispensable to the economic prosperity of the nation. On the other hand, the South seemingly was economically independent and could get along very well by itself. In other words cotton was king and with it the South could, if necessary, easily maintain itself independently.

John Brown's Raid

The third crisis of the 'fifties seems at first glance almost a trivial incident hardly worthy of the notice of today. But at the time it appeared to many to have catastrophic proportions and its influence was disastrous. The anti-slavery crusade found in its ranks many zealots, and of some of them it may be well said that their zeal outran their discretion. Such an one was John Brown. He had been actively engaged in a varied series of episodes, not all of them too creditable, trying to force Kansas to be free. But after 1858, Kansas seemed no longer to need to be freed and Brown's imagination had leisure to conceive new plans for promoting abolition. The resulting scheme was an elaborate plan of penetrating into one slave community after another, forcibly freeing some of the slaves and organizing cities of refuge to which others might flee. By this means he hoped to make slavery impossible in region after region until the South gave up the institution in despair. Such a plan today seems absurd and chimerical, but in those days it motivated John Brown and less than a score of followers to attempt to put it into effect. Sunday night, 16 October 1859, he sought to inaugurate his scheme by capturing Harper's Ferry at the junction of the Potomac and the Shenandoah. Here he expected to seize the government arsenal and its weapons, free the slaves in the surrounding district and start a Negro republic. Harper's Ferry, all unsuspecting that sabbath evening, was easy prey to the little band but the slaves were not eager for freedom, the local militia soon gathered and by Monday evening the marines had arrived. The episode passed into history when John Brown, convicted of treason, was hanged, 2 December.

This ill-judged foray filled the South with apprehension and indignation. John Brown had received financial help at various times from prominent abolitionists some of whom were in close touch with Republican politicians. Although there is no proof that any of them had any particular knowledge of this last scheme of Brown's, nevertheless, many in the South were convinced that the Republicans were engaging in a plot to produce this most diabolical of all dangers in the slave states, namely, a slave insurrection. The memory of the Negro uprising in Haiti in 1791 had been kept alive through all the intervening years and it now flamed up into terror. Nothing could be worse than the fear of the possibility of fire, murder, and violence which would be sure to accompany such an outbreak. To emphasize the terror the governor of Virginia, when he found a number of murderous pikes among John Brown's equipment, sent one to each governor in the southern states to be exhibited as an example of what the Republicans were trying to do. Surely the Union if controlled by such plotters was unsafe for the South. If the Republicans should ever gain control, more John Browns would be hired to foment servile insurrection and to destroy civilization in the South.

In the North, on the other hand, the hanging of John Brown was but another evidence of the barbarity of the South. When an apostle of freedom sought to save the South from its shame, that wicked section hanged him. Thoreau wrote, "Some eighteen hundred years ago, Christ was crucified, this morning John Brown was hung." Both sides held the exaggerated opinions of troublous times. Nerves were jangling, blind fears were unleashed, fanatic zeal was abroad, judgments could not be sober nor eyes clear-sighted. Jealousy had bred fear and now fear was begetting hate. In such wise was John Brown's crazy foray a major disaster.

The Decision of 1860

As the year 1860 approached there were few who did not realize that the Presidential election of that year was to be crucial. Upon its result probably would depend the continued existence of the Union. The South was becoming more and more apprehensive of Republican success; for after John Brown's raid, it was widely believed that the Republican party had backed Brown and that his raid was part of a plot to destroy the South by organizing a series of slave uprisings. There was no such plot but the important fact is that many people believed there was and were determined to act accordingly.

The South, therefore, strengthened in the false economic assumptions of its panic experience and frightened by the growth of the Republican party and the raid of 1859, was coming to the point where it was about ready to take a stand before the nation and make an imperious demand. The Republican party must be defeated in 1860 or the southern states would leave the Union. The only institution which could seek to enforce this demand was the Democratic party. But that party was in an harassed and distressed state and events shortly were to demonstrate that it was in no condition to cope with the Republicans. The Democratic party in power with hardly an interruption since 1828 and victorious even in 1856 was on the verge of schism and disintegration.

The Republican party had made politics more complicated. Hitherto the major parties had been national with membership drawn about equally from northern and southern states. Hence the platforms had been compromises which favored neither section widely. Now the Republican party came forward representing but one section, the North. It had no southern wing, nor could it expect to gain any support in that region, consequently it was free to appeal directly and completely to northern interest. Such an opponent placed the Democrats in a difficult position. They must carry states in both sections to win national elections but how could they carry northern states if their platforms were in any sense satisfactory to the South, yearly more fearful of northern motives. The Democrats had adopted the formula of "popular sovereignty" which declared neither for nor against slavery extension but left the question to the vote of the people in each new territory. Upon this platform they had won by a narrow margin in 1856. However, this doctrine had been discredited since that momentous election.

In the first place, the Supreme Court had decided, in effect, that popular sovereignty was unconstitutional. In March 1857, the tribunal rendered its decision in the Dred Scott Case. This case had been brought

to the Supreme Court for political purposes by some anti-slavery men
and it was used by the Supreme Court justices themselves in similar
manner. The case could have been easily decided without much thought
or the preparation of extended opinions but one of the northern justices
seemed to consider it an opportunity to give a decided dissenting opinion
which would benefit the Republicans. Thereupon the chief justice,
Roger B. Taney of Maryland, was persuaded to write a lengthy decision. It placed in convenient form certain comforting doctrines for the
South and it was hailed by their leaders as the final word. In effect
Taney gave his opinion that slaves were property and could not be
excluded from the territories by Congress or by popular vote because
of the Fifth Amendment. This not only discredited "popular sovereignty" and the demand for congressional prohibition of slavery in the
territories made by the Republicans, but it encouraged extreme southern
leaders now to demand protection of slaves in all territories as their
"constitutional right." They would be satisfied no longer with "popular
sovereignty." It had been only a delusion to them and ammunition to the
Republicans.

Furthermore, "popular sovereignty" had been greatly damaged as a
political asset by the final outcome of the Kansas question. Shortly after
the election of 1856 the pro-slavery legislature in Kansas had begun to
arrange for the making of a state constitution. The free state settlers
had refused to have anything to do with this move and the result
was that the pro-slavery group controlled the convention that draughted
the constitution in 1857. Under Douglas' interpretation of popular sovereignty this instrument should have been submitted to the voters in the
territory. However, the pro-slavery convention submitted only one clause,
namely the question of whether more slaves might be admitted into
Kansas in the future. The rest of the constitution, which included a
clause guaranteeing slave property already in Kansas and which could
not be amended before 1864, was not submitted. The free state people
would not vote on a constitution thus proposed and the result was the
adoption of the slavery clause by the small group of voters who did vote
late in 1857.

A slavery constitution thus was sent to Congress as the will of the
people of Kansas. It had been perfected by all the legal forms but it
was apparent that it was the work of a pro-slavery minority and that
the anti-slavery majority in Kansas was opposed to it. Nevertheless,
President Buchanan urged Congress to admit Kansas with this slavery
constitution. His chief object in so doing was to take the Kansas question
out of politics and to prevent the Republicans from making political use
of it in 1860. Senator Douglas refused to follow the President, his party
leader, and attacked this plan. The outcome was a heated congressional
contest which resulted in the resubmission of the constitution to the

voters of Kansas by an indirect method.[1] The people of Kansas refused
to accept the constitution and in leisurely fashion made another, prohibiting slavery.[2] This result proved to the South that "popular sovereignty" would do nothing but produce civil war and the final expulsion
of slavery from any territory in the Northwest. If "popular sovereignty"
continued the South could expect nothing from it.

This contest in Kansas split the Democratic party. Senator Douglas
had the support of a great following of northern Democrats while President Buchanan could only rally the southern Democrats and a minority
of those in the northern states. Nevertheless Buchanan tried to "purge"
Douglas and failed. Douglas after an exciting contest for re-election to
the Senate with his Illinois Republican opponent, Abraham Lincoln,
won a close victory. But in that same election period of 1858, the Democrats again lost the House of Representatives. They were badly split
between the northern Democrats with Douglas as their leader and
"popular sovereignty" as their platform and the administration forces
led by Buchanan and a group of southern senators who were trying
desperately to find a platform and a candidate for 1860 which would
unite the party. Could the Democratic party survive? Its success seemed
vital to the continuance of the Union. For if it broke up Republican
victory seemed assured and a Republican victory would mean an attempt
at least on the part of the South to break up the Union.

As the convention of 1860 approached a group of southern leaders
were planning to demand a new platform from the Democrats calling
for protection of the slaves in territories by federal power. This demand
was strengthened by the fear engendered by John Brown's raid, and
seemed to have the endorsement of the Supreme Court. But how could
realistic national politicians accept this demand? Southern votes alone
could not elect a President, northern states must be carried. The four-
square northern appeal of the Republicans made that well-nigh impossible but northern Democrats had one hope, namely, Douglas of Illinois.

---

[1] This was provided for in what is known as the English bill. Besides making a constitution, the Kansas convention had demanded a great part of the
public lands belonging to the government in Kansas. Some such gift was always
provided for a new state but never in such large quantity. The English bill
ordered that this land request be resubmitted to the voters of Kansas. If they
refused to reduce it, they must remain out of the Union for some time, otherwise
they might come in with their slavery constitution. The people of Kansas voted
to stay out of the Union, not because they would not accept less land, but
because they did not want to be a slave state. The indirect method of permitting the voters to pass on this question was due to Congressional politics.
Northern Democrats insisted that the people be given a fair opportunity to
vote. Southern Democrats who did not believe in popular sovereignty refused.
The devious plan in the English bill was the only method which the South
would accept.

[2] Kansas was finally admitted in January 1861 after the first southern states
had seceded.

Douglas to the southern mind was unavailable because he had broken with the Democratic party leaders on Kansas and still claimed that in spite of the Supreme Court, in the end, only the people of a community could decide on their institutions. If they saw fit to freeze out slavery by unfriendly local legislation it could not survive notwithstanding any constitutional interpretation of the courts. In spite of southern protests, northern Democrats were adamant in their insistence on Douglas and his doctrine as presidential nominee and platform; without him their cause in the North was lost. Whereupon the southern Democrats left the convention of 1860 and nominated candidates of their own.[1] With the Democrats split, the success of the Republicans was inevitable.

The Republicans were quick to realize their opportunity. They nominated an "available" candidate, Abraham Lincoln of Illinois and enlarged their platform. Hitherto they had stood on a program of prohibiting the further extension of slavery and subsidizing a Pacific railroad, now they added two planks of great significance, namely, one providing for a free homestead for every citizen who wanted it and the other calling for a protective tariff. Western promoters and eastern industrialists still somewhat bruised by the late panic could not help but be attracted by these generous proposals.

The North responded with great enthusiasm and Lincoln was elected by the electoral votes of the northern states. The South had failed to prevent the triumph of the party which they had come to believe spelled destruction to white supremacy and slave property and the loss of the political domination they had long enjoyed. It was evident when the result was announced that a crisis was at hand. During the preceding months many southern leaders had been threatening, just as they had in 1856, that if the Republicans won the southern states would secede. The question now had to be faced, was the South going to carry out its threat? Was the Union at length to break up?

South Carolina hesitated not a moment but took the lead and on December 19 left the Union. What was to be done? President Buchanan was opposed to secession but pleaded lack of authority to prevent it and passed the responsibility to Congress. Congress considered the matter and the question of a Compromise of 1860 was at once agitated. Senator Crittenden of Kentucky, Clay's old state, came forward with a proposal to extend the Missouri Compromise line to the coast and permit slavery south of that line. This, however, the Republicans refused; they were pledged to prevent further slave territory and could not agree to an

---

[1] The nominees of the southern Democrats were John C. Breckinridge of Kentucky and Joseph Lane of Oregon. The northern Democrats nominated Douglas and Herschel V. Johnson of Georgia. A remnant of the old Whigs formed a Constitutional Union party and nominated John Bell of Tennessee and Edward Everett of Massachusetts.

arrangement which would permit slavery not only in the then existing United States but in as much of Mexico, the West Indies, Central and South America as the nation might hereafter acquire. So congressional hope faded, and as that died six other states left the Union in January and February 1861, Georgia, Alabama, Mississippi, Florida, Louisiana, and Texas.

Buchanan refused to surrender what little Federal property he could hold, most notably Fort Sumter in Charleston harbor, and made a vain attempt to provision that fortress, which was defeated 9 January 1861, when the South Carolina batteries fired on the ship and compelled it to

The First Guns of War: Firing on the *Star of the West*

turn back. Buchanan's chief aim continued to be to prevent bloodshed until Lincoln should be inaugurated and he pinned his hope on a peace convention of delegates from all states called by Virginia. This body met at Washington but failed to find a way to peace.

The seven states which had seceded, in the meantime, formed themselves into the Confederate States of America. Their provisional congress adopted a constitution recognizing slavery and states rights but otherwise closely resembling that of the United States. Senator Jefferson Davis of Mississippi was chosen provisional president of the new republic and organized a central government and an armed force. The great disappointment of the enthusiastic experiment was the fact that but seven of the fifteen slave states had joined the Confederacy. The future depended in great part upon the policy of the administration to be formed by Abraham Lincoln.

The new President of the United States assumed office with a determination to yield no ground to the South and although his inaugural was conciliatory in its spirit, still it left little room to doubt that he would give way to none of the southern pretensions. But his cabinet was not a unit. When upon the morning after his inauguration an urgent call came from Fort Sumter for reenforcements he began to study plans to provide them in spite of the fact that his cabinet was five to two against it. Several weeks elapsed before the decision was made but finally the force of events seemed to be with the President and his cabinet agreed to the project. Seward, the Secretary of State, still felt that Sumter was not worth bloodshed and if it were surrendered a plan for a war against Great Britain, France and Spain which he had devised might bring the South back to its loyalty. Lincoln felt otherwise, Sumter must be reenforced and he notified the Confederacy that the attempt would be made. The Confederate cabinet must now decide whether they would precipitate a civil war by firing upon the approaching relief expedition or yet preserve peace. The Confederate government did not hesitate. The success of their move for independence was at stake. Their sense of honor demanded that they drive the garrison from Sumter; besides they may have hoped that if they took firm action the other slave states might be rallied to join the Confederacy. So the die was cast. Sumter was bombarded and as the relief expedition was too weak to render effective aid, the fort was surrendered. When President Lincoln called upon the states for volunteers to recapture federal property, four of them refused to obey and left the Union rather than coerce their sister states. Virginia, North Carolina, Arkansas and Tennessee joined the Confederacy.[1]

The orderly procedure of American democracy had been abandoned. Rather than acknowledge the authority of a President regularly elected as prescribed in the Constitution, seven states had withdrawn from the Union. They had set up an independent government and resorted to arms to prevent the Federal authority from caring for its own property. Rather than join in reclaiming this property by force, four other states had likewise seceded. From the Federal point of view, these eleven states were joining in insurrection against duly constituted authority. From the Confederate point of view, they were but following the example of their Revolutionary forbears in resisting dangerous tyranny. Only force of arms could decide which was right. Democracy meanwhile must stand aside.

[1] After some hesitancy and under powerful federal pressure, military and otherwise, Maryland, Kentucky and Missouri decided not to secede. Delaware, of course, could not act unless Maryland did. Also the western counties of Virginia refused to go out of the Union and the Virginia troops which sought to hold them were driven out. In 1863 these counties became the state of West Virginia.

CHAPTER XIV

WAR

The bewildering series of events which culminated in the firing upon Fort Sumter produced an unprecedented situation. Within the bounds of the republic large groups of men speaking the same language and thinking in terms of the same traditions, were arming themselves and preparing to fight each other. The North was determined to prevent the southern states from destroying a great nation, and there was much talk of punishing traitors and whipping rebels; a great deal was said also of destroying the curse of slavery and there was some hope of breaking the power of the oligarchic planter class. The southerners on the other hand felt that their lives and property were in danger, and that their power and even white supremacy itself were threatened if they remained in a republic controlled by men with the ideas held by the Republican leaders. They must protect themselves by seeking independence just as their ancestors had done in the American Revolution. Each side was supremely confident of the righteousness of its cause and naturally as both were of the same nation and tradition the struggle was bound to be long and disastrous. Much blood must be shed, much property destroyed, with much excitement, suffering and sorrow.

The Strength of the Opponents

Two groups, one of about 22 million people, and the other 9 million, including 3 million Negroes, were entering each upon a tremendous community enterprise. The 22 million were to supply about 1 million men who were to devote a part at least of four years to the business of fighting while the 9 million were to contribute about 850,000. More than 5% of the population was to take up arms. But the remainder were by no means to be exempt from the struggle. Hardly a community or an occupation but was affected and even the many who took no direct part could not fail to realize that they were living in times that were out of joint. All paid psychological toll of one sort or another to the conflict.

The first problem in each section was mobilizing an army. The North had the small regular army for a nucleus and the administrative system of the War Department to provide direction and equipment, while the South had only the state militia systems to build upon. The resignation

THE YEAR 1860: A COMPARISON

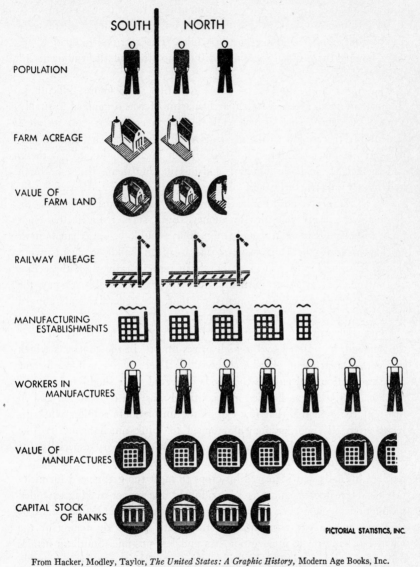

SOUTH   NORTH

POPULATION

FARM ACREAGE

VALUE OF
  FARM LAND

RAILWAY MILEAGE

MANUFACTURING
  ESTABLISHMENTS

WORKERS IN
  MANUFACTURES

VALUE OF
  MANUFACTURES

CAPITAL STOCK
  OF BANKS

PICTORIAL STATISTICS, INC.

From Hacker, Modley, Taylor, *The United States: A Graphic History,* Modern Age Books, Inc.

from the Federal army of prominent officers and bureau chiefs such as Robert E. Lee, Joseph E. Johnston, Albert S. Johnston, Samuel Cooper, and P. G. T. Beauregard did much to help the South and to hinder the mobilization of the North. Lincoln, on 15 April 1861, called for 75,000 volunteers and two weeks later he summoned 42,000 more; also he increased the regular army of 17,000 by enlisting 22,000 raw recruits. The Confederate Congress authorized President Davis to accept 100,000 troops and soon extended the number indefinitely. In both sections volunteering in the first months of the war was enthusiastic and continuous so that by 1 July 1861, on paper at least, there were 250,000 men enlisted in the hostile armies. The recruits, most of them, were having their first experience with camp life and the rudiments of military drill.

Munitions and supplies in great quantity were more difficult to obtain than men. The Federal War Department was organized to supply 17,000 men and when it was called upon to equip 150,000 it failed lamentably to respond to the pressing need. There was shortage or lack of even the most essential things, confusion in attempting to get them, and inefficiency in both obtaining and distributing them. But the North had money and factories and could rise to the occasion. In the South, however, there was no organization or supply of any sort to begin with, neither were there factories or money. Both sides realized that supplies, especially of cloth and munitions, could be purchased most quickly abroad where extensive stocks were on hand, so agents were sent to Europe for that purpose. Southern representatives got there first and made contracts but in many cases they were unable to pay the necessary deposits and installments, so that the Federal agents slipped in and took the goods for ready money.

In the meantime northern industry was working feverishly to meet the demand, stimulated by the high prices offered in the contracts which the War Department distributed lavishly. There was much waste and some corruption and part of the goods delivered were shoddy and below specifications.[1] But so hurried and confused was the distribution and so insistent the demands that few except the unfortunate soldiers who suffered from the poor equipment stopped to think much about it. The great pressure stimulated invention and new machinery especially for sewing uniforms and making shoes came into extensive use. The farmer too had his calls and increased his crops to meet the great need for army rations. Here too machines were invaluable, the reaper making extended production possible even while many a farm lad was enlisting. Lack of machines was a great handicap to the South as the tightening of the naval blockade made importation less and less possible. Southern armies had to depend on improvised industries and their not inconsiderable captures from the North in battle; the lack of equipment was to prove well nigh fatal.

Even more difficult was the problem of the navy. There again the North had the advantage in the possession of the Federal Navy Department and most of the navy yards. Only a few vessels, most notably the *Merrimack,* fell into the hands of the Confederates. However, the Fed-

[1] The Federal War Department spent $1,184,300,000 for supplies.

eral fleet numbered but 90 with only 29 steam vessels; these ships manned by 9000 officers and men were entirely inadequate to undertake the chief naval objective of the Federal government, namely, the blockade of Confederate ports. Many of the vessels were not in condition or were at distant stations in European, Asiatic, or African waters. The first task was to improvise blockading squadrons and the department went into the market for vessels of all sorts while the navy yards began to build as fast as they could. Inventors and ship-builders began experimenting especially in ironclads for throughout the world naval construction was being revolutionized and wooden vessels were giving way to armored craft. During the war 313 steamers were bought and 203 were built, including 60 ironclads. The personnel of the navy was

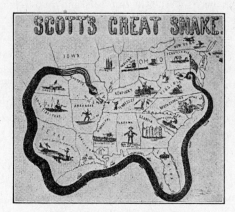

The Strangling Anaconda

increased to 59,000 officers and men recruited liberally from the merchant fleets. By the end of the fiscal year 1861-1862, the blockading fleets were in position and the cotton export, which in 1860-1861 had been 2 million bales, for the year following was reduced to 13,000.

Naturally the Confederate problem in naval matters was almost insoluble. The southern states had no merchant marine and no shipyards; building or chartering a navy within their bounds was impossible, so the attention of the southern government was turned immediately to the possibility of building abroad. Agents were despatched to make contracts and several war vessels designed to roam the seas were built in British shipyards. Some of these, notably the *Alabama,* caused much damage to American commerce and brought an increasing asperity into the tone of the protests which the American minister made to the British foreign office. At home the Confederates succeeded in getting a few vessels in shape, such as the *Merrimack* which was made into an ironclad and the ram *Albemarle,* but generally the local exploits of the Confederacy on the sea were confined to blockade running which profitably employed small swift steamers. These blockade runners succeeded quite frequently and their commerce kept the Confederacy supplied with quantities, all too inadequate, of medicines, percussion caps and a variety of other things sorely needed. The war, however, was by no means a naval war and in the North the naval expenditure was but 9.3% of the cost of the conflict.

The war machine thus created functioned with varying degrees of efficiency for four years, years of fluctuating hope and despair for until the last few months the possibility of conquering the Confederacy seemed often very remote. The South started with the advantage; not only did the Confederacy have the best officers of the old army but also had the benefit of fighting a defensive war on familiar ground. On the other hand, the North was superior in numbers and resources. Both sides, at the start, were too confident; in the North particularly did the belief prevail that one battle would decide the issue and press and public were eager to have it over. Despite the well-grounded fear of the Federal commanders that a raw army could not be depended upon in battle, pressure was so great that in July 1861 McDowell was ordered to march into Virginia and meet the Confederate army there assembling. The result was a Union defeat at Bull Run and the realization that this war was going to be neither brief nor one-sided.

The Diplomacy of the War

After this initial reverse, all hope of ending the war in ninety days was destroyed and both sides settled down for a long struggle. A human machine had to be trained and in the meantime increasing attention paid to diplomacy for there is more to war than battles and this war was to be no exception. While the armies were drilling and fighting, the diplomats were carrying on a duel which at times reached spectacular limits. The Confederacy confidently expected European aid in the early days of its career and the State Department in the North feared that such help might be afforded. England, the Confederates firmly believed, needed southern cotton and to insure such a supply would recognize the seceding states. As soon as the Confederate government was organized it ordered its cotton kept at home while it sent various agents abroad to secure official recognition in return for cotton. If England led the way France at least would concur and the ear of European capitalists would be obtained for loans.

Lincoln's Secretary of State, Seward, as soon as he entered office undertook to protest vigorously against any such recognition. Lincoln appointed Charles Francis Adams, Minister to Great Britain, but the appointment was not made right away and the new minister delayed starting, so events had raced ahead ere he reached his post. Great Britain realized the strength of the southern move and refused to accept the northern contention that these were rebel states with whom the outside world could have no concern. Therefore, seeing the reality of the situation, England on 13 May recognized the Confederates as belligerents (that is as a group of sufficient strength to be fighting under the rules of civilized warfare and not as rebels or pirates to be hanged as captured) and issued a neutrality proclamation. American protest at this action was of no avail.

In November 1861 when a zealous American naval officer stopped a British mail steamer and arrested two Confederate diplomats, James M. Mason and John Slidell, the nations nearly came to blows. Lincoln, despite popular approval of the act wisely apologized to the British. In the meantime, Confederate agents secretly let contracts in British and French shipyards for war vessels and the Confederate government continued to hope for recognition, holding back cotton importation as a sort of pressure to hurry the favorable action.

Europe in fact was generally sympathetic to the Confederate cause. The monarchical governments had no love for the republican form and would secretly rejoice if a republic proved unable to stand. Also the United States and England were commercial and political rivals and the mercantile and aristocratic classes of the latter realm had no love for this growing American competitor. Two nations would be easier to deal with than a united people. Nevertheless it was safer to wait and in the meantime the American navy grew stronger and more dangerous to British commerce. Still Confederate war vessels were built in British shipyards and were permitted to leave in spite of the neutrality proclamation. At length after the *Alabama* and the *Florida* had been demonstrated to be effective commerce destroyers to the great harm of the northern merchant marine and when it seemed that three more war ships were to be permitted to set sail, the crisis came. Charles Francis Adams in effect threatened war if these ships were not detained and in April 1863 the British Ministry put an end to this clandestine aid. Napoleon III in France was even more unfriendly, a large loan was floated by the Confederates in Paris and Napoleon used American distraction as a convenient time to establish a French empire in Mexico. Spain also made an opportunity and reoccupied Santo Domingo. Only Russia seemed at all friendly although her gesture of sending her fleet on a friendly visit to American waters was largely due to a desire to keep it safe from a possible blockade in her own ports by British and French.

The Confederacy was never successful enough to command recognition. Furthermore, the government would not offer commercial concessions to foreign powers and continued to boast of slavery. This was not a practical program in a very practical world. After Lincoln's Emancipation Proclamation liberal opinion in Europe generally swung in a northerly direction and the Confederacy's last gesture in the final days of 1865 to offer the abolition of slavery in return for recognition came too late.

The Varying Fortunes of Arms

Long before this tortuous course of diplomacy had developed, a desperate military conflict had raised alternate hopes and fears as the fortunes of both armies fluctuated. After the initial reverse at Bull Run the Federal command settled down to really train the army and George B. McClellan was chosen for that purpose. Meanwhile, a plan was devised for extended operations of conquest. One objective was to be the Confederate capital at Richmond. A second field of operations was to protect Kentucky, free Tennessee and gain control of the Mississippi. A third plan was to organize joint military and naval operations at various points along the coast and capture the seaports. The initial results were encouraging. By February 1862, Grant had opened up the Tennessee and Cumberland rivers by his victories at Forts Henry and Donelson and Pope by capturing Island No. 10 had begun the conquest of the Mississippi. The coast defenses of North and South Carolina had been penetrated and in April, New Orleans was captured.

McClellan was not equally fortunate in his drive on the Confederate capital. He had gathered a grand army and advanced on Richmond up the Peninsula between the York and James rivers. Much to the dismay of the North he failed utterly after a series of costly battles and by 1 July 1862 was in retreat. Pope was brought on from his victories in the West to take McClellan's place, and he failed in a third attempt to approach Richmond in the second battle at Bull Run, 30-31 August. Lee then started to lead the Confederates in a northern invasion and McClellan, hastily restored to command, barely defeated him at Antietam, 17 September. McClellan failed to follow up his advantage and was permanently suspended but his successor Burnside was even more unfortunate. His attempt to march on the Confederate capital was stopped at Fredericksburg, 12 December. The year 1862 which had started out so auspiciously closed in disaster, even in the West attempts to hold Kentucky and Tennessee had ended in the bitterly fought stalemate at Stone River from which neither side could gain much credit.

In the spring of 1863 Grant went into active operation to complete the opening of the Mississippi now controlled by the Confederates at but one important point, Vicksburg, undertaking the tedious and difficult task of besieging this town. Meanwhile the army of the Potomac now under its fifth commander, Hooker, started out over the ground covered by three unfortunate predecessors with the same result, a disastrous defeat at Chancellorsville, 1-3 May 1863, in the course of

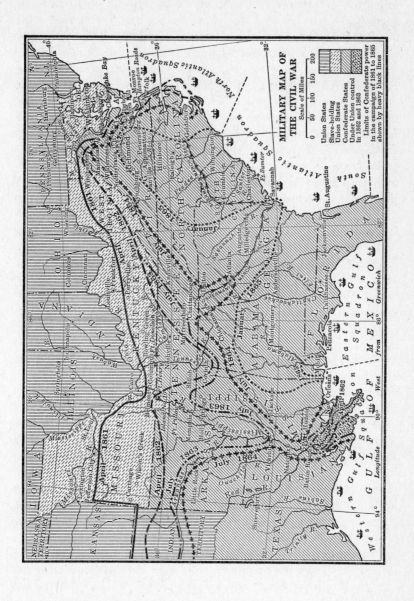

MILITARY MAP OF
THE CIVIL WAR

Scale of Miles

0 50 100 150 200

Union States
Slave-holding
Union States
Confederate States
Under Union control
in 1862 and 1863
Limits of Confederate power
in the campaign of 1861 to 1865
shown by heavy black lines

which, however, the Confederacy suffered an irreparable loss in the killing of one of its ablest generals, "Stonewall" Jackson. Heartened by this great victory, Lee now planned a second offensive and crossed the Potomac once more into Maryland and thence into Pennsylvania where his advance riders got within sight of Harrisburg. To stem this invasion, Lincoln chose a sixth general, George G. Meade, who succeeded Hooker on the eve of what all sides conceded was to be a decisive contest. The war's most famous battle was fought July 1-3 in the vicinity of Gettysburg. Lee was turned back but Meade was too exhausted to follow up his victory. Then as the North was rejoicing over this great triumph came the news that Grant had captured Vicksburg.

These successes did not spell the end. Tennessee was still undelivered in spite of much campaigning and when Rosecrans proved unequal to the task at Chickamauga on 4 September 1863, Grant, Sherman, Sheridan and Thomas all joined to undertake brilliant operations around Chattanooga at Christmastide. Success was theirs and focussed attention on these generals who unlike so many others seemed able to win battles. Evidently the time had come to capitalize their genius. In February 1864 Lincoln made Grant a lieutenant-general and gave him full command of all the armies. A scheme of grand strategy was worked out by Grant and Sherman and their forces prepared for what was hoped would be the final offensives. Grant was to lead the army of the Potomac once more against Richmond, while Sherman was to move from Tennessee into northern Georgia with the railroad center of Atlanta as his first objective. Thence he was to march to the sea and come up behind Richmond through the Carolinas. A union with Grant would complete the strangling of the South.

Grant's initial moves were not encouraging. After desperate fighting in the Wilderness, at Spottsylvania Court House, Cold Harbor and the Petersburg mine, by 30 June 1864 he was still far from capturing Richmond and had to settle down to a siege of Petersburg. Sherman meantime had made a slow but steady advance into Georgia, ably resisted by Joseph E. Johnston. His ultimate triumph in the capture of Atlanta 2 September 1864 was the first good news to reach the North in many a weary month. That victory was the beginning of the end. Sherman cut loose from all communications and began his triumphal march to the sea, living off the countryside. Sheridan, too, had been active and after the last Confederate advance under Early had reached the outskirts of Washington and been turned back, the dashing cavalryman succeeded in clearing out the Shenandoah valley, scene of so many Union defeats. Christmas day brought the tidings that Sherman had captured Savannah. The end was near.

Nothing could stop Sherman now, his victorious army marched through South Carolina and by March was in the old North state.

He was almost to his task's end and so near home was he that he determined to seek Grant and hold final conference. At City Point, Virginia, therefore in the last days of March 1865, Lincoln, Grant and Sherman laid the plans for the final offensive. It was brief and on 9 April Lee surrendered to Grant while on 26 April Johnston capitulated to Sherman. The war was over.

Civilian Participation

Though the military and diplomatic features of the contest were spectacular and served as a visible gauge of conflicting fortunes the real importance of the war lay in its effect upon the civilian pursuits of the sections. The war provided many opportunities as well as many dangers, it produced violent changes in the lives and fortunes of many who never shouldered a rifle or boasted a shoulder strap and it vitally affected the future development of the nation.

In the first place there were four years of civilian conflict. Many opposed the war and by speaking and writing voiced bitter disapproval, some even went so far as to organize in secret such orders as the Knights of the Golden Circle which spent much energy in discouraging enlistments, opposing the draft and spreading defeatist propaganda. These people were generally classed as "Copperheads" and social ostracism, imprisonment and political persecution were often their portion. The Federal government took drastic steps. Lincoln early suspended the privilege of the writ of habeas corpus and in many instances arbitrarily arrested the traitors; on one or two occasions the government actually suppressed newspapers. The worst manifestation of this opposition was in the dangerous draft riots in New York in the summer of 1863 when several hundred were killed and some property destroyed. Confederate agents operating on the Canadian border were sometimes in touch with these disloyal orders and plotted raids and other means of hindering Union war making, generally with slight success.

The Confederacy, too, had similar opposition to deal with and in some sections the opponents of the war turned marauders and carried on guerrilla warfare; for in both sections the draft was administered in such fashion as to emphasize the ease by which people of even moderate property might escape military service. In the North all who could pay $300 were exempt and much of the bitterness in the New York draft riots was caused by violent resentment among the poor against this glaring privilege of those who could command some money. In the South plantation owners and overseers were exempt on the theory that they were needed to control the slaves and keep up the agricultural production. There was a consciousness of class not congenial to the atmosphere of democracy.

As bitter as this opposition to the war, and even more spectacular, was the political conflict waged against the presidents of each of the governments by their partisan opponents, generally in the legislative branches. Lincoln evolved two policies in the first month of the war which brought him into conflict with a violent and determined wing of his own party. Lincoln made it clear that he held the war to be fought to preserve the Union, not to free the slaves and furthermore he sought to gain the aid of all parties in order to insure united effort and quick results. To Republicans of the radical type, his refusal to advocate abolition of slavery and his attempt to fraternize with the Democrats were both political heresy. Even worse in their eyes than his policies were his practices. Lincoln realized that in times of emergency action must often be taken at once to be effective and that legislative bodies were frequently ineffective and slow. Consequently he interpreted his powers as commander-in-chief very liberally. He called for volunteers, he increased the army, he declared a state of war and a blockade, he authorized expenditures, he suspended the privilege of the writ of habeas corpus, he permitted arbitrary arrest and imprisonment without trial, he suppressed newspapers. Congress generally validated these acts after their promulgation but the President's independence of Congress gave his radical enemies many opportunities for attack.

Of all these policies and practices the one pressed by his enemies most effectively was the question of the slaves. There was continual pressure for abolition. In 1861 and 1862 Generals Frémont and Hunter tried to force the issue by ordering slaves within their lines freed but in each case Lincoln overruled their orders, reiterating his stand that this was a war for the Union and if the Union could be saved without abolishing slavery he was ready to so restore it. Finally, however, pressure from his party, the realization of the hopelessness of peaceful reunion and the knowledge that liberal opinion in Europe was withholding support of the Union cause because he had made no move against slaves convinced Lincoln that the time had come to act. At a time when his enemies were attacking his arbitrary use of power and his refusal to sanction abolition he confounded them with a single act. He declared the slaves within the Confederacy emancipated, by his own proclamation as commander-in-chief. In this way he made himself stronger than ever, he had taken from his enemies their chief criticism and had increased his own power. After issuing a preliminary proclamation in September 1862 he finally decreed that on and after 1 January 1863, all slaves within the Confederacy would be free, except in parts of Louisiana and Virginia held by the Union forces. His action was later ratified by the Thirteenth Amendment to the Constitution freeing all slaves, declared in effect in December 1865.

In spite of his continued victory over his political enemies which was manifested in numerous ways, the lack of definitive victory to Union arms caused many to feel the war a failure. In 1864 Lincoln succeeded in reorganizing the Republican party into a Union Party embracing the loyal Democrats and in renominating himself with a war Democrat, Andrew Johnson of Tennessee, as his running mate. So dark were his prospects during the summer of 1864 that even Lincoln himself became convinced that his Democratic opponent George B. McClellan would be elected. Sherman's capture of Atlanta, however, is credited with turning the tide and in the November balloting Lincoln carried all states save three. Thus triumphant, however, he must prepare for another battle over reconstruction. He had already started in Louisiana, Tennessee and Arkansas to restore the state governments by granting amnesty to those who would take an oath of allegiance and agree to accept emancipation and he was planning to restore civil government as soon as possible. His opponents, however, thought this too easy and wanted to punish the seceded states. What the outcome would have been must ever be a mystery. Booth's pistol shot spared Lincoln the impending conflict.

In the South there was similar battle between Davis and many of the southern politicians. War must be waged by a strong central command and Davis realized it. But southern politicians had been preaching states rights so long that their vision was blinded and they fought centralization as vigorously as they had fought northern attempts to limit slavery. Conflict then was Davis' lot and state governors like Brown of Georgia and Vance of North Carolina in the name of states rights did much to hinder effective war making and contributed not a little to the defeat of the Confederacy. Davis, lacking Lincoln's tact and political shrewdness, never could turn his enemies' attacks to his own advantage. The southern leaders were trained to attack not to cooperate and that fact was a fatal weakness.

In contrast to this spirit of strife and contention there was great cooperation and self-sacrificing effort on both sides to support the armies in the field. Much civilian aid was rendered the armies. In the North it was early evident that the army medical service was inadequate and that the sick and wounded must be cared for in more effective fashion than the army could provide. In June 1861 the United States Sanitary Commission was recognized by the government. This organization functioned throughout the entire war, collected much money, procured great quantities of hospital supplies and comforts and enlisted the aid of thousands of men and women. It supervised all hospitals and worked vigorously to make them sanitary and to provide proper nursing and diet for the wounded. A great number of women went to the hospitals to act as nurses and many more made bandages and preserves at home to be sent to the front. Their task was arduous for 318,000 were wounded in the four years in the northern army and about 10% of the army was sick throughout the war.

Another organization was the Christian Commission which sought to provide religious worship and desirable recreation in the many hundreds of camps where temptations were by no means lacking and a moral atmosphere sometimes difficult to maintain. This group functioned in a manner similar to the Y.M.C.A., Knights of Columbus, Salvation Army, or Y.M.H.A. in later time, just as the Sanitary Commission anticipated the Red Cross. These organizations provided an outlet for the patriotic enthusiasm of multitudes of non-combatants and gave them the satisfaction of a feeling of active participation in the cause.

The war did much to galvanize religious activities. Many a church parlor was turned into a sewing room for soldiers' supplies and surgical dressings. Women's religious organizations of all sorts did much to plan and mobilize aid particularly for the convalescent. The pulpits too were forums from which to preach a holy war. Both northern and southern clergymen were fervent in blessing the arms of their young men and fast days and seasons of prayer and humiliation were proclaimed by the highest authorities. In the midst of the conflict, too, came revivals which reached their height in 1864. Anxiety and sorrow brought many to the churches.

As the war penetrated into the enemy's country a new call was made upon philanthropy. The Negroes who fled to the Union lines or whose masters had abandoned them were in many respects in need of aid. As early as the first winter of the war the charitably inclined in large cities like New York, Boston and Philadelphia organized Freedmen's Relief Associations. In spite of much benevolent confusion relief camps and freedmen's colonies were established. Not until March 1865 did the government assume its share of the responsibility by organizing a freedmen's bureau.

While the military and charitable energies of both sections were so mobilized by war, the economic system was submitted to tremendous strain and pressure. At the outbreak of the war, northern business was in panic. The northern financial structure shook, millions of dollars' worth of southern debts seemed lost and the future of the nation was in doubt. Public confidence in public credit was shaken, securities of all sorts declined in value and many stopped economic planning; business seemed at a standstill. But such a condition of panic was brief. Opportunities followed in amazing succession. The armies must be fed, clothed and equipped in a hurry with no questions asked about expense. Enormous sums of money had to be raised by the government and in so doing the financial system of the nation was entirely transformed.

The war was to cost in the immediate four years some 3 billions in the North and 2.7 billions in the South. Such a vast outlay was a

severe strain upon the resources of both sections and placed a premium
upon the financial ingenuity of financiers and politicians. Heretofore the
annual expenditures of the federal government had been less than 70
millions and the debt in 1861 amounted to but 75 millions. Before the
war had advanced very far the Federal government was called upon
to spend 2 millions a day, and extraordinary means of raising revenue
had to be devised. Imposing taxes was undertaken, but collection would
have to be slow and besides there is always a limit to taxation. Because
of the unpopularity of such levies, politicians are apt to set this limit
rather low. In the course of the war, however, a direct tax was levied
upon the states according to population as the Constitution provides.
Also, an income tax was voted. Internal revenue was collected by
means of a wide variety of stamp taxes so that hardly any sale or other
business transaction failed to yield some revenue. To compensate American manufacturers for this burden, high protection was placed upon
manufactured goods, in fact before the war was over the manufacturers
were permitted practically to write their own tariff schedules. By this
great variety of means, 667 millions in taxes were raised, or 20% of
the money expended. Most of the remainder of the funds were borrowed. During the four years nineteen different forms of certificates of
indebtedness were issued bearing five different rates of interest. The
total amount thus obtained amounted to 2 billions or 75% of the
immediate cost.

The need for such large sums in cash found the currency system of
the country entirely inadequate. The coin of the nation amounted to
only 160 millions and of this 28% was in the South. The bulk of the
business of the country was done with the notes of the 1496 banks.
These notes were unregulated by the government and often insufficiently
backed, in fact the banks had but 87 millions in coin to meet note obligations amounting to 459 millions and in December 1861 government
and banks alike suspended specie payment. Gold became a commodity
and the nation was faced with the use of state bank notes of uncertain
value or a resort to barter. To provide money for the extraordinary war
expenses the government in 1862 issued 150 millions worth of greenbacks or legal tender notes and required all to accept them in payment
of debts. This amount was later increased to 450 millions and the government paid out these notes and then reissued them many times during
the course of the struggle. As the government would not redeem these
notes, their value fluctuated with the fortunes of the Federal armies
and in one of the dark hours of the war a paper dollar fell as low in
value as 39¢ in gold, never were they at par.

Such a currency was unstable and as the war dragged on, bonds did
not sell very readily so a new scheme was devised which it was hoped
would provide a stronger currency and a market for bonds. In 1863,

1864, and 1865 a series of acts was passed establishing a system of national banks. Hereafter such banks bought bonds, deposited them with the United States Treasury and were then given national bank notes to the amount of 90% of the market value of the bonds. Furthermore the government taxed the state bank notes out of existence, thus forcing banks which desired to issue currency to become national banks. This plan was not prepared in time to create an extensive national bank system under government supervision before the war closed; it grew up afterward and remained in operation until superseded in 1913 by the Federal Reserve.

These vast financial operations and their accompanying spectacular derangement of ordinary business were paralleled by equally great demands and startling changes in the productive system. The manufacturing resources of the nation were strained to the uttermost to meet wartime needs for munitions and other equipment. In order to aid industry in its unexpected task the government inaugurated policies which were to have lasting results. To compensate manufacturers for high internal taxes, Congress raised the tariff to high protective levels. Besides, in order to provide an adequate labor supply, a law was passed permitting the importation of contract labor from Europe. Agriculture too was met by the same demand and here again the government stepped in. As the southern representation was no longer in Congress to block the move, the national legislators were now free to push westward expansion. So in 1862 they passed the homestead bill so long debated giving all citizens or intended citizens 160 acres of land and subsidized a Pacific railroad by grant of land and a bond issue. By the Morrill Land Grant Act, land was given to each state to aid in the establishment of colleges to teach agriculture and the mechanic arts. Immigrants were attracted by these free lands and the farming areas of the West developed rapidly.

Oil was discovered and new supplies of gold and silver unearthed so that much activity occurred in these lines, new companies sprang up hastily and their stocks began to have a ready sale. Business itself took on a feverish tone not only because of the increase in production but also because of the unstable character of the currency. After the early months of 1862 most business was done with "greenbacks" which fluctuated violently and showed a general downward trend. Money became cheap, prices rose and speculation was the order of the day.

The possibility of combining profit with invasion was easily understood. As the armies entered the cotton district they found large numbers of cotton bales. There was a cotton shortage in the North. Evidently this cotton should be used. The treasury licensed certain individuals to go in and bring it out. Army officers took an interest and helped locate cotton, for a share in the proceeds. Also numerous southerners saw opportunity and got their cotton to the Union agents in return for money and even military supplies. In fact the traffic became so large as to amount to half a million dollars a day through military lines on the Mississippi. Northern greed furnished much aid to southern armies. Equally unpleasant are the sordid tales of graft, which show Union soldiers suffering from cold and disease because contractors had supplied shoddy uniforms and pasteboard shoes, which tell of diseased horses sold for cavalry and artillery purposes, bad rifles for good, cotton blankets for wool, and many other items of like shameful practice. Profiteers fattened.

Large fortunes were being made in industry, and agriculture was profitable, there was a great deal of money for investment and so the speculators flourished. While the thousands were being killed or wounded on the battle fields, the hundreds were reaping a rich reward in supplying the armies, opening up new business or agricultural enterprises, or in speculating on the chances of victory or defeat. But wages did not rise as fast as prices and the poor suffered in the midst of plenty. It seemed "a rich man's war and a poor man's fight."

Economic conditions in the South presented a different picture, for the South was but poorly equipped to meet its problems of finance and production. The South had infinitely greater difficulty with finance than the North. The South at the beginning of the war had few banks and little gold; only 20% of the nation's banking capital was located there and the gold supply amounted to about 40 millions. Worse, there was little industry or commerce and the greater part of the wealth of the section was invested in land and slaves and devoted almost exclusively to the raising of cotton. The South expected to finance its enterprise with the proceeds of cotton sales abroad. However, in the early days the Confederates held back their cotton expecting to use the threat of cotton famine as a weapon to enforce recognition by the European powers. That plan failed and when southern statesmen were ready to export, the Federal blockade was too strong. Therefore the South never realized on its great crop except in a very limited way through blockade running and more or less illicit trade with the North. With the chief resource gone the Confederate government borrowed as much as it could and issued ever increasing amounts of paper currency. Without gold or without means of getting it, only one result was possible, the voluminous paper currency amounting to at least 800 millions fell to 3¢ on the dollar in the final days of the war. Taxes brought in little with the currency so valueless and in order to keep going the Confederacy impressed supplies and levied taxes in kind to be paid in produce. The war closed with an outstanding indebtedness of nearly 1 billion all of which was a total loss to its holders. But on both sides the cost of the war had only begun when the war ended. The amounts spent in war pensions alone in the years that followed to say nothing of loan funding and many other expenses, made the billions of cost pile up.

As in finance so in production, the South suffered under severe handicaps. That section had developed relatively little business interest before the war, and had little material from which to stimulate enterprise during the conflict. There was no immigration, no westward advance, no new mineral wealth discovered. The South continued in its agricultural state and though a great variety of small industrial attempts were made, no permanent advance was accomplished. Confederate currency became practically worthless and barter oftentimes took the place of regular buying and selling.

Some speculators flourished in the South. Though the blockade prevented the expected large import and export business, it was from the blockade that some profitable speculative business developed. The blockade runners brought an uncertain and miscellaneous amount of merchandise into the country and took out an equally uncertain amount of cotton. Speculating on the precarious foreign trade permitted some profiteering and created a few wealthy, a number of whom traded with the enemy. Most disillusioning was the absolute failure of the South to develop any creative or organizing talent in meeting its needs. The South had iron and fuel but it never exploited them. It devoted its whole mechanical energy to munitions and while the vital transportation system broke down, ruining chances of mobilization and supply, not a bar of railroad iron was rolled.

The strain of warfare left an impression upon American life which was to last long after the guns ceased firing. For four years there had been anxiety, sorrow, enthusiasm, the satisfaction of patriotic effort, the call to duty, sacrifice, loss of health and death. On the other hand there had been profit, speculation, wealth, extravagance and dissipation. The ebb and flow of the tide of victory made all life uncertain and many sought to relieve the strain or to enjoy their newly acquired gains by an extravagant search for amusement and excitement. A crazy spirit of carnival had flourished in some of the Northern cities even as the newsboys hawked the black-bordered columns listing the dead and wounded. Emotions of all sorts were keyed up abnormally and the reaction was to be feared.

There was much in the life of the nation during the war to give those who looked into the future, grave concern. In the North there was much that was crass and corrupt. Crime flourished. Licentiousness seemed a phase of military glory. The soldier on furlough must be amused and exhilarated; liquor, gambling, vice of all kinds pandered to this phase of warfare. Corruption and the use of money flourished when valuable contracts were to be disposed of by government. A sordid materialism which heretofore had not been so apparent now became blatant. Taste suffered, the monstrous and extravagant in display crowded out finer things and artistically the hideous, if it were large and expensive, attracted the untutored eye of the *nouveaux riches*.

The war which so disturbed and altered the lives of millions in the North hurried on the various tendencies toward social change which were in the process of reorganizing society. Rivalries and divisions within the North were given new causes to feed upon. After an initial shortage the ranks of labor swelled under the wartime demand. Hordes of immigrants were encouraged to come over. Women, too, took many places left by men and Negroes were also brought North. But the great reward paid to industry was not shared in large part with labor and this injustice was not unnoticed. The war contributed much to a growing class consciousness of labor. It also changed the position of women. They were never to return entirely to the home. One profession, at least, school teaching, they captured and having made their appearance in man's public world they would not retire.

In the South there were also disquieting signs of wartime damage to the future. The South had been isolated, invaded, its fields laid waste, its property destroyed, its leaders sadly depleted by death. Worst of all hope had died. The southerners had been forced to watch the destruction of a cherished ideal, to lose their great confidence in their own ability to stand alone, to see their power beaten down by despised northern clerks and store boys. The South came to the point where it lost the will to fight, the human spirit could stand no more. Such a defeat was to leave wounds that only long time could heal.

The war period continued the unpleasant growth of a new sectionalism. Rivalry developed betwixt West and East. The great industrial boom in the East was much more profitable in terms of money and fortunes than the agricultural boom in the West. The eastern capitalist piled up cash reserves while the western farmer extended his acres at the expense of mortgages. The two sections split on taxes and subsidies. To western leaders the war taxes and tariffs were one-sided. The East profited as the West paid. The railroad grants even were objects of suspicion, they were to make the western prairies vassal provinces of the East. But as yet these signs of social cleavage were hardly great enough to attract much attention.

A Tragic Introduction to Peace

Most significant was the final tragedy that occurred in the midst of the dawn of peace. When news of the surrender of Lee flashed through the North a great weight was lifted and the tension was snapped. The North entered upon a wild orgy of celebration. From Palm Sunday until Good Friday that sense of freedom was delirious. Then came

John Wilkes Booth, insane avenger of the South's defeat, who assassinated President Lincoln and plunged the nation into gloom and apprehension. The great joy of the people was turned to mourning and the shouts of victory became cries for vengeance. Such a shock was not a propitious inauguration of reconstruction. "With malice toward none and charity for all" was a sentiment driven from the northern mind by Booth's bullet.

The assassination of Lincoln had a greater significance than its immediate emotional effect. This martyrdom placed Lincoln definitely in the small group of national heroes. The struggles of the reconstruction period might have withered his laurels, in the popular mind at least, but the manner of his death insured his fame. More than anyone else did he seem to be the epitome of the potentiality of the American. Born as he was in the humblest circumstances he had risen to the greatest place. But so had others. His great hold upon the popular admiration came from his rôle as the nation's spokesman in wartime. He stood first of all for humanity, he was merciful and patient, he was humble, he had a sense of humor and yet he could be ruthless and implacable in pressing the war in the face of odds and almost insurmountable obstacles. It was not by efficiency of administration but by shrewd knowledge of men and the weight of ideas that he achieved his greatest fame. For it was in his expression of the nation's thought, sensed in almost uncanny fashion, that he excelled. In his inaugurals, in his messages to Congress, in published letters and in his Gettysburg address he made the people realize the righteousness of their cause and the high purpose of the struggle. Without such inspiration victory would have been much more difficult. He was also the Great Emancipator, his fiat broke the shackles of the slaves. Finally he was the prophet and also the personification of the Democratic experiment which was to "elevate the condition of men—to lift artificial weights from all shoulders; to clear the paths of laudable pursuit for all; to afford all an unfettered start, and a fair chance in the race of life." His idealized figure was to become symbolic in the national ethics, a force for the preservation of the Democratic idea.

THE NEW SECTIONALISM

1865-1878

CHAPTER XV

REORGANIZING THE SOUTH

The end of the war began a new era in the history of the American republic. The stress of the conflict had accelerated the speed of American advance and had reorganized its directing forces. First among the new conditions was the changed position of the South. The war had dragged this section from a position of power, had destroyed much of its wealth and had drastically altered its social system. The normal processes of reconstruction of the devastated section were prolonged and complicated by the efforts of the Republicans, in control of the federal government, to punish the South for its so-called "war guilt." The old South was destroyed, and the building of a new South was a painful process. Despite the discouragement of defeat, the southern people turned with determination to the difficult process of recovery.

A Terrific Problem

When General Robert E. Lee bade his remnant of troops farewell (he had remaining scarcely half the men with whom he began his last campaign), he urged them to set themselves immediately at the task of rehabilitating their home localities. Unfortunately, the men who carried his message back home with them found small encouragement for constructive labor in the conditions which stared most of them in the face. Defeat of the southern cause released approximately 175,000 soldiers to join the non-combatant population, at this time amounting to nearly 5 million whites and 3.5 million Negroes. The majority of all these people were in a disheartening situation. The chief means of prosperity formerly known to them were well-nigh exhausted. Agriculture, their main reliance, was most dilapidated, with fields neglected, implements worn out, stock gone, seed scarce and poor, and a general barrenness in some parts so extreme that it was said a crow, crossing these areas, must carry his provisions with him. In the matter of clothing, as well as food, the war sacrifices had left the populace in a sad state; garments which had not been patched nearly out of use were made rudely of such materials and cut as war necessities had allowed. Hungry men and women beginning over again could not fortify their struggles with a spruce appearance.

Nor found they happy inspiration toward effort beneath the roof-trees which sheltered them; for the dwellings they had been used to call home had been stripped of many of their family treasures. There remained marred furniture, clocks long since stopped, cemented dishes, forks half-tined, broken hairbrushes and combs, worn out toothbrushes and bent pins—an environment likely to foster more bitterness than hope, more apathy than energy. Their first courageous efforts to acquire cattle, horses and crops made some of them victims of guerrillas and ex-soldiers, white and black, who stole and killed recklessly during the months immediately following the peace. Of course most of the population did not thus take advantage of the general breakdown in social restraints; but they all, even the most law abiding and industrious, lived in an atmosphere of nervous unsettlement which retarded their work, warped their point of view, and jeopardized the peaceableness of community life.

It was the cotton crop which was most important. To it were tied the fortunes of nearly everyone, because the industrial, urban population was relatively small. Had the southerners the means to raise a crop, they had none to move it to market. Their foreign commerce had been ruined by blockade. Some important railroads to the ports and toward the north were falling apart from lack of repair where not already dismantled by the invaders. Others, which had been reconditioned by the victors for the use of advancing northern troops, remained under the control of a federal military railroad department during several months after hostilities ceased. For return to their owners, it was required that the new management be loyal and furnish bonds guaranteeing payment to the federal government for rolling stock supplied by it. Almost none of the railroads were able to meet the obligations on these forced purchases. Furthermore large debts owed them by the Confederate government were now beyond collection, while debts they had paid the states during the war had now to be paid over again, because the courts declared payments in Confederate currency null and void. Use of the river steamboats was risky on account of the broken down condition of the wharves, levees, channel markers and boats. Gangs of desperadoes on some rivers lay in wait to steal cargoes and rob passengers.

Rebuilding waited upon capital. But capital was fugitive. A capital investment of nearly 2 billions had been wiped out by emancipation of the slaves. Investors in the bonds and notes of the Confederate States also found their holdings made worthless by defeat and repudiation. Nevertheless, the ex-citizens of these same states at the same time remained liable for their personal debts, which most of them were totally unable to pay. Many a northern merchant was now known to be looking to the federal courts, aided by federal troops, to collect bills long overdue. The only people with money were the few who had used the war for their own speculations and profiteering. Business concerns and productive enterprises were at a standstill where not completely killed by bankruptcy. A man's former associates were either dead or maimed, or suffering like himself from the discouraging effects of the physical and moral ruin around them. The places of 250,000 men had been vacated by death due to the hazards of warfare. A moratorium was in practical effect, where not officially declared. In sum total, there were everywhere present mortgages and debts.

But there was one obstacle to rehabilitation greater than all these— the old slave labor supply had been wiped out and a restless horde of misguided and confused freedmen had been substituted. The most tyrannous fact of southern existence became the continued presence of about 3,500,000 persons recently in slavery. The Negro's vengeance was to prove complete. Obviously, all possibility of rebuilding the South on the old foundation had been destroyed. A new economy and a new social order must be devised.

The Solution First Attempted

The immediate pressure was for the first harvest, for rural rehabilitation. Such urban centers as Richmond, Mobile, New Orleans and Atlanta in the fall of 1865 were becoming very busy with a thriving trade in the necessities, but this reborn prosperity of the cities would dissolve into thin air if basic credit were ruined by crop failure. The crop did not promise well in the early summer of '65; it proved, indeed, a virtual failure, but the best must be made of it. The returned soldiers and the men home before them undertook first to utilize the labor of their former slaves by making contracts with them. They wanted the Negroes to agree to help get in the crop while waiting payment until it was sold. But the colored man's notion of his new freedom did not embrace any idea of working regularly for anyone, much less his former master whom he suspected of conspiracy against him. He could not appreciate the emergency because he was unacquainted with the first principles of farm management, land ownership and community cooperation. Furthermore, he believed that at the end of the year the federal government would give him a Christmas present of "forty acres and a mule," for wild proposals had been made in Congress that the plantations would be taken from their former owners and divided among poor whites and Negroes.

Pending that happy event, why work? There was that new, wide world beyond the bounds of the old plantation, beckoning them to wander at will. They might find a meagre forage for the taking, because the general debacle had brought down, with everything else, the police system. They might indulge in that aspect of their new freedom which most appealed to their warm emotions, unrestricted attendance upon religious exercises of their own race, luxuriating in ecstasies which sometimes were translated into immoral excesses. They could hold colored campmeetings and baptisms galore, usually evidenced by pillaging roundabout, for their ideas of property ownership were nebulous.

So, they followed their natural inclination to take their new contracts lightly, to wander off in groups through the country-side, sometimes to constitute themselves predatory bands for terrorization of the whites. A part of them wisely migrated into the Southwest. Having lived always in the country, the thought of cities was irresistibly attractive to many of them who wandered northward or into southern cities. Soon many of this immature race, ignorant alike of decent sanitation and the means of self-support, found themselves struggling with disease and starvation. In 1865 more lives of these colored people were lost, it was estimated, than of the southern armies in battle throughout the war. During several years, smallpox, tuberculosis and horrible living conditions took heavy toll of them and especially of their children. Fortunately, the men had in many instances left their wives and numerous children back on the plantations, expecting the planters to provision them as of yore, and in distress they returned to their old homes as to a haven. Yet they could not be relied upon to remain.

Consternation filled the hearts of the planters. What little of civilized living the war had left them seemed to be threatened by this new "Black Terror." So desperate a situation required community action and they resolved to pass legislation which should force the labor supply to stay where there was work to be done and to do it. The ex-Confederates hurried to take the oath of loyalty and apply for pardons, in order to be in time to participate in the activities of the new state legislatures. These bodies were about to meet, because the new President, Andrew Johnson, was trying to hasten the reign of peace. He was copying Lincoln's plan for recognizing repentant states as soon as enough of their voters should take an oath of loyalty and accept emancipation. Under his provisional governors constitutional conventions were called to prepare for resuming statehood. Most of the men in these conventions were obscure persons who had avoided active participation in the rebellion, for Johnson had excluded the political and economic leaders. However, while these conventions were repealing the ordinances of secession, repudiating the war debts of the states and accepting emancipation, as Johnson required, the President had been pardoning the former leaders in large numbers.

The result was that when it came time for the new legislatures to assemble, the men formerly prominent had reassumed leadership in their respective communities, had secured election to the legislature and to the important offices and had divided much upon old party lines into two political groups. The southern leaders, assuming that the conditions of readmission to the Union, as laid down by the President, would be final and complete, undertook, after they had fulfilled them, to deal decisively with the local situation.

To rescue industry and property from the "Black Terror" they devised the "Black Codes" based upon the belief that the Negro would not work unless forced to do so. These laws obligated the former masters to protect their ex-slaves to a certain extent, but they permitted them to restrict the freedman's liberty of action and to inaugurate semi-compulsory systems of labor. In most cases the Negroes were not to be allowed military weapons or participation in court processes other than those affecting their own race; their right to hold property was restricted.

As it happened, numerous features of those codes were substantially similar to regulations laid down by an entirely different group of persons, those associated with the Freedman's Bureau, which Congress had established on the eve of Lee's surrender to help the Negro socially and economically. In its inception it was unsympathetic to the planters, because its higher officials were northerners and its subordinates were such southerners as could take the iron-clad oath. Moreover, many of its lesser officials tended to encourage the Negro in wild dreams of land partition and ownership, thus augmenting delusion and suffering. Some ex-slaves were made chronic paupers by largesse from the Bureau and from northern philanthropists. But some of the more responsible, higher officials wrestled in good faith with the problem of metamorphosing the slaves into independent, self-supporting individuals. They dealt with them in special courts, judicial and administrative, gathered the wandering ones into camps and fed them, established hospitals and dispensaries and doctored them. It was in the progress of these contacts that the Freedmen's Bureau had prescribed compulsory codes governing the Negroes. This fact, however, did not keep the South from getting into trouble over her black codes immediately.

Political Hindrance to Economic Reconstruction

In their efforts to save their property and their racial prestige, the planters (especially in South Carolina, Mississippi and Louisiana) failed to consider the psychological condition of their conquerors, the northerners. Few of the victors in that section could appreciate the hard facts of southern economic and social conditions. Those northerners who were animated either by their emotional benevolence toward the freedmen or by their partisan prejudices against the South, or by their political ambitions for themselves, utilized the black codes as a rallying cry. To many northerners the codes signified a refusal to acknowledge defeat, an attempt to re-establish the institution which the war had been fought to destroy. The churches, which had been wholeheartedly working for the abolition of slavery, generally took the side of radical Republicans. Moderate Republicans who had tacitly approved Johnson's lenient policy looking toward a speedy rehabilitation of the South (and there were many such) became alarmed; they discounted a well-considered statement of the situation which the historian, George Bancroft, wrote into Johnson's message to Congress on its convening in December 1865.

Their fears were heightened by the fact that southerners chose former Confederate officers for prominent political positions. For example, the Georgians sent the vice-president of the Confederacy, Alexander H. Stephens, as one of their senators. The northern members of that august body included moderates as well as radicals, but they jointly entertained a suspicion of Confederate power and a jealousy of northern prestige which moved them to delay admitting to Congress men lately prominent in the councils of the enemy. Moreover, they felt that the executive had been too free. His pardons had set aside the iron-clad oath stipulated by Congress; he was reconstructing state governments without congressional sanction. The Radicals could overturn Johnson's reconstructed governments if they got control of Congress and events inexorably moved toward that end.

The Radicals were galvanized into feverish activity by the likelihood that southern members, once admitted with their representation enlarged by emancipation, would ally with northern Democrats and westerners to overturn the protective tariff, the national bank system, the railroad land grants, and the debt settlements arranged by the Republicans. Their bondholding constituency was aghast at the prospect of greenback and legal tender inflation. An entire economic program was in jeopardy. By strenuous efforts, and under the acrid leadership of the vindictive Thaddeus Stevens in the House, and the doctrinaire Charles Sumner in the Senate, the Radicals created a Joint Congressional Committee of Fifteen, which could be trusted to debar the southerners while subjecting their future fate to mercies none too tender.

Johnson was unable to keep the support of the moderates; rather, he antagonized them, by ill-advised acts and utterances. By April of 1866 the Radicals had won the moderates over. Thereafter the allies passed over the President's veto such measures as one for perpetuating the Freedmen's Bureau (defeated by veto earlier) and a Civil Rights Bill declaring the Negro a citizen with rights equal to those of the whites. In order to force the South to accept these principles, and to place them beyond the reach of shifting congressional and judicial majorities, they pushed through Congress, and sent north and south for ratification, the 14th Amendment to the Constitution, highly significant then and more so later (p. 554). By this measure, the southerners were asked to ratify an instrument which in substance declared: that the ex-slaves were citizens and could not be deprived of property without due process; that any state denying them the vote would have its representation reduced accordingly; that the ex-Confederate leaders could not hold office until their individual disability was removed by a two-thirds vote of Congress; and that while all federal debts incurred during the war were to be paid in full, all of the Confederate obligations were worthless.

This overwhelming sum total of disabilities challenged the political foresight of southern leadership. Tennessee ratified the amendment promptly and was readmitted to the Union without further ado; but all the other governments set up under the Johnson plan indulged in the luxury of an indignant refusal. Thereby they played directly into the hands of the Radicals, who were making an opportune use of the pending congressional elections, so manipulating the campaign that by a frantic waving of the "bloody shirt" they were able to re-arouse war prejudices and make them more venomous. Further, riots in Memphis and New Orleans in which Negroes were killed gave the extravagant warnings of the Radicals the color of reality; and when the unlucky President, in a "swing around the circle" endeavored to present matters more fairly his malapropos speeches only dyed the radical convictions a redder shade. Thus events conspired to place a premium upon animosity. The outgoing Congress, accepting the popular dictum, devoted its last hours to punitive, "thorough" measures against the President and the South. They passed a Tenure of Office Act designed to keep Johnson from ousting the radical Secretary of War, Stanton, from his cabinet. They placed on the statute books a Reconstruction Act, designed to substitute for southern home rule a Republican patent of military control.

Out went the Johnson state governments and in came five generals, commanding each his portion of the ten southern states, with power to replace civil officers and courts with military rule. Under such surveillance were the southerners to take their oaths of allegiance and qualify as registered voters, selecting as delegates to constitutional conventions such "citizens" as remained eligible after the wholesale disability imposed by the Radicals. Their new governments must favor both Negro suffrage and the 14th Amendment; and when they had accepted these conditions, the reconstructed states could send Representatives and Senators (presumably Republicans) to sit in Congress.

Thus were the former leaders of the South thrust aside while their communities were regimented under a scheme of reconstruction compounded of military law and Negro citizenry. The higher federal officials, legally in control of affairs, varied in efficiency and disinterestedness. Inevitably they could not keep within bounds the large body of underlings and hangers-on surrounding them. This latter group included two classes of opportunists destined to prove especially obnoxious—the southern white trimmers derided as "scalawags" and northern visitors aptly described as "carpetbaggers."

They cleverly took advantage of the Negro's inability to distinguish between his political prejudices and his religious emotions. Northern churches, imbued with the conviction that the Civil War was a moral and religious struggle, had cordially cooperated in its prosecution and endorsed congressional reconstruction. They set up Freedmen's Aid Societies under whose auspices missionaries and teachers went into the South to work among the freedmen. As the ex-slaves were suspicious of churches set up for them by their ex-masters, they flocked into the new congregations financed under northern auspices, Presbyterian, Congregational, Methodist and Baptist. The Baptist church irresistibly attracted them because of the ease with which it could be established and the dramatic pleasures of its immersion ceremonies.

The ministers of the colored churches and the teachers in the mission schools naturally became Republicans and accepted election to office under the carpetbag regime. They opened their schools and churches to party meetings, so that the congregation heard from the pulpit of the sanctity of the "Union League" and the "Lincoln Legion." Ingenious carpetbaggers "preached to the blacks in their churches, kissed their babies and told them that Jesus Christ was a Republican." To the freedman's mind, the identity of the Christian religion with the Republican party was for a time well nigh complete.

The legislatures set up by these persons, consisting of them and their colored associates, complied with the congressional stipulations for securing readmission to the Union. In all states except Texas, Mississippi and Virginia they achieved readmission by fall of 1868; their struggles for recognition in the last three dragged out two years longer. However, the seating of their senators and representatives at Washington signified no approach to political stability in affairs back home. There, local government in the hands of the parvenus demonstrated how dishonest politicians can greedily utilize ignorant classes to inaugurate an era of extravagance and waste; it "went so far it left little more to steal." The grossness of most carpetbag legislation obscured meritorious efforts at public improvements, relief and education. By 1872 a burden of debt had been piled up conservatively estimated at nearly 132 millions.

The South Saves Itself

The former Confederates were not without resources to combat this new leadership. They went to work in secret and by 1867 many whites were members of a thriving secret society, the Ku Klux Klan, a brotherhood of property-holders whose members donned a white-hooded uniform and operated at night. They aimed to punish carpetbaggers and frighten the Negro out of politics and back to work. Other similar societies sprang up in various parts of the South. Unfortunately these orders became addicted to violence; and when the better class of whites attempted to disband the Klan in 1869 they were not entirely successful. Bands of nightriders long continued to terrorize.

The overthrow of the local carpetbag governments was destined to come from within. They were growing so heavy with corruption that they would soon "break down under their own weight." Their white members became irked by the social ostracism resultant from their Negro affiliations. The Negroes themselves became less certain that benefits were accruing to them. The leaders quarrelled with each other over the diminishing spoils. The several white secret societies symbolized to the northern mind by the term "Ku Klux" craftily intimidated colored voters. In 1869 Radicals lost the legislature in Tennessee and there were unmistakable signs that other states were also on the way to home rule.

The Radicals in Congress took alarm and determined anew to ensure Republican returns in the lately rebellious states. They showed their temper by temporarily rescinding Georgia's readmission to the Union and they passed the 15th Amendment, specifically insisting that men of color should not be denied suffrage. That Amendment received enough ratifications to put it into effect the following March (1870) and Congress bolstered it with a Force Act, invoking heavy penalties against the violation of it and of the 14th Amendment. But these strenuous efforts did not prevent the Democrats from winning the legislatures of Virginia, North Carolina and Georgia during that year and the next. Before the close of 1870, in fact, all the southern states were undeniably secure in their recognition as states of the Union, after nearly six years spent in achieving that status. But six more years were to elapse before they all regained home rule and control of their own elections. Reconstruction was finally completed when as a result of a bargain over the disputed election of 1876 the troops were entirely withdrawn from the South in 1877.

The fact was that the radical attempt at reconstruction was failing socially and economically, as well as politically. The southerner had to find all his own solutions. As his section was to continue, for some time, essentially agricultural, solution of the crop problem remained most important.

The Negro gradually was adapted to his free status. Although deprived of political influence by such devices as poll taxes, ballot box stuffing, literacy tests and "grandfather clauses" his economic condition was bettered. His functioning in agriculture improved in proportion as he came to realize that he could not eat if he did not work. The more intelligent had given ear to the urgings of the better officials of the Freedmen's Bureau, like General Howard and General Armstrong, that work was part of the lot of a free man and that one might profit by signing contracts and keeping to them. Also, the Negro improved as a workman because he became less illiterate. His eagerness for the education which had been denied him was pathetic, and teachers of his own race were made available through the establishment of normal schools and colleges open to Negroes. These institutions were supported by funds from the southern legislatures, the Freedmen's Bureau (until it was disbanded in 1869) and northern philanthropists, which went into the establishment of such schools as Howard, Atlanta, Berea, Straight, Shaw, Fisk and Hampton.

The psychological attitude of the white southerners became more healthful. Of those who could not reconcile themselves to post-war conditions, some of the elder emigrated to England, France, Mexico and South America; younger disconsolates sought their fortunes in northern cities. But for the most part of course the planters had to stay on in the South, pulling themselves out of despondency, struggling against antiquated methods, and learning to use free colored labor. In the border states, the process was accelerated by the fact that there was more cash to pay the Negroes. In the hill country amity was retarded by the presence of poor white laborers who feared competition and who on this account were certain to give the Freedmen's Bureau much less cooperation than the former slaveholders extended.

Through the South in general, several negative factors had to be taken immediately into account. The planters could not rent their land outright, because the Negroes had no cash to pay rent and no understanding of farm management. Nor could the planters hire the Negroes outright, for the planters lacked capital to pay wages and the Negroes for their part disliked to work steadily, day after day. They found a way out by substituting for the plantation system a system of share tenancy or "cropping," adapted to the psychological and financial handicaps of the Negroes and the planters' lack of capital. The former furnished their labor and the latter such supplies as food, tools and mules, and parcels of land from forty to eighty acres in size. The crop was apportioned between them, often in the ratio of 1 to 2, until the Negroes supplied their own food, when the division became equal. Money wages were paid chiefly to the seasonal workers—to the spring cotton-choppers and the fall pickers; but on the whole money was seldom in evidence. Such necessities as had to be obtained from the neighborhood store were charged through winter, spring and summer, to the fall crop. When the Negro brought in his share, the value of his cotton was balanced against the total of his bill to date; and as he often was neither provident nor literate the balance frequently lay on the wrong side of the ledger.

The planter not infrequently found himself in similar fix. The bank had advanced the amounts due for machinery and supplies, and the proceeds of his share of the crop did not always meet the note. He might suggest to the banker that another year better returns would show if they tried a little diversified farming, bred more cattle or changed their methods of cultivation. But the wary banker preferred the ills of the crop he understood to those of others strange to him and his section. Thus the perpetual chain of indebtedness from Negro through planter up to banker retarded improvements in agriculture under the share-cropping system.

However, in spite of these difficulties, cotton production advanced. The planter might complain of the Negro's readiness to desert crops for camp meetings or political rallies, and the Negro might complain that the planter cheated him; yet the planters' land was at least partly in use and the Negroes were getting a living out of a relationship which was one stage advanced from slavery toward individual self-support. Money-making became somewhat less rare and debt less universal. All classes felt a little easier financially after the large crops of 1869 were marketed at a good price, estimated at 300 millions; and they promptly invested some of it in refurbishing their homes and improving their farm equipment. The feeling of hope was further encouraged while crops continued good several years thereafter, with cotton selling for almost twice the cost of production. Thus the small-lot share basis contributed to a steady recovery in cotton production, which after 1875 regularly exceeded the pre-war crop—that crop of the halcyon days of slavery when "Cotton was (supposed to be) King." The actual yield per acre under the share system was less than before, because tenancy was wasteful; but free labor, by reducing the overhead expense, helped to increase the number of acres under cultivation.

It was unfortunately true that cotton acreage expanded at the expense of less popular crops. Tobacco, for example, did not recover from the war until the late 'eighties; production fell off in all the Atlantic Coast states except North Carolina and leadership shifted from Virginia to Kentucky. Even tardier were rice and sugar, which did not meet former quantities before 1890, after which Louisiana staged a strong advance in both. Diversification came first on the small farms tilled by white owners, who progressed with a little corn, cattle and fruit. Fertilization was adopted. The poor whites were now buying small parcels of good land very cheaply, because the heavy taxes had brought the price of land down within their reach, while the high price of cotton was attracting them from their former occupations as hillbillies, overseers or tiny store-keepers.

The expanding farmer class, especially in South Carolina and Missis-sippi, furnished, by 1875, the membership of at least 10,000 local granges, where they learned better to understand their situation and experimented in cooperative efforts for their political and economic welfare. Room for the most rapid farm development was afforded in spacious Texas and neighboring Arkansas, whose rich acreage, easy farming and fluid social conditions attracted hundreds of the most ambitious whites and Negroes. These native southerners were much more successful in taking advantage of the cheap lands throughout the South than were the northern fortune hunters who invaded the section in considerable numbers. About 75% of the latter failed as plantation owners because they were not acclimated and did not understand the Negro. As diversification under these auspices increased, importations of general food products from the West, which formerly had sent in so much via the Mississippi, gradually were cut down and their places taken by supplies of southern origin.

Relatively, the large southern planter was becoming less important in the class scheme of his section, in proportion as the land which he sold or lost was divided into smaller parcels held by individual farmers. The number of individual farms increased by about 60% within the decade after the war. Smaller farms meant the incursion of new classes of persons to meet the wants of those farms. Whereas the large slaveholder used to order his supplies from a distant wholesale house, the small farmer bought his from a local storekeeper. Whereas the one obtained his credit through a single "factor," the other borrowed from a village money-lender. The one sold his entire crop from his many acres to a large commission firm in a city; the other sold his to a local dealer, especially after railroad building improved transportation.

Thus, small farms brought into local communities merchants, money-lenders and buyers of crops. These people created a demand for more goods and more different kinds of goods than were brought into the community before the war. To this trade the colored people added their moiety, for they craved to own more things than their masters used to buy for them. Thus the change in marketing conditions, the rise in the standard of living and diversification in industry interacted with changes in land holding. The emerging middle class of town dwellers pushed themselves into prominence as ambitious merchants, lawyers, and commercial people, undertaking to gain both a respectable living and recognition in public affairs. Thus, actual power and wealth gradually shifted from the hands of the families who had been large landholders into the hands of an incoming middle class, unfortunately a class unused to leadership.

New Economic Interests

Industrialization came very, very slowly to the postwar South; its factories in 1860 had produced 10% of the nation's manufactures, but the percentage was not recaptured until the end of the century. Considering the lack of capital and business stability it is remarkable that there was any postwar advancement whatever and it was chiefly due to the abundant water power, labor supply and raw materials near at hand. Northern capital experimented a little while new mechanical industries raised their heads. Southern capital groped its way into cotton manufacture, which became substantial by 1880, as the result of local contributions of small sums.

Refinement of raw products obtained from their natural resources was included in Lee's economic preachments and found application notably in experiments at Chattanooga. There the Southern Iron Company tried out an open hearth process for smelting inferior southern ore, so as to make it eligible for use in the best steel production. Lumber manufactures were encouraged by the desperate need of re-building; naval stores, phosphate and coal served as capital producers, too. Such centers of general trade as Atlanta, Charleston and Richmond by 1870 were bustling with an absorbing activity, in spite of political machinations. New cities appeared almost miraculously. In the lower Mississippi Valley there was more available capital than might have been supposed; for that region had enjoyed a brisk wartime trade with the enemy under a loose system of "executive permits." Powerful interests had convinced the Federal Treasury that this trade was more valuable to the North economically, than its cessation would be strategically. Consequently, speculators in southern foodstuffs had reaped huge profits while the United States provided a market for that part of the blockaded Confederacy.

In southern cities and towns congregated men, women and children who seldom before had known the feel of hard cash; they now helped to make cotton seed oil and oil cake in the factories of Louisiana and Texas, cotton goods in the five states to the eastward, tobacco products in North Carolina and refined sugar in Louisiana. The poor white did not always improve his mental and physical status by turning from the field to the factory, but the opportunity appealed to him as a release from long-endured drudgery and isolation. Women as a class tended to approach economic independence to a degree formerly unthought of. Among the more fortunate strata, after the carpetbag governments were ousted, increased comfort brought increased display and the resumption of social life for its own sake.

As to literacy, the carpetbaggers had nearly starved higher education to death, but they laid a partial foundation for free public grade schools. This the southerners built upon, meanwhile reviving their colleges and universities as white institutions. The munificence of George Peabody gave Tennessee its Peabody Institute. Southern education had become more national in that some states now included United States history as a compulsory subject of study. Creoles, slaveholding aristocrats and Negroes of pre-war days moved among the stories and poems of *Scribners*

Magazine, for George W. Cable, Thomas Nelson Page and Irwin Russell obtained recognition as local color writers for their section.

As a concomitant of her agricultural revival and her industrial and educational stirrings, the postwar South improved her transportation. Immediately upon the coming of peace the railroads then in a condition to operate did a profitable business bringing in returned refugees, and made money on freight by carrying hoarded cotton to market. The prosperity of these lines stimulated rebuilding of others. The South's prize railroad, in Mississippi, was rebuilt by General Beauregard with astonishing speed; and other southern railways quickly came to share in the flush times enjoyed by all lines before the panic. Even the huge body of corrupt legislation on railroads had left at least a residuum of liens which some states had shown the forethought to require as security for state loans to the companies and these liens became increasingly valuable as the lines approached completion. Georgia lines became prosperous enough to pay dividends varying from two to ten percent.

Pennsylvania railroad capitalists were attracted. They formed one of the earliest holding companies, which they named the "Southern Railway Securities Company," to acquire control of the chief lines south of Richmond, buying in the interests formerly held largely by individual states. They inaugurated a policy of expansion, improvement, integration of small units and north and south traffic. By 1872 their holding company was paying a semi-annual dividend of three and one-half percent. But initial success was forgotten under the stress of a long-continued depression beginning in 1873, and the Pennsylvania capitalists abandoned their plan of making southern transportation an integral part of their northern system.

As the panic wore off other financiers resumed expansion and the net result, by 1880, was a vast improvement in the situation of the southerner with products to sell. Planters living in the rich agricultural center of South Carolina, and tradesmen of Columbia, Augusta and Charlotte obtained rail connections clear to Richmond. The same were acquired by Atlantans. People of Tennessee and Alabama could look toward the exploitation of their coal and iron; where a cotton field had been, Birmingham could rise. Owners of Arkansas's yellow pine forests could ship out boards to a wider market. Tidewater townspeople were less dependent upon the vagaries of uncertain sailings, and the hinterland was hearing the whistle of the northbound locomotive.

A respectable beginning had been made toward providing southern industry with the arteries essential to economic health, two main trunk line systems (the Southern Railroad, the Atlantic Coast Line) with northern outlets. Southern mileage doubled, between 1860 and 1880, while that of the nation at large was being trebled. Thereafter, with the infusion of more northern capital, southern mileage increased at a rate more rapid than in the United States as a whole. Thus in the field of transportation as in many others, the South demonstrated recuperative powers of no mean proportions; but certain psychological aftereffects of reconstruction long retarded advance.

Aftereffects of Reconstruction

Indeed, the most unfortunate aspect of reconstruction was the unhealthy atmosphere which it bred. Temporary disfranchisement of that class of the population which included the South's most cultured citizens involved a general lowering of the standards of public behavior. Suffering under a regime of low political morality made it respectable to endorse dubious means for questionable ends. Such of the South's old political, military and religious leaders as survived the war worked heroically through the twelve weary years of reconstruction and carpetbag government to solve the race problem and clear away the debris of conflict. They accomplished a great deal; but it was not humanly possible for them to escape bitterness of spirit.

Out of their subjection and accompanying inferiority complex they developed a defense mechanism, which they bequeathed to their section. To protect themselves against their northern critics, they drew themselves together proudly as a South of one party, regardless of economic self-interest, sensitively holding aloof from national streams of progress, immediately "against" forward-looking movements proposed from the outside. Behind their wall of exclusion southerners suffered a most unhappy internal strife. As one of themselves courageously has stated their problem, they had "conflict between races, between classes, between denominations, between visible and invisible government, between dominant demagogues and their following."

Such was the environment in which the postwar generation was nurtured. The children of the veterans gained their earliest impressions from the poverty and crudeness of the South's transitional stage, when control was in the hands of an unholy alliance of political demagogues and religious dogmatism. Their schools suffered a setback from an abortive attempt to mix whites and blacks in education; their colleges could be financed only by appeals to religious prejudice and local pride. In such a state of insularity the advance of science and knowledge as such could make little headway among teachers and students. The experience and opportunity necessary for first class leadership were denied them. Southerners who attended northern and western universities would prove their potential ability there; but most would remain away, living out their lives in an environment more sympathetic to the display of their superior talents.

The lesser leaders remaining at home would prove too slow to make adjustments as the quick changes in the social scheme called for them. Their accomplishments must rank as second, third and fourth rate. Thus, members of the South's oncoming generation would reap a barren harvest from Reconstruction. Inevitably they must show the results of their lack of opportunity; they must fail to achieve high leadership and distinction, "in education, in wealth, in public health and public welfare, in the development of the people and homes and farms of the country-side, in literature, in art, and in many other fine things." The preponderating national influence of the old South had been lost, apparently irretrievably; the task of regaining regional prosperity was left as the pressing objective.

CHAPTER XVI

THE ECONOMIC AND POLITICAL DOMINANCE OF THE EAST

As the war had humiliated the South, it had exalted the East to a new position of economic, political and cultural dominance. The people of this section, occupying the region east of the Ohio and north of Virginia, lived in America's midstream, where tremendous changes were working themselves out, practically unnoticed. They felt most powerfully the currents of incoming population and industrial change and their lives were turned into new channels thereby. Among them appeared a horde of immigrants invited to America by lucrative labor contracts and the approach of peace, immigrants who swelled the population with their high birth-rate and seized the jobs of the unskilled on account of their even lower standard of living.

The Theatre of Most Rapid Change

The cities and countryside of the East absorbed much of this incoming horde before the remainder passed on toward the Middle West and even toward the far frontier. Into the East also came ambitious young men from the prostrate South, passing enroute optimistic entrepreneurs from the East who thought they saw opportunity in the devastated region. Also the West in some measure turned back its tide toward the East. This jumble of population movements made for fluidity of sections and of classes:—each moving person overlaid his former narrow sectionalism with attitudes determined by his new environment; and the mobility of opportunity sent men and women moving from one class into another, keeping the social system of the United States fluid, maintaining the national optimism.

Here were no landed gentry, or other hard and fast castes or guilds to lock people into tight compartments. The humblest immigrant workman, fast crowding in, still had leave to climb out of ordinary labor into the company of bankers and business men, who had set him the example. Like their predecessors in the new hemisphere they found an astounding abundance of natural resources enticing them to devise means of exploitation, but they experienced a more rapid succession of changes in daily life. Multiplying new inventions uprooted them more forcefully and speedily, taking them out of ancestral trades into new occupations overnight, perhaps stimulating their imaginations so that they could make their own contribution to the country's rapid industrialization. As Mark Twain declared in 1873, aptly accounting for this dynamic era, events

uprooted institutions that were centuries old, changed the politics of a people, transformed the social life of half the country, and wrought so profoundly upon the entire national character that the influence cannot be measured short of two or three generations.

The new factory economy was inundating the East and the frontier spirit was sweeping backward from the West. Men restless in industry or in agriculture could seek their fortunes over the face of a reunited country without encountering slavery, national barriers, or tariff walls to keep them or their goods confined. An unparalleled fluidity, then, was the dominant characteristic and privilege of all groups. And this was to continue for nearly thirty years more.

Preoccupation with Gain

After the Emancipation Proclamation the moral crusade of abolitionism could no longer engage the enthusiasms of the citizenry and their emotions swung into a mundane fervor—for money-getting and wealth enjoyment. Although the issue of .reconstruction was placed by main force in the center front of the political stage, there supposedly to occupy and divert the public mind, the abundant energies of the North focussed so sharply upon material things as to hasten readjustments and quicken everyday life among practically all classes. Persons with strong creative instincts, exploiting their exceptional opportunities, found them now greater than they had dreamed; their success made yet more extreme the general material trend of thought and expression.

The roots of a new prosperity had been growing deep in American soil and the war had been unable to halt certain inevitable economic trends. The people long had been in a mood for eager, unconservative exploitation of opportunity. They had pushed out along the old trails and canals to gain access to regions of vast agricultural possibilities and valuable mineral resources, they had begun to build railroads to hasten their impatient advance. Being free from inherited and over-conservative ideas, their attitude toward machinery and industrial change was one of enthusiastic adaptation. They were finding and using in increasing quantities such basic mineral products as coal, iron and petroleum, powerful agents for the new industrial advance. The Bessemer process was pointing the way from an iron to a steel economy, which meant more effective machinery as well as faster and heavier transportation. People were too busy taking advantage of their opportunities to realize the immensity of the prospect. From the day when eastern tariff advocates and western farmers won the election of 1860, business had sung with swelling volume in the key of "prosperity and more prosperity."

The worship of money-getting and the money-getter permeated all classes. Many of the commonalty had handled more money of late than ever they had seen before, because of soldiers' bounties and pay, high prices and some wage increases. Transactions formerly leisurely were become hurried, as attested by establishment of a postal money order system and free city mail delivery. Although spending was enormous, savings also accumulated. The greenbacks had sharply diminished the number of bankruptcies; so many mortgages were paid off that the insurance companies had to take over government bonds to absorb their plethora. Banks had multiplied and savings institutions were swollen with profits.

The bankers profited from the national bank system, under which many of their institutions were chartered (p. 266). The heterogeneous, unreliable welter of private bank notes which previously had hobbled business was replaced with a uniform issue of national bank notes placed in circulation by the new banks, which earned the right by purchasing bonds from the government. Since the national banks could issue the notes up to 90% of the market value of the bonds which they purchased, they received interest threefold on the transaction; the government paid them interest varying from 3% to 6% on the full face value of the bonds; borrowers paid interest from 6% to 8% on the face value of the bank notes loaned out to them; and the government paid the banks interest a second time, by accepting depreciated greenbacks in payment for the bonds, although the law arranged for payment in gold. The fact that the bonds had a gold value far in excess of the greenbacks given in payment for them aroused class feeling as a case of unfair discrimination; but debtors did not excite themselves about it as long as the supply of greenbacks was continually augmented and money was cheap.

While the war was enhancing the wealth of the bankers it enhanced their prestige and power also. In a sense, their partnership with the government through the National Banking Act caused them to be more "looked up to," and at the same time their help became more necessary to business expansion—in commerce, transportation and industry. Washington contacts brought special opportunities to shrewd profiteers, as Jay Cooke and others fully proved. Money fairly cried out for investment and the men who had gained by the lucrative war contracts, by the land grants, and divers financial speculations, being strange to great fortunes, were intoxicated by the power they possessed. It could scarcely be otherwise, when the nation as a whole was convinced that America represented an unregulated, free-for-all competition in the exploitation of opportunity.

This great supply of money of course flowed toward the centers of business and of feverish speculative activity, chiefly New York, Boston and Philadelphia. From thence emanated a flood of legitimate and spurious stocks and bonds, which the cautious, small capitalist was inclined to buy because the government lately had introduced him to bonds as an investment. Abiding faith in prosperity would mount ever higher and higher—until the debacle of 1873.

In the meantime, manufacturing advance proved inescapable; wartime contracts and high tariffs had not originated, but greatly accelerated, the expansion. The natural increase in population coupled with the horde of immigrants flowing into the cities and out through the rural regions multiplied the number of potential producers and consumers. The feverishly expanding West and the exhausted South absolutely required huge quantities of goods, while in many other people the war had fostered a spendthrift psychology which converted former luxuries into necessities. Thus to the increased number of buyers was added an increased inclination to buy, among poor as well as rich. It was a period of ebulliency in all things.

As long as money had the quality of fluidity which comes from a general faith in prosperity, capital was poured into young enterprises as well as established factory businesses. Petroleum, which was estimated to have a capital greater than half a billion by the close of the war, continued attractive. Paper manufacturing was set afloat by a concern starting in Philadelphia in 1866. New patents in agricultural machinery absorbed much capital on the middle border, at Chicago and St. Louis. The newly mechanized industries, and the railroads, made insatiable demands upon exploiters of coal and iron. Between 1864 and 1869 there were more than in any previous five year period of:—iron furnaces erected, bars rolled, steel made, coal and copper mined and gallons of petroleum collected, refined and exported. The same astounding activity was true of cotton spindles in motion, manufactures of different kinds started, lumber sawed and hewn, and houses and shops constructed.

But to both the capitalist and the small investor the shrinking of the globe was the most attractive investment. The war had disqualified the merchant marine as a field for profits, while railroads were catching the public imagination and offering entrepreneurs an infinite variety of wealth-getting schemes. So, while the transcontinental lines were being constructed, little lines in the East multiplied and were assembled into four trunkline groups, after much fighting and sharp practice. After the adoption of a uniform gauge, the union of the New York Central and Hudson railways with their connections, and the extension of the Erie, the Baltimore and Ohio and the Pennsylvania affiliations, enabled the public and its goods to travel any one of four different routes to Chicago, without changing from one line to another four or five times before completing the journey. There were twenty-eight railroads in 1869, with a total capital stock around 400 millions and the next year Vanderbilt had assembled nearly a quarter billion of capitalization for his lines alone. In the four years following the completion of the transcontinental line, 1869-1873, 24,000 miles of railroad were built. The manufacture of "Pullmans," and invention of the automatic air brake and car coupling widened the field of gainful manufacture. The "Western Union" was emerging as a virtual monopoly of telegraph facilities, with its duplex (1872) and quadruplex (1874) instruments amplifying the number of business transactions transmissible on the wires simultaneously; and as Cyrus Field's efforts with transatlantic cables blossomed into permanent success, business abroad was also expedited.

In achieving these economic ends little concern was had for the means employed. Business was shifting into a form of organization peculiarly adapted to minute divisions of responsibility and large scale manipulation of funds. The shift from partnerships to corporations had been accelerated by the war and by large capital commitments. Misappropriation did not necessarily follow but the unfortunate laxness of some state legislatures in granting incorporation pulled down the standards throughout the country. Until the investing public had learned its lesson by bitter experience, few legal restrictions were enacted to protect the trustful.

A New Labor Movement

As eastern capital was advancing, so was the army of labor which was congregating in the urban centers of industry. The mechanical industries, shifting from the water power sites of the rural districts to the steam power and labor supply centers of the urban areas, left behind them in the country many a picturesque ruin of a deserted native village and built up around them in the city a conglomerate assortment of crowded tenements occupied by a mixture of native sons and foreign newcomers. Some rural labor the industries took with them cityward; but they did not long retain the farmers' daughters who formerly had welcomed the local factories as places to earn "pin money." These shrank before the tide of immigrants and retired into more poorly paid, if more "respectable" work, such as sewing and school-teaching. Their factory and mill places were filled from city sources, partly by native labor and partly by Negroes, Italians, Irish, Slavs and Orientals, the latter groups constituting the great horde of unskilled laborers whose arrival upon the American scene had been facilitated by the labor contract law of 1864.

This historic measure had been passed at a crucial moment from the standpoint both of workmen and employers. The advance of retail prices in 1861 had put nearly nine-tenths of the wage-earners in a worse position than they held in 1860 and through the next five years their situation did not materially improve, although industry lost more than a million workers through enlistment. The widening spread between their wages and the cost of living, combined with the demand for labor and the pervasive spirit of restlessness to make them attempt a united front. The number of their local unions, in the crafts of skilled workers, increased nearly 400%; and they formed several national unions which flourished most in those crafts which best expressed the tenor of the times, the building trades and transportation. Among the national unions springing up during the period of intense activity toward the close of the war were the carpenters and joiners, the bricklayers and masons, the painters, the heaters, plasterers, ship carpenters and calkers, coach makers, journeymen carriers and the Brotherhood of the Footboard (locomotive engineers).

Organized labor, nevertheless, could not prevent enactment of the contract labor law, for employers could cite the loss of labor through enlistment and secured Lincoln's backing. The law permitted business representatives to contract with prospective immigrants for controlling their wages the first twelve months after arrival in consideration for transporting them here. The manufacturers promptly began importing cheaper foreign workmen and when the soldiers returned to look for peace-time employment, they found the labor supply overabundant. Repeal of the law was secured in 1868, the same year in which an eight hour day was specified for government workers, but as the repealer did not declare the contracts absolutely illegal, the practice persisted. When the panic of 1873 befell, 460,000 immigrants were entering annually, threatening the native workers in the less skilled trades and imposing a mounting handicap just when laborers were beginning to crave more means for entertainment and excitement. Their imaginations had been stimulated by the broadening experiences of the war; it had filled them with a restlessness which economic distress could scarcely fail to aggravate.

However, beginning in 1867 an advance in money wages had set in, slowly for two years, and then faster during 1870-1871. Furthermore, American workers had broad avenues of escape. Some few took the radical step of cutting loose from their familiar haunts and occupations and letting off steam in that so-called national safety valve, the West. Others, showing skill and adaptability as tool users, met inventions and industrial changes with accommodations to division of labor, and entered new trades. Still others showed their resistance by affiliating further with unions; by 1870 there were more than thirty national unions worthy of the name, with more than 200,000 enrolled members, besides thousands of local unions.

This attested growth in the workingmen's need for organization and their realization of it. They had a few leaders gifted with the peculiar equipment essential to any organizer who would attempt to overcome the special, American obstacles:—the continual influx of foreigners with their strange tongues, lower living standards and eagerness to work at less wages and under worse conditions. W. H. Sylvis among the iron molders, R. F. Trevellick among the ship carpenters, and Thomas Phillips among the shoemakers urged collective bargaining. A special labor gospel was the eight hour day, preached so fervently by Ira Steward that it culminated in 1872 in a great New York City strike. The union movement supported several organs, of which *Fincher's Trade Review* was perhaps the ablest.

Sylvis and a few others realized that the logical objective of local and national unions should be a national federation. While industry was receiving from the war the greatest stimulus toward productivity, Sylvis had led an attempt at federation in the "Industrial Assembly of North America" convened at Louisville (1864). At Baltimore two years later, trade unionists and reformers under his leadership organized the "National Labor Union" in which representatives of more than half a million workers, at one stage, participated. This brought several state laws for the eight hour day in 1867, and the ambiguous law of 1868 for government employees. But instead of emphasizing strikes and other means of building up industrial solidarity, the union stressed the reform of society by such means as producers' cooperatives, monetary legislation, and a national Labor Reform party, founded in 1872. The union lost its labor support, which proved fatal, and its political party proved too radical to survive the one campaign it entered.

This was because it dared to be articulate upon matters to which the vast majority of Americans were indifferent; it took the position of debtors against creditors on the greenback question, landless settlers against speculators and corporation owners on public lands, consumers against manufacturers on the tariff, workmen against employers on the eight hour day. These planks, with civil service reform and railroad rate regulation, completely removed them from the practical political performance of that day.

After the demise of the "National Labor Union" an "Industrial Brotherhood" was formed (1873) on the principle of straight unionism exclusive of politics. How far along the path of national federation this group might have advanced was left a matter of mere conjecture when the panic wrote "finis" on it.

In the meantime, a second important attempt at a nation-wide labor organization was made by the "Noble Order of Knights of Labor," a secret society first founded in 1869 by Uriah S. Stephens and his associates among the Philadelphia garment cutters. This all-labor organization became the first to attain much national influence, in the effort to offset large scale organization of capital. Unlike the craft unions, the Knights aimed at industrial unionism—of all workers regardless of skill, occupation, color, citizenship, or sex. They worked for social and industrial reform through arbitration, rather than by strikes. Unlike the National Labor Union, they persistently refused to be captured by a political party; but from the outset they attempted to influence legislatures. Claiming that labor was the sole creator of values or capital, they undertook to make public opinion sympathetic to labor, to support their demands in industry and politics.

They failed to secure such things as the eight hour day, abolition of child and convict labor, weekly pay and mechanics' lien laws, equal pay for women and men, and the legal recognition of unions. In vain they demanded government ownership of public utilities, abolition of the contract system on public works, income taxes, abolition of national banks and establishment of postal savings banks, national health and safety laws and the restriction of land sales to actual settlers. But they obtained establishment of several state bureaus of labor, which gathered statistics demonstrating the truth of their contention that industrialization was having a pauperizing effect. Only a small portion of labor was organized and the forces at the disposal of capital seemed almost too great to defeat; but labor was gaining militancy, as the panic proved.

Panic of 1873

The truth of the matter was that the great boom period of the war and the flush years which followed was almost over. The slow round of the business cycle was approaching the point of disaster. More fertile ground never lay fallow for the seeds of panic. Speculation, excessive and wasteful production, reckless extravagance, fluctuating prices, unsound banking, huge indebtedness,—all were bringing their inevitable consequences. The faith of foreign investors, made wary by the excess of railroad and mining securities and the Union Pacific scandal, was forfeited many months before the bubble burst at home.[1] The faith of investors nearer by, unsettled by exposures of political and social corruption and worried by conflagrations in Chicago, Boston and Portland, trembled on the brink of destruction.

It needed but the crash of one concern, overloaded with securities realizable only in the distant future, to be destroyed utterly. This concern proved to be Jay Cooke and Company of New York, London and Philadelphia, an investment house which had banked upon future

---

[1] Some 1.5 billions in United States securities were sold abroad, adding to the strains of a continent suffering from prolonged war-making, Suez canal outlays, French indemnity payments, overbuilt railways and speculative iron manufacture. Europe was in no condition to run to America's rescue.

occupation, by generations yet unborn, of the area served by the Northern Pacific. On 18 October 1873, this firm closed its doors in the United States. When so reputable an institution collapsed, the business of the entire nation must soon reveal its instability. Prices of securities fell so rapidly that the stock exchange was closed for ten days to stay their descent. Money was so hard to get that "clearing house certificates" were invented to take its place. Nearly every businessman proved to be in debt far beyond his capital. Speedily, marginal concerns fell into the hands of receivers and long-established, more conservative, houses saved themselves only by amalgamation, labor displacement, and half-time operation.

At first, the sanguine habits learned in the boom years made employers and employees proclaim that recovery was just around the corner; but as year after year passed without sustained improvement in the manu-facturing, banking, railroading and allied businesses, the national optimism grew frayed from the continuous strain. It developed that the depression was world wide and not to be gotten over so easily.

In the United States, each person in his measure felt the stringency. Capitalists had to accept lower interest rates and were lucky if they did not lose their investments entirely in business failures, which mounted past the high point of 10,000 annually. Manufacturers had to cut prices down closer to cost and sometimes below it. Pig iron, the world's trade barometer, fell from $53.00 to $16.50 per ton. Property owners found their land worth less than the mortgages on it. Buyers of imports ceased buying them, on the ground they were luxuries, to the detriment of people whose livelihood depended on foreign trade. Small depositors were particularly hard hit by the failure of weak savings banks. Each family knew more illness than before and children had a poorer chance at education. The lawless fringe of society widened to admit the un-employed and destitute, who in New England particularly terrorized the semi-rural population with their thefts and violence, and in the cities added new names to the rolls of vice mongers. Since democratic America no longer seemed a land of promise, immigrants turned about face.

To employees the years following 1873 brought uncertainty and dread. The ground was cut from under them and their unions when employers in marginal businesses were wiped out and surviving concerns went on a half-time basis. Men, women and children who kept their jobs felt the constant pressure of unemployed thousands behind their backs, eager to step into any places they might vacate, no matter how low the wage. Long bread lines stretched before the soup kitchens month after month, waiting for business to stagger to its feet. With buying severely limited to necessities, mere maintenance of existence absorbed most energies. Money wages and the cost of living declined at about the same rate, between 1873 and 1876, but as employment steadily fell to new lows there was a serious decline in real incomes. Then, during the second three years of the depression, while employment was slowly rising, wages fell more rapidly than retail prices, so that workmen continued to lose ground. In membership and effectiveness the unions suffered immense losses as the depression dragged on, with numerous strikes ending in failures as endurance diminished. Misery deepened among families in such hard-hit occupations as mining and textiles. In their bitterness some listened with friendly ear to the gospel of international radicalism—Marxism—while others divided allegiance between craft unions with their collective bargaining principle, and secret organizations like the Knights of Labor with their doctrine of political intervention.

In the basic industries the industrial unrest necessarily took its most violent form. There, the ideals of laissez-faire had had the fullest play, and initiative and freedom from restraint, so admirable in the individual, had proved dangerous in the corporation. In the Pennsylvania anthracite coal region, so important to the machine age, a virulent expression of opposition to the capitalist system was worked up among the Irish laborers, apparently with some encouragement from employers eager to discredit them. 1874 brought a reign of terror, which made their common appellation—"Molly Maguires"—a synonym of fear and violence, and it lasted until federal troops arrived the next year.

Transportation fell upon evil days, with railroad defaults and receiverships. As the work of construction stopped, all the foundries, machine shops and steel mills dependent on construction had to close down. Firemen, brakemen and engineers, chafing under irregular work and lowered wages, resolved to strike; and with some success early in the depression. Then the executives determined to crush the Brotherhood of Locomotive Engineers, and in midsummer, 1877, decreed a flat 10% reduction in pay, widely imposed east of the Mississippi. Workmen rose in protest all along the network of lines reaching from New York and Philadelphia far into the West. They organized the most powerful labor resistance up to this time.

At such strategic centers as Baltimore, Pittsburgh, Buffalo, Chicago, St. Louis and San Francisco, the larger groups of trainmen participated in wide-scale disturbances. Rioting, loss of life, sympathetic strikes in other industries, and general outcry ensued. Traffic was tied up and militia called out. Federal judges committed strikers for contempt of court. Here was the labor injunction foretold, for commitment under receivers in effect was the same. The trainmen had to go back to work at the reduced wage; they had failed to force employers to recognize labor organization and collective bargaining. But the moral effect of their protests proved enormous, for public criticism was not all aimed at the rioters and labor leaders dared hope that in time they might upset the classical contentions of the business men.

Meanwhile, strike failures and punishment of union membership sent more workers into the secret Knights of Labor. Broadly speaking the only trades which increased wages then were those organized for collective bargaining in unions or under the Knights. But the Knights' greatest strength did not materialize until the middle 'eighties, after various changes of policy.

The years of uncertainty and tribulation emphasized one great attribute of America. Hard times could not alter the youthful capacity of the nation for healthy rebound from adversity. The Centennial of 1876 conclusively demonstrated this quality but the trait did not confine itself to one exhibition. Inventors busily responded to the demand for improved appliances; in almost annual succession appeared the typewriter, telephone, talking machine, arc light, and practical incandescent lamp. The engineering profession was led on magnificently by Washington Roebling, carrying the Brooklyn Bridge toward completion against the most fearful odds.

Among individuals, the panic probably gave no one more stimulation than J. P. Morgan, who emerged from it with the bit in his teeth. Cutting loose from his father, Junius S., he went full tilt for railroads, battling with those slippery knights Jay Gould, Jim Fisk, and Jay Cooke. When next a panic should lay the nation by the heels, Morgan would prove able to impress his will on the national government itself. In the oil industry, John D. Rockefeller masterfully undertook to end the regime of cut-throat competition. Andrew Carnegie, yet another of the panic opportunists, learned from it to employ chemists, who showed him how to make tidy profits from products discarded by his competitors as waste. The success of these promoters in reducing the costs and dangers of competition inspired directors in the coal and railroad industries to follow suit. Hence the traffic agreements for shutting out small plants and defenseless lines. The old days of free-for-all competition were definitely on the wane, but just what new form business would adopt, no one knew.

Nature, too, intervened to dispel the depression. The summer suns of 1878 and 1879 shown upon bumper crops in the United States, just when Europe's own food supply was failing her. The money she paid for America's grain quickly found its way into the main arteries of the industrial body, which had been purged by the violent paroxysms of deflation. Indebtedness had been erased by insolvency and timid capital had accumulated in thriving savings banks. Rock bottom prices had destroyed inefficient concerns, and had forced surviving businesses to run without profit to keep going at all and to devise uses for waste products. The huge fatality among little partnerships had been accompanied by increasing adoption of the corporate form of business, better fitted for long life and large investments. No longer propped by the home market, manufacturers had found outlets in newly developing lands, especially for machinery; consequently the balance of trade turned again toward the United States and the incoming gold began to build up a reserve in the treasury at Washington.

Indubitably the nation was growing up to fit the clothes which had been cut for it during the speculative boom, justifying a resumption of railroad building and a return of immigration. By the middle of 1879, there was employment aplenty for money and for men. That subtle thing called "confidence" had been restored.

Eastern Control over the Tariff

The concentration of wealth and economic power in the East was matched by a similar concentration of political power. Eastern dictation was very largely accepted by the Republicans, and that party kept control of postwar legislation by shutting the Democrats of the South out of Congress. Therefore, the all important readjustment of the national economy to peace-time conditions was determined chiefly by partisan and sectional considerations, with eastern capitalists most successful in pressing solutions to their own interest.

The first of the problems was the tariff. Upon it, as well as all other economic legislation, the war had exercised a demoralizing effect. Legislators quite lost sight of that vague line which separates private profit from public obligation. Moreover, many sincere apostles of new doctrines were giving respectability to the theory of subsidized business. In the place of a government run by laissez-faire, they would have a paternalistic power in Washington, dispensing favors like a magic geni, on the principle that in proportion as each individual exploits his own opportunities, "Progress" and "Prosperity" trickle down through all classes. Ergo, special favors to manufacturers would benefit the nation at large.

This doctrine Horace Greeley in his New York *Tribune* and Henry Carey in his flood of pamphlets preached to the people earnestly and long. To ensure the national welfare, the government must nourish the "infant" industries. As a like individualist philosophy then animated the midwestern representatives of agricultural constituencies, they did not interpose strong opposition to the eastern manufacturers' high tariff proposals. They, too, would pre-empt their opportunities and exploit them without governmental hindrance and with governmental connivance. Since to them cheap lands and access to markets seemed of paramount importance, they were minded to swap votes favoring eastern tariff schedules for votes favoring western homesteads and railroads.

These complaisancies had made the Morrill tariff increases of 1861-1862 and 1864 contemporaneous with the homestead and railroad acts of those years. Rates on dutiable commodities were elevated in 1862 to 37.2% and two years later, in view of vastly multiplied internal taxes, the average rate became 47.06%. Industries profiting especially by war tariffs included rifles, woolen cloth and shoes much in demand for the army, and those products increasingly desired by the stay-at-homes, such as agricultural instruments, sewing machines, cotton cloth, refined sugar and, last but far from least, whiskey.

Within five years after the coming of peace, Congress repealed the obnoxious internal levies, but curiously enough left untouched the compensatory import duties based upon them. Together manufacturers and Republican partisans guarded the protection ramparts. Opposition to retention of the high rates could not become effective as long as southern Democrats were barred from Congress and thus prevented from forming a union with midwest anti-tariff members. Republican control of political perquisites could not be ended as long as the Radicals succeeded in excluding the southerners. Economic and political legislation must receive their joint impress.

This unholy alliance of political ambition with business cupidity gave the congressional reconstruction program its extreme virulence. Thaddeus Stevens led his group in Congress toward the consummation of a plan for usurping control of national affairs by overturning Andrew Johnson and installing Benjamin F. Wade as President. They boldly unseated northern conservative members and refused to seat southern Democrats, so as to maintain their majorities. They kept the saddle through three vital years (1865-1868). Their influence ramified afar, because the general unthinking public of the victorious North entertained an emotional bias which permitted, if it did not sanction outright, the excesses of the Radicals. It seemed disreputable to oppose them, and their impeachment of Johnson came within one vote of conviction. It made a senator like E. A. Ross of Kansas suffer a lifetime of obloquy for refusing to vote against Johnson; and long after Stevens and his band had departed, the bias persisted.

That the manufacturers could realize definite positive and negative benefits from their alliance with the Radicals was demonstrated in 1867 when they discouraged reduction of the tariff at a moment favorable to it. Although unable to secure enactment of a house bill for general increases, they defeated, narrowly, David A. Wells' mild proposal for tariff reform from a protectionist point of view. One group of them, certain wool manufacturers led by the astute John L. Hayes, obtained separate enactment of wool increases by uniting with certain sheep breeders on terms to benefit both. The main provisions of their wool schedule were retained in the general tariff acts of 1883 and

1890, only temporarily abandoned in 1894 and reaccepted in 1897. Thus, in the wool industry, the device of log rolling on the farmer's product effectively neutralized his opposition to real protection for the manufacturer's product, through most of the next forty years.

When the southern members began to get back in their seats in 1868, the time for effective union between South and West against the radical eastern faction was safely passed. In spite of the depression which thereafter settled upon agriculture, western congressmen and senators, nearly all of whom desired lower protective duties regardless of party, were unable to obtain them. The act of 1870 limited most of its reductions to revenue articles like coffee and tea, the only consequential protective reductions being in pig-iron; it gave considerable increases to numerous protected items, making the law as a reform measure a sham. Within two years the national exchequer overflowed because of the extravagant tariff levies, in spite of disbursements for retiring bonded indebtedness, and it appeared that a majority of the Republicans in Congress, who greatly outnumbered the Democrats, would vote for modification. But once again the House was persuaded to discard genuine reform; it accepted a Senate proposition for a 10% reduction because the entire weight of the protected interests had been marshalled by Mr. Hayes behind the latter proposition, as the lesser of two evils in view of the temper of the times. It was stipulated that the revenue duties on tea and coffee should first be abolished by a separate act, which was done.

The opponents of the protectionist compromise were not well united, while their rivals were carefully kept together by Speaker Blaine, Chairman Dawes of the Ways and Means Committee, and Congressman Kelley of Pennsylvania. So the best organized forces won, then, as again and again in succeeding years. While the compromise act permitted downward trends in salt, coal, hides and paper stock, it left the chief manufactured goods in a strong position, in view of the fact that tea and coffee no longer contributed to the treasury. A few short weeks and Republicans had written into their party platform a formal identification of the protective tariff with Republicanism; their opponents, the Liberal Republicans, were so divided that they could not come out frankly against it. Then came the panic, reducing importations and the revenues dependent upon them. No important non-protective duty being left to maintain sufficient funds, it was possible to repeal the 10% reduction without much trouble or attention. Before another tariff reform movement could gain headway many more businesses dependent upon the war rates had been established. In fact, each year of high rates made them more of an accepted fixture in economic life. Thus high protection had ample time to set its face firmly in the direction it followed sixty years, evolving from a temporary war expedient into a nearly permanent economic policy. Eastern industrialists had won.

There is room for doubt whether manufacturing would have been hurt appreciably by a concerted union of South and West for lower rates —whether it might not, on the other hand, have derived benefit from a halt in tariff increases. The extremely high rates encouraged wasteful manufacture, thus subjecting whole industries to the malign influence of marginal producers, whereas lower rates would have discouraged inefficiency in production. At the same time, the home market was widening so fast that the manufacturers needed less protection against flooding than they supposed.

Eastern Financial Policies

As the battle over the tariff was being waged, another struggle more spectacular and of wider interest was engaging political gladiators in such moments as they could spare from wreaking vengeance on the South. During the war the government had created a great debt represented by a variety of bond issues and had emitted a voluminous depreciated currency, greenbacks. Now that the war was over plans had to be made to stabilize the dollar and to pay off a debt of six billions. The greenbacks alone represented a sum in dollars greater than all the other forms of money in use put together and the actual amount of money in circulation was the greatest the nation had ever known. The existence of so much legal tender involved, with its depreciation in value, a corresponding increase in the cost of goods and in the price of gold.

All business transactions suffered from uncertainty, because prices moved erratically up and down as public confidence vacillated; a lender never could tell, when taking a borrower's obligation, whether it would be met in a cheaper or dearer currency. Contraction would lessen speculation, besides bringing creditors on outstanding mortgages a handsome, albeit unfair, profit, as $100 in gold became as valuable as $145 in paper. Secretary of the Treasury McCulloch determined to stabilize by sharply reducing the volume of the paper circulation. Business conditions at the moment were sufficiently prosperous to enable him to get through Congress the law of 1866 permitting retirement of 4 millions in greenbacks monthly and an approach toward total retirement within about a dozen years. In so far as the law lessened inflation, it lowered prices, made money dearer and advantaged the creditor class in general. Thus the Radicals in House and Senate capitalized their position with the capitalists.

They consistently aided the bondholders at the same time, resisting propaganda that the federal government pay interest and principle in paper, instead of gold. On many kinds of securities the bondholders had had to accept depreciated returns during the war; consequently that struggle had punished them severely from the standpoint of fixed income and they contended they should be allowed to recoup their losses by receiving gold for government securities they had purchased with paper. The credit of the United States would undoubtedly suffer if the nation's debts were paid in greenbacks, and so the federal government did not adopt "repudiation" (as the bondholders called greenback payments) although many cities and states did so.

Scarcely had the opponents of the greenbackers won their victory in 1866, however, when the nation experienced the temporary depression of 1867. Congressmen heard from their humbler constituents in the West and South (for many southern seats were reoccupied in 1868), and eastern debtors shared the view that contraction was nothing less than extortion. With them were allied certain optimistic business promoters who feared that contraction would hinder their schemes for exploiting the West's lands, mines and railways and the South's rebuilding activities. These entrepreneurs insisted that the natural growth of the country would soon absorb the increased currency. Thus did the greenback become the symbol of class animosities and the contest grew so close that Congress teetered first in one direction and then in the other throughout this period.

Republicans sensitive to western urgencies, such as John Sherman, decided it were better to stop retirement than rouse further support for the entire "Ohio idea," involving as that plan did, the payment of all debts in greenbacks and increases in greenback issues. So, the February before the campaign of 1868, Congress repealed the obnoxious retirement act (thus stopping contraction in greenbacks) and left a loophole through which the Secretary of the Treasury might reissue the 44 millions which had been withdrawn under it; greenbacks were continued as legal tender for debts. The Democrats determined to capitalize the growing animosity toward "Wall Street" and inserted in their platform a plank favoring payment in paper; but this was offset by their choice of the easterner, Horatio Seymour, as presidential candidate. He boldly repudiated the paper plank, thus alienating western support.

The successful Republicans and President Grant demonstrated eastern dominance by subscribing fully to the capitalistic contentions. The Republican-controlled Congress passed a resolution in 1869 declaring the intention to redeem the bonds in gold and in 1870 passed a funding act arranging such payment. But businessmen preferred to meet their own obligations in greenbacks. After the Supreme Court in 1870 (Hepburn vs. Griswold) declared the greenbacks unconstitutional so far as applied to contracts made before enactment of the legal tender act, two Republican justices were added by President Grant and the decision was reversed (Knox vs. Lee). The question whether there should be more greenbacks or less and whether they should be redeemable in gold was still to be fought out.

The panic of 1873 revived the drive for inflation. Those who favored "greenbacks" gained new allies in a group of "silver" men who represented silver producers and inflation politicians. The producers wanted silver coinage to raise the price of the metal; the inflationists wanted it as cheap money (p. 335). The general unrest of the panic and disgust at corruption in the dominant party brought the Republicans their first bad beating in the congressional elections of 1874. They therefore reassured the capitalists, with the Resumption Act of 1875, as a parting gift. The greenbacks in circulation were not to be further reduced, but they were to be redeemable in gold on and after 1 January 1879. To this extent the creditor influence won; both bonds and greenbacks were to be paid in gold.

Political Corruption and Reform

In the meantime other aspects of eastern domination were all too apparent in politics. The careless ethics of contemporary financiers and speculation were reflected in a devastating wave of political villainy and corruption. As early as 1866, James Parton satirized the situation in his *Manual for the instruction of Rings—Rail Road and Political;* but the gamesters showed no need for instruction. While representatives and senators were accepting gifts of stock as perquisites of legislative favors (as in the notorious Crédit Mobilier) those typical entrepreneurs, Jay Gould and James Fisk, Jr., were utilizing President Grant's brother-in-law to give the appearance of honesty to a corner on gold. On the "Black Friday" of 24 September 1869 Gould and Fisk pocketed their profits and escaped from the infuriated mob, whilst Secretary Boutwell dumped gold on the market and many a broker plunged into bankruptcy. Fisk next turned his talents to despoiling the Erie Railroad in a fashion so bizarre that he elicited the high talents of Charles Francis Adams and his brother, Henry, to describe his peculations. In this spectacular warfare over watered stocks, Commodore Vanderbilt and Daniel Drew assisted in making sport of the New York police. Men who gambled thus in public utilities reflected the prevalent psychosis of Boss Tweed of New York, Boss Shepherd of Washington and all their ilk in politics and out, obese buccaneers who led raids on the treasury and on the morals of city, state and nation.

Through the eight years from 1869 to 1877 there was maintained in the highest office Ulysses S. Grant, who typified his time in his reverence for the money getter. He tolerated gross malfeasance in American officialdom and his credulous blindness made it easier for men like Secretary of War Belknap, and Vice-President Colfax, to mention but two, to line their private pockets through misuse of public office. As long as Grant held to such a criterion of friendship the spoilsmen ousted from office appointees unfriendly to jobbery, undoing what little there was of reform in the Civil Service, perpetrating salary grabs and frauds on the mail routes. The whiskey ring, for example, cleverly undertook to undermine the Secretary of the Treasury because, forsooth, he was determined to enforce the tax on whiskey.

Upper left, Tweed Ring; upper right, Milking the Erie; lower left, Blind Man's Buff; lower right, Civil Service a Bitter Dose

None of these colorful exploits can be untangled from the closely interwoven pattern of national life in the period. The resident of Philadelphia, Cincinnati, Chicago or St. Louis experienced in his own community the same subserviency of politics to capital which made the warp and woof of life in New York City and Washington. In almost every city boodlers seized control of the machinery of government to mulct dividends from it through dishonest granting of franchises, contracts and appointments, to mention only the most lucrative implements of graft. In New York banking and insurance misappropriations were of gigantic proportions. In Philadelphia, a "gas ring" fattened on public plunder.

Attempts were made to end the dominance of this exploiting mood.
A number of Republicans as early as 1872 determined to defeat the
reelection of Grant. Reform movements had been gaining momentum in
some of the states. In New York, Thomas Nast of *Harper's Weekly,*
and George Jones of the New York *Times* had broken the Tweed
Ring. In Missouri, Carl Schurz and his associates, calling themselves
Liberal Republicans, had gained control. Liberal Republicanism spread
and brought reformers from various sections of the country to a Cincinnati convention in May. They nominated Horace Greeley against Grant.

Sentinel Hayes Guarding the Civil Service

Greeley was endorsed by the Democrats and conducted a vigorous and
impressive campaign. But his backers were not gifted with organizing
ability; many Democrats, too, could not wax enthusiastic over Greeley,
the arch-Republican. Grant's well-oiled machine functioned smoothly
in spite of exposure of its chicanery. The people preferred to reelect
their military hero and take the consequences.

The second Grant regime was worse than the first. Corruption was
traced even to the President's private secretary though Grant himself
was innocent. The most vicious results of southern reconstruction became apparent and the depression contributed its demoralizing influence.
The weight of it all brought the Republicans their congressional defeat
of 1874, and the Democrats their first real chance to elect a president

since the Civil War. However, dishonesty practiced by both factions, especially in southern precincts, made it possible for the party which was in power to stay there.[1] Samuel J. Tilden, the Democrat with a plurality of popular votes, lost in 1876 to Rutherford B. Hayes, the Republican, by decision of an Electoral Commission. Civil war over this disgraceful decision was freely predicted, but the good sense or indifference of the vast majority prevented serious disturbance. Hard times were pressing and political double dealing could not stir deeply when bread and butter were to be thought about. There were, however, some efforts to restore the nation's confidence in the honesty of its leadership. Individuals among the legal fraternity organized in 1878 the American Bar Association, and lesser societies for keeping up legal standards multiplied thereafter. Grant's successor, Hayes, once safely installed, strove manfully to restore honesty to government.

His Secretary of the Treasury, John Sherman, meanwhile aimed to assure stability to business. In spite of the depression and Democratic congressional victories in 1874 and 1876, the Resumption Act of 1875 remained unrepealed; a Bland-Allison Silver Purchase Act of 1878 (p. 359) had diverted inflationist intentions. Therefore, Sherman must be ready, 2 January 1879, to pay gold to all comers demanding it in exchange for greenbacks. He bent all his energies to building up an adequate gold reserve but realized, as the date approached, that there was not enough to match all outstanding paper. Yet, when the day fell, there was no great rush to the treasury. The relieved Secretary discovered that business men were so occupied with using their greenbacks that they had not time nor wish to exchange them. Specie payments were so easily resumed.

Altogether, the new, exploitive, expansiveness of the East had given that section, during the Reconstruction period, a position of phenomenal dominance over both economic and political life. Through a dozen years after 1861 it had operated almost without check. However, economic exploitation received a severe setback from the depression of 1873-1878; and political exploitation had seemed near to destroying the American representative system itself. By a single vote in the Senate the President had been saved from ruthless destruction in 1868, and the disputed election of 1876 almost precipitated a barrack revolt. Fortunately, American institutions were so firmly established as to survive these tests; but the battle for the purity of republican government had only begun. The question remained: could Democracy survive continued exploitation at the hands of ruthless financial power concentrated in the East?

[1] A third group, the greenback party (p. 358), did not show in the electoral returns.

CHAPTER XVII

THE URBAN CULTURE OF THE EAST

Culturally as well as economically and politically the East dominated the postwar nation. Here the concentration of population, earlier evidenced and influential, became yet more powerful. The pace of the process of urbanization, and the area of its operation, became highly significant facts—which the census revealed.[1] Twenty years after 1860 the United States had fifteen cities over 100 thousand in population and the growth of each was phenomenal.

The East had eight of them, the South one, Far West one and Middle West five; in these proportions the sections felt the metropolitan influence. In the East it was a lively influence, unhampered by the defeat which crushed the South or the hard agricultural conditions sobering the Middle West. The East knew hardship—in the situation of certain workmen—but before 1873 the section as a whole knew little of dismay.

The trek of poor and rich to the cities for subsistence and well being not only changed their daily lives but also made them more articulate about their manner of living. Workman and employer, business man and banker were participating in the swift and powerful changes in culture which come to aggregates of humanity.

Changing the Face of the Countryside

The pushing of native and foreign workmen into cities, places of relatively small area totally unprepared for such an influx, starkly revealed the discomforts and dangers of life in such surroundings. The habits of immigrant workmen tended to lower the standards of living of all workmen, with the evil further aggravated by employees lately from the country, unschooled in the challenge the city makes to sanitation and content with crude facilities tolerable only in open spaces amply aired by sun and wind. Filthy streets, bad sewage, and public

[1] (ooo omitted):

	1860	1870	1880				
New York	806	942	1206	Cincinnati	161	216	255
Philadelphia	563	674	847	San Francisco	57	149	234
Brooklyn	279	420	599	New Orleans	169	191	216
Chicago	109	299	503	Wash., D. C.	61	109	178
Boston	178	251	363	Cleveland	43	93	160
St. Louis	161	311	351	Pittsburgh	49	86	156
Baltimore	212	267	332	Buffalo	81	118	155
				Detroit	46	80	116

pumps invited epidemics of disease, while the cheaply constructed tenements stood waiting to serve as tinder in gigantic conflagrations.

Native metropolitans of long standing were slow to interrupt their preoccupation with private affairs by considering problems of public health and safety. Those, they left to the politicians, who were interested chiefly in their potentialities for graft. Finally, holocaust forced a semblance of civic virtue upon the larger cities; Chicago, Boston and Portland were scourged with great fires. Onslaughts of smallpox, scarlet fever and typhoid attacked the defenseless populations of New York, Philadelphia, Boston, Baltimore and Washington. The cities in self-protection devised water mains, sewers and pavements, and added to their new police forces, bands of resplendent professional firemen. Attention being drawn to the fact that crowded tenements jammed the slums unmercifully, the idea of city parks gained currency and they came to be thought essential. F. L. Olmsted's splendid planning of New York City's central park inspired emulation in Boston, Brooklyn, Philadelphia and St. Louis. Yellowstone, the first national park, was set aside for the people who could travel.

The general unsettlement of the period was also expressed by the external and internal appearance of public and private buildings. Dignity, repose or distinction could not be reflected in architecture and interior decoration at a time so absorbed with change that few thought of refinement, grace, and harmony. Change, indeed, went to the roots of life, destroying spiritual unity and thereby affecting all the arts.

The mid-Victorian builder, with few exceptions, lacked time to assimilate the vague knowledge of the history of art which he explored, and as he was anxious to be creative he combined in his structures earlier classic forms and later Gothic details; and wherever he had no inner sense of the fitness of things he created chaos. Some of his hybrid monstrosities he styled "French," others, distorted applications of Renaissance ideas, he called "Italian." In the "carpenter Gothic" of many churches he unintentionally demonstrated the dire consequences of building a Gothic structure of wood, then considered more fashionable than stone, unless it be soft brownstone which in itself bespoke the dominant color of the age. Such inventive "architects" as G. B. Croff and C. Graham and Son, for example, contrived to popularize "art." They built up a boom in "house-plan books," effectively flooding the country with "elegant and picturesque villas" and "French roofs of any size or description" with a "mild trace of the peaks of Normandy thrown in."

To architectural uses the builder eagerly sought to adapt the multiple products then being turned out rapidly by the improved machinery and mechanical processes, not sensing that they challenged him to appropriate them fittingly. From the bandsaw and the lathe he took curious brackets, finials, scalloped and patterned shingles and fantastic piazza posts. Cast iron provided him with entire building fronts which he could erect in sections, with balustrades which he could paint and sprinkle over with sand to imitate stone, with roof crestings to emphasize turrets and "observation towers," and with all manner of ferocious beasts and other metallic monstrosities for the decoration of lawn, porch, and summerhouse, He reversed the law of nature, placing the larger and heavier parts of his structures high up and the smaller and slighter parts below them, meanwhile bracing gables that needed no bracing.

If a man were rich enough to ape the fashionable, he built his city house high up with a brownstone front; around his country "villa" he entwined a sinuous veranda and he made the roof "mansard"; without and within he plastered jigsaw decorations in a riot of flamboyant and fanciful details. The same vainglorious spirit of the Gilded Age which moved senator and congressman to orate in highfalutin' periods, moved the architect and interior decorator to build as ornately and ostentatiously as possible, using "false" doors and windows to enhance largeness, and gilt engraving over walnut to simulate richness. Dark wainscoting, wallpaper and furniture cloaked in charitable shadows some of these awsome "effects." Similarly, in decoration, furniture, dress and the general behavior of "polite" society, flagrant banality gave satisfaction. The piling up of topheavy excrescences higher than one's neighbors, was the thing, whether for cupolas outside the houses of the well-to-do, what-nots within, or bustles to wear on the streets.

While the acquisitive mood of the Gilded Age did not stress the less ostentatious forms of culture, there did persist certain culturally minded individuals, who expended some of their abounding energy in the direction of improvement in art. The public knowledge of such activities was extremely meagre, but men of wealth like Belmont, Blodgett, and Stewart built up good private collections, two art schools became sturdy institutions and the notion of public galleries became familiar. Between 1869 and 1879 Corcoran presented one to Washington, and Peabody to Baltimore, the Boston Museum was incorporated and the Metropolitan Museum of Art opened. Holmes tried to express the recent conflict on canvas; illustrators like Parsons, Pennell, and Pyle were engaged by *Harper's Weekly;* wood engraving was happily perfected by *Scribner's;* Mary Cassatt did notable etchings; LaFarge, Sargent and Whistler went abroad to study; and Harvard University established a chair of Art.

Honest portraiture was dared by Thomas Eakins, even to painting President Hayes working in his shirt sleeves—a realism which the Union League of Philadelphia confined to limbo. Likewise some architects of the temperament of H. H. Richardson, R. M. Hunt, and John and Washington Roebling designed structures aesthetically satisfying by keeping constantly in mind their actual function, whether railroad stations or bridges. An improving knowledge of art was expressed in some Gothic church structures, in the completion of the national capitol and in a few other examples of federal construction. Richardson's Romanesque Trinity Church built in Boston and decorated with John LaFarge's murals, and the work of Richard Upjohn and James Renwick showed that a new sense of standards was emerging.

Weakening Hold of the Church

As urbanization affected the daily life of the populace it profoundly modified certain time-honored habits of thought. This was particularly true in religion which had always played so important a rôle in the formulation of American ideas, prejudices and emotions.

The widening of economic gaps caused by the growing industrialization involved the widening of spiritual gaps likewise, again most marked in the cities. Most of the peers of business were regular church members and the churches increasingly availed themselves of the talents of these rich men, appointing them to church boards and other official positions, substituting them for ministers as trustees of educational institutions and acknowledging their leadership in laymen's organizations known as "Social Unions." Their money built elaborate town edifices, hired trained musicians and made the services more orderly and aesthetic. But the "Tin Pail Brigade" of laborers never had been enamored of the expenses and inferiority complexes implicit in city church worship, and were now repelled by the enriching of its ritual; they became less and less inclined to join in church services.

For the immigrants church affiliation was frankly on a class basis, with home missions established for them in their own poorer quarters of the town. Where the newcomers were largely Catholic or Lutheran, they tended to displace the Puritan Sabbath with the "continental" Sabbath—so much so that a Baptist writer complained that Chicago had become "A Berlin in the morning and a Paris in the afternoon." Business no longer ceased entirely on Sunday.

There was no general acknowledgement, however, that the Puritan practice was on the wane; churches of all denominations remained literalistic with but few leaders sensing the need for a new appeal or daring to preach a more liberal doctrine with special effort to attract youth. Horace Bushnell of the Hartford Congregational Church was one of the brave liberals and he influenced H. W. Beecher and Phillips Brooks. Young people were showing interest in the Darwinian theories presented by John Fiske, Henry Drummond and Lyman Abbott (Beecher's successor); and the desire to hold the oncoming generation within the fold led to a multiplication of the Y.M.C.A.'s which had become favorably known through their aid to soldiers, sailors and the Sanitary Commission during the war. Unfortunately the Methodists, Baptists and Presbyterians retained their wartime divisions, but the Evangelical Alliance formed a United States Branch in 1867 and furthered cooperative church enterprise until the end of the century. It was not easy, however, to overcome sectarian prejudice.

Abuses rising from the new forms of industrial life, springing up on every side, were not sufficiently familiar to the general public to arouse concern over them, especially as the period was not one of social sensitivity. Even the avowed social reformers were little troubled by laboring class hardships. The emotionally attractive target, for altruistic instincts left idle by emancipation, was Demon Rum, for the war-time

Women's Crusade

federal liquor tax, continued thereafter, had made the liquor business more respectable and the heavy immigration greatly increased liquor consumption. Capital invested in this business mounted between 1860 and 1880 from 29 to 190 millions, with a corresponding extension of political influence, especially after the formation of the National Brewers Association in 1863. Some brewers, in states with German settlers, boldly boasted of their political prowess, an indiscretion which stirred the drys to organize in their turn for stimulation of the public conscience. Thus were brought into existence the Prohibition Party in 1869 and in 1874 the Women's Christian Temperance Union, of intense interest to women in many a Protestant family. The female contingent, indeed, was feeling a new access of power, the very bravest ladies uniting under Elizabeth Cady Stanton's leadership in a National Woman's Suffrage Association just fifty years ahead of fulfillment.

The reverses of the depression intensified religious feeling among the middle classes naturally inclined to church attendance. Dwight L.

Moody and his singing helper, Ira D. Sankey, utilized this flare of interest to activate spiritual stirrings in this stratum of society, concentrating upon the young people in the colleges. Results materialized in the "Intercollegiate Missionary" movement and the "Collegiate Young Men's Christian Association." Also in the midst of the depres-

The Bar of Destruction

sion Mrs. Mary Baker Eddy emerged from retirement to establish a "Christian Scientists' Home" and offered the ailing nation her first edition of *Science and Health*.

New Amusements

Among the many forms of social intercourse and diversion with which the churches now had to compete, were the expanding theatre and the recently organized sports. Evening entertainment was lively, if not always elegant, and widened in appeal, for to city dwellers the theatre became "respectable" long before the country would tolerate it. Stock companies were being replaced by a less costly star system, where shone Mary Anderson, young John Drew, Joseph Jefferson, Modjeska and Adelaide Neilson. Mediocre plays like "After Dark," "Black Crook," "Saratoga" and "Rip Van Winkle" played to large and delighted audiences. Mark Twain with his "Colonel Sellers" (adapted from *The Gilded Age*) and B. E. Wolf with his "Almighty Dollar" lampooned the current corruption in society and politics. A "Parisian Ballet" brightened Niblo's Garden in New York City seventeen months. The Germans had their own beer gardens, rathskellers, and sängerbunds. The musically-inclined supported symphony orchestras imported under Theodore Thomas and Leopold Damrosch or, if less elegant in their tastes, consorted with their kind in innumerable "concert saloons." If native Americans were too occupied with getting ahead to produce superior drama or music of their own, their enjoyment of the various imported varieties was no less hearty—until the panic. That depression darkened many a place of public amusement; and the remainder were subjected, early in 1876, to the rigorous and highly successful competition of Moody and Sankey's religious revivals, which set them back several months and many dollars.

Dignified relaxation was enjoyed by certain groups, chiefly in the East, who thought literary culture should be deliberately sought after and enjoyed. They found entertainment in keeping alive the antebellum lyceum, as a combination of debating club, lecture course and concert. Some personable individuals used it as a stepping stone to their social, political or cultural ambitions. Many young men at work during the day participated in its debating rivalries at night as a means of acquiring knowledge and useful acquaintanceships. Others found it simply an agreeable pastime, in the days before theatre going was respectable as entertainment and before numerous lodges and commercial clubs satisfied man's instinct for gregariousness. James Redpath gave the institution a new lease on life in 1867 by establishing an efficient booking office, which kept the lyceums supplied with speakers and artists and raised the income of these entertainers considerably, besides netting the founder a tidy profit.

Thus, through a few years more the lecture platform broadened the influence of the nation's literati, performers and reformers; but by the middle 'seventies city folk were turning elsewhere for entertainment and enlightenment. Among the old favorite lecturers scandal, death and new occupations took their toll and the musical entertainers proved ineffective competitors with the new Gilbert and Sullivan operas. That part of the old lyceum clientele intent upon self-improvement and instruction, turned then to the Chautauqua, an institution which broadened out from its original function as a training course for Sunday

School teachers, into a vehicle of polite and instructive entertainment for the more conservative and puritanical part of the public.

Vigorous forms of relaxation and entertainment appealed to the generality, who went in for rages, each according to his station. Men of modest means who had been wont to exercise in the militia had learned baseball during the war and now devoted themselves to a hometown nine. Cincinnati in 1869 fathered the Red Stockings, an early professional team on a money-making basis. In the midst of the depression, Hulbert and Spalding succeeded in organizing the oldest of the major baseball leagues, the National. Thousands of people tumbled about delightedly on roller skates, a rage lately brought into this country from the pioneer precincts of Australia and persistently popular through the next generation. Skating rinks like that in Brooklyn became

Championship Cup Races

popular social and political centers. The more sedate attached no less importance to croquet, so that the *Nation* gave dignified space to detailed rules for its pursuit as a high art. The champion at the first national croquet convention in 1882 received a prize Spalding mallet. Mallets, in fact, like skates, became part of every child's education. A fourth possibility in the realm of sport came from Hartford where Colonel Pope began to build his Columbia bicycles. Bicycle riding, too, became a fad and supported academies, clubs, and race meets. At Chicago, the National Archery Association opened a series of tournaments in 1879 and rifle shooting was also popular. A number of the veterans kept their acquired skill in peaceful post-bellum days.

Vigorous sportsmen unequipped with skates, bicycles, bows and arrows, or mallets, distinguished themselves in pedestrian contests as did those who energetically walked toward the purse and belt waiting at the goal, in Madison Square Garden. German immigrants and the Y.M.C.A. sponsored "athletic clubs" for the increasing number of city dwellers whom the machine age was confining to sedentary occupations. The growing class of wealthy, leisured men devised athletic clubs of their own, and the founders of the New York Athletic Club undertook to organize amateur contests in a variety of field events. In 1871 it began holding annual field days. In all this activity lay some hope that women might abandon their ideal of delicacy and dyspepsia and share in the enthusiasm for open air exercise. After the turn of the century they showed a marked trend in the new direction.

The money complex of the period tinctured sporting interest. Horse-racing was extremely popular and the wealthy patronized the races of the American Jockey Club at Jerome Park; but the infiltration of a cheap sporting element threw racing into disrepute and made it dependent for existence upon financial profits rather than support by reputable society. The extremely wealthy elite cultivated the costly pastime of yachting and racing with Englishmen, who tried in vain to get back the trophy they had lost to an American clipper ship in 1851. The Westminster Kennel Club staged the first of a long series of dog shows. Fifth Avenue took to parading in coaches. Fortunately for the national health there were those in all classes who were learning again the possibilities of vigorous exercise or recreation in the open air, which their forbears under frontier conditions had taken for granted. It was high time.

Reading Habits

The mass contacts and broadening interests of city life whetted the public appetite for news, so that daily newspapers and weekly magazines grew in favor and importance and soon had many people reading regularly instead of rarely. Undoubtedly the strongest cultural influence had become the printed page. The war had encouraged a large number of half-literate people to read, because their eagerness for battle news was matched by the newspapers which maintained reporters at the front. News on Sunday came to be demanded in no small quantities, with the result that reporters became competitors for space, the papers were issued seven days instead of six, and circulation, resources and expenditures jumped together.

The end of the war by no means lessened the popularity of the papers for the Associated Press and the Western Union telegraph system co-operated in perfecting speedy delivery of news and the sapient editors changed the emphasis of their papers from editorials to current events. The Hoe printing press was improved to permit printing 10,000 to 12,000 eight-page papers an hour and stereotyping became common in large plants, thus further enlarging newspaper profits and influence. In quality that influence shared the extreme partizanship and venality of the age; Boss Tweed could intimidate Bryant's *Evening Post* and the pious Jay Cooke could purchase endorsement from the churchly *Independent*. But in the same period George Jones of the *New York*

Times and Thomas Nast of *Harper's Weekly* proved the press could be an instrument of exposure.

Next to newspapers, the vast majority found their chief reading in periodicals. Many of these continued highly moral in tone, sentimental to an extreme; and many a farm and village family long remained content with their religious weeklies as sources for outside information and reading enjoyment. Through the nation at large, however, a profound change was at work, slowly and haltingly turning American literature from romanticism, through local color, toward realism. As the period was in flux, none of its great, sincere writers fitted any sharp definition; but the influence of the frontier, of expanding agriculture and of industrial invention was away from the sentimental. Men of business and finance subscribed to the first, great, financial weekly, the *Commercial and Financial Chronicle*. Readers interested in science and invention bought R. L. Youngman's *Popular Science Monthly*. Brilliant literary criticism and fearless political comment were offered the intelligentsia by the *Nation,* edited weekly by E. L. Godkin.

Writers gradually turned from foreign, romantic locales to more realistic, native scenes, enroute later to a more penetrating portrayal of characters upon the scene. The middle of these three stages, lasting from the Civil War to the turn of the century, emphasized "local color." The nation had grown to the point where it was not only more aware of sectional peculiarities but more tolerant of and interested in them. The effect upon magazine writers, novelists and poets was dynamic, far-reaching. Striking innovations came to the monthlies with the establishment in 1870 of *Scribners*. The astute Dr. J. G. Holland, aiming at an organ influential upon political and social ideals as well as literature and art, devised *Scribners* as "An Illustrated Magazine for the People" with vastly improved pictures, better paper and more widely interesting subject matter. He encouraged originality and realism in literary and artistic contributors from all sections. The new magazines, and publishers like Scribners, Dutton and Holt put American authorship for the first time on a paying basis.

The conservative *Atlantic Monthly* was liberalized. Long the organ of the eminent, aristocratic verse and prose writers who congregated near Boston, it at first rejected the new literary movement and abashed young talent. Elderly and rather sterile upholders of the "Genteel Tradition" were repelled by the unloveliness into which American culture had descended and found it difficult to discern anything vital and significant in Whitman's "yawping" or in the low literary standards of the commonalty. Many of them turned with a shudder from the American scene to translate foreign classics, while such fastidious persons as Aldrich in Boston, Stoddard and Stedman in New York and Boker in Philadelphia tried to maintain a decadent cultural dictatorship over

American letters. They showed, as one brutal commentator put it, that "The New England conscience was tired."

About 1870 the Boston Brahmins and their organ began to take heed of the new currents. Even New England readers were demanding some local color, which Harriet Beecher Stowe and Sarah Orne Jewett attempted to satisfy with tales of commonplace life in deserted seaports and of the trek from New England to the West. Local color finally appeared in Southern treatments also. There proved to be less popular appeal, however, in gentle stories of decadent civilizations, than in robuster narratives of life nearer the frontier. So the *Atlantic* obtained W. D. Howells of Ohio, a "genteel" realist identified with the local color movement, as editor, and he inaugurated a regime of more democratic literature. His most noteworthy novel was his sympathetic and faithful portrait of his fellow Americans in *The Rise of Silas Lapham*. He has been called "our first conscious realist of major proportions."

Oddly, the magazines showed a common obliviousness to the new forms of industrial life multiplying on every side. Factories and mines simply did not appeal as literary subjects; Rebecca Harding had published in the *Atlantic Monthly* (in 1861) a Pennsylvania story, "Life in the Iron Mills" and Elizabeth Stuart Phelps ten years later tried a sentimental treatment of New England mills, *The Silent Partner,* but in the main this rich field of industrial realism remained unexploited until the turn of the century. It lacked the romanticism which the Gilded Age relinquished reluctantly. The majority of readers were not questioning the benefits of industrialization.

In novel reading, likewise, taste shifted gradually. Formerly, worship of Dickens and eminent Victorians had been the style among the elite. Of American novels, women had been the chief readers and their uneducated taste (college women were very few) was for the moral, commonplace and "instructive." There were very few public libraries and bookstores, and purchasers ordinarily knew little of any volumes except those offered by subscription agents. Novels of sentiment remained very popular. At the battle front, however, men and boys had passed from hand to hand the thousands of dime yellowbacks edited by Erastus Beadle of the American News Company; and after peace, western humor, folk literature and local color expressed the growth in national consciousness and boosted the book trade. Beadle's company built up a profitable distribution business and Mark Twain, despite the lords of literature, became the most widely read novelist, because he understood "the shirt sleeve life of the average American" and was by turns romanticist, local colorist and realist. The cocksure and extravagant nation joined uproariously in the irreverent, lowbrow fun he poked at Europe in *Innocents Abroad* (1869); in its preface he defined all his work "I am sure I have written at least honestly, whether wisely or not." He caught the color of life.

His more serious portraiture, of the current scoundrelisms at Washington scathingly satirized in *The Gilded Age* (1872),[1] little pleased a public not yet given to self-criticism. He reacted to rebuff like a true son of his period; he abandoned serious treatments until a more sympathetic day, filling the interim with profitable local color novels.

One of Clemens' more sensitive literary compatriots, Henry James, fled from the simple, crude American environment to Old World culture, as a better place to write; but he remained anxious to present his native land in the best possible light, producing *Daisy Miller* (the story of an early American flapper), *The American, The Europeans,* and *The Portrait of a Lady*. This aristocratic genius, engrossed in the inner realities, was scarcely appreciated by the majority of readers in the democracy.

The third outstanding literary genius of the Gilded Age was the romantic idealist, Walt Whitman, who had such sympathy for the common people and such interest in the ordinary stuff of life that it made him, also, a realist, concerned with the "here and now." Spiritually reborn by experiences as a nurse during the Civil War,[2] he added to his deep convictions of the unity of the American nation and the solidarity of America with all the globe, a third conviction—fraternity among all classes. This was his final phase and through the lush, postwar period, with its increasing tendencies toward the separation of society into economic classes, this poet retained his faith in democracy and his insistence upon a frank portrayal of common people. He conceived his mission to be that of critic and prophet—critic of the unbrotherly individualists, of the "hoggish, cheating, bedbug qualities" of the Fisks, Goulds and Drews of the Gilded Age—prophet of manhood growing in a broadly social state, the kind of state to which the United States was growing less like, each day of developing materialism.

Attention to Educational Needs

The crowding of foreigners into the cities brought out the alarming fact that the majority of the newcomers were illiterates and threatened to engulf the native population under a vicious wave of ignorance. Inasmuch as the nation as a whole had a healthy faith in the efficacy of education for democratic purposes, and realized that current methods for enlightening those born within the country were not perfect, public opinion supported expansion of educational facilities.

---

[1] Written with Charles Dudley Warner, a writer more in the general tradition.
[2] The northerner Whitman, and the southerner Sidney Lanier, were the only poets to surmount sectional prejudice and denounce war.

In the lower range of city education postwar growth was almost entirely in quantity rather than quality. The women who as a result of the war had begun to replace the men as teachers worked in the cities under a curriculum little changed in recent years. But there was a healthy desire outside the largest centers to imitate such changes as had been inaugurated in them since about 1850. Organizing of pupils in grades became more common in small towns. History (largely as a by-product of the war) became a regular subject in village elementary schools; elementary science, leading to physiology, music and drawing further enlarged the lists. Most important was the effort to replace rote question and answer instruction with teaching by objects, orally; and this effort blossomed into lively results in geography, mental arithmetic and language. Pupils more frequently were taught speech usage of English instead of formalistic grammar. In the cities kindergartens multiplied, chiefly under private support, so that there were some 300 of them by 1880, and about a dozen schools for training their teachers. There was much promise for the future of the public elementary and secondary institutions throughout the country because normal schools started their effort to elevate the fitness of teachers, and the general attitude was not one of complacency. The democratic trend in education was also indicated in displacement of many old tuition academies by free public high schools.

The most marked postwar advance in education was achieved by the colleges, for the field of higher education was not dominated by the artificiality which marked men's activities in more popular fields. The number of citizens directly concerned with collegiate advance necessarily remained relatively small, what with the influence of the war upon enrollment and the lowering, by the influx of immigrants, of the absolute percentage of students in college attendance. But this smallness proved advantageous, as lessening the inertia which hindered reform, and as permitting a deepening of culture far beyond the general trend and disposition of the age.

One of the first signs that the colleges were rousing from their long-standing state of depression, appeared in the increase of state colleges and universities made possible by the passage of the Morrill Land Grant College Act, and in the resuscitation of languishing institutions by funds from that measure. The private colleges also increased because war fortunes inspired generosity, toward both sexes. Persons of wealth, like Matthew Vassar, Ezra Cornell, George Peabody, Henry Wells, and Sophia Smith, turned their originality and creative energies into the organization and endowment of schools for women, for people bent toward the practical arts, and for students of science, which in its evolutionary aspects was now warring sturdily with the current belief in a six-day scheme of creation. Religious organizations also founded colleges, the most notable of the decade being that of Hicksite Friends, at Swarthmore, Pennsylvania.

In these private endowments, as in the Morrill law, was evident the urge to widen the field of knowledge at the same time that higher education was made more available, to both sexes, in all sections. To the classical studies were added others in "agriculture and mechanic arts" and in "science." Necessarily, there was much stumbling in attempts to broaden curricula, because of their experimental nature and intense opposition from clerical conservatives loathe to lose control. But relative success attended the efforts of bold executives like James B. Angell, Daniel Coit Gilman, Charles W. Eliot and Andrew D. White, who set to work to give their courses of study sufficient fluidity to fit them into the changing needs of the nation.

Over the broad expanse of the elective system immature students wandered and lost themselves, but it rooted out the old regime so thoroughly as to make room for the planting of healthy new ideas in education. In institutions headed by such leaders, the teaching staff became more scholarly, the work deeper and more thorough, while respect for scholarship increased. While few notable scientists as yet had been produced, the collegiate group eagerly acknowledged such foreign leadership as that of Darwin, giving Spencer's work on evolution, for example, a far readier sale in the United States than in England.

An exceptional educational experience came to Americans in 1876, when the Centennial of Independence was celebrated in the city of its birth. From this great display of domestic and foreign products no mere financial depression could keep the nation away, for interest in it and efforts to make it possible extended from East to West. The general public was intensely interested in self-improvement, whatever that might be. The railroads reduced their rates and no less than three million perspiring people (for the summer was exceptionally hot) managed to visit Philadelphia. Every day in the week except Sunday and all day long until dark (for the Fair was unlighted) they stormed the gates. Their reports of the strange people and things they saw reached practically the entire nation. A very few Americans may have expressed regret at the bad architecture of the buildings, and with the exception of England, at the poor showing in art; but the vast majority were quite carried away by the mechanical prowess of their native land, whose exhibits took up three-fourths of the space in "Machinery Hall." They gazed spellbound at machinery turning out familiar articles of daily use, and at strange inventions demonstrated before their wondering eyes. In these fields American ingenuity justly showed its preeminence.

Even more important, from a cultural standpoint, was the visitors' view of foreign displays. A new heaven and a new earth opened before them in the curious Oriental wares, the fine European furniture, the

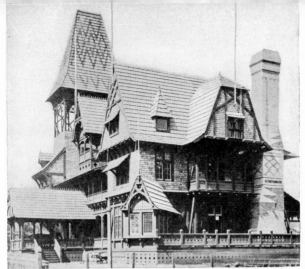

THREE GENERATIONS OF EXPOSITIONS

New Jersey Building, 1876 Centennial, Philadelphia; Machinery Hall, The Columbian Exposition, Chicago; Trylon and Perisphere, 1939 World's Fair, New York

porcelains, textiles, watches and innumerable other products of beautiful workmanship, badly needed as a corrective influence upon local artistic standards and understanding.

Some few there were who tried to escape the current artificiality and find sincere expression of America's artistic potentialities, but for the most part Mr. Average Citizen saw perfection in his period. The portly gentlemen who adorned their faces with the heavy beards favored at the time, they who disguised their hickory shirts with the accommodating linen dickeys, or encased their city feet in polished topboots reminiscent of the western cowhides, were immensely concerned with outward appearances of a sort. They observed that they were living in a time of change, and talking it over among themselves locally, perhaps before the glittering bar of a favorite saloon in the city, or around the stove in the pleasant tobacco-juice atmosphere of some rural general store, they concluded that this change must be progress. Were not they of America, of the East, at the hub of the universe?

CHAPTER XVIII

RISE OF THE FAR WEST

The primacy of the East was not to remain unchallenged. A new sectionalism was in process of evolving; it was to produce new rivalries and conflicts; it would affect profoundly the onward march of democracy. In the years of war and reconstruction the Far West was growing rapidly with frequent aid from the East, where it was looked upon as a fair field for exploitation as a source of wealth. This vast expanse of plain, plateau, and mountain began at the agricultural frontier and extended to the Pacific Coast. From the middle of the century it had been shrinking in size steadily, as its population multiplied and diversified on its eastern edge; and its western edge had acquired centers of city life, at San Francisco and Portland where capital concentrated and industries beyond the frontier stage ambitiously raised their heads.

Government Aid

The task of developing the Far West was so huge that it seemed almost impossible for private capital to undertake it. Efforts to gain aid from the government before the war had been blocked by the South. After the withdrawal of the southern congressmen, the friends of subsidy could put their plans into statutes. The Homestead Act, the Morrill Land Grant College Act and the Union Pacific Railroad Acts had bestowed great gifts of land on people, states and corporations. A flood of bona fide settlers, of speculators and corporation owners availed themselves of these gifts. For the horde moving westward Congress established at Washington a department of agriculture headed by a commissioner and under the Morrill Land Grant College Act aided each state in maintaining a "college of agriculture and mechanic arts." After these institutions developed instruction and technique they would aid the farmers as would the state departments of agriculture established at the same time.

But the most immediate need of the would-be homesteader was for railroads to take him to his homestead and to carry his crops to market after he had grown them, just as the railroads needed the farmers to furnish the crops for paying freight. In fact, the strength of the homestead push against the frontier line was largely attributable, outside of population pressure, to the mechanical improvements symbolic of the new industrial era—to the new implements and new steel rails—and their interreaction upon the people. The inhabitants of North, South and West had been sharing in railroad enthusiasms before the war, placing in operation 30,600 miles divided equally among their sections and in each outstripping the actual needs of the population at the moment. The inefficient and expensive character of this rail transportation, due to lack of uniformity in such important respects as time, gauge and fuel, became apparent during the war when water routes were used extensively to offset rail deficiencies. But even as it was, emergency war uses, coupled with the European demand for food products, so doubled and

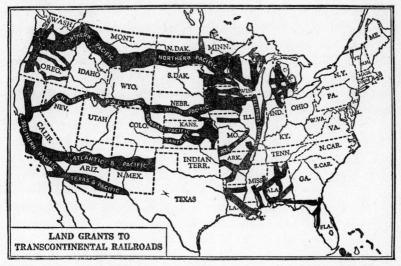

LAND GRANTS TO TRANSCONTINENTAL RAILROADS

From *American Economic History* by H. U. Faulkner, by permission of Harper & Brothers, publishers.

tripled rail earnings as to lay the basis for a spurt of both legitimate activity and speculation when there no longer should be a war to check construction.

All classes felt the enthusiasm for a transcontinental railroad. Establishment of the transcontinental telegraph in 1861 had whetted the universal desire for improved transportation of goods and people. All over the United States the tempo of life was quickening and it was generally conceded, even by people who had not the slightest chance of going west, that thirty days for a traveller to cross the continent and eighteen days for a letter by "fast" pony express were entirely too slow.

The statutes chartering the Union Pacific and Central Pacific Railroad corporations (scheduled to construct trackage west from the 100th meridian and east from the Pacific coast) gave free rights of way, *carte blanche* to take from nearby lands any construction material required for the work, and gifts of five alternate sections of land per mile on each side of the track, selected by the recipient from within ten miles of it. Since for each mile constructed the government agreed to loan 6% federal bonds, at the rates of $16,000 across the plains, $32,000 across the plateaus, and $48,000 across the mountains (these bonds to be secured by a first mortgage on the property) the impetus to building seemed considerable; and when two years later the nation's representatives increased the alternate sections to ten, to be selected from within twenty miles of the track, and changed the government loan from a first to a second mortgage, rapid construction could not be far away.

It went forward with a rush in 1865 with both railroads in financial difficulties and competing for the lion's share of the mileage bonus, a situation which made tracklaying as circuitous as it was careless. This was especially true of the Union Pacific, because of the machinations of its construction corporation, the "Credit Mobilier" which was promoted with congressional connivance to take the profits of the government bounty from the railroad corporation itself. The Central Pacific's "Contract and Finance Company" built somewhat less hastily and dishonestly. During the winter of 1868-1869 the interest of the entire population rose to white heat, with the competing forces employing 20,000 workmen, with the Union Pacific laying tracks on ice and snow, and the Central Pacific filing a tantalizing map registering their intention to build east of Ogden into what their rival considered their own territory. Neither side stopped to finish tunnels or spare expense, the Union Pacific sometimes paying as much as 18% for loans. Defense against the Indians, and the requirement that only American iron be used, further increased costs.

The rival lines actually passed each other for a distance of ten miles, before they turned and met near Promontory Point, Utah, 10 May 1869. The Central Pacific had annexed about three-fifths as much mileage as its opponent. Their meeting was signalized in the typical, ebullient spirit of the frontier, a golden spike was driven at the meeting place, and the sound of the hammer was telegraphed across the vast uninhabited spaces to the east and west; Chicago staged a parade miles in length, New York's Trinity chimes rang out, and Philadelphia listened to the sacred Liberty Bell.

The general pride of the nation in this achievement was felt among all classes, those who could not travel as well as the few who knew from experience that crossing the continent was now cut to eight days. The fate of the United States, it appeared, was bound up with the number and speed of construction of railroads. Although Congress did not duplicate the direct financial aid of the Union and Central Pacific in the case of other railroad corporations, it continued to charter them with huge land grants. Notably there were:—the Northern Pacific, to connect the Great Lakes with Puget Sound and, after war heat had cooled, the Southern Pacific and Santa Fé to tie the Mississippi Valley with the Pacific Coast through areas south of the route of the Union Pacific, besides the Denver and Rio Grande to cut through the Colorado mountains and cross the "Desert" to Salt Lake City. Cities, counties and states followed the lead of the federal government in subsidy, so that by 1870 one-half the cost of the original railroad construction had been contributed by these four public agencies. When the panic year befell, the gifts in land of the government to the railroads amounted to about 35 million acres and about 145 million more had been promised to the Pacific railroads alone. Such open-handedness could scarcely have come from popular representatives if the electorate had not been optimistic, railroad-mad for the nonce. This was the peak of the period of aid to railroads. Regulation, another story, was on the way. That lesson would be learned from adversity.

In the Middle West railroad building was undertaken to make connections with the Union Pacific; the Chicago and Northwestern stretched to meet it at Omaha, Nebraska; the Kansas Pacific went round by Denver to meet it at Cheyenne, Wyoming Territory. Minnesota, Iowa and northern Missouri in particular multiplied their lines, with construction most rapid in the three years before the panic (1869-1872) and in the year following recovery from it (1879-1880). Between 1860 and 1880 mileage trebled through the nation at large, doubling even in the secession area, and the network of railways which had stopped at the Mississippi twenty years earlier extended well past the Missouri. This pulled the true boundaries of the Middle West far west of what they had been, as shown by the list of the 12 states having the most mileage in 1880. Illinois came first, and then after Pennsylvania and New York ranked Ohio, Iowa, Indiana, Missouri, Michigan, Kansas, Texas, Wisconsin and Minnesota.

To the termini and junction points of the blossoming railroads flocked the venturesome and shrewd, multiplying the settlements and changing the face of the countryside. Their hegira so stimulated inventors that they made yet more radical the changes in the actual appearance of tracks, engines and cars, changes which the war had inaugurated. Steel replaced iron rails, large steam engines replaced tiny wood-burners, a gauge of four feet, eight and one-half inches replaced seven others, bridges took the place of ferries and sleighs, gas lights supplanted oil lamps, steam pipes ousted wood-burning stoves, and a second track began to appear alongside the single one. In 1864 George Pullman had placed in service the first comfortable sleeping car, which he aptly named "The Pioneer" and four years later the patrons of the Chicago and Alton viewed the scenery of Illinois from the windows of the first genuine dining car, travelling in the better security afforded by the new air brake invented by George Westinghouse.

Railroad Promotion

The voluntary influx of settlers was extremely large, and farmers westward-bound were joined by demobilized soldiers and workmen formerly employed in war industries. Artificial stimuli also were applied. A federal act of 1864 exempted immigrants from military service and aided them in travelling westward at little expense and trouble. All the railroads invited immigrants and settlers on their own behalf, adding to the Irish and Chinese who had laid the first transcontinental line, hundreds of citizens from the East and Germans, Scotch, Irish, English and other settlers bidden from abroad by avid advertising propaganda. Perhaps the most strenuous colonizing activities were those sponsored by the optimistic Jay Cooke for settling lands belonging to the Northern Pacific, first in the Minnesota region and thence in Dakota and Montana. Swedes, Norwegians, Finns, Hollanders, Mennonites from South Russia, Bohemians and Germans rode to the "New Northwest," attracted thither by facts, figures, need for work, and a climate advertised as so salubrious that the only pangs of the residents were those from over-eating. The astute Mr. Cooke's land department employed as promoters of emigration abroad, Swedish and Norwegian clergymen, a Danish bishop and an English organizer of farm laborers. The close competition among watercarriers and among landcarriers forced steam-rail alliances. They had to cultivate goodwill and subsidize each other to secure profits.

In the United States, promotion schemes cleverly utilized the existing organization of Civil War veterans for advertising the Northwest and for influencing Congress. Major Hibbard, Cooke's superintendent of immigration, organized the "Army of the Cumberland and Tennessee Colonization Society," which helped to get from the Congress facing election in 1872 a measure which doubled, for the Civil War veterans, the government acreage which they could take up within the limits of railroad grants, and counted toward their five year title period whatever time they had served in the army or navy. This remission may have been the speedier because up to this time scarcely one-third of the pioneer farmers had been able to endure the necessary five years of residence.

Hundreds of immigrants would congregate simultaneously at the main foci of settlement, temporarily accommodated at cost in company "reception houses." If they were bona fide purchasers transportation was free to them and their families and they had seven years in which to pay for their lands, with interest as low as 7%. They were paying, just before the panic, from $2.50 to $7.00 an acre, depending on nearness to the railroad. Land sales for cash were of course rudely disrupted by the failure of the firm of Jay Cooke and Company and the ensuing panic; and in their place a trade sprang up in exchanging land for depreciated land-grant bonds, at par value. Thus speculators were attracted and at the same time bona fide farmers were informed that the price to them could be cut anywhere from 20% to 60% according as they contracted to put the land under immediate cultivation. Such terms attracted men of means who established the so-called "bonanza farms" of eastern Dakota, huge areas devoted to wheat crops and immensely effective in attracting investment and settlement. Their ingenuity mitigated the evil effects of the panic to such an extent that, between 1873 and 1878, about 3000 purchasers bought 1,724,000 acres of Northern Pacific land. In so far as the purchasers were speculators, who bought only for a rise, they retarded the development of the region; but the decade closed with the railroad company finances sufficiently strong to push both construction and colonization west of the Missouri. Soon the energetic Henry Villard acquired control and embraced this movement in his gigantic schemes for peopling with farmers the Pacific northwest, not alone the Willamette Valley but also the far-flung "Inland Empire" of Washington, Oregon and Idaho east of the Cascades.

Henry Villard's investments in the Oregon Steamship Company and allied enterprises carried him into a broad immigration campaign, working through agencies strategically placed in such centers as Boston, New York, Topeka and San Francisco, besides others in England, Scotland and Germany. He loosed floods of propaganda,—newspaper notices published as reading matter, circulars, booklets, translations and exposition displays—to praise the region and demonstrate its productivity. The panic gave his bureaus the cooperation of agencies for the relief of the unemployed and bad seasons in California, Nebraska and elsewhere in the United States and Europe turned disaffected farmers toward his lands. His ingenious campaign manager, T. R. Tannant, cleverly secured cooperation from eastern railroad officials, helped immigrants obtain through tickets properly routed, persuaded others to change their destination from San Francisco to Portland, and recruited shiploads at a time. Some immigrants received half-fare tickets. They paid from $1.25 to $7.00 per acre with 10% discount for cash payment and a ten year time allowance. In 1876 the Villard immigrants were estimated at 7500 and the next year at 18,000. After he organized the Oregon Railway and Navigation Company in 1879 to build tracks on the south bank of the Columbia up to the Snake River, his populating efforts were further intensified. Villard, like Cooke, splendidly demonstrated the new opportunism in the westward movement as engineered by railroad interests after the Civil War.

The people moving into the Far West included three main groupings. First, the rumors of mineral wealth attracted miners who wandered widely at will; to meet their needs, came owners and drivers of mule trains who freighted supplies, and dealers in supplies, liquor and social pastimes who set up pine board towns where the trails crossed or navigation ended. Second, a sudden development of the fresh beef industry brought cowboys, ranchers and the cattle-town people, who maintained a sporadic existence at the trail and rail heads and profited by the rough businesses auxiliary to breeding, selling and shipping cattle. Third, came pioneer farmers, more concerned with grain and hogs than with beef or sheep, a stable element interested in the ownership and fencing in of farms and in the erection of banks, schools and churches at their community centers. This group was the active force in pushing the agricultural frontier westward from the line of 1860 and eastward from the river valleys of Washington, Oregon and California.

The Indians

Before settled life could really be secure the original inhabitants had to be dealt with. When the robust energies of the nation turned to play actively in the Far West some 300,000 redskins were scattered over it, occupying lands granted to them by the government, receiving annual supplies from the "Great White Father," and pledging themselves to remain peacefully in their areas and to permit other people to pass through. The arrangement had been working passably well but as increasing numbers of white people entered their vicinity contact inevitably brought conflict. Upon fertile areas, careless of whether or not the government had paid the Indians for them, would-be agriculturists would squat unceremoniously, pre-empting claims. Again, natives would find that sums long due their tribes on land they had ceded, had been cancelled by the debts of individual members while ownership was irrevocably lost. Elsewhere, prospectors passing through Indian lands would turn off the beaten trails to search for gold, and if they found it, would set up a claim on the spot. The Indians saw their hunting grounds ruthlessly overrun and the whites clinging to stakes along the routes of travel into the mining districts, particularly in Colorado and Idaho.

The continued presence of these people disturbed the savages, especially such younger braves as maintained the old blanket existence and distrusted tribesmen who took up farming or other civilizing pursuits. Worst of all, along the lines of the railroads and elsewhere, the newcomers proved unable to resist the temptation to shoot into the great herds of buffalo, upon which plains Indians depended for large supplies of meat, clothing and crude equipment. The whites amused themselves with the easy sport of wanton destruction, while the Indians saw their most useful animals wiped out in short order.

Furthermore, the railroad builders, the ranchers, the miners and their ilk were certain that the Indians had no rights which they were bound to respect, because the resources of the region were obviously in disuse,

awaiting exploitation, and the savages stood in the way. The frontiersman naturally could conceive of no good Indian but a dead one, and
acted accordingly. To their theory the War Department, sending out
troops to protect the whites, heartily subscribed. Other branches of
the government were scarcely more humane in attitude. Political agents
resident in the Indian country by appointment generally regarded their
charges as fair prey and helped traders cheat them outrageously in the
blanket and general supply business. In these far-distant depredations
the administrations in Washington inclined to a policy of acquiescence;

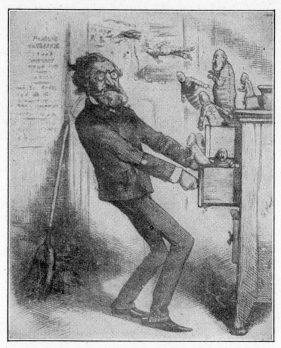

Secretary Schurz Cleaning Out the Indian Bureau

the war, or politics nearer home, seemed so much more important. Only
a few officials of the Department of the Interior and the few honest
Indian agents could see both sides of the argument; they ordinarily were
unable to persuade the War Department that it was unnecessarily ruthless, because they were regarded as misguided and impractical altruists.
The Indians exerted little political pressure.

Confronted on all sides with overwhelming odds against them, the
Indians resolved that their best lands should not be taken over by
farmers, their hunting grounds should not be ruined by railroads, miners
and wagon trains crossing them, without a struggle. They adopted the
only weapons they understood—ambush, pillage, massacre, as horrible
border warfare as possible. When the Civil War was well under way,

the time had seemed propitious. There ensued five years of as determined an effort as they could make. In hundreds of forays, large and small, they harried the frontier, levying a toll on life and property in the main regions of white incursion.

Over the farming lands of the Minnesota valley, through the summer of 1862, the Sioux under Little Crow had contested, with pillage and slaughter, the advance of settlers; they were quelled in the fall and the next year they were relegated further west to a less inviting domicile. In Colorado 1864 found the Cheyenne and Arapahoe in the way of the Pike's Peak mining camps; again scalping and burning proved futile to stop the advance of United States troops. Colonel Chivington adopted in this case the thoroughly savage expedient of surprising and destroying a peaceful Indian camp on Sand Creek. This severe "lesson" made it none the easier for the government to persuade Red Cloud and his Plains Sioux of the advisability of a fortified road across their best hunting grounds for the benefit of the miners of Idaho and Montana. In this case, the Indians and their allies temporarily won their point, in the dropping of the project in 1865 and when it was resumed the next year they forced the troops at Fort Kearney to pay for their temerity with their lives: two years later the government definitely deserted the fort sites on this road.

In the midst of the carnage and cost, when the troops on the whole were getting the better of the contest, sentiment against the way Indian affairs were being conducted was aroused among friends of the savages and their intellectual supporters in the East. Although many of these advocates were considered misguided idealists of the savage character, which in truth knew no civilized standard of conduct, Congress consented to investigate whether the military principle of annihilation were the only solution. A temporary, mixed civilian and military commission, appointed in 1867, worked to clear away the tribal obstacles in the path of the railroads and the pioneers, and succeeded in peaceably shunting numerous bands into less inconvenient locations, while a Bureau of Education began to consider the savages' enlightenment. While these pacific agencies were getting started, General Custer down in Indian Territory had broken the back of the Cheyenne and Arapahoe resistance by a night foray which destroyed their main camp and killed their leader, Black Kettle.

Then ensued some eight years of relative peace from 1868 to 1876, which gave Grant an opportunity welcome to him. Though a military man he was no enthusiastic follower of the doughty commanders in the border warfare, Sheridan, Chivington and Custer, who had been fighting the Indians with their own weapons; and a few weeks after he became President he appointed a permanent board of Indian Commissioners representing several religious sects and both political parties to keep a watchful eye upon the expenditures of the wily Indian agents. The agents themselves he tried to choose from candidates nominated by missionary groups, and he permitted religious organizations to maintain representatives on the reservations. The futile practice of trying to deal with the Indians by treaty as independent nations was abolished and roving tendencies were combated by assembling the tribes in definitely limited precincts.

The Far West continued to invite immigration and its economic expansion progressively crowded the uncivilized Indians toward the wall. Persistence of hard times in the East fostered some migration into the promising West, marked by search for gold in Dakota. Plains Sioux, resenting invasion of their Black Hills reservation, in 1876 were led by Sitting Bull to turn the tables on General Custer at the storied battle of the Little Big Horn, known among the whites as a "massacre." The Indian victory, however, was but a prelude to defeat. Some fled into Canada, where the Royal Mounted Police got on with them with less friction. Chief Joseph and his Nez Perce in the Snake River valley fared no better than the Sioux; they were bound for a Canadian haven when Colonel Miles revenged Custer upon them, and relegated them to an "unhealthy" part of Indian territory. The courts had proclaimed that Indians were not citizens within the meaning of the 14th Amendment; but Congress sensed no great gap between the two stages of culture and proposed speedily to metamorphose these 250,000 semi-savage, hunting people into civilized farmers, the miracle to be worked on reservations.

There they were herded as tribesmen, with excellent opportunity to adopt the white man's vices and very little chance to keep the Indian's self-support. The government made a little effort to educate the children, teach adults agriculture and facilitate individual landownership and citizenship; but Congress, influenced by selfish white interests, refused a comprehensive program. As the advance of settlement and railroad construction diminished the Indians' past means of livelihood and their chance of escape, some of them made disastrous efforts to flee the reservations.

Their cruel predicament inspired Helen Hunt Jackson to write *A Century of Dishonor* (1881), whereupon eastern humanitarians organized the Indian Rights Association and the Lake Mohonk Conference of Friends of the Indians, and President Cleveland entered office actively interested. The Apaches, crowded into New Mexico and Arizona reservations, were making (1882-1886) the final, great protest. The upshot was the so-called "Dawes" Act of 1887, known as "The Emancipation Act of the Indians." It signalized a temporary union of the lobbies of the humanitarians and the land-hungry, who agreed upon its terms; it encouraged Indians to abandon the tribal relationship and enter upon land ownership individually [1] as citizens and provided funds for educating and civilizing them. Although the newly liberated redmen were preyed upon by politicians and cattle interests desiring illegal land privileges, and although liquor sale victimized the weak, and protective legislation hindered the progress of the strong, the Indians gradually ceased to constitute a problem, for the savage barrier to economic advance had been removed. Their number increased and a few became very wealthy through oil discoveries.

Mining People and Cattlemen

Without waiting for the Indians to be disposed of, an acquisitive horde of miners was penetrating the Far West. Those of the forty-niners who had traversed the region in their rush to California had given much of it a forbidding name—the Great American Desert—by reason of the dangers and privations they had endured at the hands of the Indians and climate. Thereafter a decade elapsed without revealing much of the true resources. Then came the discovery of gold at Pike's Peak in the region of the Colorado and of silver at the far-famed "Comstock" lode in the Nevada country (1859). The miners and the soldiers within the next four years made gold and silver finds in the mountain portions of what later became known as Idaho, Montana, Wyoming and even Arizona. Copper and lead were also discovered in important quantities. Immigration was vastly stimulated. Placer gold mining in western Montana, for example, developed with a rapidity which started a tide of population into that region twenty years ahead of time.

The miners dashed from one discovery to the next, scarcely less migratory than the redskins, setting up lawless communities, known as "boom towns" over night and deserting them just as quickly. By necessity adept at individual action, they could also unite effectively upon what they considered community essentials. They were as one in their demands upon Congress for territorial organization to protect their mining claims, for wagon roads and railroads to lessen their privations and bring markets closer, and for protection against the Indians whose lands they over-ran. They were quick to resent efforts to victimize them wholesale; for example, when the miners of Virginia City, Montana Territory, were faced by a corner in flour, which raised the price of a ninety-eight pound sack from $26.50 to $90.00, they met the situation by raiding the stores and carrying off what they needed, not forgetting to leave payment at the regular rate. Again, when shootings became too frequent and indiscriminate, "necktie parties" were summarily meted out to the worst offenders. The miners gave their communities a lim-

[1] They could have 160 acre tracts, citizenship and the protection of territorial and state laws.

ited amount of social control by setting up a crude governmental machine known as the "mining district," which embodied the early, accepted practices and taboos of the industry and influenced the content of the federal laws on mining enacted in 1866 and 1872.

At the same time, the sparseness of population allowed a very wide latitude in standards of personal behaviour. They naturally adapted their social usages to their rude environment, reverting to primitive methods and outlook. Nature around them was harsh and they reflected her harshness—to women, to children, to each other and to animals. Life had a low value, a man often was solitary and therefore usually suspicious, and in his actions he felt fairly free of group inhibitions.

After the initial stampede into a region, the metal which could be washed out or dug up cheaply by two or three prospectors working in cooperation played out, and mining entered on its next stage, wherein eastern capitalists provided the funds and organization to carry on expensive operations working large deposits. Miners came to live in company-owned towns where life was less picturesque and independent than in the typical prospectors' community. The energy of the efforts of prospectors, miners and operators was so stupendous that between 1860 and 1873 they together increased the national silver output from $150,000 to $36,000,000 and silver fell in price.

This over-supply drew attention to the fact that the silver dollar had been demonetized. The silver producers joined cheap money advocates in urging the government to purchase and coin silver in unlimited quantities. While the price continued to fall through two decades (p. 449), the controversy between West and East over silver subsidy continued. The representatives of the mining interest, therefore, were found, like their opponents in the House and Senate, repeatedly utilizing pending legislation as an opportunity to strike bargains for their constituent industries.

That part of the Far West which consisted of wide rolling plains covered with grass became, during the postwar period, the scene of a peculiarly transitory form of food-producing industry, for cattlemen swept across the stage before farmers pre-empted it. These convenient grazing lands were discovered by Texans, long engaged in breeding for hides, and before the outbreak of the war they had begun to drive cattle up to St. Louis where they shipped them east for food. The comparative isolation of the Civil War period left Texas "brimming over with cattle"—even enough to stock much of the region to the north. When the transcontinental railroad builders brought their rails as far as Abilene, Kansas (1867), in the heart of the grass country, the ex-Confederates seized the opportunity to drive some 35,000 of their longhorns up there for shipment, fattening the herds enroute upon the same grass which the buffalo had found so succulent. Railroad building progressed and cattle driving increased. In two years the size of the herds had multiplied by ten; two years more and their numbers had passed half a million. They were driven to the shipping corrals of the Kansas Pacific at Abilene, Ellsworth, Hayes City, and Dodge City, to the Union Pacific cattle trains at Ogallala, Nebraska and Cheyenne, Wyoming Territory and at the heighth of the industry even as far north as the grasses grew, to Montana and into Canada.

The prosperity of the Texans brought competitors, convinced that a region adapted to fattening cattle must also be convenient for breeding them. The railroad and mining camps were creating a demand for fresh meat far west of the earlier shipping depots and what was not needed nearby could be shipped on the hoof to Kansas City, Chicago, Milwaukee and lesser centers. As fast as the trans-Missouri plains and plateaus secured railroad connections with the East the market was further enlarged. So, into the suitable parts of new territories and states, into Colorado, Dakota, Kansas, Nebraska and Wyoming, came stockmen to settle. Immense cattle ranges, unfenced domains thriving upon free land and forage, claimed sway over more than a million square miles of plain and upland. The stockmen fought among themselves over branding and cattle thefts and together opposed the "Long Drive," the sheep herders, horse thieves and pioneer farmers.

Pastoral life, which formerly occupied a comparatively narrow strip of land in the process of United States expansion, now speedily spread over an area larger than that occupied in the East by agriculture, influencing American life stupendously if briefly. In the food habits of countless Americans beef took the place of pork. After canning of meats became common, and G. F. Swift introduced the refrigerated car, meat packing concentrated at the larger centers, thus creating a highly industrialized population in the midst of agricultural pursuits. As a consequence Chicago by 1880 had 503,000 inhabitants, St. Louis, 351,000 and Kansas City, 56,000. Even in literature the cow country made a place for itself to the delight of eastern readers.

New governmental forms were invented for the cattle industry since the legal machinery of the territories and young states could not take care of unprecedented situations. The stockmen formed pools, and local, district and inter-territorial associations to attend to their mutual needs. The Colorado Stock Growers Association was formed as early as 1867 and a powerful organization came into existence in Wyoming half a dozen years later. The "Association" regulated the round-ups (in themselves highly cooperative enterprises), had jurisdiction over strays and unbranded animal (mavericks) and engineered petitions for lower freight rates. A very important function was the maintenance of forces of secret "detectives," so efficient that criminals feared the long arm of the "Association" reaching far across the ranges, more than the local

authority of sheriffs. Relations with the Indians were smoothed by a
special type of skillful diplomacy adapted to their situation.

These organizations enjoyed social affairs at their annual meetings,
when large and small owners, cowpunchers, managers, foremen, freight
agents and commission men intermingled jovially, making useful acquaintance. Of course association members were elected to legislatures
and placed their mark upon law-making. As far away as Washington
they influenced the enactment of the law of 1871 regulating conditions
of cattle transportation. But in spirit these extra-legal organizations
existed primarily to protect property, not to safeguard individual liberty.

The profits of the stockmen were enormous as long as free land kept
their capital investment down to the relatively small costs of breeding,
branding, rounding-up and driving. Often the fresh beef brought them
five times its cost. Rarely had industry in the United States or elsewhere reaped such profit and the middle plainsmen determined to cut
off the Texans from it. The Texans bred cattle so fast they imperiled
the forage supply in the north; furthermore, at the end of the Long
Drive they glutted the market. Their competitors therefore did what
they could to cut off the trails from Texas. They interposed barbed
wire fences around the best supplies of food and water and by corralling
their own steers within these same fences after their roundup, they were
able to delay their own sales until the glut in the market was past. The
Texans were at too great a disadvantage and by the middle 'seventies
the end of the Long Drive was definitely forecast; a decade later, the
door against the southern cattle would be finally shut by quarantine
against "Texas fever."

Meanwhile, the question intruded as to how long the stockmen would
be allowed to monopolize the open, unowned range. That depended
upon the speed with which the government sold large areas, and as early
as 1879 the Public Lands Commission was making inquiry of westerners
as to their views on land sale. Cattlemen and the newly-arrived sheepmen
fought each other but against the former made common cause. In no
uncertain terms stockmen urged that the existing system be maintained,
or that the government should erect safeguards against the sale of large
tracts. Yet the future inevitably held disappointment for them. The
instruments of their great prosperity would work their undoing—the
railroads would bring in trainloads of would-be grain farmers, bound
to take up land from the government and fence it in against the tram-
pling hoofs of the herds. These forces, combining perchance with hard
winters and bad management would make a greedy industry suffer.

The process of the intrusion of farmers on cattlemen was foretold at
a typical cattle depot, Abilene, Kansas. There as early as 1877 one of
the more imaginative and resourceful of the populace secretly, in an out-
of-the-way place, began to experiment with hardy grains. He and his

kind were looking forward to a time when they might figure as landed proprietors in a crop-producing region, rather than as vicarious profiteers by a seasonal and violent influx of cattlemen. In spite of their income from their visitors they rebelled at being taken possession of by the will of paymasters and cowboys. These settlers were of the type which was going to cling to equities in the cattle and railroad towns, ageing there while the floaters passed off, increasing as property-holders and organizing for "law and order" to protect their investments. Where they took root the frontier passed beyond them; theirs was the outer fringe of farming, with the cattlemen beyond or confined within fenced areas among them.

Farmers

The process of pre-emption of the far West was retarded by the rigorous extremes of climate on the wind-swept plains. Travellers over them during the Civil War published accounts generally perpetuating the notion of a "Great American Desert"; and Pope reported to the War Department in 1866 that along the line of the 99th meridian the rich agricultural region of the Mississippi Valley gave place to a province "of high, arid plains, without timber . . . beyond the reach of agriculture." It extended, he wrote, to the mountains, and "must always remain a great, uninhabited desert." The worthy general, however, was contradicted by some travellers who followed him shortly, with such effect that by 1870 only the reckless blanketed as a desert an entire region 1200 miles long and 800 miles wide. The slight demand for homesteads out there grew for a few months, but suffered a setback from the report of the Geological Survey of 1872, which described the region as unattractive. Western Dakota was said to afford grazing grounds, but to have insufficient rainfall for profitable agriculture; western Kansas and Nebraska, it seemed, lacked not only rainfall but building materials, fuel and running water adequate for livestock; Montana and Wyoming were thought to be even more impossible, from the agricultural standpoint; and in Colorado the industry had not established itself beyond Denver's vicinity.

As the 'seventies passed, the potentialities of the plains became more generally known; but writers continued to heap ridicule upon interested agents endeavoring to establish farmers on the "alkali wastes and barren, sunscorched plains." Even the good old American custom of giving a party of editors an excursion, failed to achieve its object completely in this doubtful area, for editorial warnings issued against settling west of the 100th meridian on land which "a fierce sun baked into sterility."

However, the adverse recollections of uncomfortable travellers could not entirely quell land agents, who devised special enticements whereby spirits rugged by nature might be further emboldened to face life in a region of climatic vagaries. In the region of Utah the Mormons aped the railroads in attracting immigrants of Scandinavian extraction, hardy enough to take up lands readily relinquished by farmers who had been disillusioned by bitter winters and parching summers. The railroads through the central and southern sections of the Far West also bid what they could for producers of freight along their lines. The pioneer farmers soon made their influence felt here, also, becoming identified with the more settled populace as enemies of the open range and laboring to destroy the typical frontier aspects of their environment. Land legislation expedited settlement; the timber culture act of 1873 and the desert land and the timber and stone acts of 1877 carried the homestead traditions to the point where one person could acquire title to no less than 1120 acres.

The westward virus infected optimistic crusaders in the religious and educational fields, so that home missionary groups were soon forming Church Extension societies. The Baptists had the forethought to elicit from the managements of the Union and Northern Pacific Railroads promises of deeds to land for churches and parsonages in every city and town along their routes. For the Methodists, "Chaplain" C. C. McCabe went from coast to coast establishing churches and setting his congregations singing to the task. The Congregationalists concentrated upon colleges, establishing Washburn in Kansas (1865), Carleton in Minnesota (1867) and Colorado at Colorado Springs (1874).

By the rapid interaction of such social, political and economic forces there were taken up, by 1880, some 56 million acres and the number of farms had increased from more than 2 million to twice that number, while the effect upon grain growing was stupendous. Dakota, Kansas, Minnesota and Nebraska multiplied their populations of 1860 more than three times by 1870 and more than eight times by 1880. Thus, the agricultural part of this immense area was permanently populated with miraculous speed, the mining regions more sporadically. As the field for farming widened toward the West, it became evident that the agriculturists through many a long year would stamp their influence indelibly upon the course of national affairs. The reactions of farmers to every issue, whether economic, social or political, would be felt throughout the republic. Leaders in Congress, perforce sensitive to groundswells, would find they never could afford to ignore the agricultural quotient in their calculations. In particular, the west north central region, as graingrowing and population overspread it, would feel an accompanying access of power.

The doings of the pioneers, whether miners, cowboys or homesteaders, interested intensely people back East and western writing affected the reading habits and literary output of all sections. Erastus Beadle found in the Far West pocket-filling subjects for dime novels. The prince of all the West's raconteurs came to the boom towns of Nevada and California in the person of Samuel Clemens, "Mark Twain"; and his first magazine appearance was on the rollicking frontier subject of "The Notorious Jumping Frog of Calaveras County." Twain gave the nation that classic of the California frontier, *Roughing It* (1872), a use of western experience which made him a lion in English society and a well-paid contributor to American periodicals.

The "Laughter of the West" was loosening, sideshaking—a skillful compound of surprise, common sense and sheer exaggeration. It rose from realities—from the hardships, democratic irreverence and barren social life of the frontier and from the urge to prick, with humor's sharp point, the inflated bubble of Gilded Age pretenses. The West gave also local color inspiration to a host of eastern and middle western imitators, for Bret Harte charmed with his "Luck of Roaring Camp," [1] "Tennessee's Partner" and "Outcasts of Poker Flat." The vanishing race was interpreted by the poet, C. H. ("Joaquin") Miller, a real westerner who was born in a covered wagon; in his "Last Taschastas" was a frontier grand, picturesque, roamed by Indians in fateful majesty. The West was helping to lay the foundation for realism in American literature, by its distinctive humor and its contributions to folk literature and local color. Merely factual accounts of what was transpiring in that alluring section were dramatic, for so were the experiences befalling its various denizens.

Political Organization

The growth of the Far West with its adventure and romance created not only a new section but one with political power. To be sure the process of organizing it was not as dangerous as similar processes in the bitterly contested pre-war days, but the consequences of its organization were significant. The establishment of more new territories began as soon as the southerners left Congress. The five immense western territories undivided since 1854 began to be sliced into smaller units, still immense in themselves. Utah gave up (1861) a western portion to form Nevada Territory and an eastern to contribute part of Colorado Territory to which the old Nebraska, Kansas and New Mexico also yielded contiguous areas. The northern three-fourths of the old Nebraska became (1861), with the adjoining unorganized region, Dakota Territory, for a short time; but that in turn was so huge that its western part was cut off territorially three times:—its further part was joined with a mountainous section of Washington to form Idaho (1863), from

---

[1] Published in California's own literary medium, the *Overland Monthly*, 1868.

this Montana was taken the next year, and in 1868 the lower western part of what remained (quickened into life by the Union Pacific) became Wyoming Territory. Meanwhile, old New Mexico had lost its western half to form another new territory called Arizona (1863) and the two territories of Nevada and Nebraska had blossomed into states (1864 and 1867). Thus, in the short space of seven years, across the face of the recently unorganized Far West had been drawn the boundary lines of all the states in that immense area today. When the end of the decade was reached, the population had multiplied by 160%. This whole process conclusively demonstrated that the United States could expand vigorously even while engaged in intersectional warfare.

The territorialists in their far-flung areas experienced their own interplay of political, economic and social forces. Men holding the higher offices often had little economic stake in the region and perpetrated the misdeeds common to carpetbaggers, taking their cue from interests concerned solely with the speedy exploitation of resources and restrained only by the watchfulness of the pioneers. Taxpaying propertyholders long feared the financial burdens implicit in statehood. The Nevadans found themselves propelled into it in 1864 because Lincoln's Union administration needed their votes for Negro emancipation. The Nebraskans received statehood at the moment when the radical Republicans hoped to unhorse President Johnson and passed the bill over his veto as a part of their schemes. The Coloradans refused the political bait in 1864 although Congress and leading territorial politicians like Henry M. Teller favored it, but swallowed it eagerly in 1876 after several years of sturdy growth, thereby helping the Republicans to elect Hayes over Tilden by a narrow margin. Among the other territorialists statehood was delayed while voluntary associations such as those of the cattlemen and miners assumed such functions of government as the territorial machinery could not fulfill. This condition was to persist through a quarter century following the Civil War, until conservative Republican leadership in Washington chose to grant statehood to six territories, supposedly Republican, almost simultaneously. It will be seen later how their action reaped the political whirlwind.

Except for professional proponents of statehood, during the post Civil War period the miners and ranchers interested themselves more in their economic and social conditions than in politics. The frontiersmen, like the middle westerners, were cold to practical application of political doctrine which ran counter to the facts of their environment. Their conglomerate origins, coupled with the knowledge of each other which the Long Drive gave them, made them exceptionally broad-minded, tolerant of marked differences in viewpoint and sympathetic to experimentation, whether religious, social or political. For example, the few women in Wyoming received the grant of equal suffrage rights with the men from the first and other political experiments were tried. Although the westerners lacked weapons of capital and organization as mighty as those of the easterners, who not infrequently could impose conditions upon them, they were highly articulate. They would be heard in the not far distant future when the new sectionalism was further advanced and they were in a position to challenge the dominance of the East.

CHAPTER XIX

THE VALLEY OF DEMOCRACY

The new sectionalism, which was to be the most striking characteristic of the reconstructed nation, was marked by emergence of the Middle West as a definite entity. This area was to play a vital rôle in a new conflict. Before the War Between the States, a dominant South and an unorganized and highly conglomerate North had struggled for the privilege of developing the wide, western country. After peace, the ruthless capitalists and corrupt politicians of the East were set to milk all sections. Would the East make vassals of the rest of the nation? The South was prostrate, the Far West too young for effective challenge of flagrant exploitation. The Middle West, however, was more mature. Its rural populace were tenacious of their own modest, vested interests. They highly cherished the ideals of democracy and fair dealing. From the Middle West the challenge was to come.

Emergence of the Middle West

In the valley of the great rivers lay an agricultural region which extended roughly from the Appalachian rim, north of the Ohio River, across the Mississippi to a vague and wavering further boundary line. That line ran unevenly up through central Texas and along the western edge of the Mississippi states, except where it bulged out into eastern Kansas and Nebraska. This region remembered the frontier but was no longer close upon it. Never definitely fixed, externally nor internally, it moved westward along both its borders. Its eastern boundary edged nearer the Mississippi as fast as more and more manufacturing plants crossed the Appalachians. Its western edge moved nearer the Missouri as more and more farmers pre-empted the wide spaces, formerly roamed by cattlemen, but soon invaded by the harvesting machine which pushed the frontier westward at the rate of thirty miles a year. It became neither East nor West. Its demands became confused and contradictory, forcing its congressmen to become chronic fence-sitters.

In this section, before the war, easterner and southerner had met, clashed and compromised. The result was a community spirit, progressive, tolerant and firmly wedded to democracy. Agriculture was the chief occupation at which the enterprising could produce a surplus; there was enough for all, with few large cities, few great fortunes. The individual was regarded as possessing rights which all must respect. Thus had grown the valley of democracy. In the post-bellum epoch, the rate of change accelerated; industry, large cities and great captains of wealth burgeoned threateningly. Here industrial capitalism and agricultural democracy were to come to grips.

The tide of migration and the forces which promoted it swirled over the Middle West and left many newcomers who went no further. As the people of the section multiplied, their industries diversified, and a class arose who did not earn their living by farming. They lived in the young manufacturing centers growing up at points convenient for the exploitation of nearby resources. Western Pennsylvania already had Pittsburgh with her iron and oil products, while Ohio had Toledo and Cleveland, engaged in similar types of manufacturing; Michigan had salt, wool, lumber and the growing town of Detroit.

In Illinois, the farmers' corn-hogs economy together with the beef-raising on the further plains were developing the stockyards at Chicago, and when energetic railroad exploiters made through connections with the East and perfected the refrigerated car, that city speedily achieved meat-packing supremacy. There at the foot of Lake Michigan the general Great Lakes business in iron, steel and lumber was contributing to the organization of other industries. In Wisconsin lumber brought the board mills; in Minnesota the wheatlands sponsored flour mills so rapidly that an infant woolen and cotton goods industry soon arose to clothe the rapidly multiplying population. Even in Kansas, at Lawrence, small-scale factories were starting up. Thus, although almost all of the Middle West's population was agricultural in occupation and sympathy, and bound long to remain so, its mushroom cities cherished industrial ambitions likely to create some sympathy with the eastern viewpoint.

Certain other trends of trade and finance pointed inevitably toward closer relationships with, and bitter antagonisms toward, the East. In the 'twenties the Erie Canal had tied to eastern capitalism that corner of the old Northwest Territory which was too distant from the Ohio-Mississippi waterway to share in the market to the south along these rivers. But the rest of the Middle West until the midcentury continued to market their corn, oats, flour, pork, horses and mules almost exclusively by flatboat and steamboat southward, with Cincinnati proudly bearing the title of "Porkopolis" and with New Orleans as the great outlet. Then came freight trains, connecting the depots of trade on the Ohio and Mississippi with Baltimore, Philadelphia and New York.

By 1860, the North and West together had twice as many miles of railroad in operation as the South, and they were turning the outgoing freight of the Middle West from the South toward the East, through Chicago and St. Louis. Steadily the Middle West's commercial interest in southern prosperity waned and the Civil War accelerated the shift, although an astounding amount of river trade persisted in wartime contraband. The time was not far distant when the farmers would realize their growing dependence upon the industrial East, for their place of sale was becoming identical with their place of purchase; the railroads would tax both transactions. Disquieting implications of this readjustment were shortly to come home to them, and they then would take the place of the Southern planters in offering opposition to the East.

The Farmers' Heyday and Disillusionment

The farmers were optimistic while the war lasted and as long as good prices prevailed thereafter. The loss of man power through enlistment and the excess of land over man power were offset by advancements in agricultural machinery which the ordinarily conservative farmer welcomed in this money-making emergency. Had there been no war, adoption of innovations would have been much slower. The heavy demands and improved facilities made agriculture so profitable that the value of improved land rose to the point of speculation; farmers eagerly borrowed more money to buy more machinery and more land to raise more wheat, corn and hogs. By the end of the war decade, they had produced a crop of more than 200 million bushels of wheat and a billion bushels of corn. Fast as the population grew, grain production grew twice as fast.

On the whole, good fortune faithfully remained with most of the farmers of the Middle West through the 'sixties, affording opportunity for life to assume a less severe aspect, especially in localities with the more convenient outlet facilities toward the East. In these favored regions, frontier hardships were somewhat replaced by an existence less rigorous, both mechanically and socially, although still far from a bed of roses. The preparation of the land for the crops was made easier by plows with moldboards of chilled iron, which cut the soil without sticking, and by harrows adjustable to uneven levels. The labor of raising corn was lightened by machinery especially adapted to planting, cultivating and shelling it. Grain growers profited by the expiration of patents on grain drills, by horse rakes, mowers, and the improved reaper especially, which evolved into the much-advertised "complete harvester" and threshing machine. Farmers found it an immense relief not to have to bind the grain by hand with raw and bleeding fingers. They also took up deep plowing, manuring, crop rotation, fruit culture and vegetable raising. Entire communities showed the beneficial effects of the harnessing of steam engines and windmills to farm duties. No longer must the farmer be a "Jack of All Trades, good at none," for the railroads brought things from the "store" to replace crude, home-made articles.

By the conditions of their home life one could gauge the degree of release of farm people from frontier hardships. The most prosperous showed their rise in status by the increasing variety of the kinds of food they ate, the softer texture and more becoming cut of their clothing, the greater number of pieces of "store" furniture in their homes, and the enlargement of their houses. Their younger children went to school more months out of each year than it had been possible for older brothers and sisters to attend. Some of them even had an opportunity to practise tunes on a "parlor organ." Women, whose unpaid work, with children, on the farms supplied most of the funds for living expenses, worked in the fields less continually; and their afternoons in the house had a bit of leisure after the coming of the sewing machine. Men had a chance at a farmers' club occasionally, to exchange ideas about crops and politics. The entire family emerged from an almost complete isolation into pleasurable and stimulating contact with other farmers' families—at the Fourth of July picnic, the circus, the county fair, or Grange gatherings.

The nearer to the frontier that a farming family lived, the less its members had of comforts, conveniences and cultural contacts. The far plainsmen were the poorest, living in sod houses, with less of tools, stock, furniture, or neighbors; they knew little variety of outlook or experience except as the blistering summer sun took turn with winter blizzards in dictating discomfort to homesteaders. Perhaps the flowers which spring brought to the prairies were the only softening influences in their lives. The more westerly of them also had to guard against the Indians, until the middle 'seventies. Moreover, over wide areas scourges of droughts, blizzards, grasshoppers, locusts and prairie fires recurrently descended upon hapless farmers and wiped out whatever they, by back-breaking toil, had accumulated. Still, in general, prosperity was marked until 1868. Then a fall in the price of breadstuffs set in abroad and in the East, harbingers of disaster. When the price of wheat fell 50% in 1870, real depression settled upon the section.

A glut in the world's grain market became evident. Gold fell in value and further depressed prices. The Franco-Prussian War could bring wheat up only temporarily. Further down travelled farm products while machinery and supplies stayed up. Taxes, alas, remained high, for the community dividends on the railroad securities purchased so enthusiastically were not forthcoming and local treasuries languished. Farm wages declined from $17.45 with board to $10.43; but interest on capital remained as high as 15% to 20%. Since the farmers could not find enough buyers to maintain prices at the level on which they had borrowed, prospects for paying off their mortgages disappeared. It became woefully apparent that they had expanded too far in the face of factors working against them on the world scene.

Since fortune no longer favored the brave, the farmer developed an acute sensitivity to his environment. He noticed that the hardship in his section was not common to all the United States. He examined, as he said, "the relation of northwestern products to those of the rest of the country," and found that the eastern industrialists, manufacturers, commercial people and speculators were still riding the high wave of prosperity. Ergo, he concluded that money was being taken from the pockets of the West to fill those of the East, by insidious devices favoring powerful monopolies. Among his enemies he classed the bondholders, at whose behest Congress kept government bonds free from taxation while the farmers' real estate remained exposed to the eagle eye of the assessor. President Johnson, in his last annual message, had advocated retirement of the national bonds, and the withholding of further interest, because the bondholders already had received, in gold, more than their original investment; but Congress had denounced these recommendations.

Another class unduly influential in the national councils, from the point of view of the farmer, embraced the creditors, who held the farmers' mortgages and had obtained from Congress such measures as the loan contraction law of 1866 (p. 303) for retiring some of the greenbacks. As it forced western debtors to pay, in dear money, obligations incurred when money was cheap, some farmers joined other debtors and expansionists in fighting the law; and economic conditions aided them in forcing its repeal in 1868. But they could not obtain an increase over the number of greenbacks thus left in circulation for the contraction in greenbacks had been somewhat neutralized by issues of national bank notes, and not all farmers were ready to declare for cheap paper money. Those who thought it had limitless possibilities for prosperity believed it raised prices and would enable them to meet notes with values inflated as when debts were contracted. They followed George Pendleton in his so-called "Ohio Idea" program for paying all debts in greenbacks and increasing the volume of paper money. Other farmers followed the lead of Ignatius Donnelly of Minnesota who at this time argued that dear money, by making foreign exchange uncertain and by raising interest on capital, lowered the world price of agricultural products. Several years passed before he and his followers changed their viewpoint.

Meanwhile according to other farmers the world market for agricultural produce was suffering from the ill effects of the high tariff enacted at the behest of yet another eastern group, the manufacturers. It raised the prices of farming machinery and other necessaries above the European level [1] and at the same time prevented Europeans from exchanging their manufactures for American agricultural produce. Particularly did the rates on iron come close home to the farmers, as raising freight rates

[1] Patent abuses also raised American prices; patents were clapped on machines already in common use and fees exacted from users.

by retarding construction, as making new machinery less attainable, and as enhancing (to the amount of an extra bushel of oats) the produce required to pay for such a common necessity as a horseshoeing "all around."

The agricultural viewpoint could not cope effectively with manufacturers' propaganda at Washington, where but 7% of the Congressmen were farmers, and they indifferently organized; so the high rates were retained upon the whole, reductions obtained in 1872 (p. 302) being inconsequential. But Congress occasionally made gestures agreeable to the Middle West, abandoning Canadian grain reciprocity in 1866 and proposing a paper protection for agricultural products in the abortive tariff bill of 1867. The latter measure, however, contained obnoxious increases and was defeated partly through farmer influence. The Wool and Woolens Act which then secured enactment did so partly through the sagacity of John L. Hayes, at that time the Secretary and later the president of the National Association of Wool Manufacturers. He inserted in the bill a device ostensibly designed to protect wool-growers in Michigan and Ohio, and it passed. Canny lobbyists later profited by his example.

But Michigan and Ohio wool-growers were only one element in the Middle West, and that one perhaps the more favored economically by reason of nearness to eastern markets and competitive rail and water routes. Many farmers were suffering severely because of the distance products must travel to market and the lack of competitive carriers. Almost all the freight carried east by the four main line railroads out of Chicago (in 1873) was farmer freight, nearly 40% of it cereals and nearly 45% animals and animal products. The intimacy of the relationship was obvious. Here lay the heart of the farmers' grievances, and they turned to legislation for relief.

In Washington the Senate was less responsive than the House and so the federal position was slow to shift from aid, through negative, to positive regulation of the railroad. The laissez-faire East hesitated to adopt the nationalistic attitude of the West toward economic political problems (although a Massachusetts man was president of the National Cheap Transportation Association in 1873) and sought to prevent rebates rather than regulate rates. Consequently, prior to 1880 the few measures obtaining federal enactment, such as the livestock traffic law and various land-grant-road regulations, were mere palliatives. Apparently the farmers could no more expect to determine the broad lines of national policy on railroads than on the currency and tariff. But they could hope to affect railroad rates and regulations within the purview of their local legislatures. Given sufficient provocation to force them to organize, the agriculturist's influence would be felt directly, in the state capitols of the Middle West.

As to the provocation, it was ample. Exorbitant and discriminatory rates for freight and storage were levying such a charge upon everything the farmers bought and exacting such a discount upon everything they sold, that they speedily lost their earlier enthusiasm for railroad grants. Influential shippers were getting preferential rates over insignificant ones; and communities with a choice of land and water routes, or two different rail routes, enjoyed better rates than all others. The railroads were demanding high prices for the land which they had from the government as a gift, and from lands they arbitrarily selected prior homesteaders were unjustly evicted. Farmers fought to repossess lands and wrested millions of acres from railroad speculators.

Railroad lobbies were proving extremely successful in state capitols and at Washington, with legislators, executives and judges enjoying liberal pass privileges; when county supervisors were "taken care of," the evil came very close home. The sway of corruption was somewhat aggravated by the fact that the Middle West, like the South, was being governed in part by carpetbaggers. Men who had failed in the struggle for preferment eastward had found it in this region of kaleidoscopic development and were none too particular about employing corrupt politics for personal gain. The fact that the western carpetbaggers failed to work a damage equal to that of their southern cousins was due to the fortunate absence of freedmen and ex-Confederates as victims. That the railroad managements were losing public respect was obvious as early as 1866, when the group, which four years earlier had sponsored the Homestead Act, opposed the Northern Pacific Railroad grant, and existing railways were authorized to carry interstate traffic without interference from state monopolies. Then, as later, the railroad problem overtaxed ingenuity.

Middlemen were as obnoxious as railroads. When produce had run the gauntlet of the freight charges it fell victim to the onslaughts of the middlemen and warehouse people who sometimes juggled the market to pay the farmer the lowest possible price and then staged a "corner" to line their own pockets. Meats were so grossly manipulated as to make the "livestock ring" of the Chicago stockyards a generally execrated institution; and storing of grain tempted the rates no less. Furthermore, the middlemen who sold agricultural machinery enjoyed a commission agreement with the manufacturers which gave them 20% to 40% as agency fees and added just that much to the farmers' costs.

Attempts at Cooperative Remedies

Given the enlightenment, efficient organization remained essential to betterment. Would their plight drive the Middle West farmers to abandon their characteristic individualism and suspicion and seek succor in cooperation? Many Germans among them had brought over to the United States the liberal concepts of the Revolution of 1848 and entertained a predilection for self-defense and leadership. But it was an Irishman, O. H. Kelly, working arduously over a period extending from 1866 to 1875, who gave the men and women of the post-frontier an opportunity for improved acquaintance, better understanding and practice in self-expression. Travel through the South had convinced this government clerk, with a background of farming life in Iowa and Minnesota, that what the farmers of the nation most needed to improve their processes and position was the intellectual stimulus derived from social intercourse.

He concluded that they could be brought together best through the medium of a secret society, of a non-political character, to which the women as well as men might swear allegiance. Its members were to be advantaged by a mutual education process. On this theory, with William Saunders of the Agricultural Department and a few other Washington associates, he organized in 1867 [1] the national "Patrons of Husbandry," better known from the designation of its local chapters as "The Grange." The founders of this organization offered farmers and their wives the delights of membership in a "secret" society and fellowship with their neighbors.

This first nation-wide organization of farmers powerfully affected their daily living. Men and women who attended the Grange meetings began to show more care in their manners and dress; they cultivated more cheerfulness and practiced more consistently the solid virtues of industry. They evidenced a more charitable attitude of mutual helpfulness toward each other in time of distress. The Grange stimulated leadership among them, encouraged educational agencies such as libraries, fairs, and schools, developed the habit of reading agricultural journals and newspapers, and provided mutual benefit and fire protection companies.

A few months' experience proved that the Grange could not attract the farmers powerfully if the economic problems of their daily existence were ignored; and so, in September of 1868, some Grangers in Minnesota widened the project to permit of appeal to the pocketbook. Grange literature began urging farmers to unite in self-defense against the corporations and to engage in cooperative buying and selling. As a result granges multiplied. They now offered members both the solace of voicing their dissatisfactions before a sympathetic audience and the comfort of united action against a common enemy.

The Grange first reached maturity in the States of Iowa, Minnesota, South Carolina and Mississippi, but during the next two years it was

[1] This was just a year before workmen began to find refuge in a secret society, the Knights of Labor.

best rooted in the community life of the upper Mississippi valley, where also its greatest strength later was developed. This location was to be expected because Illinois, Iowa, Wisconsin and Minnesota together were producing by 1870 more than one-third of the nation's wheat; and Illinois and Iowa already were the two most important corn states. Through the next four years the Grange spread widely until some 30,000 local societies were formed and more than 1,500,000 persons (by very conservative estimate) became members, all states being represented except four. The rush to join had the effect of loading the Grange with a certain amount of dead wood, since persons with but a

A Grange Meeting

remote connection with agriculture insinuated themselves into the organization. In the Middle West, railroad lobbyists posed as farmers and grangers.

Everywhere commission men and merchants felt alarm at the strong current toward the Grange and tried vainly to stem the flood. In the South, they punished grangers by choosing them for foreclosures, a policy which defeated its own object, for it convinced the farmer that the order was powerful. In Boston and New York the same class of opponents tried to bore from within by establishing their own chapters, a scandal which caused the revocation of their charters. The coastal phase of grangerism, however, could not assume great importance, because the farming classes of the Atlantic seaboard were naturally averse to a movement primarily devised for the benefit of their competitors.

The sectional and class spirit behind the movement was capitally illustrated by William Williams, representing Indiana in Congress, who on 20 December 1869 introduced a significant resolution. He pled that Congress determine whether the commerce clause did not empower them to take steps to protect agriculture from the monopolistic railroads and the selfish eastern manufacturing interests. Although the constitution of the order expressly forbade partisan activity it at the same time urged members to perform their political duties as citizens, and wherever the Grange was preeminent, as in Minnesota and Iowa, the farmers nullified the restriction by technical evasions.

Elsewhere, the situation spontaneously gave birth to divers sorts of agricultural clubs, non-secret and frankly political, and to various minor political parties, such as the "Farmers'," the "Anti-Monopoly," the "Independent" and the "Reform." In Texas flourished a "Farmers' Alliance" similar to the Grange and in all there were at least twenty-eight such organizations rising out of the same basic conditions, contemporaneous with the Grange and thriving most during its period of prosperity. Through the nine prairie states (as well as California and Oregon) the farmers organized for political action, stressing state control of corporations, (especially railroads), and reform and economy in government. Their leaders were not professionals in reform or politics, but mainly outstanding farmers, such as W. C. Flagg of Illinois, J. G. Vale of Iowa, W. R. Taylor of Wisconsin, and that dialectic genius, Ignatius Donnelly of Minnesota. Where politicians took control the movement was checked by farmers' distrust.

This virile farmers' movement could have been utilized as the backbone of a strong political party opposing the status quo; but in reality the agricultural clubs served as little more than weapons of the two great political parties against each other. Where the Democrats were in a minority in a western state, such as Wisconsin and Kansas, they tried to make common cause with the farmers against the Republicans; and the reverse transpired in Missouri. Some times both parties declared against an abuse particularly obnoxious to the grangers. But in general neither of the two dared to embrace the farmers' cause officially. The abortive Liberal Republican movement made the same mistake, for when that group of independents, predominantly from the East, summoned disaffected Republicans and Democrats to help oust the corrupt Grant administration, they made slight effort to capitalize the Grange. Their national platform opposed land grants to "railroads and other corporations" and a few western liberals like Donnelly, A. S. Sloan of Wisconsin and Newton Booth of California actively championed the farmers' cause; but such prominent western liberals as Schurz and Trumbull held aloof from the farmers.

Moreover, the liberal ranks in the East included many like E. L. Godkin of the *Nation* who ridiculed the agricultural viewpoint, largely for its soft money leanings. Ridicule the farmer never has relished; and in the emphasis of the Liberal Republicans upon reform of the national civil service and removal of political disabilities in the South, the men of the upper Mississippi felt small interest. The party's straddle on the tariff and its advocacy of specie payments alienated many farmers, and the Democrats among them did not appreciate the candidate's (Greeley's) record of enmity to their party or his high tariff sentiments. The farmers as a whole were sceptical of the probable performance in power of a group which could not unite successfully under the stress of campaigning. The sad result was that liberalism was defeated, for lack of enlistment of its strongest individual proponents.

The very nature of their grievances thrust the Grangers prominently into county and state politics, if not national. They, and farmer politi-

Greeley Whitewashing Tammany

cians, secured election to the lower range of offices. The railroads' money was fought with farmers' votes; they forced the state legislatures to enact (1869-1874) the so-called "Granger Laws." However, it should be noticed that the Grange and these laws were not simple cause and effect. Some of the most stringent of the laws were passed before the farmers' movement reached its full strength, and the laws helped to a certain extent in bringing the Grange from infancy to maturity. The real relationship between the Grange, allied clubs, and the "Granger laws" was one of contemporaneous interaction, the trend of events in general creating them severally and mutually.

The Grange legislatures concentrated upon the railroad grievances, especially where transportation was most in ill repute, in Illinois, Wisconsin, Minnesota, Iowa and Ohio. Into the statute books were written mandates on such subjects as passenger and freight rates, long and short haul, railroad commissions, incorporation, grain elevator rates and transportation conditions. The urgent mood of the farmers was capitally illustrated in Illinois, where as early as 1867 they forced the passage of a warehousing act forbidding railroads to refuse to deliver grain to warehouses they did not control. These canny agriculturalists, failing other legal remedy, in traditional American fashion had determined to secure "appropriate legislation." They observed with unwonted perspicacity that "nothing can be accomplished for the enforcement of our rights, and the redress of our wrongs, without an efficient organization on the well known principles that give the great corporations such tremendous power."

They rewrote the state constitution (in 1870) to give the legislature the specific power of rate making, which it obediently exercised the next session by specifying maximum rates, while it also forbade discrimination in handling and storage. When the state Supreme Court declared the act unconstitutional the farmers presented themselves in convention at Springfield, so that the affrighted legislature warily enacted a yet more thorough and efficient law. At the ensuing election, some of the offending judges suffered retirement. In the van of Illinois followed Minnesota, Iowa (host to an Anti-Monopoly Convention), and Wisconsin. Fate conspired to make these laws temporary, for a panic was imminent. The farmers were approaching the peak of their power but were soon to lose it.

The panic which descended upon the United States early in 1873 had the immediate effect of strengthening the farmers' movements, and aggravating sectional and class animosities. It caused eastern creditors to come down hard upon western debtors, foreclosing mortgages, sometimes without giving credit for improvements made by the mortgagees. Ousted farmers found little betterment in a hegira further westward, for they must raise the same staples out there where the railroads held them in a yet firmer grasp. Some farm owners had to become renters and face a lifetime landless. Those who had mortgaged their farms to buy railroad stocks and bonds found their paper securities depreciating on their hands and short term loans difficult to negotiate, even at interest ranging from 15% to 28%.

Small wonder that the farmers were goaded to a degree of cooperation such as they never before had achieved. The active Grange workers ousted timid bureaucrats from control of the National Council and then pushed more aggressively such programs as that which had been successful in Illinois. 4 July 1873, dawned as "The Farmers' Fourth of July." Throughout the communities of the Northwest on that day farmers assembled at political picnics, listened to the reading of a farmers' "Declaration of Independence" and felt their strength rise within them. Concerning their status, they declared, "it becomes necessary for a class of the people, suffering from long continued systems of oppression and abuse, to rouse themselves from an apathetic indifference to their own interests, which has become habitual." They vowed to "use all lawful and peaceful means to free ourselves from the tyranny of monopoly."

The Grangers widened the scope of their activities beyond the railroad legislation then so pervasive. To offset attacks upon them as radicals, they disavowed "personal, local, sectional and national prejudices." They emphasized improvements in standards of farm man-

A Farmers' Picnic

agement and home life and particularly stressed cooperation. Since the abuse closest to them, next to transportation difficulties, was extortion by middlemen, their cooperation took a strenuous form in efforts to eliminate that group. They set up their own stores to sell to grangers at reduced rates. They established cooperative creameries and elevators which successfully saved them money in disposing of their produce. Some of them subscribed to stores which sold at trade rates but paid subscribers a dividend, and divided profits according to amounts purchased. They made arrangements with manufacturers and retailers for special rates to Grangers and pooled orders where they could not get reductions as individuals. They bought patents and went into the manufacture of farm implements and sewing machines on their own account, determined to eliminate the agent whose fees had raised prices; and it was this situation which gave Montgomery Ward and Sears, Roebuck and Company the idea of starting the mail order business.

The high price of farm implements, such as reapers at from $200 to $225 and mowers at from $100 to $125 was the subject of many pamphlets and books, the one of greatest influence perhaps being

E. W. Martin's *History of the Grange Movement,* which depicted Cyrus McCormick as charging from 50% to 100% more than his machinery was worth. Mr. McCormick, in spite of reduced sales, and in spite of the combination of competing companies against him, refused the pleas of Grangers and his own agents that he follow the lead of other chief implement makers in granting Grangers special reductions. A slight decline in his prices, he declared, was due solely to the general decline. He was certain that the Grangers could not hold together long enough to force him to recognize them and was bold in opposing public opinion in his own section because he was finding a market abroad. He was, in fact, president of the Chicago branch of the "Mississippi Valley Society," an organization of middle western manufacturers devoted to the encouragement of foreign trade and reporting a business abroad of 600 millions a year. Obviously, a new factor was being injected into the economic life of the Middle West.

The Depression Brings Greenbackers and Silverites

In the meantime, most of the cooperative ventures approached failure by reason of the farmers' confined individualism, ignorance and lack of business experience. Grange stores lost their patrons when other stores temporarily lowered prices to freeze them out; and Grange patents and manufacturing plants involved the organization in lawsuits and business competition it could not meet. The panic was particularly fatal to young businesses. And so, in a general atmosphere of recrimination, misunderstanding and impatience, the movement worked itself out. As early as 1875 it was clear that cooperation was doomed to an early death and by the end of the decade the Grange had lost four-fifths of the membership it boasted half a dozen years before.

Even in that field where the Grange was for a time measurably successful—railroad regulation—it rapidly lost ground after 1875. The United States Supreme Court did indeed rise to the occasion with a warehouse decision in *Munn vs. Illinois* declaring that businesses such as warehouses, commoncarriers, etc., were "affected with a public interest," that they were customarily regulated by law, and that the right to fix rates was implicit in the right to regulate. But this decision could not be capitalized for the railroads were in a bad way financially by reason of the panic. They lowered freight and passenger rates and stopped construction, while they conformed to the rate laws in a manner calculated to make those laws obnoxious. The state legislatures, except that of Illinois, repealed the measures before they were fairly tried and the theory of state regulation was vitiated by lack of uniformity of action. Therefore, in the one field where the Grange was most successful it appeared to have failed. Yet it had accomplished something. A legal basis had been provided on which the right of the states to fix maximum charges became a recognized part of public policy, even though subjected later to limitations. The way had been paved for interstate control. The railroad commissions continued to function after a fashion and the Granger states later enacted further legislation.

Of much future significance was the fact that Congress felt compelled to take up the question. A special committee investigated railroad abuses and submitted a mine of information in the Windom report (1874). In 1878 Congress passed the Thurman Act creating a sinking fund for Union Pacific securities, to protect the United States government as a creditor, and the same year saw the establishment of the important office of auditor of railway accounts. Also there were signs of aid from the East. There manufacturers and shippers were worried by the unfair discrimination in rebates. The farmer was going to have important allies.

It was a strange phenomenon which the Middle West farmers had shown the nation. They had interfered as a class on the side of governmental protection against oppression, imposing at least a temporary check upon those mighty entities, the public carriers. Through their attempts to deal directly with producers and manufacturers, without the aid of middlemen, they learned valuable lessons regarding the intricacy of business functions and obtained a better balanced notion of the basis of credit. The manufacturers for their part learned that organized farmers could be formidable. From the experience the farmers took some recollection of practice in cooperation and business usage, to be capitalized at a future date in the Farmers Alliance, Populism and other lineal descendants of the Grange.

Even before the farmers had tired of their struggle against the railroads and middlemen, they had turned to money and credit as offering panaceas for their woes—first to greenbacks and later when its bullion price had fallen, to free silver. Greenbacks, during the Grange enthusiasm, had not attracted many farmers, although there had been enough interest among them to cause the Democratic party to write a greenback plank into their platform in 1868. Some of the farmers supported the "National Labor" party in 1872 when it advocated paper money and opposed the resumption of specie payments.

In fact the farmers' independent parties had been usually opposed to inflation, but began to change about 1874. Congress, facing a campaign, proved sensitive, and passed the inflation bill increasing the volume of greenbacks to 400 millions. Grant's veto brewed the storm in which the famous "tidal wave" of Democratic votes swept away the Republican majority in the House and cut deeply into their two-thirds majority in the Senate. But before the newly chosen members could take their seats outgoing Republicans had pledged resumption of specie payments for 1879 (p. 305). This pledge the greenbackers were determined should never be fulfilled; and under the leadership of James Buchanan of Indianapolis, they captured important independent political groups in Indiana and Illinois. This was followed, under the leadership of "Brick" Pomeroy, with a campaign of "Greenback Clubs." They sprang up in rural regions particularly, they conducted their proceedings in secret, and they attracted the more radical farmers (especially the ex-Grangers) to Greenbackism. The farmer-debtor was persuaded that if money were cheap his products would command higher prices and his debts be easier to pay, while if holders of government bonds were paid in cheap paper (euphoniously called "lawful money") instead of gold, they would not enjoy advantages over farmers.

Tilden and Hendricks Facing Both Ways

As the campaign of 1876 neared, a greenback party was organized. The farmer-debtor had allies in addition to eastern wage earners. Men like the conservative protectionist, Henry C. Carey, became inflationists. The tightness of money convinced Carey that manufacturing needed the fluidity of capital that remonetization of silver would bring, and from this position he advanced to espousal of greenbacks. That party nominated the philanthropist Peter Cooper of New York for the Presidency and fought Wall Street for a "democratic" monetary system. The election showed, however, that the greenbackers could expect little from the East; Pennsylvania and New York were the only eastern states to give Cooper more than 800 votes. His largest votes came from Illinois, Indiana, Michigan and Iowa.

Gradually, as the resumption of specie payments approached with greenbacks rising in price and produce falling, the Middle West farmer-debtors became more numerous than the industrial debtors, in the fiat money crusade. In 1877 nation-wide railroad strikes sent additional laborers into the movement. By this time silver money had become a token of inflation. The silver dollar had been demonetized in the United States and parts of Europe in 1873, while the metal was still too expensive to permit of coinage at the old ratio; but thereafter output continued high while the price fell until the silver content of the dollar amounted only to about ninety cents. The producers now demanded that free coinage be resumed at the old ratio, approximately 16:1, so that they might exchange 90¢ for $1.00 at the Treasury until their product rose in the market. The debtors were interested in a rise, not of the price of silver but of the amount of cheap money.

The frightened politicians facing the election of 1878 determined to meet the inflationists partway. They passed over Hayes' veto a "Bland-Allison" act, directing the Secretary of the Treasury to purchase at the market price between 2 and 4 million dollars worth monthly and to coin it at 16:1. The coin could be exchanged for silver certificates of $10 and higher. This measure possibly satisfied the miner wing of

Rescuing National Credit

the insurgent group but just how many farmers' and workmen's votes were thus deflected from "greenback-Labor" or "National" candidates is difficult to estimate. The grand total of the coalition party in 1878 was one million votes and about two-thirds of them were cast by middle-westerners who sent to Congress six of the fifteen greenbackers elected to that body, including that stout defender of the section, General James B. Weaver of Iowa. This was the peak of the Greenback movement.

Yet the relatively small size of the Greenback vote showed that the first national political party adopting the agricultural position could not break the habit of most farmers (and workmen) of voting for one or the other of the two major parties. Inflation as a cure-all was not so convincing to them that they were willing to give the Greenback party a chance at solving the problems of the Middle West, and that party made its last official appearance in national politics in 1884. The thing which actually killed the farmers' interest in inflation was the abundance of corn, wheat and oats sold at good prices as the 'seventies closed, just when renewed industrial activity lessened the workmen's anxiety for inflation.

Economic and Cultural Recuperation

In truth, between 1875 and 1880 the harassed middle western farmer found conditions at home and abroad sometimes working toward his temporary satisfaction. Several crop failures befell Europe, and as they left America unscathed, and there was little competition from the Argentine, Russia, or India, the United States achieved a wheat export of 150 million bushels. It became in fact the greatest grain producing area in the world. The cereal yield rose from more than 1500 million bushels to more than 2400 million. This was accomplished partly with the help of more efficient machinery—with the heavy gang plows, spring-toothed harrows, cross-row corn planters, self-rake harvesters, and hay loaders. Not only were wheat and corn from America demanded by Europe, but also something of cheese, bacon, pork, corned beef and (after 1875) refrigerated meats.

Prices, though unsteady, were usually much better than during the first half of this decade. When wheat was lowest (1874-1875) corn rose to offset the disadvantage; and even in the worst depression years, 1874 and 1878, No. 2 spring wheat averaged in the eastern markets around $1.35 a bushel, thus showing an almost complete independence of the general panic sag. During the particularly bad industrial year of 1877, marked by nation-wide strikes and severe unemployment for both labor and capital, the wheat growers of the whole north central region averaged a gross return per acre of $15.11; and those in the eastern part of the same census area obtained $20.72 in 1879. These were very good returns indeed, considering the current high purchasing value of the dollar. Some acres which had cost farmers but $10 apiece now repaid them with a yield worth twice that amount in one year.

Moreover, those of the farmers who lived no further west than Chicago, were less irked than formerly by the extortions of the elevator men and commission dealers, because they could forget them in a feeling of pleasant relations with the railroads. The Chicago-New York rate for grain fell from twenty to twelve and even nine cents per bushel, while the competing lake and canal carriers reduced their rates to the point of extinction. The farmer further west did not do anywhere nearly as well because his railroad, elevator and interest rates all remained relatively high. But although he still suffered much poverty, as in Minnesota, he shared somewhat in his more easterly brother's prosperity, by reason of the active market for agricultural produce, reduced price of manufactured articles, lowered wage scale, rise in the value of his acres, and his own developing knowledge of the science of farming. The first agricultural experiment station had been established in 1875; control of pests was becoming a possibility. Many farmers in the midst of their prosperity remained keen to improve their methods and showed it by eagerly reading Emerson and Flint's *Manual of Agriculture*. The improvements they made were more secure, also, for laws of 1875, 1876 and 1880 protected land entries within railroad grants.

Regardless of the terrific hardships yet met on the further farming frontier, it remained a mecca for some of the people thrown out of employment by the hard times in eastern industry.[1] As consumers they had complained of the price of meat and some went westward with much faith if little capital. Since they had to save money before they could buy land, they passed through a novitiate as renters; and together with the tenants in southern Negro districts they made up one-fourth of the nation's farmers in 1880. But most of the Middle West renters were destined to become land owners. They filtered through the pre-empted areas across the old borders of the Middle West, along the river courses and over the more arable lands, stretching the farming area over into what had been cow country. At the same time the cities of the section perforce shared in the general growth, especially at the meatpacking centers of Chicago, St. Louis and Kansas City and the grain centers of Minneapolis and St. Paul. Lesser aggregations of citizens grouped themselves at other smaller, but very lively, centers. Thus it transpired that the total effect was an increased complexity in the social and economic life of the section, so that the farmer's point of view became less dominant. But one thing continued certain, whenever production outstripped demand and prices fell, agricultural misfortune would depress the tone of this area and would make its people contribute again to new movements for relief.

In the election of Lincoln, political leadership had been seized by forces from the Middle West. As the imagination of the nation veered westward, writers of the Mississippi Valley took their cue from the Far West, as did Mark Twain, adopting its brand of humor and adding their own folk literature and local color. Readers of newspapers and some magazines delighted in the tall lies, dialects and genial philosophies of humorous commentators, essayists, lecturers and story tellers. They were discovering America. They echoed the "hoss sense" of Henry W.

---

[1] Recent research has indicated that the West was less of a "safety valve" in hard times than formerly supposed, because of the cost of migrating.

Shaw as "Josh Billings" in *The Farmer's Alminax* (1860-1870). They so relished the columns in the Cleveland *Plaindealer* by Charles F. Browne, ("Artemus Ward") that he assembled them as *Artemus Ward: His Book* (1862) and *Artemus Ward in London* (1867). They had their union sentiment strengthened through similar use of humor and satire by David R. Locke, ("Petroleum Volcano Nasby") in the Toledo *Blade;* and they gave their support to the comic weekly *Puck* founded in St. Louis in 1869.

Mark Twain obtained a most profitable contract with the *Atlantic Monthly* for seven reminiscent sketches of "Old Days on the Mississippi." The mighty river he had known in the heyday of steamboats and the swift changes befalling the West of his youth moved him to write a saga of the pre-railroad days. Came the great "American Odyssey," *Tom Sawyer* (1876), *Life on the Mississippi* (1883) and *Huckleberry Finn* (1884). These rollicking tales, especially the last named, expressed Twain's personal philosophy, his rebellion against sham and his preference for the individualist and contempt for the conformist. Whether writing as humorist, romanticist or realist, he expressed the dominant movement of the time—the West pushing back "to Americanize the Atlantic seaboard," overwhelming the East with frontier psychology, gaiety, optimism, acquisitiveness.

Other novelists and some poets exploited the local color of the Middle West. Constance F. Woolson wrote of the Great Lakes area; Will Carleton wrote *Farm Ballads*. Perhaps the ablest novelist in local color next to Mark Twain was Edward Eggleston, who delineated frontier life as it was lived by the very poor. His *Hoosier Schoolmaster* (1871) and *Circuit Rider* (1874) wakened instant response in the recollections of many a family. So did John Hay's *Pike County Ballads*. By such faithful portraiture was the middle class throughout the nation slowly weaned from taste for romantic literature and made eager to take stories of life as they and their neighbors had lived it.

These writers introduced into the national literature the Valley of Democracy, the section where the people were laboring to preserve the spirit of pioneer individualism against the inroads of eastern power, and to keep themselves free from vassalage. The Middle West was to be the citadel of the national faith in democracy and the keeper of the nation's conscience.

THE IMPACT OF LARGE SCALE ORGANIZATION

ORGANIZATION

1878-1900

CHAPTER XX

BIG BUSINESS EMERGES

As the depression which engulfed the United States in 1873 gradually lifted, the attention of the nation was drawn to new developments; by the beginning of 1879 a tide of prosperity had mounted. It pushed Americans along toward subjection to a dominating characteristic of modern living—large scale organization—which thoroughly permeated American life by the end of the next panic and depression period, 1893-1898. Formal acknowledgement of its sway was signalized by the organization of the giant corporations which emerged at the turn of the century. During these two decades, the correlation of growth in population with availability of natural and mechanical resources pushed leaders in all important fields of activity into schemes of monopoly. Some of these schemes had been in the making before the epoch began; others became significant only after it ended; but in the main this period was dominated by a mighty urge for organization on a national scale. That became its predominant characteristic.

Momentum from Growing Population

The area of the United States remained the same—3,025,600 square miles—but the density of population increased greatly. With this increase other increases were involved; the whole correlated the activities of the growing nation. A few population figures suggest the momentum of growth.

Year	Pop. in Millions	% of increase	Prop. urban to tot. pop.	Westward movement of center of population	Density of Population per sq. mi.
1870	39 —	23	20.9	42 miles	13.0
1880	50 +	30	22.6	58 miles	16.9
1890	63 —	25	29.2	48 miles	21.2
1900	76 —	21	32.9	14 miles	25.6

Thus, the cities of the nation grew greater in number and size, while the farming population was appropriating new areas to the west. A closer association in cities and a survey of wider regions beyond stimulated the most intelligent and the most ruthless leaders to appropriate the national resources and to exploit the human market which the growing population placed at hand. The results accumulated in geometric ratio, and on a nationwide scale, involving the organization of economic and social groups in units crossing state boundaries and exerting an influence more pervasive than that first conceived by the organizers themselves. Whenever large scale organization was achieved by ruthless means, as often it was, it ultimately challenged thinking men and women to devise means whereby the national government might control forces which the states proved helpless to handle. Upon the great swell of American development the individual was swept unthinkingly, and awareness came only in extremity.

In the movement of population native and immigrant were commingled, in shifting proportions. The cities did not lose many of their workers to the country, for the cost of land, equipment, and moving exceeded their slender capital. They packed into the densest area, chiefly the states of the North Atlantic Division, New England, New York, New Jersey, and Pennsylvania—14.5 million people in 162,000 square miles. To them were added those immigrants who were caught, beyond release, on the Atlantic seaboard.

The great fluidity was in the farming population, equipped by training and predilection for the trial of strength with nature, and by 1878 in possession of almost one-third of the national area. Native farmers who had failed to succeed in New England, in middle and western New York, in Pennsylvania, in Ohio's Western Reserve, or yet further west, moved on to search for soil that was not stony or need not be cleared of trees, or to find change and adventure, or to justify their chronic optimism. They moved chiefly in times of relative prosperity for, contrary to the opinion held through many years, the farmer who suffered in hard times rarely was able to migrate until they were over. In their new locations they found their own venturesome, unsettled kind, whether Missouri men moving into the Red River country, Kansans into Colorado, or Carolinians and Georgians into Florida: and the communities they built reflected the aspirations and ebulliency of the founders, as affected by such difficulties as their new locations imposed upon them.

To the native farmers was added an important percentage of farm families from northwest Europe; German, Scandinavian, English and Welsh, Scotch and Canadian, whose coming was eagerly sought by the federal and state governments, the railroads, steamship lines, and land companies. The national government which still owned approximately a million square miles of land or one-third of the nation's expanse, had legislated on the theory that the vast western area could be peopled with an independent farming population, such as already had established themselves in the Mississippi valley, through the sale of small parcels of land on easy terms. But the laws had been evaded with such success

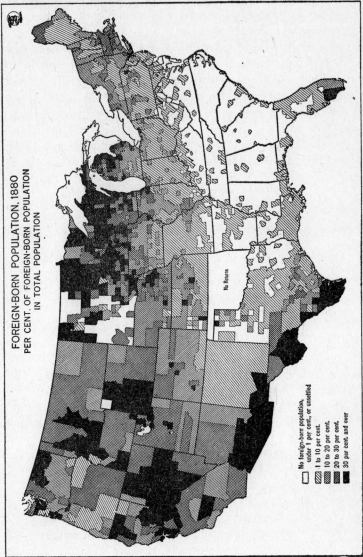

FOREIGN-BORN POPULATION, 1880
PER CENT. OF FOREIGN-BORN POPULATION
IN TOTAL POPULATION

No foreign-born population,
under 1 per cent., or unsettled
1 to 10 per cent.
10 to 20 per cent.
20 to 30 per cent.
30 per cent. and over

No Returns

From Charles O. Paullin, *Atlas of the Historical Geography of the United States* (1932), edited by John K. Wright; Carnegie Institution of Washington and American Geographical Society of New York, joint publishers. By permission.

that much of the trans-Mississippi area was seized by absentee owners holding large units. In the struggle to develop their unused lands, state governments established their own immigration bureaus, to furnish information, aid and inducements to prospective settlers. The Immigration Bureau of the national government had been established in 1891 as a part of the Treasury Department.

But the most strenuous and effective immigration work was done by the private corporations with tickets and lands to sell, and future freights to hope for. Their personal representatives showered attractive literature and promises upon the peasants of all Europe. In Italy they were aided by the interests which were establishing new steamship lines from southern ports; in regions like Russia and Poland, persecution of the Jews played directly into the hands of the ticket salesmen. Their success and their move southward were indicated by the census figures.

	1871–1880	*1881–1890*	(*Figures in thousands*)	*1871–1880*	*1881–1890*
Total immigr.	2800	5247	Canadians	383	393
Germans	718	1453	Hungarians	73	354
Eng., Welsh	460	757	Italians	56	307
(incl. Gr. Brit., not spec.)			Russians, Poles	52	265
Scotch	88	150	Danes	32	88
Irish	437	655	Dutch	17	54
Norwegians, Swedes	211	568	French	72	50

The vast majority of the immigrants settled in the northeastern and north central states, avoiding the South with its Negro competition and low economic scale. In the western states and territories the number of foreign born was not large, but their proportion to the total population was very heavy. As most of the immigrants had passed childhood and had not yet reached old age, the United States had a double advantage: it got people who had been reared at the expense of their home countries and who now were giving their productive years to their adopted country.

The migratory movement grew by what it fed upon, for relatives sent back to kinsmen glowing accounts of prospects, backed up by the wherewithal for more steamship and railroad tickets, and these sprouted in the village gossip of the old country, opening wide the door for personal representatives of the transportation and land companies, who cooperated closely for their mutual gain. The end of the journey might be far out on the line of the Santa Fé, the Southern Pacific, the Union Pacific, or the Northern Pacific. If it was along the route of the Great Northern, the pioneer found that James J. Hill's organization was ready to guide and help him in laying out towns with their banks, schools, churches, and stores, with their hinterland of farm homes; for Hill sought to apply the sound principle that a railroad takes its sustenance from the area it feeds.

Such long range planning, unfortunately, did not inspire most of the speculators in immigration. Many of them were business men wanting cheap workers to lay railroad ties, dig ditches, and perform unskilled labor in cities and mines. The progress of invention and manufacture enlarged the market for this kind of illiterate newcomer, setting him down in his own "little Ireland," "little Italy," "little Russia," or "Chinatown," where for a time he fulfilled his destiny as a contract laborer, meanwhile unconsciously challenging efforts to assimilate him in an independent scheme of American democracy. His heavy impact upon American life is suggested by the census figures of the percentage of foreign born in the population: in 1880, 13.3%, in 1890, 14.7%, and in 1900, 13.6%.[1] Nearly one-third (20,676,046 persons) of the entire population by 1890 were persons whose parents were foreign born. This one-third, living largely in sections dominated by people of their own race and tongue, offered in the mass the maximum resistance to "Americanization"; they showed the unruly, undisciplined temper of the second generation in America.

But they comprised a "selected" group, because their families had felt themselves misfits in the old world and had dared risk what little they had on a move to the new. Many of them again would fall victim to the modern scheme of civilization. But among them must be determined leaders, daring and resourceful, who would deflect American trends into directions suiting their needs. As few of them settled in the agricultural areas, they were affected chiefly by conditions of city life and in that fertile field sowed the seed of their influence.

The full implication in American history of the rapid increase of population during this period can be realized only if one stops to consider the interaction of expanding population with developing resources. The United States was not unlike a huge turkish towel, which could absorb wave on wave of immigration because it had the requisite unfilled spaces. Ten of the present states were not yet in existence and many areas in the remaining thirty-eight were capable of supporting a larger population. The national wealth in minerals, water power, lumber, grazing lands and food-growing areas was understood just enough to create the conviction that it was boundless. Here were coal, oil, iron, gold, silver, lead and copper—to mention but few of the most valuable resources—challenging the inventiveness of the engineer and scientist and the acquisitiveness of ambitious men of vision. The employment of

[1] Immigration was retarded in the 'nineties by the American decline in economic opportunity and land supply and by improved conditions in western Europe.

electricity, for which stupendous resources in water power awaited, was in its early infancy. On the western ranges there was yet room for more cattle and sheep to feed and clothe the incoming hordes. Billions of feet of timber still stood, awaiting conversion into houses and newsprint, and of almost all the kinds needed for industrial and domestic purposes. Even the so-called "Great American Desert" had sufficient occasional rainfall to tempt farmers on the great plains to over-optimism and their ruination.

West and East furnished ample justification for an inflationary point of view, keeping Americans a nation of incurable speculators. The wealth available for use had increased in the past twenty years—despite both Civil War and depression—from a little over 16 to near 44 billion dollars. While it was most concentrated in a few heavily populated states—New York, Pennsylvania, Ohio, Illinois and Massachusetts, it was most strikingly augmented west of the Mississippi: in Kansas, Nebraska, Colorado and California—concrete justification for boundless faith in resources. Even the city-bound family, which could not own land, or go West to take it up, pleasantly beguiled its imagination with tales of the new discoveries. To this large class of the dissatisfied the West was a psychological, if not a physical, outlet. Possibly these gave to the nation stronger injections of optimism than did those who actually tried their fortunes beyond the "frontier line" and experienced its disappointments.

Back of that line was reason enough for loyalty to the concept of the "land of opportunity." The increase in population offered the farmer, builder, manufacturer and railroader progressive expansion in the demand for their goods and services:—for food, clothing, houses and transportation. Outside the range of bare necessities, the providers of education, entertainment, religion, luxuries and innovations could count upon an active demand. It was the more active because much more than half of the population was under forty years of age, was still in "the age of acquisition." Moreover, they were located in an area with ample waterways and an extended coastline, convenient for commercial purposes. These expanding demands brusquely challenged America's potential leadership in every field of activity.

The budding capitalists needed no conscience to prosper. Their cupidity was aroused and their ingenuity challenged by the economic developments which swirled about them, nerving them to fabulous feats of exploitation. As the crude individualism of the frontier was rampant through the nation, they felt no inhibitions against the use of ruthless methods; no compulsions to moral scruple. What more convenient philosophy than that he who could seize wealth and organize production should be rewarded with special privileges at the expense of an envious, admiring, emulating public? Did not everyone get ahead who deserved

it and was willing to work? Were not the poor in that class for lack
of brains and ability?

The far seeing seekers for wealth developed their skill as organizers.
They learned how to bring order out of the chaos of men and materials
in competing industries so that waste and competition should disappear
and the market be milked efficiently. Thus they imposed their will over
wide areas and millions of people. They achieved results—good and
bad—which exceeded imagination. The means, ends, and consequences
involved in the process are best understood by examining typical cases
in the major fields.

Exploitation of Oil Furnishes a Pattern

Large scale organization was earliest perfected in the exploitation of
natural resources. The essential tools were waiting:—a large and sturdy
laboring class, rich and easily preempted resources and a wide market.
In the oil industry were these first effectively exploited. That industry
well typified all aspects of corporate organization—the industrial, social,
political and legal. The facts of its history are largely known. Its
organizing genius had the originality and ruthlessness requisite to cut
a pattern for beating one's competitors at their own game in modern
business. Rising capitalists in other fields were duly instructed.

When John D. Rockefeller took up oil refining near Cleveland during
the Civil War, the new business (recently graduated from quack medicine) was typical of western development—speculative in nearly all its
branches. The supply of oil fluctuated violently as gushers came in and
wells went dry. The operators who sank the wells were gamblers—
theirs was no stable industry with modest profits fairly rewarding
effort, but one in which a drilling might bring a man a million or
nothing. The refiners were the sharpest kind of competitors—because
the cost of refining equipment was small enough to open the field to
many people and the possible profits were tantalizing. Since the entire
industry was speculative, prices gyrated wildly; a barrel of oil could
be quoted at fifty-two cents in 1861 and at more than $8.00 in 1863.
The only certain sure aspect of the industry was an increase in the
public demand for the product, because foreign and domestic users of
kerosene for light and lubrication multiplied rapidly.

Rockefeller and his associates, foreseeing the demand, undertook to
control the supply; that involved controlling all branches of the industry. The means ready to their ends had the dubious quality then
current in business and in their expert hands were used quite too efficiently to meet present day ethical standards. Ruthlessly and thoroughly
they destroyed their competitors and systematized the business under
their own control, cutting a pattern for trusts of all kinds. They reached

their goal through four stages: first refining; second transportation; third selling; and last well drilling and pumping; until in 1899 Standard Oil temporarily controlled them all.

Refining began in 1862 with a small investment in a Cleveland concern, a company of his own in 1865 and a Standard Oil Corporation chartered at $1,000,000 in Ohio in 1870 with such associates as H. M. Flagler and S. V. Harkness. This third company was but one of twenty-six concerns in the Cleveland area alone, which with others of Pittsburgh, New York and Philadelphia engaged in murderous competition. Efficiency, elimination of waste and improved processes could not alone cope with the industry-wide disorganization. The Rockefeller group, together with others in the four cities mentioned, therefore joined themselves in 1870 in a "South Improvement Company" which made a deal with the oil-carrying railroads, themselves competitors, to eliminate competitors. The New York Central, Erie and Pennsylvania were to raise freight charges by agreed amounts, but were to give South Improvement shippers rebates on both their own shipments and on those of their competitors, while the traffic was to be regularly apportioned. The outcry of outsiders against this discrimination forced the Pennsylvania legislature to annul the South Improvement charter in 1872; but by that time Standard Oil had acquired the property of twenty of its twenty-five Cleveland competitors and controlled 20% of the refining capacity of the nation. Also, it had entered a career of regularly demanding and usually receiving secret rebates invaluable to it.

Next the Standard Oil built pipe lines, with which it forced railroads to grant more rebates, and competitors to hand over their businesses; it proved futile for the Pennsylvania Railroad or for outside refiners to try to compete by organizing their own pipe lines. Among all competitors there was cajolery, lying, intimidation, spying, destruction of property, theft and sometimes murder. When the fight abated the Standard Oil organization had control of more companies. Forty of them, embracing control of 90% of the refineries and pipe lines of the nation, were organized under a trustee certificate plan in 1879 into the "Standard Oil Trust" which was formally created three years later.

While thus winning control of the refining and transportation of oil, the same genius for organization was applied to selling agencies, to force merchants to sell only Standard Oil output, to keep prices at a high profit level, while occasionally cutting them drastically, to eliminate other sellers, and meanwhile to build an enviable reputation for delivery of a standard quality product regularly, on time as ordered. The system effectively reached into the smallest hamlets. It contributed its quota to the maintenance of high prices at huge profits.

Control of drilling and pumping was attended to last, beginning on a large scale about 1887, and practically completed within ten years. Before 1900, therefore, large scale organization as applied to the oil industry had placed absolute control for the nonce in the hands of Standard Oil.

This, however, could not be accomplished without ruthlessness and cruelty, violent protest, social upheaval and the enlisting of ingenious legal and legislative talents. The services which the corporation rendered the consuming public were of a high order to which they were by no means accustomed, but the approach of absolute control, coupled with high prices, brought public support to competing producers as they struggled against their ultimate fate. Men who had been eliminated filed suits at common law, and attracted public attention to the evil practices of competitors:—to rebates, spying, tampering, destruction of property and the fomenting of labor troubles. Their interest in reform rose from their adversities.

Public interest, the United States being a democracy, had political effects. As noted, the Pennsylvania legislature annulled the charter of the South Improvement Company: a committee of Congress denounced it; the House Committee on Commerce at Washington investigated the Standard Oil Company in 1876; the Hepburn Commission in New York followed suit in 1879. The federal Anti-Trust Act of 1890 was followed the next year with trust investigations, undertaken by a commission for the New York State Senate and by the Committee on Manufactures of the national House of Representatives. In 1892 the Ohio Supreme Court ordered the Standard Oil Trust dissolved, and in 1898 an industrial commission looked further into it.

All of this had importance, as expressions of social discontent were fomented by competitors of Standard Oil and other dominant corporations, and transmuted into political and judicial responses. But it interfered very little with oil control or profits. The House inquiries of 1876 were guided by H. B. Payne, father of the O. H. Payne who was treasurer of Standard Oil. When the trust was ordered dissolved in 1892, the charter of the company remained unimpaired. It turned out that the dissolution order could not be enforced. The men in control proceeded to perfect a new device, a holding company, and Standard Oil, which had a charter from the complaisant New Jersey legislature, obtained in 1899 an amended charter highly significant in American corporate development. It was good for almost any sort of undertaking.

Eager imitators of Standard Oil multiplied during the 'eighties:— the cotton seed trust in 1884, linseed in 1885, in 1887 the cordage, lead and whiskey trusts, in 1891 the American Sugar Refining trust. These of course remained unaffected by the Ohio decisions and the general term "trust" kept its meaning. Before January 1, 1898, eighty-two trusts capitalized at 1197 millions had been organized. The cumulative force of this movement showed in the organization of 236 more trusts, with a total capitalization of 6000 millions within the next six years. Mightiest of these were Amalgamated Copper, American Smelting and Refining and the Standard Oil of 1899, Consolidated Tobacco and United States Steel of 1901 and the International Mercantile Marine of 1902. America's industrial and agricultural prosperity of 1898-1902, a world situation which contributed to a trade balance favorable to the United States, and the complaisant attitude of the public and charter-dispensing legislatures—particularly New Jersey, Delaware, West Virginia and Maine—made these consolidations the easier and more profitable.

The charters were the perfect product of the nation's keenest legal lights, led by such attorneys as Joseph H. Choate, James B. Dill and Elbert H. Gary. They found their high-paid calling in protecting private corporations from restrictions imposed by public will. The large scale organization of business had reached the point where it undermined the government of the democracy itself. The public soon would be made aware of the fact.

Iron, Coal, Copper and Electricity

Iron and coal offered an opportunity hardly less stimulating than oil for the talents of large-scale organizers. These two natural resources could be utilized in the manufacture of steel to furnish a product indispensable to American industrial advance. In this great field Andrew Carnegie was the leading spirit and accumulated a fortune next in size to that of Rockefeller.

The United States as a "land of opportunity" found its living embodiment in Carnegie who between 1848 and 1900 ran the gamut from destitute child immigrant to the nation's second richest citizen. A persistent and unyielding application of competitive energy, courage, optimism and foresight made possible this feat. Carnegie's difficulties were made less because he had a personal charm and romantic temperament which could find in America response extremely gratifying to the ego as well as to the purse.

The Civil War afforded him opportunities in telegraphy and railroading which led on into bridge building and iron manufacture. Oil dividends brought funds for investment. When he was selling American railroad bonds abroad the vision of steel appeared to him; in Britain he grew to know Bessemer, observed his process for converting brittle iron into strong steel, and studied operations of the world's leaders in the industry. His enthusiasm was concentrated from 1873 upon smelting operations in the coal, limestone, and iron area near Pittsburgh; in sixteen years (with the help of a high tariff) the United States had become the largest producer of steel in the world and Carnegie the biggest steel manufacturer in the United States.

The United States and Carnegie attained these eminences because he and his associates as well as his competitors in steel were working at the center of American economic development. Outside of Pittsburgh the principal producing regions were in Illinois, Tennessee, Alabama and Colorado: Carnegie's three principal competitors in unfinished steel were therefore the Illinois Steel Company, the Colorado Fuel and Iron Company, and the Tennessee Coal, Iron and Railway Company. As to resources, Carnegie benefitted by Henry Clay Frick's development of the Connellsville coke area, coke being superior to ordinary coal for smelting; he obtained for $2.50 a ton better coke than British manufacturers obtained for $4.50. Carnegie aligned Frick with him in 1882 and finally yielded to the younger man's tardy urgency that he investigate the rich iron ore deposits lying practically on the surface of the shores of Lake Superior. The best of these deposits had been acquired at a cheap depression price in 1893 by Rockefeller, and from him in 1896 Carnegie leased ore lands at a price so low as to make him practically invincible against all rivals; there would be no way out for his warring competitors but large scale combinations of their own.

As to markets, all the steel manufacturers benefitted by the feverish railroad building and multiplication of inventions for farms and factories. This, whether or not Carnegie realized it, was the reason why his scheme of mass production, low profits and continual expansion of output worked. Thus did transportation, agriculture, westward expansion, manufacturing in general and steel interdepend.

Being at the center of American economic development, steel making was infected by its ills—by business cycles, pitiless competition, railroad malpractice and labor unrest. The cycles, severely felt throughout the nation, moved the more violently because Carnegie set a production pace which his competitors strove to emulate, periodically glutting the market. He not only insisted that his workmen compete with rival firms, but also with each other. In depression years when weaker concerns let their equipment run down, the optimistic and far-visioned Carnegie expanded plants at minimum construction cost: he could supply the market the moment buying recommenced at figures below those of hapless competitors with boom-time building charges. During the resulting warfare pools and other trade agreements common in railroads and oil were tried in steel, and failed on account of the same mutual suspicion. Carnegie was producing steel too cheaply to bind himself very often to an arbitrary allotment.

The competitive frenzy for tonnage, with all its evil effects, worked four great benefits. It caused quick scrapping of obsolete machinery, lightning development of inventive aspects of the industry, rapidly improved processes and lowered prices. For low grade ores the Siemens-Martin open-hearth process was devised and by 1900 was producing more steel than the Bessemer method. Carnegie kept competitors continually trying to meet his underselling, thus giving the public the priceless boon of cheap steel.

Railroad abuses beset steel differently than oil. Because the Pennsylvania railroad enjoyed a near monopoly at Pittsburgh, Carnegie could not secure rebates and preferences in the Rockefeller manner. He and his Pittsburgh competitors were discriminated against in favor of Chicago and Cleveland. He fought the Pennsylvania—his old employer—hard, building some trackage of his own and shipping his Lake Superior ore via Rockefeller steamships and railroads.

For labor, Carnegie felt more sympathy than many of his fellow industrialists; but his associate Frick felt less. Strained relations which had become serious by 1887 culminated in 1892 in the notorious Homestead Strike and a complete rout of the union (p. 388). Thus, in the basic industry of steel, large scale organization of capital whipped large scale organization of labor. This year of 1892 was the same in which various Carnegie holdings in coal, coke, limestone, iron ore, ships and railroads were combined as the Carnegie Steel Company, Limited. It was by far the strongest of the concerns producing crude and semi-finished steel.

Meanwhile, in the production of finished steel, large scale organization was applied in almost every nook and cranny. Pitiless competition had been alternating with pools, in nearly every steel product in use; but by about 1898 J. P. Morgan of New York and W. H. Moore of Chicago, had engineered gigantic combinations:—in wire, nails, tubes, hoops, tin plate, sheet steel, and bridge steel, to mention but a part of the products. They strengthened themselves by combining into the Illinois Steel Corporation.

Then Carnegie, who now wished to retire and devote his time to charity and leisure, vigorously commenced to invade the finished steel field. Frightened, Morgan and millionaire associates, with the legal aid of E. H. Gary, bought up Carnegie's great holdings. They managed this by setting up a 1400 million dollar corporation—United States Steel—through which they consolidated his holdings with theirs, paying to him 447 millions in bonds and to themselves large blocks of preferred and common stock. As their combined properties were conservatively estimated to be worth only about 682 millions, it was clear that they weighted down the new corporation with more than 700 millions of watered stock, based upon nothing but future hope. Fortunately for them, their dominance in steel was so complete, and American prosperity then was so pervasive, that the corporation paid dividends on its water, thus soaking it up. The water formula of large scale organization was commonly and profitably practiced by the consolidators of this period.

Incorporation of the steel trust in 1901 marked a new era in steel manufacture. Away went Carnegie's old partnership organization, wherein steel stock was owned and controlled exclusively by executives actually working in the industry, with speculation definitely ruled out. Ever since, executives have been hired, and stock manipulated. More important, from the standpoint of the public weal, when Carnegie departed competition in steel departed with him. This probably had effects reaching beyond and counteracting his efforts as the incorporated philanthropist, the giver of libraries and founder of technical institutes and foundations for the advancement of knowledge.

In the exploitation of copper is found a further illustration of the remarkable inter-relations between individual talents for large scale organization and contemporary developments in related fields. After silver mining in the 'seventies lost its strongest appeal in Montana, came the realization that copper was more valuable than silver. Copper proved indispensable to the growing electric industry and rivalry over control of the metal brought the "War of the Copper Kings" among William A. Clark, Marcus Daly, and Augustus Heinze, three of the most colorful personalities in the mining industry. With the help of daring investors like George Hearst were founded the Anaconda and other companies which monopolized the copper field.

They hesitated at no forms of political corruption and utilized most of the known means of speculative manipulation. Their rivalry in and out of legislative halls wrote a disreputable story, but at the same time contributed to a social order which hastened the admission of the mountain territories as states and vastly increased the influence of that area in national politics. At the close of the century one of the contestants, Marcus Daly, tiring of his long warfare, prepared to sell out his copper interests to the Standard Oil Company. Thus control of the extractive industries was falling into the hands of a few business giants from whose will few important industries would be left free.

Other natural resources besides oil and metals were brought to use by large scale organization. Water power was applied to the manufacture of electricity on a large scale, for business and for private consumption, and thus began its long career of direct influence upon American life. Following 1877, dynamos and arc lights developed by C. F. Brush and John Thomson led to Edison's incandescent lamp of 1879, which Drexel-Morgan wisely financed. By 1886 Westinghouse was ready to market alternating current, against the bitter opposition of Edison and others. Its adoption splendidly illustrated the far-reaching influence of changes in this industry. The introduction of alternating current had such significant consequences as the re-financing of electric companies, construction of municipal plants, flagrant franchise corruption, the forcing of the displaced gas companies into the heating business and the development of the huge industry of electric appliances.

The application of electricity to traction proved difficult, with Edison and Thomson advancing but slowly. Leo Daft and C. J. Van Depoele were doing somewhat better but it was not until Frank J. Sprague succeeded at Richmond, Virginia, in constructing a traction system permitting a great many trolley cars to consume electricity at the same time that success was assured. His company was promptly absorbed by the Edison Electric system and capitalistic control of public utilities was assured for many years. Just as there was no precedent in American experience for electric traction itself, so there was no precedent for government control of that traction; and the same thing proved true with other American electrical developments.

Vitally important in the field of electrical advance were the telegraph and telephone, which evolved in such a manner as to keep rapid communication—a vital aspect of large scale organization—under private control. The Western Union Telegraph Company emerged from a combination of fifty companies before the Civil War; but in 1878 it entered upon a new era under the presidency of Norvin Green. Three years later its two chief competitors, the American and the Atlantic and Pacific Telegraph Companies, were absorbed by it. There followed the indispensable contracts with the railroads, which accomplished huge savings by exchanging the use of office space and telegraph wires for the sending of train despatch messages.

Following an unsuccessful strike in July 1883 came an outcry for public ownership of this vital utility; but it was defeated by the gift of free franking privileges to legislators, state and national, who could send their telegrams free, just as they could ride on the trains without cost. Herein the lobby technique of the telegraph companies showed an interesting parallel to that of the railroads. Agitation led to encouragement of the formation of the competing Postal Telegraph Company, but within four years the Western Union had made an agreement with it which effectually ended the rate-cutting and competition alike; they became as one in the distribution of franking privileges among potential rate regulators.

Meanwhile large scale business received indispensable aid in the annihilation of distance through the efforts of entrepreneurs in the telephone business. As an avenue of wealth-getting, telephony attracted Western Union leaders who had refused to buy Alexander Bell's patent rights and launched a competing company with Gray's patents. They met their match when T. M. Vail assumed charge of the American Bell Telephone Company and forced Western Union (in 1879) to stop infringement and retire from the field. There were many small com-

The "Party-line Telephone"

Rural Free Delivery

GROWTH OF INTERCOMMUNICATION

Part of an Overseas Switchboard

panies in various localities, some of them formed simply for fake stock-
selling and most of them infringing the Bell patents. The scandals
penetrated the cabinet of Cleveland whose Attorney General, A. H.
Garland, was found to have invested unwisely; but the Bell litigants
repeatedly won their cases and in 1885 prosecuted far-reaching schemes
for long distance consolidation of companies, which greatly quickened
communication in American business.

Many small town units survived at the end of the period but their
relative importance was so slight as to make the trust absorption only a
matter of time. Fortunately, the Bell concerns were financed conservatively, without the gross stock manipulation typical of most virgin
industries. Telephony vastly increased employment because it stimulated manufacture and distribution in innumerable fields. Successive
inventions aided engineering, with such things as underground wiring,
copper wiring, and the fabrication of cables adapted to multiple messages over long distances.

Railroad Consolidation

No phase of American enterprise felt the effects of the demand for
large scale organization more than did railroading. Successful consolidation required the growth and spread of population and the mobilization of wealth. The map was a constant inspiration to railroad promoters.

In the region west of the Mississippi there were by 1880 four long
lines linking the Mississippi valley to the Pacific seaboard, besides
numerous lesser lines built across more sparsely settled areas to connect
points of promise. From San Francisco, Portland and Seattle, from
Denver, Salt Lake City and Cheyenne, from Atchison, Topeka and
Santa Fé, from Duluth, St. Paul and Minneapolis, from Kansas City,
Sioux City and St. Louis it seemed eminently desirable to construct
railroads, and many of them. They performed a national service,
accelerating the speed with which the continent was exploited and
settled. But the operators did not regard theirs as a career in social
service, but as one for making money, as quickly as possible.

The rivalries of many builders and stock manipulators, together with
the faith of investors that the future of the railroads could be realized
in the immediate present, caused rail-laying where there was no traffic
in sight and where existing roads were adequate. In the early 'eighties
the favorable balance of trade helped to bring in a plethora of foreign
investment funds and the orgy of building was feverish. By 1883 competition and the growing demand for some return on investments led
to ruinous rate wars; the depression descending in 1884 brought to the
weaker roads the inevitable deflation and receiverships.

By 1884 there were four times as many miles of railroad in the United States—of one sort and another—as there had been in 1865, and the more farsighted of the managers were consolidating their holdings. Collis P. Huntington had followed up his work in building the Central Pacific by uniting in the Southern Pacific system a gigantic network extending from New Orleans, through California to Portland, with branch lines in Texas, connections with St. Louis, and control of a steamship line from New York to New Orleans and Galveston. To these he later added control of steamships operating from Oregon to the Isthmus and across the Pacific.

Scarcely less magnificent, but not as successful, were the plans of the Union Pacific. It expanded eastward to St. Louis, northward into Oregon and cross-country into Wyoming, Colorado and Texas; by 1893 its mileage exceeded 8000. Unfortunately, the Union Pacific typified the mischances of the average American railroad, expanding so rapidly and managing so extravagantly that it could not meet obligations. The panic of 1893 plunged it, and many another railroad, into bankruptcy, sometimes by malevolent prearrangement. J. P. Morgan refused to help pull it out, because its sparsely settled territory and its partial control by the government seemed to him to cloud its future. The road had to wait until 1898 when Harriman came forward in its behalf.

Further north Henry Villard (who had been developing Oregon rail and steamship lines and was backed by German capital) expanded the Northern Pacific system to about 2300 miles before the depression of 1884 embarrassed it. He later found an entrance into Chicago, but payment of dividends from surplus, while fixed charges increased, brought the usual receivership and loss of valuable feeders during the panic of 1893, ending with a new and significant development. J. P. Morgan, who had successfully undertaken the refinancing of several eastern roads (the Erie, Reading, Baltimore and Ohio, Southern and Hocking Valley system) but had thus far held aloof from the Far West, now cooperated with the American and German interests on the Northern Pacific. The stage had been reached when big banking (as distinguished from speculative banking) determined the destiny of transcontinental railroad systems.

Beyond the Northern Pacific was a railroad which made better use of its opportunities. James J. Hill, with Scotch-Canadian backing, had begun in the midst of the depression of the 'seventies to push a railroad westward across Minnesota; by economical construction and profitable operation he had avoided many ills that railroading was heir to; when he and his associates watered their stocks and bonds on the basis of "good will, earning power and future prospects" the Great Northern, as it came to be named, throve. Amidst the 1893 panic they reached the coast and 5% dividends were not only paid but earned. Hill, like

Huntington, proved that the tremendous obstacles to railroading reared by the mountainous West were puny when matched against the resources of that same region.

Meanwhile, east of the Mississippi, railroad consolidators enjoyed the tremendous advantage of operating in a more populous, industrialized region with maximum freights and shorter hauls, in addition to linkage between the West and eastern seaboard market: five great trunk lines—the New York Central, Grand Trunk, Erie, Pennsylvania, Baltimore and Ohio—by 1880 were providing through connections from the Atlantic to Chicago. They carried the scars of mismanagement, rank stock speculation, bitter traffic wars, and panic strain. Without remarkable increases in population, industry and wealth in this area, neither the B. & O. nor the Erie probably could have been consolidated, for the Garrett family badly mismanaged the first, and Drew, Vanderbilt, Gould and Fisk kicked the Erie around as a speculative football until in 1896 a drastic reorganization was insisted upon by J. P. Morgan.

The magnitude of the profits at stake in eastern transportation made more disreputable the weapons employed in a disreputable era. Lines like the West Shore along the Hudson were blackmail roads, strung practically parallel to existing lines for the object of sale. In railroad wars, as in the oil industry, no quarter was given; the devil took the hindmost in the game of stock manipulation, rebates, and drawbacks. Sometimes rate wars were abated by formation of pools, but these were weak because there often was no honor among thieves. All charged as much as the traffic would bear, especially where competition was absent or the haul short.

In this situation the need for large scale organization was as obvious as in the oil industry. Ambition for wealth and power, economy and convenience made consolidation inevitable. Accomplished usually by the methods of highway robbery, by theft of the management of the stock of a company, it steadily progressed, eliminating the weaker, less efficient or more unlucky.

In railroading, as in oil, the democratic basis of American government sometimes forced operators to consider public sentiment. Although federal courts had declared the state Granger legislation unconstitutional, operators could still be put on the defensive by a drastic change in railroad management. One of them was rescued by banking aid and a new era was reached in railroad control.

William H. Vanderbilt personally owned over 87% of the 100 million dollar capitalization of the New York Central system. He had to fight continually against Jay Gould and other competitors as well as the public while he built up his New York-Chicago system. The size of his fortune, much of it acquired within 10 years, became known and he was credited with the phrase "the public be damned." He became the target of an investigation by the New York legislature while he was fighting a rate war and was upset by a Gould raid on his traffic. In acute distress, he enlisted the help of J. P. Morgan who quietly secured English buyers for 25 millions of Vanderbilt's stock without depressing the market; Morgan's syndicate profited by approximately 3 millions, whilst Vanderbilt reinvested his proceeds, largely in tax-free United States government bonds.

A legislative and financial emergency thus was overcome, but the means employed had long time effects upon the lives of millions of persons. The banking house of J. P. Morgan became financial agent for the New York Central system, which was one of the two richest railroads in America, thanks to the thickly populated cities in its reach. Morgan thenceforward handled its expansions and consolidations, functioning fully on its board of directors. Large scale organization in railroads and finance had joined hands. The result was a power more than the sum of the two, affecting the fortunes of a huge aggregate of people. American banking control came to be divided, roughly, between two groups: Morgan's affiliates with their heavy interests in railways and steel, and the Rockefeller group founded on oil, financed through the National City Bank, possessing their own railways and ambitious for further conquest in gas and electric utilities.

More than 65% of the railroad mileage of the United States went into the hands of receivers, 1893-1898, but not the Central or the Pennsylvania. They (unlike the Erie and B & O) survived the seaboard-Chicago rate wars of 1877-1889 without serious weakening in credit or position and went through the difficult 'nineties without defaulting a bond or passing a dividend. An early president of the Pennsylvania, J. Edgar Thomson, was like J. J. Hill in preferring businesslike operation to stock manipulation. He formed in 1870 what was probably the first "holding company" in United States history—to control and manage leased lines in the Pennsylvania's interest.

His aggressive successors, T. A. Scott and G. B. Roberts, saw clearly the princely opportunities which America's resources, population and legislatures offered her railroad operators. There, invitingly, lay oil in western Pennsylvania, soft coal for manufacturing purposes in Indiana, Ohio and western Pennsylvania, the growing manufactures in the country's largest cities, farm products in the Middle West; all awaiting transportation. There were the state legislatures, not too friendly in the mass, but frequently sensitive to pressure as individuals. By intensive application of the principles of large scale organization to the Pennsylvania's benefit and the detriment of competitors and public, Scott and Roberts, between 1874 and 1897 stretched the Pennsylvania lines from New York to Iowa and Missouri, from the Straits of Mackinaw to Chesapeake Bay with intricate networks in regions of richest traffic.

The Pennsylvania owed much of its success to that combination of natural resources and manufacturing development which made the Pittsburgh district the center of iron and steel manufacture. It was the first American railroad to lay steel rails and the first to lay Bessemer rails. The work of Andrew Carnegie and George B. Roberts was complementary. Whereas the New York Central exemplified coordination of transportation with high finance, the Pennsylvania coordinated transportation and manufacturing.

Consolidation Among Manufacturers

Inevitably manufacturing responded to the growing needs of the nation by resorting to large scale methods. These needs grew more varied in kind while they swelled in total volume. They challenged inventors, capitalists and executives to fill more factories with more machines, to make more money in more different ways. Thus mechanization of the nation was quickened during the 'eighties, by a manufacturing development far greater than in any previous decade. Manufacture spread westward, in pursuit of raw material, usually as fast as the supply of labor, transportation and capital permitted. The number of employees increased about twice as fast as the population; capital invested in manufacturing more than doubled, as did the value of the net product of manufacturing.

But this did not mean that the number of factories and the number of employees increased as fast as the capital and the product. On the contrary, their growth was somewhat less rapid, due to the greater size of manufacturing establishments and the increased use of machinery in them. Machinery was displacing workers, at the same time as it vastly enlarged their output.

Not less pervasive in its effects was the tremendous increase in the proportion of the population living machine-made lives. Those affected were of all ages and both sexes, because machinery increased employment of women and children. Unskilled laborers tending machines at some endlessly repeated stage of manufacture could have little of that very important sense of satisfaction which comes from completing a product. Life became something much more narrowly restricted than craftsmen in the old handicrafts had known, did not teach them balance or discrimination. Unguarded, powerful machinery caused serious accidents and a sense of daily danger. In their play as well as work, in religion as well as politics, in fact in all aspects of their lives they become easy prey to the superficial, the violent and the transitory. The vast majority of the men, women and children employed in the United States came to belong to this class of unskilled, underprivileged laborers.

The gap between these automatons and their employers was far wider, even in boom times, than the distance between pre-war artisans and shopowners. Whatever there had been of personal acquaintance, approachability and mutual liking, was by the 'eighties, well nigh destroyed by growing differences between the nature of activities and extremes of poverty and wealth. The employee tended to lose his identity in the machine he tended; the boss came to assume toward his flesh and blood workers a less careful attitude than he showed for his vital machinery. This tendency grew more marked as expensive machinery displaced cheap labor, as factory floors came to be crowded with steel giants. The attendant of course could not own any of the machinery (as the artisan owned his tools); nor could he cultivate much personal pride in its careful use and productive efficiency, for it was his taskmaster. It increased his output and his employer's profits rather than his own wages.

These tendencies became aggravated whenever a fresh trade rivalry or a depressed market threw industrialists into a new frenzy of competition; then labor and machinery became alike commodities, to be got at the lowest possible price, to lie idle, untended in time of slack; but with this significant difference; the manufacturer's outlays for machinery gave it a place in his idealization of property values, made its destruction or injury a personal loss and involved its careful repair. In his workers the manufacturer had invested only the little capital required to train them. They did not equal machines in implicit, unquestioning obedience. Just as many of them were suspicious and discontented, so their employer often-times despised them as weaker persons, cheap instruments, and felt little compunction about discarding and forgetting them when worn out.

Manufacturers, offered capital, machinery and labor in abundance, overestimated the domestic market, which they monopolized behind high tariff walls—walls watchfully guarded by such national organizations as the American Iron and Steel Association, American Wool Manufacturers Association and the Association of American Manufacturers. They turned second to foreign buyers, expanded their plants and sharpened their wits to meet demands of the world market. This in turn made American industry more sensitive to world trade fluctuations; under the conditions of competitive machine manufacture all the great industrial nations—the United States, England, France and Germany—were likely to find themselves in a slump almost simultaneously, to the extent that local and foreign demand moved up and down together.

Americans failed, lamentably, in 1884 and 1893, to absorb their own output; the entire nation felt the pinch. Among the results were overproduction (from the standpoint of the seller, not of the consumer), lowered prices and wages, and unemployment—the acute sufferings that go to make up a depression. These had more drastic effects than formerly because the mechanization of industry made variations more extreme, while it imposed a manner of living which left the laborers with less resource for combating unemployment. They worked ten and twelve hours for low wages; they paid high rents for an existence in squalor. During the depression of the mid-eighties skilled men competed for jobs paying only $1.00 per day, and women for fifty cent wages. The price fall then partly compensated them for low wages, but there were too many jobless days for decent living.

The various forces at work by 1890 had brought 1% of American families more wealth than all the other 99%. Of the city population (largely foreign-born) 10% then were living in poverty; thus industrialization and poverty marched together. Yet Andrew Carnegie in 1886 denied the existence of poverty in America; so did William G. Sumner, whose researches as professor of economics and social science at Yale left him as blind as the average comfortable person. Others less blind thought poverty always was due to laziness, wastefulness, drunkenness or illiteracy. Most Americans tenaciously cherished the belief that theirs was still "the land of opportunity," that the unprosperous had but themselves to blame. It was heresy to assert that pauperism could be imposed "in the land of the free." Class fluidity did indeed remain far greater than in Europe; but it was far less than when Carnegie started to rise. To uproot such preconceptions, invalidated in fact by large scale organization of capital, labor must perfect its own organization. At this it worked blunderingly and persistently during the 'eighties and 'nineties.

Labor Organizes

Early in this period the Knights of Labor were approaching their ascendancy. They established their general assembly of 1878, on the upswing of the country's return to prosperity. The next year they abandoned secrecy (due in part to the Molly Maguire disclosures) and, electing T. V. Powderly as Grand Master, they entered an aggressive phase in which they abandoned their former dislike for strikes. As national and local craft unions also were very active in this period, there were, 1880-1885, over 500 strikes and lockouts annually. Union membership grew with union effectiveness and the hard times beginning in 1884 brought more radical recruits. Two years later the Knights alone had nearly 750,000 on their rolls.

With strikes and boycotts they made their mark in two fields. In industry, they proved less unsuccessful than before in fighting wage reductions, forcing the eight-hour day, and securing recognition of the Knights; their most decisive victory was over the Gould railway management in 1885. In legislation, their state victories brought a factory inspection act in highly-industrialized Massachusetts (1879). Nationally, they got exclusion of Chinese (1882) and contract labor (1885). Machinery to assist their propaganda efforts was set up within the national government in the form of a standing committee on labor in the House of Representatives (1883) and a national Bureau of Labor (1884). Their gains were insignificant compared with demands; but they made themselves a force to be reckoned with, politically and industrially.

However, 1886 brought disaster. Following a May Day movement for an eight-hour day, a mass meeting was held 4 May in Haymarket Square, Chicago. Someone, who never has been discovered, threw a bomb. The results were conviction of eight anarchists (on general principles since their direct connection with the outrage could not be proved) and a storm of public disapproval of the Knights when they asked clemency for the condemned men. They and their agitation for an eight hour day were thus thoroughly discredited, although they were not responsible for the bomb-throwing.

Worse, their ideal of one organization for all labor proved unworkable. Producers' cooperatives did not compete successfully with private business. Their conglomerate membership lacked the organization, discipline, and funds essential to successful union policy. Their manner of concentrating power in a central group ran counter to American democratic practice. Against their country-wide strikes employers wielded the lockout, blacklist, and iron-clad oath. Their skilled members, who could not float from one job to another as easily as the unskilled, were heavily penalized; they of the cities withdrew back into the more conservative craft unions. The Knights turned increasingly toward the farmers (p. 405).

Meanwhile, a new labor federation destined to come down into the present, was being built on a narrower principle—one better calculated to succeed in the America of those years. Units of skilled craftsmen had formed in 1881 a "Federation of Organized Trades and Labor Unions of the United States and Canada." Skilled craftsmen, said they, should combine solely for their own benefit. So, within two years they and the Knights of Labor were at war. After the Haymarket affair, the Federation reorganized as the "American Federation of Labor"; with unaffiliated unions preferring them to the Knights of Labor and with disaffected craftsmen coming over from the Knights, the Federation ultimately succeeded in displacing its predecessor as the strongest labor organization.

Chances of success in securing nationwide recognition of skilled labor depended upon the quality of union leadership and membership and their skill at forging and wielding weapons. Leadership here was assumed in many cases by immigrants, who were not inhibited from the outset

by heritage of American perfectionism. Samuel Gompers and his associates had learned by experience that industrial warfare was a far more
effective instrument than political programs and currency reform! They
were imbued with the European concept of class struggle but had the
sense not to attempt any basic reordering of American society. They
accepted the capitalistic system and respected American traditions in
self-government. That historic entity, the local union, was accepted in
the Federation as a practically autonomous "city central" run demo-
cratically and frugally and tied into the national body by the familiar
device of a state federation. Each national craft union kept complete
autonomy, was apportioned representation in the federation according
to its membership and contributed annually to the central war chest a
3¢ per capita tax.

Furthermore, Federation leaders had learned from others' failures
not to push demands beyond public tolerance nor to concern themselves
too deeply with the general welfare. They therefore kept their imaginations under control, kept their social understanding as limited in scope
as did the capitalists they opposed. When they supported such propositions as municipally-owned utilities, large public school appropriations,
woman suffrage and popular election of senators, they helped to advance
social democracy, but officially they rejected socialism. Their main interest and weapon was collective bargaining. They paid little attention
to "isms" or political organizations to promote them. Their main constituents were local unions in railroading, mining, metal-working, building, and manufacturing which varied greatly in vision, methods, and
success. Union autonomy weakened unionism because locals of various
crafts quarreled over jurisdiction on big jobs. The Federation worked
mainly among the relatively small proportion of labor which was skilled,
teaching them allegiance to the union label. They quite frequently organized effective boycotts of goods or employers who refused to use the
label, particularly between 1881 and 1891. Strikes advanced beyond
the limited hour-pay objective to a demand for union recognition—for
the principle that industry should not be run without periodic trade
agreements between capital and labor.[1] Gompers' policy of high dues
and benefits enabled unions in 1893, for the first time, to pass through
a panic without loss of membership. The fact that organized labor held
its own, 1893-1898, against the modernized capitalistic warfare of that
depression, proved its growth in strength. By 1900 the Federation had
a labor press of some 500 editors and over half a million members.

Such activities in the industrial field brought forth fruit in legislation. The contract labor law was strengthened in 1891, when also
federal control of immigration was established. Chinese exclusion was
renewed in 1892. A federal law attempting the eight hour day for gov-

[1] Iron moulders in 1891 made the earliest trade agreement of importance.

ernment workers proved ineffective, however. Among the states, labor by 1895 had accumulated fifteen arbitration statutes. But trade unions were still illegal as corporations and therefore subject to national and state conspiracy laws; nor had labor obtained national laws satisfactory to them for cutting down the labor supply in respect to children, apprentices, and contract immigrants.

Among the craft unions organized upon a national or international scale were important bodies which added much dignity to the cause of labor, although they held aloof from the Federation. The aristocrats among these were the Railway Brotherhoods. They had about them much of the paternalism of the medieval guilds; and as they were a very highly trained, selected group they had a value to their employers which the ordinary industrial worker lacked. They developed their organization cautiously, in accordance with habits inbred in them by their responsible occupation, and four conservative brotherhoods resulted:—the Locomotive Engineers, the Railway Conductors, the Firemen, and the Trainmen—which finally achieved a national unity. They got little in national legislation—a railway arbitration act of 1888 proved unusable and another of 1898 was unpopular; but they amassed funds for accident and death benefits, and as men of resource, not easily replaced, won concessions in working conditions and wages. Outside of their ranks was a more radical and less successful organization, the American Railway Union.

All these efforts at organization on a large scale were characteristic of labor's contribution to the history of American development during the two final decades of the nineteenth century. Between 1881 and 1900 labor staged approximately 24,000 strikes; 1190 annually involving nearly a third of a million workers. The strikers won 35%, compromised 17% and lost 48% of these engagements.

Three of these defeats illustrated vividly how large scale organizations of capital, already achieved in key industries, could defeat large scale organization of labor in the making. At Homestead, Pennsylvania, in 1892 an exceptionally strong union—the Amalgamated Association of Iron and Steel Workers of the United States—challenged Frick (and Carnegie) over reduced wages and the closed shop. In the middle of a struggle relentless on both sides, an anarchist once more damaged labor; Alexander Berkman, attempting to assassinate Frick, deprived the Amalgamated of the sympathy of the public, and the Carnegie Corporation not only broke the strike but also wrecked the Amalgamated, killing unionization of the industry.

At Chicago in 1894 a union of pullman car workers living in a "company town" struck against a wage reduction. The American Railway Union espoused their cause, with a boycott spreading through the Middle and Far West against handling trains to which pullman cars were attached. To the aid of the Pullman company came the General Managers' Association, representing the executive branches of twenty-four railroads, and the thousands of laborers grasping for any kind of job in the depression. Also President Cleveland was a conservative on labor and Attorney General Olney was committed to capital; when the strike involved interruption of government mails federal troops were sent (against the wishes of Governor Altgeld) to defeat the workers. Their leaders, including Eugene V. Debs, were removed from the scene by court action, through injunctions.

Labor leaders earlier had been subject to jail sentences for calling strikes, under the conspiracy laws; but in 1894 the Sherman Anti-Trust Law against combinations in restraint of trade was invoked for the first time without recourse to a jury trial; and another weapon of labor, the boycott, was declared illegal. Since Pullman underscored the illegality of trade unions as corporations, it was a tremendous setback for labor. This was a mass defeat, with nearly 750,000 workers—even more than in 1886—involved. Added to this disaster, came a defeat for the United Mine Workers, who lost a strike in this same calamitous year. Recovery for labor must wait until the depression passed.

Thus, the last two decades of the 19th century were marked by large scale organization in every field of business. The economic opportunities afforded by America's growing population and abundant resources had been exploited in the mines, at the waterfalls, along the railroad lines and in the factories. The profits from organization had been greatest for capital; but labor had not been entirely without advantage. A third great class lived on the American scene. Did agriculture share in the trend?

CHAPTER XXI

THE FARMER'S STRUGGLE TO COMPETE

The agriculturists, at the same time as the other classes, became entangled in the American trend toward large scale organization. But to them it failed to bring either a place of great power or a prosperous position; and it swept away the foundations of their thinking. The American farmer had always felt that agriculture was the great national mainstay, and that his occupation was an independent, self-sufficient, ideal manner of getting a living. In his optimism and self-reliance he had been committed to laissez-faire (as were most Americans), convinced that uncontrolled exploitation of the national resources by individuals, without government interference, was the great guarantee of his well-being. It proved his undoing.

The Great Migration

Between 1862 and 1889 a migratory movement unequalled in world history established more than a million farms in a heretofore unpopulated

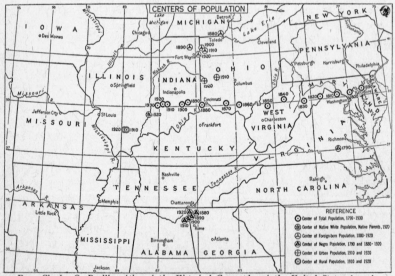

From Charles O. Paullin, *Atlas of the Historical Geography of the United States* (1932), edited by John K. Wright; Carnegie Institution of Washington and American Geographical Society of New York, joint publishers. By permission.

America Moves West

region. The 'seventies had seen farm settlements in the eastern third of Kansas, Nebraska, and the Dakotas; into their central and western sections and into Colorado,—west of the Missouri—farming was carried during the 'eighties, at a speed which within about six years covered a larger area than the thirteen original states. Some Americans were habitual migrants—the same family might settle successively in state after state, as did the Hamlin Garland family. Their hopes and those of immigrants were fired by the uncensored optimism of railroad advertisements, of land companies and speculators. The speculators helped to make the 'eighties the period when agricultural migration reached its

EXTENT OF EROSION IN THE UNITED STATES

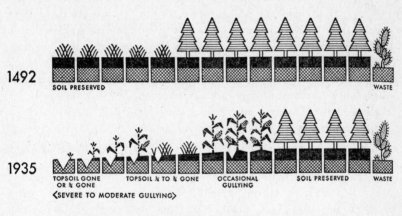

EACH BLOCK REPRESENTS 135 MILLION ACRES

PICTORIAL STATISTICS, INC.

From Person, *Little Waters: Their Use and Relation to the Land,* Government Printing Office.

Waste of the Soil

height, by availing themselves more generally of the "commutation" privilege whereby land could be purchased by persons with no intention of farming or ranching.

The migration movement was further accentuated by extravagant habits of cultivation. The Homestead Act, by offering land free, had "signed the death warrant" of prudent land use (land use had been none too prudent even before); and harvesting machinery (like the cotton gin earlier) had put a premium on land wastefulness. Farmers did not expect land to support one family more than twenty years; thereafter the eldest son took the old farm and the other sons went beyond to new acreage. Precautionary crop rotation and fertilization scarcely belonged in this picture; they existed, to a limited extent, only because horses and mules remained the farm motive power and required hay and oat acreage. The farmers of this period in the American West were skimming the cream off of the agricultural resources.

They did it, unthinkingly, for two reasons:—the world was making an imperious demand for more foodstuffs, and the means of supplying the demand were available. On the demand side, was the industrialized population of the United States, Britain, and parts of Europe; the town and the factory required the farmer to concentrate his efforts upon food production. Thus the flow of American wheat, corn and pork facilitated an economic revolution in Europe late in the nineteenth century, as had Spanish-American gold and silver in the eighteenth.

Also, there were the British, German and French investors in American railways and other undertakings, who were the creditors of the United States and took their interest payments chiefly in food export balances; they could not take their pay in sales of manufactured goods because the United States tariff was keeping foreign articles out, so that home manufacturers could control the domestic market. In addition, foreign producers of such daily necessities as coffee and tea, and such manufacturing essentials as dyestuffs, based their American sales on balances created through food production. All of these in effect challenged the American farmer to maintain the debt payments of the United States. He was able to meet the demand so vigorously, between 1879 and 1883, as to create then a favorable, "visible" balance of trade which contributed to prosperity through the entire nation.

Through the bad times and the good, of the two decades prior to 1900, the activities of the farmers totalled into a precipitous rise in food production—a rise more rapid than the increase in population. Foodstuffs became much the largest element in agricultural exports, with cotton second and tobacco third, while agriculture furnished seven-tenths of all American exports. Thus important was agriculture in the national economy. Few if any of its leaders realized that manufactures might in a later period preempt first place, although by 1900 agriculture was furnishing little more than half of America's total exports.

Accumulation of Liabilities

The most powerful agents of agricultural supply (as of population movements) up to 1890 were the free public lands, the low price acreage, the influx of labor to work them and the railroads to provide outlets to markets; the functioning of these agents is a familiar historical fact. But less familiar and almost equally important as affecting farm efficiency was the new machinery. Most of the successful machines came in the latter part of the nineteenth century. Their effect upon sheer bulk of output was of course tremendous: but that was only one aspect of their intricate influence. They led the farmer to substitute for diversi-

fied farming and home handicrafts the growing of staple crops adapted
to machinery; his well-being he rashly entrusted to the price of staples
grown in huge quantities. They increased the supply of food without
a proportional increase in the number of persons to whom they afforded
employment; these increased more slowly and sometimes declined. They
lowered the cost of food to the consumer by making it more abundant;
but they meanwhile increased the liabilities in farming as an occupation.

Liabilities accumulated disproportionately, not only because the machines themselves were expensive but more because they called for larger
farms; as the supply of land diminished, speculation in it made acreage
(rather than livestock, seed, fences, buildings, and other equipment)
become the heaviest part of the agricultural investment. Climatic changes
encouraged unsound finance. In the trans-Missouri states exceptionally
adequate rainfall from 1879 through 1886 made for good crop yields
and a false sense of security; this at the same time that capital was
accumulating in the hands of impatient eastern and foreign investors.
Their imaginations were fired by the western rates of 6 to 12% on real
estate and 10 to 20% on chattels. At first western investment companies had taken the place of timid banks in loans; then insurance
companies and state banking systems came to participate with the farmer
in his huge gamble on land and weather. To mortgage companies and
irresponsible agents eager easterners entrusted their funds; while the
value of lands and improvements temporarily skyrocketed, farmers were
bombarded with offers of loans.

Before drouth conditions returned, in 1887, more than 45% of the
farms in many of the states of the boom area had been mortgaged, and
frequently "up to the hilt," with their village and county seat communities as heavily loaded for public improvements. This had involved
a steady increase in the proportion of the crops lost to interest and taxes.
The farmer could carry such liabilities only as long as the values of his
land and crops were held correspondingly high. As values fell, the farmer
complained of the high interest rates and taxation, of the heavy renewal
charges and five year terminal dates of his mortgages. He found that low
prices of land and food spelled foreclosure. Those in the western part
of Kansas, Nebraska, and the Dakotas, hardest hit by drouth, chinch
bugs and frost, began moving back eastward in great numbers. But
those in the central portions of these frontier states, although heavily
involved, had some resource remaining and considerable faith in future
weather prospects; the majority of these "stayed on and suffered," and
revolted.

In the nation at large there had not been a farm boom, but conditions
of competition were reducing many farm owners to tenancy, while farm
laborers and tenants found less encouragement to work and save toward
purchase of their own farms. Since 1880 the percentage of agricultural

laborers working for wages has remained nearly stable, around 47%, with many mere migrants from one ripening crop to the next. The lessening likelihood of a rise to ownership made for less careful tilling and less initiative in devising ways to break out of the vicious circle made by cultivating staple crops on a large scale with machinery. In 1880, 25.8% of cultivators were renters; in 1890, 28.4%; in 1900, 35.3%. Even within the tenant class, status fell; among wheat and corn tenants, renters for cash tended to give place to the less affluent and less independent renter "on shares."

In the cotton belt the trends established through, and after, reconstruction largely continued. By 1880 the sharecropper dominated the scene. With his perpetual debts to merchant and landowner and his chronic inability to break the tyranny of his own staple, he became the symbol of capital-less tenancy. His absentee landlord was often a merchant or lawyer. His situation was more precarious than that of the northern or western farmer, for through the periods as a whole cotton exports decreased both absolutely and in relation to other agricultural exports of the nation. Domestic consumption was rising, but not enough to take up the lag. The cotton-growers were unlearned in science, unskilled in processes and management, their adaptability stifled by worship of the post-war fetish of the "lost cause." Some sharecroppers changed to a cash income by putting themselves and their families to work in the new mill towns coming to the South, for both the consumption of cotton and its manufacture began to move there during this period. But the "company store" soon held these mill village workers in the same vise of debt as the country crossroads merchant held the sharecroppers. Escape from the vicious circle seemed impossible.

With farm machinery came industrial machinery adapted to farm products; together they affected city as well as country life, influencing the history of crops, enlarging the national debt, altering the day's work of both factory employee and farm laborer. For example, oil machinery glorified the cotton-seed and its by-products in the South; the cream-tester, the separator, and other machinery used in dairy factories of the middle states widened the market for cheese, butter, and condensed milk; sorghum syrup machinery affected corn growing in the Southwest.

Unfortunately machinery put the farmer at a special disadvantage. He still had to sell in a sharply competitive market, for he could not combine effectively to control the price of crops; but he could not buy his machinery or other necessities in the same kind of market, for competition among manufacturers was reduced. Over a hundred large machinery manufacturers competed for farmers' patronage in 1879; but by 1900 the makers of drills, harrows, harvesters, and various other kinds of essential machinery had combined until there were but fourteen large concerns and these had found abroad an outlet for 12% of their product. They were in a far more independent position than the farmers to whom they sold.

Grain and Meat Problems

The stimulus which machinery gave food production was further increased by adaptation of new varieties of grain to various soils and climates in the United States. Hard red spring wheat, with improvements for milling fine white flour from it, opened Minnesota and Dakota. Hard red winter wheat put Kansas among the first ten wheat states by 1889. Wheat then was the pioneer crop—with its yield of twelve bushels to the acre it belonged with cheap land, with labor scarcity, and lack of credit; and so it moved West—except where aridity barred it—close behind the frontier line. Pushed by rising land values it spread to the Pacific Coast, reaching bonanza proportions in California before 1890 and thereafter making the Columbia River basin the last wheat frontier.

By the end of the 'eighties, however, wheat farmers of the United States had to struggle to keep their share of the world market, fighting against competition from cheaper acreage areas of Russia, India, Argentina and Canada, and against tariffs imposed upon American wheat by France, Germany, Italy and Spain. Worse, while machinery had built up the exportable surplus at a fast rate world conditions were lowering the price at a faster: through the 'eighties and 'nineties Americans doubled to quadrupled their output of foodstuffs and fibers against an almost continuous world fall in prices.

The American grain grower was at the mercy of international forces, because grain was a world product which had to be held until needed and he could control neither storage nor marketing. The railroads had devised a highly organized elevator system to store and handle millions of bushels of grain in bulk at large terminals. By 1880 the grain elevator business at Chicago had standardized a body of practices governing the grading, storage, transfer and sale of grain reserves so huge that their existence affected the economy of the entire nation. Uniform warehouse receipts representing these reserves expanded credit, expedited trade and made trading in futures possible. The opening up of the grain states was facilitated, routes of trade were determined, markets and whole industries were affected.

Cities grew like Chicago; Milwaukee, Duluth, Minneapolis, Kansas City and St. Louis developed as primary grain markets. To these terminals came buyers who acted as brokers for the millers, eastern distributers and exporters. Chicago for a time remained the greatest grain market of the world, and the Chicago Board of Trade the outstanding exchange, with its machinery copied in many other world centers. This machinery made for grain one big world market, in respect to supply, demand and price. The price was determined in Chicago, Minneapolis and Liverpool. This fact farmers resented.

The large scale organization perfected by the buyers and traders in grain levied harshly on the grain growers; their troubles multiplied in the 'eighties when the railroads took to selling their elevators to chains. Within twenty years the chief buyers were a limited number of terminal elevator companies, enjoying special railroad favors and often operating in agreement against the growers. They paid storage to themselves and mixed bad with good grades of grain. Their futures trading decreased price fluctuations but angered growers.

Some of the grangers had been accumulating through the 'seventies considerable experience in resisting the older elevators allied with the railroads and through the 'eighties and 'nineties their successors—Alliance men—fought the burgeoning terminal system with more aggressive schemes of cooperation among themselves. To their cooperative elevators and stores they added in 1889 certain penalty clauses against buyers which won some encouragement from the commission men. During the last decade of the century the grain growers' cooperatives exercised an influence out of proportion to their numbers in lessening the dictation over them. They materially increased the price of grain at country points, standardized their product, disseminated information, and advertised and extended the use of cooperative devices.

But the wheat growers in the mass suffered from lack of capital and from a chronic tendency to act as individuals, which enabled the enemy to wield against them price-cutting, boycott and ground-leasing schemes. Their insuperable obstacle was the worldwide range of agricultural competition, which prevented growers from affecting terminal prices or restricting production. The better world crops, the worse their situation.

Behind wheat in its westward march followed—where rainfall permitted—crops repaying larger capital investment—corn, potatoes, diversified farming, dairying, fruit. Planters, harvesters, huskers, and shredders did for corn what threshing and mowing machinery did for grain and hay; they carried the corn belt west from Illinois into Kansas. Corn growers of the eastern and central areas adjusted themselves to competition from western growers by using 90% of their corn as fodder for dairy cattle, quality beef, and fat hogs, which they raised at a profit greater than they could make by selling corn. Where dairying could follow the retreating staples, it proved a more permanent type of agriculture. With the aid of cream separators introduced from Sweden in 1882, with testing machinery and the right type of foreign immigrants, Wisconsin was transformed, by 1890, into a dairy state. Dairy farmers, like growers of vegetables and fruits, enjoyed a prospect of stability denied the staple farmer, for they could exploit the local scene in the coming era; this was the period of the rise of the city, where grew the demand for a more varied diet.

Among the foods for which American agriculturists found a rising demand was meat, due to the growing population at home, the foreign demand, and the cheapening of price, following increased production and improved transportation facilities. Beef and pork were by 1881 major factors in export trade, and until 1900 cattle increased faster than the population. Most of the cattle were raised on the small farms of the humid region, around 1880; the plains states then produced only about 15.4%, Texas about 12.3% and the Pacific states about 6.3%. However, the vast area stretching between the one-hundredth meridian and the mountains, from the Rio Grande to Canada, was known as the "Cattle Kingdom," and it was destined to exercise an influence upon American politics and habits out of all proportion to its economic production. It had its own peculiar problems of large scale organization.

The depression of 1873-1878 had cheapened Texas cattle and had pushed expansion of the cattle business to the north. The trail from the Texas panhandle, bent westward by the barriers of the Kansas farmers, the Indians and the Kansas-Missouri quarantines, found its way through the corridor of the eastern third of Colorado to the northern ranges. There, mining stampedes, Custer's defeat and the military campaigns following it, advertised the Yellowstone lower country and cleared the way for stockmen. The close of the 'seventies brought an end to the frontier conditions on the old Oregon trail; the Indians had to give up nationhood and accept reservation life. As the 'eighties opened, the cattlemen were changing the mining frontier as far north as Montana into a stock frontier, with the Northern Pacific and the Union Pacific building the necessary railheads while the national government bundled the Indians out of northern Wyoming and eastern Montana. Lands set aside for Indian reservations were opened to the whites by the Dawes Act of 1887.

When Colorado (where sheep-raising was taking hold) became overstocked, Wyoming and Montana received the surplus. The demand on the northern ranges reached extreme limits. Farmers of the upper Mississippi Valley, Illinois, Wisconsin, Michigan, Iowa and Missouri, began to ship stock to western breeders. Although Texas now shipped many cattle directly east, an eager rivalry of drovers for the northern trek continued. As the cattlemen were using free the grazing land owned by the government, almost their only outlay was for stock. Exceptionally abundant rainfall and mild winters insured easy feeding and their profits were fabulous. Railroad advertising, and lurid literature on "How Cattlemen Grow Rich" encouraged an orgy of speculation. Money from the East and from England and Scotland (following

Europe's tradition of profits in American land speculation) poured into cattle companies, run under absentee ownership, while the quick profits of the boom years of 1882-1883 made lucky operators "Cattle Kings" and "Cattle Queens." The growers in this area then had no great quarrel with the packing industry. Although the "big four" packers in 1880 had made a "gentlemen's agreement" for monopoly, ensuring great economic and political power, in the early 'eighties they supported the price of beef and pork despite an export collapse.

The phenomenal prosperity of the cattle magnates could not last; its end was hastened by the fact that the cattlemen were extreme individualists, who had to be taught by bitter adversity before they could learn to combine for their own advantage. Farmers of Europe, who were not blessed with free grazing lands, had determined to protect themselves from American competition and the cattlemen blindly furnished them with a convenient excuse. There had been evidence of pleuro-pneumonia disease among cattle on the Atlantic seaboard, and of Texas fever in the Southwest; and the stocking of the open range to the west and north from these sources threatened the industry. Despite pleas from states and territories which sought to escape infection, other cattlemen had fought and long prevented establishment of a federal quarantine. Therefore, British farmers in 1878 and those of other countries thereafter persuaded their governments to impose regulations covering importation of American livestock, which cut the profits of American exporters of healthy no less than of diseased cattle. By 1883 Germany was piling her restrictions on top of those accumulated.

Clearly, this interstate and international problem could be solved only if American agriculturists consented to violate their long-standing tradition of independence. The Commissioner of Agriculture, to whom the control of quarantine was transferred from the Treasury Department, called a convention of live-stock breeders at Washington in 1883 and, to salvage their export market, they accepted the principle that the "general welfare" clause of the Constitution empowered the Federal Government to restrict the freedom of the individual for the public good. They put pressure upon Congress to establish federal inspection and quarantine.

Consequently, 1884 saw a Bureau of Animal Industry established in the Department of Agriculture by congressional fiat. Within five years it had practically wiped out the pleuro-pneumonia and Texas fever, and was making progress on the trichinosis and hog cholera which plagued pork breeders of the Mississippi valley. Its discoveries concerning "host carriers" would prove invaluable to medicine, on the yellow fever problem of the Panama Canal. Its achievements so improved the reputation of the Department as to raise the Commissioner to cabinet rank in 1889. But more important than the magnitude of the operations of the Bureau of Animal Industry was its significance in our social and constitutional history. It was one of the first cases where an interstate problem brought about the restriction of private business by congressional fiat for the common good.

Unfortunately, the stockmen meanwhile were suffering other dire effects of their own unrestrained competition. The open range had become badly overcrowded. Cattlemen had avoided the expense of land ownership and had opposed a leasing system for themselves and fencing by would-be farmers; now shortage of grazing land led some cattlemen to erect their own fences, enclosing alternate sections purchased from the railroads and by this device enclosing also the government sections in between. Next, the cattle, prevented from drifting before the wind of winter storms, froze to death by the hundreds of thousands along the lines of the fences. Furthermore, fencing of stream courses and monopoly of irrigation was posing the terrific problem of water rights peculiar to this region of scant rainfall. Obviously, large and open acreages were essential to this industry; but popular sentiment against land monopoly killed a bill for the large "pastoral homesteads" which a congressional commission sagely recommended.

Out of their very pressing need for self-protection came the formation of cattle-growers' associations, which received general support wherever their industry was dominant, as in Wyoming. But where mining and agriculture also were important, as in Montana, the stockgrower was outweighed and there was war. With the realization that they were victims of their own overexpansion came a scourge of drouth, pests, fires, and the blizzard winter of 1886-1887 when between 40% and 50% of the cattle in some Montana regions were frozen to death. The industry was deflated by huge forced sales, gradually lost its frontier aspect and after 1890 was rebuilt on a sounder basis. The open range economy was displaced by enclosed ranches. Cattle no longer could be expected to find free food for themselves summer and winter. The grower now had to own private pastures for summer grazing; and he had to raise, with the help of irrigation, forage crops to make hay stacks for winter feed.

Problems of Aridity

The defeat of the old range cattle companies had been dealt by a combination of two other agricultural groups whose coming the cattlemen disputed—the small rancher and the farmer. The owner of a few cattle and the tiller of a small acreage had come on to the Great Plains at the invitation of a Government which tried to "legislate the farmer westward" regardless of the aridity of the region and of the necessity for free range for stock. These farmers, in the heyday of Populism, built up an "anti-stock" agitation strong enough to keep vacant through two years one of Wyoming's seats in the Senate. Congress was unfriendly to the range cattlemen because it reflected the preconceptions of the great body of American farmers of the Middle West, South and East, who exerted tremendous political pressure.

These were determined that the rules of land ownership familiar to them and denominated as democratic should not be undermined by the establishment of a large ranch regime, although over land they might never use. Their resistance was fortified further by the knowledge of longstanding abuses under which the homestead and bounty lands had been misappropriated. They knew that railroad, land and mortgage companies, speculators, politicians, government agents and dishonest surveyors in one way and another had fattened off the public lands; that lumber barons had stolen timber, and that mining corporations stole minerals. Land abuses disclosed by Commissioner Sparks and attacked by President Cleveland confirmed the people's knowledge. To them legislation for large land holdings smelled of monopoly.

The partisanship of Congress for the farmer was unintelligent. Congress (despite vociferous demands from the far regions) had difficulty projecting its imagination past that transition zone, which lay in general along the one hundredth meridian, and over into the region beyond. There, except for the North Pacific coast and several districts in California and in the northern Rocky Mountain region, was an area in which life was conditioned by rainfall and topography or altitude, rather than by soil and temperature or latitude. On the other hand the agriculture most Congressmen knew was humid-climate farming based upon tilled crops, corn, small grains, tame hay and pasture; stock was fed in barnyards or fields, with shelter at night, and agricultural regions followed parallels of latitude, extending generally East and West. A permanent class of farm tenants was secured by fairly dependable crops.

Conditions in the Far West, as Congress found, offered violent contrasts. There were dry and irrigation farming, winter crops in certain localities, wild hay and grazing; stock was mostly grazed on the open range, and agricultural regions were determined by the mountain ranges, extending generally north and south. Tenants often could not be permanent; lacking financial reserves they had to move back East, from areas of temporary rainfall, when the drouth struck. East of the one-hundredth meridian 160 acres or less might support a family; west, a like amount would more than suffice where ample irrigation was available, but dry farming required at least two to four times as much land and stock-raising two thousand acres or more. Such violent contrasts have made it well-nigh impossible for Congress to legislate satisfactorily for the arid region.

Farmers on the High Plains were slow to realize that scarcity of water dictated the conditions of their survival, for between 1877 and

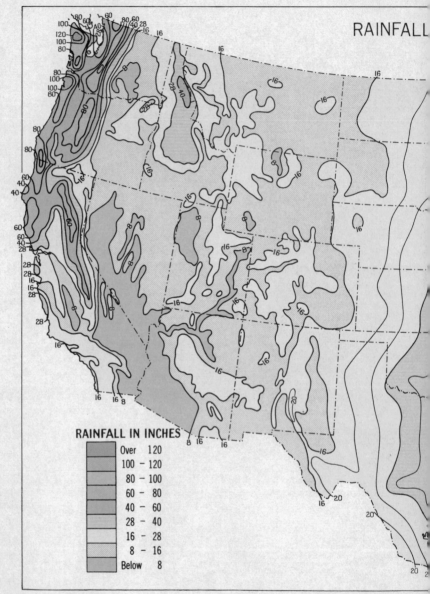

RAINFALL

RAINFALL IN INCHES

	Over 120
	100 – 120
	80 – 100
	60 – 80
	40 – 60
	28 – 40
	16 – 28
	8 – 16
	Below 8

Lith. A. Hoen & Co.

From Charles O. Paullin, *Atlas of the Historical Geography*
Institution of Washington and American Geographi

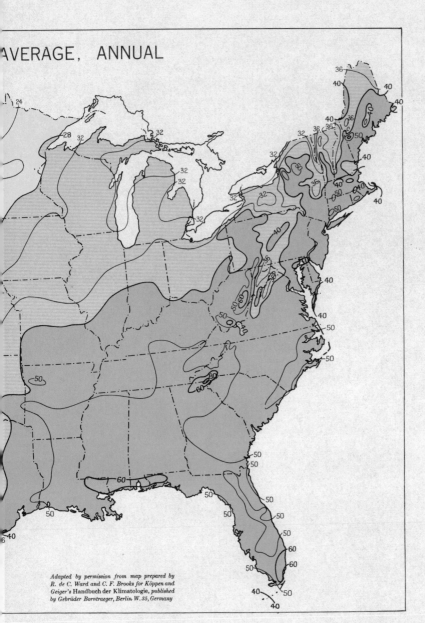

Adapted by permission from map prepared by
R. de C. Ward and C. F. Brooks for Köppen and
Geiger's Handbuch der Klimatologie, published
by Gebrüder Borntraeger, Berlin W. 35, Germany

United States, (1932) edited by John K. Wright; Carnegie
iety of New York, joint publishers. By permission.

1886 they enjoyed a period of exceptional rainfall. Even with its aid they could not have penetrated very far without the invention of barbed wire and the introduction of well drills, windmills and irrigation. In this region of scant rains and hot winds farmers did more experimenting than on all the other farms of the United States combined. For them, Europe, Asia, and Africa were combed by agricultural specialists for plants to meet high plains needs. Agriculture was "literally created" in western parts of Texas, New Mexico, Oklahoma and Kansas. When the federal government failed to make the definition of a homestead elastic and to abandon rectangular surveys for the hydrographic, the resourceful dry farmer and rancher acquired land by extra-legal means; and they abrogated the English common law on water control and substituted their own arid-region doctrine of prior appropriation.

Congress, dimly realizing that the Homestead Act fitted only humid areas, had passed the Irrigation Law of 1877 providing for 640 acre holdings; but these were to be paid for at $1.25 an acre and carried an obligation for irrigation (at private expense) within three years. As this made the law inoperable, Major Powell of the Geological Survey came forward after two years with well-considered plans for scientific development. Unfortunately public awareness came too slowly to give him government cooperation and there ensued the irrigation boom of the 'eighties, run by private speculators and marked by overdevelopment, bad management and wretched financing.

Retribution descended, upon the evil and the good, with the end of the exceptional rainfall. The drouth decade beginning in 1887 led to abandonment of private irrigation but did not quite establish federal responsibility. A series of government resurveys and irrigation conventions under mixed federal and private sponsorship led up to the Carey Act of 1894. In Carey's state, Wyoming, the legislators had progressed to the point where they actually considered the amount of water available and the area it would irrigate; therefore this law entrusted, to such states as would undertake settlement and irrigation, new grants of public lands.

The salvation of the agriculturists on the Great Plains, and indeed wherever during the 'eighties and 'nineties severe hardships befell farmers, was their faith in their own ability to invent remedies. That optimism, which always had given to individual self-reliance the credit for a farming prosperity due chiefly to virgin and cheap soil, yielded reluctantly. Long after good land became difficult to hold and markets hard to keep, the farmers clung to the tradition that native ingenuity could work miracles, that failure must prove temporary, that farm possession meant independence and comfort. Abounding faith in any case must be the temperamental equipment of those in an occupation largely dependent upon God's will with the weather. An emotional system of ethics somewhat fortified them in adversity—for were not they the "honest sons of toil"; were not the commission and elevator men, the bankers, creditors, and Wall Street operators, "robber barons"? For the righteous, seeming miracles had worked before and might again; one agent in the miracles was the Department of Agriculture, expanding on a nation-wide scale.

Help from the Department of Agriculture

In their agricultural problems of local scope the farmers received help from their state universities, colleges and high schools, where short-winter and correspondence courses reached persons otherwise unreachable. Wisconsin's pioneer "winter course" established in 1885 was widely imitated, was most important in building up her dairy industry and was the first such course to have a continuous history. To handle interstate problems, however, the farmers and the Department of Agriculture must learn to coordinate their efforts. On the one side suspicion and a clinging to the old ways of individualists, on the other, some show of arrogance, hindered cooperation. Farmers and seed-sellers denounced the Department's seed distribution as political graft (although Congress was to blame for perpetuating this abuse); they found its bureaucrats lazy and wrongheaded, its claims extravagant and its research too technical and impractical. The farm press resented the competition of government bulletins and reports and regularly gave space and voice to criticism.

For its part, the Department at first was so engrossed in its scientific research as to neglect its educational function, thus sadly restricting its economic and social usefulness. Until it put forth an effort to popularize scientific knowledge and to cooperate with local agricultural schools and movements it could not foster the general enlightenment of farmers. Of the early crop reports, for example, the average farmer unversed in economics could make little use; the reports helped most the speculators and middlemen they were aimed to hinder. Chemistry experiments helped the sugar refiners, and the meat packers also had the acumen to obtain expansion in the Department's functions.

The farmers in the mass had to be taught to exploit the Department; the pressure for its expansion came to be furnished by some of the more progressive specialists within the Department, cooperating with leaders in the Association of Agricultural Colleges. The East furnished one of the propaganda groups—the Society for the Promotion of Agricultural Science. Some leaders of the Grange, until the late 'eighties, and then Alliance leaders, acted as liaison officers. Some advance along the lines of forestry, chemical analysis, agricultural statistics, veterinary investigation and study of injurious insects had preceded the establishment of the Bureau of Animal Industry (1884), which so quickly proved a great boon to cattle and pork growers.

In 1887, the year in which the decade of drouth commenced, came a second significant extension of the authority of the federal government to provide for the general welfare in terms of the farmers. Officials of the Agricultural Department and educators of the American Association of Agricultural Colleges directed upon Congress a deluge of petitions from citizens, farmers' associations, and schools, for experiment stations. Several college presidents came to Washington to help Representative LaFollette organize pressure on Congress. The Hatch Act resulted. It carried the theory behind the Department of Agriculture to its logical conclusion, recognized both the joint responsibility of federal and state governments for agricultural development and the inability of the Department to cope with the problems peculiar to state boundaries. It appropriated $15,000 annually to each state and territory for experiment stations (of which a few had been established by some states) and specified means for making the findings available to the public. Soon experiment station experts were forming an Association of Economic Entomologists, which developed and correlated their scientific work, and heartened them to continue it.

Under the Hatch Act and another in 1888, state work was coordinated, supervised, and enlarged. The two laws could not make the experiment stations popular with farmers (who did not fully accept them much before 1910) but they gave new impetus to agricultural research throughout the country and lifted that done by the Department to a higher scientific plane. The Department was freed for concentration on vastly more important national and international problems. Solution of them was the more difficult and pressing because of their far-reaching application and the farmer's inability to comprehend them.

As the agricultural depression deepened after 1887, the functions and usefulness of the federal Department increased; farmers showed growing confidence in it and general approval of its expansion. In the vague hope of lifting the depression, rather than in a visioning of potential scientific gains, they approved the campaign of Department officials and college professors to elevate the Secretary to cabinet status; and after the House had three times passed such a measure the Senate in 1889 permitted it to become a law. In that year, Kansans were burning corn for fuel, wheat was 30% below its 1870 price, and cotton 73% below; the antagonism between agriculture and industry was mounting, and the Department of Agriculture Act reflected the farmers' feeling that they should have more weapons to resist the influence of industry on legislation. They set more store by knowledge, obtaining in 1890 a supplement to the Morrill Act which allotted federal funds to agricultural schools; within ten years, sixty colleges were teaching agriculture and the mechanic arts (at least one in every state and territory), and instruction was increasing in Negro schools and short courses.

The expanding Department accepted the challenge of farmers' agricultural distress in the 'nineties. The Bureau of Entomology attacked the locust and bollweevil; the Bureau of Plant Industry explored afar for crops adapted to rainless regions; the Weather Bureau was taken over from the War Department. American concern over exports was reflected in establishment of a division on Foreign Markets, and in the aggressiveness of the Bureau of Animal Industry which helped to bring laws for meat inspection and better animal quarantine. A Division of Publications set out to disseminate the information collected by all these groups.

The rigors of the drouth years had a selective effect upon farm population. It declined in the worst hardship areas of eastern Colorado, western and central Kansas, Nebraska, and South Dakota; and also in humid regions in northern New England and in the backward areas of New York, Pennsylvania, Ohio, and Michigan. It sought new regions and new crops in Florida, entering the Disston drainage area, the De Land orange development and the Tampa phosphate exploitation. It became more intelligent at the same time. Interest in soil fertilization, heretofore limited chiefly to eastern and southern farmers (the cotton growers of Georgia and North and South Carolina and the truck gardeners of the Middle Atlantic States), grew in the West as free land was exhausted. Americans since 1880 had been rapidly exploiting Chilean nitrates and after 1890 they became the largest consumers of German potash and showed an appreciation of United States phosphate supplies. With the advance of the boll-weevil north across the Rio Grande in 1892, Negro migration to the North commenced, in a small way, and white labor increased in the South. In the West, as well as the South, farmers learned during the depression more thrift and better management.

But these lessons could not create a prosperous market. In such crucial matters as low prices and farm foreclosures the Department of Agriculture was worse than impotent; it aggravated the crisis by its scientific stimulus to overproduction. Not through scientific investigation but through social and political pressure, hard-headed leaders undertook to close the gap between farm income and farm debts.

Rise of Populism

The gap between farm income and farm debts was blamed by farmers upon the monopolistic influences obviously at work in American land ownership, transportation and finance—influences immoral because unfair. A moral crusade for the full restoration of the age of competition, they thought, would restore their status. An attack upon the capitalistic system at its foundations they had no desire to make, for they either owned property or hoped to own it and expected to make money on it. Nor did they clearly appreciate the effect upon them of the fact that the agricultural depression was world-wide. They did not blame over-production. Hence their program was palliative, not extreme :—invoke government aid to enjoin laissez-faire only so far as it was victimizing the farmer, equalize railroad rates either through government ownership or operation; check collusion in the middleman's purchase of farm prod-ucts and in the manufacturer's sale of farm supplies; shift the burden of taxation from real estate to cash income; ease credit by lowering interest rates and expanding the currency with the population. These were the principle alterations which the farmers of the 'eighties and 'nineties wished to make in the American manner of living.

The farmers expressed their demands in a variety of terms, of course, and exerted their influence through various channels. The influence of the Grange had declined sadly by 1880 because of careless mushroom organization, poor cooperation between members, Granger jealousy of the national government, and the public's tendency toward impatient repeal of Granger laws before they were fully tried. The Knights of Labor also had become in most areas little more than an agricultural social group. Most important in quieting farmer agitation had been the comparative prosperity of 1879-1882. The return of uncertain con-ditions revived interest in freight rates, and caused the Grange states to enact railroad laws on similar but better organized principles.

Next an "Alliance" movement flourished. Alliances originally had much the same appeal as the Granges, emphasizing cooperative enterprise and social betterment; and they suffered from much the same difficulties; but they usually had new leadership, and eventually proved more aggres-sive and sophisticated in attitude toward national finance and politics. They had the strength and the weakness of all movements which spring spontaneously direct from the soil.

Texas farmers as early as 1875 were forming a secret county organ-ization which first emerged in 1878 as a Grand State Alliance. It ex-panded into adjoining states under the direction of C. W. Macune, who with his *National Economist* exhorted cotton raisers to ape, in their own defence, the national trend toward organization. It joined with the Farmers' Union, which originated in Louisiana, to form the "National Farmers Alliance and Cooperative Union." It annexed an "Agricultural Wheel" which had started rolling in Arkansas, and other societies and clubs; the whole came to be spoken of ordinarily as the "Southern Alliance," which Macune pushed as a "strictly white man's non-political, secret, business association." By 1890 it claimed a million members.

Meanwhile, near Chicago, Milton George was promoting with his

Western Rural another group which, vitalized by a Kansas Alliance and by recurrent hard times, grew into the "National Farmers' Union," generally distinguished as the "Northwestern Alliance." It engaged in cooperative enterprises somewhat less than the Southern Alliance and in politics much more. It stressed railroad and land reforms; the Southerners, finance.

The two groups made an effort to unite, by convening at the same time and place, 5 December 1889 at St. Louis.[1] This meeting had threefold importance. First, sectional prejudices, northern fear of southern dominance, and diversities of interests and attitudes toward rebels, Negroes, secrecy and third parties prevented fusion; the number of agricultural societies was not diminished greatly then, or later. Second, despite failure to fuse, both memberships nevertheless presented a united front *as a class;* they demonstrated their sympathy one with another upon the vital issues of monopoly, money supply, railroad control, and land ownership. Both denounced trusts, national banks and trading in grain futures; both demanded inflation, free coinage, government ownership or operation of the railroads, and landownership restricted to Americans.

Third, the Southern Alliance endorsed a significant commodity credit scheme, for freeing the farmer from the tyranny of gold prices, bank credit and fall sales. This was to be managed through a "sub-treasury plan" under which the currency would be expanded at harvest time, crop sales would be spread through the year, and the government would market the agricultural surplus. Forty years later, part of this commodity credit program would be inaugurated from Washington. Dissension over it, between 1890 and 1891, almost split the Southern Alliance in two; but the superior organization and leadership in the southern group was attracting more than two and one-half times the northern membership. They joined from as far west as the Pacific Coast and as far east as Ohio, Pennsylvania and New York. Kansas and Dakota alliances virtually seceded from the Northern to join the Southern Alliance; and some northerners supported the sub-treasury scheme "more or less" to win southern support for government ownership of railroads.

Thus, although alliance men failed to merge their organizations, and in spite of the fact that financial and political difficulties were rising which were destined to send the alliance movement into its decline, its basic principles meanwhile had won a degree of popular support which made for effective political pressure. In addition to the land laws earlier mentioned, the farmers, with the help of other reform elements, forced from Congress three significant concessions—relating to railroads, money and trusts. The land laws had proved disappointing in their effects because, although they dealt with a somewhat less complicated

[1] Several lesser farm groups also met simultaneously.

set of factors, the complications yet proved too intricate for congressional mastery. The interstate commerce, anti-trust and silver legislation of 1887-1900 proved yet more intricate, and disappointing (p. 448).

The continuing difficulties of the farmers and the disappointing results of pressure upon Congress led the various agricultural leaders into another attempt at fusing their forces for political action. Unrest was abroad in the land beyond the Mississippi as the "heart-breaking nineties" began. The frontier, by its imperious mandates, had forced the frontiersman to become an innovator; and economic ills were inspiring his children to concoct radical remedies. Thence came, to South and North, "the alliance summer of 1890."

This movement was native, mobilized close to the soil; it expressed two resentments. One, against economic inferiority—against a fall in total return on farm produce at a time when manufacturing groups were enjoying a degree of relative prosperity. The other, against psychological inferiority—sons and daughters were deserting to the city, attracted by its cash return; even the new immigrants, agriculturalists born and bred from southern and eastern Europe, were becoming urban in the United States. Agriculture no longer was the occupation of greatest national value. These farmer resentments were accompanied naturally by a greater toleration for lawlessness, and a greater susceptibility to demagoguery, which attracted also some urban workers pinched by the McKinley tariff.

Western Alliance men and women, angered anew by a United States Supreme Court decision invalidating a Minnesota railroad rate law, became impatient to influence the 1890 election with their own political party. Their orators had had a rigorous training in frontier experience and in lecturing before sharp-witted Alliance audiences at schoolhouses, public squares and exciting picnics. Ignatius Donnelly of Minnesota and James B. Weaver of Iowa were long-practiced at marshalling the arguments of discontent. The sweep of oratory and song was cyclonic, especially in the western third of Kansas, which by deflated land values was made the stronghold of a new political enthusiasm called Populism.

There intense and purposeful evangelists like Mrs. Mary Elizabeth Lease exhorted the farmers to "raise less corn and more HELL": while "Sockless" Jerry Simpson, an habitual third-party heretic, and long-whiskered, inflexible William A. Peffer preached in a pentecost of politics which sent the one to the House of Representatives and the other to the Senate. The Kansas "People's Party" elected also four other congressional representatives and a majority of the legislature. South Dakota's "Independent Party" elected Reverend James H. Kyle to the Senate while obtaining the balance of power in the legislature; and Nebraska's "People's Independent Party" working in a formerly solid Republican state, won a majority of the legislature and one of the congressional seats. In Minnesota, Michigan, and Indiana, Alliance politics diverted 1890 victory from Republicans to Democrats. Eight westerners frankly carried the Populist or Independent label to the national House, besides old-party men who modified their behavior if not their labels.

In the South, fear of aiding Republicans deterred Alliance men from forming third parties; and so they undertook to pledge Democrats to Alliance policies. The capable and ambitious president of the Southern Alliance, L. L. Polk, led the North Carolina Alliance men in placing four of their members in Democratic congressional seats. The wrathful, one-eyed Ben Tillman, as South Carolina's gubernatorial candidate, won the Democratic nomination for himself and for his entire ticket. The suspicious and combative Thomas E. Watson led a hot Georgia campaign which gave Alliance men the governorship, a majority of the state legislature and six of the state's congressional districts. Also, they affected events in Alabama, Florida, Kentucky, Mississippi, Missouri, Tennessee and Virginia. Altogether, they won three governorships, legislative control of eight states, and sent to Washington two Senators and forty-four representatives pledged to Alliance policies. On the political horizon a large black cloud had arisen. It drenched enough Republican candidates in 1890 to give the Democrats a huge majority in the House, while in the Senate certain western members showed little gratitude to the party which had given their states a premature statehood and themselves the senatorial toga. To Populism, direct descendant of the Granges and Alliances, were flocking throngs of people long in pursuit of reform.

Encouraged especially by third party politicians who chronically "don't know what they want and will never be satisfied until they get it," delegates from southern Alliances, from the Farmers' Mutual Benefit Association and from the Colored Farmers' Alliance met simultaneously in December of 1890 at Ocala, Florida. Again they reaffirmed the familiar principles, with some widening of the scope of their reform planks; but again southern reluctance to abandon a war-bred Democratic label prevented their united participation in the formation of a national third party. Also the actual achievements of the Alliance legislatures were proving meager.

However, the third-party trend could not be stopped in the West. Alliance and Knights of Labor members, with a majority hailing from Illinois, Indiana, Kansas, Nebraska and Ohio, convened at Cincinnati 19 May 1891 and put forth a platform enlarged to attract non-agricultural voters, such as veterans, laborers and liberals in general. The action at Cincinnati pleased all radicals and "let in on the ground floor" of this new movement the professional third party men. They got "surprisingly slender results" in the elections of that year, but professed satisfaction. The next step was a Washington's Birthday Convention at St. Louis in 1892 which launched, with some southern Alliance support, a "People's Party of America"; and the job of organizing was completed with a July nominating convention at Omaha.

Arduously, hesitantly, and after great travail, hundreds of thousands of farmers were brought to accept leadership in a great protest movement, challenging the major parties at a nation-wide poll. Only the extremity of their disadvantages could have carried them thus far; and it did not carry the majority of the farmers in all sections, for very many (perhaps 50% in the South) refused to divert their Alliance activities into third party politics. In all sections both old parties tried to throw sops to the Populists.

Among the leadership at Omaha, however, was a determination to inject a rare realism into platform making. They used as planks the principles stressed by the Alliance conventions of the past three years, for their People's Party was "born a party of principle"—the principle being that the government must control selfishness and the people must control the government. Refusing to listen to stale rantings on the bloody shirt and the tariff, they issued a clarion call to industrial workers to unite with farmers in demanding reforms in finance, transportation and land. For their benefit all currency should be given full legal tender, national bank notes should be discarded, free coinage of silver should be resumed, and the circulation should be expanded to not less than $50 per capita; also, taxes should be limited to the costs of economic administration, incomes should be taxed, postal savings banks should be established.

To their transportation plank the delegates gave their wildest enthusiasm:—the railroads, as well as the telegraph and telephone, should be owned and operated by the government "in the interest of the people." Concerning land, ownership should be restricted to citizens and actual settlers; nor should natural resources be monopolized for speculative purposes.

In addition to the platform as such, the convention accepted an "expression of sentiments" attractive to various electorates:—to soldiers seeking pensions; to workmen opposing contract labor, Pinkerton troops, and immigration and demanding an eight hour day; to reformers seeking the Australian ballot, the initiative and referendum, and direct election of Senators. Southern votes were invited by the nomination of James G. Field of Virginia, to run with Weaver of Iowa, as vice presidential candidate, a device not very successful in Field's own state.

In the November result was reflected the growth of the farmers' discontent since 1880. Then, Weaver as Greenback candidate in a year of good crop sales had received less than 309,000 popular votes and no electoral votes. In 1892 as Populist candidate, in spite of his record for defeat, he won more than a million popular votes and, in addition, that which no one had obtained since the Civil War, a place in the electoral column for a third party, with twenty-two electoral votes. This he did at a time when radical agrarianism was moving West of the old Alliance states, and when Populists tended to fuse with Democrats in the North and West, with Republicans in the South. If the South had gone Populist, Weaver would have won. But southern Democrats had adopted Populist planks to prevent the Populists from uniting with the Republicans; while the Republican force bill, with its threat to white supremacy, had made southern Populists vote for Cleveland instead of Weaver, thus defeating the objects of both Republican and Populist leaders. As it was, Populism paved the way for the political emancipation of the poorer class of southern whites, but the election of 1892 shattered the Southern Alliance.

In the states of the middle border, the weather played tricks on the Populists; although hard times were not ended and little money-making was possible, still the harvests were sufficiently adequate to make the farmers less hopeless than in 1890. Farmers of the humid area between Iowa and New England, the upper South and Canada, were not deeply impressed; and laborers of the East, although Alliance and Populist platforms from the outset had championed labor reforms, were not greatly attracted. They were conscious of a conflict of interest and Gompers opposed the Populists.

Genuine Populist votes proved thickest in the Dakotas, Kansas, Minnesota and Nebraska; they elected governors in Colorado, Kansas and North Dakota. In several western states they won enough offices to experiment with their own policies; but they in no instance obtained complete control of a state government, and their following in silver areas had interest only in their silver position. In Nebraska, they helped return to Congress William Jennings Bryan, who from his two terms there gained an experience and prominence which would bring him the Democratic and Populist nominations in 1896 and make him the instrument of the destruction of the Populist party. In the nation at large, they won three or four senators, eight to ten congressmen, and claimed fifty state officials and 1500 county officers and state legislators. Exact measurement was made impossible, by the confusion of fusions and designations. The significant facts were two:—the number owing their election to various liberal deals was extremely large, and the diversion of votes helped Grover Cleveland regain the White House.

Populism Killed by Free Silver

Populist hopes ran high, with plans for no more fusion with the two old parties. But again a world situation conspired to destroy the prospects of the American farmer. A crisis abroad was spreading into American business and May of 1893 saw a panic on the New York stock exchange. This was but a forerunner of worse distress to befall the nation. The Treasury itself was hard pinched, because the high tariff, pension and pork-barrel legislation of the Harrison administration were draining the gold reserve at the time that the Sherman silver purchase act forced continued purchase of that cheapening metal and issuance of paper money upon it. Steadily the United States was being forced to a silver standard.

This alarmed both the Treasury Department, which wanted to maintain government credit and sell government bonds, and the creditor classes in general, which had no mind to receive interest and principal on their investments in a cheapened currency. To offset this influence, the silver propagandists in 1893 held three conventions of their "American Bimetallic League." But Cleveland would not follow them; against the outcry of Populists, debtors, inflationists and other classes expecting to gain by a silver standard, he forced through repeal of the Sherman act at a special summer session of 1893. Thus were the wishes of the Populists immediately set at nought on finance. The continued high rates of the Wilson-Gorman tariff law, next enacted, affronted them again (p. 457).

The total Populist vote increased by 42% between 1892 and 1894, when seven congressmen and six senators were elected as Populists, of whom four each were to wear the label openly at Washington; but they actually had gained little, if any, ground. In the West, fusion with the Democrats diminished because the latter now were on the defensive; most states which had given the Populists a majority returned to their old allegiance; and all the silver states repudiated Populism because Republican votes seemed a more certain rebuke to Cleveland's gold policy. In the South, fusion with Republicans remained unabated because the latter held the attacking position; but southern Populists were only slightly more successful than westerners. Nevertheless, Populists saw in their total vote a portent of victory to come and made confident plans for 1896.

Easterners were amused, or alarmed, according as they thought Populist confidence justified. Oftentimes ridicule was a thin veneer on a genuine dread. Some eastern liberals took Populism very seriously; they long had realized the strain which large scale organization was placing on the little man—upon the individual competitor, the consumer and the worker—and saw in Populism some chance for the fruition of hopes dashed many times.

Influential among these persons who were struggling to make Americans aware of their changing economy, was Henry Demarest Lloyd, who had begun to reach readers through the Chicago *Tribune* and the magazines. His "Story of a Great Monopoly" had proclaimed in 1881 some of the ramifications of large scale organization in the railroads and Standard Oil; monopolistic developments in wheat marketing also concerned him. He had undertaken defense of labor in successive emergencies—the Haymarket affair of 1886, the coal strikes of 1890, and the Pullman strike of 1894. The dire suffering of the nation during the latest depression moved him to make another effort to arouse Americans in their own defense. In *Wealth Against Commonwealth* he again used the Standard Oil for dramatic exposition with the hope that a popular uprising might follow.

It did not follow, but Lloyd and his kind were nevertheless affecting the American trend. Lloyd, for example, was heartening such younger men as Louis D. Brandeis, Robert M. LaFollette and Ethelbert Stewart, in the habit of a bold insistence upon a broad view of social problems; they and their brother liberals would influence the making and interpretation of laws sympathetic to labor and ordinary citizens. The thinking of countless Americans was affected, for Lloyd planted the seed of that literature of exposure which attained a rank growth early in the nineteen hundreds. Meanwhile, Lloyd supported Populism as a steed to ride against monopoly.

Unfortunately for the broad objectives of social justice, Populism was on the point of destroying itself. Following the example of Greenbackers, Populists were allowing their ranks to become dominated by a single idea—cheap money—which displaced the sub-Treasury plan in popularity. At the outset they had used free coinage planks to capture votes for their platform as a whole, to unite southern and western debtors; now free silver threatened to capture Populism. Such an outcome was particularly opposed by southern Populists who had fused with Republicans and by two ex-Republicans of the West—Senator Peffer of Kansas and ex-representative Donnelly of Minnesota. But they contended against agricultural forces far stronger than party leaders.

In the central and western areas of the agricultural frontier, farmers between 1887 and 1897 did not get enough rain for a full crop in eight years of the ten, and practically no crop at all during five years. In Ohio, Michigan and Indiana a drouth during 1895 raised the expectation of a compensating rise in prices; but foodstuffs came in from the westward. In but few localities did agricultural prices reach cost of production. Certainly farmers' profits were far below those of manufacturers who had their trade agreements, monopolistic devices, advertising and high tariffs, with which to juggle supply and price. Yet, since industry took its own beating at the hands of the depression, with labor deprived of jobs and manufacturers of markets, the industrial areas had their own inflation factions. Since nearly all debtors, large and small, were infected, farmers could not be immune.

So great was the appeal of free silver that certain Democratic leaders —politicians of far greater influence than the Populist organizers—

WHOLESALE PRICES. 1791-1930
1913 = 100

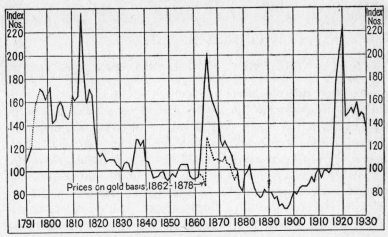

From Charles O. Paullin, *Atlas of the Historical Geography of the United States* (1932), edited by John K. Wright; Carnegie Institution of Washington and American Geographical Society of New York, joint publishers. By permission.

were planning to use it. As the Populist creed set principle above party, and its breed were habitual breakers of political ties, they naturally deserted Populism for Democracy on the principle of free silver. Thus in 1896 they met defeat, as will be seen (p. 461).

In 1900 two groups of Populists tried to run candidates, but they polled not more than 20% of their 1896 vote. The volatile electorate had deserted them. In the brief and badly-hindered period of their experiments, Populism had been judged a failure. The farmers' party was dying. But that did not signify an end to farmers' movements. They had learned that in prosperity and adversity they must organize to promote their welfare. In subsequent legislation concerning election reforms and labor, as well as land, transportation and finance, the American nation would go far toward accepting the cardinal Populist principle—that the voice of the people is the voice of God.

CHAPTER XXII

THE SPREAD OF URBANIZATION

Since large scale organization of industry crowded factory workers into cities, the manner of life in this part of the population (and by 1900 32.9% of the people lived in cities over 8000) was drastically changed. The rapid adjustments which city people made to urban environment gradually affected the habits of the rural population, so that large scale organization influenced daily living in the entire nation. The cities drove the nation into change in a manner sometimes brutal and sometimes beneficent but always dynamic, for close association powerfully stimulates activity among mankind. That activity varied in the different sections of the United States, during the twenty years before 1900; but as the nation retained a democratic form of government, its well-being was most affected by the developments in home life, education, recreation, in religion and crime, and in private and public standards of living and behavior.

Lessening Influence of the Home

Most important of the influences at work on the rising generation was the home. Home life was most affected by city growth, new types of work, and strange inventions. It had been the custom, particularly in the country and small towns, for young men and women to marry early, and soon to remarry after the untimely death of either of them. In the cities, with their more numerous diversions, the employment of the poorer women, and advancing education for middle class women, marriage was later and less nearly universal. Also it was less permanent; neither propaganda from the National Divorce Reform League, federal investigation of lax state laws or tightening of those laws could prevent divorce from increasing three times as fast as the population, during the 'nineties.

Industrial life in the cities strained family unity by giving women a chance at self-support and a feeling of independence. In most states they could now hold property, control it, keep their own earnings, and make contracts of their own volition. But they still had grave disadvantages in such matters as control of children, divorce rights, conditions of work and suffrage;[1] and they became increasingly aware of

[1] Except in Colorado, Idaho, Utah and Wyoming.

414

these important lacks as they learned self-respect through self-support.

Women long had been in housework, factory work, and teaching; now large scale industries were multiplying openings in the telephone, publishing, typewriting, newspaper, social service, legal, and medical businesses and professions. College and university experience were adding to their skills, South and North. The total consequence was that employed women increased from the two and one-half millions of 1880 to five and one-third by 1900.

Some women were learning to organize. They made beginnings at voting rights for local, school, city and tax elections. Militant feminists, led by Mrs. Stanton and Carrie Chapman Catt, with some support from masculine leaders and organized labor, united forces in 1890 as the National American Woman Suffrage Association. The first international congress of women was held at the Chicago Fair in 1893 and gave wide impetus to feminine organization. The leaders and those opposing them were struggling to sway that indifferent majority of American women who were too busy with children or jobs, or too conservative, to take excursions beyond the thinking of their own male kinsfolk. That majority seemed little interested in suffrage late in the 'nineties. But part of them, women of the conservative middle class—were getting the time, money and inclination to unite in clubs:—art, dramatic, book, sewing, religious, musical, scientific or athletic. This trained them for broader activities without the home. They organized nationally in 1889 as the General Federation of Women's Clubs; and their influence became a thing to be reckoned with in social legislation affecting their households. Households were smaller than formerly, for industrial life was spreading the knowledge and practice of birth control.

Families of small means sat down to supper in the kitchen near the "cookstove"; it might now boast a steamcooker, doubleboiler, or other new utensils such as the lighter iron with a cool, removable handle invented by Mrs. Potts to replace the old, heavy, hot sad-iron. This iron was the more appreciated because only the more comfortable families of the city were able to patronize the new commercial laundries. The frying pan still reigned supreme on country stoves.

City folk, encouraged by cooking schools and women's pages, were branching out in the variety of foods and their preparation. They provided a huge market for refrigerated fish and fruit, for "cereals," canned foods and synthetic products like oleomargerine and shortening. Their shopping habits were changing in the 'eighties. Department stores stocked a larger variety of goods, the Chicago mailorder houses of Sears Roebuck and Montgomery Ward appeared and the Kresge, McCrory and Woolworth chain stores were in operation. Large scale manufacture and distribution diffused responsibility and encouraged adulteration, as proved by an exposé 1200 pages long printed in 1887 by the chemical division of the Department of Agriculture. The manufacturers' lobbies succeeded in killing pure food legislation because the American family had yet to become constructively critical as a consumer. Vegetable, meat, and fruit growers near cities were building up a market for fresh foods. Candy and the improved, cheaper tobacco were bought more heavily than before, with cigarettes almost nine times as popular as cigars, although "respectable" women were not supposed to smoke. Small dealers in these things multiplied.

After supper, which was "dinner" in a dining room for the few, the family adjourned to the sitting room or back parlor. The front parlor (especially in rural regions) remained sacred to funerals, weddings, and the more important courting, if done in summertime. It usually displayed a marble mantel and marble-topped table, crowded with china statuettes, false flowers, paintings by ambitious kin, stereoscopes and fat, plush albums of family photographs. A "base burner" coal stove in the sitting room, with the pipe enlarged into a "drum" where it passed through a bedroom above, ensured comparative winter-time comfort in at least these two rooms. The affluent boasted a hot-air furnace calculated to warm the downstairs and take the chill off the upstairs except when the wind was "wrong." This class was more likely, also, to have attractive bathrooms, for plumbing improvements were ousting sewer gas and zinc tub-linings, at a charge—per bathroom—of eight to sixteen times the former cost.

In home furniture city householders were escaping gradually from horsehair and topheavy walnut and mahogany, for the art museums and schools made suggestions on use and beauty which the *Ladies Home Journal, Good Housekeeping* and World's Fair popularized. Manufacturers of metal beds and Morris chairs made furniture innovations. More windows, lighter wallpaper and hangings, and some use of rugs simplified household routines, otherwise complicated by a growing servant problem.

Simplification did not extend to women's clothes, however; heavy layers of full garments continued to hide the female figure. Dragging skirts, ridiculed as the "street-cleaning style" gave way slightly to shirt-waist suits for business women and divided skirts for bold bicyclists; but advocates of "health waists" could not destroy the popularity of tight, high corsets.

Children customarily were dressed as mimic adults but their deportment belied their appearance, according to critics of their manners. City boys and girls were the ones whose life changed, for their range of experience was widened by sights and sounds striking them at the city's quickened pace. Their right to a place off the streets for play, and to a knowledge of nature, came to be recognized by establishment of playgrounds and of "fresh air funds" for giving poor children one week of country life in the summer. A very few well-to-do city boys learned woodcraft in summer camps.

Children of the poor, however, often knew nothing of play or the country. A million boys and girls between 10 and 15 years of age were by 1880 a part of the ranks of labor; and by 1900 they had increased to one and three-quarters millions. Textile mills, stockyards, newspaper selling and sweatshops chained them. Few laws against child labor were enforced; children of Italian immigrants were sold into slavery as beggars. To combat some of these slum abuses, city people formed during the 'eighties societies for the prevention of cruelty to children.

New Rôle of Education

Parental responsibility was somewhat relaxed because of an outburst of enthusiasm for, and faith in, education. Upon schools, the indispensable perquisite of democratic living, the influence of the city was most beneficent. The accumulation of taxable wealth, with the economic recovery following 1878, created funds whereby the number and kinds of free schools, their equipment and the length of their terms could all be increased. Americans tolerated taxation for these purposes because they had abounding faith in the desirability and utility of education; it was expected to raise the political morality of the nation and the money-earning ability of the citizenry. Such a compound of democratic idealism and practical ambition is typical of the republic. Compulsory attendance laws by 1900 adorned the statute books of thirty-one of the states and territories in the North and West. They ordinarily included only children between eight and fourteen, and annual terms of only twelve to sixteen weeks; also they were not enforced outside of the better-established states. But they were an earnest of intention, as was the fact that ten of these states invested in free textbooks by state edict. Despite the influx of emigrant children, the number of pupils cared for in the common schools increased a little faster than the population.

In urban communities, where were extremes of wealth and poverty and masses of children desperately in need of schooling, the urge for educational improvement was most felt. Advances along the line of kindergartens, better buildings, longer school terms and higher salaries for teachers, set an example for slower communities, and forecast large scale organization of education for the masses. City teachers were led to depend less on the hickory stick and more upon interesting subject matter, to maintain discipline. Drawing, music, nature study, cooking, sewing, carpentry, commercial subjects, civics and science were introduced into the more progressive schools. There they stood stoutly against the charge that they were merely "crazes," until village schools in the next century generally followed suit.

City improvements helped to raise the professional standing of common primary school teachers. Their advance was retarded by poor wages, which sent most of the capable men into business callings and made the women (who came to compose two-thirds of the staff) regard their jobs as temporary stepping stones to something better. When the average time in the profession was only four years, great proficiency could not be attained. Some few women obtained administrative advancement as superintendents, but the vast majority remained in the humble ranks, receiving a monthly salary averaging (for the country as a whole) only about $38.14, or some $4.00 less than the men teachers. They knew too well that their jobs were jeopardized by political favoritism and interference from textbook publishers; but their status improved as cities came to demand normal-school training and teachers organized in self-respecting associations. Further prospect for advancement in the profession was opened by the urban rise in tax-supported high schools. These secondary schools, by extending the school age for middle class children proved that property owners were accepting responsibility for the training of leadership and taking pride in the acquisition of further culture by the offspring of their class.

Immigrants presented obstacles to education because of language differences, but those from northern Europe were accustomed to the idea of a popular education—even where they objected to using English in place of their native tongues, and the majority settled in cities where school facilities were most advanced. Also, Catholics accepted (in 1884) the challenge which immigration raised for them, and projected a program which rapidly expanded their parochial system in industrial areas. Altogether, by 1900 American born children of immigrants had become more literate than white children of native parents, and were often extremely ambitious.

Rural schools (and over half the population was rural) remained sadly deficient in most respects. Almost everywhere country districts clung to their poor, isolated, ungraded schools, conducted for short terms by untrained teachers paid less than farmhands. Struggling schoolmasters and schoolmistresses, "boarding 'round," performed a community service out of all proportion to the respect they received. State commissioners of instruction pointed out the rural deficiencies continually but ineffectively, for the farmers were slow to apply to their children's schooling the principles of united action and organization with which they were experimenting in the marketing of their crops. To pool their resources in consolidated schools seemed like a renunciation of their liberties. Village schools varied in primitiveness, between district and city status, according to local cultural differences depending upon racial elements, nearness to a large city, and sectional trends. Backward areas were encouraged by the national Bureau of Education, which under the better commissioners supplied school people with inspiration as well as information.

Particularly difficult was improvement of schooling in the South. There the higher birth rate, for the white population was increasing much faster even than the Negro, and the large adult illiteracy made essential the enrollment of a higher percentage of the total population than in other sections. Unfortunately, the section needed time to recover from federal muddling with local affairs, was lightly supplied with taxable property, heavily supplied with children and had the extra expense of separate schools for white and colored. Alliance organization improved somewhat the facilities but southerners in general did not yet feel deeply the obligation to supply free education to the lower classes, and Congress was no longer shouldering colored problems.

Negro education was advancing with the aid of private philanthropy. Booker T. Washington, an ex-slave schooled at Hampton Institute, Virginia, assumed responsibility. He established in the heart of the Alabama black belt, in 1881, his famous "Tuskegee Institute" for teaching trades and occupations. Also northern millionaires, J. F. Slater, Daniel Hand and George Peabody, provided funds to educate Negroes. Results appeared when, notwithstanding their social, political and economic disadvantages, 20% of them acquired ownership of their own homes; despite lynchings they grew in self-respect. Talent emerged, with a colored poet, painter, novelist and an inventor. Negroes in classes more than doubled between 1878 and 1898, but still about half of them had no schooling; this retarded the national advance in literacy.

Illiteracy declined, 1880-1900, from 17% to 11%, with the cities chiefly responsible; and the average of knowledge seemed so much higher than that of other nations that it won the praise of foreign observers. But literacy means no more than the ability to read and write; and the schooling of the average American had advanced but one year—to a total of five. The national literary output (books, magazines and newspapers) showed a tendency to be pulled down toward the fourth or fifth grade level of taste and understanding. However, there were forces pulling in the opposite direction:—to some extent the high schools, attended by a minority of the children between thirteen and eighteen years of age, and to a much greater extent the colleges and universities, attended by the sons and daughters of men and women who assumed some obligation for social and intellectual leadership.

The growing faith of Americans in higher education was abundantly demonstrated between 1878 and 1898. The number of colleges and universities increased from 350 to 500 approximately, and their students from 58,000 to 100,000 approximately. Ten more states of the West and South overcame sectarian opposition sufficiently to set up their own tax-supported universities, and allocated public funds for ambitious projects.

The University of Michigan set an example in large scale organization of higher education. High school students were invited in, under an accrediting system which dispensed with entrance examinations; political interference sometimes was defied; new methods were dared and in the West co-education was generally accepted as necessary and proper. While the national proportion of co-educational colleges was growing from around 50% to 70% the East came to acknowledge the right of women to higher education, and college work of superior quality was undertaken at Bryn Mawr and Mt. Holyoke while "coordinate" schools were opened at the side doors of Brown, Columbia and Harvard. At the same time the possibilities in higher education so intrigued millionaires that they endowed whole universities, special departments, and particular chairs of learning.

In and near urban centers the complex, driving quality of this period challenged the ingenuity of the educators who were developing the big colleges. Presidents and faculties struggled with two difficult problems: with what subjects and methods should they meet the pressure for large-scale organization in higher learning? At Harvard President Eliot popularized the elective system, trusting the students at that highly selective institution to choose from an expanded curriculum courses more closely connected than Latin and Greek with daily life. Harvard led also with summer school courses, which President Harper at the University of Chicago elevated to a quarter part of the academic year. Extension courses and self-government experiments on the campus increased the number of persons who could take college work and permitted some students a hand in the business of managing college life. The kind of oratorical and debating opportunities provided by college societies and by intercollegiate rivalries determined the early training of such future political leaders as Beveridge, Bryan and La Follette. The spread of fraternities and sororities, with the musical, dramatic and literary societies found on most college campuses, supplied the basis for subsequent cultural leadership.

Fortunately, as the stream of higher education was broadening it was raising its level also; for mechanical experiments in industry and elective experiments in education encouraged scholars to specialize, to discover new "laws" in science and history. Technological schools expanded and improved their standards, with the East emphasizing engineering, the Far West mining and metallurgy and the South and Middle West agriculture and horticulture. Laboratory methods greatly improved. Out of agricultural difficulties had grown research at state universities; through governmental and private aid, through practical utility and competitive stimulus, science branched out widely into such fertile fields as applied chemistry, mathematics, astronomy, geology and physics. American scientists cooperated with others in international undertakings.

Graduate study received its chief impetus from Germany, where during the 'eighties the number of American students doubled until they reached a total of over 2000. Fellowships and the growing diffusion of wealth had made it possible for middle class young people to enjoy study abroad. They returned to permeate American scholarship with German traditions of thoroughness. The emphasis upon graduate work which Johns Hopkins had begun in 1876 was copied at Catholic University, Clark and Chicago, while the growing appeal of such work expanded it at Columbia, Cornell, Harvard, New York University, Pennsylvania, Princeton and Yale. Many a "college" became a "university," sometimes more in name than fact.

The professors offered a contrast to the average American. They were men either without taste or aptitude for wealth-getting, teaching usually at salaries of $2000 and seldom getting more than $4000, meanwhile looking with some askance at the business ethics of the period. Historians among them produced huge, detailed histories of particular periods; economists often found in the existing capitalistic system justification for all its major workings. But there was a growing tendency for political scientists and sociologists to explore the usefulness of government to mankind; and William James led some of the philosophers and psychologists away from the metaphysical thinking of Josiah Royce and into a frank consideration of the individual and the immediate results of his conduct.

Professors violating the mores of special pressure groups in their localities had to face possible dismissal. Most of them banded together in various national associations (like the American Historical Association founded in 1884) to get from their own large scale organizations and quarterly publications the necessary assurance of recognition, comradeship and professional dignity. They enjoyed the realization that the United States now contributed its share to world learning; and they found their greatest satisfaction in a thoroughness of knowledge which contrasted sharply with the general superficiality.

They had excellent reasons for contempt of the superficiality, for a thriving business in fake labels was lining the pockets of men who sold all kinds of degrees from fictitious colleges. Interest in the professions multiplied professional students faster than the population. Medicine attracted the greatest number; but deplorable standards ruled even at respectable universities and charlatans in healing mulcted the gullible with secret remedies of dubious efficacy. A multitude of non-medical groups emerged, with the osteopaths winning wide recognition. This forced establishment of state boards of health to license practitioners, which led to improved instruction. Further acquaintance with germs, antiseptics, nervous disease and finally x-ray made possible more healthful living in crowded cities. With city and state boards of health to safeguard food, water and sanitation, the average American longevity rose, 1890-1900, from thirty-one to thirty-five years.

Theology remained the longest-established American profession, second in popularity until the early 'nineties and kept high standards. Ministers had to confront advances in evolutionary thinking and new religions reflecting the quickening pulse of national life. The law superseded theology in second place; it enjoyed high repute despite careless teaching, poor entrance requirements and inadequate restrictions upon admission to the bar. Incomes of lawyers serving large scale business mounted. The only considerable effort to make a profession out of business itself was Joseph Wharton's endowment of the Wharton School of Finance and Economics at the University of Pennsylvania.

Conscious Striving for Culture

The general level of education and the range of exploration into the higher learning were reflected in a new striving for culture. Writers, and their friends the artists, gathered in colonies like Greenwich Village, New York, for work and play together. Boston, Philadelphia, Chicago, Cincinnati, St. Louis and San Francisco had each its nucleus of literary and artistic men and women who, either by responding to the popular taste or by endeavoring to raise it, affected the cultural level.

General interest in art was increased by mechanical improvements in photography and reproduction, so that books and magazines subtly conveyed art appreciation, through illustrations. Thus came a gradual improvement in domestic decorative forms, like glass and tableware, pottery and fabric design. The sway of cast iron "fronts," dogs, deer and mounted military statues—the war foundry work—was not yet ended, but art leadership consciously sought to end it. A young "New School" of American artists trained abroad in the best European traditions returned to dispute with the "Old School," and sometimes fled back again in despair. Courses in "art appreciation" acted as a leaven and pretentious public and private buildings, at unprecedented cost and under millionaire patronage, gave mural artists their first important American opportunity.

In sculpture, St. Gaudens showed restless Americans the beauty which rests in dignity and repose, while his pupil, MacMonnies, excelled in sculptured motion, and Daniel Chester French in allegory. Whistler, Sargent and Pennell won from foreigners further praise for American achievement in painting and illustration; McKim and White, pupils of Richardson and Hunt, designed beautiful public and university libraries. Domestic architecture remained largely mediocre; but business structures in expensive rental areas evolved into skyscrapers, after elevators were invented, thanks to the imaginative genius of Chicago archi-

Roebling's Brooklyn Bridge

ARCHITECTURAL ACHIEVEMENT

Richardson's Trinity Church at Boston

tects. In the midst of the panic year 1893, the finest American architects and engineers cooperated in creating at Chicago the buildings of the "World's Columbian Exposition," structures which by their classic loveliness amazed, awed and instructed the nation. Here was abundant proof of the educability, even under stress, of the people in the great hinterland of the United States. Twelve million persons, young and old, went to school at Chicago that summer.

Self-improvement long had been a favorite pastime of adult Americans, who formed voluntary associations for that purpose. Outstanding was the annual summertime meeting at Chautauqua, New York, started in 1874 by a manufacturer and minister as a sort of Sunday-school camp meeting. Enthusiastic support and the cooperation of leading American and foreign scholars during the next quarter century expanded "Chautauqua" into a succession of Round Tables on literature, science, government, economics, temperance and other subjects, with concerts, prayer-meetings, gymnastic exercises and cooking demonstrations enlivening the grove. The middle class clientele liked it so well that a "Literary and Scientific Circle" next was organized for a four-year course of study through books written for this purpose; a monthly magazine, a "college," and an offspring chautauqua in almost every state multiplied the persons influenced. In nearly all small towns a "star course" lecture series interrupted the winter's dull gossip.

In larger towns and cities librarians inspired by the American Library Association were learning how to circulate efficiently quantities of books among thousands of readers. Europe had neither the readers nor the efficiency. Books and buildings were financed by private donors and tax money, until by 1900 Boston, Chicago and New York had outstanding facilities and the nation as a whole had at least 9000 free libraries— over half of them in the Middle and Far West. Alliance groups in the North established circulating libraries which introduced farm families to the gospel of social betterment as written by Bellamy, Donnelly, George, Peffer, Powderly and Weaver. At the national capital Congress had proudly appropriated for the biggest and most expensive of the world's libraries. Fortunately, the most avid library users were the most impressionable class—young people. Few of them had at home more than an occasional "set" of books bought by "subscription" through agents or the mail; but the book trade was gradually discarding its antiquated distribution scheme and the department stores were pushing book sales as bargain merchandise.

Literature could enter the lives of more Americans and writing could become a decently paid occupation because of the mechanical aid of inventors, and the financial aid of advertisers. The inventors improved the presses, picture-making and color-combining; they devised capital and lower-case typewriters (1878), fountain pens (by Waterman in

1884) and linotypes (1885). Advertisers took some 40% of the space in important dailies besides large sections in periodicals. The length of magazine subscription lists and the size of newspaper circulation figures became unimportant as direct income producers and most important for their sales value with prospective advertisers. Retail stores bought much space in newspapers; but patent medicine manufacturers took much more in many mediums, became the most important group of general advertisers and found the columns of religious magazines especially lucrative. The irresponsible competition among advertisers revealed and changed in countless ways the habits and standards of the people, often without much awareness of the process.

Their appetite for books was voracious, surpassing all records. Fiction, then as now, was first in sales, and the typical taste remained for sheer, romantic sentimentalists like Frances H. Burnett, Mary J. Holmes, and E. P. Roe. Some sentimentalists like F. Marion Crawford, Helen Hunt Jackson, Frank R. Stockton and Lew Wallace rose above mediocrity. Children's books were "goodie-goodies," dime novels, and success stories, with a few in the better manner of such authors as Louisa May Alcott, Mark Twain, and Kate Douglas Wiggin. In general, problems of sex were kept taboo, by survival of a mid-Victorianism which supported Anthony Comstock and various societies "for the suppression of Vice" in indiscriminate destruction of pornographic, literary and medical works. Even the poets found it extremely difficult to get away from romanticism.

By this time local color had spread among southern writers of fiction —children of the pre-war aristocracy whose stories supplanted "westerns" in height of popularity. They fostered national unity:—the Uncle Remus, Marse Chan and Colonel Carter characters created by Joel Chandler Harris, Thomas Nelson Page and F. Hopkinson Smith: the plays "Shenandoah," "Heart of Maryland," and "Alabama"; and editorials by Henry Watterson in the Louisville *Courier-Journal* and by Henry W. Grady in the *Atlanta Constitution*—all these helped to reconcile North and South. Mary N. Murfree ("Charles Egbert Craddock") portrayed the mountaineers of Tennessee; and the New Orleans creoles inspired differing interpretations by George W. Cable, Lafcadio Hearn and Grace E. King.

The Middle West further developed humor: artists in the droll, like Bill Nye, Eugene Field, Marietta Holley, James Whitcomb Riley and Maurice Thompson provided very popular novels, poems and cartoons. But whether literature centered South, West, or East, in urban or rural locales, most of it was at the intellectual level of the average, common-school-trained citizen. Editor Robert Bonner, who paid Mrs. E. D. E. N. Southworth $10,000 annually for sweet stories for his *Ledger* magazine, obtained nearly half a million subscribers; due, he thought, to the fact that in the *Ledger,* "there never appeared one line which the old lady in Westchester county would not like to read to her daughters."

Nevertheless the trend toward realism, evident since the Civil War, continued. Unlovely aspects of city, town and country life were pictured by Joseph Kirkland and Brander Matthews. The literary pattern of Populism was furnished by Hamlin Garland out of his own experience in *Son of the Middle Border* and *Main Travelled Roads.* As America lost her frontier she became conscious of it, and Professor Frederick Jackson Turner of the University of Wisconsin read before the American Historical Association in 1893 his historic paper on "The Significance of the Frontier in American History." The panic, strikes and general unrest of the period thrust the class conflict upon the attention of the literati. William Dean Howells acknowledged the influence of Tolstoi and mildly criticized the American situation in *A Hazard of New Fortunes* (1890) and other works; Mark Twain's developing pessimism found expression in *What Is Man, The Mysterious Stranger,* and *The Man That Corrupted Hadleyburg* (1898 and 1899). Utopia tales like Edward Bellamy's *Looking Backward* partook somewhat of the nature of political tracts, and during the 'nineties the place second to fiction in popularity (which had been first religious and juvenile books and secondly legal volumes) was taken by histories and treatments of government and social problems. A few Americans became sufficiently self-critical to study such foreign novelists as Tolstoi, Turgenev and Hardy.

Literature became so thoroughly established as to permit of very serious criticism of technique, in which Henry James excelled. American authors worked at a tremendous disadvantage, however, because the lack of an international copyright agreement gave publishers on both sides of the Atlantic the chance to line their pockets with profits from pirated editions. Finally, in 1891, authors and some publishers made a bargain with the printers' unions whereby the latter consented to an international copyright law on condition that foreign authors were required to reprint their books in America for domestic distribution; as a result, in 1894 novels of American authors for the first time outnumbered those of foreigners in domestic publication.

The magazines had grown to national stature, by filling a triple function:—supporting writers, preserving the record of social development and furnishing a democratic form of literature. This period knew a generation of great editors, such as Beecher, Bowen, Curtis, Gilder, Godkin, Holland, Howells, and Rice. The prestige periodicals—the twenty-five and thirty-five cent *Atlantic, Century, Harper's* and *Scribner's,* carried further the serialization of some of the best fiction. They encouraged the literary output of that class which most deserved support and which could not expect an adequate income from books.

Interest in literary criticism, outdoor life and current events justified establishment of the *Dial, Public Opinion, Current Literature, Literary Digest,* and *American Review of Reviews;* and the *Arena* and *Forum* found prosperity in a pre-muckrake policy. Monthlies between 1878 and 1898 were increasing 50% and quarterlies 100%; but the significant facts were two:—the greater part of the new periodicals concerned transportation, business, trade and fraternities, and the general magazines did not increase so much in number as in circulation. Such clever publishers as Cyrus H. K. Curtis,[1] Edward Bok, S. S. McClure and Frank Munsey enlarged the number of magazine buyers, by the simple expedient of producing popular ten-cent and fifteen-cent monthlies, filled with warm, daily life and human nature. For polite essays and travel sketches they substituted current affairs, short stories, women's articles and serialized novels. Some three million people thus became magazine buyers —a six-fold increase.

Newspaper editors, meanwhile, far outstripped magazine and book publishers in exploiting mass education in the United States. Ready to their hands was the largest literate public in the world, with a reading ability approximating that of the fifth grade. The "average" American was curious about daily happenings, business, politics, government and finance. He and his wife developed much more interest in sports and women's concerns than in humanitarianism, religion or "culture." Cheapness, also, they demanded.

All these things they got, in a sprouting variety of weeklies, semiweeklies, dailies, morning and evening issues, special, extra and Sunday editions; for in this era technical and industrial advance were so conjoined with large scale organization as to make possible quick, efficient newsgathering and cheap news printing, all at a profit. Competition for this profit so challenged the ingenuity and cupidity of its creators that they all hastened to multiply and vulgarize the press. The demands they made upon reporters schooled the better ones, like Samuel Hopkins Adams, Richard Harding Davis, Will Irwin, David Graham Phillips and Jacob Riis, to contribute their own books to the literature of their era. Newspaper readers increased faster than the population, dailies were multiplying by over 200%, weeklies by 50%; until by 1900 the United States had more than half the world's newspapers.

To get news to fill their front pages, competing editors had to learn to cooperate in subscribing to newsgathering agencies, the chief of which under Melville E. Stone became dominant in 1897, as the Associated Press. "Patent insides" were syndicated first by S. S. McClure in 1884 and gradually a wide sale for syndicated stories, articles, serialized novels, women's and children's features, was built up. Propaganda agencies, such as the Republican National Committee in 1896 used syndicate methods to put partisan cartoons and arguments before voters as news. Large

[1] The *Ladies Home Journal* was started in 1883 by Mrs. Cyrus Curtis.

scale newsgathering and dispensing led logically to more intimate connections between papers; the Scripps brothers before 1890 had leagued together a chain of Midwestern units.

About one-third of the people, it has been estimated, were within a fifty-mile radius of city dailies; and although three times as many Americans were buying weekly and semi-weekly papers as bought dailies, the city papers, and magazines were the stronger moving force in American journalism. Continually they impressed their large-scale contents and far-reaching practices upon country papers. City subscribers cared but little to read of agriculture—rural subscribers enviously read of "store clothes" and city excitements. The steady, relentless impact, well defined as "urban imperialism," heightened the resentments which built up the Alliances, Populism and Bryan, demonstrating again the complicated interdependence of economic, social and political forces in the history of the United States.

Most forceful in editorial and educational influence upon the masses in this period were Joseph Pulitzer and William Randolph Hearst. Pulitzer, beginning in 1883 with the New York *World,* showed how a following could be built up by appealing to the masses with sensationalism. His clever use of "human interest," cartoons, Sunday colored supplements, and evening editions; his invasion of the privacy of all and sundry; and his crusades against corruption enlarged his circulation and those of editors who complimented him with imitation.

He had no serious competition until William Randolph Hearst undertook in 1896 to out-pulitzer Pulitzer, with the New York *Morning Journal.* Their titanic struggle for supremacy led to numerous inventions of the press, among them the term "yellow journalism," which grew out of their bitter lawsuits over use of the "Yellow Kid" cartoons. The reading public was enlarged if not enlightened and the damage which their sensationalism did to public taste was offset somewhat by the purgings which their exposures occasionally gave business cheats and grafting politicians. In 1884 Pulitzer had helped elect Cleveland by printing Walt McDougall's and Valerian Gribayedoff's series of political cartoons—the first such series to appear in newspapers of the United States. Hearst in 1896 added considerably to Republican difficulties through Homer Davenport's cartoons of Hanna, garbed grotesquely in dollar signs.

Use of Leisure

The influence of education and its literary allies was extended and strengthened in part and in some ways hampered by the increasing leisure which a goodly portion of the population enjoyed. These hours of leisure (except for farmers, their wives and children) were now being increased:—for the rich, by reason of their mounting wealth, for wage earners through shortened hours in the workday, for salaried persons through summer vacations. This city leisure challenged the inventive capacity of its possessors; for the most part unaware of the challenge, they hurried *en masse* to spend their spare time imitating each other's recreations, furnishing the patronage for a large scale organization of recreation built on the common desire to escape from a humdrum existence.

Most complete escape was found in the secret fraternal orders, of which the United States had more than all other nations. There had been only seventy-eight before 1880; but by 1901 the delight of over six million men and women in romantic ceremonials and regal robings had fostered 490 more fraternities, ranging all the way from the Knights and Ladies of the Golden Rule to the Concatenated Order of Hoo-Hoo. Most promised sick and death benefits, as a practical attraction. Organized on the largest scale were the "big four": the Odd Fellows, Freemasons, Knights of Pythias and Ancient Order of United Workmen, with one-third of the total membership. In large cities, lodges were far more numerous than churches; in the South, they completely fascinated the Negroes; in rural areas they softened the bitter struggle of farm life.

Other societies shifted the appeal from secret ritual to patriotic exercise. There was a great flourishing, at patriotic centennials and celebrations, of the Sons of the American Revolution, the Daughters of the American Revolution, and Societies of Mayflower Descendants, Colonial Dames, Colonial Wars, and the War of 1812, in addition to the Grand Army of the Republic and the Confederate Veterans with their feminine auxiliaries, the Relief Corps and the United Daughters of the Confederacy.

Since these various societies met but once or twice a month, they left city and townsfolk (who did not need to rise at farmer's dawn) with an amplitude of evenings for leisure activities. More were spent than formerly in reading and study, as education and publication records show, but for the vast majority of the populace evening diversion was found, not at home, art institute or library, but at the many places of commercial entertainment supported on a large scale by city people. They made New York preeminent in the theatre, with Daly, Palmer and Wallack, Belasco and the Frohmans, the great play producers of the 'eighties and 'nineties. They increased the number of actors from five to fifteen thousand; and the foremost of these, such as Booth, Barrett and Ada Rehan, figured in an international exchange of talent. They encouraged the famous Drew-Barrymore dynasty. To meet their demands the finest dramatic productions were included in the large repertoire of talented city stock companies.

Out from the largest centers into the hinterland, with its typical local "opera house" went offshoots of stock—travelling companies with one "star" supported usually by much less brilliant luminaries. They fed the popular taste, which turned from Hamlet and Camille toward the sentimental heroics of native drama. Theatregoers in the mass did not demand the realism of "Shore Acres" by James Herne, exceptional American dramatist of the period. Rather they liked to weep and laugh over "The Old Homestead," "County Fair," "Way Down East," "Uncle Tom's Cabin" and "The Heart of Maryland." Audiences which were supporting the new journalism and the popular magazines, thrilled to the dime novel, western plays and metropolitan melodramas.

More than half the theatregoers were habituées of vaudeville, which took over features from the minstrel show, dime museum, variety hall and circus, refined them and made a 15 or 20 "act" combination, admirably adapted to city restlessness. Keith, Proctor and Considine exploited "continuous" vaudeville profitably in circuits, and musical comedy actors there got their training. Male theatregoers of less "refined" taste were supporting another type of inexpensive entertainment, the burlesque, featuring vulgar music, jokes and posturing. Many of the persons hired wintertimes for the city's 10-20-25¢ shows and dime museums went through the countryside summers appearing at "amusement parks" and in circuses. Circus popularity reached its peak when some forty big tents were on tour simultaneously. Barnum and Bailey joined their gigantic extravaganzas in 1881; and, like Buffalo Bill with his new Wild West Show, they took their freaks, tricksters and menageries on tour abroad, to their great profit and the amazement of curious foreigners.

In American entertainment music assumed new importance, as evanescent, popular tunes became the rage. Sentimental songs about misplaced affection were unwound on city streets by organ grinders, and tooted through the land by itinerant German bands. With songs about tenement life, with jig tunes syncopated from Negro melodies and with the "ragtime," which began a long vogue in 1896, popular music entered large scale production and consumption. Its sway was vastly extended by Edison's phonograph, which about 1878 raucously commenced its long career of recording the vagaries of American emotions, morals and manners. Sheer delight in musical entertainment was a sensation given the polite public by the production (beginning in 1878) of light operas, such as those of the Englishmen, Gilbert and Sullivan and the most popular American operetta, "Robin Hood," with its perennial favorite, "Oh Promise Me." In comic opera Lillian Russell and David Warfield got their start.

Whether or not the phonograph and light opera were mainly responsible, Americans gave evidence of serious interest in music, and women did much to foster it. The subject was admitted to city grade schools; no middle class parents were left wholly content without a "square" piano, or at least a "parlor organ," at which their protesting progeny must take lessons from a private teacher; and young and middle aged common folk enjoyed the contacts and vocal exercise of singing schools. Nearly every town boasted a "brass band," with a few like Sousa's Marine Band known throughout the country.

German communities developed choral societies which sometimes fostered interest to the point of annual music festivals like those at Cincinnati, which raised middle westerners' music appreciation. Artists, native and foreign, now could "tour" profitably. Most important cities boasted at least one conservatory, some of high excellence, and these, with college and university departments, provided training formerly found only abroad. The finest symphonies now could be heard by middle class and rich people, in New York, Boston and Chicago, albeit the orchestras which played them and the conductors were usually foreign-born.

In New York were wealth and taste sufficient, in 1883, to open the costly Metropolitan Opera House, and to bring there the world's. finest singers, and heavy German opera, where light Italian had sufficed. New Orleans with its French companies was the only other city boasting grand opera; but general musical interest was sufficient to encourage composers of orchestral, choral, choir, art song, piano and band compositions. John Philip Sousa, Victor Herbert, Ethelbert Nevin, Edward A. McDowell, Dudley Buck and John Knowles Paine were some who showed Europe that America now was making her own musical contribution.

Since concert and theatre going were confined chiefly to evening, indoor and inactive leisure, they left unsatisfied the great need of city dwellers for bodily activity out-of-doors. Realization came of the physical handicap in urban occupations and fostered indoor gymnasium work for a few people in Turnvereins, city clubs, Y.M.C.A., Y.W.C.A., colleges and schools. Basketball—an American invention of 1891—was one of the consequences.

In the great outdoors the commonalty participated, directly or as spectators, in sports. Among them, baseball, bicycling and football attained high popularity and therefore reached the proportions of professionalism and large scale organization; the public, in fact, was said to "have sport on the brain." In baseball the American Association, founded in 1882, joined the National League (of 1876) in developing individual skill and team play, with World Series games, from 1884 to 1891, as the climax. In bicycling, the new, safety-type machine, with pneumatic tires, by 1893 had a million users, pedalling over automobile-less roads improved through the lobby pressure of the League of American Wheelmen. In football, colleges under pressure hired non-students as players and changed the game from Rugby to a much rougher spectacle; alumni and the public enthusiastically appropriated the show and made it the occasion for excited betting and unrestrained outbursts of "loyalty."

Roller skating intermittently had its devotees; even gentle croquet—then a courting sport—organized (in 1882) its own national association, as tennis players had done a year earlier and canoers the year before that. Rifleshooters' and anglers' associations with sportsmen's clubs so put birds, fish and beasts on the defensive that other associations—like the Audubon Society of 1886 and the Boone and Crockett Club of 1887—were organized to protect them.

Racing organizations spent lavishly on larger clubhouses, faster tracks, greater stables and bigger stakes; but their frauds and betting gave racing some ill repute. Even less respectable was prizefighting, illegal in most states; nevertheless, the size of the winnings of Sullivan, Corbett and Fitzsimmons, the length of their bouts and their invention of "scientific boxing" and the "solar plexus punch," made them household news and city boys' idols. So much for the commoner recreations.

For rich families, with leisure scarcely interrupted by work, social pleasures adapted to mass use on evenings, Saturdays and holidays were too inadequate and common. Therefore the rich set up in large cities and at expensive resorts their own exclusive cliques called "the 400" who outdid each other in novel and lavish devices for conspicuous spending. They had their international yacht races, and travel, and at their own country clubs enjoyed polo, golf, archery and trap shooting. Their various displays, duly detailed by the press, were imitated in small ways by the well-to-do of the county seats. Their arrogant wastefulness aroused resentment chiefly among the few who had not hope of imitating it, for most people defined success in terms of money and the things it could buy; they felt a certain sense of patriotic pride in such transactions as those of 1895, when three wealthy American women annexed husbands with foreign titles. The "gold standard" of the New York, Chicago and San Francisco brand was displacing the culture and family standards of the Boston and Philadelphia brand as the urban determinant in social destiny. Its worst effect was to encourage poor taste.

Awakening of the Social Conscience

Notwithstanding the momentum of educational and cultural advance there remained slums, social evils, vice and crime. Murder in the United States increased (1881-1895) six times as fast as the population and was thirty times as frequent per million as in the north European countries. Americans habitually thought of themselves as altruistic, but they preferred foreign to home missionary outlay because their sympathies and understanding were outdistanced by the rapid workings of large scale industrial organization. While city and factory conditions challenged the well-to-do to accept social responsibility, most of them clung to the familiar and comfortable practice of religion as a strictly individual matter, permitting insulation of church and prayer-meeting thoughts from workaday actions. Support of the expensive metropolitan churches and expanding home missions by the new group of wealthy industrialists thickened the insulation.

From pulpits came sermons revealing a blindness to the human effects of monopoly and a lack of sympathy for labor. A few religious organizations were known to own and collect rent from slum property. Only six out of five hundred New York and Brooklyn clergymen responded to an appeal from New York bakers to preach against compulsory Sunday labor. Even the successful team of preaching and singing revivalists, the popular Dwight L. Moody and Ira A. Sankey, reached out for respectable backsliders more than for unregenerates beyond the church; they often found them apathetic and evangelism unappealing to the city sinful. As former humble denominations became rich and formalized, their poor and uneducated members left to form such sects as the Holiness group, to serve as a "poor people's church."

Churches in general, particularly the Protestant, turned their backs upon industrial problems physically as well as mentally. Out of crowding city neighborhoods comfortable parishioners moved their residences, and often times their meeting places, leaving behind churches which were abandoned or too few in number, too luxurious in appearance and too undemocratic in viewpoint to do service for the ill-dressed masses living around them. Even the Jews and Catholics—who aimed to attract and hold the workers—could scarcely keep pace with city crowding. The number of church members increased faster than the population, yet more slowly than the number of wage-earners. James Bryce judged that church influence was deeper and stronger in the United States than in Europe, but the president of the American Federation of Labor, Samuel Gompers, justly charged church people with neglect of the working class.

The trouble lay in the fact that the vast majority of Americans preferred a static religion, although they were addicted to change secularly. They continued to accept, implicitly, that sort of revealed religion which had seemed to promise enough for rural and middle class people. They by now had more than 150 different sects from which to choose according to taste; but these were based upon similar, familiar concepts, and congregations had abandoned their bitter rivalry. Members convened in a mood of social rather than spiritual communion, and resented the intrusion of dynamic factors. Fiercely the majority of church officials denounced those scientists and scholars who persistently disturbed the religious waters with winds of Darwinism, the Higher Criticism, and comparative religion. South, North and even West (where churches were fewest and creeds most fluid) "heretic" preachers and professors were punished by trials, suspensions, and dismissals. Schisms among Lutherans allowed a large majority of the Swedes, Norwegians and Danes to become lost to that church.

Religious resentment over change found its most violent expression in the American Protective Association—popularly known as the Anti-papal Association, which focused upon Catholics the fears felt by certain non-Catholic farmers, city-dwellers, and workers. The Catholic organization, due to immigration, had by 1890 a far larger membership than any Protestant denomination, with 200,000 more communicants than the Protestants in old Puritan New England. Catholic immigrants settled chiefly in cities, where they ran political machines, competed successfully for jobs, and agitated for public funds for parochial schools. Chicago had become the most Catholic city in the United States; but the Middle West over which that city dominated had had a Puritan background. Various and confused elements of strife readily found expression (between 1887 and 1896) in this secret order, which swore its members not to employ or vote for Catholics and exchanged with its enemies the most fantastic charges and counter-charges. The disgracefully warring factions could not be diverted until class rivalry found new expression in the excitements of the campaign of 1896.

The resistance to change in the bourgeois churches aroused revolt among important leaders and the masses. The intellectuals and their minority following supported with high sale figures such things as the revised version of the King James *Bible,* J. F. Clarke's *Ten Great Religions* and W. Gladden's *Who Wrote the Bible?* Some novels denouncing intolerance became best sellers. Dynamic ministers like H. W. Beecher and Lyman Abbott accumulated influence until in 1893 the New York Chautauqua included a lecture series by the prominent Scotch evolutionist, Henry Drummond, and a World's Parliament of Religions was held at the Columbian Exposition. Other groups collected around Ingersoll and his agnosticism, Adler and his Ethical Culture Society and Mme. Blavatsky and her Theosophy.

City workers of the North in search of recreation on Sunday defied the blue laws, thus forcing Sabbath labor upon trainmen, trolleymen and other servitors. Farm influence in most legislatures prevented repeal of the laws, but neither national nor international Sabbath Associations could force city Germans, Catholics or Jews to treat Sunday according to the rural American tradition instead of the continental. The A. F. of L., the Brotherhood of Locomotive Engineers and the Knights of Labor would cooperate with the American Sabbath Union in lobbying for laws against Sunday work, but not against Sunday play.

Yet were thousands of people eager for a religion which should alleviate their daily lives. To the spiritually and physically starved of "rumdom, slumdom and bumdom," the Salvation Army (beginning in 1879) offered regeneration through repentance and reform. To nerve-wracked city people of the middle class (after a beginning among the poor) Mary Baker Eddy offered health and happiness through Christian Science. For the mass of urban immigrants in general the most liberal Protestant leaders were socializing their churches, supplementing Sunday sermons with week-day sewing, gymnastics, reading, carpentry, child care and club activities; "institutional" expansion brought membership expansion. Into a few theological seminaries and universities crept courses in economics and sociology with practice in social work; some denominational lines were bridged by large scale home missionary activities. The Christian Endeavor Society founded by Francis E. Clark in 1881 expanded into several denominations, becoming an international organization and bringing together for discussion many thousands of young people. Out of the Y.M.C.A., Y.W.C.A. and Student Volunteer movement evolved in 1898 the World's Student Christian Federation.

Labor troubles focussed the attention of a few liberals, as individuals and as minority groups, upon industry's challenge to the church. Washington Gladden, Ohio's Congregational liberal, during the coal strike of 1884 and the street car strike of 1886, confidently preached the right of labor to organize. He and Josiah Strong emphasized the social teachings of Jesus; and a political party of Christian Socialists was formed in 1889. Cardinal Gibbons of Baltimore in 1886 persuaded the Pope not to condemn the Knights of Labor and he successfully defeated less liberal Catholic clergy in their effort to place Henry George's *Progress and Poverty* on the Index. The year after the Haymarket riots liberal Episcopalians formed their Church Organization for the Advancement of the Interests of Labor; and in 1889 under W. D. P. Bliss of Boston they launched the Society of Christian Socialists.

The papal encyclical *Rerum Novarum* two years later encouraged Catholic liberals, although it denounced socialism. Archbishop Ireland of St. Paul helped settle two of the big railway strikes of 1894; but the Methodist, W. H. Cawardine of Pullman, suffered disgrace that year for denouncing the reigning corporation of Indiana and Catholic priests and laymen, friendly to labor, sometimes were excommunicated. Through the early 'nineties a sympathetic minority of Congregationalists, Baptists and interdenominational agencies was essaying to cope with social and economic problems and the depression following 1893 spurred their efforts. The public grew so interested in the application of Christian doctrines to modern life that when Reverend C. M. Sheldon of Topeka put out in 1896 his *In His Steps* they bought up hundreds of copies of it.

The growth of general interest in schemes for combating the evils aggravated by industrial life was particularly stimulated by a few women. They led in setting up, outside of the churches of which most of them were members, organizations for rescuing the individual from the worst effects of his association in the mass. They selected for concentrated attack four major evils—poverty, disease, drunkenness, and crime.

To make any headway whatever against poverty, charity had to adopt large scale proportions. Charity as such long had been an accepted part of American life and the number of existing public and private agencies was legion. Bryce judged that the United States was spending more, in personal effort and money, for charitable objects than any other country. But the various agencies were disorganized and inclined to jealousy, and their conflicting efforts were ill adapted to discourage fraud and chronic pauperism. So, during this period some score of state boards of charity were set up to coordinate the work of tax-supported institutions; and some integration between their work and that of private agencies was achieved by the organization of "associated charities" at the heart of the problem, in 138 cities.

As the city was the heart of the problem, the core of that heart was the slum district; and straight into it a few women and men moved, to set up settlement houses. Imitating Toynbee Hall over in East London, Dr. Stanton Coit in 1886 opened the Neighborhood Guild in New York, and Jane Addams with Ellen G. Starr in 1889 opened Hull House in Chicago. By 1900 approximately one hundred of these settlement houses were operating in northern and western cities, their workers trying to help immigrant groups to take better care of their children, to exercise, to save, to find employment and to play wholesomely. They tried to touch the daily life of the underprivileged on as many sides as possible and the contact in turn instructed the college boys and girls whose idealism was stimulated by the hard work among the very poor. The houses became focal points for gathering support for all kinds of social betterment movements.

Among these movements the conservation and restoration of health proved especially important, for the poor of the cities had the worst possible location in all America. If they were so fortunate as to live in New York or Boston, where sewage and drinking water systems were made superior to those of other cities, they yet had to live in the terrible "dumbbell" tenements, so called from their shape. These were "walkup" buildings, five or six stories high and ninety feet deep, with narrow, dark halls, inadequate and unsanitary toilet facilities and many rooms without direct light or air. With whole families crowded in each room or two, they proved admirably adapted to the breeding of vermin, tuberculosis, diphtheria, child diseases and immorality. New York City—with the worst congestion on the face of the globe—within these twenty years doubled the number of her firetraps of this type and trebled the number of human beings she jammed into them.

Preparation of food in such surroundings could never be cleanly and the initial risks were multiplied by difficulty in enforcing the pure food laws, with the exception of milk inspection which was more vigilant. To combat such terrific obstacles to health and well-being, the Association for Improving the Condition of the Poor and other charitable groups ceaselessly agitated. They were helped by a growing familiarity among the medical fraternity and some of the public with the habits of germs and the uses of antitoxins, quarantine and isolation hospitals. Continual propaganda gave people a personal, selfish interest in their own cleanliness.

After the Gulf Coast epidemic of yellow fever in 1878-1879 extended north into cities of Kentucky and Missouri, twenty-seven commonwealths roused to the necessity of State Boards of Health. These agencies made possible a more or less systematic campaign against city ills. Meanwhile Jacob Riis, with his *How the Other Half Lives* in 1890 re-awakened the public conscience. This New York *Sun* reporter "gently led and fiercely drove" a tenement commission into decisive action. Hospital dispensaries, wards, clinics and ambulance service began to help share the burden of the sick poor; and beginning in 1881 the American Red Cross under Miss Clara Barton undertook to provide emergency care and rehabilitation in sudden, wholesale, disaster.

A permanent threat to health in the cities was the large scale organization of commercialized immorality, which built up its intercity white slave traffic, and its tie-ups with liquor interests, corrupt politicians and black-mailing police. Its exploiters profited by the fact that the city aggravated the temptation both to enter the profession and to patronize it. Periodic investigations like the Parkhurst-Lexow in New York and the Stead in Chicago (1894) could accomplish little, as long as the general public—women as well as men—accepted the double standard. Immorality was increasing in amount, but it was not spreading widely and moral standards in America averaged higher than abroad, with ostracism a feared punishment.

Not less pressing was the movement for temperance. City living, with its heavy strains, increased the desire for alcohol as a means of release, especially as the saloon served as a sort of poor man's club; also, a habit of daily drinking was brought over from many sections of "the old country." Brewers and distillers expanded their market further by large scale organization and clever development of saloon appeal through free lunch and other features. The number of persons employed directly in manufacture and distribution, the number of industries indirectly involved in liquor profit-taking, and the splitting of profits with corrupt politicians, the police, criminals, and vice rings made the liquor business almost impregnable in the cities.

The capital invested multiplied in the twenty years almost four times and annual consumption per capital more than doubled; growth in number of teetotalers was offset apparently by increase in drinking to excess. This built up the dry movement. It had originated with rural people and with the Methodist, Baptist, and Presbyterian churches strongest among them; now abstinence societies were established by Protestants in most of their city churches, while Catholics had their own Total Abstinence Union and appealed (1884-1885) to their membership to get out of the business. Large scale organization of the drys was perfected under the leadership of Francis Willard who, becoming president of the W.C.T.U. in 1879, welded it into a strong, modern weapon. Subsidiaries were established in every community; emphasis was shifted from moral suasion for individual abstinence to wholesale legal prescription against sale.

In defence the wets had to form their own National Protective Association (significantly omitting the word "liquor" from their title). Unable to get much effective statewide prohibition, the drys forced widespread experiments in the effects of high license. The result of this was disappointing. They failed to put the Prohibition Party in the electoral column, or the woman suffrage states in the dry column, or prohibition in the Constitution. But they secured local option in a great many rural villages and counties of the Middle West and South, and they forced the legislatures of all but two states to make temperance instruction a compulsory part of the common school course. Finally, in 1895, the Anti-Saloon League took over a twenty-year task of belaboring the national government.

Closely connected with the temperance movement was an effort to discourage crime, which found its large scale development in New York and ten other of the greatest cities. The frontier might still have its picturesque desperadoes, like Billy the Kid and the James Brothers, but they—like the frontier—were a passing phase. The permanent school for crime, and its shelter, was in the large city. With the city it grew, flourished and sent its influence ramifying into the life of children and grownups all over the land. Between 1881 and 1898 the absolute increase in murders and homicides was more than sixfold, the increase in proportion to population more than fourfold. In other "civilized" countries criminality was declining. Americans, however, did not feel particularly disgraced by lawlessness.

The period started with an American prison population of which one-fifth was under twenty. American-born children of Irish and Italian immigrants, lacking respect for parents who knew less of English than they, and lacking homes from which they could unconsciously absorb a knowledge of American traditions and laws, went out into slum streets to play. There they took for childish imitation bad practices of older people around them; and slipped into the corner saloon to display their antics, satisfy their curiosity or get liquor to carry home for the family.

They might observe the deference accorded robbers like George L. Leslie, credited with four-fifths of the nation's bank burglaries of the early 'eighties. They might hear men talking of how some of the new inventions could be adapted for use in crime. All about them was the ceaseless moil of restless slum life, day and night.

If their father, uncle, older sister or cousin "got caught," the children learned that the police or the judge might be "fixed" with the help of the political boss in the ward, or that the same crime might carry a different penalty in different states, different courts, or on different days in the same court. If a relative did go to prison, they learned that wardens were politicians too, that rules were stupid and hard, and that prisonmates boastingly gave full instructions for successful crimes. Thus was the experience of punishment thoroughly divorced from a respect for justice.

A novice in crime soon learned that the law-abiding majority were more his prey than his enemy, for the nation long retained its post-frontier tolerance for violence. Tolerance was abandoned for investigation and reform only under the strongest provocation and briefly; for organized crime could be crushed only through eternal vigilance by the majority of the electorate, and they would not continually interrupt their individual pursuit of gain and pleasure with the arduous duties of social responsibility. Even the tramp-hobo nuisance required for its eradication more thought and outlay than the railroads or rural folk cared to give it. Tong, gang and black-hand rivalry sometimes killed off criminals whom the police did not eliminate. Public tolerance of the maintenance of crime was encouraged somewhat by automatic protection due to inventors and manufacturers of yale locks, burglar alarm wiring and street police boxes. Real advance against criminality was made by establishment of free, intercity exchange of rogues' gallery pictures, and by the recording of the exact measurement of criminals, under the Bertillon system.

A thoughtful few in this period attacked the problem of crime from the angle of reform rather than retribution and, organized as the National Prison Association, established reformatories in nine states for segregating young culprits and liberalized also the treatment of older convicts through plans for probation, parole, state farms and sanitary construction of cell blocks. The number of federal crimes subject to capital punishment was reduced from eighteen to three; and New York pioneered in electrocution. Unfortunately, efforts to help prisoners by keeping them employed were hindered by union opposition to prison-made products; and the city and county jails, with their indiscriminate mixing of old and new offenders remained perpetual schools of crime, sending innumerable graduates out to become habitual criminals.

This was but another evidence of the complexity of social problems growing out of the evolution of urban and industrial society. The public conscience had to be much more sensitive and alive before social sores could be healed. While urbanization had to its credit appreciable advances in education and culture, it had to its discredit alarming increases in poverty and crime. With these contrary and inseparable trends politics was closely identified.

CHAPTER XXIII

LARGE SCALE ORGANIZATION IN POLITICS

The impetus toward large scale organization which in this period powerfully affected Americans, economically and socially, no less affected them politically. The forces upsetting politicians were many and mighty, compelling organization of an unprecedented size and complexity upon both the major parties.

Gigantic Problems Facing Politicians

To the sheer increase in number of voters, caused by growth of population, was added increase in the breadth of area to be controlled, caused by establishment of new states, and increase in the density of voters, caused by city crowding. To these were joined growing complexity of life in all areas, as new inventions marched in to overwhelm old occupations and raised a babel of voices where formerly local constituents had fairly agreed as to what to expect of their congressmen. Politicians competed fiercely for the favor of the new economic groups, while their ears were assailed also by loud-voiced racial and sectional demands. Politicians became prey to organized pressures as never before. No party long could retain power which awkwardly juggled the political effects of diverse oddments:—such, for example, as the effects of barbed wire fencing in the cattle country, machine manufacture near Chicago and Anglophobia among Irish New Yorkers.

Organization must be carefully perfected indeed, to handle such wide confusions. National party lines must be maintained, with an infinite variety and inconsistency of appeal, down from national into state, county, city, and ward elections. For such organization a large purse was indispensable, to meet both the recurrent costs and campaigns and the uninterrupted outlays of permanent organization. The politicians had to run machinery with two delicate systems of gears: one set adjusted to persuade the masses to continue national support in spite of conflicting interests of sections and classes; the other capable of satisfying at least a minimum of the demands of men with more dollars than votes. This required intelligence and integration of no mean order. Failure brought political destruction.

At the same time, the rewards for those who should best perfect their national political organization loomed gigantic, for whatever party won power would possess an economic influence wholly unprecedented in range. When in control at Washington, it could direct legislation into the very nooks and crannies of the nation:—into the crevices of burgeoning manufacture through tariff provisions; into the boundless store of known and dimly guessed natural resources through laws affecting exploitation of such things as coal, oil and lumber; into the bloodstream of national economic life through measures governing mighty public utilities like the transcontinental railroads, steamship combines, telephone, telegraph and electric power. Thus were politicians crowned potentates, whether they received their investiture with a sober sense of responsibility or as an opportunity for blackmail.

Whichever their attitudes, the politicians who strove to perfect organizations, large enough to function in dealing with ever larger forces, worked without the inspiration of generally accepted high ideals of public service. Business ideals of control for gain continued to dominate thinking in most avenues of life during this period. Blinding disparities of race, language, religion, economic and sectional interest were delaying that national likemindedness which is necessary before the general electorate can have a wide vision of the common weal.

Would-be reformers contended with a farflung electorate neither well informed on the true course of events nor easily aroused for "righteousness." Voters were preoccupied usually with personal advantage and wealth getting, and accepted a like usual preoccupation in other walks of life. Although they proved less tolerant than formerly of political corruption in the highest individual offices of the nation, they moved with painful slowness against forms of graft which organized on a wide scale to filch funds from city, state and nation. Only very gradually did it become possible to say that the majority were no longer amoral, politically.

As individuals, people in the United States took democratic privileges for granted, but ignored their obligations as voters in a democracy. They themselves had a supreme confidence in national abundance which made them wasteful of resources; and therefore they the more easily condoned waste among politicians. They expanded the popular adage, "All's fair in love and war" to read "All's fair in love, war, business, and politics"; therefore they customarily treated business dishonesty as a necessity and political dishonesty as a joke. The South as a section did not exert its influence for ideals of public service, for it was obsessed with separatism, denying the obligation to function in a widening field which its states rights tradition held should be kept narrow.

In the nation as a whole, industrial leadership rather than statesmanship won the loudest acclaim; the amassing of wealth rather than the doing of service spelt highest distinction. Therefore people of superior executive ability were repelled from politics and attracted to promising industries, although the one stood much more in need of constructive and imaginative talents than the other. Thus Carnegie and Frick exercised and developed their abilities through acquisition of millions in organization of the steel business; Armour in meat packing; Drexel and Morgan in banking and finance; Whitney, Widener and Yerkes in public utilities.

These industrial leaders did not, in the last analysis, face responsibilities or opportunities as large as those facing the politicians; but the industrialists nevertheless held themselves as superior to the politicians, whom as inferiors they would use and control, raise up and destroy according to their usefulness to industrial potentates. Often those politicians who were not cowed as individuals were overborne by a majority facing the other way, especially when interests hired newspaper editors as well as politicians to direct public opinion. Persistent agitators for high ideals of public service were relegated to the sidelines as editors or to minor political positions divorced from lawmaking. Organized groups preyed on politicians as never before.

The politician who managed to retain public office over a long period of years oftentimes was referred to as "keeping his feet in the trough"; but it is scarcely fair to class him with swine. He had the almost insuperable task of aligning a diverse population and had to struggle desperately to grasp the concept of size as it faced him continually in national legislation. He had been trained, perhaps, as a lawyer or business man, to deal with businesses amounting to ten or twenty thousands of dollars; in Congress he had to handle matters involving millions of dollars. Or perhaps he was in reality retained in Congress by heads of corporations who counted upon his loyalty to the businesses in which they had invested millions and which employed thousands of his so-called constituents. In the latter case the Senators or possibly the Representatives, sometimes were granted opportunities to amass great wealth as a silent partner in these businesses.

But in either case able Congressmen seldom escaped paying an economic penalty for their political prominence. The business man in politics, like Senator Aldrich or Senator Sherman, undoubtedly would have been wealthier if he had given up his time entirely to business. His brother politician without business talent was receiving a salary of some $6,000 a year to which he added usually a little more than 10% and in a few cases as much as 25% through gainful use of his political position. But while he was getting this modest sum the entrepreneurs outside of politics were amassing millions. Most politicians observing business achievements competed to extend the necessary cooperation in legislation and to divert some of the proceeds into political profits. They too subscribed to the doctrine of "trickle" prosperity:—

let the rich, large organizations flourish, and prosperity must trickle down through the lower strata of society until even the grateful laborer received his mead. They levied on business to maintain their political machines, but they also passed such legislation as the Inter-State Commerce and Anti-Trust laws. They were not so much rascals as men dealing with the map, mixing honesty and chicanery in their objects and deeds. Somehow they contrived to preserve the republic, largely unrewarded; and democracy would be safe as long as the honesty outweighed the chicanery.

The offspring of the marriage of large scale business and politics were ill-favored, especially in the urban areas. Cities had grown too fast and conditions of living there changed too rapidly for knowledge of municipal science to keep pace. For lack of training in city government even honest officials committed colossal blunders; while the dishonest lined their pockets by the sale of franchises to the new water, gas, electricity, and trolley companies. Traffic in liquor licenses and vice protection knit the corruptionists together in a closely coordinated machine, while individual aldermen tapped private sources, by introducing "strike bills" so that threatened interests would bribe them to withdraw the bills.

It was difficult to pin responsibility upon them or oust them, when the framework of city government was kept unwieldy and they barricaded themselves behind national party labels which had no legitimate application to city politics but aroused public loyalty. The grafters themselves knew no loyalty except to their own interests. In fact, they were careful to share graft with "insiders" of the chief opposing party, so that a shift in the majority vote should not disturb the system on which they alike battened. The continuous circulation of the spoils among them, regardless of surface political upheavals, gave their system the expressive title of "the ring."

The schools of city politics in America during this period offered complete courses in corruption, so that city government became the worst in American history and the most expensive, corrupt and inefficient in the western hemisphere. At the elbows of local boodlers sometimes stood grafting members of state legislatures, who passed laws forcing cities to set up unnecessary offices, to construct unneeded public works and purchase unwanted property. Insofar as the right to pass laws governing the ever larger and mightier corporations rested with the states, their capitols were the hard-fought battlefields over decent and indecent methods of issuing stock and allocating profits.

Certain states, particularly New Jersey, Delaware, and West Virginia, became notorious for their lax standards in granting charters to shady corporations. To these capitols promoters flocked for broad grants of power which they then could exercise with impunity, in any and all of the states. Corruption of state legislators was on the whole less common than of city councilmen, partly because of farmer resistance; but in both graft reached proportions which could not escape at least temporary interference. Corrupt practices acts—written upon the statute books of seventeen out of the forty-five states between 1890 and 1900— indicated that about 38% of the state electorates could be aroused to declare the practices illegal, whether or not they remained so continuously watchful as to enforce their laws. In any case, the maze of large scale organization hid many approaches to graft, often leaving the giver unaware that he had been party to the granting of unsavory favors; lobby skills of this sort gave lobbyists immunity.

In the cities, reform was discouragingly spasmodic. Philadelphia in 1881 briefly ousted their gas ring while Buffalo was managing to elect a stout reform-mayor, Grover Cleveland, whose reform policies won him enough support to make him governor of New York in 1883 and Democratic nominee for the Presidency in 1884. In that year New Yorkers investigated Tammany corruption with sufficient earnestness to improve conditions for two years, only to let Richard B. Croker establish himself and his ring in 1886. Eight years later, Reverend C. H. Parkhurst aroused New Yorkers to a three year reform period, ended by the election of Mayor Van Wyck. A real long-time record for city government was made by Mayor H. S. Pingree at Detroit from 1889 to 1896.

Most of the other large cities meanwhile tolerated bad rule most of the time; Cincinnati had G. B. Cox, Minneapolis, Boss Ames, St. Louis, Ed Butler, and San Francisco, C. A. Buckley. At the National Capitol itself the talented A. R. Shepherd kept a real estate ring in the saddle. These organizers busily and profitably demonstrated during this period how the expanding fortunes of an American metropolis could be bent to the will of a boss and his ring.

Attack on the Spoils System

The subservience of the major parties to special interests in national legislation was due in large measure to new difficulties in meeting the expenses of those parties as national organizations; and those expenses were increased, ironically enough, by reform movements. Political leadership and the responsibilities of citizenship, curiously enough, were not stressed in the schools of the democracy, but a few capable men including such personalities as G. W. Curtis, and D. B. Eaton, E. L. Godkin and T. H. Higginson, Carl Schurz and F. A. Walker were struggling to inject the ideal of public service into current political practice. Their reiteration of reform propositions which pedestrian politicians considered "impractical" educated the public and chastened the politicians. Their continued existence forced precaution, if not purity, on both the major parties and their principal henchmen.

Beginning in 1878 their attack upon the spoils system was aided by such powerful and graphic organs of public opinion as *Harper's Weekly* and the New York *Nation*. Levies on office-holders for campaign expenses in 1878 and 1880 were so flagrant and open that the prostitution of the Civil Service became a matter of public knowledge; and after a disappointed office-seeker assassinated President Garfield the local civil service reform societies blossomed forth into the National Civil Service Reform League of 1881. Under the presidency of George W. Curtis it pressed for destruction of the spoils system; the movement was aided by incompetence among political appointees, and by the demand for scientific and technical work under government auspices. Large cities gradually passed civil service laws and sometimes enforced them.

Political Toe-Warming

Finally the Pendleton Act of 1883, drafted by Dorman B. Eaton, forbade political assessments on federal officers. This "Magna Carta of civil-service reform" stipulated a bi-partisan National Civil Service Commission to maintain competitive examinations for filling government offices under what was called the "classified list." At first only the executive departments at Washington, the larger post offices and the custom houses were to have their new vacancies filled in this manner; but Cleveland and other presidents extended the service to other departments and when a party was overturned, the departing Administration gladly enlarged the Civil Service to establish its recent appointees.

Although these were scarcely worthy motives for good acts, and although state and local salaries continued to finance many of the lesser elections, the spoils system was kept almost continuously on the defensive. New York and Massachusetts legislated for the merit system in 1883 and 1884; and the old open ballot which was so easy a device for the purchase of votes began to be displaced by the secret ballot, which forced the purchaser of a vote to trust the honesty of the man whom he was paying to be dishonest. Louisville, Kentucky, established the secret ballot in 1888, Massachusetts soon made it state-wide and the New York spoils system took refuge in secrecy between 1889 and 1895, while Theodore Roosevelt was active as a Federal Civil Service commissioner. Before 1900 the merit system had some legal recognition in such important centers as Chicago, Philadelphia, and New Orleans.

Since campaigns and permanent organizations could not be financed regularly by patronage and assessments of the spoils, party managers turned to more dependable sources, the corporations and the rich. For example, in 1888 the old bloody shirt was obviously incapable of reinstating the Republicans, and they (with Cleveland's help) eagerly seized upon high protection as a lucrative agent for victory. Similarly Mark Hanna in 1896, when the silver issue was forward, levied systematically upon leading banks for contributions equivalent to onefourth of 1% of their capital and surplus, while Bryan's collectors levied upon silver producers. The principle seemed a good one to both from the political standpoint. In any case economic questions no longer could be shunted from their rightful place in the forefront of American political issues.

The revolt against big business in politics was sponsored only in part by the Civil Service reformers. They were one element in a larger group—the Mugwumps—whose tendency to vacillate between Republican and Democratic tickets infuriated regulars like Roosevelt and Lodge. Mugwumpery was encouraged as the Republicans lost preeminence with the end of reconstruction. The Golden Age of complete consecutive Republican control of the national Congress, which began in 1861 had met a sad end in 1875. The solid South, after Hayes had removed the northern troops from their polls, could be counted upon to give its ninety-five electoral votes to the Democratic candidate and the Irish in cities like New York often followed suit. Republican leaders desperately took to twisting the lion's tail, for Irish hatred of England diverted more votes than the wildest waving of a bloody shirt, about which the new generation cared very little.

From 1875 until 1889 the Republicans controlled but one House, (that of 1881-1883); and they had even lost their stronghold, the Senate, 1879-1881 and were tied with the Democrats 1881-1883. Losses in the Senate had been more apparent than real, because certain influential Democrats were as closely affiliated with big business as were the Republican managers, and because sectionalism and undisciplined individualism fomented disunity in the Democracy, creating an erroneous impression of Republican independence of election returns. But the Republicans felt keenly the inconvenience, worry and danger in legislating across party labels. Both the major parties became much more sensitive to minority demands. At least three "third" parties appeared at every election, bidding for votes with platforms for social and political reform, thereby sharpening rivalry between the two major parties, liberalizing Republican and Democratic political promises and performance, and appealing particularly to the pocketbooks and imaginations of westerners.

Republican and Democratic platform makers aped each other and straddled the vital issues in unison. So the actual difference between the principles and performance of the two parties usually was very slight, and the chief significance of some elections was the interest of the voters, rather than genuine conflict over issues. The unheard of and never surpassed figure of 80% of the eligible voters was reached in the elections of this period and they made a questionmark of Washington. Between 1876 and 1896 Democrats won a majority of the "popular" vote in four out of the five presidential elections, although they put their own candidate in the White House only twice. They lost the election of 1880, when General J. A. Garfield defeated General W. S. Hancock, by only 10,000 votes; and the Senate that year was a tie. Between 1874 and 1896 the Democrats had the majority in the House of Representatives all but twice. Altogether, shifting votes prevented either party from controlling the Presidency, House and Senate more than two years at a time.

St. Nick's Visit to Washington

This political instability beset Chester A. Arthur of New York when the assassination of Garfield in 1881 placed him in the presidency without a sympathetic Congress. Continuing uncertainty made possible the defeat in 1884 of the outstanding Republican James G. Blaine of Maine, who had been Speaker of the House and Garfield's Secretary of State. Blaine was a magnetic, popular personality; but he had carried the reigning principles of co-ordination between politics and business so far that he had smirched himself in a railroad deal.

The Democratic candidate, Grover Cleveland of New York, by contrast was a blunt, uncompromising personality, disliked by corruptionists. His personal history included a relationship which violated American mores of domestic respectability; but the Democrats argued that Cleveland as the honest politician should enter the White House and Blaine as the exemplary family man should retire to private life. This shifting of rôles was accomplished, partly with the aid of a Reverend Dr. Burchard, who, on a New York platform in Blaine's presence and without rebuke from him referred to the Democracy as the party of "Rum, Romanism, and Rebellion." Enough Catholic votes shifted to help give the Democrats New York (by 1149 votes) and the election.[1] Rapidly the day was approaching when the managers of the major parties must confront a campaign on a vital issue.

As the electorate of the democracy gradually became aware that large scale organization was fastening them in the grip of big business, they intermittently undertook to arrest the economic process by political means; they further enlarged the scale of government functions. Their representatives in Congress expanded the everyday work of the government to include such agencies as the Bureau of Labor, the Office of Education, the Bureau of Immigration and many other new units in the executive departments. Appropriations voted for scientific and technical work in the Department of Agriculture and the Interior Department often were extremely significant. While these amplified functions were not on a scale commensurate with growing needs, they pointed the way.

Much more important was the effort, against almost insuperable odds, to extend the application of democratic theories in wider fields—fields in which strong sectional, political and economic forces long had been entangled. Varying success met the struggle to control the four primary concerns: transportation, trusts, the currency and the tariff.

Railroad Regulation

The momentum behind federal regulation of railroads had been accumulating through two decades, while the farmers, joined by eastern manufacturers and merchants, struggled to exert sufficient pressure to push back the very powerful railroad lobby. Its members were past masters in the art of corrupting local, state and national legislators. They long violated the traditions of democracy with impunity but their political activities were so deeply resented, South as well as West, that the railroad interests preceded the trusts as the best-hated foe of the commonalty. It was said that no passengers paid fares except those who could not well afford to pay.

Faced by the imperious facts of transcontinental lines and widespread railroad systems, the agitators quit advocating competition and turned to fight discrimination and rebates. These last particularly incensed eastern manufacturers, who through their tariff lobbies had acquired a skill at intimidating lawmakers greater than that of the railroad representatives. Grangers and Alliance men had their own techniques, perfected by practice on state legislatures. So, at Washington, from 1874 a series of committee investigations (especially those under Senators Windom of Minnesota and Cullom of Illinois), of bills (especially in

---

[1] Other New York Republicans who lessened Blaine's chances included his enemy, ex-Senator Roscoe Conkling who refused active support and the blunderers who staged a party banquet at the luxurious Delmonico restaurant.

the House) and of presidential recommendations (especially a message from Arthur), pointed in the direction of federal regulation.

The fact that state regulation was unworkable had been proved to the discerning by the ineffectiveness of state laws and commissions; the courts were not sympathetic and the products of American industry and agriculture were finding their markets across too many state lines. Corporations had grow greater than states. The fact had to be admitted universally when the United States Supreme Court, in the Wabash case of 1886, outlawed state regulation of interstate commerce. The Court in effect deprived the states of functions they had been performing badly and took unto itself supervision of legislation on property and labor. Even before this, considering the temper of the times, a federal law seemed inevitable; and the lowest common denominator, of congressional compromise under conflicting pressures, found its expression in the terms of the famous Interstate Commerce Act of 1887.

This historic measure forbade pooling, traffic agreements and rebates; all charges should be "reasonable" and no more should be charged for a short haul than a long one, under "substantially similar circumstances and conditions." Uniform accounting and filing of tariffs were required, and annual reports. The law read nicely, but enforced badly. The Commission had to appeal to the courts to uphold its decisions and the courts gave the law a narrower interpretation than the apparent intent of the legislators. The railroad lobby proved able to keep the Commission from obtaining real authority over them and continually checkmated proposals from agricultural shippers. Abolition of pooling spurred consolidation—through purchase, lease and stock control—almost continuously until 1904; resulting gains in efficiency were offset by loss of competition.

Silver, Tariff and Trust Bargains of 1890

A stronger attack upon monopoly was staged in 1890 in the three fields of the trusts, silver and the tariff; because events long had been building up a triple mandate for action.

Republican managers filled with trepidation by President Cleveland's popularity on the eve of the 1888 elections, had hatched two schemes to salvage their party security. First, to sew up for a long time their majority in the Senate, they expedited the admission of six new Northwestern states, so that North and South Dakota, Montana and Washington, entering in 1889, and Idaho and Wyoming in 1890, should write twelve Republican names on the Senate rolls. Thus they would enlist on their side the leaders of politics in the no-man's land of western disaffection.

Secondly, they undertook to obtain a campaign fund, adequate to put a Republican in the White House, by levying upon manufacturers with the understanding that tariff rates would be raised. This sort of bargain was agreeable to both the signatories, for there was a threat to both in a determined Cleveland demand for a low protection measure. In 1887 the President, alarmed by the increasing surplus piling up in the Treasury, had devoted his entire annual message to a demand that tariff duties be lowered. Senators Aldrich and Allison, both intensely loyal Republicans, the one of Rhode Island and the other of Iowa, drew a trans-sectional protection measure to use as a foil to the Democratic "Mills" bill. The two bills were publicized on the Senate sounding board until near election, while W. W. Dudley, national treasurer of the Republican party, organized floating voters under a scheme of wholesale bribery and the successful merchant, John Wanamaker, devoutly levied upon industry for a Harrison majority. With much aid from corruption in Connecticut, Indiana, and West Virginia Harrison won a majority of electoral votes and the Presidency. Cleveland received a plurality of popular votes.

The manufacturers proposed to collect promptly, at the first session of Congress under Harrison, that is, between 2 December 1889 and the election of 1890. But the Republicans were in .danger of proving unable to deliver the increased tariff rates, for they had an advantage of but seven in the House and two in the Senate. A few of their more extreme and shortsighted members planned to deliver through the threat of a "Force Bill" for perpetuating federal control of southern elections; but members from the West as well as the South realized that tariff increases had to be explained to farmers. They knew that anti-trust and cheap money promises were better vote getters with farmers, debtors, and large elements of the population. Out of this delicate situation resulted, during the session before the congressional election of 1890, three acts significant in the history of farmers and of all other classes in the United States:—the "Sherman" Anti-Trust, the "Sherman" Silver Purchase, and the "McKinley" tariff laws.

First to secure passage was the Anti-Trust measure. Anti-monopoly legislation had been gathering momentum throughout the country, because of a sharpened awareness of the power of large scale organization to take toll of the unorganized. Both major parties and two minor ones of 1888 adopted planks demanding either the regulation or the abolition of trusts. A House committee submitted testimony on the practices of the American Sugar Refining Company and the Standard Oil Corporation which further galvanized public sentiment. By 1890 fourteen states and territories had anti-monopoly provisions in their constitutions; thirteen had anti-trust laws.

Finally, three eastern senators (Edmunds of Vermont, Evarts of New York, and Hoar of Massachusetts) revamped a Sherman bill and it passed 2 July with but one dissenting vote. The act feebly responded to the popular demand; it declared the common law principle that trusts or other combinations in restraint of trade were illegal. Congress, however, could not destroy trusts by declaring them illegal; and the terms of the act were left too loose to apply with accuracy. The law provided no precise definition of "trust" or "restraint" and did not specify whether it applied to combinations of labor as well as capital. In reality Congress was afraid to handle this big issue and deliberately left such vital questions for the courts to decide. However, the act had real importance as an effort to regulate private property in the public interest; it was not so much the result of private pressures as of public realization of need for political action. It forced trust makers to adjust their devices somewhat to aroused public opinion.

Silver Compromises

Secondly, Congress produced the Silver Purchase Act of 14 July. It was thought of as an attack upon another form of monopoly, the monopoly of money and credit by bankers. Three classes were most prominent in securing this law:—farmers, silver producers, and debtors in general. In it were bound up bitter class antagonisms, smouldering and flaring alternately through fifteen years of a falling price level, and warring over efforts of the federal Treasury to keep United States credit on a gold basis. So much of economic and political experience was affected by the silver issue that a study of it illumines the entire period.

Expansion of the currency gradually was becoming one of the strongest tenets of the agricultural creed, for economic distress was dissolving the instinctive conservatism of the farmers as property owners. They resisted resumption of specie payments and in 1878 helped to obtain the "Bland Allison" silver law (p. 359). A minority of them, raising doubts as to the beneficent effects of laissez-faire as applied to economics and politics, had furnished the largest element in the greenback movement at its high water mark in 1878; two-thirds of the million greenback votes that year came from the Middle West and one-third from the East. Then came a temporary prosperity from 1879-1882, due mainly to shortage of foodstuffs in other countries; this helped to cut by two-thirds the Greenback vote in 1880 and to kill the party.

The new prosperity however so affected the volume of money as to encourage both the demand for more of it and the animosity between creditors and debtors. Around the campaign of 1882 centered conflicts over the currency and the tariff which were prophetic of future trouble for the entire nation. The silver purchases had proved moderately inflationary; although people would not carry silver dollars they eagerly accepted the $10 certificates based upon them. The banks worked for contraction; they sold back to the government at a premium [1] bonds on which their bank notes were based and retired the notes. The treasury published some of the figures of this currency retirement; and as the masses are hurt by contraction the bankers who caused it increased the unpopularity of their guild. This made it more difficult to pass legislation for perpetuating the national banking system in 1882, when the charters expired. Tremendous revenues, in gold and in silver certificates, piling up unspent in the Treasury, bolstered a campaign for destroying the banks through paper retirement of the government debt.

As mounting gold revenues were due to continuation of the wartime tariff rates, the protectionists came within farmer displeasure. The high duties were denounced by farmers and some urban workers as class legislation for the benefit of the rich manufacturer at the cost of the consumer, and agitation for their reduction became portentous enough to alarm both the protected interests and congressmen facing the election of 1882. Congress effectively disposed of large lumps of the surplus by extravagant pork—pork so ill-smelling that it ultimately contributed to the defeat of the Republicans that November—and shunted the tariff issue to a Tariff Commission. Its chairman was John L. Hayes of the steel industry and a majority of its membership favored protection. This commission, fearful lest the system be undermined if they did not retire an appreciable distance, advocated reductions amounting to about 25%.

After the election came the big surprise! The departing Republican majority, and Democrats from the industrial areas by the Tariff Act of 1883 gave the protected interests rates approximately 95% of those under attack. In other words, as so often happens, the lobbyists exaggerated the courage of the legislators while the legislator exaggerated the political influence of the lobbyist. Thus were the rates left high, the surplus fed continually, and the basis laid for further difficulties. Thereafter the farmers of the United States again found themselves caught frequently in the downward cycle of world agricultural prices. Their class in England, France, Germany and Scandinavia tried unsuccessfully to get relief through various Royal Commissions, tariff, currency and land laws. In the United States an exceptionally large following was built up for currency expansion.

For this there were special reasons. American farmers after 1875 were particularly oblivious to the interplay between world and domestic price levels. In their immediate vicinity the rise in the value of the dollar was forcing them to raise more bushels of wheat or corn, more pounds of beef, pork or cotton than formerly to get the dollars to pay their debts. The long-time appreciation in the dollar was accompanied

[1] Gold imports and a rising treasury surplus had so far elevated credit that the bonds went above par and other factors also made the sale profitable.

by short-time fluctuations in its value during a given year, aggravating the evils of uncertain currency and prices. Therefore farmers talked of price stabilization and of expanding the currency to check falling prices.

Confident that an expanded currency—a cheaper dollar—would bring more money for their products with which to pay off their debts, they refused serious consideration of other factors, including the possibility that in the long run a corresponding rise in other prices might put them back in their old predicament or a worse one.

The issue was further confused by its connection with foreign loans and the credit of the government. A very large part of the American securities held abroad had been dispensed there by the house of Morgan and other strong firms; the names of the leading American bankers were synonymous for "debt" and had all the opprobrium heaped upon them which a debtor likes to bestow on his creditor. The bankers' arguments against destruction of the banks, against retirement of bonds with greenbacks or silver, rather than gold, were countered by the charge that bankers were actuated by unpatriotic motives—that they were the creatures of British capitalists. The ease with which American prejudice against England could be capitalized for political purposes was never forgotten by astute politicians. Therefore Administration pleas to save the "credit" of the government by ending silver coinage until Europe should resume it, played into the hands of flag-waving inflationists.

Nor was Europe minded to aid the American treasury by entering into a silver agreement; for the Presidents who asked it at the same time lessened the chance of it. Arthur and Cleveland urged that America cease purchases of silver pending European agreement, at the same time as they demanded a lowering of the tariff. To lower the tariff, however, would remove what inducement existed for Europe to cooperate on silver.[1] Furthermore, all of the proposals and counter-proposals on silver were made against the background of the existing Bland-Allison Act. Europe knew perfectly well that Arthur and Cleveland were not persuading Congress to stop coinage—that American support of silver was likely to continue for a time to ease the silver market for them.

As the certificates issued under the Bland-Allison Act were good for payment of duties, they were bound, eventually, to displace the gold in the customs channels; but they had not yet had time to do this. The warnings of Hayes and Arthur, Sherman and Folger, that the certificates would destroy the gold reserve, on which the resumption of specie payments so arduously achieved in 1879 was based, meant little to the

[1] The lowering would mean increased exports to America and a lessened loss of gold (which loss had been embarrassing Europe) to America in the form of duties.

average citizen; and the thoroughgoing inflationists saw no need for a gold reserve in so rich a country. A fall in the value of the dollar or of government bonds peculiarly delighted the farmers as punishing their traditional enemies—bankers and bondholders. If accused of taking a narrow, class view, they pointed to selfish policies of manufacturers, railroad operators and bankers. They could show that the existing currency was inadequate, inelastic, and manipulated through the banking system in the interest of organized creditors. They argued that their only recourse against this large scale organization was to insist upon more money issued in amounts equal to the "reasonable demands" of business and trade and kept "safe, sound and flexible" by popular legislation.

Furthermore, they were conscious that many Americans in other walks of life clung to a way of thinking which was sympathetic. Debtors in industrial areas, real estate operators and other groups eager for a price rise joined farmers in emphasizing the popular, and in principle sound, American doctrine that increases in population and in business require increases in available currency. Since they did not appreciate that availability is affected by business confidence and rapidity of circulation, they placed faith in a quantitative increase, regardless of the amount of business under way. Since it was obvious that population and industry were on the increase, it was easy to argue that failure to accelerate the current rate of currency increase was tantamount to contraction. Arguments that the Bland-Allison Act increased the currency faster than population multiplied were disbelieved. They called themselves anti-contractionists, rather than inflationists, and secured wide support from millions of Americans committed to the national creed of expansion in all things.

The policy pursued by Congress amounted to the lowest common denominator of the domestic influences. The bankers won the renewal of their charters in 1882, but the coinage of silver was not ended, nor the purchase of it, despite pressure from creditor interests, from all the Presidents and from every Secretary of the Treasury, and despite the accumulation of most of the bulky and unused dollars in an idle, storage lump. Successive campaigns indicated that the silverites knew how to frighten the politicians and platform makers. They reiterated on behalf of silver the bondholders' conspiracy charges earlier emphasized by the Greenbackers. Republicans and Democrats through two decades felt compelled to equivocate.

Europe lost all notion of cooperating with America on silver, and the perpetual purchase of the metal, with circulation of the certificates through customs channels, indicated that the United States was moving ever closer to a silver standard. This trend was accelerated by the shift of emphasis from paper money to silver, as the medium of expanding currency. To many small property holders, who had been ingrained with a fear of greenbacks, inbred by their fall in value during the Civil War, silver as "hard" money—even though its intrinsic worth fell below the paper dollar—was "sound" money, in the American tradition. This made the mine-owners' lobby the direct beneficiary of national faith in expansion and in hard money.

Out of the legislative jam of 1890, especially out of the drive for tariff increases, numerous types of inflationists tried to get free and unlimited coinage of silver. They obtained instead the so-called "Sherman Silver Purchase Act," which increased the fixed amount of silver money, or the paper representatives of silver, which the Treasury was forced to inject into the channels of national life. The law of 14 July enlarged purchases from a minimum of $2,000,000 and a maximum of $4,000,000 monthly to a flat monthly amount of 4,500,000 ounces, calculated to absorb all the national production of the metal. Two million ounces of this must be coined monthly until 1 July 1891. More important, these purchases must be paid for with "Treasury notes," redeemable in "coin" on demand, reissuable after redemption, and legal tender for both public and private debts; and the Treasury was advised to follow such a policy of redemption in "coin" as should maintain gold and silver on a parity. This the Treasury interpreted as forcing the repeated redemption of the notes in gold, whenever demanded, because redemption in silver would destroy the parity.

Furthermore, as the amount of the notes could be neither more nor less than the cost of the bullion and the dollars made from it, a continuous currency expansion was effected regardless of the fluctuating needs of business or of diminishing gold reserves. A fall in the price of silver in any given month would decrease the amount of forced emission of the notes, but any relief which that might give the Treasury would be offset by the ill effects of the falling value of the silver hoard already accumulated. This was indeed such an inflationary act as a Republican, considering that party's creditor affiliations, could be moved to pass only when hard-pressed; all of the Republicans and none of the Democrats, in House and Senate, voted for it. They gave far more to the farmer and debtor classes than any important foreign government was granting, and for "purely" political reasons. They paid this high price in part return for the enactment of tariff increases denied them until something was done for silver.

The "McKinley" Tariff

The "McKinley" tariff law—the third significant measure revealing the disparity between effective organization in business and ineffective organization in farming—was enacted as a result of this log rolling war of the sections just on the eve of the election, 1 October 1890. Actually in large measure the Aldrich-Allison bill, it gave big business a vast enlargement of the protective principle; restrictive duties should not be abolished when businesses became firmly established but should remain into the far future, giving domestic manufacturers leave to set their own prices regardless of world prices.

To watchful farmers and other ordinary consumers such provisions opened an alarming prospect. The increases required sugar coating, and so duties were raised on the farmers' wool, barley, hemp, and flax; and wheat, corn, potatoes and eggs were given petty levies although these could have no important effect. To please consumers and the sugar refining trust, raw sugar was made free; to compensate sugar cane and beet planters, who produced but one-tenth of the sugar Americans consumed, a bounty of two cents per pound went on their products. A curious Blaine provision for back-handed reciprocity provided that if any countries exporting sugar, molasses, tea, coffee, or hides into the United States (where they could enter free) dared to impose unreasonable duties upon United States exports, the President could promptly retaliate with duties on the five products. This was supposed to enlarge the South American demand for United States grain, flour, provisions, and manufactures.

Unfortunately for the Republicans, the electorate of 1890 did not entirely applaud prompt discharge of their 1888 debt. All the concessions on silver and anti-trust legislation, not to mention lavish pork barrel and pension appropriations, could not save their seats when housewives were convinced—by Democratic peddlers—that the tariff had raised the price of tinware. In the Valley of Democracy were Congressmen who had been whipped into support of the schedules at Washington and now apologized for their humiliation at home. There and elsewhere were Mugwumps vaguely resentful of such blatant pragmatism in politics. The election severely chastised the Republicans; but it settled no issues.[1]

Bryan's Campaign

The ferment in the hinterland continued as the "Alliance" orators abundantly demonstrated; and Grover Cleveland in 1892 was returned to Washington to try to mitigate the consequences of the Republicans' ill-advised tariff and currency legislation. As world trade conditions were taking a bad turn, he was assured of the heaviest obstacles. Panic struck the stock exchange in May 1893 and a five year depression

[1] Only 88 Republicans were sent to the House, as against 231 Democrats and 14 Independents. The Senate was left with 47 Republicans, 39 Democrats and 2 Independents.

dragged its weary length into American experience, exposing the harsh outlines of illbalanced industry and agriculture, and putting the political sense of the democracy to severe test.

The first thought of the second Cleveland administration was to protect the disappearing gold supply of the Treasury, on which national credit rested. Cleveland drove through repeal of the Sherman silver purchase act after a terrific struggle with the silver senators, which left his store of patronage persuasion very inadequate for his tariff reduction project. The Wilson-Gorman tariff law of 1894 therefore travestied tariff reform, for the manufacturers' lobby was the strongest then in Washington and industrialization was proceeding apace in the Middle West and South. Genuine reduction by the House was transformed into near-Republican rates by a bi-partisan, protective combination in the Senate. Cleveland allowed the bill to become law without his signature.

From the abyss of the depression, in 1894, the silver issue was springing to new life, under the leadership of a political messiah. For him the way had been well prepared by the farmers' attempts to organize and by the silver producers. The 1893 repeal had not sufficed to kill the movement, for it had been sired from strong stock. The extremely able Senator Jones of Nevada (where silvermining practically ceased from 1890 to 1900) had elaborated useful arguments back in 1876—arguments which the silverites had burnished with continual restatement. An effective propaganda organization for silver had been maintained since 1889 by the American Bimetallic League. The League first battened on the drought condition in the West and then upon the nationwide depression.

That depression was exploited most astutely by one of its victims, William H. Harvey, who had lost what he had saved at ranching and prospecting in Montana and had failed as a journalist in Chicago. In 1894 he sprang to fame with an illustrated pamphlet, *Coin's Financial School,* in which he presented with consummate cleverness the arguments for free coinage. They were seized upon as gospel by hundreds of thousands of dissatisfied people. Politicians fed with their oratory an inflation sentiment which silver producers gratefully helped to finance. They had no notion that forty years would elapse before their subsidy would be restored, and under a Democratic President. The fall of 1895 it was obvious that Cleveland's party had deserted him for the debtor position and silver producers seemed justified in optimistic expectations of the Democracy.

The leaders of the free silver movement had little to fear from sober second thought upon the long-time effects of a silver standard, for among the groups to whom they appealed the immediate advantage to the debtor was obvious, and future evil was optimistically exorcised. Typical was the psychology of Nebraska, which bred three of the great apostles to the farmer in this period:—W. E. Smythe and H. W. Campbell working miracles in irrigation and dry farming and W. J. Bryan painting a new heaven and a new earth, made new by "free and unlimited" coinage of silver.

The tall, handsome, black-haired young Bryan (he was born in 1860) had caught some radical contagion from an apprenticeship in the Chicago law office of the very independent-spirited Judge Lyman Trumbull. Two terms as a Nebraska Representative at Washington during the turgid years of 1891-1895, and an editorial connection with the Omaha *World-Herald* had taught Bryan and his wife Mary that the tariff and kindred issues were but poor stepping stones to fame compared with

A "Coin" Harvey Illustration

free coinage—a philosophy nicely fitting their temperaments, talents, environment and personal situation.

Evidently they were not disturbed over the conflicting objectives of silvermen; it gave them no pause that the mine owners expected free coinage to make the metal more expensive, that the debtors expected it to bring cheaper money and the Populists expected it to pave the way for a fiat currency of paper. The point was its popularity. From lecture platforms in every section they looked down upon audiences which gave indubitable evidence of the magic and power in Bryan's oratory when the subject was free silver. They could see that it had made the widest appeal of all the Populist planks, rising to domination of that party. They could observe that leaders among southern Democrats were afraid to oppose free silver lest they lose control of the South; and that southern and western Democrats were planning to bring the entire Democratic organization under control of silverites. A convention at Memphis in June of 1895 made this doubly clear.

Through the nation, however, were many debtors who were also creditors. They joined others with conservative interests, the bankers, investors and Treasury leaders, who saw personal and national ruin in a depreciated standard. Among these the Democrats could not follow Bryan, and the Republicans could dictate a creditor gold plank to their party. When the Republicans convened at St. Louis, 16 June 1896, they were forced to abandon their habitual equivocation on gold and silver and declare themselves "unalterably opposed" to currency depreciation. There could be no free coinage of silver "except by international agreement with the leading commercial nations of the world, which we pledge ourselves to promote." They expressed their opposition in terms all the stronger, because Marcus A. Hanna, the Cleveland iron manufacturer and capitalist, had been building up his friend William McKinley for the nomination. He collected votes for him by pretending to be giving up an evasive currency plank.

McKinley's skillful balancing on the currency, while an Ohio Representative and Governor, had left enough uncertainty as to his "soundness," in the minds of eastern seaboard capitalists, to enable the astute Hanna to make sport of such anxious gold senators as Lodge of Massachusetts and Foraker of Ohio. When the various eager platform-makers had done with their real and fancied phrase-making, they had accepted McKinley as their standard bearer (with Garret A. Hobart of New Jersey as the eastern running mate), and had fabricated a platform which promised free homesteads and vague benefits from the tariff and reciprocity, but otherwise ignored the farmers' distress.

When the Democrats convened at Chicago, 7 July, they were ready to throw the words of the Republicans in their teeth. They declared themselves "unalterably opposed" to the gold standard, and demanded free coinage at 16 to 1, "without waiting for the aid or consent of any other nation." They offered the disaffected farmer and laboring classes planks against interest-bearing government bonds, national banks, high tariff, lavish appropriations, injunctions and high railroad rates. In scathing terms they denounced the Cleveland administration. They rose to a state of exultation when they heard Bryan make the reply to the Republicans which he had practised before many another smaller and less important audience:

Having behind us the producing masses of the nation and the world, the laboring interests and the toilers everywhere, we will answer their demand for a gold standard by saying to them: "You shall not press down upon the brow of labor this crown of thorns—you shall not crucify mankind upon a cross of gold!"

The convention wildly acclaimed Bryan as their standard bearer, taking the precaution at the same time to name an eastern banker and railroad director who espoused silver, Arthur Sewall of Maine, as their vice-presidential nominee.

The Democratic nominees were happily endorsed three weeks later at St. Louis by two groups. The smaller of these, calling themselves the "Silver Party," and led by producers of and dealers in the metal, hailed this "patriotic" fruition of their persistent propaganda. The larger was the Populists. As has been explained (p. 410), they had allowed free silver to overshadow their major program. When they convened, too late, at St. Louis 22 July, they were faced by an accomplished fact —the Democrats had stolen their thunder; a Populist candidate against Bryan might divide, and possibly defeat, that free coinage which Populists no less than Democrats demanded. Republicans were on hand, lobbying against such a fusion, and Democrats for it. It was resisted particularly by Southern Populists who had burned their bridges in their fight against the old-line Democratic Bourbons. Finally western fusionists, Allen of Nebraska, Taubeneck of Illinois and Weaver of Iowa defeated Donnelly and the other "middle of the roaders."

For nominee they passed over their long-time leaders and named Bryan, although they substituted the Georgia Populist, Thomas E. Watson, for Sewall. The platform became chiefly a face-saving device; first they reiterated the program for the social and economic well-being of the people which long had held their loyalty, (much of which today is on the statute books), and promised to maintain their organization for the vindication of those principles. Second they acknowledged that "the pressing issue" was financial; wherefore, "we cordially invite the aid and cooperation of all organizations and citizens agreeing with us upon this vital question." Thus feebly they attempted to describe the Democratic party as a tail to the Populist kite; and committed party suicide.

Upon so vital an issue as inflation no nationwide party could hold all classes of its membership. From the gold-standard Republican convention departed thirty-four silverites under the leadership of Senator Teller of Colorado, declaring for free coinage. After the "16 to 1" Democratic convention, gold-standard Democrats organized the "National Democratic" convention to endorse the Cleveland Administration and nominate gold Democrats, John M. Palmer of Illinois and Simon B. Buckner of Kentucky. Even the Prohibition party, which never obtained enough votes to be represented in the electoral column, sent off seceders who as a "National" party endorsed free coinage. Only the "Socialist-Labor" party, almost equally obscure, managed to avoid both a pronouncement on silver and a split over it.

America presented the novel spectacle of a whole people intensely engrossed in serious debate on money. The gold Republicans in the next six weeks had a bad fright because they proved unable to divert public interest from the currency to the tariff and the full dinner pail. They were saved by the weather and Chairman Hanna of their National Committee. Fall crops proved of a character to ease farm anxieties in

From N. Y. *Advertiser*

Which Way, Miss Democracy?

important localities: Hanna levied systematically on frightened creditor interests for sinews of war. From industrial workers votes were secured by a system of terrorism, under which they were warned that they would find factory doors closed the day after election, if Bryan were victorious. The silver mine owners contributing to his campaign could not match Hanna's finesse.

Victor Gillam in *Judge*

Don Quixote Bryan Unhorsed by the Dinner Pail

With the market and the money against him, no amount of special combinations between Populists and Democrats, or Populists and Republicans, could save the eloquent and indefatigable Bryan. He lost five states west of the Mississippi and four south of the Mason and Dixon line, which he required to offset McKinley's lead east of the Mississippi and north of the Ohio. The former Grange areas of the old Northwest, with Iowa, Minnesota and North Dakota, were not sufficiently unprosperous to follow the Populist leadership. Of the nearly 14 million votes cast, silver got about 6.25 million and gold about 7.1 million, with the electoral votes divided 176 and 271.

McKinley had the distinction of being the only President elected in this period who obtained a majority of the so-called "popular" vote. There was free silver versus sandwiches and coffee—and the coffee won.

The Dingley Tariff

Unfortunately, business did not at once endorse Hanna's victory; some factories opened on faith in the gold standard had shortly to close again. During the winter of 1896-1897 political promises again succumbed to economic forces. The tactful McKinley, from Ohio, well versed in the political uncertainties of the hinterland, and uneasy, hoisted water to both shoulders. He at once sent Senator Wolcott of Colorado on a futile European mission to investigate that elusive agreement for international bimetallism which the Republican platform had pledged him to promote. Second, in his inaugural address he stated that he considered his election a mandate (not from certain campaign contributors but from the electorate) for immediate tariff legislation; he promptly called Congress in special session, 15 March, to fulfill this pressing obligation.

The economic and political situation made inevitable an extreme protective tariff. Business interests which had submitted to Hanna's systematic levies for the Republican exchequer, especially manufacturers, were impatient to collect on their political investments. Exporters wanting renewal of negotiations for reciprocity to enlarge their foreign markets also clamored for tariff action. With Democratic opposition thoroughly discredited by that party's increases in the Wilson-Gorman Act, and by Bryan's dramatic defeat over silver, little chance remained for effective opposition to an arrogant attitude. Also the fiscal situation, with the federal treasury's deficit mounting annually since 1893, lent to upward rates the appearance of budget necessity, a necessity quickly ignored in setting prohibitive rates.

Some of the party's leaders did not wish to ignore the fact that the country at large supposed the election had been fought over the currency. They had made pledges against extreme protection to gold Democrats who helped elect McKinley but opposed high tariff. They paid polite attention to Wolcott, Chandler and other international bimetallists of their own party who did not know how the Klondike and South Africa would quiet their fears and therefore were scheming to entice France into a bimetallic agreement by giving her tariff concessions. Meanwhile Chairman Dingley of the Ways and Means Committee and Speaker Reed, both of Maine, used the majority machinery of the House (which the Republicans had won in 1895), during the short session, to prepare for quick enactment a tariff which was little more than a restoration of the McKinley rates.

As finally enacted, the tariff of 24 July 1897 raised the average level to a new high of approximately 50%, regardless of any pledges to the contrary. The map made the method ridiculous. The American system of determining rates, by committee hearings of interested parties and by trades between senators, revealed its preposterous effects when thoroughly applied to the vast, conglomerate reaches of the United States. The plains and mountain areas of the West, through their fourteen members of the Senate secured concessions beyond the reach of their paltry House membership. Their senators proved apt pupils of eastern members in the art of pressure politics.

The tendency of western-eastern trades to raise rates beyond reason was best demonstrated by vital schedules of food, clothing and metals. In the wool schedules, sheepmen of Ohio, Michigan and Pennsylvania obtained increases on combing and clothing wools, the herdsmen of Montana, Wyoming and Idaho (natural competitors of the other states) received increases on carpet wools; and the woolen manufacturers of the East and elsewhere were "compensated" with increases on their finished products. Similarly with shoes; cattle interests obtained a duty of 15% on hides, which had been free since 1872 and manufacturers using leather received "compensation." The sugar schedule was a group of compromises arranged to satisfy the conflicting interests of western beet-growers, Louisiana cane-growers and the American Sugar Refining Company which enjoyed a near-monopoly of refining in the United States. Thus did the producing and manufacturing interests of varied sections impose double levies on 75,000,000 consumers.

The metal schedules gave western senators a restoration of the duties of 1890 on lead and lead ores. There was little pressure from iron and steel manufacturers, however, because earlier favors and improved mechanical processes had placed them in an easy position to meet British competition.

Campaign pledges for reciprocity were met in part by three provisions. One stipulated, in effect, that if Latin American countries discriminated against American goods their tea, coffee, tonka beans and vanilla beans would be taken off the free list; this led to treaties favorable to the United States. Another, authorized the President to reward concessions with reductions on such things as brandy, wine, pictures and statuary; this brought agreements with France, Germany, Italy, Holland, Portugal, Switzerland, Spain and Bulgaria. A third empowered the President to make treaties—with Senate approval—for reductions up to 20% on all articles; but when some eleven treaties thus negotiated had been rejected by the Senate, it became clear that reciprocity sentiment could not prevail against Senate backscratching. The Republican party's "backhanded reciprocity" was a temporary response to demands for world markets, rather than a permanent success in obtaining those markets.

Business stubbornly refused to leap into emphatic prosperity at the touch of the Dingley rates; and early in 1898 some Republican politicians felt concern over those fall elections which from the further distance of 24 July 1897 had seemed so safe. Tariff prosperity like Bryan-defeat prosperity, failed to come up to expectations. Early in 1898 silver senators, their power strengthened by six Populist victories in 1896, and by the slow recovery, showed themselves still powerful; they put through the Senate a resolution that the government had the option to pay its bonds in silver dollars and that to do so was no violation of public faith; also with the help of twenty-five third-party men elected to the House in 1896, they forced into the war revenue act a provision directing the Treasury to coin monthly not less than one and one-half million silver dollars out of the bullion accumulated under the Sherman Act. Boss Brayton of Rhode Island sent Senator Aldrich, who with great men of business was opposing needless interference in Cuba, an earnest plea for a war to save the fall elections. He did not persuade the Senator, but other conditions (p. 477) ensured hostilities and by the time the war had reached its quick and successful conclusion trade was definitely acknowledged to be better.

The difficult job of recovery was being accomplished mainly by natural resources. Gold discoveries in Australia, the Klondike, and Nome areas of Alaska, and the Rand section of Africa proceeded to inject enough new activity into lagging world business to hasten prosperity in the United States. To agriculturalists rains and good crops brought comfort. To the fagged nation at large emotional and moral stimulus was provided by the Spanish War.

The sense of national well-being was reflected in a victory by banking and commercial interests, after the 1898 election had returned to the Republicans that control of the Senate they had lost in 1892. By making concessions valued by the small fry among bankers, they obtained the so-called "Gold Standard" Act of 14 March 1900, which was supposed to administer the *coup de grace* to silver agitation for all time to come. This law declared the gold dollar the standard of value (as indeed it had been since 1834), and provided for redemption of paper in gold, without special legislation by Congress. It stipulated a minimum treasury reserve of 100 millions—granting the Secretary of the Treasury authority to sell short-term bonds whenever ordinary gold receipts should be inadequate to hold the reserve at that figure—and gave permission for a reserve of 150 millions. Small bankers were gratified by a reduction, from 50 thousands to 25 thousands, in the capital necessary for establishing a national bank; and the profits of all bankers were raised by an expansion in the permissible bank note issue, from 90% to 100% of the government bonds purchased to secure the issue privilege of note issue. It appeared that the currency, at least, had been settled for all time. Although politics is a kaleidoscopic profession, lawmakers, being human, fool themselves with static hopes.

At the close of the century, therefore, the Republican party, representing the new tendencies toward large scale organization, business dominance and centralized control, was back in power. It is easy to decry the collective cupidity, cowardice and short-sightedness shown in the politics of 1878-1900. But such judgment is hardly fair. The politicians who had to formulate policies to meet the unfamiliar emergencies of this age with its new sectionalism and its preoccupation with large scale organization probably were no more unintelligent or grasping, in the long run, than the voters who elected them or the corporation directors who so frequently dictated to them. In their United States, the new sectionalism was breeding new interests and antagonisms and the all-pervasive urge to organize in a big way was setting up aggregations of wealth and power which in the last analysis victimized their creators. The history of the democracy during these years is the history of the swift creation of these forces and the slow realization of the need for their control.

CHAPTER XXIV

AMERICA'S APPROACH TO IMPERIALISM

The nature and extent of America's excursions into the field of foreign relations, between the Civil War and the end of the century, were determined in the main by two influences:—the nation's economic status and the attitude of her people. England, France and Germany, during the last third of the century, were engaged in an outburst of rival imperialistic ventures, reaching out for supplies and markets. The United States, however, was slow to join them. Her doubling population had made ample room at home and ensured an expanding domestic market for her products; her resources provided abundant raw materials; her phenomenal development brought tempting opportunities for internal investment of her savings. Witness her production of huge surplus crops and her development of large scale manufactures behind tariff walls. The urge for national prestige found much satisfaction in safe, domestic achievements.

Liquidation of War Issues

The popular attitude of aloofness was endorsed by a highly preferential position, which gave Americans a considerable sense of security and superiority. Safe remoteness from attack and dangerous alliances seemed guaranteed by two oceans. Economic independence was underwritten by that wealth of agricultural and metallic resources which gave the United States richer prospects of prosperity than any other nation then could anticipate. Political superiority was attested by a Union victory which had demonstrated conclusively that the American experiment in democracy could withstand even the acid test of prolonged civil war. The sense of pride in America, which was the heritage of her revolutionary descent, burned the fiercer in the immigrants who had fled from a worse to a better situation. Economic facilities and national attitudes ultimately would develop into influences toward war on a grand scale; but before 1890 they on the whole continued to insulate.

America's regular international relations remained mostly routine, non-political and little-appreciated. She participated in agreements concerning the Red Cross, weights and measures, patents and trademarks, the slave trade, exchange of publications and publication of tariff schedules, submarine cables and protection of industrial property. She cooperated in polar exploration, famine relief, a meridian conference and some peace, missionary and arbitration movements. The turn of fortune in successive administrations frequently made the State Department govern its policy by domestic, political opportunism: but by each foreign engagement ties with Europe were drawn a little closer, for American economic growth pointed toward a leading political rôle among world powers of the future. In their more conspicuous negotiations prior to 1898 America's officials usually cultivated her prestige and economic gains—which are the chief concerns of international policy—along lines projected during earlier administrations.

First came liquidation of war issues. In 1863 the French Emperor, Napoleon III, had ventured into Latin America for political purposes. Against a waning prestige he schemed to win over both the clerical and republican parties, by establishing French influence in Mexico, which should glorify him as the protector of church property and the provider of opportunities for trade and investment. He essayed to set up Archduke Maximilian, brother of the Austrian Emperor, as Emperor of Mexico, counting on American preoccupation with fratricidal strife. Officials high in the French government who were speculators in repudiated Mexican bonds applauded Napoleon's purpose. But Appomattox freed Seward to protest to the French government, while President Johnson resisted the temptation to strengthen his own political position by diverting popular attention to a warlike venture. Abroad, the movement for German unity and other European miscalculations forced Napoleon III to abandon the Mexican project. This left the Archduke to die in Mexico and raised American prestige through Latin America.

Next in importance came settlement of the wartime dispute with Britain, where lay through this period the most serious and numerous conflicts. Although Britain's ministerial rule was something of an approximation toward the American ideal of self-government, the traditions of Anglophobia nourished by the Revolution, the War of 1812, trade disputes, fishery quarrels and Celtic immigrants, made it profitable for hard-pressed politicians recurrently to twist the lion's tail. Yet, the two powers managed to continue that policy of mutual conciliation which since 1815 has permitted the settlement of all Anglo-American disputes either by arbitration or (in the case of the Isthmian and Panama Canal questions) by diplomacy.

Americans of 1865 and after resented not only the accumulated prewar differences but also the losses inflicted upon the Union cause and the merchant marine by the Confederate cruisers—the *Alabama, Florida, Shenandoah* and other vessels—built, equipped and manned in British territory. The damages, according to Senator Charles Sumner of Massachusetts, chairman of the Senate Committee on Foreign Relations and persistent schemer for Canadian annexation, were huge. For her part, Great Britain was faced by serious complications in Europe and the Far

East: she well realized her need to destroy the bad precedent she had created, for she was bound to suffer if the United States should perform a like service for Britain's enemies. Therefore she listened sympathetically to Secretary of State Fish, when President Grant's obsession with a Santo Domingo scheme left the Secretary relatively free to urge a reasonable settlement. He asked that Britain express regret, make an acceptable declaration of the principles of international law involved, and pay the claims for the vessels' depredations.

A Political Pastime

Britain duly expressed her regret, for failure to exercise "due diligence,"[1] in the great arbitral convention of 1871 known as the Treaty of Washington. This treaty, irrigated through the Senate by a flow of champagne, registered the sensible determination of both governments to settle peaceably accumulated differences. It announced reciprocal agreements on fishing privileges, use of rivers and canals and bonding of goods; more important, it entrusted other issues to arbitrators. Under it, the German emperor determined the Puget Sound boundary favorably to the United States, and a commission of five—an American, a Brazilian, Briton, Italian and Swiss—conducted the famous "Geneva Arbi-

[1] America expected the rules of due diligence would be included in an international code, but they were not so accepted until the Second Hague Conference of 1907.

tration." That court (with the British member dissenting) awarded the United States 15.5 millions for the Confederate cruiser damages, while a general claims commission and a Halifax fisheries commission, sitting under the same treaty, allotted Britain approximately 7.5 millions in counter-claims. Thus did Britain invest some 8 millions in American good will; it paid her high dividends. The two nations, drawn together by racial and economic ties, established an invaluable habit of compromise which repeatedly hurdled serious obstacles to cordial relations.

Expansion Continued

Expansion had ever been a strong characteristic of the American people; but the war between the states had wiped out the two classes—slaveholders and merchant shippers—who might have pressed for acquisitions off the mainland. Not until after the supply of rich, free land gave out and the source of immigration shifted from northern to southern Europe (both about 1890) and investments abroad grew considerable (about 1898) would the tempo of acquisition greatly accelerate. Meanwhile, Americans were content with simple protection of modest commercial interests and expansion proceeded very slowly, along lines earlier suggested.

Secretary Seward and Senator Sumner particularly led those who clung to the long-standing hope for annexation of Canada. Any cooperation of the Canadians to this end, however, was sacrificed when Fenians raided Canada and Congress tried to force her to come in by terminating a reciprocity trade agreement; Britain cleverly countered by encouraging the plan for Canadian Union which materialized in 1867 in the establishment of the Dominion, which has continued into the present.

Beyond Canada lay the territory of Alaska. Russia knew she could not defend it in case of war, and that it would be a buffer state between her Asiatic holdings and British possessions if it were United States property. Therefore, although only a few Americans, such as those interested in fishing and fur trading, had any desire for Alaska, Russia cleverly brought the negotiations (which had started in 1854) to a sudden head in 1867. She capitalized her record of friendliness to the Union during the Civil War, she attended to a few mysterious gratuities, and she received a purchase price of 7.2 millions for a territory which since that time has paid for itself more than 100 to 1.

Thereafter, Alaska furnished two fields for Anglo-American mutual conciliation:—the fur seals and the boundary. To protect the seals from complete destruction by rival fishermen, the two powers agreed to the arbitral convention of 29 February 1892 which denied Blaine's legal claims but endorsed his objective by prescribing fishing restrictions. As this still left the seals to be decimated by other nationals, it was not until Russia and Japan joined in the quadruple sealing convention of 1911 that the herd was saved from ultimate destruction, by international regulation and profit-sharing in this industry.

The Alaskan boundary became important through the discovery of gold, when Canada moved Britain to claim that the line cut across the fiords, instead of lying ten leagues within the coast line around the inlets. As this claim was not consistent with the maps of long standing, the United States was unwilling to accept a British proposal for arbitration and suggested instead a commission. The matter dragged along from June of 1898 until 1903, when President Theodore Roosevelt consented to an ostensible arbitration by a Boundary Commission of six members, with a majority of four to decide the issue. That majority was carefully picked to ensure defeat of the unjustifiable Canadian demands and so the American position was upheld.

Successive American Secretaries of State attempted to seal Anglo-American friendship with a general arbitration treaty pledging postponement of any hostilities pending action by a tribunal or mediation by friendly powers. Parliament proved willing, but the Senate was loath to give up the right to pass on particular disputes as they came up. So the treaty failed. Inconsistently enough, the United States ratified without reservation three conventions agreed on at the first Hague conference of 1899; and ten years later entrusted to the Permanent Court of Arbitration at The Hague the settlement of the long-standing and harassing dispute over the North Atlantic fisheries. In like spirit of comity, the two powers in 1914 signed one of Bryan's cooling-off "treaties for the Advancement of Peace."

Meanwhile, Seward's and Grant's expansionist activities proceeded elsewhere, without benefit of public interest. At the same time that Seward was closing the Alaska bargain before Americans were scarcely aware of it, he was advancing another step toward Asia by raising the American flag upon the uninhabited Midway Islands. At this point his annexationist proclivities were definitely discouraged by the complete lack of public interest and by an economical phase in Congress. With difficulty he secured the appropriation to pay Russia. The Senate blocked plans for Caribbean purchases—Seward's for the Danish West Indies as a naval coaling site, and Grant's for Santo Domingo, which a speculative clique urged upon him. Hostility to expansion in the Pacific was gradually overcome in the case of Samoa and of Hawaii.

The Samoan islands, another Pacific ambition of Seward's, are as important in the southern Pacific as Hawaii in the northern, because they cover the water approaches to the British antipodes. They possibly could have been acquired, up to about 1875, without serious objections from Germany or Great Britain; but American opinion remained unready. The Hayes administration, however, obtained control of the fine harbor of Pago Pago, on the island of Tutuila, second only to Pearl Harbor and Manila Bay. Next, rivalries with Britain and Germany over concessions and dummy, native kingships were resolved by the tripartite protectorate arranged at the Berlin Conference of 1889. A decade later, when Britain withdrew, taking compensation from Germany elsewhere, American interest had been raised by the victory over Spain. So, the islands were divided between Germany[1] and the United States, which obtained Tutuila and all the islets east of it.

Expansion to Hawaii neatly illustrated the imperial thrust of successive missionaries, traders, investors and militarists against popular indifference and opposition. Hawaii's location on the sealanes of the north Pacific assisted the strategists. Since as early as 1840 Honolulu had been quite familiar with New England merchandise and ministers, for traders in sandalwood and whalers followed the missionaries; Secretary of State Marcy nearly accomplished annexation, but that waited until the sugar crop tied the island to the United States. Here again, executives went faster than the electorate; five successive administrations took steps to insure that Hawaii should not become the perquisite of any other power, while other nations showed comparatively little desire to challenge American interests.

Hawaii's white population, largely descendants of American missionaries and traders, was led by a few planters who acquired ownership of about three-fourths of the private plantation lands. They manipulated the native rulers into pledges of an exchange of special trade privileges with the United States and a guarantee that no third power should infringe Hawaiian sovereignty. The Senate finally (1875) ratified such a treaty. Garfield's Secretary of State, James G. Blaine, perpetuated this policy and Arthur's administration obtained (1884) exclusive right to a fortified naval base at the splendid location of Pearl Harbor. Cleveland's Secretary of State, Thomas F. Bayard, managed to sidestep a Franco-British proposal for guarantee of Hawaiian independence.

Reciprocity brought prosperity to the sugar growers through near-free trade with the United States, which by 1890 bought 99% of Hawaii's exports. The growers tired of their continual struggle to protect their monopoly of the island's resources from the political ambitions of native rulers sensitive to the aspirations of natives, white laborers and coolies. The McKinley tariff deprived Hawaiian sugar of its preferred position and the next year Queen Liliuokalani ascended the throne with the firm intention of breaking American ties. Soon the United States Minister John L. Stevens was conniving with the growers, who deposed "Queen Lil" and prepared a treaty of annexation which Secretary of State Foster signed. Then Harrison lost the election to Cleveland, who

[1] The New Zealanders obtained Germany's share during the World War.

exposed the scheme, withdrew the treaty and tried to reestablish the somewhat bloodthirsty Queen. She tactlessly refused to spare the heads of the conspirators and they set up a new republic, under a constitution authorizing annexation when practicable. They made their republic a going concern, forcing recognition from Cleveland's administration and thereafter from other governments, while waiting a change of party at Washington.

Senator Lodge and other annexationists stressed the importance of Hawaii to a future isthmian canal and the danger of Japanese control until McKinley, 17 June 1897, hurried a new treaty of annexation to the Senate. But that body was so uncertain on outright imperialism and farflung naval stations that a ratification majority of two-thirds did not appear. Not until the Spanish war and Hawaii's eager tender of her facilities for a naval base, did they achieve their object. Even then they accomplished it, 7 July 1898, only by using a joint resolution of annexation, patterned after the Texas example, requiring only straight majority votes. Two years later Hawaii was made a fullfledged territory, eligible for statehood, with its polyglot population, largely Malaysian but including Orientals also, made citizens of the United States.

Supporting the Monroe Doctrine

Toward Latin America the basic policy remained normally one of peace. Through many years most of the republics to the south were for all practical purposes further from the United States than was all Europe. As the United States grew in economic and political importance she assumed bolder leadership and promoted commercial relationships; but her investment stake was not yet large enough to attach a severely dictatorial amendment to the Monroe Doctrine. The only approach to war with a South American republic came when an Irish-American minister to Chile, Patrick Egan, allowed his anti-British sentiments to place him on the minority side, in a Chilean revolution of 1891 which enjoyed British support. The victorious revolutionaries, incensed at Egan, attacked sailors ashore from the *U.S.S. Baltimore,* inflicting a few casualties. Secretary of State Blaine, fortunately, exercised restraint and the *Baltimore* was called home. After investigation, apology and reparations were demanded of Chile; she tendered them upon a change in the personnel of her government.

The gratifying rôle of arbitrator came readily and frequently. The United States helped to bring to a legal end in 1871 Spain's prolonged war with the Pacific Coast republics of Bolivia, Chile, Ecuador and Peru. President Hayes acted as arbitrator on the Argentine-Paraguay boundary; President Cleveland on that of Argentine-Brazil; W. I. Buchanan (American minister to the Argentine) on Argentine-Chile;

and the controversy over Tacna-Arica, which from 1883 divided Chile and Peru, was finally settled some forty-six years later through the good offices of the United States.

The more vigorous rôle of sponsor of western democracy, as against European autocracy, well suited the government which had proclaimed the Monroe Doctrine. The rôle was best glorified in the Brazilian incident. When a bloodless revolution in 1889 overthrew that Empire, the United States was the first government outside Latin America to recognize the new republic. European powers, however, extended aid four years later to the monarchists, who seized the Brazilian navy and undertook to reestablish themselves. Cleveland refused to recognize them and United States manufacturers dispatched munitions for the republican forces. Germany had many nationals in southern Brazil, did not realize how rapidly the population was being welded into one nation and particularly feared the republican government might displace German with United States influence. British battleships joined hers in a blockade to prevent delivery of munitions to the republicans. Thereupon, the American admiral took a firm stand prepared to attack, the English ships withdrew rather than antagonize the United States and the German vessels, left alone, retired. This signalized defeat of the monarchists; it won for the United States the friendship of Brazil and a higher respect abroad for the Monroe Doctrine.

Not so glorious was the exploitation of the Monroe Doctrine in Venezuela. When gold discoveries during Cleveland's second administration made the line between Venezuela and British Guiana important, Britain claimed a boundary which would have increased Guiana's area about 40% and Venezuela counter-claimed at least half of Guiana. Britain was not particularly moved when Venezuela broke off relations and Cleveland recommended arbitration. But during Cleveland's second administration domestic discord tempted him (as it did other Presidents) to seek compensation abroad, especially as British seizure of the Nicaraguan customs to secure payment of a claim had aroused resentment. A joint congressional resolution of April 1894 supported Cleveland in another plea for arbitration. A year later, while a declaration of war (which would much embarrass the United States) by Venezuela against Britain threatened, the President permitted Secretary of State Olney to make an extremely brusque demand for arbitration, with the assertion that the Monroe Doctrine was involved. Olney rashly declared it had become a "Doctrine of American public law." "Today the United States is practically sovereign on this continent and its fiat is law upon the subjects to which it confines its interposition."

To this undiplomatic language and farfetched assertion, Britain waited for months before making reply that the imposition of arbitration by the United States was unreasonable and unjustified by international law. Thereupon Cleveland with congressional support, and confident that British consent was near, created a fact-finding commission whether Britain would or no. A few sensible leaders on both sides opposed war but jingo sentiment was strong. At this strained juncture came the Jameson raid into Boer territory; and the aggressive, congratulatory telegram from the German Kaiser to the Boer leader, Kruger, revealed German hostility to British colonial expansion. London was moved to conciliate Washington with an arbitration tribunal; it decided mainly in Britain's favor. Ever since, with an eye for an ally against other powers, she has avoided intrusion in the American hemisphere.

Olney's assertion that the United States was "sovereign" over the continent harmed such beginnings of cordial relations with Latin republics as had been cultivated. Primarily interested in export markets, Blaine had sought to check the infiltration of European influence into Latin American trade and politics, by inter-American treaties of reciprocity and arbitration. But the delegates of the 17 Latin powers who accepted invitations to the first Pan-American conference, convened at Washington in 1889, would not ratify Blaine's propositions except to agree to establishment of an information center, the International Union of Latin American Republics. It became the Pan-American Union, which Andrew Carnegie housed in a palatial structure in Washington. Pan-Americanism proved a tender plant, easily wilted by southern fear of northern aggression.

The ease with which United States exploiters secured control of Mexico's resources from the eagerly cooperative President Diaz (in office thirty years) was bound to add to Latin suspicions; nor did trade expand sufficiently to allay them. Between 1860 and 1900 the percentage of total United States imports from South America grew from 9% to 11% but exports to South America fell from 4% to 2%. Reciprocity treaties negotiated under the tariffs of 1890 and 1897 were blasted by protectionist influence in the Senate lobby. British and German salesmen proved better than Americans at studying the southern temperament. Most important, the period closed with a dramatic expansion of northern political power down into the Caribbean, verifying the suspicion that the United States now took, from the fact of her widely separated coast lines, a command to acquire a protective sphere of domination to the south.

The Spanish War

As the 19th century drew to a close, Americans were restive. They had been engrossed in filling up the West, building railroads, exploiting resources, developing great industries, meeting demands of the domestic market and struggling with a depression. Now the frontier was gone. There was some weight of boredom with matters mundane. Without

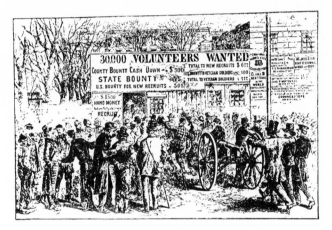

Loyalist Appeal, 1776

Civil War Recruiting Station, 1863

Recruiting Poster, 1917   The Philippines a White Elephant, 1898

WAR MAKING

realizing exactly why, people were eager for post-panic emotional outlets. Bright young men were full of activity. New York City Police Commissioner Theodore Roosevelt, Senators Henry Cabot Lodge and Albert J. Beveridge, and other ambitious Republicans, Democrats and Populists were unwilling to rest under Bryan's youthful challenge. There was a new navy the efficiency of which the staff was eager to demonstrate; and the public which had gaped at the *U.S.S. Illinois* at the Columbian exposition was growing navy conscious. Altogether here was a psychological ripeness which clever politicians could richly harvest. Trade, too, pointed sharply outward. Since 1876 exports regularly had exceeded imports every year except 1888, 1889 and 1893. Moreover, the increase in exports was more marked among manufactured articles than among foodstuffs, although the latter continued to overshadow the former; and manufacturers were more skilful than farmers at pointing out such matters to Presidents.

The direction which venturesomeness should take already had been determined upon by eager expansionists. Such men as Lodge, Roosevelt, Minister John Hay in London, Whitelaw Reid, editor of the New York *Tribune,* and Albert Shaw, editor of the *American Review of Reviews,* pressed forward the arguments of the naval historian, Captain A. T. Mahan. He preached that United States coastal defense, trade, prestige and power required a big navy, an isthmian canal, control of the Caribbean and acquisition of Hawaii and Samoa. Each need seemed inseparable from the others, with Caribbean openings wide to the eye. Sidelong glances they cast toward the Philippines and trade with the Orient. From outstanding professors of history, sociology and economics came endorsement of these views. In magazines, public speeches and private communications they were pressed.

A Cuban situation was ready at hand. That unhappy island had experienced an exhausting contest with the mother country, Spain; during their crisis of 1868-1878 Secretary Fish had been hard put to it to prevent President Grant from following Congress in recognition of Cuban belligerency. Filibusters, conveniently led by naturalized American citizens, had wrongfully flown the American flag at the masthead of vessels operating in aid and comfort to the Cubans. The summary execution of the crew and passengers of one of these vessels, the *Virginius,* had aroused a great deal of excitement in 1873 and easily could have brought war. Then the United States was in a position to have waged it with some ease and without European intervention; but public interest did not reach fever heat and Fish was able to avoid war. Exhaustion ended the revolt of 1878; they were contending against a depression greater than that behind the American Revolution. Ex-filibuster politicians found a restless refuge in New York, Florida and Louisiana, whence they established some tradition of popular interest in Cuba, whilst lobbying in Washington, selling bonds and outfitting expeditions. American investors proceeded to acquire in eighteen years a direct property interest of 50 millions, mostly in sugar, iron and tobacco; but their stake was small compared with British, German and French holders. More Americans —shippers, manufacturers, exporters and importers—were interested in trade connections, for the annual amount reached 103 millions in 1893.

By 1895 the Cubans were revolting again; to the burden of Spanish misrule and exploitation were added a serious depression with a crisis in the sugar industry. The export trade was smashed by the hard times in the United States and by the end of reciprocity, for the Wilson-Gorman tariff reimposed the 40% sugar duties and Spanish schedules retaliated. Tobacco had not recovered from an increased duty in the McKinley tariff. The Cuban-American trade dropped to 63 millions in 1895, while all kinds of property on the island were wrecked by the insurgents, who ended work operation by terrorism and levied assessments on planters. The owners hated the thought of an American intervention which should turn them over defenseless to native control; and Secretary Olney was fully apprised of their attitude, particularly through E. A. Atkins, prominent American sugar planter.

To crush the guerrillas, the Spanish General Weyler, called "Butcher Weyler," resorted to "reconcentration," placing all non-combatants— men, women and children—in a few camps and treating the remainder of the population as insurrectionists. Reconcentration later was practised by Britain in South Africa and the United States in the Philippines, but Spain lacked foodstuffs and sanitation adequate to keep alive all the reconcentrados.

Also in 1895 William R. Hearst and Joseph Pulitzer began their journalistic rivalry. The color, emotion and cruelty in the Cuban situation had high news value, and lent themselves readily to vivid picturization, manipulation and untruth, while the *Journal* and the *World* madly competed for circulation. The sales of lesser editors who bought their stuff also jumped, while other editors took up the cry on the basis of its popularity and the Associated Press lent its influence to sensationalism. Americans proceeded enthusiastically to confuse their desire for expansion with their altruistic emotions. Did not the poor Cubans need deliverance from the Spanish yoke? Would not the western hemisphere, including the United States, be better off with the Spaniards out? Thus did the yellow press come to the aid of the ardent expansionists while the public went to the aid of the Cubans.

Against this muddy current, Cleveland set himself. Considerable care and funds were expended to stop filibuster use of numerous Atlantic ports. He and Olney followed the precedent established by Grant and Fish, insisting upon protection of the treaty rights of American citizens, and tendering mediatory services. Disavowing any designs against Spanish sovereignty, they proposed mediation toward a peace based on home rule. The congressional majority, however, was less defiant of mass sentiment in an election year; they passed the concurrent resolution of 6 April 1896 proclaiming their opinion that the belligerents should be recognized and that American mediation should look toward Cuban independence. As theirs was not a joint resolution it neither required the president's signature nor had the force of law, but Madrid knew that Cleveland had lost political influence, that Republicans were less tolerant of Spanish rule, and that politicians of both parties might see advantage in a foreign diversion.

Many of the Spanish people were intransigent, knew not the weakness of their navy and threatened to unseat the government if they should compromise too hastily. Late in 1897 a Conservative was followed by a Liberal ministry which finally offered the Cubans liberal propositions approximating autonomy. The gesture came too late; loyal Spaniards in Cuba opposed autonomy as giving the Cubans control over them; the revolutionists rejected autonomy because now they had high hopes of United States intervention and independence.

Intervention was made sure—mysteriously. Hearst published in the New York *Journal,* 9 February, a stolen letter written by the Spanish Minister, Enrique Dupuy de Lôme to a Cuban friend: "McKinley is weak and a bidder for the admiration of the crowd, besides being a would-be politician who tries to leave a door open behind himself while keeping on good terms with the jingoes of his party." This was not likely to stiffen the presidential spine against a Spanish war. Six days later, the United States battleship *Maine,* which had been stationed in Havana harbor for reasons never made clear, was blown up killing 260 men. Regrets of the Spanish government over this disaster, for which it apparently had no responsibility, could scarce be heard against the hysterical American cry, "Remember the Maine!"

The Madrid government, desiring peace, belatedly revoked the reconcentration orders, granted suspension of hostilities and urged the Pope to save their faces by pleading for peace. They promised Washington to go in this direction "as far and as fast" as their public opinion permitted. But the Cubans wanted no peace, and the American public (unlike Wall Street, the Republican high command and investors in Cuba) was eager for a war of liberation. McKinley, fearful for his party leadership, reported the Spanish capitulation to Congress very sketchily, and left the decision to the popular body. It passed the war resolutions of 19 April 1898,[1] hesitating only long enough to include the famous self-denying ordinance of Senator Teller, which reflected the missionary mood of the moment by disclaiming any intention to annex Cuba. United and happy, the leading democracy of the new

[1] The Senate vote was 42-35, the House, 311-6.

world was going to war against Spain as the symbol of all old world autocracy. Only the few expansionist schemers intended the war should embark the United States upon an imperialistic policy.

The conflict proved short and decisive. With plenty of martial spirit the sea and land forces (the latter after some delay) were ranged against those of Spain in and about Cuba, Puerto Rico and the Philippines. The United States navy had a skill and aggressiveness which made it vastly superior to the Spanish armada, even with half the North Atlantic fleet left to guard the little-fortified Atlantic seaboard. The small United States army had to contend against politician-management in Washington, but showed abundant courage and resource and was aided by the failure of the Spanish Captain-General to send more than a fraction of his troops to oppose their advance. A more than adequate contingent of newspaper correspondents kept American readers fully informed of the real and fancied exploits of their forces against a weak and discouraged enemy.

Theodore Roosevelt, lately become Assistant Secretary of the Navy, had been busily laying the groundwork for just such an eventuality; he had seized the occasion, when Secretary Long was absent one afternoon from the Department, to station Admiral Dewey at Hongkong in readiness for a run to Manila. Previously he had managed to place Dewey in command of the Pacific fleet.

For his part, Dewey had established at Hongkong friendly relations with an exiled insurrectionist, Emilio Aguinaldo, who understood that his friend was pledged to Philippine independence. Aguinaldo happily cooperated with Dewey and General Merritt (commander of the land forces in that area) to defeat the Spanish. Dewey also enjoyed the cooperation of the British Captain Chichester, who effectively discouraged a blundering German admiral from hindering Dewey's operations. Dewey with ease destroyed the Spanish squadron in Manila Bay, 1 May and ten weeks later a combined attack by American naval and land forces and Aguinaldo's insurgents forced surrender of the city of Manila.[1] These victories on the other side of the world were completed 13 August, one day after the signing of an armistice at Washington.

Americans had taken comparatively little note at the moment of the unaccountable Pacific excursion. They had been excited over the war around the Caribbean. Over Admirals Schley and Sampson blockading Cuba, while the Spanish fleet under Admiral Cervera took refuge in Santiago harbor. Over the daring Lieutenant Hobson sinking the *Merrimac* in the harbor in an effort to "bottle up" Cervera. Over the fleet's long wait for the delayed army to help capture Santiago. Over the three-hundred-pound General Shafter, struggling to move troops ailing

[1] The vacant Wake Island and the Spanish Island of Guam were conveniently occupied by American forces en route to the Philippines in the summer of 1898.

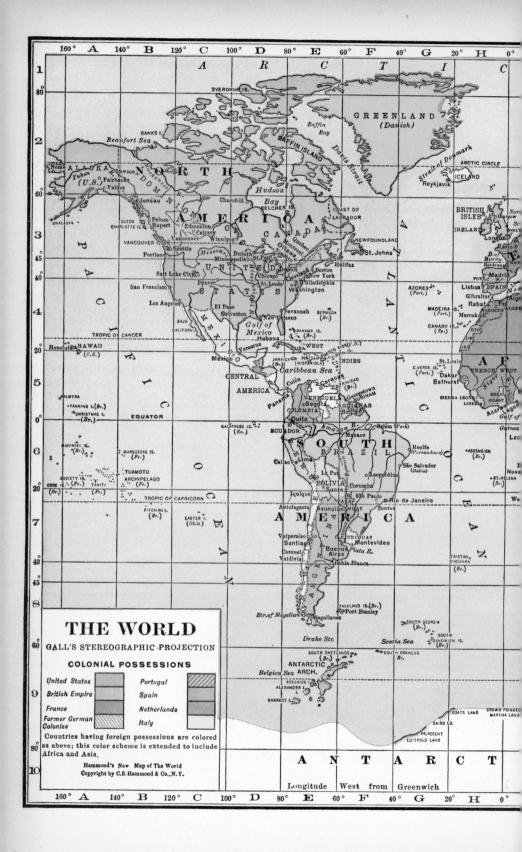

THE WORLD

GALL'S STEREOGRAPHIC · PROJECTION

COLONIAL POSSESSIONS

United States
British Empire
France
Former German Colonies

Portugal
Spain
Netherlands
Italy

Countries having foreign possessions are colored as above; this color scheme is extended to include Africa and Asia.

Hammond's New Map of The World
Copyright by C.S. Hammond & Co., N.Y.

Longitude   West   from   Greenwich

from the ill effects of winter clothing and poor food and medicine issued for summer use in subtropical territory! Over Colonel Roosevelt leading his "horseless Rough Riders." Over the army's capture of three heights overlooking Santiago, San Juan Hill, Kettle Hill and El Caney— within twelve hours of fighting. Over Cervera's escape from the harbor and the destruction of his fleet in the four-hour battle of 3 July which made for a Glorious Fourth! Over General Miles' joyful progress through Puerto Rico to the huzzas of the natives.

An armistice was signed 12 August. The crude had saved the lives of numerous Spanish soldiers, Cuban insurrectos and civilians who would have died during a dragging civil war. It is estimated to have cost, eventually, the lives of about 5500 Americans (many dead of disease, not bullets) and a total of more than 1300 millions in expense, including pensions. But these sacrifices were readily entered upon, for American expansion in the Caribbean was a logical trend, dictated by geography, and there lay public interest.

Oriental Entanglements

The terms of the armistice suggested, however, a hand pointing toward Far Eastern expansion, for in addition to certain expected Caribbean terms it specified that the United States was to hold Manila until a peace conference settled the status of the Philippines. The imperialists planned to inject American influence far eastward of its natural limits and business men dreamed of profits in the China trade. Britain was encouraging American imperialism as one means of balking Germany. The fact that Great Britain, Germany and Japan were all known to be interested in the archipelago gave it an attractiveness which was enhanced by the enthusiasm of victory.

How would the President instruct the delegates of the United States waiting upon his decision, at Paris? They had been well-chosen (unlike the Paris peace commission of 1919) for their strategic influence at home. Chairmanship was entrusted to William R. Day, who had resigned as Secretary of State for this purpose; the other Republican members were the chairman of the Senate Committee on Foreign Relations, C. K. Davis, the Senate's president *pro tempore,* W. P. Frye, and New York's most influential Republican editor, Whitelaw Reid. Senate opposition was scantily recognized by inclusion of a lone Democrat, George Gray of Delaware.

Upon the kindly and well-intentioned McKinley the imperialists concentrated their arguments, stressing civilization, morality and trade (although the Spanish government was both civilized and Christian). On these grounds he painfully reconciled himself to instructing the delegates to demand all of the Philippine Islands. Consequently, when the

Treaty of Paris finally was signed, 10 December 1898, Spain ceded all of these. With them she gave up to the United States the island of Guam near Hawaii, and the expected Cuban areas:—Puerto Rico and all of the other Spanish West Indies except Cuba, over which she simply renounced sovereignty. Also, she was forced to assume the Cuban debt of 400 millions. She received from the United States consolation money amounting to 20 millions, ostensibly for a speedy departure from the islands.

Such a treaty posed the new and fundamental question of American imperialism. Would the Senate ratify? The Anti-Imperialist League, led by Senator Hoar of Massachusetts and supported by prominent persons from all the different occupations and parties, questioned the value of the insular possessions. Why subject Americans to competition with cheap agriculture (as in beet sugar and tobacco), with cheap oriental labor and with madly extravagant imperialistic powers? The Philippines would be difficult if not impossible to defend, would saddle the United States with a heavy liability and would involve the government in the unfamiliar mazes of Far Eastern diplomacy. To seize the Philippines was contrary to the ideals of the Declaration of Independence, would violate moral obligations to the Filipinos and ensure the ill-will of Aguinaldo and his Independence Party. Indeed, they already were fighting the perfidious Merritt, as they regarded him, and would so continue through two years.

The anxieties of Senator Hoar and of the interested and disinterested backers of the League were shared by enough members of the Senate to make it possible for a Democratic leadership to deprive the Republicans of their necessary two-thirds vote. A confused Democratic leader was Bryan. He disapproved of imperialism and wanted the nation to have an opportunity to defeat it in 1900. Like many another American politician, he did not ascribe to foreign relations an importance which would debar their use as a football in domestic politics. His oratory and understanding had been spent earnestly but fruitlessly on the currency issue in 1896. Might not a crusade against imperialism save America in 1900? With the help of his advice, not yet fully explained or measured, enough Democrats voted for ratification, 6 February 1899, to save the treaty by a margin of one vote. For good or ill the United States had undertaken to maintain her influence in the eastern hemisphere, 7000 miles from her Pacific Coast and neighbor to an awakening yellow race. A new era was acknowledged in foreign relations.

THE PROGRESSIVE ERA

1900-1914

CHAPTER XXV

RESPONSIBILITIES OF PROGRESS

The Progressive Era was a period in which the American public became aware of a remarkable sense of knowledge and power. Belonging to a lusty, secure nation which had expanded across a continent, they prided themselves on past and future achievements, as never before. The sight of gigantic forces harnessed to mankind's will expanded their assurance, and their interest ramified into more aspects of their economic, social and political environment than formerly. The majority of vocal, middle-class people felt secure in prosperity, and came to think of themselves as greatly enlightened and as committed to the principle of social betterment, of progress. Such attitudes are by no means common to world history at all epochs and places. They were greatly reinforced among Americans by the rapid pulse of change, in daily living among all classes.

A New Era of Power and Communication

As the twentieth century opened, an augmented flood of inventions revolutionized industry, making intercommunications vastly easier and home life far more convenient. Water, coal, steam, electricity and gasoline were more securely chained to service—to do heavier work in settled places and to annihilate further distances on the earth's surface, underground and in the air. An intensive exploitation of physical resources and manpower stimulated production; it changed habits, spread ideas and altogether so heightened the tempo of daily living as to work effects beyond computation.

One of the sharpest impulses came from electricity; the possibilities in it now began to be more fully realized. Nicola Tesla's researches after his immigration from Austria, and those of his successors had lengthened transmission wires to more than 150 miles. At Niagara by 1900 and Keokuk, Iowa, by 1914 vast hydro-electric plants were setting a pace for hundreds of others at less favorable sites. The 2000 power stations of 1898 grew in number by 1914 to 5000, delivering current to homes as well as factories, undertaking to meet continual demands for more electricity.

Unfortunately, the resourcefulness shown in producing current was not matched by intelligence in dispensing it. Experiments of twenty years had cheapened production but the huge profits were not used so to lower charges as to expand the market and the profits to the outer limits of potential consumption. A nation which long had practiced private ownership and control of national resources would be slow to require a sharing of the gains from them. Nevertheless, electric lights and telephones moved out of the class of luxuries for thousands of families in the less affluent sections of cities and in small towns where people never before could have either lights or telephones. They became necessities for business and the middle class, increasing the output of work, and multiplying the uses of leisure.

Thanks to the inventive and managerial abilities of Alexander G. Bell and Theodore N. Vail, Americans by 1900 were using more than 700,000 telephones (more than twice as many as in all Europe) and by 1915 about 6,000,000. Long distance communication reached its farthest range in direct connections between New York and San Francisco by overhead wires in 1915. Meanwhile along the Atlantic seaboard underground wires beneath the Hudson and between the largest cities were insuring continuous service in bad weather and in spite of natural obstacles. Wireless telegraphy was proved practical over the Atlantic by 1901; and all large ships had this equipment inside of half a dozen years. An American, Lee De Forest, contributed much to this improvement.

As the delivery of current was perfected, the largest users became the trolley and elevated railroads. They aroused the enthusiasm of the riding public in the cities and between towns, and attracted the genius of engineers, financiers, and executives. Trolley tracks increased over 2000 miles annually, 1902-1907, and about 1000 miles, 1907-1912. Electric trains displaced steam railroads on the elevated lines of New York, Chicago, and Boston, beginning in 1901; and American subway construction, imitating London, came to Boston, New York, Brooklyn, and New Jersey (1898-1908). The enthusiasm for trolleys built them between most of the towns in the heavily populated areas, and threatened the fare schedules of the steam railways so that some of the latter purchased the trolley lines and electrified their own railroads. The cleaner and faster electric motor was admirably adapted to the needs of New York people.

The steam railroads continued to expand their annual mileage construction until 1907, when interurban competition and declining profits resulting from watered stock and mismanagement cut down construction. Furthermore, most of the new tracks were built to unite existing lines. Only the Los Angeles-Salt Lake line of 1905 reached out to tap new areas—important mineral deposits. As this line also cut twenty-four hours from the time of express trains carrying fruit from California to Eastern tables, it modified national diet habits. Railroads continued to reflect the ingenuity, imagination and aspiration of Americans in many ways. One symbol was pride in stations. At Boston, Washington, Chicago and Kansas City huge structures rose, while the Pennsylvania and Grand Central at New York (1910 and 1913) outshone all others in combining beauty, immensity and usefulness.

Americans in these years of prosperity demanded huge canal facilities, to offset railroad abuses and inadequate freight lines. The example of successful barge canal developments in Europe, and the Panama venture, heightened interest and made digging dramatic. Imaginations were intrigued by the fact that Panama would cut thousands of miles from the distance between the west coast and Europe, and between the east coast and the Orient. Down at the Isthmus Colonel Gorgas was controlling yellow fever and malaria; there engineers were removing a mountain in one place and building another elsewhere. Feats in canal building seemed limitless. Huge outlays, therefore, were undertaken lightly.

Although military uses were stressed in projecting Panama, commercial uses appealed more to business-engrossed Americans. Nearly 50% of the original canal mileage in the United States had sunk into abandonment heretofore, but in 1907 Roosevelt responded to the renewed interest by appointing an Inland Waterways Commission. New Yorkers enlarged the Erie canal to cheapen rates from the Lakes to the Atlantic, mindful of the fact that over two-thirds of the state lay within fifty miles of the canal. An intercoastal waterway along the Atlantic was again agitated, until the Cape Cod canal was built as the first unit of it. Illinoisans started to dig southward from the Lake toward rivers connected with the Gulf. To improve the Ohio River the national government, in one year, appropriated about 60 millions. Interest in canals, however, soon passed.

Much more influential was the automobile, for it was becoming a practical adjunct of daily life. On "horseless carriages" many minds, especially European, had been working during the past 150 years. Since 1879, when the American G. B. Seldon had obtained his first patent for a gasoline vehicle, numerous American mechanics had experimented with electricity, gasoline, steam, compressed air, carbonic acid gas and alcohol, as motive power. A gasoline car contrived by Henry Ford during the 1893 panic made twenty-five miles an hour; and many fundamental principles were embodied in a vehicle patented by Seldon two years later. With the lightening of the depression in 1897 came various successful demonstrations by Ford, C. E. Duryea, Elwood Haynes, and R. E. Olds; and by the end of the century some eight thousand automobiles were registered, nearly half of them driven by electricity and nearly half by steam.

The hard-won Seldon patent of 1895 had embodied so many fundamental principles that manufacturers who, unlike Seldon, had capital to venture, agreed to pay him a modest royalty and organized an exclusive Association of Licensed Automobile Manufacturers, to protect their patent. They successfully sued Henry Ford, and other independents, for infringement. But the latter group fought the decisions up from the lower courts until in 1911 the Federal Circuit Court of Appeals decided that they were not infringing the patent in the test cases. This signified that American automobile manufacture would be less retarded by patent monopoly.

Keen competition for profits drove rival manufacturers to breakneck speed in devising such mechanical improvements and cheapened production as should bring cars within the reach of ordinary citizens who had neither mechanical training nor large means. The low speed and narrow range of the electrics, and explosive propensities of steam automobiles, swung manufacturers toward gasoline. Mechanical difficulties which interrupted nearly every ride in the high, wind-swept, vehicle of early years gradually were eliminated to a practical simplicity. Jerky, "one-lung" motors evolved into smoother-running "fours," "sixes" and "eights." By moving the engine from beneath the car to in front of it, and by equipping it with a self-starter (1913-1914), looks and convenience were doubly served. As air-filled tires displaced hard rubber and as roads were paved motion became smooth and rapid.

American manufacturers were applying to the underlying inventions of other nationals a standardization of process which cheapened production. Ford, who had been charging from $850 to above $2000, in 1908 began progressive reductions; there came a general tendency for the manufacture of cheaper cars to increase. Total registration, of business and pleasure vehicles in America, jumped from 8,000 of 1900 to 2,500,000 by 1915, for the automobile was passing from a plaything of the wealthy to an indispensable of business and a pleasure necessity of the middle class. When an invention which is convenient also feeds the instinct for showing off, exerting power, and surpassing one's neighbor, it becomes so desirable it calls for mortgaging the home or the farm if necessary; and it becomes a powerful educative influence. Proudly families motored from the city to the country and vice versa; rural isolation was becoming impossible in many areas and suburban development was powerfully stimulated.

Increased speed of locomotion accelerated many other aspects of living. Automobiles were bought so rapidly as to surpass the increase in other manufactures. Capital invested in them multiplied about seventy times. Production and purchase were diverted from other articles. The automobile created a tremendous amount of work. Jobs in manufacturing the car itself, plus jobs in all the industries which feed automobile manufacture (such as copper, oil and steel), helped to keep the United

States free of wide panic between 1898 and 1929; for capital was being created at least as fast as the increase in population. More than any other invention since the Civil War, probably, the automobile has changed the situation and behaviour, the daily life, of Americans.

Alteration of daily living through the use of airplanes, however, waited while French, English and American inventors experimented with them as instruments of war. S. P. Langley, secretary of the Smithsonian Institution in Washington, devised models which in 1898 won a War Department appropriation of $50,000 for a man-sized experiment. He just missed success in the fall of 1903, only a few days before two bicycle mechanics who had been experimenting with gliders, Orville and Wilbur Wright, made successful flights of twelve and fifty-nine seconds' duration in North Carolina. On this encouragement, Americans and Europeans set to work anew, with the latter making most of the advances during the next decade. G. E. Curtis in 1911 made an American contribution in a successful hydroplane flight over the Hudson, and an airplane flight across the Atlantic was in preparation when in 1914 war intervened.

The cost of airplanes kept them far removed from the experience of everyday citizens, whose intimate concern was for better roads. Automobiles took up the pressure where bicycles had left off, because nearly 2,210,000 miles of road in the United States were dirt. As dirt, gravel and water-bound macadam proved incapable of standing up under automobile traffic, bituminous macadam became a standard material, until adoption of concrete. In this field, as in so many others, the initial agitation came from private sources and the movement thus started led to an expansion of public functions. Some Americans attended an International Good Roads Congress at Paris in 1908, and two years later the American Association for Highway Improvement was founded.

Long stretches of road continually in hard use proved too expensive for little, local, political units to construct and repair; so voters shifted responsibility to state governments which made appropriations and appointed highway commissions to finance and engineer the undertakings. Stronger and wider bridges made necessary by automobiles were aided by the cheapening of Portland cement. A cement craze caused its temporary use for domestic architecture and led to its use, in the form of reinforced concrete, for public and large structures requiring inexpensive fireproofing. The most obvious beneficiaries of better roads were the farmers, whose horizons were widened and living standards raised.

Rising Living Standards

In fact the greatest service which mechanized power did for the democracy was its elevation of living standards, rural and urban. To farmers came a new degree of self-confidence and hope, inspired by returning prosperity and widening opportunities. The value of farm property doubled, 1900-1910, while the price of farm products increased nearly 50%; dangers in the disparity between the two attracted little attention as long as the farmers' new assurance was endorsed by a rising standard of living. Few of them now had to live in sod houses on the prairies, for the majority, except in the South, had substantial houses, capacious barns, new equipment and improved roads. The ex-Populist enjoyed an expansive mood as he rode in a spring buggy, sat on upholstered furniture, telephoned his neighbors, listened to his gramophone and heard his daughter practice on the piano.

Of his rising status he and his associates were daily conscious, for in addition to their better roads they acquired more frequent train services, regular free mail delivery and, quite gradually, automobiles. Instead of spending two hours to drive eight miles with a load of produce, a few well-to-do farmers of 1914 could take a truck to town in half an hour. Their wives and daughters were livelier, better dressed and more interesting, as septic tanks, heating and lighting systems and new gadgets lessened back-breaking housework. New profits financed a college education for some of the young people.

It was this class of the more fortunate farm folk, and the villagers who shared their economy, who furnished the backbone of the progressive movement in the middle border, supporting bold interlopers in politics and innovations in legislation.

In the cities Americans felt most the dynamics of change. Seven-tenths of the 16 million increase in population between 1900 and 1910 was urban, that is, poured into towns over 2500 in population. Most of the newcomers were from foreign lands but approximately 3 million of them hailed from the country, sent by the new machinery which made fewer farm hands necessary, and drawn by the city's multiplied opportunities. Unfortunately, this often meant that the more intelligent and desirable of the rural people were drained off the land, leaving farm areas depleted morally and physically as well as numerically. A "Commission on Country Life," established in 1908, recognized and studied the problem but could not solve it.

Every state except Montana and Wyoming, between 1900 and 1910, found its towns growing faster than its country districts. This meant more cities in farming states as well as spectacular expansion in industrial states. Immigration and the overflow from centers like New York, Boston, and Philadelphia built up farflung suburban areas in neighboring states. Expanding markets for iron developed cities like Birmingham; autombiles built up Michigan and Ohio cities, and electricity Schenectady. California and Florida enjoyed the twin stimuli if citrus fruits and well-to-do winter visitors.

As between states, also, movement accelerated change. Over 20% of the people in 1910 had moved outside of the states of their birth, a slight increase over the mobility of 1880 to 1900. The main stream faced West. California had residents from all states and a greater proportion born outside, than since 1870. New Jersey and Florida reported the heaviest influx east of the Mississippi. Southern Negroes continued to move North and West, and the "talented tenth" joined the manual workers in this trek, chiefly to the colored districts of the great northern cities.

The city pulse was further quickened by family outside employment. As more members of each family earned their living and found amusement and mental stimulus quite outside the home it was reduced to little more than a place for hurried meals and sleeping. Meals became less in bulk and simpler in kind and preparation, thanks to indoor occupations which reduced appetites, corner delicatessens, canned goods, pure food agitation and cleverer advertising of prepared foods. Breakfasts became little more than a form, the noon-day meal a light lunch, and the main, evening meal had less meat than the old-fashioned noon-day dinner.

Home furnishings changed markedly, for the middle class. Families abandoned gradually their huge nineteenth century dwellings; building and rent costs, servant problems and shrinking families dictated more compact dwellings or division of the old home into flats. Apartment buildings in the larger cities increased in size and height with the servicing of electric elevators from street conduits, and individual apartments grew smaller. The comfortable found hardwood floors with rugs easier to clean than carpets, and improved their taste in furnishings and dress. The entire family came to accept as a matter of course improvements in heating, plumbing, bath and kitchen fixtures, and electrical aids brought through telephones, lights and home gadgets. The restricted quarters put a premium upon obviously useful things. Among the things effectively crowded out of the small apartments were guest rooms for relatives and storage space for family lares and penates. This helped to break the sense of continuity with the past and lessened respect for old standards and traditions. Also it led people to destroy family papers valuable to future historians.

In this era the family was diverted by a greater variety of recreations, for to Americans of the early twentieth century recreation was more important than ever before. The rise in numbers and self-consciousness of the urban population helped to make it so. City people feeling the need to forget their work-a-day environment found varied means for transporting themselves out of it. Their nostalgia for rural benefits could be indulged with the aid of the bicycle, trolley and automobile; and press publicity given sports was both a cause and an effect of public interest in them. Propaganda for exercise, as a means to efficiency, influenced many.

Admitting their responsibility, city governments marked this era with wide extensions of the acreage of play areas, creating park belts and systems in and near cities, while state and national governments provided "reservations" at a distance. The ambitions of such places as Boston, New York and Philadelphia, Cleveland, Chicago, St. Louis and Seattle, brought to park engineers and landscape architects, like J. C. and F. L. Olmsted, Jr., an unprecedented opportunity for the exercise of their ingenuity. Private, commercial interests, particularly trolley corporations, exploited the urge by moving to the outskirts of cities popular amusement parks, which provided not only merry-go-rounds, freaks, shooting galleries and dancing, but also large auditoriums where music and other programs were heavily patronized.

In exercise itself Americans were developing an interest which amounted almost to "an athletic renaissance," because of wide participation by all classes, either directly or as onlookers, in "championship" contests. Professional baseball with players' salaries at new highs became more commercialized throughout. To the old National League, formerly successful in killing promising competition, the American League gave a challenge which in 1903 forced compromise and stabilized the industry for the next decade. The public watched through the summer while Chicago or New York usually won the National pennant and Philadelphia or Detroit the American; then cheered and bet through the world series between the champions. Professional gamblers, however, gave their support chiefly to the horseracing carried on by the rich, while with the underworld and sporting fraternity boxing was most popular; but neither horseracing nor boxing had a large enough following to raise its repute and save it from adverse legislation.

The middle aged of the middle class now had the leisure to transform golf from a "dude" fad to an inexpensive obsession enjoyed on public links. It and motoring were the most notable additions to outdoor life of the era. By 1914 more adults were said to be playing golf than any other outdoor sport, its popularity enhanced by publicity given the "open golf championship." "International Davis Cup" contests were helping tennis to regain the popularity of which bicycling earlier deprived it; and American victory in international yacht competition with Sir Thomas Lipton made the public observe with interest a sport open only to wealthy participants.

Professionalism in college football, and play so strenuous as to cause fatalities, drew attention to the harm football was doing. Some smaller colleges depended upon it for support; others erected monster stadiums, for the benefit of sporting alumni, with funds badly needed for educational expenses. The National Collegiate Athletic Association, formed in 1906, began a long series of efforts to revise the rules, to save life and education. The reformers hoped athletic coaches could be absorbed into the faculty and the mass of the student body could be made to share in intramural sports. They built huge gymnasiums to house basketball and track teams, which broke records and won laurels at the Olympics in 1896, 1900 and 1904.

A new recreation, destined to become one of the greatest national industries, gradually was growing from the crude, animated films, which during the 'nineties had been shown in makeshift quarters for 5¢ admission. These curiosities had reached even the small towns, as travelling exhibitions. In 1905 Edison set up a rude studio for indoor picture making; and within the next five years money was invested in elaborate studios, where outdoor pictures, especially ranch plots and slapstick comedy, were manufactured for sale to a rapidly multiplying number of theatres patronized by ever larger audiences. Movies took theatrical entertainment to places formerly without it and brought to third and fourth-rate areas a rise in theatrical standards. Movies became a part of vaudeville performances, which like burlesque and light opera strongly attracted popular audiences.

Music and girls became increasingly important to the American theatre, through development of musical comedy; with its romances, foreign settings and musical scores it reached a climax of popularity in productions like "The Merry Widow," "Chocolate Soldier" and "Babes in Toyland." The minstrel shows, lacking female actors, were losing out to Revues and Follies, based almost solely on pulchritude; through these, popular songs were floated and dancing was enlivened, substituting for the two-step and waltz the tango, one-step, fox trot and turkey trot. Like the Hippodrome spectacles and cabaret shows they sold uneven talents to heterogeneous audiences. Although most actors in burlesque, follies, minstrels, musical comedies, revues and vaudeville dropped out of sight with the passing of transitory beauty or personal magnetism, some showed talents which made them long-time stars. There emerged such skilled artists as Ina Claire, Marie Dressler, DeWolfe Hopper, Al Jolson, Will Rogers, Lillian Russell, Fritzie Scheff, Fred Stone, Fay Templeton and Weber and Field.

As music and girl shows became elaborate and costly spectacles, huge profits became essential. The modest performance, formerly considered successful with $6000 to $7000 weekly receipts, lost out to musical comedy profits. The serious drama suffered most from capture of the theatre by ambitious profiteers; most of these had a minimum of that sense of artistic values which had prevented complete commercialization under actor-managers. A central booking office had been established by Daniel Frohman and others in 1896; and Klaw and Erlanger bought up many theatres. The few in control of bookings and buildings acquired the power to "railroad" a play to death with one-night stands. The Schuberts in 1900 began a competing trust which ultimately extended to some 1200 theatres and broke down Klaw and Erlanger. There were various efforts to offset materialism. An "endowed" theatre in New York failed through over-elaboration; a Drama League established in 1910 undertook to foster the better production through the support of clubwomen; a "little theatre movement," copied from abroad, increased interest by amateur participation. Percy Mackaye led an effort to restore pageantry and at Harvard and Carnegie Institute of Technology in Pittsburgh were established study courses and laboratory work on the theatre.

The subject matter used in the serious drama was first historical romance of the sort written by Clyde Fitch and produced by David Belasco; then the height of the progressive urge brought the problem play and psychic fantasies. Clyde Fitch, somewhat in the mood of Mark Twain, satirized social climbers and tourists in "The Climbers" and "The Girl with the Green Eyes." Interest in the native scene grew enough to lay the basis for a future O'Neill; and stock and road dividends helped out playwrights, before the movies decapitated both stock and the road and made playwrights dependent upon amateur and movie rights.

Despite box-office producers and frequently mediocre playwriting, acting remained of a high order, with excellent schooling in the stock companies of the provinces. Maude Adams, the Barrymores, John Drew, Mrs. Fiske and David Warfield led the best. Shakespearean drama was supported as given by Mantell, Marlowe and Sothern. In drama for the masses, swashbuckling was succeeded by mystery, comedy and sentiment. George M. Cohan, a remarkable technician in this field, skillfully mixed laughter, tears and thrills in the proportion best liked by the multitude.

The small town, with its "opera house," could not usually attract the large commercial producers and suffered from the controlled booking system. Except for travelling burlesque, melodrama and circuses, it supplied its own entertainment with the familiar neighborhood activities. Men and women of large towns and small continued to glory in lodges, raising the membership by 1914 to about 15,500,000, distributed among 57 groups. To these was added a new type of organization reflecting the national obsession with commercial ideals—lunch and dinner groups such as the Kiwanis, Lions and Rotary Clubs.

In national diversion the Chicago Exposition had set an example irresistible to ambitious lesser cities. Local pride, sectional rivalry, commercialism and propaganda stirred them to achieve amazing things, with the aid of electricity. Beginning with a Trans-Mississippi Exposition at Omaha in 1898 there followed the Pan American Exposition at

Buffalo, and the Interstate Exposition at Charleston, South Carolina, in 1901; in rapid succession St. Louis, Portland (Oregon), Hampton Roads (Virginia), Seattle, San Francisco and San Diego offered to Americans an entertaining display of their own national resources. Most of these expositions involved financial losses to the communities giving them; but the educational gain was tremendous, for Americans will undergo considerable sacrifice during part of the year for the sake of travel at vacation time. Thus, to the many influences modifying daily life in the progressive era, the expositions must be added; they weakened resistance to change and strengthened faith in betterment.

A Quickened Conscience

Splendid as were the achievements of this era, there was a dark side which stimulated the more sensitive consciences. The life of the very poor was out of step with the rising standard of living. The slum was a sore that cried for healing. New York slums in 1900 were worse than those in most of Europe then and as bad as those in Manchester and Liverpool in 1800, because of flooding immigration, mushrooming cities and concentration of wealth in the hands of a few. More than $2\frac{1}{3}$ millions of the $3\frac{1}{2}$ millions living in Greater New York were crowded into about 90,000 tenements, where only four rooms of the fourteen on each floor had direct light and air and fewer of them had privacy and sanitation. The Charity Organization Society at the time of the Spanish War started propaganda for housing laws adequate to combat vice, disease and crime. New York state three years later defied speculators and tenement owners with a law requiring ventilation in all rooms and hallways, sanitation, firescapes, running water and decent-sized rooms. The "dumbbell" apartment was to be replaced with "court" apartments built under the eye of a State Tenement House Department. New Jersey, Pennsylvania and Connecticut followed the New York state example and elsewhere individual cities imitated it.

The association of the slums with liquor selling, gambling, police corruption, crime and prostitution led a committee of New Yorkers in 1900 to explore these murky areas. The facts thus uncovered concerning widespread and complete organization of the prostitution business shocked their city; a ten-year crusade against "Raines Law" hotels and other forms of vice greatly reduced the number of disorderly houses and forced them to abandon open operation. This movement led into reform of minor courts. Vice conditions in other cities, exposed by G. K. Turner in *McClure's* (1907-1910), shocked the nation. Several cities following the example of New York regulated amusement places, established juvenile courts, separated the saloon business from prostitution, and passed laws against white slave traffic. City and state efforts at cleansing

finally led the federal government to announce adherence to the international white slave treaty, and Congress legislated to debar immigrants
in the business and to stop interstate traffic in it.

The urge for moral uplift characteristic of the progressive era accumulated its greatest momentum in the field of temperance, because it
interested women and church circles. The Women's Christian Temperance Union succeeded in making anti-alcoholic propaganda an integral
part of public school instruction, with chapters on evil effects of intemperance included in grade school physiology texts, implanting a vague
conviction that drinking was bad for health. Each denomination set up
a temperance organization and the Temperance Society of the Methodist
Episcopal Church came to be hated and feared by organized liquor
dealers. The American Anti-Saloon League, winning support from all
Protestant groups except the Episcopalians and Lutherans, became the
most militant dry organization. Led by Wayne B. Wheeler, and
W. H. Anderson, the League undertook (1) to establish that drinking
was morally wrong, and (2) to end it by political compulsion.

By 1908 their 100 main offices and total campaign budget of $400,000
was frightening politicians. Courts upheld state dry laws and Congress
by the Webb-Kenyon Act of 1 March 1913 prohibited liquor shipments
into dry territory. Rural America was dried up, legally, as were nineteen states of the South, Middle West and Far West (by 1 January
1916). Total liquor consumption, however, was not reduced; evidently the League was failing in its first objective. But it forged ahead
on its second, and by capitalizing war urgencies obtained the Eighteenth
Amendment and the Volstead Act of 1918, making it illegal for Americans to drink for pleasure. The question remained, however, as to how
permanent this victory could be, since the League had failed in its
first and basic objective.

The temperance agitation was but one aspect of expansion in the lives
of women, who in urban centers, particularly were developing more initiative. A few of the wealthy and middle class women remained too conservative, timid, uninformed, or self-indulgent to do anything with their
leisure except waste it; yet even they came to flout convention with
forgetful frequency because the strict restrictions of European chaperon-
age had never been popular outside of a limited class. Most of
the underprivileged women were held too fast by poverty to break
loose.

But the great bulk of American wives and daughters, at leisure or
employed, were in this period groping for new avenues of self-expression
in personal improvement and community service. Inroads upon higher
education opened many avenues and a few won popularity and wealth as
authors. While fewer women were lawyers and ministers than formerly
and physicians did not multiply greatly, the number of professions entered

by women increased and in teaching their percentage continually enlarged. Into home economics, industrial studies, athletics, social welfare, patriotic projects, club activities and any number of "movements" women plunged. Leadership from Jane Addams in settlement work heightened their interest in public affairs. Membership in groups affiliated with the General Federation of Women's Clubs grew from 50,000 in 1898 to 1,000,000 in 1914. Since women's clubs often were the only community organizations pressing for civic improvement, they made a large and immeasurable contribution to the progressive era.

Styles reflected the new interests. Ventures in business, golf, tennis and other sports turned the venturesome to something simpler and more convenient than large picture hats, trailing skirts, numerous petticoats and massive corsets. Huge, artificial pompadours and tight-sleeved, high-necked dresses of the very early twentieth century gave way to separate shirt waists, shorter skirts, simpler, lighter corsets; costumes likely to reveal that they clothed living, breathing people. Hobble skirts proved a fleeting aberration; America's contribution to the world of fashion—the Gibson Girl of the magazine covers—proved temporary.

Because active women of the progressive era were increasing their importance in the scheme of daily living, the legal status of the sex could be raised, unevenly, in the South most slowly. They made sufficient progress in winning control of their own earnings, equal control of their children and admission to the bar, to convince militant suffragists that they should concentrate upon equal suffrage. For it a few women had been agitating through three-quarters of a century; but only four states —Colorado, Idaho, Utah and Wyoming (where women were at a premium) had granted full suffrage by 1898. Progressive advances between 1910 and 1914 added Washington, California, Oregon, Kansas, Arizona, Montana and Nevada; but only Illinois further east. Passive indifference from most women and men, with active hostility from a minority of women, corrupt political groups and liquor interests proved the main obstructions to suffrage through state legislation.

When the militant faction decided to concentrate upon a federal amendment as a short cut, and revived the Susan B. Anthony amendment which had been pending since 1878, Congress, Roosevelt, Taft and Wilson successively, sidestepped. 1912 brought Roosevelt a change of heart and Wilson's inauguration gave publicity as well as abuse to the suffrage paraders led by their lobbyist-in-chief, Alice Paul. As her preference for militant, English tactics was not shared by Dr. Anna Howard Shaw and other leaders of the majority of the National Woman's Suffrage Association, Miss Paul organized her own "Congressional Union" which helped to force Congress to its final surrender on an equal suffrage amendment in 1919.

The majority of American mothers, wives and daughters were indifferent to suffrage; but most of them were well aware of a vastly more important trend—the falling rate of population growth. In spite of huge immigration, each decade since 1890 showed further shrinkage in the size of families, a shrinkage greatest in the upper middle class and persisting to various degrees through the white collar proletariat and down through the second generation of immigrants. Investigation and report indicated that the more affluent class of the population was committing suicide.[1] This highly unfortunate trend was deplored by most people, who endorsed clerical protests; and Roosevelt fulminated against it. Federal laws against distribution of contraceptive information were in some places enforced more rigorously; and in 1906 an editor was sent to Leavenworth for publishing a serious discussion of the marriage relation.

But family limitation was due to deep-seated economic and social causes:—among them, delayed marriage of working women, work after marriage, higher living standards, small apartment house life, and unwillingness to sacrifice economic and social opportunities to continual parenthood. The modern movement for scientific limitation—loosely described as "birth control"—grew. Some twelve states passed eugenics statutes for sterilization of mental defectives and habitual criminals and the indomitable Margaret Sanger in 1912 began her campaign to legalize dissemination of contraceptive information. Work as a nurse on New York's East Side had convinced her that children had a right to be wanted and to be properly spaced and that the poor stood peculiarly in need of that scientific knowledge which the well-to-do already possessed. She began to study methods, publish propaganda and be arrested. She had to flee the country; but she and Mrs. Mary Ware Dennett were laying the foundation for the American Birth Control League of the next period. Although they failed to change the laws they were accumulating support.

Extremely complex factors were making daily living more rapid and intense in many ways so that marriage became less of an obligation and more of a convenience. The divorce rate rose from 73 per 100,000 of population in 1900 to 112 in 1916. The United States had the highest divorce rate, with the exception of Japan, of all civilized nations; and granted more divorces than all the rest of the world except Japan. A large majority of the citizenry deplored this situation, publicized in another federal investigation and report, and divorcees in most towns were in poor repute. Yet it proved futile for statesmen and clergymen to denounce divorce, for it was an even more complex matter than the desertion, drunkenness, non-support, adultery and cruelty usually aired

[1] Only half the college women (among native girls of the central part of the United States) were marrying; they married two years later than their less-educated sisters and averaged less than two children apiece.

in the courts. Varying standards of state legislation made the divorce situation chaotic; but wide divergence of opinion over what constituted just cause for divorce prevented federal legislation.

Interest in National Health

Divorce and the shrinkage in families helped to make children, individually, more important, so that some Americans of the progressive era became intensely interested in safe-guarding childhood. Basic to this interest was the faith of all classes that with foresight their children might go far in the America of the future. The crusade to save children carried its advocates into legislation on delinquency, food, medicine, amusements, housing and labor—family legislation affecting daily life.

For delinquent and defective children, juvenile courts began to be established in 1899, and spread to every large city within one decade. Benjamin B. Lindsey, most notable of the children's judges, advanced all kinds of child welfare by his court procedure, his lectures and articles. His widening reforms aroused against him the closely interconnected corrupt interests—those committed to franchise exploitation and vote buying as well as child labor. He finally was defeated for reelection; but the cause gained publicity, for the new psychological discoveries were confirming the principle that dire punishment did not necessarily deter bad children.

Of primary importance was the extremely high infant mortality, possibly half of it preventable as due to ignorance, malnutrition and filth, scourges of the cities. The crusaders forced private interests and craven politicians to permit enactment of milk codes and appropriations for baby clinics, for visiting nurses, prenatal care, midwifery and wage-earning mothers. To ensure to children amusement, health and crime prevention, the Association of Day Nurseries, founded in 1897, led the cities to establish supervised community playgrounds. To direct into healthful channels the instinct for group play, the Y.M.C.A. and Y.W.C.A. expanded their activities. The Y.W.C.A., awakening to the need of group action to better working conditions, began in 1912 to attempt to organize its industrial membership on a national basis.

The Boy Scouts of America was formed in 1910 by Ernest Thompson-Seton and Dan C. Beard in imitation of the British plan of Sir Baden-Powell for training boys in self-reliance, citizenship and manliness. It fitted American ideas so admirably that in three years it had about 300,000 members. Although scouting was taken up more by children of the middle and upper class than the poor, it helped to Americanize some immigrants, through teaching their children Indian lore and woodcraft science. The Campfire Girls and Girl Scouts, founded in 1912, helped to promote interest in everyday tasks, thrift and health.

Health was becoming a major interest of Americans. Although they showed much less interest in exhaustive scientific research than in spectacular pseudo-science—such as Commodore Peary's dash to the North Pole in 1909 and F. A. Cooke's claim (never completely established) that he had preceded Peary by a year—they proudly acclaimed certain practical discoveries. The scientific researchers themselves, indifferent to their lack of notice, now were reaping a rich harvest of findings which carried America into the world stream of scientific advance. Like other nationals they utilized foreigners' discoveries—English and Italian in malaria, German in X-ray and sex determinants and French in radium —working them over for American purposes in endowed institutions and private college and commercial laboratories.

Courtesy of Minneapolis *Tribune*.
Governor Wood Begins His Duties.

The disease-ridden subtropics acquired through the Spanish War stimulated preventive medicine. Dr. Walter Reed and Major William C. Gorgas, with others, attacked yellow fever through mosquito infection— to the quick benefit of Cubans, Panama Canal workers and residents of New Orleans. Dr. H. T. Ricketts of the University of Chicago and his associates attacked Rocky Mountain fever and typhus through the tick and body lice. Major B. K. Bashford and the Rockefeller Sanitation Commission attacked the anaemia of Puerto Rico and of the southern states through the hookworm. Chemists and bacteriologists, keeping in touch with European advance, worked together upon bacilli, antitoxins, gland secretions, calories and vitamins. This stimulated further efforts for the cure of scourges like diphtheria, syphilis, scurvy, beriberi, rickets, and pellagra.

These scientific discoveries harmed as well as helped the public. Manufacturers learned how to disguise rancid butter and stale meat; how to fool consumers with artificial preservatives, colorings and flavors. Patent medicine makers invented new nostrums to exploit new fears.

Finally, to protect Americans from the dangers of daily living, Congress was forced to pass a pure food law. More important, pressure from community leaders was forcing city, state and national governments to establish laboratories, to war on mosquitoes and flies, to quarantine infectious diseases, to administer antitoxins, to inspect milk, and to watch over school children. Regular dental and medical inspection began among city schools, with the dual objects of lessening existing misery and preventing future contagion and disease. Cities reduced other hazards by improving sewage elimination and by chlorination of water. The American Public Health Foundation in 1912 (forty years after its founding) began publication of its *Journal of Public Health*.

Making heaviest inroads upon young people was tuberculosis, long thought incurable. In the fight on it the United States led, under Theobald Smith of Harvard and Dr. E. L. Trudeau, who preached rest in special, private and public sanitariums. Local societies and state commissions, the National Tuberculosis Association (1904) and the nationwide sale of Christmas seals (a scheme copied from Norway in 1907) began to teach the public the first principles of prevention and cure. The now familiar sign, "Spitting is unlawful," posted in public places proved again that although Americans proclaimed the principle of individual liberty they in practice were requiring their local and national governments to assume continual watchfulness over their behavior. Most federal departments were contributing some quota toward disease alleviation; and the Marine Hospital Service, with its quarantine and immigration inspection and precautions against interstate contagion, expanded into the Public Health Service.

The horizon of the medical profession was immeasurably widened by such private subsidy as the Rockefeller Institute (1901) and Rockefeller Foundation (1913). Members of the profession improved the education and practice at their medical schools, while the standards of trained nurses were protected by registration, boards of examiners and state associations. The effectiveness of the various efforts toward better health was measured by a fall in the death rate—from 17 per thousand in 1900 to 15.4 in 1910—and by an increase in the average length of life from 49 to 51. Typhoid, diphtheria, croup, tuberculosis and scarlet fever were taking fewer lives; but in cancer, influenza, diabetes, cerebral hemorrhage, softening of the brain and heart disease were proofs of the hazards of existence in the twentieth century.

Outside the field of medicine, American chemists were following Europeans impelled by greater scarcity of raw materials. Business men financed industrial laboratories where experiments in coal tar led all the way from high explosives to coloring matter for frosting cakes; wood pulp was converted to sell on the market as sausage casings and rayon underwear. Scientific discoveries, practical and theoretical, had a width and depth of range which the public could but dimly sense.

Among the distinguished scientific contributions were those of the American immigrant, A. A. Michelson, in astro-physics. The physicists, with X-ray and radium, were rudely upsetting the comfortable notion that all fundamental principles had been discovered; mechanics, they proved, no longer explained everything. This was a most disturbing thought, in a very disturbed period.

Religious Inquiry

The general unsettlement, the flux of ideas and experiences, could not but affect religious attitudes of clergy and congregations. Further scientific discoveries heightened the trend, begun by the evolutionary hypothesis, toward "higher criticism" of the Bible and old familiar creeds. Protestant conservatives were overborne at large theological schools. Among Congregationalists, modernism was ascendant by 1898; Baptists heard liberal teaching at their Chicago Divinity School; Episcopalians got it from Bishop William Lawrence at Cambridge; northern Presbyterians (but not Southern) were led by H. S. Coffin of Union Theological Seminary to repudiate infant damnation; when Methodists tried Professor B. P. Bowne of Boston University for heresy he was acquitted.

But when young clergy went out to their charges, liberalism was discouraged by the relative conservatism of the congregations who faced them weekly and paid their salaries. Not modernism, but shorter sermons, less theology and more Billy Sunday dramatics were the demands of many congregations. Ministers had little energy for pushing doctrinal innovations where they were hard pressed by competing diversions and changing communities. Sundays they struggled for the momentary attention of parishioners attracted by livelier excursions, ball-games, pictures, newspapers, automobiles and golf. Week-days they saw their congregations moving away under their noses. Immigration filled former Protestant neighborhoods with a flood of Catholics; cityward treks emptied country churches once established in the enthusiasm of schism and competitive sectarianism. Many a church building lost its steeple, to be converted into a business or tenement structure; others stood as derelicts. At the same time, where population crowded in, the need grew more desperate for contributors to establish more churches, hospitals and schools.

Unity—integration of effort—now was recognized by a few leaders as the crying need of Protestantism. The old prejudices and the habit of dissent, accumulated through generations, deterred Protestants from important mutual concessions before 1900. But the following decades saw three marked efforts:—particular subsects of Presbyterians, Baptists, Methodists and others united under more general denominational banners; the large denominations learned to cooperate successfully in special fields, such as the Christian Associations, Sunday Schools, Bible and Tract Societies and Missions: they also joined in local, city and state federations.

This led to the most significant Protestant step of the period—the cooperation of thirty-three evangelical bodies, representing 17 million communicants and more than half the population, in establishing in 1908 the Federated Council of Churches of Christ in America. While its functions at first had to be limited to study, recommendations, and acting as a clearing house for Protestant activities and as a rather tentative spokesman for American evangelical churches, it earnestly strove for unity. More important, it proved effective as a progressive influence which led Protestants into constructive criticism of the *status quo.* To liberalized theology and unified organization it helped to add a third influence—emphasis upon social relations; the three together during this period interacted to modify Protestantism.

The majority of the clergymen, who tended to float with the tide, accept a comfortable definition of respectability and shrink from direct attack upon special privilege, became the target of certain playwrights, muckrake magazines and novelists. A more realistic Christianity was preached on the stage by C. R. Kennedy's "Servant in the House" and J. K. Jerome's "Passing of the Third Floor Back." C. E. Russell in *Everybody's* exposed the inhuman tenement policy of Trinity Church, and R. S. Baker in the *American* blamed churchmen for "The Spiritual Unrest." Winston Churchill's novel, *Inside the Cup,* was a best seller, among the pleas for a new Christianity of which Americans were reading during the years just preceding 1914.

The main body of clergymen gradually followed bolder spirits beyond the spiritual into the physical and intellectual welfare of their parishioners. Many joined in progressive campaigns for political reforms and projects for social redemption. Official recognition of organized labor was given by Congregationalists in 1901, Presbyterians in 1903 and Methodists in 1908. City groups of ministerial associations and labor unions were exchanging "fraternal delegates" by 1905 and the Federal Council from the outset supported labor legislation. Religious therapy was stimulated by the mental and physical strains of modern life. Episcopalians established the Emmanuel movement. Christian Science reached an expansion of 100 new churches annually, and its daily, the *Christian Science Monitor* (begun 1908) soon had a fine reputation for foreign news and a huge circulation. Mystics flocked to New Thought cults which superimposed eastern philosophy upon transcendentalism. Americans craving religious showmanship got it in New York from Elbert Hubbard and his Roycrofters, and in Illinois from J. A. Dowie and his Zionists.

Against these and other innovations most Roman Catholics stood steadfast, so firm in historic doctrine that the conservative papal decree, the Pascendi of 8 September 1907, was here given readier acceptance than in France and Germany. Their church in America obtained from Rome full ecclesiastical status in 1908 and three new cardinals in 1911. Cardinal Gibbons of Baltimore was supporting the American Constitution and the doctrine of separation of church and state with an enthusiasm which tended to make the American church national. His denomination was getting the lion's share of the increasing membership through its watchfulness over immigrant members, through the Catholic Extension and Colonization Societies, and through priests of recent immigrant stock.

Of the total church increase of about 16 million members, 1900-1914, the Methodists with 2 million had the largest Protestant portion; Baptists and Lutherans came next. Increase in southern membership was due largely to colored evangelism. The Protestant Church in the rural South and West was holding its importance, but in New England it was losing influence. Throughout the nation the religious outlook inherited from Puritan forbears was still strong, even with many who no longer acknowledged its influence. There was still an instinctive dislike of sin and injustice, still sensitive consciences to urge people on to reform. Poverty, suffering and disease did not fit in with progress. Something must be done about it.

CHAPTER XXVI

SEEKING WELL-BEING

Since the majority of Americans felt during the progressive era a strong urge to deliberate change and betterment, certain acknowledged agencies of enlightenment—schooling, literature and art—assumed added importance. On every hand the supremacy of big business had created conditions which challenged both professional educators and that part of the public interested in enlightenment. A minority of thoughtful leaders welcomed the challenge; a majority of the public still believed in the necessity of free education—still saw in youth the great hope and great concern. Thus were provided the leadership and following for a strong educational impetus early in the twentieth century. It aided immeasurably in carrying the nation over into the main current of the progressive era.

Progressive Education

It was essential that educators become greatly interested in America's immediate environment. The realization must come that the schools should Americanize because of the heavy immigration, should discipline because of the decline in home and church influence, should recreate because of crowded slums. To meet these and other pressing needs, educators should devise new curricula and methods; the public should finance, build and organize for expanding school systems.

Leadership in making a realistic approach to education came from William James and John Dewey, believers in pragmatism and empiricism, who argued that the value of an idea depended upon how well it worked, and that one must arbitrarily select ideas for trial. Outstanding psychologists like G. Stanley Hall and Edward L. Thorndike added their contributions and some researchers stressed psychotherapy. Sociology became important in the graduate schools. Economists turned to inductive examination of actual economic institutions. Political scientists stressed structure and theory less, and function and practice more. The problem of fitting the law to actual social conditions engaged a few progressive lawyers like Brandeis, Kirchwey and Pound. Historians, building upon foundations laid by McMaster, Rhodes, Osgood, Channing and the authors of the *American Nation* series, now were led by Frederick J. Turner, Charles A. Beard and James Harvey Robinson into more realistic formulations.

Out of the effort to think realistically in many fields emerged a new psychology and philosophy, applicable to education. When accepted by certain educational leaders (mostly city-connected), several states and numerous cities made educational surveys under this leadership. Thus Dewey's thesis, that the object of education was social efficiency and that its method was cooperation in work and play, received practical application. Experiments by William Wirt at Gary, Indiana, in making the school a social center for all ages, daytimes and evenings, in classrooms and workshops, received wide attention and some imitation. Progressive elementary schools paid enthusiastic attention to music, drawing, domestic science and manual and physical training. In some high schools college preparatory courses began to be shifted from prominence, and vocational training—in agriculture, industry, trade and commerce—was added. A few high schools devoted themselves entirely to vocational training.

These adjustments recognized the basic fact that 90% of the children never reached high school; since the average pupil had little more than six years at school, the vitalization of his work there was essential. The next largest group included those who went only up to the tenth grade; for them curricula in large cities (beginning about 1910) were broadened, to allow for individual differences by making the seventh, eighth and ninth grades into a junior high school, with courses taught by special and departmental instructors. For the next stage came the senior high school; and beyond, the junior college, emphasizing the democratic principle as applied to college education, accommodating with two years near home those who could not afford four at a greater distance, and relieving some of the older colleges of unwieldy freshmen and sophomore classes. More than fifty of these were in existence by 1914, located chiefly in the South, the Middle and Far West, and approaching the European secondary school in scope.

Quantitatively, educational expansion set new highs. The number of pupils in elementary schools was increasing, 1898-1914, more than 25%; in high schools more than 100%. Old, private academies declined while a new public high school was established for each day of the year from 1890 to 1918. Although the national average of attendance per child by 1914 had reached only 6.16 years—of 200 days—this represented an increase in the length of the school period from 143 to 158.7 days; and an increase in the average attendance from 68 to 86.7 days. Southern states, with a rising income, could now respond to the pervasive educational movement by acceptance of the high school as a part of the state system; by strengthening educational features of their laws; by doubling or trebling their school funds; by greatly expanding their white enrollment.

Rural communities in a few progressive states began to pool their resources to finance better buildings, instruction and grade division, and transportation of children by the new school buses, for which they had to improve their roads. Even in the old, one-room, ungraded schools they somewhat improved the teaching, by raising requirements slightly; teacher-training courses in high schools aimed to help. Among the normal schools, growth in number and enrollments stimulated some increase in understanding. All along the line, acceptance of the obligation of education for all launched Americans upon broadened programs of community cooperation. Without stopping often to realize it, they were readjusting their democracy the better to stand the strains of modern life in the United States.

Assuming that the majority were fitted for college and would profit by the experience, Americans between 1893 and 1916 multiplied by five their contributions to colleges, and trebled the number of students they sent, until by 1914 at least one person in every twenty-five, between the ages of 19 and 23, was in college. On a similar assumption state universities, especially Wisconsin's, undertook to carry higher education beyond the campus, providing study centers, lecture and correspondence courses, travelling libraries and exhibits. A few of the smallest colleges passed out of existence, while the largest ones established professional schools of education, journalism and business, which transformed them to departmentalized universities.

In all this, thoughtful educators perceived dangerous tendencies. To the colleges and universities now came many who were neither interested in, nor fitted for, higher education. Academicians feared education was losing its meaning. They did not all welcome the School of Journalism attached to Columbia University by Pulitzer's money in 1912. Some charged that multiplication of departments and application of business methods made universities little more than "degree factories." For their part, businessmen themselves showed suspicion of the friendliness of the Harvard School of Business, established in 1908 as the first such school since Joseph Wharton in 1883 endowed one at Pennsylvania.

Education could not escape the influence of big business. The schools were getting huge endowments and multimillionaire trustees, who often expected professors of economics and history to justify all the practices of big business. Professor Scott Nearing at Pennsylvania and W. C. Fisher at Connecticut Wesleyan raised a challenge for academic freedom. Some critics deplored the indebtedness of education to John D. Rockefeller. His General Education Board, endowed with 53 millions (1903-1909) ranged over a wide field; it aided higher education through the University of Chicago, Rockefeller Institute of Medical Research, and endowment of medical schools and small colleges. It aided lower education through Negro schools, aid to federal and state secondary programs, to farm demonstrations, and especially to the South. Such endowments encouraged other millionaire imitators and public allotments, but seemed to some critics more paternalistic than democratic in their implications.

To cope with their uncertainties as to freedom of speech and tenure, professors in 1914 called for organization of the American Association of University Professors. To offset the growing heterogeneity of student bodies, presidents tried various devices. Woodrow Wilson stressed the preceptorial system at Princeton. C. H. Van Hise defended professors against reactionary politicians at Wisconsin. H. P. Judson distinguished Chicago for educational experiments. A. Lawrence Lowell injected the tutorial system and the general examination into Harvard procedure. At Columbia graduate schools of education and the social sciences, under the Burgess and Dewey stimulus, dared considerable innovations.

For the struggle to loosen the dominance of special privilege over American life, a few colleges had been breeding liberals who, at the turn of the century, were leading the nation into its progressive era. They had approached their prime in the decades when small colleges abounded in Ohio and other states of the Mississippi valley, in areas but a generation or two removed from the vital experience of pioneer cooperation. These colleges but recently had been chiefly training ground for ministers; but Ingersoll's nation-wide lectures had created many an agnostic; and the secular trend had been vastly accelerated by the Morrill Land Grant Act. Its emphasis upon training in agriculture and mechanic arts had invited a new type of student and stirred the hopes of farm parents for sending their sons if not their daughters to get a new kind of college education.

The hard struggles of these families to keep one member at college gave the rising generation a personal experience in cooperation for the common good—an experience which emphasized and underscored community traditions of cooperation. Such boys and girls absorbed from their environment that belief in the educability of common citizens, and that faith in their ability to replace old maladjustments with new opportunities, which made the progressive era possible. This type of college contacts injected some potential leaders with a concentrated solution of such faiths and beliefs; this gave them a high resistance to corporate poisons, equipping them as donors of democratic blood to the sick public.

While a very large part of instruction at post-frontier colleges was necessarily quite uninspired, many an institution had on its faculty one or two members who raised the coming issue. Was the United States on the way to rule by wealth, rather than by men? The concept that the government was being subverted, and should be restored to control by the people, was deeply implanted by instructors of that type. Some of them had been inspired as graduate students by the tutelage of such teachers as Brice, Ely, Howard, Shaw and Wilson at Johns Hopkins. William G. Sumner, Yale's pioneer in sociology, who hoped to reverse the trend toward plutocracy by restoring primitive laissez-faire, was a great mind-opener; this in spite of the fact that he could not realize how laissez-faire was destroying democracy by fostering a bitterness of competition which resulted inevitably in huge combinations.

At the University of Wisconsin was built up the "Wisconsin Idea" which spread over large areas. The influence of John Bascom, long teacher and thirteen years president of the University, ramified very widely because of the long friendship between him and Robert M. La Follette. He ever stressed the importance of moral victory, whatever the outcome. Men of his sort were likely to prove uncompromising as well as progressive; they urged action on conviction and emphasized the obligations of citizenship. Wisconsin acquired R. T. Ely from Johns Hopkins in 1892 and J. R. Commons from the National Civic Federation in 1904. C. R. Van Hise, of La Follette's class of 1879, maintained a continuous connection with the University from the time of his graduation, became its president in 1903 and identified himself also with conservation. Bascom, La Follette and Van Hise were but three of the University group which built up the "Wisconsin Idea."

More obscure, but certainly important, were liberal individuals in very small colleges, such as Charles H. Rammelkamp, a Cornell Ph.D. who taught history and government at Illinois College; and Professor Charles Hurd who at Knox left an indelible impression on a poverty-stricken student named S. S. McClure. At the University of Nebraska the conservatism of the economics professor was counter-balanced by an ardent democrat, Howard Caldwell, himself inspired by Johns Hopkins tutelage and finding kindred spirits in colleagues in the philosophy and German departments.

Daring thought at colleges alarmed big business and therefore small politicians. University of Chicago students gathered as much from their Washington Day orators. McKinley, the 1895 speaker, deplored "the influence of the professors in some of our institutions of learning, who teach the science contained in books, and not practical business." So did Theodore Roosevelt in 1896. Not so La Follette in 1897. He seized the opportunity to make a plea for the direct primary, describing to the students "the Menace of the Machine." La Follette well remembered how he, as a youth of eighteen, had been stirred at a Wisconsin Commencement when he heard Chief Justice E. G. Ryan (author of a decision sustaining a Granger law) warn the graduates of the danger to democracy from plutocracy. Thereafter La Follette re-echoed Ryan's warning on the stump, the platform, and in the Senate; three years after his death it echoed again, as progressives of Wisconsin used as their slogan, "Which shall rule, wealth or man?"

The boldest of progressive leaders must have cried down the wind in vain—but for the practical economics taught adults of America outside of formal schools and colleges. A combination of Redpath lectures and Chautauqua features was brought to small towns. The popular Chautauqua, which with the Lyceums and lecture courses painlessly mixed entertainment with instruction, proved an active agent for propagation of liberal ideas. This was its golden age (1899-1915), when its programs were improved and it maintained an International Alliance. In hundreds of communities, for a week every summer, folk flocked to hear music, see plays and listen to discussions of current affairs. The Chautauqua was based upon a belief in community of interest, equality of understanding and educability of the democracy; its audiences were peculiarly responsive to liberals who proceeded upon the same assumptions.

La Follette's favorite Chautauqua and Lyceum subject, "Dangers Threatening Representative Government," drew such crowds that from this one lecture the course managers some years realized enough to finance their entire series. His direct, confident attitude, clear explanations and dramatic approach to audiences on the plane of their personal experiences, convinced them and stirred them to action. Too much emphasis cannot be placed upon his lecture skills; they assured him of independent funds with which to finance his political organization. They carried his thought and ideals far ahead of his political ambitions.

Adult education was popularized all along the line, with group study in women's clubs, with forums, correspondence schools, schools for immigrants and with broadening of library functions. Libraries increased in numbers [1] and equipment, expanding from routine circulation of books to an aggressive effort to meet public needs and improve public taste.

Newspaper and Magazine Influence

The inseparable relation between education and the printed word gave the printed output of the progressive era, whether magazines, newspapers or books, major significance. On the newspaper level, editors profited from mechanical improvements on such earlier inventions as the speedy power press, linotype, typewriter and telegraph; newly come to their aid were the wireless, printing telephoto machine and motortruck. To the existing newsgathering agencies Hearst added his International News. Sunday editions were swollen with feature articles, special departments, and the rotogravure introduced by *The New York Times*. The dailies added special pages including "Advice to the Lovelorn" which performed a social service beyond the grasp of those who ridiculed it. The demand for humor increased the number of comic strips and engaged special humorists like George Ade with "Fables in Slang" on the Chicago

---

[1] Libraries of more than 5000 volumes increased approximately from 1700 to 3000, while the New York Public Library alone threw out sixty-five branches.

Record, and Finley Peter Dunne with "Mr. Dooley" on the Chicago *Journal.* Carolyn Wells, Irvin Cobb and Ring Lardner also amused Americans with some of the national pretenses and laughed them out of a few. Growth of women's interest in current affairs modified news presentation and gave some women careers on the dailies. Columnists began to occupy columns left vacant by departed editorial owners:— in New York Don Marquis on the *Sun* and "F.P.A." on the *Mail* and in Chicago B. L. Taylor, were of the first. Such stellar contributors acquired political and cultural influence.

The great loss to newspapers came through standardization. Syndication of articles, joint use of press services, dominance of editorial policy by economic and political views of stockholders, and single ownership of many papers destroyed most of the remaining individuality. To the earlier Scripps-McRae chains were added transcontinental purchases by Hearst and Munsey. Brisbane as editor for Hearst beginning in 1897 entered upon a long career in which yellow journalism was largely devoted to the degradation of taste. However, it had the excellent effect of forcing respectable papers to brighten up, and encouraged concern in the welfare of the common man. A few papers kept their identity by some special characteristic; real power therefore still was exerted by such editors as W. R. Nelson of the *Kansas City Star,* Henry Watterson of the *Louisville Courier-Journal* and Fremont Older of the *San Francisco Bulletin.* Under the editorship of Frank T. Cobb the *New York World* made definite contributions to the progressive movement: it forced the life insurance investigation of 1905, and the publication of campaign contributions thereafter; it exposed political corruption in 1912 and not infrequently aided La Follette.

These contributions by the *World* were the more significant because the press was losing the confidence of the people through its venality and subservience to advertisers. News was tainted at its source, according to those who accused the Associated Press of ultraconservatism and the United Press of ultraradicalism. Gross frauds perpetrated through advertisers' dictation of press policy became matter of such common knowledge that Scripps-McRae established their own censorship (1903) and the Associated Advertising Clubs of America set up a vigilance committee (1913). Public attention had been fixed upon it largely through exposures of patent medicines written by S. H. Adams and Will Irwin for *Collier's* (1905-1906 and 1911). State and federal legislators passed laws on truth in advertising and on libel; the courts attempted to suppress sensationalism and the postoffice tried to prevent delivery of mail to fraudulent concerns. The *New York Herald* was forced to pay a fine of $30,000 for printing prostitution advertisements. The campaign for truth brought political attacks upon the freedom of the press; President Theodore Roosevelt forced the federal government to sue the *Indian-*

apolis News, but lost the decision. The New York *World* was sued for exposing the seizure of Panama.

The reform legislation of the progressive period would not have been possible without the publicity given to abuses by some "muckrake" magazines. During the 'nineties a few magazines had entered the field of publication with material less polite and restricted in scope than that of the *Atlantic Monthly, Century, Harper's,* and *Scribner's. Munsey's* had been founded as a twenty-five-cent magazine in 1891, *McClure's* at fifteen cents in 1893, whereupon *Munsey's* became ten cents. These developments enraged the American News Company which had a monopoly of distribution; but Munsey in 1899 finally forced the Company to accept a seven-cent wholesale rate on a ten-cent periodical. By that time McClure was approaching a realization that consolidation had become the biggest fact of American life. He acted on the principle, with far-reaching results.

He undertook to finance an investigation of various forms of consolidation:—to do it thoroughly, dispassionately, and factually. The process educated the public and lined McClure's pockets simultaneously. He put Ida Tarbell on research in the field of Standard Oil, Lincoln Steffens on city government (beginning with St. Louis) and on state government, and Ray Stannard Baker on ramifications of the railroads and handling of the Negro problem. The public grew interested and excited and the articles reappeared in book form as *The History of the Standard Oil* (1904), *The Shame of the Cities* (1904), and *The Struggle for Self-Government* (1906).

In 1904 Baker, Steffens and Tarbell took over the *American Magazine* and infused it with the spirit of their articles. The field was entered by the *Cosmopolitan, Everybody's* (a significant title), *Hampton's, Munsey's* and *Pierson's.* Life insurance graft was exposed in articles by Burton J. Hendrick; frauds in patent medicines and other advertising by Samuel Hopkins Adams; vice conditions in New York and Chicago by G. K. Turner and Alfred Henry Lewis, Judge Ben Lindsey wrote of injustices in juvenile laws. Charles Edward Russell described the beef trust, and the tie-up between the Southern Pacific and the California state government.

These articles constituted an attack on a very broad and vulnerable front and as presented by McClure and his early staff they avoided overstatement and were thoroughly investigated. The fact that neither the magazines nor the authors lost important suits for libel based on these articles added to their impressiveness and influence. But Hearst purchased the *Cosmopolitan* and gave it a yellow tinge in the method of presentation of David Graham Phillips' articles. Less patient with the expense and delay of painstaking research than was McClure, Hearst could not resist a sneer at him and proclaimed his own intention to initiate "virile" exposure. Crass sensationalism had entered the field when *Everybody's* published Lawson's "Frenzied Finance," an exposure of Wall Street, and Hearst published Phillips' "Treason of the Senate."

The latter threw so lurid a light on the control of the Senate by big business, especially in the person of Chauncey DePew, that it frightened Roosevelt, who felt keenly the necessity of Senate cooperation if he were to complete his executive program. Therefore at a gridiron dinner, 17 March 1906, he referred to the exposurists as "muckrakers." The label thus applied at an unreported affair spread by word of mouth and proved so popular that Roosevelt determined to announce his authorship publicly. In characteristic fashion, he seized the occasion of the dedication of the House Office Building, 14 April following, to attack both big business and the "lunatic fringe" of muckrakers.

The title stuck to all the exposurists, McClure's writers as well as Hearst's, and to the era as well; but the difference must not be overlooked. The factual Steffens, unlike Lawson and his tribe, was supplying information on home truths which was sadly lacking in current texts on American government. With him it was special privilege, whether applied to big business or little business, which was the basic evil.

After Roosevelt's derisive labeling muckraking gradually trickled out. Baker in 1911 turned to helping La Follette with his autobiography; Steffens became a Christian socialist, Miss Tarbell became conservative. Russell, however, continued exposure while joining his loyalties to the Socialist party. The magazines themselves either died or changed their character, because advertisers boycotted magazines exposing fraud, and a union of manufacturing and banking interests bought up what survived. The public did not maintain sufficient interest in their own protection to support the exposure magazines without advertising. Muckraking, however, had performed an inestimable service, by demonstrating the need for the protection of mankind from special privilege.

A more comfortable success came to a larger number of editors who accepted the status quo, and simply filled their pages with selections to fit special sectors of the reading public. The widening range of magazines displayed on news-stands testified that unprecedented numbers of Americans of both sexes and all ages were keen to read about the passing show. This much, at least, compulsory grade schooling had done for them. For practically every industry, pastime, religion and social group a periodical was printed, ranging all the way from children's magazines, through those devoted to movies, crime and sports, and on up to such journals of public affairs as the *Independent, Literary Digest* and *Outlook.* Feminine appeal par excellence was found in the *Ladies Home Journal;* and conservatives addicted to ardent nationalism and worship of financial success delighted in that mirror of their viewpoints, the *Saturday Evening Post.*

Stimulus from Books

The reading of books also became habitual. Serials in cheap magazines had familiarized readers with the book type of fiction; improved type-setting and binding made books more attractive to the eye; display ads reached more prospective buyers than the old book agent system; and the shortening of novels to a length of but 150,000 to 200,000 words helped sales. Came the "fat years of fiction" in which a circulation of 100,000 was no longer uncommon. The percentage of fiction, in total published literature, rose. It ran the gamut, from historical romance through bourgeois aspects of the American scene and on into revival of the social revolt and realism.

Since more Americans were high school and college graduates, better-written fiction was demanded; but progress toward realism was arrested by a post-war reversion to historical romance, which was encouraged by emergence from the depression, entrance into Spanish War enthusiasms and dawning awareness that America had a history. This demand was met by such novels as S. Weir Mitchell's *Hugh Wynne,* Henry Sien-kiewicz's *Quo Vadis,* Charles Major's *When Knighthood Was in Flower* and *Dorothy Vernon of Haddon Hall,* and Mary Johnston's *To Have and To Hold.* Other good sellers were Paul Leicester Ford's *Janice Meredith,* Maurice Thompson's *Alice of Old Vincennes,* Emerson Hough's *Mississippi Bubble,* John Fox's *Little Shepherd of Kingdom Come,* George Barr McCutcheon's and Hugh McGrath's imaginary kingdoms, and Winston Churchill's historical romances.

This type lost preeminence as taste became more heterogeneous. Around 1904 American authors (men and a growing number of women) took to emphasis upon bourgeois aspects of the native scene, some presenting village morality and others city sophistication. They managed to take most of the American trade with novels of sentiment by Kate Douglas Wiggin and Mrs. Rice, northwoods stories of strenuous super-men by Rex Beach and Jack London, college tales by Owen Johnson and stories of gentility by Margaret Deland and Mary Wilkins Free-man. W. S. Porter, known as "O. Henry" pleased many with short stories of city types. Such literature, however, was not realism in the sense of the social revolt.

A "literature of getting-on," which glorified business ethics, compli-mented the successful and stimulated the ambitious. The gospel of acquisitiveness was popularly presented in Edward N. Westcott's *David Harum,* George Horace Lorimer's *Letters of a Self-Made Merchant to His Son* and George R. Chester's *Get-Rich-Quick Wallingford.* Edna Ferber's *Roast Beef Medium* first portrayed woman in business. The extreme materialism brought satires of it, written by Clyde Fitch, Robert Herrick and Edith Wharton.

For the most part, fiction suffered from comfortable backgrounds. Booth Tarkington may be taken as an example. He, like the poet Riley, came from Indiana's region of democratic neighborliness far removed from industrial stresses, and clung long to a superficial, optimistic belief in success. Theodore Dreiser, from the same locality, was saved from superficiality by a harsh boyhood. Establishment in decent comfort, as in Garland's case, often turned writers "soft." Formal education and privileged, decent upbringing often proved handicaps to realism. However, a harsh realism was achieved by Frank Norris, who exposed the strangulation of the California farmers by the Southern Pacific Railroad in *The Octopus,* and grain speculation in *The Pit.* Theodore Dreiser dared present modern problems of sexual morality in his first novel, *Sister Carrie* (1900), which was so far in advance of public tolerance that a decade of hackwork followed for him; publication by Harper and Brothers of his *Jennie Gerhardt* and *The Financier* showed public advance in realism, although his *Titan* was suppressed in 1914.

The factual picturization of social, economic and political conditions provided by McClure and his kind came to the novelists with difficulty. The "kidglove" type of political reformer, earlier presented in local color by Ford, Garland, Twain and Warner, was finally followed by types foreshadowing the muckrake magazine movement. Francis Williams produced *J. Devlin, Boss* and Brand Whitlock *The 13th District* in 1902. A. H. Lewis pictured Richard Croker of Tammany Hall in *The Boss* and Elliot Flower told the story of the Chicago utilities in *The Spoilsman* in 1903.

The exposure articles in *McClure's,* sandwiched between artificial fiction, gradually awakened novelists to the connection between special interests and politics. Men like Winston Churchill, who had been feeding his large public such romance as *Richard Carvel, The Crisis* and *The Crossing,* turned a little to the left to problem novels and political reform. Trying to comprehend the real sources of power in America he wrote *Coniston, Mr. Crewe's Career, Inside the Cup* and others. London and Herrick tried to expose capitalistic society.

Their contemporary, David Graham Phillips, who has been termed "the Roosevelt of American Literature," tried to get spot news across in fiction, writing twenty ephemeral novels in ten years. He succeeded in catching the sense of grievance from the air and making fictional capital out of it; but when its news value was gone, he went with it. Lincoln Steffens tried to deal with political negotiation and human beings in indecision, in his *Dying Boss, Reluctant Driver* and *Boss Who Was Bossed.* The most powerful novel, in its immediate effects, was Upton Sinclair's *The Jungle,* which so mirrored stockyard practices as to clinch the passage of a pure food law. Such novelists educated readers who lacked the inclination or the ability to follow the more precise magazine exposures. Typical of the progressive generation, they identified the "cause" of the little fellow with morality in general and assumed that he, though poor, would have the stamina to turn out the rascals, though it involve temporary starvation. This assumption exposed them to the literary criticism of such writers as Paul Elmer More.

Booth Tarkington's *Gentleman From Indiana* showed his failure to realize that America needs good men in back of politicians even more than good politicians. His strongest attempt to expose dirty politics, *In the Arena,* led President Theodore Roosevelt to ask him not to help to crystallize the feeling that politics is no place for a gentleman. The incident poses the question of Roosevelt's influence upon realism. His denunciation of muckraking somewhat discouraged realism but tariff agitation revived it. Its subsequent decline came when the nation assumed that Congress had shouldered the duty of investigation and that reform had been secured, when bold magazines were destroyed or purchased, and finally when the World War came to swing the country back to conservatism.

An enlarging minority of readers bought books on economics, politics and philosophy. Progressives who sought to get social and economic reform by strengthening national government found in Herbert Croly's *Promise of American Life* a presentation of the inseparable connection between their belief in democracy and their faith in human perfectability. The best presentation of economic behaviour was Thorstein Veblen's *Theory of the Leisure Class.* Outstanding philosophical observations on religion were William James' *Varieties of Religious Experience* and Henry Adams' *Mont-Saint-Michel and Chartres.*

The progressive era, meanwhile, had inspired a few poets to abandon hackneyed expression for more serious artistry. By the pens of these few, poetry passed from Edwin Markham's restless questioning in *The Man With the Hoe,* through Edwin Arlington Robinson's frustrated characters to the dominant realism of Vachel Lindsay, Carl Sandburg's western portrayals and Robert Frost's New England pictures. Amy Lowell's excellent pioneering in free verse was too good not to make that form more respectable. Belated recognition came to the posthumous printing of Emily Dickinson's unique verse.

Participation in Artistic Trends

Like America's educators and writers, her artists reacted variously to the challenges of the twentieth century—some responded to surface trends —some to deeper undercurrents. Neither in music, painting, sculpture, dancing nor architecture were developments extremely startling; but national pride increased, participation widened and a few leaders took long strides.

In music, as might be expected, this period was marked by wider participation. While ragtime, sentimental ballads and musical comedy "hits" satisfied the general public; and while American composers lagged in building a native music upon Negro and Indian melodies, nevertheless musical appreciation was stimulated. The National Federation of Musical Clubs became active (in 1898), New England and New York conservatories kept their influence, and phonograpth recorders canned good as well as bad music. Alexander McDowell's influence was perpetuated by a colony in New Hampshire and Frank Damrosch established in New York an Institute of Musical Art.

Enthusiastic American audiences greeted Caruso, Kreisler and the ever growing number of visiting artists. The symphony idea spread over the country with new orchestras founded at Philadelphia, Minneapolis and St. Paul, New Orleans and Seattle, and with specialization in Russian and children's music. Grand opera was benefited by the brilliant efforts of Oscar Hammerstein to establish permanent competition with the Metropolitan Company in New York and Philadelphia.

In other artistic forms—such as dancing and painting, Americans showed their conservativeness. Their native-born dancer, Isadora Duncan, attempted to restore, by simple draperies and flowing movements, the natural, classic dance; but Americans would not give her the full support Europe extended. Artistic immaturity was also indicated in painting, where purchasers liked imitation better than originality. Realism, however, was by no means wholly absent; and although the European school of "expressionism" found few followers in the United States, the "post-impressionists" began to win admirers about 1914. Of a high order, fortunately, was American mural painting, for the many new public buildings were lavishly adorned. John Singer Sargent and Edwin A. Abbey, classicists, distinguished themselves on the walls of the Boston Public Library, Violet Oakley at the Pennsylvania State Capitol, Edward Simmons at Minnesota's, Edwin H. Blashfield at Wisconsin's and several good artists at the Library of Congress.

Whistler's influence diverted many painters to etching, in which Joseph Pennell, by turning to American subjects, best reflected the changing United States. But few Americans appreciated illustrations by artists of such technical skill as Abbey, Frost and Pennell. Readers of the ten-cent magazines and Sunday supplements liked better the handsome and healthy heroes standardized by Maxfield Parrish, Howard Chandler Christy, Charles Dana Gibson and James Montgomery Flagg; their "types" had a better influence upon dress and health than upon artistic taste. The best illustrated magazine, the *Masses,* reached only a very limited and popularly distrusted clientele.

In sculpture, American artists turned principally to United States history for subjects and portrayed them with such power, skill and realism as to raise American sculpture to the level of the world's best. Augustus Saint Gaudens, George Grey Barnard, and Daniel Chester French, now at the peak of their powers, were but leaders in the van of many who together made the period notable.

Toward the historic past turned also some of the architects, who diverted suburban construction from the overly-ornate Mid-Victorian styles to reproductions of the earlier New England farmhouse, or the gambrel roofs of New York's Dutch relics, or stone houses of Pennsylvania, Georgian styles of the South and mission lines of Spanish America. For smaller, cheaper and quicker building, the West enthusiastically adopted the flat, nondescript, six-room bungalow, which quickly infested other sections. Very few adopted the more modern architecture of Sullivan and Wright, who emphasized glass and horizontal lines.

American communities, city and country, showed themselves generally indifferent to a lack of variety in architecture; but the foremost architects were encouraging education in taste and craftsmanship, stimulated by the establishment of architectural schools, courses of study, travelling fellowships and professional journals. Congress was persuaded to incorporate the American Academy at Rome (1905). Architecture diluted for mass appeal was provided by illustrations and colored photographs on women's pages and in popular magazines. In the largest cities the leaders were gathering courage for the bolder exercise of originality and imagination in adapting steel and glass to the imperious demands of fabulous land values. Leaving far behind the twenty-storied Flat Iron building of 1902, they constructed such super-office buildings and gigantic industrial structures as the Woolworth, Singer and Metropolitan buildings in New York City and the Larkin Building in Buffalo.

The number of Americans who consciously associated art trends with their daily living was of course almost negligible, although the influence was there and cannot be ignored. Changes in reading habits and education, on the other hand, came closer home to the general public, by reason of their own participation in them, and influence upon them. The almost infinite variation in individual experience in daily living makes exceptionally risky the always daring venture of generalization. But at least one outstanding trend marked daily living of Americans during the progressive era. It was generally changing at a faster tempo than before, and the changes were of a character to increase the general awareness of participation in change. The problems which these changes raised were not to be left to educators, writers and artists to solve. The public interest in progress was to be sensed and promoted by politicians and public men, who were to exercise the kind of leadership which gave the period the name of the progressive era.

CHAPTER XXVII

THE VALLEY AWAKES

Those politicians and progressives who undertook a critical appraisal of trends in this era found themselves face to face with special privilege as a dominating factor in American life. They found it to be an integral part of that large scale organization which had given speed and pervasiveness to change. The resources, capital and manpower of a rich nation had lain open for exploitation in a period of invention when the social conscience was not functioning very effectively. This had placed a premium upon ruthless application of the principles of laissez faire, regardless of heavy costs to humanity. It had bred a race of aggressive, talented and greedy captains in industry whose competition eliminated the least ably ferocious. By the time large scale organization had evolved into combinations of combinations—into the trusts—the nation at large was gradually awakening to facts which only a minority formerly had perceived.

Taking Stock of Special Privilege

There came a tendency to take stock; and restless, uncomfortable persons, middle class people including farmers, laborers, professors and politicians, showed the effects of the long strain imposed by the falling price era of the 'eighties and 'nineties, and of the passing of the idea of free land. Special privilege, they saw, had given strength to capital and imposed weakness upon the worker and consumer. Faith in the benevolence of the American scheme of things, in the limitlessness of resources and opportunities, became sufficiently shaken to spread a belief that reform was overdue. The social conscience was awakened.

On every side inquiring minds discovered evidence that the wealthy sought to control politics in order to preserve special privilege in economics and society. Members of the middle class with a Puritanical heritage were tremendously shocked by disclosures of dishonesty, particularly when highly respected and "successful" personages were discovered to have been intimidated into bribery transactions. They joined with the laboring class in denouncing aggregations of great wealth; and undertook to exert their balance of power on the side of reform. Since they were democratic as well as moralistic, they believed in the infinite educability of the individual and, through him, of the mass.

They assumed that by placing honest individuals in office they could work political reform, and in turn economic and social reform. So believing, they undertook to educate the voters in enlightened self-interest so that they should cooperate in keeping honest individuals in office, under whose leadership the nation should progress in prosperity and happiness. Upon this basic philosophy the "progressives" built their movement and dominated the trend in America between the Spanish War and the outbreak of the World War of 1914.

When the progressives came to consider the application of their democratic philosophy to a concrete program for industrialized America, they made optimistic assumptions. They assumed that good men in office could maintain the delicate balance between capital and labor to the advantage of all. They tended to forget that politicians good and bad must continually endure buffeting from warring factions of capital and labor, that the balance must always be precarious, with the weight at any given moment a little heavier on the one side or the other. Furthermore, the few people in control of American economic life had by this time entrenched their position so that it was almost impregnable against the assaults of reformers attempting to act as instruments of good government.

A popular scheme of attack was to use anti-trust laws as projectiles which should blast the trusts into small, competitive corporations. But that kind of competitive production had involved a terrific waste in resources and human values, a situation in itself unstable. Some American liberals, pondering upon the difficulty of keeping the instruments of production permanently scattered among large numbers of competitors, ventured to assert that the only alternative to the trusts would be some form of a socialized state. But the main body of the reformers of the progressive era conditioned their logic by their loyalty to past institutions and past concepts of respectability. To them socialism was not respectable; their age was not one of drastic revolt, but of tentative reform, of palliation.

So the progressives, denouncing the constitutionalism of the Hamiltonians went back to the spirit of Jefferson and the Declaration of Independence. Swearing fealty to the little man in business, the small farmer, and the honest debtor, they determined to restore the balance between industry and agriculture. For these, opportunity should be made more equal, conditions of work should be pleasanter, safer, and more democratic, and social justice should approach nearer. The progressives undertook to apply to industrial America the remedies of a past agrarian age.

Furthermore, since the vast reaches of the United States were simultaneously in many transitional stages, progressivism had to be a relative thing, meaning many different degrees of awareness of objectives in different sections. While the middle class progressives at long last were willing that their class should march with the agrarians to slay the ogre of business consolidation, their discontent was voiced in a babel of tongues. Could their many voices rise with the might of one, against the highly organized and unified special privilege which they had to fight?

The Heritage of Faith in Democracy

It has been customary of late to criticize the men and women who were called "Progressives," because of their optimistic faith in palliative devices. But there were many and excellent reasons why the Progressives enjoyed the luxury of abounding faith in the betterment of life in America.

The pioneer experience, contrary to common notions, was permeated with an abiding social sense. Children and adults experienced in the daily life of frontier living a continual exercise in the importance of cooperation. While they had a high respect for each other as individuals, they were continually depending upon cooperative effort for their comfort and survival. Family life and neighborhood relations had an importance which we of the present generation scarce can grasp; and this training in cooperation, this drill in the mutual dependence of mankind, in enlightened self-interest, was an essential element of their democracy, a part of their natural education which had a lasting influence upon the children of the frontier and of the post-frontier, farming communities.

At the same time, the development of the United States made exacting demands upon self-reliance and individual courage; it afforded a rigorous training in the power to form one's own judgments and to act on one's own conclusions. Of it was born a courage and competitiveness which would stand in good stead when the Sons of the Middle Border undertook to re-establish in a trust-ridden country respect for the rights of common individuals. With such an equipment would go a distaste for compromise and for evasions, which must force some action upon the most unwilling of politicians.

To the Granger and Populist movements, the Progressive movement was heavily indebted. A significant number of leading Liberals at the turn of the century had been born either in 1854 or 1855, had reached their majority at the height of the Granger movement and had been in a position to experience intimately the conditions which fostered Populism. Also the farm boys and girls who were born between 1855 and 1875 took the hard impress of their adolescent years from the difficulties which beset their struggling parents during the following decades of falling prices. To the members of these families, the railroads were the symbol of all that was unjust and such legislation as they early obtained for railroad regulation remained an abiding proof of their own prowess and a stimulant for further effort. In this sense, the Interstate Commerce Act of 1887—despite its fate at the hands of the courts—stood

as a charter of their liberties. It was concrete evidence of victory over
their worst foe. Some of them considered it the direct result of their
Granger agitation; and similarly they later came to the conclusion that
the reforms of the Rooseveltian decade were won through their Populist
pressure.

Regardless of the lack of skill of the farmers as lobbyists, the earnestness of their convictions remained indisputable. Their doctrines were
imbibed by such promising youth as LaFollette in Wisconsin, U'Ren in
Oregon, and Cummins in Iowa, to mention but a few. Their experiences,
recollections, and impressions were underscored by the hard times which
began in 1893 and which gave rise to such things as Coxey's Army and
Bryan's awakening. There were many other armies besides that captained by Coxey and the marchers in them included such talented young
men as Lincoln Steffens. In the year of the panic and the World's Fair
at Chicago, there had convened in a Methodist church of that radical
city a convention of free silver advocates who held their stand in spite
of ridicule; and while their prescription for the nation's ills was arousing
tremendous enthusiasm for cheap currency it was also familiarizing hundreds of thousands of people with the fact of economic injustice and
encouraging the revolt against it. Coxey himself had risen from the
ranks of the mill workers to those of the well-to-do businessmen; but
he had had a greenbacker father and during the winter of 1893 to 1894
he had had as a guest in his home Carl Browne, whose resentments went
back to the "financial conspiracies" of the Civil War. This is but one of
many significant examples of infection with liberal ideas.

The true significance of the Bryan awakening lay in the fact that it
dramatized the common man, who adopted silver as the symbol of his
revolt against falling prices, low wages, and the intimidation of labor.
The excitements and the price rises which came with the Spanish War
diverted Bryan's following, so that their demands obtained no immediate
satisfaction; but the Spanish War itself was popularly imagined to be a
charitable undertaking and therefore provided some stimulation as an
exercise in humanity.

The Progressive Breed

The elderly Mugwump leader, Carl Schurz, who had helped to direct
Wisconsin political opinion into independent channels at an earlier critical time, thought of La Follette as his political heir. The younger man
could adopt an even greater degree of independence against more difficult obstacles, because Wisconsin farmers were cultivating self-education.
In the practice of the new leadership under the encouragement of the
old Mugwumps, there were other active personalities during the 'nineties.
In Illinois the Democratic governor J. P. Altgeld, the iconoclastic attor-

ney and legislator, Clarence Darrow, and Judge E. F. Dunne, by their questioning of the assumptions of corporate privilege helped to keep Chicago the most radical large city in the United States. In Texas, Governor James S. Hogg was securing a state railway commission and was checking security issues, city extravagances and gigantic land-holding companies. In Ohio, Tom Johnson at Cleveland, and Sam Jones at Toledo, were preparing to inject progressivism into that most graft-ridden of political and social entities, the American city. In Indiana, Eugene V. Debs was making the American Railway Union an effective obstacle to wage reductions during the depression, until President Cleveland interfered at Pullman and Debs went to jail for violating an injunction.[1] His six months of leisure there gave opportunity to read Karl Marx; next, Debs led his followers in the support of Bryan, and following that failure turned left to form a Socialist party.

Many Americans could not abjure their traditional allegiance to the Republican or Democratic labels, they had had much more social and political education. Before 1900 the men who were destined to assume progressive leadership were showing the influence of three nineteenth century theorists:—Henry D. Lloyd, Henry George, and Edward Bellamy. To these, foreign theorists could not be added to any large extent because the Marxists, Fabian Socialists and anarchists could not be very influential as long as the American majority were content with reform instead of revolution. The progressive movement would prove to be not a conflict between the haves and have-nots, but between the have-lesses and the have-mores. Even Bellamy, with the Socialist state described in his *Looking Backward,* had lost much influence with the rise of Populism.

The father of the muckrakers was H. D. Lloyd, the Presbyterian minister's son, who in his exposé of the Standard Oil Corporation set a pattern for much later writing. As his brother David had exposed the Erie Canal graft of the 1870's, so Lloyd took the cue, and undertook a documentary study of the industrialism of the nation. His data on oil, the railroads, the trusts, and the Haymarket riot led him to become a socialist in the 'eighties, while he left for future writers a challenge to carry exposure much further. His oil exposé in its earliest *Atlantic Monthly* version reached a wide audience. Charles E. Russell, a boy student in St. Johnsbury Academy in Vermont, received from it an impetus which carried him deeply into exposure writing during the nineteen hundreds. The same article by Lloyd came to be used habitually by certain campaigners.

Most influential of the theorists was Henry George. His *Our Land Policy,* a foretaste of *Progress and Poverty,* was read by a blacksmith, who loaned it to young La Follette, and by all manner of inquisitive

[1] The United States Circuit and Supreme courts ruled against Debs in United States v. Debs et al., 64 Fed. 724, (1894) and In re Debs, 158 U. S. 564, (1895).

opponents of monopoly. Among these were numerous urban reformers who feared the regimentation of party discipline because they knew the evil wrought by boss rule. Henry George did not show them how to seize power, but since he reduced the state to little more than a tax collecting agency, he made a special appeal to people of independent political viewpoint, such as Clarence Darrow, at work in the Illinois legislature, Sam (Golden Rule) Jones of Toledo, and Tom Johnson of Cleveland.

"Golden Rule" Jones (a Welshman), like Altgeld, was a successful manufacturer who once was worth half a million; but he became convinced that government should be by the Golden Rule; and as one of the first Henry George mayors, he tried to bring to Toledo freedom from domination by the street railway and electric lighting corporations. His agitation from 1897 to 1904 made it possible for his satellite, Brand Whitlock (mayor for four succeeding terms) to obtain a new charter providing for the initiative, referendum, recall, and direct nomination.

Another Ohio mayor who had been converted by Henry George and undertook to fight for public ownership of public utilities was Tom L. Johnson. The wealth he acquired as a steel producer and inventor made him a stiff competitor of Hanna in Cleveland traction. But a reading of *Social Problems* followed by *Progress and Poverty,* converted this manufacturer to free trade and the single tax. He shared the belief common to progressives that the electorate was educable; and at the behest of Henry George he went to Congress (1891 to 1895) where he fought high tariff and read George's *Protection or Free Trade* into the *Congressional Record.* He widened his influence by gathering around him a circle of young and middle-aged liberals who helped this native-born Kentuckian to leave his mark on municipal government in Ohio, and indeed throughout the United States. As mayor of Cleveland from 1901 to 1909 he waged such a fight for home rule, just taxation, and the three-cent fare that Lincoln Steffens called him "the best mayor of the best governed city in America." He helped Mayor Dunne in Chicago and Henry George in New York.

Among Johnson's aides were Newton D. Baker and Frederick C. Howe who, significantly, had studied at Johns Hopkins under Ely and Wilson. Baker secured the mayoralty two years after Johnson's 1909 defeat and saved much of the Johnson program. Meanwhile other cities obtained mayors with courage to oppose boss control and to make a continuous and factual attack upon special privilege in taxation and the courts, in spite of opposition from pulpit, press, and chambers of commerce. St. Louis had Joseph W. Folk, 1900-1904. The Ames Ring at Minneapolis was uncovered by Hovey C. Clarke as grand jury foreman in 1902. Denver's boss rule was fought by Judge Lindsey of the Children's Court. Jersey City's control by railroad and trolley interests was fought by Mark Fagan. In New York the reformer Seth Low, president of Columbia University, was elected mayor in 1901. Texas established an effective pattern in municipal efficiency by the commission form of government, which the tidal wave disaster in 1900 forced on Galveston; Houston followed suit in 1905 and the commission form slowly spread thereafter. A more radical departure was made by Milwaukee in 1910 with the election of Emil Seidel, the Socialist mayor.

The fight against control by utilities and bosses widened out from the circle of the cities into state governments. In Oregon, U'Ren between 1891 and 1910 typified the progressive's faith in the ultimate wisdom of the electorate. He engineered adoption of most of the favorite, progressive, political devices. The Australian ballot, registration of voters, initiative and referendum, direct primary, corrupt practices acts, and the recall were supposed to enlist citizens in perpetual watchfulness over government. But if citizens were to remain continuously watchful they needed watchful governors. The most outstanding were La Follette in Wisconsin, 1900-1906, Folk in Missouri, 1905-1909, Cummins in Iowa, 1902-1908, Hughes in New York, 1906-1910, and Wilson in New Jersey, 1910-1912.

The wide scattering of city and state reform movements from Oregon to New York indicates the reach of progressive influence. In each state reforms became possible only after severe struggles by disinterested citizens and disappointed office seekers, backed by brilliant journalists and by a few capitalists of generous instincts. For example, Wilson's achievement in New Jersey owed a debt to George Record, protagonist of the "new idea movement" there, and to the well-to-do Charles R. Crane and James E. Pope.

In Pennsylvania progressive advance was aided by a German immigrant, Joseph Fels, the millionaire who in 1905 announced his retirement from the soap business with the explanation that since one could not get rich without robbing other people, "I am proposing to spend the money to wipe out the system by which I made it." Fels had been interested in humanitarianism by an acquaintance with George Lansbury, begun when Fels visited England to stimulate the export trade of Fels Naptha soap. He lavished huge sums on single tax propaganda in many countries and in the United States contributed liberally to La Follette's campaigns.

Among the early journalists pushing the liberal, single tax view was Louis Post, who had been taken from the Presbyterian church by a reading of Paine's *Age of Reason*. Backed by Tom Johnson and Joseph Fels, and with the active collaboration of his wife, Alice Thacher, he edited at Chicago (1898-1913) the liberal weekly, *Public*. He helped the program of Mayor Dunne by membership on the Chicago School Board and carried over his influence into the job of Assistant Secretary of Labor for eight years in the Wilson administration.

Banding Progressives Together

The contenders against entrenched wealth and privilege in America could not have kept up their morale, in the ruthless fight in which they were engaged, if they had not been in continual communication with each other. Among the Fels single-taxer group—Johnson, Howe, Steffens, Daniel Kiefer and Post—round robin letters distributed vital inspiration and information. There was much writing back and forth and in times of stress an exchange of platform cooperation. For example, the Republican La Follette campaigned for New Jersey liberals; the Democrat Bryan several times helped the La Follette campaign in Wisconsin.

But more essential for progressive purposes was a sympathetic press which utility control of most newspapers put almost out of reach. For this purpose, the Scripps family proved invaluable in the daily newspaper field. Edward W. Scripps had been born in Illinois in 1854, the year of the birth of Joseph Fels and Tom Johnson, the year before La Follette and Debs were born, and five years after the birth of Louis Post. Edward Scripps with his half-brothers, James and George, and his half-sister, Ellen, had the imagination to start cheap and popular evening newspapers, which they established in Detroit, Cleveland, St. Louis, Cincinnati and elsewhere. They had the first daily newspaper chain in the United States. Subsequently, E. W. Scripps with M. A. McRae organized the independent gathering of news for a league of papers, which led finally into the United Press news service. After Scripps moved his residence to San Diego, a Pacific coast chain of papers was established.

Ellen Scripps became a personal friend of Robert and Belle La Follette, on their visit to La Jolla in 1898—a significant friendship because Scripps papers then practiced political independence, sympathy toward unions and liberality of view. They were, as E. W. Scripps explained, designed for the "95%" of the population. Much of the fortune they won was devoted to research in such fields of social welfare as population, biology, and science. Their press in Cleveland supported Tom Johnson and permitted some latitude to Bob Paine in his reporting of the La Follette undertakings, at a time when other papers were almost universally hostile to him. Scripps papers supported progressive presidential candidates—Roosevelt in 1912 and La Follette in 1924.

Achievements of the muckrakers cannot be separated from those of the progressive leaders. The bold fight of a few men against the boss system helped to create a demand for muckraking articles and by the same token the articles helped to embolden the politicians. The result was a temporary re-direction of political thought and action. The deepening and strengthening of the reform movement in its various facets, by articles on honest advertising, meat inspection, pure food and drugs, and improved insurance practices involved a significant realignment in politics.

The new interest in liberalism worked its political effects chiefly during the administrations of McKinley, Roosevelt, Taft, and Wilson, although it of course had long range repercussions which reached far forward into the present. Insofar as a few progressive leaders proved incorruptible and immune to discouragement from defeat, they surprised and embarrassed such old-line politicians as had found corruption and defeat the most effective instruments for political control. It was almost impossible for the latter to believe that a politician could consistently adopt positions against his own immediate advantage; nor could they understand men or women who believed that honest effort to serve the public interest is seldom lost, even though the immediate end is not obtained.

Such attributes, which to corruptionists seemed to define weakness and sheer folly in a politician, were elements of strength and wisdom to the few progressives capable of exercising them consistently. It is extremely difficult to destroy the influence of reformers who wear the impenetrable armor of inner peace, for their life cannot be spoiled by the ordinary chances of politics. That was the true secret of the power of a few of the sincere progressive leaders.

The quest for social justice was pursued by the liberals at the turn of the century through the political means available in platforms and candidates. First came victories in political platforms, when the major parties were forced to take on planks which only the minor parties previously had dared to endorse. These planks were of three main types:— first, those which gave the voter a more direct influence in the choice of candidates and the subject matter of legislation by means of direct primaries, direct election of senators, the recall, and the initiative and referendum; second, those which challenged that control over legislation which long had been exercised by the manufacturing and transportation lobbies; third, those aiming at more equable taxation. It must be noted that all of these types of planks were based on the assumption that the American electorate had the interest and the intelligence to maintain watchful supervision over their representatives when once they were accurately informed on the character of the issues involved. The true progressive thought his major task was to equip the electorate with this information.

Men of conviction, who were effective speakers and prodigal of their strength, by unremitting toil instructed the local conventions and caucuses in the principles of the new democracy. Thereby they liberalized the personnel of the local, district and state conventions until they were able to force their planks into state platforms. At the same time they pushed the process of public education by becoming candidates for nomination for office when they had but little chance of selection. For example, when Nils Haugen of Wisconsin ran for the gubernatorial nomination in 1894 on a reform ticket, he was defeated; but the campaign demonstrated the influence of the La Follette group, especially over young men, and the state machine was made aware that the fight against it had commenced.

The education of the public spread through the influence of temporarily defeated candidates, so that at the turn of the century the electorate in many states was showing a new independence of the old party managers. The results were seen in the planks of major parties, in the membership of state legislatures and in choices for governors. There was of course nothing unusual about adoption of liberal planks for decorative purposes. But the new legislators were often young men who had not lost their sympathy for change and who were not yet firmly tried to organized business. Some were congenital progressives and others entertained a willingness to challenge the reigning machine in direct ratio to their thwarted ambition to be a part of it. Both the new politicians and the old knew that youth held the key to the fate of both parties.

The actions of the interlopers could not always be predicted by the seasoned lobbyists; and insurgency was encouraged by disappointed hangers-on of the old regime—Republican and Democratic soreheads—North and South. The happy optimism of the progressives joined with the bitter resentments of the soreheads influenced a third group—the chronic fence sitters in legislation—to slide off on the left side into support of progressive measures. Since this breed of politicians is barometric, registering changes in the political climate, their liberal decisions testified to the platform prowess of the progressives and the muckrake activities of the magazines.

The trend was revealed strikingly, 5 September 1901, when President McKinley in his last speech hinted at tariff reform, the doctrine dear to progressives of the Middle Border. It assumed a double significance coming from the lips of that Republican who as representative had given his name to the tariff increases of 1890, and who as President had signed the yet higher tariff of 1897.

During the following decade, the sense of independence mounted in Washington, fed by the streams of progressivism that were rising in the forty-eight states, some scarcely more than a trickle, others a flood. Their volume mounted until in 1910 it wiped out the Republican majority in Congress and unseated the legislative symbol of the old regime, Speaker Joe Cannon.

Two years later the flood was at full tide with the election of a Democratic President, Senate, and House committed to "reform" in the major fields of public polity:—the tariff, trusts, transportation, high finance and social welfare. The movement had not burned itself out, but rather was developing prospects of a new freedom for the commonalty of the United States, when Europe blazed into war. American interest, so painstakingly aroused, and laboriously directed into channels for readjusting the balance between capital and labor, was suddenly and completely centered upon a world war. The loss to American democracy was incalculable and has yet to be regained. That loss can be appreciated only by an understanding of the influence of the Progressive movement upon politics, legislation and workaday living.

CHAPTER XXVIII

TRANSFORMING NATIONAL POLITICS

The curious irrelevance between political labels and the actual facts of American living was never better illustrated than during the sixteen years between 1897 and 1913. Through eight congressional campaigns the Republicans remained technically in continuous "control" of the Senate and, with the exception of 1911-1913, of the House also. The relative prosperity of this period handicapped Bryan, whose peculiar genius for espousal of the rights of the common man was most effective in times of distress. Also the fatter political purse of the Republicans helped to sanctify the denunciation which they had poured upon the party of Bryan and free silver.

Illuminating the Republican Label

Consequently, until near the end of the Progressive era, the Democrats suffered comparative subsidence, helping to goad Republicans into reform legislation but failing to win sufficient endorsement to become the majority party. Furthermore, as the accompanying table shows, the Republican majority often was of a size which would appear to have permitted them to practice arrogance without limit. They had the tremendous prestige and power of successive victories at the polls. Their security was made the more secure by that percentage of the American electorate which is notorious for unwillingness to vote for a probable loser.

But although the official Republican party appeared to be master in politics it remained a servant in economics. Its long-standing leadership —the Cannon group in the House and Aldrich group in the Senate, often supported by influential Democratic veterans in both bodies— maintained their habitual interest in the welfare of big business. Theirs continued to be the "trickle" philosophy:—the wealthy win eminence chiefly by superior ability and only as they make money can the middle classes and the poor prosper and receive their salaries and wages. Believers in this doctrine underestimated the contribution to prosperity made by natural resources, which were the big pawns in the game; they permitted the resources to be appropriated rapidly by private beneficiaries.

Many legislators continued blindly to accept this doctrine as a sort of natural law, giving their votes to legislation based upon it, without other reward than their own reelection. A smaller number of legislators

POLITICAL RETURNS 1892-1916

			Senate				House of Representatives			
Year	Congress	T.	R.	D.	I.	V.	T.	R.	D.	I.	V.
1892	53d	86	38	44	3	1	357	126	220	8	3
1894	54th....	86	42	39	5	..	357	246	104	7	..
1896	55th....	90	46	34	10	..	357	206	134	16	1
1898	56th....	90	53	26	11	..	357	185	163	9	..
1900	57th....	90	56	29	3	2	357	198	153	5	1
1902	58th....	90	58	32	..	..	386	207	178	..	1
1904	59th....	90	58	32	..	..	386	250	136	..	..
1906	60th....	92	61	29	..	2	386	222	164	..	..
1908	61st	92	59	32	..	1	391	219	172	..	..
1910	62d	92	49	42	..	1	391	162	228	1	..
1912	63d	96	44	51	1	..	435	127	290	18	..
1914	64th....	96	39	56	1	..	435	193	231	8	3
1916	65th....	96	42	53	1	..	435	216	210	9	..

Key: T—Total; R—Republican; D—Democrat; I—Independent;
V—Vacant.

continued deliberately to add personal, financial gain as their price for
support of the system. These two groups together followed and made
possible the Cannon-Aldrich leadership. They maintained so long the
integration between big business and their party that a chasm widened
between them and the nation at large, for their lengthy sway perforce
encouraged corruption insofar as it destroyed fear. They acquired the
moral disabilities of the "Party in power," so that their party came to
need to be saved from itself. That service was performed by progressives,
who tempered triumphant Republicanism in the fire of their reforming
zeal. They bent the reigning party somewhat to their will and prevented
it from being broken by the impact of a rising social consciousness until
the days of Wilson. This practical accommodation to the representative
principle aided the nation no less than the party.

The resentments against special privilege, which Bryan, Debs, La
Follette and other leaders of protest hoped to implement into destruction
of the dominance of wealth over American life, were not resentments
bitter enough for their objects. The rising price level of these years confounded reformers with apparent prosperity and optimism. These were
years of economic and social surge, but the United States had not yet
enough starving and unhappy people to destroy the foundations of special
privilege erected on the ruins of the Civil War. However, during the
administrations of Theodore Roosevelt, Taft and Wilson, resentments
accumulated sufficient momentum to make the political reaction of Americans highly significant. Therefore, the campaigns of the progressive era
are here traced in succession, to show how, under such circumstances,

political majorities were contrived in this democracy. And these majorities are found so intimately associated with the tariff that its history must be considered with the campaigns. Many a candidate painfully learned the connection.

The election of 1898 was significant of the condition of the Republican party. It had pledged new allegiance to protection by the Dingley tariff and it had embarked upon a new colonial venture. While the House majority was reduced, the Republicans gained sure "control" of the Senate for the first time since they lost it in 1892. In the light of future events, the election was even more significant, in that war enthusiasm catapulted into the governorship of New York a young and ambitious Republican, who had more of an ear for the groundswell over the nation than had many of his practical party associates. Theodore Roosevelt cut a dashing, zestful figure attractive to the "average" American, because full of engaging surprises, but by the same token disturbing to older men of the machines who were less adaptable to changes in popular sentiment.

To a better known public favorite, Bryan, the war finally proved to be more of a liability than a political asset. When the Spanish treaty hung precariously in the Senate balance that winter, Bryan had assisted ratification (p. 480) ; apparently he was making sure that the Republican record bore the "taint'" of imperialism. Through that policy he dealt anti-imperialism a body blow, by helping to establish Philippine annexation as an accomplished fact; when in 1900 he placed his party on a platform stressing anti-imperialism, it did not suffice to elect him president. For their part, the Republicans banked on public pride in military glory and public pleasure in the quixotic rôle of big brother to the new colonials. When they came to write their campaign platform in 1900 they used it to praise annexation of Hawaii, to reassert the gold standard, to promise Cuba to the Cubans, and to proclaim the right of Americans to the Philippines.

Thus, imperialism proved no compelling issue for either party in 1900. Nor did free silver. Bryan's party again demanded it; but the Republican managers feared silver sentiment less than importunities of creditor and conservative groups, who had insisted upon pre-campaign enactment of a gold standard law (p. 464). Other interests significant for the coming progressive era were receiving some attention that year. The Republicans offered the voters an ambiguous trust plank, promised marine interests a subsidy and gave labor a plank for immigration restriction and against convict labor.

The Democrats perforce were more specific, declaring war against monopoly, denouncing the tariff as the mother of trusts, and excoriating government by injunction. Their bid for votes included enlargement of the functions of the Interstate Commerce Commission, direct election of senators and construction of a canal through Nicaragua. This platform induced the Populists, Silver Republicans and Anti-Imperialists to endorse the Democratic candidates. But more radical protest was not stilled:—four other groups (insignificant in numbers) registered their dissatisfaction by selecting separate candidates and platforms; and the disillusioned Debs started on its long career that highly significant party, technically named the Social Democrats but usually referred to as the Socialist Party.

None of these anti-Republican aggregations could cope with the efficient Hanna, as long as there was a further rise in agricultural prices and quite a popular relish for paternalism in the islands. When miners of the anthracite coal fields threatened to mar election prospects, Hanna as chairman of the Republican National Committee persuaded the operators to grant a wage increase of 10% and a reduction in the price of blasting powder. Thus

F. Opper in N. Y. *Journal.*

Skinning the People

Mamma Hanna smiles while little McKinley says: "Papa doesn't kill them; he merely skins them and lets them go, to grow more skins."

victory came to the Republicans, and Hanna was able to return to business interests some of the funds he had levied to secure it.

Bryan in 1900 got electoral votes only from the solid South and the mining states of Colorado, Idaho, Montana and Nevada; to more than this the silver interests could not help him. McKinley kept the presidential chair and his party held comfortable majority seats in the Senate and House. But in popular votes McKinley beat him by little more than 860,000 out of a total of more than 13,500,000. Thoughtful observers might note that neither rank inconsistency nor gold discoveries could weaken greatly Bryan's hold, as long as millions of people were interested in him as a symbol of social justice. That was his contribution to the progressive era.

Their own personalized symbol of social justice came to the Republicans out of the 1900 campaign, thanks to Boss Tom Platt of the New York machine. He and his henchmen were willing to go to any lengths to get rid of the restless, sensitive and able politician who had climbed San Juan Hill into the governorship. Theodore Roosevelt was not wholly averse to running for the vice presidency, under the circumstances of 1900; and while the campaign was acquainting him further with the progressive stirrings in the westward (for which he had shown some sympathy as New York's governor), he was demonstrating that he knew how to get on, politically, with the Middle Border.

Growing Progressive Pressure

But in the last analysis even Hanna was defeated at this election, for Robert La Follette that same fall was elected governor of Wisconsin; his unquenchable crusading zeal and dynamic personality eventually would force the Hannas of the old guard to a new definition of Republican obligations. "Fighting Bob" in 1892 had vowed that the 1894 campaign should launch a persistent attack upon the old Wisconsin machine maintained by the railroad and lumber interests. During the following six years, as he addressed great crowds at chautauquas, county fairs and lyceums, upon the subject of "Dangers Threatening Representative Government," he had been educating himself as well as his listeners. The governor had progressed far beyond the understanding of that representative who had supported the McKinley tariff. By an unending stream of progressive speeches, by exploitation of liberal literature, and through a modest beginning of newspaper support, he in 1898 had forced a liberal platform upon Wisconsin Republicans. Two more years, and he won the party's gubernatorial nomination and the state election.

The victories of 1898 and 1900 did not mean to La Follette and his wife (a woman of remarkable faith with resilience to adversity) that the machine had altered its true character; but that public sentiment was changing—that the rank and file would make themselves heard "if they understood." So they set themselves to the patient industry of digging up public information.

The beliefs and faiths stirring in Wisconsin liberals of 1900 were important because they were not unique. The young insurgents rising in several states in revolt against arrogant machines were led by men and aided by women with the social imagination and political ingenuity to feed and use resentment against corruption. Revolt came first in cities, where democratic government can be its worst and where uprisings stand the quickest chance of success. As mayors were infected, so were governors. The progressivism of these ambitious leaders was sharpened by their desperate conflict with relentless opponents. Their real enemy was entrenched business, which pulled the strings for puppet politicians to dance; progressives could not afford to weaken themselves by quarter-way compromise. They must travel at least half the distance.

A sense of the rising trend, and of the political pitfalls involved, was the fortunate possession of the new Vice President. Consequently, when the Russian anarchist, Leon Czolgosz, on 6 September 1901, took advantage of McKinley's attendance upon the Pan American Exposition at Buffalo to remove from the scene the kindly, unaggressive and acquiescent President, he catapulted into Republican leadership a genius who knew how to play with the political dynamite of his period.

Roosevelt proceeded to make his first message to Congress a roomy, twenty-thousand word discussion housing vague references—pleasant to the eyes of people in the intra-party movement for social justice—references to greater regulation of corporations and trusts, to extension of the Interstate Commerce Commission's powers, more reciprocity, development of conservation and irrigation, and extension of civil service. He mentioned also —for no less cogent reasons— subsidy for the merchant marine, an immigration policy, extension of the consular service and a militaristic program including a bigger navy, a better army and "justice" to Civil War veterans. With comments on the Library of Congress, the census and colonial policy, there were not many types of sentiment to which Roosevelt made no general appeal.

Macauley in New York *World.*

The Balancing Act

In July of 1902 Iowa suggested that Roosevelt grow more specific. The farmers of the Middle Border were daring to question protection and insurgent Republican leaders must needs join in sponsoring protest. Governor Albert B. Cummins at the state convention in July endorsed the so-called "Iowa Idea"—that the tariff was the mother of trusts and that the way to prevent monopoly was to revise the tariff downward. This was the Middle West's teasing interpretation of guarded and general statements earlier made by Roosevelt; but would he go that far? In some of his ensuing campaign speeches, he endorsed the notion of a non-partisan commission, which should advise Congress in the maintenance of flexible schedules, for neither he nor the Iowans worried overmuch as to the practicability of obtaining a non-partisan commission in the first place or persuading Congress to accept its advice in the second. Commissions were becoming popular.

But before seconding Iowa's demand for downward revision, Roosevelt cautiously called a September conference at Oyster Bay, of Mr. Aldrich and other senators intimately conversant with their party's business alignments. Their arguments convinced him that the tariff was a political explosive, with which he did not care to blow up his own administration. He soon announced at Logansport, Indiana, that too frequent changes were unwise. He found compensating activities in energetically inducing Morgan and other financiers concerned in a coal strike (p.

577) to temper their intransigeance to the necessities of a Republican majority.

However, the Republican majority in Congress was somewhat reduced at the election of 1902 and liberal commentators assumed that the President would seriously undertake revision downward and further government supervision of trusts. Speaker David B. Henderson of Iowa, a pronounced protectionist, had refused to run again, possibly because of dissatisfaction with the liberal trend, yet more likely because of loss of popularity in his own district. But his successor in the speakership, Joseph G. Cannon, certainly was not chosen for any reform leanings; and Senator Aldrich and his conservative associates on the Senate Finance Committee still believed that their party's compulsions were not toward revision.

They reiterated their convictions when the uneasy President called another conference, at his White House office early in 1903. Roosevelt, listening, knew that he wanted to remain on cordial terms with these conservatives, for he had yet to win the presidency in his own right. So he determined to sidestep the issue then. Nor could he bring himself to come to grips with it after his 1904 re-election. The issue grew in importance; but Roosevelt let the tariff dynamite accumulate in the Republican backyard, for his successor to handle.

Meanwhile, during the summer of 1903, after Roosevelt had turned his back on tariff reform, other issues were being stirred which he was less reluctant to face. On an extended tour of the Middle West and a journey east as far as Maryland and New York, Governor La Follette was making his chautauqua speeches on "Representative Government," an address presented as a new Declaration of Independence. At county fairs in Wisconsin he read to listening farmers railroad rate schedules demonstrating gross discrimination. His platform arguments outside Wisconsin were the more convincing by reason of his record as governor. Wisconsin, he was bound, should set a broad example to other states.

Impetus from 1904

The immediate outcome of 1904, on the other hand, most concerned Roosevelt. He was uneasy lest Mark Hanna, as a more conservative candidate, should win the nomination. But death definitely eliminated this imagined competitor, and the President clinched his own popularity by seizure of the Panama Canal (p. 595), so that the nomination came without difficulty. By espousal of popular subjects less dangerous, politically, than the tariff, such as trust busting and labor reform, he added to his value as a symbol of social justice.

Republican managers were less afraid of a Roosevelt candidacy than of a La Follette platform. Therefore, at the Chicago convention in June, they refused to seat the La Follette faction as delegates from Wisconsin, seating the conservative following of Senator Spooner instead; and they said very little about corporations, refusing to endorse La Follette's scheme for physical valuation as a gauge of railroad rates. These refusals gave the progressive position splendid publicity. McClure, under the impression that La Follette was a demagogue, sent his cleverest journalist, Lincoln Steffens, to Madison to expose the situation.

Steffens unexpectedly became so thoroughly convinced of La Follette's sincerity and soundness that he did for him in the September *McClure's* what he already had done for Missouri's progressive governor, Folk. Subsequently *Collier's, The Outlook, Harper's,* and *The Review of Reviews* featured La Follette, most of them favorably in spite of their eastern affiliations. To cap the climax Wisconsin's state Supreme Court declared, 5 October, that the La Follettites shut out by the party machine at Chicago had indeed been the regular delegation.

That fall, as in 1902, Bryan stayed out of Wisconsin because he wanted Democrats there to support progressives. His party had accepted planks for tariff revision downward and enforcement of anti-trust laws, but had dropped the income tax and free silver. Also, they had abandoned Bryan as a candidate, substituting the New York gold conservative, Judge Alton B. Parker, to signify a return to "safe" principles. Thus, in 1904 when the deeper currents of political feeling were changing direction, party managers were confused. The traditional liberal party took a conservative candidate, while the quasi-progressive candidate of the traditionally conservative party was financed by corporation contributions. The only political classes to resent this anomalous situation seriously were those Socialists, Prohibitionists, Populists, and Social Laborites who cast a total of about three-quarters of a million votes for their presidential candidates without placing any of them in the electoral column.

Roosevelt and Parker divided the main body of the votes on the approximate ratio of seven and one-half to five millions; and in the first flush of a victory which had given him the greatest popular and electoral majority in the history of the country, Roosevelt announced that "under no circumstances will I be a candidate for, or accept another nomination."

While Roosevelt was defeating Parker, La Follette was obtaining a Progressive majority in both houses of the Wisconsin legislature, together with re-election as governor and wide, national recognition of the significance of the Wisconsin movement. The legislature promptly elected La Follette to Quarles' seat in the United States Senate. But the governor-senator and his following were determined to fulfill their campaign pledges; and so they expanded the state program, and together set a record in establishing democratic election procedure and physical valuation as a basis of railroad taxation. Not until January of 1906 was La Follette content to relinquish the governorship for the senatorship.

At Washington Congress was indicating anxiety over the rising demands for economic and social legislation, and the President was extremely eloquent and painfully eager to place legislation on the statute books. La Follette prodded Roosevelt vigorously; and, since he was thoroughly familiar with the progressive advance in various states and personally acquainted with the situation and achievements of his fellow-progressives, he worked to unite these forces for national reforms. His influence doubtless increased the number of messages on interstate commerce, employer liability and the trusts, which Roosevelt sent Congress; but the basic differences between the mainsprings of action in these two men made for mutual dislike and distrust, which was bound to retard far-reaching legislation.

The President was an astute politician, with his ear to the ground and with a habit of worrying which could be quieted only by vigorous action. He had an impatient urge for immediate results which prevented him from taking thought as to long-time effects. Uncomfortably aware of his own limitations in economic theory and practice, he was thoroughly conscious of his dependence upon the legislative cooperation of the Old Guard—that Old Guard which in the last analysis represented the economic interests of the social class to which Roosevelt and most of his closest friends belonged. As a practical man, with but three years remaining to add to his legislative record, he felt compelled to compromise for half-a-loaf. Roosevelt and probably a majority of Americans were convinced that he epitomized "the square deal" and that he knew well how to "speak softly and carry a big stick" to frighten "malefactors of great wealth." His oratory and gestures alarmed enough of the privileged classes to persuade the under-privileged of his Messiahship.

The few discerning, who perceived that Roosevelt did not originate his program and did shrink from drastic economic reform, were reassured or disappointed according to their class. La Follette, starting out on a national career which it was reasonable to suppose might be prolonged, felt that permanent renown and reform were not built upon half-way legislation; he believed that by patient persistence and courageous acceptance of temporary defeat progressives ultimately could force Congress to take the "full step" for effective legislation. Given time, "the people," once well informed, would endorse his program. His twenty years of political experience, since he first entered the House of Representatives, had given him a deeper understanding of problems but greater faith in their solution.

Congress adopted the Roosevelt doctrine. Before the election of 1906 they passed tentative laws on pure food, meat inspection, railroad employers' liability and railroad regulation, described in succeeding chapters.

But they failed to purify the advertising of foods or to require that railroad rates should have any true relation to the actual value of railroad property. In so far as these measures contented the country they retarded the movement toward lasting solutions.

1908 Guarantees Schism

Despite the hectic congressional output of May and June, 1906, fall elections reduced the Republican majority in the House from 114 to 58. While control of the majority party machinery still remained with members of the Old Guard, they were put on the defensive and, overestimating Roosevelt's responsibility for their discomfort, they adopted an attitude of open resentment toward him, which he cordially reciprocated. They had to let him select the Republican nominee in 1908; and he on the other hand had to pass by his first choice, Elihu Root (because of Root's trust affiliations) and choose that friend, William Howard Taft, whose faithful service as governor of the Philippines and as Secretary of War indicated a sympathetic attitude toward what Roosevelt erroneously described as "my policies." A New York conservative, James S. Sherman, was named as running mate. Since Mrs. Taft was most anxious that her husband receive this presidential nomination instead of donning the robes of a Supreme Court Justice, as he preferred, feminine influence thus ensured that progressive politics of 1912 should be deflected by a Rooseveltian sortie against both Taft and La Follette.

Platform making at Chicago was controlled by the Old Guard, masters at putting together planks which promised a continuation of the "Roosevelt policies" without defining them. Ambiguity emasculated references to the use of injunctions, to the Sherman anti-trust law and to the Interstate Commerce Commission. On the tariff they were forced, by the widening popularity of the so-called "Iowa Idea," to promise "revision," but whether up or down they conveniently neglected to state. These Old Guard devices did not, however, keep out of the Republican campaigning state planks which took a bold position on crucial issues. A platform demanding tariff rates based upon the difference between the cost of production at home and abroad, a permanent tariff commission, physical valuation of the railroads as a basis for determining rates, popular election of senators and publicity for campaign contributions and their expenditures was constructed by La Follette and a group of twenty-eight supporters. They forced it upon the attention of the nation by submitting it to the Republican convention—for inevitable defeat.

Whether or not Roosevelt and Bliss, the treasurer of the Republican party, were alarmed at a prospect of publicizing the corporate contributions customary to Republican campaigns, it proved easy to vote down the progressive platform. Nor was it difficult to purchase southern support of the Taft nomination through the customary patronage devices, nor to crush the western opposition to him.

The Democrats proclaimed as proved the connection between big business and the Republicans, and undertook to garner the harvest sowed by the progressives. They abjured their eastern, conservative connections of 1904, staging a convention in the heart of the West, at Denver. They proclaimed Bryan as candidate and instead of an eastern man chose John W. Kern of the Middle Border state of Indiana, as vice presidential nominee. They let Bryan insert a plank explicitly demanding destruction of trusts; and they called for an income tax, an end to injunctions in labor disputes, and removal of duties on trust-made articles. Gratefully, Gompers delivered to them the official endorsement of the American Federation of Labor.

The resulting exigencies of the ensuing campaign moved Taft, on reaching the Middle West, to define the prospective revision of the tariff by the Republican party as "downward"; and 7.5 million votes were cast for him as Roosevelt's heir. Bryan accumulated approximately 6.5 million; and, thanks to the liberal offerings of the Republicans and the radical offerings of the Democrats, the "protest" vote under various third party labels totalled less than in 1904.

The outstanding victor in this election however, was not Taft, but La Follette. He persisted in his campaign practice of "calling the roll," to expose the votes on popular measures of candidates for re-election. This helped to modify the voting predilections of the House and Senate membership, from those states where public sentiment was progressive. Also it guaranteed schism among the Republicans of the sixty-first Congress, on that perennial political and sectional issue—the tariff.

CHAPTER XXIX

THE PROGRESSIVES WIN

It was during the administration of President Taft that the progressive movement attained sufficient momentum to split the Republican party. For this there were numerous reasons. Three of the most outstanding were as follows:—the demands of the progressive movement had developed past the toleration point of the Republican management; after that point was passed the movement attracted an increasing number of voters; the President to whom Roosevelt had bequeathed the tariff issue was too honestly inept and unimaginative to placate the progressives. The story of how the split occurred is a warm, human document.

Use of the Tariff

President-elect Taft was not a timid man, and did not shrink from tariff conflict. He pressed the committee on Ways and Means of the outgoing Congress to begin preparation of new schedules immediately; and when Congress met, 15 March 1909, in special session at his call, the House version of the tariff was almost ready to be introduced. The insurgent congressmen for their part were quite ready to use the tariff issue and Democratic aid to unseat Speaker Cannon. This proved unsuccessful, because eastern Democrats were scarcely less conservative than the Republican Old Guard and because Taft had the sense to see that if he aided the hybrid group he would destroy all chance of fulfillment of his administration's program by the Republican majority. Therefore Cannon again was elected Speaker and Chairman Payne of the Committee on Ways and Means received the commission to see the tariff bill through the House. This job he completed after three weeks of "debate," because everyone knew that the real political battle over the tariff would be fought in the Senate.

The House bill carried an inheritance tax advocated by Taft; and the rates were a revision downward, because the Chairman and the House both fought jokers and secret increases and because progressives had been sent to the House from far-flung areas. The Far West sent Poindexter of Washington, Hayes of California, Gronna of North Dakota; the plains area Murdock and Madison of Kansas, Lindbergh and Volstead of Minnesota, Norris, Kincaid and Hinshaw of Nebraska; the Middle Border nine Wisconsin members and six from Iowa; the East, Fowler of New Jersey and Gardner and Lovering of Massachusetts. These members were the voice of the middle class, endeavoring to determine the political trend of the progressive era.

In the upper house the progressive group contained about a dozen members, most of them indebted to La Follette for campaign assistance. To the Senate in 1907 had come Borah of Idaho, Burkett and Browne of Nebraska and Bourne of Oregon; in 1909 South Dakota sent Crawford, Kansas Bristow, and Iowa Cummins, the last-named second only to La Follette in strength and popularity with progressive Republicans of the West.

Among the Senators who now voted progressive were three who were not recent newcomers to that body:—Dolliver, Clapp and Beveridge. Dolliver, at long last, voted progressive because the death of Allison and the rise of Cummins had freed him from the conservative alignments to which he had owed his advancement but with which he never had been comfortable. Until now, his political course had violated his inclination toward democracy; but, after Aldrich disappointed him in committee assignments at the 1909 session, Dolliver's loyalty to progressivism never wavered again. His intimate convivial crony, Moses Clapp of Minnesota, represented the more radical influence in his state while Clapp's colleague from Minnesota, Nelson, occasionally voted progressive. Indiana's more liberal leanings found expression through Senator Beveridge who had worked with both Roosevelt and the Old Guard and whose main interest was child-labor legislation.

The conglomerate character of the La Follette following—if it can be called a following—was highly significant. It demonstrated the confused motivation of the senators who individually and jointly dared to challenge the will of big business in politics. It forecast that they would fall apart readily.

Most of these senators came to share in the work of exposing the special interests entrenched behind the schedules of the Payne-Aldrich tariff, when it emerged from the Finance Committee, and most of them voted "nay" on the question of its final passage. Their joint influence was greatly enhanced by two policies recently adopted by La Follette:— he had established in 1908 his own weekly organ, *La Follette's Magazine,* which had such talented contributors as John R. Commons, William Hard, Frederick Howe, Herbert Quick (editor), E. A. Ross the sociologist, Lincoln Steffens, and William Allen White of Kansas. Secondly, La Follette in February of 1909 had taken a larger house in Washington and he and his wife commenced the practice of giving dinners to bring progressives of the Senate and House together in a closer personal and political understanding. Mrs. La Follette also tried to make her receptions and other social affairs function similarly.

The first gathering of progressives for concerted legislative action occurred 13 February 1909, when La Follette undertook to inspire his colleagues with the faith that by concerted action they could put through the United States Congress laws like those forced through the Wisconsin legislature. His victories in the smaller area, which had a comparatively homogeneous population and unified economic interests, were the source of his strength to withstand almost insuperable opposition in the larger and vastly more conglomerate arena at Washington. He realized that his purposes could be accomplished only through careful teamwork, and that the deep, personal resentment which Senators felt over his campaign use of the rollcalls required that other progressives should play the more conspicuous part. This fed their egos and in no wise diminished his influence upon the legislation in question. It probably lessened his personal renown and may have helped eventually in making it possible for Roosevelt to displace him in the leadership; but La Follette was one of those occasional politicians who care for definite achievement as well as for personal advancement.

The tariff bill, as it reached the Senate from the Finance Committee, had become a capital example of logrolling. Its atrocities (which went further than Aldrich himself preferred) were the perfection of political practices long hallowed by use among senators of both parties. The insurgents realized that certain increases in the cotton, woolen, silk, rubber and other schedules played into their hands and apportioned these among themselves for denunciatory analysis. Each went through the gruelling experience of hurriedly amassing sufficient data on his assignment for exposure purposes. Several shared to some degree La Follette's ability to breathe life into figures, relating them to daily tasks and common experiences, investing abstract sums with power to stir the imagination of a familiar audience. For this they won much popularity in home districts; but outside applause could not break the hold of protection lobbyists upon senators of both parties.

President Taft intervened little until Senate and House conferees appeared in deadlock, when he succeeded in enlarging the free lists to include hides; also, he welcomed establishment of a tariff board to gather information continuously along broad lines and it was provided for. But neither he nor the insurgents introduced any essential change in the United States tariff system. They attached a bad odor to the extreme protectionists and fenced them into a defensive position, where they yielded a corporation tax, an income tax amendment (p. 552) and a few reductions important enough to lower the average below 1897. All reciprocity arrangements, however, were expressly repealed and the best that can be said for the progressives is that at this point in American history they stopped the upward tide.

When Congress adjourned 5 August, after a hot, exhausting and bitter session, the evil social implications of exorbitant rates had been aired thoroughly throughout the country by various devices of dissenting Republicans, some Democrats and such magazine writers as Ida Tarbell and David Graham Phillips, who wrote human interest stories on the schedules. Against their outcry it was of no avail that the *Outlook,* with which Roosevelt was to be connected, pronounced the Payne-Aldrich law "by far the most enlightened protectionist measure ever enacted"; nor for Roosevelt to tell *Outlook* readers that it was better than Dingley's; nor for President Taft (with more boldness than wisdom) to tell an audience at Winona, Minnesota, that this tariff was on the whole the best the country ever had had. The President did improve it to the extent that he declined to superimpose 25% retaliatory, maximum rates which it put in his control. But that could not metamorphose the work of the Senate into a law in tune with the most vocal sentiment of that moment in American history. The progressives went up and down the countryside pointing out that this tariff was a gross and inequitable assumption of special privilege by entrenched interests. They convinced the Middle Border that Taft's administration was at the service of Cannon, Aldrich and all their cohorts. Such vigorous offensive tactics pushed the conservatives into a weak position.

As a political device, the fight over the Payne-Aldrich tariff did its perfect work. It fomented personal hatreds which rankled and cut deeply; and these hatreds become in times of stress the most active agents in determining the course of legislation. Those Republican Progressives who had been invading the bailiwicks of the Old Guard, reading the record of their votes and interpreting that record in terms of unfaithfulness to American democratic ideals, had adopted the only effective means for ousting the old leaders from their pathway. While firmly insisting upon their Republican affiliation, these progressives employed their imaginative and energetic talents to attract such habitual Republicans as might be persuaded to question their habitual assumption that old party managers manage well enough. The new sensation of active participation in the choice of candidates and policies was pleasant during the excitement, and made them ready to take time and trouble for serious consideration of the national welfare.

Few progressives thought in realistic terms of the lobby, disliking to admit the inevitable dominance in politics of whatever interest maintains the most efficient lobby. Rather, they thought of their legislators as persons who by their individual honesty or dishonesty could maintain "democratic" conditions, democracy being a thing in which they firmly believed. So they turned their resentments against the Cannons in office, rather than against that worship of individual success and those applications of the principle of laissez-faire which were jeopardizing the common welfare. Bryan, Gompers, La Follette, some journalists and a few of the more thoughtful critics partially realized the shallowness of the movement. So did minorities in many places and the majority in Wisconsin; but in the main progressives were content to capitalize easy resentments.

Exploiting 1910

Cannon, as Speaker of the House, was so entirely a product of his twenty-seven years of intimate connection with the direction of Republican legislation that he became the foremost target for progressive fire. He now was serving his fourth Speakership and his record of co-operation with the dominant Senators in their resistance against the social legislation of the 1900's had well-nigh destroyed that impression of homespun common sense which he had so carefully created earlier

Herbert Johnson in Phila. *North American.*

Uncle Joe the Defendant

in his career. It had long been customary for the Speaker of the House to have the privilege of appointing committees and their chairmen, and to head the Committee on Rules which determined both ordinary procedure and the special orders under which major legislation was enacted. These privileges gave practical control of House policy to the Speaker and to the small group of representatives who shared with him membership on the Committee on Rules and held the chairmanship of the other significant committees, Ways and Means, and Banking and Currency. With clever management they could practically bend the majority to their will and deliver such legislation as special interests and party managers approved.

Assuming that the House membership in the mass would have the public welfare more at heart than the old Rules Committee, thirty Republicans who in March preceding the 1910 campaign were no longer obedient cogs in the machine of their party, joined with the Democrats, who had not elected a Speaker of their own since 1893, to pass a Norris resolution for unhorsing Cannon. Without any help from Taft, they debarred the Speaker from membership on the Committee on Rules and made that Committee elective by the House. Cannon—and the Speakership for the nonce—were reduced to mere presiding units.

Where, then, was House leadership to reside? The leading progressives, of course, had their own answer; Aldrich and Hale did not like that answer, but they were hard-headed realists and knew that the happy days of the old system at Washington were gone. In New England they retained an almost impregnable position in the Republican

In Phila. *North American.*

Weeding Out the Standpatters

machine; but they shrank from the indignities of a campaign certain to bring their worst enemy, La Follette, into their home states to denounce them, before the populace. They had the sense to announce their retirement to become effective in 1911. Conservatism, it seemed, was in full retreat.

The Congress which had demoted Cannon passed several election laws proclaiming its faith in the honesty and interest of the electorate and the perfectibility of the bureaucracy. An economy and efficiency commission was appointed to investigate the administrative departments with an eye to ending waste. Publicity of contributions to federal campaign funds, with names of donors, amounts contributed and the manner of their expenditure were stipulated in a law of 25 June 1910. A constitutional amendment for direct election of senators—another reform Taft favored—passed Congress that summer and within three years was ratified and put into effect.

Unhappily, Taft's basic tolerance for moderate reforms availed him little during this era. In June of 1910 Theodore Roosevelt was on his way home from Africa. Roosevelt had been met at the upper waters of the Nile, when his political genius was suffering from a year's inactivity, by an angry and eloquent conservationist, Gifford Pinchot (p. 583). When Roosevelt reached New York, La Follette and other progressives unburdened themselves to him. Plunging into the melee, he won a contest for temporary chairmanship of the New York State Republican convention, endorsement of the direct primary and choice of a gubernatorial nominee; but his candidate, H. L. Stimson, lost to the Democrat.

That summer and autumn Roosevelt took the pulse of the country from western and southern platforms; he found that it was quickened by his version of progressive principles, which he later labelled the "New Nationalism." He found the old standpat organization, with which he had cooperated on most essentials during his presidency, on the defensive, insurgents of his party capturing the applause and the primaries, and the Democrats making loud music with the tariff, Cannonism, and the high cost of living. His own anointed, President Taft (whose administration Roosevelt, by indirection, both endorsed and impugned), was bringing worse than no acclaim to his patron. Taft soon was engulfed in a cloud of obscurity wrapped about him by the conspicuous popularity of his predecessor.

That fall Roosevelt observed that Democrats won the governorships in many states, several in the West of course—including Ohio and Oregon—but surprisingly in Maine, Massachusetts, Connecticut, New Jersey and New York. This last was hard to bear. In the total situation there was more than enough to wound the tender pride of the ex-president. He burned for active leadership. The membership of the United States Senate was slipping from the party which had been in titular control there since 1897. Nine state legislatures which were due to elect senators, were made Democratic by the 1910 voting. The new Senate would have 42 Democrats; and of its 49 Republicans too many were insurgents to permit party harmony. Speaker Cannon had been defeated; to the House had been elected a Socialist and 228 Democrats, who with the insurgents among the 162 Republicans evidently would prove responsive to progressivism.

President Taft, who never had been elected to an office in the usual sense, since the many he held prior to his presidency were all by appointment and Roosevelt's endorsement in 1908 amounted to the same thing, cast about clumsily, for means to establish his own leadership over Republicans. Hoping to make the nation understand that he was the moderate reformer—which indeed he had become—he again laid awkward hands upon the tariff. Overestimating American interest in development of international trade, underestimating the instant resistance of sectional lobbies to measures for the general welfare, he demanded of his expiring Republican majority in Congress a measure for reciprocity with Canada. It was calculated to bring free trade in many raw materials and some food products, with reductions in tariffs on some manufactured goods. Endorsement might fairly be expected from the American Newspaper Publishers' Association because the agreement proposed duty-free newsprint; from James J. Hill's railroad interests because they would haul the goods of the expanding trade, and from Minnesota millers who wanted Canada's hard wheat to blend with American softer wheat.

Bitter opposition, however, came from manufacturers of lumber and paper and from farmers who feared Canadian competition. Interests opposed to any weakening of the protective principle supplied copious propaganda against reciprocity, to the farm press. Some progressives of North Dakota for example, who had demanded tariff reform for the benefit of farmers in 1909, in 1910 opposed it for the same class. Again Taft appeared as the farmers' enemy. He managed to obtain a large congressional majority for the agreement, but only after fierce internecine warfare with those Republicans who furnished most of the opposition. These pyrotechnics fed into Canadian politics, fostering the charge of subserviency to the United States. Sir Wilfred Laurier's fourteen-year-old government, which had hoped for a vote of confidence out of reciprocity, was ousted and the agreement killed.

The incoming Democratic majority went through the motions of passing what were called "pop" bills, which were proposals for reducing the rates on a few of the items which had great political significance:—sugar, steel, chemicals, wool, and cotton. There was no pretense that this was a scientific way to approach the tariff but it was generally agreed that it was clever politics. Taft vetoed the "pop" bills and the Democrats gleefully used this to strengthen their 1912 campaign.

La Follette versus Roosevelt

Republicans sincerely advocating reform, with those temporarily committed to progressive principles, took great encouragement from the situation. They met at La Follette's home in Washington, 21 January 1911, to form the National Progressive Republican League. La Follette, Bourne and Bristow led the van of senators; with Roosevelt drifting, watching, fearful lest the League shrink into a small group far ahead of public sentiment, desirous that the League delay nomination of a candidate against Taft. Within four months the inner group had agreed to settle upon an anti-Taft candidate and several, including friends of Roosevelt, had assured La Follette that they and Roosevelt would favor him. La Follette's candidacy was announced in June and he asked for open Roosevelt endorsement; but although Roosevelt aided the candidacy in various ways, he would not actually commit himself to it. Nevertheless, at a Chicago conference in October, La Follette progressives overbore counsels for delay and secured endorsement of the senator. To his war chest came $1,000 from Medill McCormick, $2,000 from William Flinn of Pennsylvania, and $20,000 from the brothers Pinchot.

The progressive group proposed to preserve honesty in democracy and to establish moral standards in business practice by political devices: —by popular election of senators, direct primaries for nomination of elective officials, direct election of delegates to national conventions, the initiative, referendum, and recall, and a corrupt practices act. They showed somewhat more unity in these fields the next session of Congress than they could on the tariff; for although most of them were committed to the doctrine that the tariff mothered the trusts, it went "agin natur" to cooperate with Democrats on pop bills which urgently denied the validity of revered Republican protectionism.

By January of 1912 the La Follette boom was expiring for lack of open endorsement from Roosevelt, who was reaching the determination to lead the progressive movement himself. The administration had wounded his self-esteem terribly by a suit against the United States Steel Corporation, in which aspersions were thrown upon his righteous wisdom in cooperating on the Tennessee Coal and Iron acquisition (p. 563). Roosevelt knew that an anti-Taft movement probably would give the Democrats the election, but he burned to lead it. Already the state of his emotions had drawn him into denunciation of Taft for pushing principles of arbitration and reciprocity which he earlier had espoused. Now he became obsessed with the belief that it was his duty to "sacrifice" himself to a progressive campaign.

The Roosevelt following demanded that La Follette retire in favor of the more popular candidate, who was more likely to obtain the party's nomination. La Follette, at the distance of 1938, seems to have been the ablest, most persistent and far-seeing of the progressive leadership; but his stubborn addiction to relatively drastic reforms and his tendency to reject compromises marred his availability as a candidate of a movement which perforce included many members devoted to the immediate main chance. Roosevelt, on the other hand, was less likely to jeopardize his political following by insisting upon drastic economic reforms; as President he repeatedly had accepted compromises in order to get immediate action, and that action can be convenient for campaign purposes.

Luckily for Roosevelt, at this juncture La Follette was exhausting his strength and judgment by an inhumanly heavy speaking schedule and by worries over the serious illness of a daughter and over Roosevelt's attitude. Most of his following and financial backers were only waiting an occasion to announce their shift to the more highly magnetic and available ex-president. La Follette provided the occasion. When the Periodical Publishers Association included him in their list of after-dinner speakers at a Philadelphia banquet, 12 February 1912, he inflicted upon a tired, uninterested and not entirely sober throng of publicity men a very long, critical and strangely repetitious speech. By contrast, a fellow guest named Woodrow Wilson had sat through the tedious evening at table (unlike La Follette who came in at 10:30 only for his speech), had thus measured the temper of his hearers and had advantaged himself with a very brief, felicitous talk. Next morning, the press loudly proclaimed the appreciation and the resentment respectively earned.

Promptly, Gifford Pinchot, whom La Follette had understood to have pledged that Roosevelt would not be a candidate, announced that La Follette was too ill to assume such a responsibility. Roosevelt seized the cue 21 February, with a ringing speech to a Columbus, Ohio, audience, proclaiming the progressive principles which La Follette had done more than any other one man to advance and adding thereto the far more extreme propositions of recall of judges and of judicial decisions. Three days later, he planned a formal request for his own candidacy, which was duly presented to him by seven Western governors in attendance at Oyster Bay. His "reply" was not unfriendly to "their" bequest. La Follette had been out-maneuvered.

During the four months preceding the Republican Convention at Chicago, 18 June, the new progressive leader staged a series of platform appearances over the United States, dramatizing his candidacy for the Republican nomination by a shrill attack upon his unfortunate heir in the White House and the tariff he had praised. Taft had responded to the progressive urge by supporting an income tax amendment and popular election of senators, and had ratified a parcel post system, an eight hour law for government employees and civil service expansion; but all that did not now avail him. He tried, unskillfully, pitifully, to reply to Roosevelt in kind; and the electorate, pleasurably excited, cared not at all that the campaign had descended quite completely from principles to personalities. They were enjoying the favorite quadrennial sport of Americans, heightened by a most dramatic fight for the Republican nomination.

The states which had established Presidential primaries registered their preference for Roosevelt, who was the majority choice of the Republican rank and file; but that did not give him the clear majority of the convention delegates, to which he declared himself entitled. In the remaining 34 states, Republican conventions managed after the old system endorsed Taft. Some 200 "doubtful" delegates at the National Convention were the result. The National Committee, following customary precedents and usual patronage methods, especially with southern delegates, gave the contested seats to Taft's friends, and thus renominated him. Exceeding wroth at this application of principles which he himself had employed in 1904 and 1908, Roosevelt protested the "theft" of 80 or 90 delegates, instructed his following to participate neither in the platform nor the nominations of their party, and prepared to secure his own nomination at a convention of bolters. La Follette did not join the bolters.

The progressive Republicans (each paying his or her own expenses) convened at Chicago 5 August in an atmosphere of religious fervor. Hymns, sermons, Biblical quotations, tears and solemnity, all registered the emotional state which swayed the 2000 delegates assembled from all the states of the Union. They were enjoying all those feelings and reactions which come to people convinced they are engaged in a holy cause. They nominated Roosevelt for President and made Hiram W. Johnson of California (one of the abler reform politicians who in 1910 had stepped out of the obscurity where the Old Guard had tried to keep him, and into the governorship) his running mate.

Presumably a few progressives believed that "Teddy's" primary success and personal popularity had some chance of winning for him a plurality of the votes in November. Politicians of experience, however, knew that the Republican split presaged Democratic victory. Critical liberals read on the roster of Roosevelt's campaign backers the names of millionaires like George W. Perkins of the J. P. Morgan firm, Frank A. Munsey, owner of the New York *Press,* and the Pinchot brothers. They scarcely could be expected to favor too literal an application of the new party's platform. Its makers described it as "a contract with the people" and summed up its principles as "The New Nationalism." Outside of protection, most of the planks in it were not very different from those chosen by the Democrats five weeks earlier, because both groups banked on progressive capital—upon the liberal doctrines for which sentiment had been built up through the past dozen years.

Wilson Made Legatee

The Democrats assembled at Baltimore, 25 June, had much the same sort of understanding as to what kind of contract the people wanted and called theirs "The New Freedom." Their platform stressed the popular devices for mitigating the evils of trust control, in the notion that Congress could so legislate as to substitute for inter-locking directorates a restored competition. Herein they contrasted with Roosevelt who now advocated strongly paternalistic government. Among the many specific fields in which the Democrats promised to force wealth to have regard for social welfare were the railroads whose rates were to be based on valuation, the banks which were to provide elastic credit, and the courts which were not to kill strikes by injunctions. The passing of the Spanish

War fervor was suggested by a plank promising the Philippines independence as soon as a stable government was established.

The veteran liberal of the Democracy, Bryan, had the pleasurable experience of determining the candidate, after rivalries among Democrats who had won office in 1910 as reform governors simmered down to a contest between Wilson of New Jersey and Clark of Missouri. When the Tammany Braves wheeled into position behind the Clark banner, Bryan detected signs of "Wall Street" support; and although his 1896 campaign had been generously underwritten by that section of Wall Street which placed its investments in silver, he gave Tammany support as the reason for preferring Wilson. Thomas R. Marshall of Indiana was nominated Vice-President and the New Jersey governor proceeded to spend a summer in the profitable campaign business of assuring the voters that his "New Freedom" embraced all of the economic, political, and social devices which the liberal electorate were inclined to consider a guarantee of a reformed America. It was a campaign in terms of Utopias.

Setting aside the conservative Republicans who were bound to Taft either by economic affiliation or loyalty to his label, the contest developed into one between Wilson and Roosevelt. Taft himself, in July, privately and candidly admitted the probability of his defeat, but his supporters found much solace in keeping their party machinery out of progressive control. The nearly 3.5 million people who in November cast their votes for Taft probably were well aware that in the ordinary sense they were "wasting" their suffrage. The 4 million and more voters who cast Progressive ballots registered thereby a heighth of liberal feeling which was much more significant than the 6.25 million votes for Wilson. For the Progressives were sufficiently stirred by their faith in the new nationalism to break their traditional Republican ties.

Most of Wilson's voters were old-line Democrats whose support of the New Freedom involved no grand gesture of renunciation of an inherited label. Not less significant is the fact that nearly one million Americans were sure that liberal leaders had not invented devices which could prove successful, in safeguarding public welfare against the overwhelming fact of large-scale organization; they voted for the Socialist Debs and their total was more than twice as great as in 1908. Thus they, too, reflected the rising surge for reform.

Wilson and his Democratic Senate and House proceeded to discharge their obligations to Democratic, Progressive, and Socialist malcontents by legislating in the three major fields of the trusts, finance and the tariff. The first two are described with the other progressive measures (p. 564). The tariff of 1913 is analyzed here, although it was somewhat less dominated by political considerations than were preceding tariffs.

Since the Progressive as well as the Democratic platform and candidates in 1912 admitted the necessity for tariff reduction, revision in that direction in 1913 was a certainty. The so-called "Underwood-Simmons" tariff was the first item on the Wilson agenda and he in person, one month after his election, called upon Congress to restore "effective competition" between American and foreign manufactures. As Underwood's Ways and Means Committee, according to precedent, had been engaged on a bill through the previous session, a measure passed the House at the end of a month; and by a strict party vote. The lobbies undertook to elevate the schedules with Senate aid; but the insurgent attitude of the nation made it possible for Wilson to prevent the degree of rewriting which had been done in the administrations of Harrison, Cleveland, and Taft.

Logrolling was kept at such a minimum that the average rate of duty was lowered from the 36.86% of the 1909 act to 26.67% in 1913. It was the first tariff measure since the Civil War that aimed to benefit the nation as a whole. Instead of choking off all foreign competition, it aimed at moderate protection, with plain and relatively simple *ad valorem* duties instead of the old specific rates which had been perfected as devices to raise rates secretly. Duties on chemicals and some other products went up; but farmers and the consuming public were pleased by its large free list of common daily necessities; and groups who had risen in revolt against extremes of wealth were gratified by its program for increasing revenue with the aid of income taxes.

While the passage of such a law would not have been possible without the previous progressive agitation, the reductions were due in part to the fact that heavy and unfinished steel products already were being produced by American manufacturers more cheaply than by Europeans. Iron and steel went on the free list. Also, that principle of "compensation" which had elevated the rates in 1897 and 1909, now could be worked in the opposite direction, due to the weight of public opinion. Since raw wool was free, the compensating specific duties could be taken from woolen manufacturers. Rates on these and cotton goods were heavily reduced; since nitrate of soda, boots, shoes, agricultural implements, and certain other items of foreign use were put on the free list, that list could also include corn, wheat, rye, eggs, meat, cattle, sheep, and like items.

Manufacturing interests could find some solace, at least, in an antidumping section and in penalties against bounty-supported imports; while the President was empowered to negotiate reciprocity agreements, their acceptance was made dependent upon Congress. Furthermore, the tariff board was not reestablished and exports to Cuba and the Philippines were encouraged by a reciprocity agreement in one place and complete free trade in the other.

The 1913 tariff was a significant advance in the social, economic, and political development of the American nation because of its income tax features. The states had taken nearly four years to ratify the 16th Amendment to the Constitution (p. 541) which Secretary of State Knox had proclaimed 25 February 1913. The Underwood Tariff seized upon the income tax to destroy the deficit created by the lowered schedules: all net incomes over $3000 were to pay 1% except that married men were allowed an exemption of $1000; all net incomes above $20,000 were subject to an additional tax, called a surtax, starting at 1% and reaching 6% on incomes above $500,000. Also corporations must continue to pay 1% on net incomes above $5000. These provisions meant that the historic excuse for tariff increases, the deficit, was weakened. They also meant that accumulated, invisible wealth had lost its tax immunity; it must supply funds which in part had formerly been collected from the poor in the form of tariff duties. Such provisions were an earnest of future taxes on competence and special privilege. This epoch-making tariff marks a high point in the stream of progressive accomplishment before it was engulfed in the overwhelming flood of the great war.

Since neither the Democrats nor the Republicans had emerged from the election of 1912 with a majority of the popular vote, both of them were extremely anxious to acquire the 4 million and more voters who had supported Roosevelt. Particularly was this true of the Democrats because, since the Republican Party first captured the Presidency in 1860, they had not won a majority of the popular vote. This helps to account for the record made during the first two years of Wilson's administration, a record for social legislation achieved in spite of the distractions of the Mexican War (p. 600) and the Canal Tolls (p. 596) questions.

Early in the spring of 1914, the Democratic National Committee issued literature stating the record; it showed that the legislation asked for by Progressives of all shades had been passed, regardless of party, by the triumphant and ambitious majority in Congress. When, they adjourned, 24 October 1914, after the longest consecutive session yet held in our history, it was evident that the Progressive Party as a separate entity was disintegrating. A fortnight later, the Democrats had become a majority party in very fact, with a 30 vote lead over the combined Republicans and Progressives in the House, and a lead of 16 in the Senate.

Just how much farther along the road of social reform the Wilson administration might have been carried by the momentum of public interest and political ambition will never be known. The war which broke out in Europe, in August of that year, both diverted public interest from domestic welfare and divided the Democrats on war policy. This was a severe blow to Progressives who were interested in the program regardless of party. Senator La Follette, who had found it quite impossible to join the Rooseveltian band, realized the blow the War dealt his program. It would not receive any noteworthy impetus for almost 20 years, after death had taken La Follette. The Progressive era dominated by the principles dear to the Middle Border had ended. It remains to see how far those principles had impressed themselves upon legislation.

CHAPTER XXX

WRITING SOCIAL CONTROL INTO THE STATUTES

The Progressives were motivated by the prevailing American enthusiasm for embodying social philosophy in legislation. They therefore sought to write into the statutes those ideas of social control which they had been developing in the states. This countered the established Supreme Court practice of exercising control over all attempts to regulate private business in the public interest. To this control the 14th Amendment had proved invaluable, because its framers had specified that no state could deprive any person of life, liberty or property "without due process of law" and the Court had repeatedly ruled that a corporation was a "person" in the meaning of the Amendment and not to be deprived. Thus the Amendment once supposed to be for the protection of colored persons had functioned principally as a bulwark for vested interests. Despite this legal obstacle, the Progressives prepared laws regulating transportation, trusts and finance and, after much debate, enacted them.

Transportation

When a nation rich in resources stretches across a wide continent, its transportation systems become primary instruments of public destiny and private wealth. The central position of the railroads in America's economy had kept them the object of capitalistic rivalries, the victim of manipulation and the symbol of special privilege. They became acutely sensitive to the ebbs and flows of prosperity and politics.

Thanks to government largesse, a vast network of standard-gauge mileage had projected long distance transportation far ahead of income from freight, thus raising the national wealth in real estate and other values, in advance of population growth. But now the era of phenomenal railroad expansion was closing, while consolidation continued very rapidly. The latter had reached the point in 1906 where approximately 77% of total mileage was divided among 17 systems, and of these the most influential were the 5 interlocked in the Morgan, Vanderbilt, Hill, Gould and Pennsylvania groups. Complete identification of the railroads with bad as well as good developments in American life necessarily made their regulation—in lieu of government ownership—a primary obligation of non-socialistic progressives.

On the one hand, violent fluctuations in personality of railroad control, in prices of rail securities and in rates for freight and passengers had aroused shippers and the using public over the means by which a few great railroad fortunes had been amassed through speculation, gross mismanagement, amalgamation and rate tyranny. On the other hand, most legislators were accustomed to riding on a pass, most railroads paid only minimum taxes, hectic pursuit of prosperity hurried many persons into acceptance of extortion, and frequently blackmailers introduced anti-railroad legislation for the sole purpose of being paid to kill it. Also, the courts had interpreted the Act of 1887 so narrowly as to vitiate regulation of railroad rates by the Interstate Commerce Commission.[1] Thus, the need for stronger railroad regulation was well known, while firmly established legislative and legal practices blocked it.

Legislation to be effective must apply in the broad fields where the railroads were functioning. In the field of trust regulation, because monopoly control of railroads was closely integrated with nation-wide trustification. In the field of valuation, because stock was watered to establish a base for raising rates, whilst properties were undervalued and earnings hidden as a means of lowering taxes. In the field of labor, for liability for employees' injury and hours of service; in the field of public protection, for compulsory use of safety appliances; in the field of conservation, because railroads possessed valuable tracts of coal, timber, mineral and agricultural lands. In all these fields the Progressives repeatedly essayed to be effective.

They cared most about giving the Interstate Commerce Commission responsibility and power. So complicated were the factors affecting rates, with and without justification, that a fair understanding of regulation eluded most of the electorate who demanded it and most of the legislators who were forced to acknowledge the demand. Fragmentary and fumbling approaches to the problem therefore were usual, with the tactical advantage on the side of the railroads' lawyer lobbyists.

State railroad commissions had been numerous for twenty years. Their existence in Illinois and Iowa had brought somewhat-lowered rate schedules. Minnesota investigated and uncovered railroad earnings heretofore hidden from tax assessors. Wisconsin moved toward a similar investigation, with La Follette leading on from physical valuation of railroad properties into regulation of other utilities, including telephone, telegraph and trolley corporations.

State activity inspired national action, especially when railroad con-

---

[1] The Court insisted that due process requires provision for judicial review and that rates must be high enough to yield "a fair return" on a fair valuation of the property; but a method for determining a rate and valuation fair both to the public and the companies had thus far eluded them. See Chicago, Milwaukee and St. Paul R. R. Co. v. Minnesota, 134 US 418, (1889); Smyth v. Ames, 169 US 466, (1897); and Reagan v. Farmers' Loan and Trust Co., 154 U. S. 362, (1894).

solidators made themselves notorious. In 1901 E. H. Harriman, backed by Morgan and Jacob Schiff, sought to seize control of the stock of the Northern Pacific Railroad. Morgan, since 1885, had been finding in railroad reorganizations an enlarged scope for profitable use of his surplus and expansion of his power; and he now proposed to end competition between the Northern Pacific and Great Northern, and unite their management with that of the Union Pacific and Southern Pacific. A Northern Securities Company was set up to facilitate the merger. However, James J. Hill, builder of the Great Northern and reorganizer of the Northern Pacific, raised such stout resistance that the stock was elevated, temporarily, to $1000 a share; and the stock market suffered a disturbance which would have been worse if there had not been abundant crops and a good foreign market for them.

The astute Theodore Roosevelt made his first message to Congress, 3 December 1901, a proclamation of benevolent intentions toward small industry; and during the congressional campaign of the next year he not only employed a speaking tour in an attack on the trusts, but also instituted suit against the Northern Securities Company.

The United States Supreme Court (in 1904) decided, 5 to 4, that the Northern Securities Corporation was a "combination in restraint of trade." [1] This outcome was hailed, because it seemed to indicate that prosecutions under the Anti-trust Act, which had failed through the seven years following the negative Knight decision might again prove successful. Little notice was taken of the fact that the dissolution order was so worded as to leave intact the bond issue floated against the Great Northern and the Northern Pacific; and this enabled J. J. Hill to squeeze E. H. Harriman out of the control of the Northern Pacific. Other railroads, including the New Haven and Union Pacific, were ordered by the court to relinquish some of their holdings. Bankers did not lose their skill at profitable manipulation.

While the Supreme Court deliberated, Congress passed the Elkins Act of 1903 which aimed to eliminate rebating, a practice contrary to the spirit of the Interstate Commerce Act but persisted in by violently-competing railroads and shippers. The act forbade variation from published rates and the receiving and giving of rebates. Guilty corporations and their agents were both declared punishable, with fines from $1000 to $20,000. Enforcement was facilitated by clauses permitting injunction proceedings to restrain violations, and declaring variations from published tariff rates to be *prima facie* evidence of violations. Conviction was made easier by removal of the penalty of imprisonment. The wiser railroad executives were not unwilling to end an abuse which victimized management as well as shippers. The mood of Congress that February was reflected further in anti-trust legislation, to be described shortly, and

[1] Northern Securities Company v. U. S., 193 US 197 (1904).

in an appropriation of $500,000 for the improved enforcement of interstate commerce and anti-trust laws.

Since the railroads shared with shippers the advantages of the prohibition of rebates, and since the larger problems of rate-making, valuation and monopolistic control remained unsolved by the Elkins Act, that measure did not quiet agitation. The railroad lobby was fighting wider legislation early in 1906, when La Follette entered the Senate eager for nationwide physical valuation as the basis for railroad rates. He had to contend against conservative and corporate opposition and against the vital fact that elements additional to physical valuation fairly affect rates. He inclined to overlook those elements; but his valuation principle was a closer approach to reality than other would-be regulators had reached, and his activity in the long run made it impossible for politicians to ignore him or his issues.

After a struggle Congress enacted the so-called "Hepburn" railroad law of 1906. It did not give the Interstate Commerce Commission the power to set original rates. It could merely reduce those it found unreasonable after complaint by shippers; furthermore orders and schedules set by the Commission could be suspended pending judicial review, and court sympathy for railroad contentions had been habitual. The act, nevertheless, applied enough principles of social control, in the vitally important field of transportation, to bolster American democracy against advancing plutocracy. Its great influence and significance, as the outstanding economic legislation of the Roosevelt administration, require a full listing of its provisions.

It brought within the scope of Commission regulations express, sleeping car, pipe line, bridge, ferry and terminal companies and transportation which was part rail and part water. It gave the Commission, now enlarged from five to seven to handle the load, power to standardize accounting procedure—vital for taxation and rate making. It placed the burden of proof upon the carrier rather than the Commission, thus lessening court interference. It declared illegal those hoary devices for securing special favors:—midnight tariffs and passes for non-employees. It attempted to push transportation companies out of mining and other businesses, by forbidding carriers to transport commodities they produced (except timber) unless needed for the operation of the carrier; but the court practically nullified the commodity clause by declaring that it required railroad companies merely to transfer their coal stock to separately organized corporations.

In spite of the limitations of the Hepburn Act, shippers gave abundant proof of their faith in it. They had filed less than 900 formal complaints in the two decades since 1887, but now proceeded to file 1500 within the next two years. Within five years the Commission had halved approximately 194,000 of the rates existing in 1906; and the Supreme

Court had upheld the constitutionality of the anti-rebating and commodity clauses, and had recognized the right of Congress to lay down operating principles for the commission. The carriers had to prove confiscation "beyond any just or reasonable doubt" to get relief from the courts, and a decision of 1913 reaffirmed with finality the right of the Commission both to regulate rates and to intervene in internal administration of railway companies.

While shippers and courts thus were treating the act of 1906 with considerable respect, its limitations kept the Interstate Commerce Commission a live political issue, especially after the United States Circuit Court of Appeals in 1907 set aside as confiscatory a fine of $29,240,000, levied against the Standard Oil Company of Indiana for accepting rebates. By June of 1910, the insurgent movement at its height was forcing through the Mann-Elkins Act, so that the Commission might expand with modern inventions. Henceforth, its jurisdiction was to embrace telegraph, telephone, cable and wireless companies. It could start action against a carrier without waiting for federal laws, could suspend for ten months a new schedule pending examination of its reasonableness, and appeals against its rulings must come before a special Commerce Court of five circuit judges assigned by the Supreme Court and sitting in Washington. In addition, 1910 lawmakers eliminated the clever phraseology which had vitiated the long and short haul clause of 1887:—"under substantially similar circumstances and conditions."

The special court was abolished in 1912, following implication of one justice in a scandal; but the same Congress, with the cooperation of President Taft, put on the statute books a law empowering the Interstate Commerce Commission to study the physical valuation of railroads with the ultimate view of basing rates thereon. This marked the high-watermark of La Follette influence.

While the Interstate Commerce Commission held the center of the stage, Congress registered increasing pressure from organized railroad employees. The Erdman Act of 1898, providing for voluntary arbitration of disputes on interstate railways, was followed in 1906 by an employer's liability law. When the latter fell afoul of the Supreme Court for not specifying interstate employees, a Congress whose important rollcalls were being published passed the liability law of 1908, drawn to satisfy legal criticism; it made interstate railroad corporations liable for injuries to employees. The Newlands Act of 1913 created a Board of Mediation and Conciliation to decide railroad disputes.

Close affiliates of the railroads, the express companies, also felt the Progressive lash. Liberal bestowal of express "franks" had protected the companies from legislation, by transporting free many a lawmaker's goods and even live stock, lo these many years. But the demand for parcels post, in imitation of Europe's systems, would not be denied at the high point of the progressive movement. Furious objections from the companies were overruled in 1913. Parcels post proved so useful for domestic and business purposes, especially for mail-order retailing to farmers, that it soon had its own widely vested interests strong enough thenceforth to prevent the express lobby from repealing the law.

Trusts

Railroad policy, as has been indicated, could scarcely be dissociated from trust policy. The economic fact underlying progressive protest, the poor distribution of wealth, was a situation which came to be summed up in general usage of the term "the trusts." 80% of the population lived a marginal existence, while the wealth was held by the remaining 20%. When Wilson was elected as a reform President, the nation's wealth had increased 188% over what it had been in 1890; but the aggregate income of wage-earners in the basic industries of manufacturing, mining and transportation had risen only 95% and the population to be fed, clothed and sheltered had multiplied.

The great mass of Americans, 1900-1914, were in the peculiar position of a people whose total wealth was increasing and whose consumer tastes were rising while their purchasing power—their real wages—suffered a slight fall.

This situation was created by the complex interaction of a great many factors. From a list of the more important of these one can sense the baffling complexity of the total. They included new industries made by increasing population, currency inflation caused by Klondike and Rand gold influx and by cyanide processes of ore extraction, increased use of natural resources and diminution in them, relative decline in agriculture, urban trends, high tariffs, arbitrary price-raising by monopolies, raising of wages through labor unions, social losses due to accident, disease, poverty, crime and militarism, and especially uneconomical production and distribution. For these losses the populace received some slight compensation in obligations assumed by the government (for such services as water and sewage, schooling and roads) and by some millionaires for endowment of medicine and education. The rise in total wealth and in standards of living furnished evidences of prosperity which encouraged the demand for further sharing of it.

Sharing, however, ran counter to the ambitions of the handful of multi-millionaires, who were undertaking to control every major facility of modern life, by controlling investment funds. Lesser manipulators aped the great, all infected in the early 1900's by a spirit as reckless and unscrupulous in some fields as that of the Grant era. They practiced stock swindling, railroad wrecking, security inflation and legislative corruption, with a boldness scarcely equalled today. They achieved monopolistic control the more quickly by utilizing gross corruption and flagrant waste.

The waste and corruption could not escape exposure and emphasis, when the victors imposed upon the vanquished economic disaster. Few

F. Opper in N. Y. *Journal.*

"Jingle bells, jingle bells, jingle all the day!
Oh, what fun it is to ride in a one-horse open sleigh!"

consolidations could be effected in the comparatively peaceful quiet with which Carnegie in 1901 (p. 376)) retired before the founders of the United States Steel Corporation, to his profit and their greater gain.

Bartholomew in Minn. *Journal.*

Anti-Trust Act Revived

Railroad mergers, as in the Northern Securities affair, raised a big noise. In fact, consolidation was overreaching itself, with daily sales on the stock exchange climbing from .4 million to between 2 and 3 million shares, culminating in the so-called "rich men's panics" of 1903. By their excesses the consolidators made themselves into political targets as "malefactors of great wealth"—an excellent Rooseveltian phrase.

The fracasing brought measures additional to the Elkins Act, earlier described. An "Expediting" Act gave preference to federal suits brought under the Interstate Commerce and Sherman Anti-trust laws; a Department of Commerce and Labor Act provided for a bureau of corporations designed to investigate diligently "the organization, conduct and management of corporations."

Corporations manufacturing foodstuffs became of special interest. The rising cost of living, and the indefatigable activities of Dr. H. W. Wiley, chief chemist of the Department of Agriculture and most implacable foe of adulteration, concentrated the attention of all classes upon price and quality in food manufacture. A Wiley "poison squad" of twelve men working in 1902 proved conscienceless adulteration of food and drugs; and the next year a bill was pressed in Congress to impose fine and imprisonment upon everyone who offered for sale adulterated canned goods. The bill was killed in the Senate by the united efforts of the distillers' lobby, food manufacturers and critics who deplored placing the onus on the corner grocer.

During the campaign excitements of 1904 the new Commissioner of Corporations busily investigated food from the angle of price. In a suit against a branch of the "beef trust," he charged:—that 60% of the dealers in fresh meat had agreed not to compete with each other in the livestock markets—a policy which lowered farmers' incomes; also, that they had agreed to raise prices by restricting output—which raised consumers' expenses; further, that they kept a blacklist—which lowered wages through discouragement of union organization; and that they got railroad rebates—which infuriated all other shippers. The Supreme Court, following the election returns, in January 1905 ordered dissolution of the trust.[1]

Next, *Everybody's* published a carefully documented series of articles written by Russell, on the food preparation practices of Armour, Swift and others, under the title "The Greatest Trust in the World." Upton Sinclair followed early in 1906 with his dramatic novel of the Chicago Stockyards, *The Jungle;* and Roosevelt forthwith detailed J. B. Reynolds and C. P. Neill to investigate meat packing, while Senator Beveridge introduced a bill for effective inspection of packing houses. Loathsome disclosures made by partial publication of the Neill-Reynolds report strengthened the hands of the department chemists, physicians, humanitarians and Progressives who were pushing a pure food and drug bill. The manufacturers' lobby actively opposed them, not realizing that the public would buy attractive-looking goods, in spite of labels listing

[1] Swift and Co. v. United States, 196 US 375.

adulterated contents, almost as quickly as they would buy an impure article falsely labelled.

Finally, danger to the export trade and a presidential threat that all the report might be published, brought partial capitulation by the packers' and manufacturers' lobbyists. Two emasculated laws resulted, in

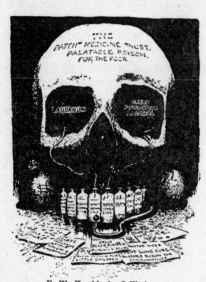

E. W. Kemble in *Collier's.*

Death's Laboratory

June and July of 1906. A meat inspection act required the packers to maintain government inspectors of carcasses converted into food products. A pure food and drug act put the burden of penalty for selling falsely labelled goods upon the wholesaler and the burden of watchfulness over the wholesalers upon the Bureau of Chemistry of the Department of Agriculture. It purported to leave a wide field of discretionary policy to the Bureau; but the President and the courts tended to limit the chemist's activities, to the corresponding disadvantage of consumers.

Consumer hatred of trusts was increased in 1907, by disclosure of the fact that the American Sugar Refining Company (which virtually controlled the nation's sugar supply) had been cheating the federal treasury, by wholesale tampering with the scales which weighed their imported raw sugar. They could not convincingly deny their guilt, when the government proved able to recover some $400,000,000 in damages, and to convict several officials and employees as criminals. Such disclosures ensured further anti-trust activity. The Roosevelt and Taft administrations instituted suit against other combinations, in important, everyday fields such as anthracite coal, harvesting machinery, oil, paper, powder, salt, shoe machinery and tobacco. Yet presidents and lawmakers were always some steps behind consolidators clever at finding legal ways to practice monopoly. This was repeatedly proved.

The stronger features of the Hepburn Act, for example, were due to the fact that almost all railroads, shipping lines and other public utilities bore the scars of the titanic rivalries which had left them with watered stock, wasteful construction and a weak morale. Nevertheless, reckless over-expansion and speculation proceeded apace, leading—in a year of deficient rainfall—to the "silent" panic of March and the "bankers'" or "Wall Street" panic of October, 1907.

These stringencies served to advance, rather than retard, the process of consolidation, for the 1907 panics like the worse ones of 1873 and 1893, gave strong corporations an opportunity to swallow up weaker ones, narrowing yet further the field of effective competition. In this outcome the "trust-busting" President was not unhelpful. Disturbed by the charge that he was blamable for the stringency, he gave tacit agreement to annexation by the United States Steel Corporation of its only important, surviving competitor, the Tennessee Coal and Iron Company, when the deal was presented to him as a market stabilizer.[1]

Speculators responsible for the panic ultimately were shown to have been guilty of criminal practices. Some of them suffered prison terms as well as loss of their wealth; but the more astute climbed to higher eminence—elevated by the additional properties they had seized through the stringency, and by the envious admiration accorded them by large groups of equally amoral but less well-endowed compatriots. One good effect of the 1907 stringency was the attention it attracted to weaknesses in currency and banking systems. This led later to an effort to democratize control of capital.

Interest in the misdeeds of monopolists became intense. It was fed by the Middle West attack upon the tariff as "the mother of trusts," which attack converged with the anti-monopoly agitation and brought the corporation and income tax features of the 1909 tariff. Taft, meanwhile, was doubling Roosevelt's record of anti-trust activity, and even reached the point of proposing that the federal government establish a Corporation Commission and license and supervise interstate corporations. Legal high lights of 1911 were the court decisions requiring dissolution of the unpopular Standard Oil and American Tobacco corporations. The court, however, issued an *obiter dictum* that the anti-trust law applied only to *unreasonable* restraint of trade.[2]

The income tax amendment, provided in 1909, was conceived as a levy upon wealth and secured such endorsement that it was proclaimed as the sixteenth amendment to the Constitution on 25 February 1913. The Democratic congress that summer proceeded to formulate a modest income tax schedule as part of the Underwood tariff. It dealt tenderly with wealth, however, levying a maximum of only 6% in surtaxes on incomes over $500,000.

More important than the income tax was the so-called "Pujo Committee," sponsored by the House Committee on Banking and Currency

[1] Apparently this was only a minor, consultation-by-courtesy aspect of a larger deal; under it, J. P. Morgan is supposed to have agreed that Rockefeller copper interests could dispose of Heinze and Morse competition, provided U. S. Steel annexed Tenn. Coal and Iron.

[2] Interesting elaborations of the "rule of reason" were provided in United States v. Trans-Missouri Freight Association, 166 US 290, (1897) and in Standard Oil Co. of New Jersey et al. v. the United States, 221 US 1, (1911).

and empowered by the Sixty-Second Congress to ascertain the facts regarding the "money trust." The committee accumulated evidence showing that capital consolidation had reached a point where money and credit were largely monopolized by the banks:—J. P. Morgan and Company, The First National Bank of New York and the National City Bank (a Rockefeller institution). The three, through seven subsidiary banks, controlled approximately 2 billions of capital; four allied institutions of New York City held 341 directorships in various concerns with resources aggregating 22.2 billions. Rivalry between these often was abandoned for profitable cross investments and interlocking directorates. They obtained control over trust companies, in which insurance companies could invest under most state laws. Morgan came to dominate in the "Big Three" of the insurance world—the Equitable, Mutual and New York Life. Billions of dollars in savings thus became available for speculative and monopolistic purposes.

Evidence abounded that the money trust was the core of the trust system of non-competitive consolidation in control of American production. Less than one-eighth of the business concerns were now manufacturing more than 80%, in value, of the nation's products, and employing more than three-fourths of the workers. This meant that the little competitive businesses (which numbered over 75% of American concerns) had sunk to insignificance in the scheme of labor policy, output, price and all the other aspects of business affecting general prosperity. Welfare hung upon the judgment of the few individuals in economic control of the nation. Chairman Pujo asked one of these, George F. Baker (banking associate of J. P. Morgan), if he considered this "a comfortable situation for a great country to be in." Baker answered "not entirely."

A remedy for this parlous state was obligatory to the first Wilson Congress, then riding the crest of the progressive wave and led by a President who recently had stiffened New Jersey's notoriously lax corporation laws. Congress responded in 1914 with two statutes intended to regulate trusts and preserve competition. The Federal Trade Commission Act, designed primarily for trust regulation, wiped out the Bureau of Corporations, which as a part of the Department of Commerce had proved flaccid in its trust supervision, and set up a bi-partisan commission of five, empowered with investigative and regulatory duties. Within their purview came all corporations engaged in interstate commerce (except common carriers and banks) and subject to anti-trust laws and court decrees. They could make public such reports as they thought best and investigate trade relations with foreign countries. They could issue certain "cease and desist orders" in cases of unfair competition and their findings as to fact were to be held as conclusive.

In other words, the Federal Trade Commission was set up as an agency for establishing the fact of dishonest practices in business; these once proved by it, the Sherman law as amplified by the Clayton law was to be employed to reestablish "effective competition." The Clayton Act attacked some of the competition-throttling devices which had been perfected during the 24 years since 1890:—price discrimination, interlocking directorates and tied contracts. Some practices it prohibited; certain remedies it prescribed; and since farmers' organizations and labor unions thus far had proved ineffective against trusts, the law expressly exempted these two groups from prosecution as conspiracies in restraint of trade.

The same Congress registered popular resentment against some of the most flagrant stock manipulation—particularly the ruin of the New Haven under Morgan and Rockefeller—by formulating the "Rayburn" bill for giving the Interstate Commerce Commission power to pass on securities of common carriers before issuance; the outbreak of war postponed legislation in this field, by two decades. Before the War, however, progressive momentum had written into national statutes far-reaching provisions governing other activities closely associated with the trusts— the activities of banking and currency control.

Banking and Currency

Experience with falling prices and concentration of wealth, through the three decades between the Civil and Spanish wars, had been responsible for the acute interest of the electorate in the volume of money. As each depression raised from the left wing of major parties and from most of the minor parties the outcry for more and cheaper money, Congress had fed the supply by retaining $346,681,000 of the war greenbacks and by injecting a larger total in silver coins and certificates. Per capita circulation had moved from $20.57 in 1865 to $21.10 in 1896, but maldistribution had more than offset the increase. The intense heat of class warfare generated during Bryan's free silver campaign doubtless would have flamed into inflationary legislation before the end of the century if it had not been cooled by the war and the upward turn of prices. Then creditor interests had secured their reaffirmation of the gold standard (p. 464), and thought the question safely settled.

Soon, however, bankers and businessmen became leading advocates of currency expansion, for the large crops, heavy exports and business vivacity of the progressive era convinced them that the money supply was inadequate for full profit-taking. The system devised when the government was floating heavy issues of wartime bonds seemed too rigid for peacetime business expanding under rising prices. Farmers and rural businessmen also complained. Farming now required larger capital investment and credit facilities; lack of funds inconvenienced movement of fall crops and the hinterland had to wait impatiently upon the East for credits. The various classes clamoring for greater currency elasticity and fluidity of reserves scarcely reflected that activity might be too great or that the real lack might be a central bank, holding larger reserves.[1]

This movement was brought nearer to a head by events connected with the bankers' panic of 1907. The panic was touched off when Wall Street speculation in copper brought revelations discreditable to the president and directors of the Mercantile National Bank, which in turn exposed weakness in interlocking directorates of the system. Country banks, alarmed, undertook to withdraw reserves from city institutions and these in turn from their correspondents in New York. There, thirteen banking institutions closed; and the stringency sent a number of manipulated railroads into receiverships. The government stepped into the breach between 29 and 31 October, with emergency deposits of $36,000,000 and the clearing house issued temporary certificates. But the affair had depressed wages, increased unemployment and upset business enough to alarm conservatives.

Their influence expedited the hasty passage of stop-gap legislation—the Aldrich-Vreeland Act of June, 1908—intended to provide currency elasticity in emergency. This measure was significant of the progressive era for two reasons:—out of the debate over it, the Middle West won some recognition of its special banking needs, and progressive influence expedited the movement for basic banking reform. In the first place, the law empowered national banks to issue notes not only upon bonds of approved states, counties and municipalities—these bonds being stock-in-trade of eastern banks—but also on four months commercial paper—heavily held by western institutions.

In the second place, while the law as finally enacted severely limited and taxed these notes, to confine them to emergency use, the intervening debate took a turn which both enhanced the prestige of the outstanding Progressive and launched the outstanding conservative upon immediate consideration of monetary reform. La Follette forced the withdrawal of an Aldrich proposal, for including railroad bonds among the securities usable for emergency note issue, and presented a detailed, factual statement on railroad control which increased his ultimate following although he won only two supporters for his filibuster against the bill. His contention that the bill was designed to prevent basic overhauling of the banking system helped to insert a clause for a National Monetary Commission. Senator Aldrich, who was growing greatly concerned over the problem, took the chairmanship himself and began, personally, a survey of banking practice and theory at home and abroad.

Some European practices adjusted to American conditions, and exten-

[1] The United States customarily used up reserves, while England conserved them for expansion emergencies.

sions of domestic clearing house practices, were incorporated in the plan finally prepared by him with the aid of H. P. Davison, F. A. Vanderlip, P. M. Warburg and J. B. Morgan—bankers representing the dominant eastern banking houses of Morgan, Rockefeller, and Kuhn, Loeb & Company, and Chicago's leader, the First National. But the regulatory institution which they proposed to set up was to operate under private control centered in New York; and their plan was not perfected until 8 January 1912, by which date the progressive tide had swept out Aldrich and his regime. Any plan was bound to be modified by the Democratic-Progressive coalition, in a direction toward decentralization and political supervision.

Now culminated the second great effort to vest control of America's monetary system in the national government. Capture of the House, Senate and presidency in 1912 made possible the Glass-Owen Federal Reserve Act of 1913. It acknowledged the obligation of the federal government to supervise banking, while safeguarding sectional, agricultural and commercial interests therein. It modified the outgrown, fifty-year-old, national bank system with a Federal Reserve establishment to which all national banks were to belong, participating in ownership of stock in regional Federal Reserve Banks. One-third of the Boards of these banks and all members of the central Federal Reserve Board must be nominated by political influence (the President)—a Bryan requirement supposed to prevent Wall Street control.

From eight to twelve regional reserve banks designed to be subsidiary to the Federal Reserve Board, were to meet currency needs of their respective sections, taking the rôle of bankers' banks, rediscounting commercial and agricultural paper of member banks, granting them loans, and buying and selling domestic and foreign exchange. They could rediscount agricultural paper for six months, commercial for three; and on the basis of this paper they could issue the new, more elastic, currency, named "federal reserve notes," up to any amount provided a 40% reserve were kept in gold. As they could not rediscount paper issued for the purpose of trading in stocks and bonds, speculation was supposed to be debarred from enjoying the currency-expansion privileges of industry and agriculture. The old, inelastic, national bank notes, dependent upon government bonds, were to be retired.

The Federal Reserve bill encountered bitter resistance from bankers opposing regimentation of their operations but the larger institutions entered the system, which within fifteen years embraced more than four-fifths of the nation's bank resources. Many disputes arose over management, political manipulation, and influence exerted by the New York Reserve Bank. Quickly the progressive era closed, while legislative amendments and administrative policy moved the system further away from the democratic objectives of some of its sponsors and toward private control. The system served, however, to increase money in circulation and the total sum in the country; and it forwarded three of the major reform demands—currency expansion, mobilization of reserves, and control for national, rather than personal, ends.

The trend toward government participation in banking functions meanwhile had caused enactment, in 1910, of a postal savings law, designed to encourage poor people to save and to assure them of safety from bank failures. The bank lobby which struggled to defeat the bill succeeded in setting the interest at 2% on a full year's deposits—a return so low as to discourage deposits during boom years of high interest. In times of depression and low bank rates small investors flocked to the postoffice, further attracted by the privilege of exchanging their postal savings certificates for small, tax-exempt, postal savings bonds bearing interest at 2½%. Bankers also grew to like the system, after the government came to deposit some of the postal savings funds in the banks. With this law, as with the Federal Reserve Act, bankers as a class continued to win comparatively favorable terms from the progressive movement.

CHAPTER XXXI

TOWARD ECONOMIC DEMOCRACY

Not only were Progressives interested in controlling certain forms of business enterprise but some of them had a more fundamental philosophy which spurred them to seek the spread of economic democracy, to insure to all workers, in industry and agriculture, an equal chance to earn a decent living. There was less unanimity and understanding of this more fundamental problem; and constitutional restrictions upon activities of the federal government made it more difficult. Popular enthusiasm for such policies was also less marked; they were considered by many as too radical.

Realizing Labor's Disabilities

Progressives who tried to restrict monopoly control over American economy—as exercised by bankers and financiers, trust magnates and railroad manipulators, were somewhat less interested in helping labor to tighten its grip on jobs. The typical progressive, a member of the middle class, long reacted to the shibboleths of the old agricultural era, long assumed persistence of opportunities which were passing. The huge size and resources of the United States had so retarded the formation of hard and fast classes that the great body of Americans were reluctant to face the issue raised by the Granger, Populist and Bryan campaigns—the issue of whether they were being deprived of their birth-right, of "opportunity."

A new leadership, around 1900, was submitting figures to show that the birthright was gone. While wages were higher than in Europe, they averaged less than $2.00 per diem and at least two-thirds of the adult males earned less than $600 annually. But realization could come only after continual reiteration by such hard-headed advocates as La Follette, Steffens and Debs. La Follette's most intimate experience, unfortunately, lay in the locale of North European immigrants, engrossed chiefly in problems vivid to the Middle West. He sometimes evaluated labor's alternatives during this period more clearly than did Gompers, and put labor in his debt thereby; but that was not the main interest or principal contribution of the outstanding Progressive.

Labor furthermore suffered for lack of an identification of interest with agriculture:—an increase in the prices paid farmers at first would penalize chiefly the laboring class; an increase of wages to labor, insofar as it raised prices of manufactured goods and machinery, at first would penalize farmers. The ultimate benefits to both from a rise in living standards were not sufficiently obvious to bring frequent cooperation between their lobbies.

On the other hand, labor found its greatest single ally in cheap newspapers as developed by the yellow journals. With lurid descriptions and stark drawings, reporters and cartoonists for Hearst and Pulitzer demonstrated the violent contrasts between life of rich and poor, educating the poor in resentment. The more moderate material by reporters for Scripps newspapers showed a sympathy for labor likely to impress more thoughtful, middle-class readers, readers whose prejudices frequently determine the balance of political power. Neither Hearst nor Pulitzer nor the elder Scripps brothers, however, exerted in this period as much political influence as the more conservative capitalistic press. Readers in general needed a long course in education before they would cease to practice an intolerance which frequently played into the hands of the least-enlightened capitalists.

The chief disability of labor was the fact that workers remained too abundant and their position too unstable, on the whole, for effective bargaining with their employers. The progress of mechanical invention repeatedly reduced the number of skilled jobs, substituting unskilled work at machinery; and when new inventions fostered new skills, the Federation had to work hard and long to organize and affiliate the latest type of skilled workmen. Nor did benefits commensurate to industrial expansion come to the unskilled, for immigration put too sharp an edge on competition for jobs.

The total of immigrants reached a new high—more than a million annually in 1905-1907, 1910, 1913 and 1914; and at least 700,000 in every year but two between 1902 and 1914. Their proportion to the entire population became greater than at any time since the 1840's. Poverty-stricken peasants of Southeast Europe, Austro-Hungarian Slavs and persecuted Russian Jews eagerly believed the optimistic tales of agents of steamship companies, land-grant railroads and labor contractors. Settling most heavily in New England and the Middle Atlantic states, by 1910 they had made the majority of the population there either foreign born whites or native whites of foreign or mixed parentage.

They were mainly segregated in their own sections in the cities; and approximately one-fourth of them planned to return to their home-lands. Slow to intermarry with the earlier strains, they very gradually injected into American stock an influence making for a shorter, swarthier, and more temperamental population—one representative of all Europe, rather than only of its western part. The prospect of competition in America with these non-Teutonic Europeans increasingly deterred from immigration the workmen and peasants of England, Ireland and Germany, especially as broad social legislation, improved agrarian policies and industrial expansion were alleviating their home situations.

American labor leaders agitating for restriction of immigration met their greatest obstacle in the nation's personal experience and national tradition of the United States as a land of opportunity for the poor and oppressed, who could be absorbed without disadvantage, a concept fostered by employers and transportation agencies. Restrictionists obtained, in statutes of 1903 and 1907, exclusion of the diseased, immoral, anarchistic and imbecile, and those whose passage was paid by some corporation, association or government; but evasion was frequent.

Restrictionists turned to accomplish their objectives through a literacy test, since 25% of adult immigrants were illiterate, as were about half of the largest single group—the Italians. Literacy planks were placed in Republican and Democratic platforms. An Immigration Commission was obtained and it demonstrated—in 41 volumes—the illiteracy and other serious problems involved. Congress twice was persuaded to put up bars against illiterates, but Taft and Wilson (like Cleveland) tore them down with vetoes.

Absolute exclusion was obtained against a minority group only, and that through the aid of the color line. Japanese were increasing from 24,000 to 72,000, 1900-1910, mostly in California; their extremely low living standards and industrious habits made them serious competitors of white labor and landowners wherever they intruded. An Asiatic Exclusion League, formed under labor auspices in 1905, fomented propaganda which led the San Francisco School Board to segregate some ninety-eight Japanese children in a separate school. The circle of agitation widened into diplomatic interchanges, until a "gentleman's agreement" was arranged between Secretary of War Root and Ambassador Takahira; Japan agreed not to issue passports to skilled and unskilled laborers wishing to go to the United States. Still the California legislature showed truculence, until federal laws of 1913 and 1920 barred Japanese from owning or leasing agricultural or other real property.

By the cheap labor of women and children, adaptable to new industries, labor solidarity was further postponed, as women wage-earners increased in total number and in proportion of all women in the United States. Wives and daughters of immigrants poured into sweatshops, but the greatest relative increase showed in office and store work:—among stenographers, telephone operators, bookkeepers, clerks in offices and five-and-ten and department stores, nurses and waitresses. Nearly half of those aged sixteen and over, working outside the professions and homes, were receiving in 1914 less than $6.00 weekly. Their low wages were blamable on their youth—with half of them in certain manufactures and trade under 25; on their expectancy of marriage which made them tolerant of bad conditions as a temporary expedient; on their inability to go from place to place because of family ties; on the status of seven-tenths of them as members of an earning family group, which permitted wages below the level needed to subsist away from home. They were difficult to unionize, and the few women's labor leaders and social workers who formed in 1903 the National Womens Trade Union League only gradually turned women toward organization.

Cheap child labor was used in cotton mills, glass and canning factories, coal mines and the artificial flower industry. Agitation against it was pushed by humanitarians of the women's clubs, the National Consumers League and the other groups aided somewhat by union officials. A few old industrial states passed legislation, working from the schooling angle, with Illinois, Massachusetts and New York advancing farthest. A National Child Labor Committee (organized in 1904) so coordinated the campaigns for minimum age and education, limitation of hours and healthful and moral working conditions that during the next two years two-thirds of the states either strengthened existing laws or initiated measures; but few adopted the committee's model law.

The national Congress in 1907 appropriated $150,000 for an investigation and report, a Children's Bureau was set up in the Department of Commerce and Labor (1912) and Congress (in 1916 and 1919) voted to exclude child-made products from interstate commerce. The Children's Bureau, however, could do little to secure enforcement of state laws; and the Supreme Court invalidated the federal legislation.

Skilled versus Unskilled Labor

Leaders of organized (skilled) labor were acquiring also a less friendly feeling toward Negro workers, as the race became more literate,[1] entered a few more occupations and became somewhat more skilled. Baiting of them was carried into such literature as Thomas Dixon's *The Leopard's Spots,* lynchings averaged not less than fifty annually for a number of years, and the increasing number of race riots reflected the rising tension. It spread beyond the South.

There were signs that they might demand a more conspicuous part in the national life, for a young minority was revolting against the doctrine of conservative Booker T. Washington that Negro salvation rested in education and hard work. W. E. B. DuBois, holder of a Harvard Ph.D., professor of history and economics at Atlanta University and a frequent contributor to magazines, undertook to lead young intellectuals of his race in a movement for equality in law and opportunity. Their Niagara Falls Conference of July 1905, failed of considerable after-effect; but in 1909 the National Association for the Advancement of Colored People took up the work of the left wing. Its

[1] Illiteracy fell from approximately 44% to 30%, 1900-1910.

organ, *The Crisis,* pushed DuBois' thesis that persistent agitation is the way to liberty.

Political and social agitation were not theses of Samuel Gompers, who continued to hold the American Federation of Labor to a comparatively conservative policy. He was busy with numerical and regional expansion. His policy seemed to be endorsed by the degree of his success in the prosperous period of 1897-1904. Then the Federation was answering trust expansion with its own increase in membership, of more than 500%, and was expanding into new industries and areas so rapidly that 92 new national and international trade unions were organized and almost three-fifths of trade-union-membership affiliated with the Federation.[1]

Growing aggressiveness of employers' associations and apparent court hostility, however, led the executive council in 1906 to decree a more purposeful political policy:—union members should regularly support candidates of either major party who were pro-labor, defeat those who were anti-labor and name no candidates of their own unless both the major parties selected anti-labor men. This policy in practice increased Federation membership and turned labor votes to the Democrats, since the Republican affiliation lay with "big business" and the Democrats had the

J. Baer in *American Federationist.*
Labor Holds the Scales

liberality of the "outs." Their anti-injunction plank of 1908 earned formal endorsement from the Federation, which in 1912 claimed credit for Wilson's election and in 1914 obtained the Clayton Anti-trust Act "on account."

Those Federation members who wished the official labor vote to go to the Socialists or some other separate Labor party were balked by the highly skilled character of Federation membership, which was more nearly committed to the capitalistic system than was that 96% of labor which was both unskilled and outside the Federation.

However, labor protest grew against the major parties after 1900.

---

[1] Organized labor centered in industrial districts as workers in mining, building, machine shops, or as members of railroad brotherhoods; the food, liquor and tobacco workers at one time were the less conservative of the membership.

Debs' Socialist party had been born of the defeat of the American Railway Union in the Pullman strike; and his group displaced recent-immigrant leadership with men who knew American conditions and could broaden the Socialist appeal accordingly. In the industrial areas of New York, Pennsylvania, Ohio, Illinois, Wisconsin, and California they interested groups of skilled manual workers and clerks, merchants and professional people. In spite of the official aloofness of the Federation and of southern workers the Socialists—as a labor party in the main—built up their vote from 95 thousand in 1900 to 900 thousand in 1912, when they placed Socialists in office in at least 300 cities and towns.

More serious than labor's dispute over politics was their split over the relative merits of craft and industrial unionism. Radical blocks in the Federation—the United Brewery Workers, United Mine Workers of America, and the Western Federation of Miners—insisted that craft unionism was both selfish and weakening. A group of advanced socialists and industrial unionists broke from the Federation in 1905 to form the Industrial Workers of the World, known as the I.W.W. In it strong leaders contended, the most radical won, and the I.W.W. under "Big Bill" Haywood accepted two principles:—that the capitalistic system must be abolished and that unskilled labor should be organized with the skilled.

These doctrines, as joined with their practice of sabotage against capitalism and their success in attracting unskilled and unorganized workers, brought the I.W.W. ruthless opposition from capitalists and hatred from Gompers' group. Although the I.W.W. had only 4 or 5 thousand paid-up members in 1912, when they became most aggressive, and probably never had over 60 thousand, the activity of Haywood and his associates gave them an influence far wider than their membership. In the East their chief appeal was to unskilled factory hands; in the West, to migratory workers—the "wobblies"—who were badly exploited but retained enough spirit to resent their persecution and to act to end it.

The I.W.W. forced betterment of working conditions on some capitalists and more recognition of unskilled labor on the A.F. of L. Successful strikes in Nevada and Pennsylvania and a stubborn fight for free speech on the Pacific Coast made them widely and favorably known among unskilled workers. They reached their crest in 1912 when unskilled workers—mostly recent immigrants—at Lawrence, Massachusetts, and Passaic, New Jersey, turned to them, after craft unions had refused cooperation, for betterments and increases. Haywood and J. J. Ettor, with others, managed to hold the strikers together whilst they struggled for the indispensable public sympathy. They offset the discredit incurred from fake dynamite planting and imprisonment of their leaders, by sending deputations of strikers' children on "Vacations" out of the city where they aroused sympathy. Victory ensued.

But a Paterson, New Jersey, silk strike of 1913 started the decline of this industrial union organization. Its leaders concentrated all their resources upon a conflict in which they contended with manufacturers intent upon a double objective. These employers wished to enter the field of cheap goods and they were determined to destroy the I.W.W. The industrial unionists could not collect enough funds or maintain high enough morale to counteract the influence of police brutality and court hostility. After five months, they went down in defeat, their rise sharply broken.

Labor advancement required public sympathy; and the anti-labor propaganda of capitalist groups proved the more effective among the citizenry whenever lawbreaking could be coupled with organized labor. The murder of Idaho's anti-labor Governor, Steunenberg (1905) was charged to officers of the Western Federation of Miners, who obtained fair defense and acquittal only through the aid of Gompers and other labor sympathizers. But President Roosevelt labelled them "undesirable citizens" and newspaper propaganda played them up as anarchistic criminals. Despite a verdict of acquittal, labor was badly smirched.

Worse in its effects was the dynamiting of the building housing the anti-labor *Los Angeles Times* (1910), which brought death to twenty-one persons. Three members of the International Association of Bridge and Structural Iron Workers were arrested for the crime; and two, at first, persuaded Gompers of their innocence. When later they joined in pleading guilty, although the Federation immediately repudiated them, Gompers was charged with prior knowledge of a crime—a charge never proved, but it blackened labor.

In reality, Gompers and his Federation in the main continued to hold themselves aloof from the vast majority of workers—from the un-skilled, less literate, ill-paid, migratory, unorganized and potentially radical conglomeration, which made up 96%, approximately, of America's laborers. The relatively skilled and conservative minority under Gompers obtained some recognition from Mark Hanna and other con-cilatory employers, who joined in the National Civil Federation in the hope of keeping labor the tool, rather than the master, of capital and politics. These industrialists signed enough trade agreements and recog-nized the craft union principle sufficiently to give the period of 1898-1904 the misleading caption, "the honeymoon of capital and labor."

Industrial Warfare

The actual fact was, however, that in the seven years following 1898 the number of strikes was doubling, with increases in violence and bloodshed on both sides, and in union instigation of strikes. The great majority of industrialists followed unimaginative leaders who thought they could kill the union movement if sufficient unity and force were employed. They organized the American Anti-Boycott Association (1902), the Citizen's Industrial Association (founded in 1903 by the National Association of Manufacturers) and the National Council for Industrial Defense (1907) to finance anti-labor litigation, to unify anti-labor policy and to lobby for capital and against labor. The trend away from competition into consolidation acted as a force for brutal selection; these who survived as captains of industry operated under conditions which sealed their determination to hold a common front against labor, and the consumer. A capital illustration was furnished in the vitally important electric field. Power producers quickly consolidated their interests with major utility companies, while the habit of the latter, of expanding beyond immediate needs, accelerated power production. With these two groups manufacturers of generating equipment worked in close cooperation. Likewise in mining, railroad control of anthracite properties gave the struggle between mine workers and operators titanic proportions.

As unions gradually built up a record for raising wages, lowering hours and bettering working conditions, strikes moved from those specific objectives to the basic one of union recognition; and as recognition conceded the right of labor to share with capital in the control of industry, it was in many cases a war to the death. The unions found the boycott the most effective weapon against producers, until high paid legal talent and a conservative judiciary smashed boycotts with injunctions and contempt of court proceedings. Against an adverse court set-up the unions could not prevail—in the American scheme of things—except as they won public sympathy, legislation and a change in precedents. Along these lines the battle was joined in the key industries throughout the progressive era, with the biggest union successes won by the crafts requiring the highest skills.

In the machinery and metal trades—vital to the age of invention—employers in the National Founders and Metal Trades Associations made arbitration agreements with international unions of molders and machinists; but soon the agreements were broken and warfare and instability returned. The International Typographical Union, however, made with the Newspaper Publishers Association a successful series of one year agreements; and the four Railway Brotherhoods—the most important unions outside the A.F. of L.—lived peaceably with their employers until the high cost of living weighed them down in 1912-1914.

In the bituminous branch of the coal industry in Ohio, the United Mine Workers secured wage increases, other concessions, and recognition of their union. In the anthracite field of Pennsylvania, however, they faced a mine-railroad-capitalist control of about two-thirds of the output and amounting practically to a trust. They turned to political weapons—the United States being a democracy—and staged strikes in the presidential and congressional campaigns of 1900 and 1902. This frightened Mark Hanna and Theodore Roosevelt into mediating between J. P. Morgan's capitalist group and John Mitchell (President of the United Mine Workers) with his 100,000 to 150,000 miners. The operators in 1902 expected Roosevelt to follow Cleveland's example at Pullman by sending troops to end the strike as a violation of the Sherman Anti-trust Law; but he threatened government operation and suggested Cleveland as head of an arbitral commission. Such devices won the miners wage increases, a nine-hour instead of a ten-hour day, abandonment of the sliding scale, and a union man to check weights. Thus much had the politico-industrial climate moderated in favor of labor, between 1894 and 1902.

But 1902 had not brought recognition of the United Mine Workers Union; and the Board of Conciliation which adjusted difficulties for the next decade was unable to prevent a strike in the high-progressive campaign of 1912. Again a partial success—a four-year contract for higher pay, without union recognition. During the next two years, despite the period's impetus toward social legislation, the United Mine Workers suffered disastrous defeat; the Colorado Fuel and Iron Company, using machine guns, private troops and dynamite, broke a strike waged there on behalf of 30,000 immigrants who labored under unspeakable conditions. Arbitration proposals from President Wilson had not won acceptance. The crushing of this strike demonstrated the narrow limits of progressive influence. The Miners' Union, building up membership meanwhile, had to wait for wartime markets to bring them recognition. Later, oil would weaken their position.

A worse disaster, than the Colorado defeat of immigrants and semi-skilled workers, had come to organized labor in the hat and stove-making trades on the Atlantic coast. There a hostile judiciary specialized in invoking the anti-trust law against unions, and declared injunctions against boycotts. A fourteen-year fight between the Danbury Hatters Union and the D. E. Lowe Company ended with a decision that a secondary boycott was illegal as contrary to the Sherman Law and that the members of the union were subject to a fine of $235,000.

In the Buck Stove and Range case, officers and members of the A.F. of L. were enjoined from listing the stove company's products in the "we don't patronize" column of their official periodical, and from mentioning the dispute in print or conversation. Gompers, Mitchell and Frank Morrison (secretary of the A.F. of L.) were sentenced to prison. The Supreme Court finally dismissed the action, as outlawed by the statute of limitations, but the court avoided the fundamental issue of constitutional guarantees of free speech, free press and peaceable assemblage.

Defeated by judges, labor persuaded Congress to exempt unions from prosecution under anti-trust laws: hence the strong emphasis upon labor in the Clayton Law of 1914. It limited use of injunctions in labor disputes, prescribed jury trial in most contempt cases, and declared strikes, picketing, boycotts, peaceable assemblage and the collection of strike benefits as not in violation of federal law. This so-called "Magna Carta" of American trade unionists was nullified in a few years by court action, which left only the provision specifying jury trial; judges persisted in injunction abuses long after they became more liberal in other fields.

Such abuses aroused concern in public spirited citizens of many professions, for the liberal tradition persisted among thoughtful, middle-class Americans. They helped to support the National Consumers League (formed 1898), Civic Federation (1901), Child Labor Committee (1904) and the American Association for Labor Legislation (1906). These variously urged adoption of the trade agreement, the right of collective bargaining and the necessity for social legislation. They tended to side with labor in their difficulties with state police. State police were almost unknown before the 20th century; but since 1900 ten states have established them and three of these in turn have disbanded them. The Pennsylvania constabulary in particular was hateful to labor, because called in regularly from other duties in time of strike to protect capital investment; and it had a reputation for cruelty toward strikers.

The sympathy of the middle class was a valuable, but incalculable asset. It was turned toward members of the International Ladies' Garment Workers' Union, led in 1909 by Morris Hillquit and Mitchell in a strike against unsavory conditions, when the police turned to support the employers. The shorter hours, higher wages and sanitation then obtained by the union encouraged the unorganized sweatshop makers of coats and suits in New York to go on strike in 1910. The Ladies' Garment Workers' Union promptly took charge, thereby raising its membership from 20 to 70 thousand in two weeks; and the outstanding liberal attorney, Louis D. Brandeis, forwarded conferences which brought higher wages, better working conditions and abolition of sub-contracting. These were important advances but the union had not reached its goal.

Again strikers failed to get full recognition of the union by establishment of the closed shop; but arbitration machinery was set up for future disputes; and these two short strikes demonstrated that it was possible to change a badly sweated trade into a highly organized and effective, self-controlled union. Since they were in clothing manufacture, which urbanization had made extremely important to American life, their influence was the wider.

Meanwhile, labor's uneven struggles with capitalistic overbalance during the progressive period failed to throw the main body of American labor into the hands of extremists—failed to destroy the middle or the capitalist class—for the progressive movement, peculiar to American psychology, had intervened to palliate the situation. Legislatures did not always disappoint the laboring electorate; much was obtained at state capitols. Laws on child labor, women's work, sweating, minimum wages, hazards, and physical conditions of employment were passed by the states in an amount far exceeding all other periods.

In workmen's compensation, the United States was the last great power to accept the principle that the industry rather than the individual was responsible for occupational accidents, of which this country had an exceptional number. The state laws in this field were soon declared unconstitutional, as violating due process of law. But more carefully framed measures, and constitutional amendments, by 1921 had placed into effect, in all but six states and the District of Columbia, employers' liability acts.

The imperfections of the laws could not alter the fact of their existence; they encouraged action in such fields as old age and mothers' pensions, sickness and unemployment insurance, and labor exchanges. America had been extremely slow to follow Europe's example in this field, in spite of her pressing need. For this the courts were largely to blame. The judges were conservative by nature and affiliation. They had slight knowledge and less understanding of the industrial realities of the twentieth century and continued to decide cases according to the legal doctrines of the eighteenth century. Gradually state courts overruled or reversed many of their anti-labor decisions; and the Supreme Court of the United States in 1908 upheld an Oregon ten-hour law and in 1915 a California eight-hour law.

There were other gains for labor. The Commissioner of Labor, who since 1888 had headed an independent department without cabinet rank, was in 1903 made head of a bureau in the newly created Department of Commerce and Labor.[1] A Children's Bureau was added in 1912 and the next year the Department of Labor was set up as a separate cabinet unit, with a most important Bureau of Labor Statistics in it. The War brought requirements for decent working conditions for seamen, in 1915, and a year later the Adamson eight-hour law for railroad workers. Thus did the progressive era bring considerable gains to labor. America, however, had another class of workers—no less important—who were slower to reap benefits from organization.

[1] Federal employees obtained a compensation act in 1908 and an eight-hour day was set for workers on government contracts in 1912.

Surface Prosperity in Agriculture

The farmer of the United States remained, throughout the progressive era, the greatest speculator of all mankind; he was becoming more class conscious, but he still was more used by the politicians than using them. His legislative winnings were mostly measures of broad, national interest obtained with and for other classes as well, because urban tolerance was essential to agrarian legislation. Laws on the tariff, transportation, trusts and currency were due in part to farmers' agitation and paid some heed to their interests; but there was little of exclusively agricultural law-making.

This was due, in part, to President Roosevelt's failure to understand farm economy and to his success in getting farm support. He never had sympathized with western radical movements, being attracted rather to the colorful and venturesome aspects of ranching life. His inherent individualism and eastern training in conservatism, joined with a certain superficiality of thought, deterred him from considering possible advantages to the common farmer in cooperative movements. At the same time, his ardent nationalism with his frequent allusions to western experiences, to his interest in nature, and to his concern for the common man, fooled him and the rural classes. This President who lauded the small land owner and hailed "the farmer who had to plow and pitch hay" seemed an eager friend. He and the majority of the nation accepted him at his own valuation.

The most important force forestalling farm legislation was a temporary prosperity. Agriculture could not respond as quickly as industry to the impetus of prosperity returning with the gold discoveries, for it had too many adjustments to make:—adjustments to exhaustion of the supply of cheap, fertile land, involving a rise in capital invested in land, labor, machinery and fertilizer—capital for which the farmer paid interest at least at 10% or 12%. But after the Bryan crusade came a series of good harvests which helped to put agriculture as a whole, from 1907 to 1913, back in the position it had occupied between 1856 and 1860, when farm prices were relatively higher than prices of general commodities.

Farmers paid old debts, and acquired new ones in improving their facilities and enlarging their operations. Pioneering days seemed well over and the West no longer seethed with unrest. Gas and electricity came to farmhouses and barns, now mostly well built, of wood or brick; the telephone "party line" and the daily paper became usual equipment of sitting rooms. Some sense of oneness with the outside world came to them. These betterments, however, could not break the cityward trek of the more ambitious and talented boys and girls, whose departure inflicted a loss which was moral and physical as well as numerical. Over 3,000,000 people moved (1900-1910) from rural to urban areas.

Surface evidences of activity and prosperity abounded. American farm property, in the first decade of the twentieth century, doubled in value while farm prices rose nearly 50%. The population meanwhile was increasing 50% while improved farm acreage rose only 15.4%. In the following four years (1910-1914) the number of cattle fell 12.9% while their total value rose 42.2%. The dangers in these disparities were obscured by the price rise. The same first decade saw rural areas receiving only 30% of the total increase in the nation's population, while New England and the eastern-north-central states were showing an absolute loss in farm population and income. These losses spread to the Middle Atlantic states in the next decade, for farming in these sections could not compete with farming in the West or with city life nearby. The different sections of the United States were finding their respective competitive levels.

Farmers on the move to other farms found the supply of good, free land practically given out, unless one migrated to Canada. The perennial American urge for land speculation, merging with the national trend toward consolidation, reached a new climax about 1900 when more than 25,000,000 acres had fallen into the hands of only 54 holders—companies and private persons. Almost half the farm land of the mountain and Pacific states by this time was held in units of 1000 acres or more, tilled by laborers or tenants, often worked by Japanese or, a little later, Mexicans. Much of the Southwest and Far West would have produced quickly a plantation system like that of the ante-bellum South if Orientals had not been barred; and the process went on even as it was, by reason of the flood of Mexicans. Exhaustion of free land necessarily ended the wide distribution of land ownership companion to it, for ordinary tillers of the soil found it difficult to acquire, and retain, ownership of increasingly expensive acres.

Reduction in the number of holdings also was due, in part, to mineral subsoil resources for which corporations of all descriptions fought, neglecting no device, illegal or criminal, in their efforts to grasp the richest deposits of coal, oil, copper, gold, silver, aluminum and iron. Public indifference to such seizures was of such long standing that only very dramatic revelations, useful in political rivalries, would move the central government to action. As free public lands had made for social, economic and political equality, so now class stratification appeared. Campaigns for means of ameliorating conditions pointed no longer to a person rising from his or her class, but to bettering their position within the class where they were.

Reclamation and Conservation

Some 570,000,000 American acres remained unclaimed, much of it usable only by dry farming or irrigation. Nevertheless, land entries were considerably more numerous during the twenty years following 1898 than during the preceding twenty, especially after the residence requirement was cut (1912) from five years to three.[1] Bona fide homesteading and private seizure of natural resources together brought about the organization of three additional states—Oklahoma (1907), Arizona and New Mexico (1912), strengthening by six votes the Far-West influence in the United States Senate.

Entries into semi-arid areas, and a growing awareness of land limits, pushed Americans deeper into experiments with irrigation, reclamation and conservation. The national psychology had been built up around the historic need for increased production. The government still was engrossed in helping people get on to raw land—was not yet concerned in getting them off. President Roosevelt, with his North Dakota experience, naturally clung to this emphasis. Unworried by thoughts of possible overproduction of foodstuffs or of submarginal farmers, he heartily absorbed Pinchot's and F. H. Newell's various enthusiasms for conservation, reclamation and exploitation, as moral obligations. Annual messages to Congress regularly featured desert irrigation and forest preservation. Congress in 1902 passed a reclamation law sponsored by Representative Francis G. Newlands (who hailed from the semi-arid state of Nevada) which led to irrigation of 3,000,000 acres within four years, and projected engineering undertakings in immensity almost as great as the Panama Canal.

Reclamation enthusiasms, awakened by agricultural needs for water, fostered more serious consideration of the bigger problem of water power as related to industry—a problem so basic to a democracy in an electric age that it became inseparable from the politics of the progressive era. No money-making scheme for control of production could neglect sources of electric power. Inventions were more than doubling the number of power stations, were lengthening to 150 miles the distance from the powerhouse that electricity could be delivered. Water power was proving much the cheapest way to manufacture electricity. Expanding prospects of profits in hydro-electricity were making a battleground of the best river locations, and Niagara had been harnessed by private interests before 1900.

Private interests planned to control, among other sites, a valuable one on the Tennessee, at Muscle Shoals, Alabama; and in 1903 they

[1] This action was taken largely with reference to large-scale farming, as for example flax growing in Dakota and Montana.

put through Congress a bill for private construction there of a dam and power station. This project, however, ran counter to the awakening interest in public welfare, which in the progressive era was attaching serious political implications to the "power trust." Therefore Roosevelt, announcing that water power was public property which should be conserved for the people, vetoed this, one of a long series of Muscle Shoals bills. It was but one victory for the public interest.[1]

Meanwhile, the forestation branch of the conservation principle was proving strong enough to burst strictly legal bounds in its application. Farm settlement in treeless areas, and the washing away of farm land by water from denuded hillsides, were changing trees from enemies, to cherished friends. Pinchot and La Follette, whose worst foe in Wisconsin had been the railroad-timber combine, urged an aggressive policy of withdrawal of timber lands from entry. Pinchot's division was expanded (1905) into a Bureau of Forestry and moved from the Interior into the Agriculture Department; and Roosevelt by executive order set aside nearly 150,000,000 acres from public sale. Congress was persuaded to adopt a policy of leasing, rather than selling, coal lands and other deposits. National parks, fire patrols, and bird and animal reservations were set up. The Forestry service favored farm settlers as against large cattle and sheep raisers; the latter in 1906 were forced, for the first time, to pay for the privilege of using public land facilities. Congress legislated to improve land tenure and established a Bureau of Mines.

By means of various state and national commissions on waterways and conservation, the way was prepared for a National Conservation Commission, appointed in June 1908, which coordinated the efforts of some thirty-six state commissions and made a valuable inventory of national resources. Thus were the American people familiarized with the principle and practice of conservation of natural resources for national welfare—a valuable bequest from the progressive era to the present.

As conservation ceased to be merely a symbol of prudent land use and became the symbol of progressive principles in general, it cut deeply across the system of special privilege which was undermining democracy in the United States. Politics felt its dividing influence so sharply as to make the so-called "Ballinger-Pinchot controversy" an event of historic significance.

The controversy grew out of the fact that some of the water power sites which Roosevelt and Pinchot had withdrawn from sale were reopened by Taft and his Secretary of the Interior, Richard Ballinger. Ballinger, like Taft and unlike Roosevelt and Pinchot, had a legalistic mind and lacked enthusiasm for withdrawals. His action fanned the flames of animosity and rivalry for prestige burning between the Interior

[1] Private interests by 1913 were delivering power from a plant erected at Keokuk, Iowa, projected then to become the world's largest producer.

and Agriculture Departments, ever since Roosevelt took the administration of the vast forest reserves of the nation away from the one, and gave it to the other. Pinchot the crusader, apprehensive for his beloved conservation program, publicly drew attention to the fact that the power trust was seizing water power, and hinted that Ballinger was in the scheme.

Into this breach jumped Louis R. Glavis, investigator for the Department of the Interior, and widened it. He had been examining claims made by a Cunningham corporation to valuable Alaskan coal lands and Ballinger had withdrawn him from the task. Guggenheim and Morgan interests were operating in the territory. Glavis now announced that the claims were fraudulent and the group pressing them were personal friends of Ballinger, their former counsel. Pinchot endorsed Glavis. Taft upheld Ballinger, and dismissed Glavis and subsequently Pinchot.

In a Congress already divided by disputes over the tariff, over control of Senate and House committees and over party organization, the Ballinger-Pinchot controversy was a high explosive. It widened the split between the progressive and standpat wings of the Republican party. It posed the fundamental question of special privilege. Although a congressional committee of investigation essayed to "exonerate" Ballinger, his intolerable position forced his resignation, in March of 1911. Like Cannon, Aldrich, Hale and others he had become a symbol of that philosophy of government for the privileged which had flowered luxuriantly since the Civil War. By temperament, association and long practice men of this type belonged to the era which the progressives appeared to be about to bring to an end. They left the theater of government at the same time. Following their departure protection of national resources, in Alaska and elsewhere, became a recognized test of honest administration, and legislation in the field became an obligation of thoughtful lawmakers.

Demands for Aid to Agriculture

While the western agricultural situation was giving Americans of many classes new concepts of conservation and the general welfare, they were becoming aware that the farm no longer was in all instances the model incubator of democracy described in the panegyrics of politicians. It was discovered, belatedly, that New Jersey berry fields, Delaware and Maryland vegetable gardens, Michigan and Nebraska and Colorado beet-sugar fields, and Connecticut, Pennsylvania, Virginia and Kentucky tobacco areas were working children in twelve-hour days, often under unhealthful and immoral conditions. Farm tasks were engaging 60% of the 1,700,000 or more children under sixteen at work in 1900.

Farm prospects for adults were not growing more pleasant. An Industrial Relations Commission reported in 1914 that renting was spreading; ownership of large areas by absentee owners lowered wages, raised rents for small plots and discouraged cooperation between owner and tiller. Neither East nor West, were conditions of farm labor very attractive to intelligent workers, or well calculated to select from the rising generation an adequate supply of those ambitious and independent farmers who had been acclaimed as the "mainstay of American Democracy." Emotional interest once aroused, President Roosevelt under urgings from Sir Horace Plunkett established a "Country Life Commission" to consider palliatives. It aroused disdain among farmers and its report failed to win respectful treatment from a congressional appropriation committee; but the movement made a strong, popular impression among some other groups, which paved the way for more competent and positive achievement by later leaders.

It was from the cotton country that the demand came for more concrete aid to farmers. Southern agriculture was being challenged by a phenomenal manufacturing development. The section was doubling its steel output, while cotton mills transformed the hill towns of Charlotte, North Carolina, and Columbia and Greenville, South Carolina, into busy cotton manufacturing centers. Economic development so engrossed the more capable southerners that the poor white and middle classes enjoyed a new political importance, with the race issue perpetuated by rabble-rousers for political convenience. The more ambitious of the poor whites and lower middle class were attracted from hillside farms. There remained only those who submitted to the share-cropping system. In the lowlands Negroes continued to do most of the farm labor, many of them as virtual peons, enchained by share-cropping and by the custom of putting Negroes to work for persons who paid their petty fines.

A gradual rise in the literacy of the Negroes, however, was reflected in an increase (1910-1920) of 20% in the number of Negroes operating and owning southern farms—an increase four times greater than that in the rural Negro population. Industry was entering into competition with agriculture for Negro labor, inspiring a movement which ran both from country to city and from South to North and West. The serious handicap to cotton contentment, however, was surplus yield. Prices had fallen, 1879-1898, from 11.6¢ to 5.5¢ a pound, while production doubled. Now prices were rising (1899-1914), and, in spite of the boll weevil, cotton acreages and yields were increasing. Efforts to produce better grades, earlier varieties and higher yields, irrigation, fertilization and cotton seed uses, all encouraged production.

Always concerned in price-control of their products, farmers who in the earlier years of drouth had pushed monetary inflation devices now in years of heavy yields turned to emphasize marketing and distribution. A "Southern Cotton Growers Protective Association" began, about

1900, an ineffective campaign for reduction through diversification. In 1902 two new farmers' organizations, the "American Society of Equity" and the "Farmer Cooperative and Educational Union" (known as the Farmers' Union), were started, stressing marketing from the outset. The Equity group based its program upon the principle of controlling production and withholding surpluses.

The Farmers' Union from the beginning built its program around cooperative buying and selling, in which class feeling was so strong that membership was limited to whites, the order was secret, and bankers, merchants and lawyers were debarred. However, the record-breaking cotton crop of 1904, and the ensuing lowered price of 1904-1905, moved the Union in 1905 to cooperate with cotton exchanges, and other groups admitting the debarred classes, in a reduction program. A reduction of about 14% was achieved in that one year, when state unions existed in Alabama, Arkansas, Georgia, Louisiana and Texas. Neither group secured a membership approaching that of the Alliance or the Populist party, but since their plans were adapted to grain and livestock regions they founded a few northern groups. During the 1907 and 1909 cotton crises they secured some bankers' cooperation in financing cotton marketing.

Most of their activities were outside the legislative field; but they obtained a few state laws legalizing cooperatives. The Department in Washington, the agricultural colleges, and the farm press had been so engrossed in production that they were slow to aid the marketing agitation; but their interest heightened when the high cost of living in the progressive era established something of an *entente cordiale* between rural and urban populations, as allies against their common enemy the middleman. Congress finally in 1913 appropriated $50,000 so that the Secretary could create an "Office of Markets," and the next year passed a Cotton Futures Act, later frequently amended. The latter expansion of governmental functions was made to pass muster with the Supreme Court, as a revenue measure based upon the tax power of Congress, through the device of writing it so as to levy a tax under certain conditions instead of fixing penalties outright. Federal aid in financing agriculture was tendered by a law of 1916 for twelve regional Farm Loan Banks, designed to lower the cost and raise the principal of farmers' loans.

The progressive movement also extended farm appropriations in the familiar field of education. An Adams Act of 1906 doubled federal grants for experiment stations. A Smith-Lever Act of 1914 so expanded government aid to education in agriculture and home economics as to lead land grant colleges into active campaigns for state extension services. This latter would incubate the farm bureau movement, as it became known later.

Radical farm bureau developments, like the realization of some of the Farmers Union principles, were, indeed, nearer in time than in the congressional imagination, which was paving the way for it knew not what. The voice of the West, as it rose in the Progressive era, was a voice for regulatory legislation as conducive to the general welfare.

Altogether, legislation typical of the progressive era—whether touching transportation, trusts, finance, labor or agriculture—had consisted of a series of devices in the democratic tradition, invented to safeguard freedom under modern capitalism. Americans of the early twentieth century recognized as dangerous the control of practically all major activities by a handful of men who ran supercombinations known as trusts; but in the main they indignantly repudiated the notion of substituting for this a scheme of general control by the masses. They cherished their faith in individualism; and although it had become rampant they distrusted people in the mass. The capitalistic system, not collectivism, remained the preferred vehicle for carrying on the nation in free living.

So, Americans had gone on fighting graft, demanding the "common honesty" which had sufficed in the old agricultural regime, and failing to realize how modern living strains to the breaking point the homely virtues. They had thought to safeguard their interest adequately by passing laws "against" big business and special privilege. From this difficult task of domestic social security, their attention was violently diverted by the prospect of participation in a struggle to save democracy abroad.

CHAPTER XXXII

THE DEMOCRACY EXPERIMENTS WITH IMPERIALISM

Public attention during the Progressive Era was not completely absorbed in domestic concerns. While the struggle for purer democracy and social betterment was waged, the international position of the United States was changing. The war with Spain had swept into the orbit of American influence the polyglot of yellow, brown and black peoples chiefly inhabiting Hawaii, the Philippines, Puerto Rico, Cuba, and most of the other Caribbean areas. Their social and political institutions had not been cut after the Anglo-Saxon pattern, from which had been fashioned the United States experiment in democracy. Their economic resources, of raw material and man power, would partly complement, partly compete with, the American economy. Thus they added their quota of diversities to that sum total of differences which had made the history of the United States a long series of compromises. This basic fact was but little weighed, at first.

No less diverse was the reaction of Americans to the allotments of the Peace of Paris. Improvement was a prominent objective among beneficent persons, whose enthusiasm moved from freeing the oppressed of Spain to establishing sanitation, education, transportation, and orderliness among backward peoples. Protection was the object of military strategists, who drew the defense line from Alaska to Hawaii (some said the Philippines) through an isthmian canal and into a dominated Caribbean. Prestige was the object of those who proclaimed that the United States had "come of age" as an acknowledged world power, and thenceforth must steam across the seas to council tables in either hemisphere. Profit was the object of producers and investors. With these objectives, others became entangled, heterogeneous, opportunistic. Clashes quickly developed between parties at interest. The steps toward imperialism were to run contrary to some of the progressive ideals.

Supreme Court Definitions

Inasmuch as pursuit of the various objectives quickly carried American policy beyond accepted boundaries, the need soon arose for a judicial assignment of rights, privileges, and immunities. If Puerto Rico and the Philippines enjoyed the status of all previously acquired areas, they were enroute to statehood, their people were citizens of the United States and they could market on the mainland free of duty, to the inconvenience of sugar, tobacco, and other producers previously protected against them by the Dingley tariff. Could they not rather be given a classification new to United States experience—as dependencies? Americans hated to admit the term "colonies" to their vocabulary.

Dispute raged furiously; did the Constitution follow the flag? It became evident that, while protectionist sentiment temporarily was strong enough to insist upon its profitable perquisites, yet the American public persistently cherished the theory of inalienable rights. The Supreme Court majority (by various and close decisions in "insular cases" of 1901-1917) accommodated themselves to this situation. They decided that the dependencies were not foreign countries, but that their people were not necessarily citizens of the United States. They lived in "unincorporated" rather than "incorporated" territories. The "fundamental" rights of the Constitution, such as life, liberty, and property, applied to them, but not the "formal" rights of grand and petit jury practice; and Congress could decide how far the Constitution and the statutes applied to them. Congress proceeded to regulate duties on insular products; and for political pattern turned, after periods of military rule, to British colonial experience. Government of the Philippines and Puerto Rico, each was assigned to an appointed governor and a legislature composed of an appointive, executive council and an elected lower house, with the governor (unlike the American colonial officials) enabled to continue appropriations when the assembly proved recalcitrant. Such arrangements made the political and economic (and consequently the social) status of the colonies dependent upon the ebb and flow of pressures on Congress.

Economic Concomitants

The majority of Americans who welcomed the Treaty of Paris were confident of profits from the undertaking. Whitelaw Reid pictured the Pacific become an "American Lake" and many were certain that at least the Caribbean would become such a placid sheet. The fact that only the latter of these ambitions was achieved did not mean that American trade and investment affected foreign relations only in that confined precinct. Their ramifications require some notice.

The nation's accrued debts, held by European investors, kept the United States a net debtor in international payments until 1914; but in trade and investment Americans were making such strides as to have reached the creditor position even if there had been no World War. Between 1881 and 1897—a period of falling prices—they had increased the volume of their exports sufficiently at least to keep the total value of them comparatively stable; then in 1897 the export trend veered upward sharply, reaching 2.5 billions in 1913. European manufacturers fearing for their markets protested against the "invasion." Furthermore, American investments abroad, which totalled only 635 millions in 1897, quintupled to 3314 millions by 1 July 1914. This activity of traders and investors followed lines patterned by competing capitalists of all the highly industrialized nations.

First, as to trade; foreign sales organizations sprouted. Standard Oil by 1911 had 16 subsidiaries; International Harvester by 1912 had 53 foreign branch houses; United States Steel by 1913 had 268 agencies scattered over about 60 countries; National Cash Register by 1914 was assigning one-third of its output to foreign dispersion. Foreign areas were thoroughly penetrated also by other machinery, by meats, shoes and soap. Foreign transportation facilities, storehouses and warehouses were required for use. Branch banks, however, were so restricted under American law that exporters and investors had to depend for facilities largely upon British, French, German and Dutch branches. This proved a real hindrance.

Second, as to investments, some 1000 millions in securities of foreign governments and foreign-controlled corporations found purchasers in the United States between 1897 and 1914. Vastly more influential, in the imperial situation, were the direct investments in American-controlled ventures abroad as the United States contingent in the world scramble for control of natural resources became, with government aid, very active. They invested most heavily in those minerals closely integrated with modern industrial production:—oil,[1] copper, aluminum, lead, nickel, tin, zinc, iron—and such non-metallic minerals as nitrates, coal, asbestos, gypsum and sulphur; in these they invested eight times as much as in gold and silver mines.

Capital for agriculture went principally into tropical products needed by a nation located in a temperate clime:—sugar plantations and mills in the Philippines, Cuba, Puerto Rico and Hawaii attracted the larger part; second came fruit (especially bananas in the Caribbean area) and other tropical foodstuffs like cocoanuts, cacao, chicle, coffee, tea and spices; most of the remainder went into rubber plantations and Mexican and Canadian ranches and farms. Sisal, jute and hemp had some attractions.

Capital for branch factories had begun to engage Americans as soon as the factory came to the United States, and by 1914 most outstanding concerns had foreign factories; their stake rose from perhaps 100 millions in 1900 to about 400 millions in 1914, distributed about 220 in Canada, 200 in Europe, and almost 60 in Latin America and the rest of the

---

[1] Oil was particularly important, because the United States came to produce and use about three-fourths of the world consumption and other nationals shut her out of foreign fields; the government obtained a share for United States interests in Turkey and the East Indies.

world. In foreign railways, chiefly Caribbean, American investment rose from 143 millions in 1897 to 350 millions in 1924.

Thus, to this wide extent, were Americans locating their fortunes outside their native land. Their progress in this risky business is indicated by the figures of the aggregate value of American-controlled enterprises abroad—in 1897, 655 millions; in 1914, 2.7 billions; in 1929, 7.6 billions. But no less significant than the aggregate is the fact that it includes, besides investment of new money, subsidies given by foreign governments as concessions, unearned increments, appreciation and reinvestments. The getting of all of these, and the manner of it, largely determined the social, economic, and political dynamics of imperialism.

In the dependencies and protectorates, pursuit of profits brought with it United States government-financed improvements in the environment of work, producing roads, sanitation, disease control and some modicum of modern education and conveniences. Similarly order and stability were firmly imposed upon regions of chronic revolution and change. There the dictatorship was assumed by economic forces, which dispossessed the inefficient, and small land and property owners, using them as employees in the large, one or two crop systems—such as tobacco and sugar—with which the great corporations earned dividends from huge plantations. The agricultural classes of Cuba, Puerto Rico, and the Philippines, became landless employees of absentee landlords, virtually peons; so did the workers in Mexico and other Caribbean areas where foreign capital took over the main economic processes.

These were some of the more powerful economic processes of the developing imperialistic foreign policy. As they operated in various locales, they worked differing effects. Around the Caribbean, United States imperialism reached its height in dependencies and protectorates; in Mexico and Venezuela exploitation was curbed by native sovereignty; in the Orient neither trade nor influence reached expectations; in Europe and Africa came occasional cooperation along lines of peace. To these various ventures the public reacted according to individual opinions as to the military necessity and humanity of the policies.

Around the Caribbean

Around the Caribbean appeared dependencies and protectorates in Cuba, Puerto Rico, Panama, Santo Domingo, Haiti, Nicaragua, and the Virgin Islands. The background of the picture in this region revealed elements present also in almost every other Latin American area—elements persistently affecting relations with the United States and therefore essential to be kept in mind. First in importance was the continual expansion of investment and trade. Secondly, all European competitors here held dear one common objective:—to foster anti-United States feeling. Thirdly, to offset their hostile influence and to protect the preferential position actually won by American capital, Washington had to invent "Pan Americanism" and had to struggle through the years to give it something other than a domineering connotation.

Cuba became a virtual protectorate. There United States military rule continued four years after peace. The military did much for the social and political reconstruction of the island, substituting order for complete chaos, establishing the beginnings of self-government and sound finance, cleaning up Havana and discovering (with the sacrifice of the lives of Dr. James Carroll and Dr. Jesse Lazear) that the yellow fever scourge could be stamped out by mosquito control. Withdrawal of the troops was a foregone conclusion; the conditions of that withdrawal, in view of American interests, were the issue. The pledge of the Teller amendment, that Cuba should be left to the Cubans, had been made during the excitement of declaring war with Spain, but the pledge conformed to historic, popular, democratic ideals and stubbornly resisted the schemes of General Wood and divers expansionists to displace it with annexation.

Secretary of War Root, thoroughly committed to the maintenance of United States interests, military and economic, undertook to protect them. A so-called "Platt Amendment" to the army appropriation bill of 1901 made military withdrawal dependent upon Cuba's acceptance of a treaty embodying significant pledges: Cuba was to ratify all the acts of the United States military regime, continue the sanitation program and eschew extraordinary indebtedness; she was not to jeopardize her "independence" (nor the influence of the United States) in compacts with other nations; naval and coaling stations were to be available for United States lease or purchase; most important, Cuba was to admit the right of the United States to intervene for the preservation of Cuban independence, the maintenance of a government adequate for the protection of life, liberty, and property, and the discharge of obligations under the Treaty of Paris. The right of intervention spelt annexation to the Cubans; but Root reassured them and they signed the treaty, incorporated its provisions in a new constitution, as per directions, and thus in 1902 temporarily rid themselves of American troops.

Economic prosperity was undertaken through reciprocity treaties which since 1903 have maintained for Cuban exports to the United States a 20% preference over products from other nations; American exports to Cuba obtained preferences ranging from 20% to 40%. These arrangements aided the sugar producing companies, American sugar refiners, and American exporters, to the disadvantage of consumers. The World War carried Cuba to the side of the Allies within twenty-four hours after the United States joined them; but it so overstimulated sugar production that postwar bankruptcy resulted; American and Canadian banks holding sugar paper took over financial control. Economic domination from United States interests became fairly obvious and complete.

Political independence proved impossible to maintain in financial stringencies. Furthermore rival political factions frequently tried to ride into power on the tails of American intervention, sometimes engaging in violent disorder to bring it about and then campaigning against the "American ogre." American troops and control returned, for stays varying from three years to a few months, in 1906, 1912, 1917, and 1920. During the 'twenties, however, nationalism strengthened in Cuba while imperialism weakened in the United States; and when the depression of 1929 coincided with a revolution against the terroristic Machado the United States did not follow the old pattern. For military intervention was substituted a careful easing out of Machado; and a treaty of "general relations" in 1934 reorganized a new regime. Under executive agreement (which neatly avoided ratification by the United States Senate) new reciprocal tariffs were granted which aimed to benefit Cuba as well as the United States; the Platt amendment and the right of intervention were abandoned, and thus the protectorate was nearly abolished. Only the naval station of Guantanamo was retained. This left Cuba free to feel assured of the right to maintain her own government, except, perhaps, if other powers should attempt to intervene. As the United States came to adopt liberal expedients likewise in other areas embraced in her Panama policy, she improved upon Europe's example in imperialism.

Puerto Rico became a colony. It well illustrated how much easier it is to grant the forms of political democracy than to establish the facts of general well-being. Under congressional acts of 1900 and 1917 the government approached a territorial status and Puerto Ricans, although lacking the complete home rule many desired, attained United States citizenship. These political advances were possible largely because of stable characteristics of the inhabitants. Some social advance came with attention to education, sanitation, transportation and public works. Trade and wealth expanded with the exploitation of abundant cheap labor in the production of sugar, tobacco, fruit, coffee, and manufactured goods. But these could not lift the masses out of a dependence so extreme that in the depression year of 1930 more than 60% of them lacked fulltime employment. Since 1902 they have been inside the United States tariff system, which means free trade between them and the mainland but extension of the American high price structure over their poor purchasing power. Their overcrowded situation, their liability to hookworm and their overdependence upon the American sugar market help to push them deeper into peonization.

Panama became a virtual protectorate, by a devious route. The two-month voyage of the battleship *Oregon* in 1898, from the coast of Washington 14,000 miles around the Cape of Good Hope to Florida, had indicated that an isthmian canal was essential to coastline defense. Also the canal idea was part of the expansionists' program and appealed to western farmers as a freight-lowering device. The United States, unfortunately, had agreed in the Clayton-Bulwer Treaty of 1850 that any isthmian canal should be internationalized and neutralized. To build under that treaty would mean construction at American expense of an unfortified canal, controlled equally by Britain and shared, as to facilities, equally by all nations. This was not to the interest of the United States; Secretaries Blaine and Frelinghuysen had tried to change it, and party platforms demanded abrogation of the old treaty. The series of canal negotiations undertaken at the turn of the century came to involve questions of America's policy as a world power in both hemispheres. So closely connected are decisions near and far.

Great Britain at this juncture was prepared to make concessions. Desiring an Anglo-American alliance, needing American support for her far-eastern program, she hoped that for canal concessions she might be compensated on the Alaska boundary, and realized that her interest lay in leaving control of the Caribbean to the United States. As events proved, the Senate would not tolerate the alliance nor would the Roosevelt administration yield on Alaska (p. 470); but meanwhile Britain instructed her Ambassador at Washington, Lord Pauncefote, to follow up a first, unpopular treaty which the Senate had killed, with a second Hay-Pauncefote treaty of 21 February 1902, which the Senate accepted.

What this treaty did not concede openly it conceded tacitly, by omission. It declared the Clayton-Bulwer treaty superseded; it did not prohibit fortification by the United States nor provide for the adherence of other nations. Although its rules for neutralization prohibited any act of war within the canal, Great Britain during the negotiations admitted the right of the United States to fortify and defend it; and Britain followed ratification by virtually withdrawing from the Caribbean, removing her principal naval forces and reducing her permanent garrisons. Fortifications subsequently erected there by the United States became the key to America's defense policy.

With Great Britain out of the way, canal routing could proceed; and as French and American companies attempting private construction had gone into bankruptcy it was clearly a task for the government. Routing could cross either Colombian or Nicaraguan territory, as transit rights had been secured long since from Colombia (then New Granada) in 1846 and from Nicaragua in 1867. Three official American commissions declared for Nicaragua, where one American company had buried capital before the 1893 panic and another now hold a speculative concession; and the House of Representatives in 1902 passed a bill for construction there.

On the other hand a French company headed by the Suez engineer,

DeLesseps, in the 'eighties had squandered some 400 millions on a ditch in the Panama section of Colombia; by 1901 American speculators had taken over the wreckage. Ably managed by the J. P. Morgan banking company, by a New York attorney-lobbyist, W. N. Cromwell, and by a versatile ex-engineer, Bunau-Varilla, they undertook to salvage their investment with government aid before their franchise expired in 1904. A timely volcanic eruption in Nicaragua helped them. They pared their sale price to 40 millions, convinced President Roosevelt and Senator Hanna that Panama was best and lobbied through the Senate a Spooner amendment to the House bill, authorizing purchase of the Panama property if Colombia acceded.

Secretary Hay and Colombian Minister Herran proceded to negotiate a treaty authorizing the Panama Company to sell to the United States, granting the latter full control over a strip of land six miles wide, and allotting to Colombia immediate payment of ten millions and after nine years annual payments of $250,000. These figures were generally considered fair, but the Colombian Senate delayed, possibly for higher figures and expiration of the company rights.

The none-too-patient Roosevelt, consulting Secretary of War Root, was assured that the treaty of 1846 could be interpreted to justify intervention, if to prevent interruption of transit through "domestic disturbances." [1] All apparently required for the intervention was the disturbance. So a quiet "revolution" against Colombia was staged at Panama 3 November 1903, a few hours later than expected in Washington and while United States warships hovered conveniently near to prevent landing of Colombian troops. Inside of three days Colombia offered to accept the Hay-Herran treaty if her isthmus sovereignty were protected; but the United States recognized the *de facto* government on the 6th and other powers quickly followed.

Bunau-Varilla, now accredited Panamanian plenipotentiary, signed with Hay the treaty of 18 November giving Panama the 10 millions in gold and the $250,000 annually. Panama tendered the right to build and fortify a canal and to possess a zone ten miles wide across the isthmus. The United States promised to maintain Panama's independence but received other rights which virtually made Panama a protectorate. Canal construction was turned over, after some initial bad appointments, to Colonel Gorgas and Colonel Goethals, who respectively made a malaria-ridden region healthy and an almost impossible engineering dream an accomplished fact.

Thus Theodore Roosevelt "took" the canal. That was his own description and it is history's verdict. American attitudes in foreign relations were then so casual as to tolerate such a performance. The seizure

[1] The Hay-Pauncefote treaty provided that no change in the territorial sovereignty of the canal would alter the obligation of the signatories.

antagonized not only Colombia, which is the only government refusing today to recognize Panama, but all Latin America. It burdened the United States with a heavy moral liability. Root in vain offered Colombia three treaties tendering 2.5 millions of Panama's annuities in exchange for recognition. Next the Wilson administration negotiated a Bryan treaty which offered an apology and an indemnity of 25 millions; this was defeated in the Senate by friends of ex-President Roosevelt. Meanwhile, Britain was objecting strenuously because Congress by a 1912 law had exempted coastwise shipping from tolls; she indicated that the Hay-Pauncefote treaty stipulated equal treatment for vessels of all nations. Perhaps the United States had a case for arbitration, but Wilson had a tacit bargain with the British for support of his Mexican policy (p. 600); so the exemption law was repealed in mid-1914, shortly before the canal was opened to commercial traffic.

Finally in 1921 Colombia balked at petroleum concessions to American interests and a treaty resulted which omitted the Bryan apology but paid the 25 millions; after seventeen years more, amity between the two governments reached the point where they raised their legations to embassies. When the second Roosevelt was liquidating as much as possible of the Caribbean liabilities, needing and cultivating Latin friendship, a treaty was signed looking toward the end of the protectorate over Panama. Two facts, however, remained unchanged:—Latin America could not forget the seizure and the United States could not dispense with the canal.

The assumption of canal responsibilities brought a keener interest in the affairs of the Latin American Republics in the Caribbean. Many of them were under heavy financial obligations to European powers and often they failed to pay their debts. Some European powers threatened to intervene to force the collection of these debts and incidentally to control a landing place or naval station near the Canal. The United States could not look with equanimity on such practice. Therefore in 1902 when Germany, Britain and Italy jointly blockaded defaulting Venezuela, bombarded two ports and seized several gunboats, President Theodore Roosevelt supported Venezuela's insistence on arbitration. Germany also took note of the fact that Admiral Dewey's fleet was wintering off Puerto Rico. Arbitration was therefore agreed upon as a substitute for intervention. The incident led to adoption (in modified form) at The Hague conference of 1907 of the so-called Drago Doctrine; [1] it outlawed collection of contract debts by force if the debtor agreed to arbitrate, and served as an international supplement to the Monroe Doctrine.

The United States further undertook financial protectorates to fore-

[1] Named for its proposer, Dr. Luis Drago, Argentine Minister of Foreign Affairs.

stall intervention. In 1904 Santo Domingo got into similar difficulties and again Roosevelt acted. He conveniently invented what became known as the "Roosevelt corollary" to the Monroe Doctrine; according to it, since the United States could not allow Europe to collect western debts, she must collect them herself.[1] He arranged a treaty under which an American receiver would collect Dominican customs, apportioning 55% of the revenue to creditors and the remainder to the island government. When the Senate refused to accept either corollary or treaty, he proceeded to collect the debts anyhow under a *modus vivendi* until the Senate two years later ratified a new treaty with new loans. By an outburst of revolutions between 1911 and 1916 the Dominicans jeopardized payments on loans floated by Kuhn, Loeb and the National City Bank. President Wilson ended the disorder by an armed intervention which continued until a Dominican constitution of 1924 established a financial protectorate—significant because a terminal date was set for it.

Haiti, Santo Domingo's neighbor on the western half of the island, contended with similar difficulties. Secretary of State Knox forced an entrance to the republic for American capital. Political conditions became chaotic by 1915, and although President Wilson disclaimed any designs upon Haiti's political or territorial integrity he sent down the marines. Under a treaty ratified by a puppet government exploitation was facilitated; a protectorate broader than Santo Domingo's was set up, with most functions supervised by United States advisers under marine protection. Some few instances of atrocities helped to arouse public opinion against a too inclusive and brutal occupation and so the marines were withdrawn in 1934 and financial dictation was modified the next year by placing revenue collection under the Haitian National Bank.

Nicaragua was the Central American country of greatest concern to the United States government, because of her closeness to Panama, her possession of territory usable for a second canal, and her chronic political and financial difficulties. When these difficulties became too severe and American lives and property endangered, the Taft Administration despatched marines in 1912 to remain in Nicaragua most of the time for twenty years, and Brown Brothers and J. and W. Seligman made loan agreements without benefit of treaties. The bankers firmly thrust development and exchequer control upon the little countries, nominating customs receivers, after consultation with and approval by the State Department. Thus the United States avoided official guarantees but encouraged numerous arrangements for protecting investments. President Taft gave the policy the accurate but odorous description of "dollar diplomacy."

The Wilson administration continued it, putting through the Bryan-

---

[1] He based this assumption upon a larger one:—that in case of flagrant disregard of international obligations the United States had the right to intervene in Latin America, under the "international police power."

Chamorro treaty, paying Nicaragua 3 millions for a lease of the Great Corn and Little Corn islands and of a naval base on the Gulf of Fonseca. This was calculated to protect canal rights but was denounced by the Central American Court of International Justice, a miniature league of nations sponsored in 1906-1907 by the United States and Mexico, as an infringement of sovereignty. When revolutionists busied the marines with guerrilla warfare, the United States extended her policy of embargoes on arms to revolutionists, particularly in Nicaragua, Honduras and Cuba. The great importance of Central American order to the United States led to an effort, in 1922-1923, to strengthen the Central American Court; treaties were signed for "cooling off" before going to war, and for refusing recognition to revolutionary governments. This proved no bar, however, to further revolt in Nicaragua and a reoccupation by marines. Evacuation of Nicaragua was not completed until 1933.

As the 'twenties wore on, it became increasingly clear that the United States had few fears remaining of European threat to the Panama region and that continual intervention was impractical, costly, and bad for trade. Therefore, in one country after another intervention had been tapered off, to the delight of those Americans who thought it wholly commercial in origin. In 1929 the Department of State published the so-called "Clark Memorandum" which in effect cut from the Monroe Doctrine the Roosevelt corollary. This left non-American intervention still taboo but removed the pledge of United States intervention. A capstone on this new policy was placed by the Montevideo treaty of 1935 which conceded that "no state has the right to intervene in the internal or external affairs of another."

The only other area considered necessary to round out the Panama policy was the Danish West Indies, the three, little, poverty-stricken and undeveloped islands which the Senate had refused Seward. Enthusiastic expansionists of 1898, in the days before oil-burning ships, had committed the Republican party to their purchase. The Senate in 1902 agreed to give 5 millions for them; they were only a liability to Denmark but her Rigsdag rejected that treaty by one vote. In 1917 the German admiral, Von Tirpitz was understood to covet these Virgin Islands, as they had come to be called, and the United States, in wartime enthusiasm, paid 25 millions, an exorbitant sum.

Mexico's Challenge

Mexico has posed a most delicate problem in neighborhood diplomacy, complicated by rich resources, heavy investment, frequent revolutions, extreme differences in culture and temperament and the memory of 1848. Officially, the United States since then has shown forbearance, displaying force seldom and briefly; but Mexican politicians and people read private, foreign expropriation between the lines of every diplomatic document, and Latin Americans generally measure the sincerity of the words of the United States by her actions in Mexico. Capital from the United States and other nations got a sixty-year head start of the Mexicans in the exploitation of their country. The process was such as to ensure a violent reaction when the Mexican nation awakened to the fact.

Dictator Porfirio Diaz, who was tremendously interested in rapid exploitation of resources and totally illiterate in human values, kept political control from 1877 to 1910, while he lavishly dispensed concessions, chiefly to foreigners. They invested about 2 billions—one-half of it from the United States—in agricultural lands, electric power, mines, oil, rubber, and railroads. Diaz's absolute dictatorship had the support of the landed aristocracy, the Creoles, that tenth of the population who absorbed whatever of profits did not leave Mexico for foreign pockets. The other nine-tenths of the population, deprived of the lands they had worked on the communal system, became worse off than the slaves in the United States had been. Of Indian, Negro and other mixed blood, they sank into a condition of peonage, desperately poor, ignorant superstitious, and diseased. Of education, sanitation, and public welfare there was none. No middle class group, with the wish and power to implement representative government, existed to preserve for the nation its just share of the profits from exploitation, as the middle class in the United States had done throughout the long years of foreign investment.

Popular resentment accumulated in huge volume, not against Creoles or European investors so much as against the "gringoes" from the north. This concentrated hatred became tremendously important in Mexican emotional, cultural, and political life. No politician could ignore it; all would be tempted to use it. The overturn of Diaz by more liberal forces (apparently aided by American oil interests resentful of concessions to Englishmen) began a decade of revolution during which successive leaders fought for control. While Mexico painfully moved in the direction of constitutional liberties and social regeneration, the northern democracy showed remarkable sympathy and forbearance.

National traditions and population characteristics made impossible anything like the orderly fighting of the United States Civil War. Pillage, outrage, slaughter, insurrection, deceit and guerrilla warfare generally characterized Mexico's struggles. Bandits and honest citizens alike voiced their rivalries and discontent in terms of violent hatred of the United States, whenever a more precise statement of objectives taxed ingenuity. In a decade of revolutions between 40,000 and 50,000 citizens of the United States abandoned their property and suffered damage estimated at 170 millions (Mexican); nearly 800 lost their lives. Three perennial problems faced Presidents Taft and Wilson:—protection of lives and property, recognition of revolutionary governments, and chastisement of outrages. Always there was the painful decision:— should forceful intervention be used for these purposes?

President Wilson sympathized with the agrarian reform program planned by Madero (president of Mexico from 1910 until murdered in 1913) and undertook—against the wishes of powerful foreign capitalists—to unseat his reactionary successor, Huerta. Clumsy efforts to block arms shipments into Mexico led to shelling of Vera Cruz by United States guns; but Wilson generally handled the situation with such restraint that South America began to pay him dividends on his moderation. Argentine, Brazil and Chile offered to mediate—an innovation—and the "A.B.C. Conference" at Niagara Falls exonerated him of aggression and set up the salutary principle of an inter-American guarantee of mutual independence. Meanwhile, Wilson had reached an agreement with Britain for concessions on Panama tolls in exchange for support in unseating Huerta. Huerta finally departed.

Wilson anxiously adopted a policy of "watchful waiting," as he called it, which only American traditions of democracy enabled him to maintain. He recognized a new president, Carranza, who was favored by South American powers, and accepted his promise to punish a troublesome bandit, Pancho Villa. Villa was committing murders on both sides of the international boundary, in the effort to provoke armed invasion, exploit Mexican hatred of gringoes, destroy Carranza and elevate himself. Although Congress passed a resolution for armed intervention and Theodore Roosevelt and investors in Mexican holdings shouted for the scalps of both Carranza and Villa, Wilson limited himself to mobilization of militia on the border and despatch of General Pershing in pursuit of the bandit.

Villa was not captured, nor would Carranza recognize the foreign right of intervention, nor pledge protection to foreign citizens and property. These guarantees he probably could not give, and Wilson in January of 1917 ordered withdrawal of troops without them. Wilson wanted no Mexican war on the eve of entrance into the European struggle.

Carranza soon secured election by the Mexican Congress, which demonstrated its prejudices by hissing Ambassador Henry P. Fletcher and applauding the German Ambassador. At the moment, Germany's scheme for a joint attack by Japan and Mexico upon Texas, California and the states between had just been published; but when the United States joined the Allies Mexico followed suit. Although Wilson's self-restraint had cost Mexico's respect, it had gained him the goodwill of Latin America and prevented war. It left uncertain the property rights of foreigners:—their claims for damages to person and property, for expropriated farm and mineral lands, and for defaulted bonds.

Mexico's crucial problem remained the recovery of her resources for the benefit of her people. To solve it, a new constitution in 1917 provided for the protection of labor from capitalistic domination, for the nationalization of church property and secularization of schools and for an end to foreign concessions. The famous "Article 27" declared all lands, waters, and mineral deposits the property of the nation, which could determine conditions of private holdings and could expropriate them in the public interest; oil, formerly allowed to lie in private ownership, was to be brought into fifty-year leaseholds, under state ownership. A "Calvo clause" required foreign concessionaries not to call on their governments for support of title against the Mexican government.

Alarmed American investors, particularly oil interests aided by Senator Fall, exhausted every expedient during the next decade to secure agreement that the reforms should not be retroactive, as indeed the 1917 constitution said they could not. Intervention was demanded by American Catholics also. War nearly came in 1919 and there were no diplomatic relations from 1920-1923; but Secretaries Hughes and Kellogg found that the American public preferred patient negotiation. American demands were tempered to Mexican political realities in a series of agreements known as the "Bucareli Conferences," and satisfaction was expressed in reassuring amendments to the Mexican code.

The Mexicans gradually achieved political stability under more liberal presidents. They passed Petroleum and Alien Land Laws in 1925 to implement the 1917 reform, hitherto applied only in temporary decrees. Finally Dwight W. Morrow, a liberal member of the J. P. Morgan firm, was sent down as Ambassador. By exceptional tact and understanding he obtained compromises on the moot points of titles, the Calvo clause, the church and land claims. Amicable relations were assisted no little by the rising interest of American tourists and intellectuals in Mexico's culture and history, and by "goodwill flights" begun by C. A. Lindbergh, who met in Mexico his future wife, Anne Morrow. Strained relations did not return until Calles' successor, Cardenas, confronted the F. D. Roosevelt administration with another effort to apply the constitution of 1917 to land distribution.

Oriental Excursions

The reaction of the American people to possession of the Philippines demonstrated that imperialism came unnaturally, made them uncomfortable and could not be maintained according to the European pattern. Although Bryan met defeat in the 1900 campaign on imperialism, the treaty with Spain had been ratified with difficulty, the Senate came within a vice-president's vote of pledging Filipinos speedy independence, and from the outset Congress reiterated the intention to let them go. Maintenance of this colony, which Congress labelled an "unincorporated territory," with its 7,000,000 people multiplying to 12,000,000 "citizens of the Philippines," violated democratic mores. It put Americans on the defensive, an unwonted rôle since 1865, and gave them three disconcerting surprises.

The Filipinos would not admit that possession by the beneficent, well-intentioned United States was a privilege. They put up a bitter, three-year fight for independence against the odds of 60,000 United States troops, relentlessly captained. They demonstrated that their vast majority were not uncivilized, unintelligent, unchristian or incapable of political organization. Facts surprising to Americans were revealed by commissions sent out to learn what manner of people were being subjugated and instructed.

No less surprising was the failure of the Philippines to prove a gold mine. Their acquisition did not convert the Pacific into an "American lake." The islands proved neither a phenomenal outlet for American products nor a convenient re-export depot for the China trade, which fell rather than rose. Tariff adjustments failed to remedy this situation: —in 1902 Congress tried a 25% reduction from Dingley domestic schedules; in 1909 they tried free trade in everything except certain products, like sugar, tobacco, and hemp, competing with American production; in 1913 they established nearly complete free trade. Yet the Filipinos proceeded to sell Americans more than 30% more than they bought; and their biggest export crop, sugar, which was produced by non-American capital, competed with American-financed sugar of Cuba, Puerto Rico, Hawaii and the mainland. Nor did capitalists find Philippine investments attractive; they confined their modest outlays chiefly to railways, public utilities and government obligations.

A third surprise was that the Philippines proved a distinct liability. With lack of abundant private profits went heavy public outlays. As elsewhere, American governors with hearty approval from home spent lavishly to establish facilities considered indispensable for intelligent, progressive living; imperialism should be justified by paternalism. The Filipinos eagerly used the facilities, with little expense to themselves and heavy outlay to the United States treasury, but were not too grateful to want to be free. Worse, American naval experts knew and admitted that islands 6200 miles distant could not be defended; the United States was in an exposed position, to which prestige and moral obligations chained her!

Whatever the solution, it quickly became evident that military rule would not long be maintained without a vestige of native participation. Three Filipinos shortly were given places on the Taft Commission which established civil government in 1901; the Philippines (Foraker) Act of 1902 provided that an elective, lower house should be established after census taking, and it met in 1907. Next the Democrats, committed to independence since 1900, added an elective Senate under the Jones Act of 1916, authorized native reorganization of the government and formally promised future withdrawal. Wilson's gubernatorial appointee, General Francis B. Harrison, wisely prepared the islands for self-rule, encouraging native civil servants and state control of island development. Wilson asked Congress to make them independent.

The Republicans took no such mandate and Harding's appointee, General Wood, undid Harrison's reforms; but his successor, Stimson, practiced conciliation. The independence party received strong reenforcements, from American competition with Filipino goods and labor, and from the return of the Democrats to power. They rejected an independence act of 1932 as too unfair but accepted a 1934 law. It provided for independence after a ten-year probationary period, with the United States keeping naval privileges, barring Filipino immigration (which had been worrying Californian white labor) and shutting out Filipino goods.

The price of independence, apparently, would be economic collapse, for in 1935 80% of the islands' exports went to the United States, and they could ill compete with cheaper markets to the East. Moreover, Japanese imperialism effectively confused American oriental policy, threatening to substitute for self-rule under American paternalism an economic and political subjection under Nipponese militarism. Aguinaldo himself took second thought, on the blessings of independence, as the years of "probation" wore on into 1939.

Pacific-mindedness carried America into the "backyard of European politics"—China—where the modern powers were scrambling for the spoils. There the United States aided them more than herself, by a policy of benevolence mixed with impracticality in which missionary zeal far outstripped investments. Perry's push against the closed door of Japanese trade in 1853 had helped to awaken Japan to modern aggressiveness. Next the United States (which had insisted upon equal trading privileges in China since 1844) obtained in 1883 a trade agreement with Korea and stumbled into a most delicate situation, for Japan and China had been contending there for dominance through three hundred years and Korea, as a buffer state between China, Japan and Russia, had become the "touchstone" of Far Eastern diplomacy. The Arthur administration obtained the Korean treaty by giving her more considerate terms than other governments would have offered, and the latter hastily copied them to obtain like privileges.

The agreement also avoided reference to Korea as a dependency of China, which advantaged Japan. She was bound to exploit the scramble of the western powers over China so as to get the opportunity to expel occidental influence and substitute her own. She exposed China's weakness in the war of 1894-1895 by which Japan won Formosa and domination of Korea; this inspired France, Germany, Italy and Russia to follow Britain's example in seizing port leases and railroad concessions.

When Britain "went shopping for allies" to counter her rivalries, she proposed that the United States join her in insistence upon the "open door" in China. Secretary of State Hay was very sympathetic toward England.[1] American interest in eastern trade was forward and capitalists had no desire to throw away the Spanish victory: but joint action would seem to suggest an "entangling alliance." Therefore Hay made in 1899 an independent appeal to the powers to guarantee, in their respective Chinese spheres of influence, equality of trade opportunity, so that merchants of all nations would pay the same tariffs, port dues and railroad charges. Only Britain formally seconded Hay's doctrine but he announced that it had become established. Britain, gratified, facilitated subsequently the canal and Alaskan settlements (pp. 470, 594). She got out of the Caribbean and the United States got into Asia.

When patriotic Chinese formed a secret organization called the Boxers and proceeded in 1900 to stage an outbreak against foreign concessionaires, the United States sent troops to help rescue the whites. Hay announced in explanation that America's Asiatic policy included preservation of China's territorial and administrative entity. This amazing assumption of responsibility, without compensating advantages and impossible to fulfill, was consented to by the other powers to placate America, and Hay was able to soften somewhat the onerous penalties imposed upon China for the uprising.[2] The United States had won the friendship of China at a cost of needless aggravation of occidental powers.

The rising Asiatic power, Japan, also was aggravated. President Roosevelt helped to end hostilities of the Russo-Japanese war at a juncture more favorable to Japan than to Russia, and he arranged that the peace negotiating should be done at Portsmouth, New Hampshire, under his friendly eye. But Japanese, blaming him for their failure to obtain the whole of Saghalin Island, turned his portrait to the wall. This resentment would be one of many; including contempt of the open door and dislike of restrictions upon Japanese immigration, schooling and landownership in America, besides anger at immigration bars in Hawaii and the Philippines.[3] Roosevelt salved her pride somewhat in 1907 by the "gentlemen's agreement" which put Japan on her honor to issue no

---

[1] He leaned on an American friend, W. W. Rockhill, who leaned on a shrewd Englishman, Alfred Hippesley.

[2] Of the 333 millions of reparations the United States claimed only about 25 millions and later remitted about three-fourths of that. The Chinese allocated nearly 11 millions of the remission to a fund for educating their youth in the United States.

[3] The Senate in 1912 interposed the Monroe Doctrine against Japanese leases on the Mexican coast.

passports for entry into the United States by skilled or unskilled labor. Events proved that the substitution by the treaty of Portsmouth of Japan for Russia in Manchuria did not bring the open door there and did give Japan recognition as a world power, which she in time would use to close the door to China.

Roosevelt pursued his oriental excursions through careful avoidance of treaty-making, which would have revealed that neither Senate nor nation acquiesced. After Portsmouth he made two personal agreements with Japan. By the Taft-Katsura memorandum and the Root-Takahira agreement, America endorsed the Anglo-Japanese alliance, and approved a free hand for Japan in Korea, while Japan disavowed aggressive designs on the Philippines and made pious pledges on Chinese independence and the open door. Both knew, however, that the status quo to which they pledged themselves was transitory and that the door was closing. The United States navy made an ostentatious visit to Japanese waters while Japan seized some more of Manchuria and continued her practice of working with European capitalists particularly Britishers, to hinder American profit-sharing in Chinese exploitation.

President Taft and Secretary of State Knox first proposed that the powers renounce the special railroad concessions which were destroying China's integrity and subscribe to a joint loan, whereby China either could buy foreign-held lines or construct a competing, neutral line; cooperation did not come. Then Taft and Knox tried to open the door for United States capitalists, the former in the notion that such beneficent influence would prevent Chinese bankruptcy and dismemberment, the latter as a business-like application of dollar diplomacy. They helped American bankers to participation in a four-power railroad loan; but their project for a share in a six-power "consortium" planned for financing reorganization after China's 1911 revolution, was killed by President Wilson, and the bankers did not get into China again until 1920. Wilson was not unaware that America's stake in China was small, and he was acutely conscious of the fact that forced loans undermined Chinese independence and violated the American democratic principle.

The World War freed Japan to penetrate unhindered; she made "Twenty-one Demands" on China which victimized her, and by the Lansing-Ishii agreement of 1917 the United States recognized that Japan had special interests and Japan secretly agreed to spare the rights of friendly powers. Japan obtained Germany's concessions and practically ignored the open door while elevating herself to primacy as the imperial power of the East. The occidental powers could make little official headway against this trend.

The disarmament movement of the early 'twenties gave the United States an opening for a graceful retreat from Asiatic imperialism. At a nine-power conference convened at Washington in 1921, at the invitation of the Harding administration, Japan publicly gave the pledge secret in 1917. The old British-Japanese alliance was ended by a "four-power treaty" in which Britain, France, Japan, and the United States agreed to respect each other's rights in the Pacific and to handle differences through diplomacy. These four, with Belgium, China, Holland, Italy and Portugal, signed the "nine-power treaty," which among other things guaranteed China's integrity and the open door. Thus the United States shifted onto nine shoulders the burden she formerly had assumed to carry alone.

The same treaty, however, presaged future strained relations with Japan. It set a naval building program of 5-5-3 for Britain, the United States and Japan respectively; and a London conference of 1930 kept Japan in the same minor position although it accorded her parity with the United States in submarines. Shortly she was destroying Chinese sovereignty in larger areas, and further invalidating the open door. By 1934 she was ready to demand complete parity, and the London conference of 1936 was wrecked on the same demand. She managed to turn to her own advantage the purchase of Chinese silver by the United States and prevented some American capital from fleeing the country for safety. Her cheaper-made goods, offered as barter, invaded United States markets in some parts of the American hemisphere. Across the Pacific she confronted the F. D. Roosevelt administration with the fait accompli of her own Monroe Doctrine in Asia; its corollary was a closed door.

Africa and Europe

While the European struggle of competing governments to maintain and to upset their "balance of power," was hastening the partition of China, it operated likewise in Africa and kept the European continent on tenterhooks. In these areas, as in China, American public opinion resisted involvement, the Theodore Roosevelt administration marked an interfering phase, and small, isolated incidents led tenuously toward entanglement.

American philanthropists in 1822 founded Liberia as a haven for freed slaves, but the United States steadfastly refused to assume a protectorate and in 1847 acknowledged its independence. When the powers in 1885 established the Congo Free State President Cleveland refused to involve his people.

In the badly-managed sultanate of Morocco, however, the powers in 1880 had made a definition of extra-territorial protection to which the Hayes administration had subscribed; and in that troubled area the T. Roosevelt administration figured thrice. It connived in payment of $65,000 in 1901 to ransom from bandits an American missionary, Miss Stone. It demanded and secured in 1904 the release from bandits of

Jon Perdicaris, an alleged American. Roosevelt knew he was not a citizen, but caused publication (the Republican national convention was just meeting) of the rousing part of a cablegram to Morocco:—"We want Perdicaris alive or Raisuli (the bandit leader) dead." The unpublished part of the telegram instructed the Americans not to land marines. Perdicaris was released and the convention applauded.

Shortly thereafter, German domestic troubles required the Kaiser to demand that France and Britain consult Germany before settling the matter of control over Morocco, and the Kaiser appealed to Roosevelt. There was no real United States interest in the Morocco business but the President readily persuaded himself he could figure as one who prevented a European War; he urged France to admit Germany to conference. As the resulting Algeciras convention of 1906 gave Germany recognition and gave France a preferred position in Morocco, both sides (unlike the parties to the Portsmouth treaty) were pleased. Roosevelt was highly gratified.

The United States Senate, however, was apprehensive. While ratifying the treaty, they pinned to it a protective reservation, which from 1899 they attached to all multi-lateral treaties having the slightest political significance. They disavowed United States concern in anything other than the lives, property, and commerce of her citizens and the peace of the world. They reiterated that she had no purpose to abandon her traditional aloofness from European political settlements. This reservation relieved the United States from participation in the Agadir crisis of 1911, which Taft avoided.

The other treaties negotiated with European powers between 1898 and 1914 concerned social betterment and disarmament. Sixteen non-political instruments dealt with sanitation, public health, hospitals, drug formulas, the white slave traffic, an international institute of agriculture, war wounded and importation of liquor into Africa. On disarmament the first Hague conference in 1899 reached no agreement, but the United States subscribed to three compacts:—that neutral powers could tender peace offices, that an involved nation could call for a Commission of Inquiry and that there should be a permanent Court of Arbitration.

With five other powers America in 1904 signed conventions for submitting all but vital disagreements to the Hague tribunal, arrangements amended by the Senate in 1908. At the second Hague conference in 1907 an international prize court was set up and provision made for the London naval conference of 1908. Secretary Knox sought in 1911 to extend the field of arbitration but the Senate refused. The high water mark in peace cooperation was Bryan's negotiation of "cooling-off" treaties with thirty powers for submitting all questions, without exception, to formal inquiry before either going to war or increasing armament.

In spite of dollar diplomacy, armed intervention and the calculating character of much of American diplomacy it was not all out of line with the aspirations of the Progressive Era. There developed a somewhat belated desire to treat Latin American neighbors as equals; laudable efforts were made to promote fair dealing in the Orient and there was hope of insuring lasting peace. The American democracy as of old had a sense of world responsibility which sometimes rose above rivalry for gain.

THE UNITED STATES IN A WORLD AT WAR

1914-1918

CHAPTER XXXIII

TOWARD WAR

In the second decade of the twentieth century, as the United States reached a climax in democratic advance under Wilson's New Freedom, world events were conspiring to open a new era for the American republic. World war was to reorder the condition of mankind and the United States was to be forced into a new testing of the democratic experiment. Few Americans foresaw such a possibility as the storm broke in 1914.

Europe Goes to War

Most Americans in that midsummer of 1914 were engrossed in domestic affairs. Those who enjoyed foreign contacts and information usually apportioned their regard and admiration among outstanding persons and institutions of various nationalities, without particular thought of any one power as threatening peace and democracy. The progressive era had reenforced a long-standing assumption that mankind might continually advance toward some "bigger and better" scheme of existence. Cosmic-minded citizens dreamed of European cooperation in steps toward the common good; President Wilson in May had despatched Colonel E. M. House to interest England, France and Germany in international disarmament, a clean-up of the tropics and development of waste areas—worthy, peacetime objectives.

In Europe, however, France, Russia and England as a Triple Entente stood ranged against Austria, Germany and Italy as a Triple Alliance, in a delicate "balance of power." Imperial rivalries over trade and natural resources, secret treaties, armaments, rampant nationalism, clashing ideologies and race hatreds had set the world stage for war. Through forty-three years—ever since the Franco-Prussian War—each recurrent crisis had been deflected from becoming a major conflict; but war machinery had been perfected, while the will (and probably the power) to avoid war diminished. Finally resentments between Serb Nationalists and Austro-Hungarian Imperialists, and between Pan-Slavs and Pan-Germans caused the murder by a Bosnian Serb, 28 June 1914, of Archduke Ferdinand (heir to Austria's throne) and his wife, while visiting Sarajevo, Bosnia.

This assassination touched the match. Germany endorsed Austria in plans for rigorous punishment of Serbia; Russia went to the aid of this diminutive Slav state; France joined her ally against Germany, which promptly declared war on both and quickly marched troops across neutral Belgium toward Paris; England, vulnerably located just across the channel, joined the anti-German group—hereafter called the "Allies." Japan soon accepted British inducements. All the little Balkan states were ultimately sucked into the flames; only Bulgaria and Turkey took the German side. Italy, however, could and did refuse to take fire until the Allies later tendered big bargains in territorial pledges. Only minor Iberian and Baltic powers out on Europe's margins—Spain, Portugal, Holland, Denmark, Sweden and Norway—contrived, like Switzerland, to preserve neutrality in a war which engaged 28 "allied" nations against the 4 "central" powers.

These events opened for America a new epoch, dominated largely by external influences, although the United States was unconcerned with controversies causing the war and her diplomats were little better equipped than her politicians and people to understand its intricacies. Wilson ventured prompt offices for peace, only to be rebuffed. Americans wanted peace and endorsed him in a quick proclamation of neutrality; they would be slow to realize that their country had become too important in world economy for trans-Atlantic belligerents to leave them unmolested in the gainful pursuits of neutrality.

Prosperous Neutrality

The longest congressional session to date in American history (1 December 1913—24 October 1914) was still legislating under progressive impetus when interrupted by wartime emergencies. American exporters, of cotton especially, were hurt by Allied blockade of the Central powers and by conversion of Allied freight vessels into troop transports. Also federal revenues were suffering through a falling off of $100,000,000 worth in dutiable imports. So Congress took time in an election year for emergency laws, providing for a Bureau of War Risk Insurance, for transfer of cargo ships from belligerent flags to American registry, and for special excises to restore revenues. In the congressional campaign the Democrats were featuring America's freedom from war; but domestic factors proved mainly responsible for leaving Wilson a majority in both houses.[1]

To business the war brought relief, reversing a downward trend begun in 1913.[2] The stock exchange had closed 31 July not to resume wholly unrestricted trading until April following; but industrial and

[1] Democratic losses in the House and gains in the Senate left them majorities of 38 and 17 respectively.

[2] Federal rate-making, wage regulating, prosecutions and anti-trust laws had been met with a slowing down in industry and a practical stoppage of railway construction.

agricultural production after five months registered a tremendous spurt.
Munitions factories, some spurred by British ownership of majority
stock and control of production, raised munitions exports from 40 millions in 1914 to 1290 millions in 1916. The United States became the
base of military supplies for England. Metal and lumber industries
expanded to supply the machinery of death, houses to shelter workers
who made it and ships to carry it. All manpower diverted to destructive
manufacturing still had to be fed. Although many goods and services
were not paid for in gold, the gold in the federal treasury, approximately
1250 millions 1 July 1914, had doubled by April 1917. The United
States had become a strong creditor nation.

As the market for labor tightened, wages rose, unions prospered and

POWER

Becker in *The Masses.*

Power—in the Adamson Act

strikes increased. This situation fathered the pre-election "Adamson
Law" of 1916 stipulating an eight-hour day for railroad workers. It was
the government, rather than the workers who practiced conciliation—
until America's entrance into the war gave strikes a disloyal connotation.
The rising cost of living was penalizing persons of fixed incomes; but
factory workers, before the war ended, obtained higher real wages than
ever before.

Wartime prosperity could not have developed had America followed
European neutral example and imposed embargoes against exports of
war materials; and insofar as the Allies blocked cotton and wheat
exports to Germany, the farmers and planters of the Middle West and
South were deprived of war profits. They denounced the munitions
business of the large centers in the East as a patent violation of neutrality. Senators Hitchcock of Nebraska and Stone of Missouri tried to

place senators on record against shipments of contraband; the Speaker and Majority Leader, Champ Clark of Missouri and Claude Kitchin of North Carolina, boldly urged an embargo and a warning against shipments of contraband.

An embargo is the strongest weapon a neutral nation can wield, it probably reduces likelihood of a neutral entering a war, and a munitions embargo any time after the middle of 1915 might have destroyed Allied belligerency. The embargo advocates, however, were easily pushed on the defensive by militant businessmen, untutored in wartime foresight and fortitude; nor could a party which captured the White House through a three-cornered fight be expected to resist war profiteers. Only leadership with extraordinary insight and influence could have swung a program to jeopardize immediate profits for future benefits, especially as an embargo would have hurt belligerents for whom the President and the majority of the people had the greater natural sympathy.

Those belligerents were the Allies. Great Britain (unlike Germany and Austria) was dependent upon the United States for munitions and vulnerable to an embargo. Therefore, in maintaining the Allied blockade of Germany early in the war, Britain took some care not to carry violations of neutral trading rights to the point of driving America into an embargo.[1] Extreme measures came after United States prosperity was firmly tied to Allied purchases.

Payments for those purchases came to be made increasingly from loans of money and credit obtained in the United States. Secretary of State Bryan, who had been devoting much effort to negotiation of "cooling-off" treaties whereunder war-inclined powers agreed to postpone open hostilities twelve months, saw that war loans must imperil neutrality. He desired official discouragement of such loans, although he defended munitions exports. The Administration early warned against loans but soon tolerated credit loans; and, after Bryan's resignation (9 June 1915), withdrew what remained of opposition. Business and political pressure, exerted through Secretary of State Lansing and Secretary of the Treasury McAdoo, proved effective.

Mr. J. P. Morgan, central purchasing agent of the Allies in the United States, obtained practically a free hand to engineer purchases, sometimes amounting to 10 millions daily. Eager domestic investors absorbed 250 millions in American securities unloaded by Europeans, and bought so many English and French securities that in mid-November 1916, the Federal Reserve Board issued a warning that too many American funds were travelling beyond the reach of American business-

[1] She had not at first included in her classification of "conditional contraband" such products as cotton, tobacco, resin and turpentine, which embargoes infuriated powerful interests shipping these to Central Powers. She delayed somewhat her use of war pretexts for weakening American competition in areas her own commercial interests hoped to control.

men. By the time the United States became an "associate" of the Allies, Americans held at least 1500 millions in Allied paper; their German holdings then were down to about 27 millions.

Choice of Propaganda

Economic influences alone could not carry the United States away from insularity toward sympathy for the Allies. Social and political influences were powerful. On the one hand, America's heterogeneous population, of which one-third was either foreign-born or of foreign parentage, included about 9,000,000 persons who had at least one German parent; the Irish element also ranged against England's side, contributing to what was called "hyphenism." On the other hand, the vast majority of Americans felt drawn to Britain—by ties of language, literature, ideology and institutions. Thence stemmed most of their constitutional, legal and political customs. Revolutionary resentments had died out. In the Spanish war, Britain had shown herself friendly at Manila Bay; Germany hostile (although she had complied with a request to search a vessel suspected of carrying war supplies from Hamburg to Spain). Subsequent contacts encouraged the feeling that Germany was a militaristic power, rather than a friendly democracy, especially when she refused a "cooling-off" treaty. For France, Americans entertained a feeling of gratitude which the compatriots of Lafayette were not slow to exploit.

The "best instincts" of many Americans made them extremely susceptible. They had entered the twentieth century righteously interested in reform of their own institutions and in other nations' welfare. The progressive movement had developed the uplift urge to a very high point. The war administered a series of severe shocks, making them peculiarly responsive to proposals for transforming the struggle into a benefit to mankind. They had little information on the causes of the war and knew not the territorial bargains among the Allies. Ready to believe that Britain and France were busy saving the world from barbarism, they swallowed whole British propaganda on German "atrocities," following the example of America's notable friend, Lord Bryce, whose gullibility was communicated to many outstanding American leaders.

The British adroitly adjusted propaganda to American sympathies, prejudices and idealism. Their efficient publicity expert in America, Sir Gilbert Parker, supplied weekly war reviews to hundreds of newspapers, inspired pro-Ally articles under the authorship, usually, of native Americans and watched over the movies. Personal contacts between Englishmen and leaders of American thought and politics helped to make speeches, debates and lectures friendly. British interception of international mails and control of cables, which were strictly censored, left only the wireless for transmission to the public of Central Power information and propaganda. The British Intelligence service unhesitatingly eavesdropped on informative ciphers passing between the United States Government and her emissaries abroad. The gospel of Allied innocence and German infamy damned curious questioners as "Huns."

German propaganda was inept, blundering. Slow to follow the British "White Paper" with one of their own, in October of 1914, they gave many Americans the impression that they solely caused the outbreak. Their frank references to the Belgian neutrality treaty as "just a scrap of paper" were more realistic than American ears liked. Purchase of the *New York Evening Mail,* and other subsidizing, became known so quickly as to defeat their objectives. The British were more effective with their *Providence Journal.* The Austrian Ambassador, Dumba, with German Military and Naval Attaches, Von Papen and Boy-Ed, through sabotage of munitions plants discredited their cause. German invasion of Belgium aroused suspicions of infamy which the U boats were soon to underscore.

The anti-German cause became politically useful to highly influential Republicans. The hatred of Theodore Roosevelt for Wilson knew no bounds after the apologetic treaty with Colombia in the spring of 1914; and, as long as Wilson was supposed to be maintaining neutrality, a violently pro-Ally, Roosevelt, denounced him. Through innumerable public pronouncements, active correspondence and in the columns of the *Outlook,* he effectively undermined the respectability of peace.[1]

Although predisposed to the Allies, the American people were not quick to abandon their national tradition of isolation so far as to fight Germany. Their history showed them averse to pacifism but they steadfastly regarded themselves as peace-lovers. The arbitration treaties and Hague tribunals in which recent administrations had participated attested loyalty to the peace ideal in many walks of life, especially in the Middle West. An American League to Limit Armaments, a Union against Militarism and a Women's Peace Party were very earnest. Henry Ford transported some of their membership to Europe in December 1915, filled with the laudable but futile ambition to "get the boys out of the trenches by Christmas." Germans and Irish-Americans organized to press for an embargo and took such attractive titles as the

[1] Roosevelt (like Taft) formerly had preached German virility and efficiency to Americans; favoring neutrality immediately after the rape of Belgium, by that fall he was thoroughly committed to the Allies. Close personal friendship with Spring-Rice, Lord Bryce and others facilitated the turn; also as President he had had a secret understanding with England and Japan regarding the Orient, and had assured Edward VII, through Senator Lodge, that the United States intended working with England. His pro-British leanings had given color to rumors of a secret pledge of United States aid to England and France against Pan-Germanism.

Friends of Peace, American Independence Union, Labor's National Peace Council and the American Humanity League. Genuine peace lovers found notable leadership in the League to Enforce Peace, launched at Independence Hall, 15 June 1915, under the leadership of such men as ex-President Taft, President Lowell of Harvard and Hamilton Holt, who sought to combine realism and idealism in an international league.

Preparedness groups urging American entrance into the war had to struggle for control of public opinion. A National Security League demanded fighting equipment, an offshoot called the American Defense Society demanded American entrance following the *Lusitania* sinking, and an American Rights Committee, from December 1915, fought for immediate participation. By that time the war-minded groups had given the peace societies such ill-repute that most of them were left in control of pacifists, whose preachments increased the fervor of the militarists.

While Wilson was waiting and public sentiment was crystallizing, the presidential campaign of 1916 registered American reluctance to enter the war. Progressive and neutrality issues were curiously mixed, with neutrality bothering Democrats and progressivism the Republicans. Wilson knew the din a minority can raise against peace and events were weakening his resistance to additional military preparations. Fearing vociferous Republican charges of inadequate defense, the Democrats passed laws for gradual increases of the regular army to 223,000 and the National Guard to 450,000; they specified construction of ten dreadnoughts and three cruisers in three years, and set up a Council of National Defense for the co-ordination of American protection. But compulsory military service was defeated; Congress was taking short steps—not strides—toward preparedness. They showed greater unanimity in establishing a United States Shipping Board, to safeguard commercial profits under neutrality.

For their part, Republicans dared not ignore pro-German or progressive voters. They tried to convince Irish and German-Americans that their preparedness clamor was designed to aid the Central Powers; at the same time they alienated peace groups by criticising and ridiculing Wilson's moderation toward European belligerents and Mexico. Eagerly they welcomed progressives back into the Grand Old Party where Roosevelt threw all his strength, refusing the Progressives' nomination and thereby eliminating their ticket. Reunited, the Republicans nominated Charles E. Hughes, who became New York's reform governor after exposing insurance scandals, and as an associate justice of the United States Supreme Court had proved fairly conservative. In the West he supported national women's suffrage, a proposition Wilson labelled a state question; but he neglected to conciliate California's favorite Progressive, Governor Hiram Johnson, Roosevelt's 1912 running mate. California Republicans sent Johnson to the Senate but failed to help Hughes into the White House. Elsewhere, Republican attacks on the Adamson Act alienated labor.

When the shouting and confusion ended, Wilson had won on both the progressive and neutrality issues. His 9 million popular votes as against Hughes' 8.5 millions were so distributed as to give him 277 electoral votes against Hughes' 254. While all the industrial and financial, high-tariff sections of the North and East (except New Hampshire and Ohio) had voted for Hughes and against the "New Freedom," every state in the trans-Mississippi area (except Minnesota, Oregon and South Dakota) had joined Maryland, Kentucky and the solid South in support of Wilson. A liberal legislative record attractive to foes of capitalistic imperialism, joined with clever party use of Bryan's slogan, "He kept us out of war," had overcome the handicap of a deficient war chest.[1] Through raising his 1912 total by 3 million votes, the Executive gained the satisfaction of ceasing to be a minority president. The public did not know that peace and progressivism already were defeated,—that Wilson no longer believed he could keep the United States neutral, and that as War President he would be made the world's greatest autocrat.

How America Entered

While politics assumed that the United States was not about to enter the war, diplomacy was threading its way, through natural sympathies, profits and propaganda, toward direct intervention. The self-interest of the neutral trader dictated watchful safeguarding of that gainful position, and Americans began with the desire to enforce neutrality; but the submarine caused emotions to become over-engaged and inescapable. Counselor (later Secretary) Lansing, Colonel House and Ambassador Page were frankly pro-Ally. The President was victimized by overpowering circumstances, zealous advisers, his own theories and self-communing, and turned almost inevitably toward the Allies. A high moral tone and occasional firmness and sagacity could not weld together the confused policies of the drifting administration. As the powerful neutral responsible for neutral rights, the United States failed to distinguish herself.

American shippers long since had learned that England, as mistress of the oceans, defined the law of the sea to suit her needs:—blockades to be legal had to be effective: contraband carried by neutrals was liable to seizure. As the growing United States ceased to be a weak neutral, she enlarged neutral rights somewhat; but during the Civil War, to starve the South, she had restricted them—extending blockade rights to

[1] The Democrats had about $1,800,000 as compared with $2,500,000 of acknowledged Republican funds.

cover goods bound to a neutral port when destined for an enemy. Britain had accepted this "final destination" restriction, with an eye to its future value.

Representatives of the principal world powers in 1909 drew up the Declaration of London; it validated the Civil War contention as to munitions but protected neutral commerce in "conditional contraband" (such as food and certain supplies used by noncombatants), when bound to a neutral. Germany of course accepted this declaration as likely to replenish supplies; Britain vetoed it because of its probable usefulness to Germany; the United States accepted it, but Taft withheld ratification after the British veto. The Declaration had little chance of fulfillment at best, in a world-wide conflict. International law remained vague on controversial matters and silent on the vital, new problem of submarines.

Britain early in the World War applied the rule of final destination to foods and miscellaneous supplies as well as to munitions. Treating wheat and flour as contraband, even when consigned to neutrals, would starve out the Central Powers. Declaring the North Sea a "military zone" for searching and seizing ships enroute to natural feeders of Germany, she subjected rich American cargoes to a costly blockade. Extending the right of search, she dragged neutral cargoes into British ports for leisurely examination for British-defined contraband. Her warships hovered close to American territorial waters. British and French commanders seized "suspicious" characters from American ships. Mail between the United States and neutrals was wantonly molested; German goods needed for American industries were intercepted; some American firms were blacklisted, others cut off from neutral customers so that British traders might annex business.

American interests, incensed, demanded protests from the State department. These were couched in vigorous language but not backed up by pressure. Britain delayed her replies, yielded nothing of her position and gave the United States the minimum of satisfaction. Her statesmen were well-advised of Allied sympathies in high American places, and acted accordingly.

In fact, during October of 1914, despatches had passed between Wilson and Lansing, Page and Lord Grey, which in effect proposed that Britain declare the Declaration of London to be in force while she proceeded to do as she pleased regarding actual enforcement. Thus instructed, Britain could discount official protests long before United States investments and exports were firmly tied to the Allied cause. Sentiment thus preceded economic ties, in preventing vigorous retaliation for British violation of neutral rights.

To offset blockade with blockade, Germany, 4 February 1915, declared the waters surrounding Great Britain a war zone and ships entering it liable to submarine attack. Also, since submarines had no carrying facilities and were highly vulnerable, their commanders would not follow the old rule of international law requiring that passengers and crew be placed in safety before a ship was sunk. As Britain freely used neutral flags (a war device of long standing) it was clear that Germany would sink neutral as well as enemy ships. This she did upon occasion.

International law was silent on submarines; but Americans were not addicted to a realistic approach toward international relations and resented the use in warfare of an American inventor's outstanding contribution to ruthlessness. All their moralists, but not all navy men, denounced it. Their government asserted that a modern war machine could not modify international law; and suggested a *modus vivendi.* Germany should renounce mine laying and submarine attacks while Britain restricted use of neutral flags and permitted transport of foodstuffs to Germany's civilian population. The replies of both revealed their indifference to peace.[1] Each equally eager for starvation and economic strangulation of the other, each paid no more respect to international law than self-interest dictated. Their notes to the United States regularly made a pretext of being forced into desperate retaliation by the inhuman conduct of others; it really was a race in inhumanity. The inhumanity at first lay chiefly at the door of Germany, for her use of U boats; later at the door of the Allies, for their long blockade of foodstuffs for civilians, continued even after the armistice.

Submarine ruthlessness culminated 7 May 1915 in the sinking of the giant liner, *Lusitania,* which was a part of the British navy, carried munitions and was armed. 114 Americans were among those who had disregarded a German Embassy advertisement, published adjacent to the sailing notice in the newspapers, reminding them of war risks. The captain had disobeyed anti-submarine instructions for proceeding at full speed in a zigzag course.

The *Lusitania* sinking, by its wanton destruction of 1153 lives, boosted pro-Ally sympathy tremendously, for violations of international law by British blockades affected chiefly inanimate cargoes, while submarine sinkings destroyed also many passengers and crews; material loss paled into insignificance compared with destruction of human life. Secretary Bryan sensed here an opportunity to bargain between Great Britain and Germany for maintenance of the laws of war; serious threat of an embargo might bring both belligerents to terms. If Wilson had accepted Bryan's ideas for counterbalancing England and Germany in American

---

[1] The Allies replied that Germany could not be trusted to keep a bargain; Germany insisted that raw materials, including those applicable to army use, should be classified with foodstuffs as non-contraband and safe from blockade.

diplomacy, and against lending to belligerents and travel by Americans on armed vessels, world history might have been guided in a different direction.

But the submarine prevented Wilson and most of the electorate, from regarding Britain and Germany equally. He demanded an end to submarine ruthlessness, warning that repetition would be considered "deliberately unfriendly"; he ordered naval and war secretaries to prepare defense plans. The peace-loving Bryan resigned his place to Robert Lansing. Lansing's sympathies persuaded him the Allies were fighting the cause of Democracy versus Autocracy; his instincts assured him that submarines would turn the scale, and his policy was to send the British "wordy fleabites," instead of bringing them to book.

After three notes demanding disavowal, reparations and no recurrence, Ambassador Bernstorff notified the White House, 1 September, that Germany agreed no liner should be sunk without warning, and that she would provide safety for noncombatants, except where the liner resisted or tried to resist. The Berlin government at that time was hopeful of winning the war before supplies ran too low, was uncertain whether her fleet of 28 submarines could starve England, and hesitated to risk the effect of ruthlessness upon American sentiment.

Germany's disavowal was followed by six months without the loss of American lives through submarine activities, months marked (as events later proved) by tightening of Wilson's attitude. He clung longer than any other leader in the United States to the determination to maintain neutrality and to aid peace; but by the end of 1915 he had been driven to Allied sympathies, while the people were losing neutrality, although likewise craving peace. He knew that none of the various belligerents was especially righteous, and that Britain's interests particularly were primarily commercial and imperialistic; but apparently he reasoned that the type of industrial imperialism to which Germany wished to subject Europe was a threat to American civilization no less than to Europe's. He concluded he ought to shift his line of attack from domestic, industrial abuses to greater tyrannies on a world scale. His abhorrence of methods dominating European diplomacy flowered into an unshakable determination to inject liberalism into world relationships. So, his initial lack of confidence in his own ability to handle foreign relations was transmuted into an assumption that the powers could be moved to higher ground and that he could move them. If he took America into the war would not he be in a position to write into the peace treaty his own provisions for an end to all war?

1916 indicated his trend:—January, a western tour to transmute pacifism into preparedness sentiment: February, a proposal to England that if she would join in a world conference on peace, and Germany would not participate, the United States would "probably" join the

Allies. Britain, not yet apprehensive of defeat, and bound by secret treaties with Russia, Italy and Japan, rebuffed this overture and sent Wilson on another track. He sounded Democratic congressional leaders on United States participation in behalf of civilization. In March he exerted pressure to prevent passage of a McLemore House resolution and a Gore Senate resolution, which had support among both parties and would have warned Americans that they travelled in the theatre of war at their own risk.[1]

Germany had announced renewal (29 February 1916) of attacks upon armed merchantmen; but after the *Sussex,* a British ship carrying some Americans, was damaged by a torpedo, Wilson issued an official threat to sever relations, which drew from Germany another proposition impossible of fulfillment. She promised to abide by the rules of visitation and search—to give warning and to put passengers and crews in safety—provided that merchant ships cease carrying contraband and remain unarmed, and that the United States hold England, also, to strict accountability.[2] A submarine truce ensued, lasting about nine months, well past the presidential campaign with its preparedness legislation and its slogan—"He kept us out of war." The nation, as Wilson wrote, "seems to demand two inconsistent things, firmness and the avoidance of war."

Wilson's European scouts reported that fall some tolerance of peace propositions; hoping for a salutary stalemate, he asked both sides, a week before Christmas, to state their war aims. Among the Allies his demand lost force, because delayed until a week after a German proposal, and they saw indications of American assistance. Although their food and credit status was troubling their loan agent in the United States, their reply to Wilson stipulated peace terms so drastic as to indicate they preferred a finish fight to peace.

Wilson, helped by House, was phrasing his own peace formula, announced to Congress and the world 22 January 1917. World stabilization required a "peace without victory," guaranteeing nations large and small their rights:—to government by consent of the governed, to independent entity, to sea outlets, to freedom of the oceans and to peace by international agreement. This program was to reappear later.

The Germans, like the British, entertained a cynicism foreign to the President. After vaguely expressing willingness to negotiate, they made specifications indicating no more eagerness for peace than the Allies; and against the advice of Ambassador Bernstorff they repudiated the *Sussex*

---

[1] The vote to table the McLemore resolution stood 182 Democrats and 93 Republicans for, and 33 Democrats and 102 Republicans against; Gore's resolution was kept from a vote.

[2] Wilson in September obtained from Congress authority to prohibit loans and restrict exports to the Allies, if they did not alter their "intolerable course."

pledge and announced resumption of unrestricted submarine warfare 1
February 1917.[1]

Wilson promptly severed diplomatic relations; he and the majority
of his people found submarine warfare intolerable. But so many Americans were uneager for war that twelve senators defeated an authorization for "armed neutrality." The British Intelligence Service intervened
to galvanize opinion, particularly in the hesitant Southwest. They
handed the State Department a month-old message, filched by them
from cables passing between the German Foreign Office and its Washington Embassy over American wires; Wilson handed it to the press.
The public thus learned that Foreign Secretary Zimmerman had instructed Ambassador Bernstorff, if the United States joined the Allies,
to use bribery. Mexico was to be promised Texas, New Mexico and
Arizona—a sort of *Mexico irridenta;* Japan was to be tempted with
Pacific Coast areas.

Zimmerman's note galvanized sentiment. American resentment flamed
against Germany, just as a Russian Revolution substituted a liberal for
an autocratic regime and strengthened the belief that the Allies were
waging a "war for democracy." British emissaries arrived, insisting
England had grain enough for only six weeks and could not possibly
hold out beyond 1 November. While munitions manufacturers, merchants and other creditors of the Allies worried over a possible stalemate
or defeat for them, some peacelovers were concluding that rich old
England as victor would prove more peaceful than young, ambitious
Germany. Thus mixed sentiments of gain, patriotism and philanthropy
helped to carry America toward war.

When German submarines during February and March sank six
American ships, three carrying her citizens, they forced Wilson to go
to war or be inconsistent. After taking thirteen days to prepare a
message, the President finally, 2 April 1917, asked Congress to declare
war. Fervor by this time had mounted to a point where it was useless
for such men as Senator Stone of Missouri or La Follette of Wisconsin
to point out that the Allies in many respects were more autocratic than
democratic, and that the United States had not protested German and
British violations of neutral rights impartially. Assertions that Americans did not wish war were not compelling, although before long
rigorous conscription and espionage laws assumed a less than unanimous
belligerency. The proposition for entrance paid respect to fears of entanglement by designating America as "associated" rather than "allied"

[1] By now they had a fleet of more than 100 submarines which they estimated
could cut British imports by about 40% and end the war within six months,
before their own man power and resources were exhausted. Calculating that
American participation would not enlarge the current stream of credit and
supplies reaching the Allies and would not add man power, they decided they
could afford to alienate the United States.

with the Allies. 4 April the Senate (86-6) and 6 April the House (373-50) declared that a state of war with Germany existed.

A mighty combination of factors:—among them, democratic traditions, propaganda, profit-seeking, weak peace forces, incompetent statesmanship, and altruism—had drawn in the United States. As the problem of neutrality had not been solved, intervention had proved unavoidable. America's entrance would not only determine the outcome of the war, but alter greatly the course of world history.

CHAPTER XXXIV

THE EXPERIENCE OF THE UNITED STATES IN THE WORLD WAR

The instant the United States became associated with the Allies, they despatched delegations to speed up American aid. Here was an opportunity for the President to strengthen his hand by conditioning abundant assistance upon acceptance of his peace principles; upon the advice of House, he failed to exploit the opportunity, to the lasting detriment of the cause he held dear.

Domestic Regimentation

To assist the Allies, the entire nation was mobilized on the home front, while only about two million soldiers went overseas. Despite, therefore, the brilliant record of the forces in Europe, America's war history was made chiefly at home. Approximately 11,500,000 took up war jobs, 2,250,000 experienced military service which did not extend beyond the border, and all the rest learned that modern warfare enlists everybody. Americans expected to contribute food, supplies, transportation and money, rather than men, whom they supposed would not be needed in large numbers, or if needed could not be transported. For temporary, war purposes, their representatives in Congress (as in Lincoln's day) gave the President broad, unconstitutional powers; and the citizenry tolerated assumption of still wider functions, until he was exercising the widest powers of all Occidental rulers.

With comparatively little objection, Americans accepted minute supervision over what had been their private affairs, demonstrating their blind faith in the cause, and their sensitivity to war fervors. War entrance released pent-up feelings and abundant energies, encouraging feverish activity which many found pleasurable. The emergency taught individuals new modes of behavior while placing them in a new relation to the state. Every man and woman was made to realize they were part of the largest mass movement in history. Each male between the ages of 18 and 45 finally found himself a potential conscript. Clad in a uniform, even an insignificant person attracted attention—from both sexes. Every woman who took a man's former job found a sense of broadening power; women did practically everything except enter the trenches.

Of first importance was unity of public opinion. Patriotism in its best, truest sense burned for Wilsonian war ideals—for spreading over the world the progressive spirit. A war for humanity, to end wars, to punish autocratic German rulers but not the German people, and "to make the world safe for democracy" justified the highest zeal. But patriotism in its worst, pseudo aspect gave complete sway to intolerant emotionalism. Both aspects of patriotism contributed to war unity.

Separation from the scene of conflict had spared Americans that acute suffering which chastens the emotions, so that many ordinarily democratic citizens now were tempted to abandon all restraint, to bedeck intolerance with the American flag. Congress passed espionage and sedition acts, 15 June 1917 and 16 May 1918, forgetful of the "New Freedom." [1] Although editorial lobbies kept out of these laws that censorship of the press which the Department of Justice tried to put in, the administration found means to badger the press under the general terms of the acts, and occasionally to blacken liberals. Socialists, like Debs, Stokes and Berger, were sent to prison alongside some 450 military objectors; La Follette's enemies tried to have him expelled from the Senate. Expression of an unenthusiastic viewpoint invited bitter persecution and relentless ostracism in all walks of life.

The Department of Justice organized a volunteer American Protective League, of approximately 250,000 indiscriminate enrollees, to report evidence of disloyalty. This afforded some types a fine chance to vent personal spleen or succumb to neurotic fears. The courts and intelligence offices of the State, War and Navy Departments made complete the countrywide search for German spies and Bolsheviks. Terms of 10 to 20 years were imposed. Oddly enough, the basic loyalty of Americans was such as to provide no first-class spy or revolutionist to be caught in all this fine network.

In propaganda the United States far outdid the Allies, through a Committee on Public Information set up under the efficient George Creel to spread "information" over North and South America and even unto the Orient, in many languages. The public was asked to believe, and accepted, as violent a set of atrocities as modern times has invented. Churches cooperated with pulpit testimony, abandoning peace propaganda, to preach "a war to end war." Colleges gave courses on war aims. When a few pacific persons calling themselves "The Peoples' Council for Democracy and Terms of Peace" sallied forth toward a Minneapolis convention, they were trailed across country and efficiently discredited by a group of government emissaries calling themselves "The American Alliance for Labor and Democracy." Upon the movies descended four-minute speakers, inspired, eloquent and unavoidable.[2]

---

[1] Only 24 Republicans and 2 Democrats voted against the Sedition Act.

[2] Theodore Roosevelt did his bit with a tour demanding a vigorous offensive and denouncing La Follette and all non-conformists.

All this outlay and effort, in the best advertising tradition, was designed to sell the war to a nation which—if one may judge by its quick and easy acceptance—was sold on the war already.

Domestic mobilization at amazing speed, though at huge cost, was achieved through the pliancy of public opinion. Citizens of this great democracy, accustomed to large-scale organization, yielded the resources, leadership and following for the most colossal regimentation the world ever had witnessed. The Council of National Defense, which had been set up in imitation of European practice in 1916 under the supervision of the Secretaries of War, Navy, Interior, Commerce and Labor, assisted by seven experts, was expanded and patterned after in the states until war boards were supervising every major activity and many minor ones. A highly perfected technique of large scale organization was readily invented and applied in each major field.

Food regimentation, through the Lever Food Control Act, was delayed from April to August 1917 by progressive fears of monopoly and became possible only through emphasis upon the legislation as necessary for majority welfare. Agriculture was encouraged to finance expansion beyond the bounds of profitable peace-time farming, although the total physical output of agriculture (1917-1919) increased but slightly. In the excitement, speculation raised land prices, erosion and lack of fertilization depleted the soil, and there was much farm operation at a loss. Prices were stabilized, with wheat at $2.20 a bushel—a figure too low in view of other prices. A grain corporation and sugar equalization board saw to the purchase and distribution of these vitally important crops. Herbert Hoover, renowned for Belgian relief, excelled as Food Administrator. Through local food committees, war gardens, enthusiastic women's clubs, wheatless and meatless days, sugar limitation, pledge cards, etc., Americans so rapidly decreased consumption and increased production of breadstuffs, meats and sugar that they were enabled to export in 1918 three times their normal bulk of these vitally important provisions.

In industrial life, diversion of production to war needs and acceleration of certain outputs progressed under close supervision from Bernard Baruch, adviser to the Council of National Defense. With cooperation from the nation's Chamber of Commerce organizations, more than 500 war service committees functioned, handling relations between various industries and the government; manufacturers were forced to stop non-war activities unless approved by the War Industries Board, and the nature of industries was in some cases arbitrarily changed. The total physical output of mines and factories (1917-1919) declined. Leaders in industry gave an amazing degree of cooperation; they submitted to arbitrary fixing of contracts, prices, material distribution and the priority in which orders should be filled. Some businessmen who had spent their lives engrossed in their own plants, volunteered as "dollar-a-year" men at Washington.

Many industrialists profited during regimentation. Competitive bidding by purchasers representing various Allies made prices fantastic until a United States government and inter-allied war council set up joint purchasing agencies which reduced somewhat this type of abuse. A few American entrepreneurs were rewarded with control of valuable alien property, such as the German dye privileges. War fortunes reached heights far beyond those obtained by profiteers of the 'sixties because opportunities soared.

Organized labor also cooperated and profited, with Gompers and lesser Federation leaders conciliated by the government and enthusiastic in support of it. The war gave a tremendous impetus to their organizing activities, membership and governmental influence.[1] Given places on the labor administrative board and elsewhere, they agreed to removal of some working restrictions on the understanding that the government would not permit a fall in labor standards. Their official position was "Work or Fight." They exploited the labor shortage created by a 50% fall in immigration and a diversion of 4,800,000 men to army and navy occupations. A government employment service placed nearly as many men as the recruiting service; disputes were conciliated the more easily because public disapproval would be focused on dissentients. Housing problems obtained attention. While the cost of living rose faster than wages, for consumers in general, organized labor managed to obtain an increase in real wages. Their greatest triumph was a law won over Wilson's veto imposing a literacy test on immigrants.

Lesser war agencies were legion, among them the fuel administration for conserving, pricing and distributing coal and oil, and supplying cars to carry it. Practically every adjunct of intercommunication and of handling supplies came under regulation.

The nation's railroad systems broke down early in the emergency, with full cars choking eastern ports and empty cars desperately needed out in production areas. Government operation resulted, with extremely high rentals under guarantees of adequate compensation to owners.[2] As the government kept freights low and spent heavily to modernize the railroads the cost climbed to a total of $714,000,000. This outlay was denounced by those who forgot that government operation brought order out of chaos and made for an unwonted efficiency.

As troops and supplies depended also upon shipping, and the "farmer-labor-planter" group would not consent to private subsidy, it was a federal emergency fleet corporation which undertook to offset sub-

[1] A.F. of L. membership increased 37%.

[2] Wilson in December, 1917, issued a proclamation for government operation, which was followed three months later by legislation for federal control.

marines by building a marine; it raised available tonnage from 1,000,000 to 10,000,000. On American ships were transported all of the military supplies and 80% of the troops sent abroad, without the loss of a life by torpedoing. Here, too, costs were enormous, raised further by a "cost plus" system which made contractors agreeable to pyramiding of base figures. Prices were further inflated by the easy credit policies and lavish security issues of the government.

To meet these outlays the Democrats had to depend almost wholly on new taxes and bond issues, for tariff increases violated their traditions. The progressive element—Socialists, agrarians and Middle Westerners—disliked bond issues and opposed burdening unborn generations with past wars. But taxation alone could not finance a war costing almost $42,000,000,000.[1] About one-third of the total was raised by taxes, which compared favorably with earlier war practice. Congress laid progressive levies on incomes and inheritances with heavy rates on excess profits of corporations and partnerships. Increased excises and amusement and luxury taxes did not rouse violent protest. Although some levies were avoided by stock dividends, income from taxes increased almost sixfold over 1916 and reached an amount heavier than any other war power levied.

For the remaining two-thirds of war cost, Secretary McAdoo employed a "continuous" revenue system, with Treasury estimates of expenditures far exceeding actuality and with government finance on a "boom" basis. Every two weeks he issued short term notes, in turn taken up by proceeds from long term bonds. Four "Liberty" loans and one "Victory" loan, issued at interest of only 3, 3½, 4½ and 4¾% (only the first of which was wholly tax exempt) brought in about $21,500,-000,000. Over 65,000,000 persons contributed; for employers cooperated with the government in strenuous drives for over-subscriptions, the Treasury artificially supported the market and the Federal Reserve Banks encouraged people to borrow money to buy bonds. Liberty loan window cards, service buttons, vaudeville entertainers and popular speakers persuaded and enticed on every hand. From persons of low income, $1,000,000,000 was collected through twenty-five cent savings stamps and five dollar war savings certificates. All these issues were sold direct to the people over the counter, instead of through syndicates as in the Civil War. They made the entire nation security-conscious—a state of mind which would contribute greatly to the stock market crash of 1929. Also, the Federal Reserve was riveting its hold on commercial banking, with bad auguries for future prosperity. But few people noted the portents.

The bond campaigns were perhaps the most effective agencies for

[1] $10,000,000,000 were loaned to the Allies and associates, $26,000,000,000 were spent at home and $6,000,000,000 went in indirect outlays.

sustaining war morale. Nearly every war activity created an enthusiasm which communicated itself to another activity. Their total force became well nigh irresistible. The deep reservoir of American funds and enthusiasm was tapped eagerly by the Allies. Their clamorous competition for loans forced the United States to establish an American Purchasing Commission; and with the aid of the Interallied Finance Council, which functioned under an American chairman, it managed to lessen the misallocation of loans. Their ultimate repayment was not of particular interest at the time.

Military Participation

The naval and military aspects of American participation likewise evoked the native genius for large scale organization. The navy proved better prepared than the army. Admiral Sims had been sent to England in March and the navy forestalled German battleship efforts. It con

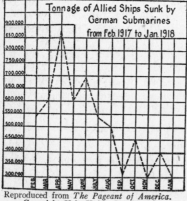

Reproduced from *The Pageant of America.*
Copyright Yale University Press.

tributed 80 destroyers to the Allied forces in European waters and laid 56,000 mines in the North Sea blockade of Germany. It convoyed four-fifths of America's troop ships and prevented any of them from being torpedoed. By the end of the war over 300 American war vessels and 75,000 sailors were in European waters and Germany had lost almost half of her U boats.

Quick upon American entrance, the Allies clamored for man power. The popular French general, Joffre, and the astute English politician, Balfour, hurried over to ask for 500,-000 troops. The extremely able Secretary of War, N. D. Baker, superintended a badly needed military reorganization and within 18 months created a force of 4,000,000 men of whom about half went abroad and 1,400,000 fought in the trenches. This achievement was effected through drafting, under a selective service act. It met strong opposition in Congress where Theodore Roosevelt's friends delayed passage because the fifty-nine year old ex-President wished to lead a "Roosevelt Division" of picked cavalry volunteers! But the draft came to be accepted almost unanimously. The riots of the Lincoln administration were avoided by conducting registration through civilians and giving registration day a patriotic significance. Altogether about 24,225,000 registered and 2,800,-000 were called from the lists. Voluntary enlistments also were accepted in the regular army, navy, national guard, and marines. Examination of the drafted men revealed disturbing deficiencies in the physical fitness of American youth.[1]

The soldiers were trained at 32 camps of about 48,000 men each, where they experienced a regimentation wholly new to most of them, under reserve officers hastily trained for the emergency. The army was provisioned chiefly by domestic products, except for English and French arms and supplies made necessary by the speed with which soldiers were sent overseas and by the inadequacy of American artillery and aircraft manufacture.

Propaganda machinery used in other war activities found its counterpart in recruiting, with service flags and Red Cross stickers employed to proclaim patriotism and generosity. American soldiers received more consideration than those of any other nation. Their pay already was highest and was raised still further; and the government paid part of it to families where desired. Government insurance was provided at low rates, in the vain effort to avoid post-war pension scandals. The public for its part supported the Red Cross, Y.M.C.A., Y.W.C.A., Knights of Columbus, Y.M.H.A. and Salvation Army (the last apparently the best managed) in the effort to lighten the strain of soldiering.

Originally the Administration planned to wait dispatch of troops until March, 1918, but upon Allied insistence, Wilson sent General John J. Pershing, his excellent choice of a commander, to France in the spring of 1917. Ports and railroads were equipped to land the troops and carry them toward the battle line. Pershing and Wilson insisted upon the principle that their soldiers should remain a separate entity instead of being scattered to fill in depleted regiments of the Allies. American pride, the morale of the soldiers themselves, and the need for continued enthusiasm in the United States dictated this course. Troops landed in September 1917 and received a course of hardening before entering the trenches. Assigned at first to quiet sectors, they exerted more moral than military effect. They might never have known the trenches if Wilson had accepted in August a plan of the Pope for condoning all the belligerents alike; but American emotions were too much engaged. Also, they were so engrossed in erecting a leviathan of a war machine that they would have resented intensely the lack of opportunity to demonstrate its running power. The Allied governments also were too confident for peace making; they forbade attendance of their citizens upon an International Conference of Socialists convened in September at Stockholm.

Confidence was shortlived and soon put a premium on American aid.

---

[1] Native whites from the country proved better endowed than alien born, colored, or city youths; boys from Middle West extending from Texas to North Dakota were 70 to 80% fit, while those from the Far West and some of the industrial states rated little above 50%.

In October the Italian line broke; in November Bolshevik Communists overthrew the liberal Kerensky regime in Russia and in March accepted from Germany the harsh peace treaty of Brest-Litovsk. These combined disasters forced the Allies to spare for the southern frontier troops badly needed to the west, just when 500,000 Germans were being freed from eastern fighting for western assault. There, by spring, the Germans had a numerical superiority and prepared to take Paris and win the war.

Their terrific assaults between 2 March and 18 July forced the

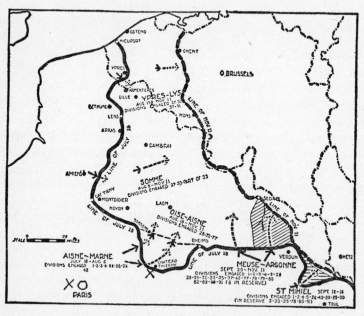

Where Americans Fought

Allies to establish the unified command (under Marshal Foch) which the United States had been urging. A Supreme War Council and Naval, Maritime, and Munition Councils were set up. Pershing and Wilson agreed to a temporary scattering of troops among beleaguered assailants. When the Prime Ministers of England, France, and Italy cabled (2 June) for 300,000 troops monthly, the war machine promptly filled the quota and so continued until November.

American aid by mid-July was turning the tide and Foch, under Pershing's urgency, undertook a counter-offensive. The American army was enabled to resume its separate status in August, and supported by a few outside troops and British and French tanks and airplanes it took over nearly one-fourth of the line. Its exploits at Chateau-Thierry,

Belleau Wood, and Soissons, and Saint Mihiel, and in the Meuse-Argonne region through that spring, summer and fall wrote American prowess into continental military annals. Before the Armistice approximately 130,000 Americans—nearly one out of every ten there engaged—had given up their lives. Insufficient training, inexperience, a preference for open field tactics and a hard-pressed sector had taken their toll. But with American aid, German morale and resource were destroyed. Mutiny appeared in her navy, revolution in her cities. A Republic was established, the Kaiser fled to Holland and an armistice, 11 November 1918, ended the carnage.

Peace Propaganda

No small part of this victory was due to President Wilson personally. The Bolsheviki published in December 1917 secret treaties proving that the Allies were fighting not for democracy, but for territorial aggrandizement; these exposures disaffected the long-suffering populaces. Desertions among French and other soldiers, restiveness among British and other laborers, turned the Allies toward Wilson for a convincing proclamation that theirs was the cause of humanity. In America, less wellinformed laboring and socialistic groups were committed to the war and doing much to help unite Americans behind it. They were carried away by their missionary zeal.

Wilson promptly, 8 January 1918, had addressed Congress and the world on the terms of a just peace. He projected a peace embodying "Fourteen Points":—five, for the general good, specified open diplomacy, freedom of the seas, removal of trade barriers, reduction of armaments and fair colonial adjustments: eight, specified territorial adjustments conforming to racial differences: the last, proposed an association of nations guaranteeing political independence and territorial integrity to big and little powers alike. Allied diplomats accepted the points in principle, but not specifically, and made no protest against them as long as victory remained uncertain. As the military situation shifted, they issued peace pronouncements vaguely referring to the Fourteen Points, which they found particularly effective as propaganda published in their own press and dropped over Germany's entire countryside. It was through Wilson, and on the basis of the Fourteen Points, that the Germans had negotiated for the armistice.

The President even then was making concessions to Britain on freedom of the seas and to France on reparations. But he required the Germans to democratize their system of government and drop the Hohenzollerns before he permitted pre-armistice negotiations to leave his hands for those of General Foch. Thrones were falling and revolutions breaking out in Middle Europe when German socialists under

Chancellor Ebert finally, 11 November 1918, signed the armistice,[1] which silenced the guns.

If the American nation were convinced that they had won the war, the President felt no less confident that the victory was his. Determined to vindicate American entrance by ending all warfare, he made meticulous preparations for a treaty of permanent peace. He wrote a draft and Colonel House and Dr. D. Hunter Miller of the State Department had worked out a plan. A host of experts labored months on details. Wilson assumed, with much reason, that his doctrines had effective support. A reorganized Republican party, in which Theodore Roosevelt participated actively, had somewhat discredited Wilson in the 1918 election, defeating his plea for a sweeping Democratic victory in endorsement of his projects; but millions of people at home and abroad were enthusiastically acclaiming his hope for a sane peace.[2]

About 150 peace societies existed in the western world in 1914, with the World Peace Foundation at Boston rich enough to afford lavish publicity. Less influential but no less earnest were the Women's Peace Party, the American Union against Militarism, and the American League to Limit Armaments. A League to Enforce Peace, organized under non-partisan auspices, had enjoyed bi-partisan support when Wilson and Lodge addressed it from the same platform in 1916. Ex-President Taft, President Butler of Columbia University and President Lowell of Harvard had prepared drafts for an international league, as had some British and French groups during 1917. Objections to a League as impractical were not current before 1917, when Senator Lodge appeared as the only prominent dissenter.

Thereafter, however, the efficient George Creel had immersed Americans in a heavy bath of hate. Acquiescing in suppression of liberalism, many had given themselves up to vindictiveness or greed. These, like millions abroad, still burned with hatreds propaganda had lighted—a fact Wilson forgot though partly responsible for it. Forced to qualify his doctrines, he still expected to overcome foreign and domestic opposition to a just peace, believing he could successfully pit his idealism against crafty, European statesmanship. Not realizing how citizens in a democracy can be more uncompromising than their diplomats, he determined to attend the peace conference and there protect the peoples from their leaders.

Wilson minimized his domestic problem, assuming that Republican support outside Congress would offset Republican opposition within. Forgetting that his bargaining position might be stronger if treaty

---

[1] Austria surrendered 3 November.

[2] The 66th Congress elected in 1918 contained 48 Republicans in the Senate, 237 in the House, the Democrats had 47 and 191 respectively; the Independents, 1 and 7.

makers had to appeal to him (as well as to the Senate), from across the ocean, he went in person to the peace conference, 4 December 1918. He took a thousand experts and the plan of a treaty. For official associates he took Colonel House, General T. H. Bliss, Secretary Robert Lansing and Ambassador Henry White—an unfortunate selection as lacking a representative Republican, a member of the Senate Foreign Relations Committee, and an American of outstanding international repute.

Peace as Obtained

Politics and psychology together destroyed the Fourteen Points. The disembarking President found imperialistic editors prepared to discount him from the outset, taunting him with the fact that the victorious Republicans had found some campaign support for a savage peace and against a league treaty. English and French candidates were campaigning on slogans of hate and retaliation; although the masses acclaimed Wilson, on a triumphal tour, as the apostle of forgiveness and magnanimity, Lloyd George found nothing magnanimous in England's "Khaki election," nor Clemenceau in relentless French nationalism. The democracies of Europe voted with their war resentments; and the bourgeois capitalist class, afraid of Bolshevism, feared to be liberal. Lloyd George and Clemenceau were not the premiers to challenge the popular resentment, the demand for security and insistence upon territorial gains, which were rife in England, France and Germany. In so jingoistic an atmosphere the only leader interested in a just peace was the American president; and he could not implement his high aspirations with political and diplomatic astuteness.

The decisions awaiting the peacemakers were the most portentous in history. Any peace at all was a feat. The business mainly lay with the three premiers and Wilson—logical heirs of a pre-armistice council of Lloyd George, Clemenceau, Orlando and House. They barred the doors of discussion to the defeated powers (an innovation in modern practice) and listened little to lesser Allies. After secret negotiations lasting until 28 June 1919 their treaty was signed. It showed that Wilson had not been defeated on all issues. He had prevented charging Germany with the entire cost of the war, although he failed to make the sum of reparations either definite or reasonable in prospect. Also he somewhat reduced territorial spoils obtained by Italy, Japan, France and Poland, although in the main (except for Russia) the bribes of the secret treaties were paid. Thirdly, he forced the League into the treaty itself.[1]

The grand object of the League was world peace, obtained through arbitration and arms reduction through League machinery. All nations

[1] The League plan was finally drafted by Dr. Hunter Miller and Sir Cecil Hurst.

were invited to participate (each with an equal vote) in a popular, lower House called the Assembly. Executive functions were allotted to a Council of nine, with five permanent members representing England, France, Italy, Japan and the United States; and temporary elective members from four other powers. Their duty was to wipe out political friction:—by planning arms reduction, publicizing treaties, exercising mandates and investigating disputes submitted to them. Legal frictions were to be handled by a permanent Court of International Justice, sitting at The Hague. A permanent League secretariat and International Labor Bureau were to function from Geneva. All member nations pledged themselves to respect and preserve three basic principles:—territorial integrity, political independence and arbitral practices; they would avoid war with nations accepting League awards, impose sanctions (penalties) on recalcitrant powers, arbitrate disputes and delay war three months.

In order to make the Covenant of the League an integral part of the treaty with Germany, Wilson yielded the vital, moral question of blame. It was all laid on Germany, contrary to the spirit of the Fourteen Points. Her economic ruin was predicated upon reparations, imposed beyond ability to pay readily, upon a gold penalty of 33 billions, and upon loss of areas producing coal, iron, potash, and other materials essential to strength. She seemed unlikely to re-enter competition for world markets after relinquishing Alsace-Lorraine to France and other strategic areas to Poland, Belgium and Denmark. Reduction of her army to 100,000 men and a fifteen-year occupation of key centers by the Allies capped her punishment.

While these terms were formulating at Paris, American politicians and publicists worried over Wilson's commitments. They made him aware of a responsible American demand that the League should recognize the Monroe Doctrine and exclude domestic concerns from its interference. Unanimity of voting in the Council and withdrawal of members at will also were pressed. The urgencies of such charitable critics as Taft, Hughes and Root persuaded Wilson to secure reservations on the Monroe Doctrine and on withdrawals from the League. But he did not obtain specifications that the United States was not to pledge sanctions, nor get that exclusion of domestic matters which would have conciliated senators interested in controlling immigration and the tariff.

During a month's interlude in the United States (14 February-14 March) Wilson gave a White House dinner to Senate and House foreign relations committee-men and made public comments; but he neither invited official Senate suggestions nor outmanoeuvered politicians inspired by political and personal animosities. Thirty-nine senators and senators-elect determined to defy the President. Irreconcilables, led on the left by La Follette, Borah, Johnson and Poindexter, and on the right by Brandegee, Hitchcock, Knox, Lodge, McCormick, Moses and Sherman, signed a round robin 2 March 1919 declaring that the League must wait until after peace. No less defiant, Wilson proclaimed the Covenant would be in the treaty, inseparable from it.

Before Wilson returned again to the United States, a newspaper friend favored Borah with an advance draft of the Covenant, which he read into the *Congressional Record*. Thus the pact was exposed to criticism a month before Wilson officially presented it to the Senate. The Republicans had filibustered against appropriation bills to make sure Congress sat that summer; and the special session beginning 19 May saw anti-League sentiment in triumphant sway over the vital Foreign Relations Committee of the Senate, controlling a majority of its members and installing the implacable Lodge as Chairman.

Realizing that public opinion strongly favored the League, the irreconcilables had recourse to delay, to interminable hearings, (held publicly, contrary to custom, and promptly published) and to long drawn out amendments and reservations. Some forty-five amendments to the treaty and four reservations, designed to protect American sovereignty and to separate the United States from execution of the treaty were gradually accumulated for Senate voting. Alexander Frick and Andrew Mellon lavishly contributed funds to help turn public opinion.

The President, who had made broad concessions to foreigners to place the Covenant in the Treaty, could not be persuaded by Colonel House or Viscount Grey to make concessions to the Senate. His type of mind plus physical exhaustion ill-equipped him to strike a balance between Versailles and Washington. He undertook a western tour to turn the flank of the opposition, with the irreconcilables dogging his platforms. In Kansas 26 September he suffered a complete physical collapse culminating in a stroke of apoplexy. This personal calamity made it possible for the irreconcilables to defeat the treaty in three Senate votes of 19 November, to the amazement of Americans and the World.

These tallies did not convince adherents or satisfy the public generally. A joint resolution declaring the war at an end was put through Congress by the irreconcilables but Wilson vetoed it. A second Senate poll had to be taken. But it was delayed four months—while political capital was being made against Wilson, while many Americans were becoming engrossed in domestic and private affairs and tiring of world idealism. Arguments that the League meant British dominance, American entanglement in European wars and perpetuation of injustice gained weight. Then, 19 March 1920, Wilson's Covenant again failed of a two-thirds endorsement.

Yet, more than three-fourths of the Senate had remained ready to accept League membership with modifications. A popular referendum was demanded; and frightened candidates prepared to hedge in 1920.

The Democratic platform did not oppose reservations; the Republican did not take a clear stand against the League. Harding even endorsed an "association of nations"—which thirty-one prominent Republicans advertised as meaning the League. But, after the Republicans won the election anti-League members interpreted the poll as a third vote against the Covenant; and Harding, once inaugurated, pronounced against it. Not since has it appeared in any national platform.

To a second, joint congressional resolution (of 2 July 1921), proclaiming the war at an official end, Harding gave his signature. This reserved to the United States all rights which would have accrued under Europe's Versailles, St. Germain and Trianon treaties, aiming for all the advantages with none of the obligations. To this, Germany, Austria and Hungary agreed, in treaties signed separately with the United States during August. America had kept herself free to watch the League experiment from a distance, while the member nations gradually proved their unwillingness to yield practical concessions toward a peace ideal, and while the League was failing as a weapon of permanent defense for England and France against Germany. None can know how the League would have fared if the United States had joined it. The war, however, had left a mark on Americans which they would not eradicate.

Post-war Treaties with Europe

The democratic missionary zeal which had animated Wilson reached too far down into America's spiritual heritage to be uprooted. Also the modern age had woven transoceanic ties—economic, social and cultural —too strong for war and politics to kill. Therefore neither the political death of the League in the Senate, nor frantic and fervent reiteration by most Americans of their distaste for European entanglements, could re-isolate America. Also lovers of world peace and militarists with surplus energies, bankers and industrialists with surplus funds and goods, and farmers with surplus crops each sought their particular objects; all were caught by a common result—world contacts. The concept of isolation remained, but (like American war debt policy, see p. 678) it was not based on reality.

Popular interest lay in the positive aspects of disarmament and peace. The government, however, awoke also to negative imperatives—the United States as a "have" nation might be affected by rearmament by the "have nots"; she could not remain unaffected by the struggle between her erstwhile allies and the defeated powers over whether victory should be static, or upset by a return of the vanquished to power and glory. Consequently, a confusion of ideal and practical considerations moved the United States in her postwar relations with Europe. The sequence of events during the double decade, 1919-1939, vividly demonstrated how this great nation continually became more involved in European arrangements.

At Washington was convened the World Disarmament Conference of 1921-1922, when the United States with Great Britain, Japan, France and Italy agreed to scrap all but a certain number of battleships and to limit for ten years new battleship construction, to the respective proportionate ratios of 5-5-3-1.7-1.7. Significantly, they failed to regulate the auxiliary shipbuilding so important in swift modern warfare:— submarines, destroyers, etc. This "Five Power Treaty" proved no more successful and no less significant than the Four and Nine Power treaties on far eastern affairs (p. 606) reached at the same Washington Conference.

The World Court established at The Hague in 1922 as a League adjunct for aiding peace through judicial decisions on international law, obligations and treaties both interested and repelled Americans. It was founded on rules which Elihu Root had helped to formulate; and although each succeeding President has proved unable to overcome Senate opposition to membership, the court regularly has kept one American jurist on its bench.[1]

The broad scope of early League activities attracted "unofficial observers" from Washington to Geneva and the existence of the League finally was officially recognized in 1923. Official American delegations attended League gatherings after 1924, safeguarding American interests, cooperating on non-political matters and encouraging some public and private financial support. They observed and reported the failure of the League, whether regarded as an implement for peace or for preventing reapportionment of the spoils divided in 1919. Although the United States never entered the League proper, she latterly maintained a secretariat at its doors. Some of her leaders hoped to mobilize world peace opinion as a substitute for the League's scheme of collective security and economic boycott.

The peace ideal remained strong in theory but weak in performance. In Europe it had sponsored the Locarno Pact of 1925 by which France, Belgium and Germany agreed always to settle disputes by arbitration rather than war; but when President Coolidge, pressed by American peace sentiment, two years later tried to implement peace through further naval limitation he failed, to the gratification of international armament interests which fought the conference.[2] Yet fifteen powers,

---

[1] John Bassett Moore 1921-1928, Charles E. Hughes 1928-1930, Frank B. Kellogg 1930-1935, Manley O. Hudson 1936 ff. The Senate in 1926 proposed membership under five reservations, of which the vital one was that the Court must have U. S. permission before considering questions in which the U. S. claimed an interest; but after the reservations were virtually accepted the Senate still refused to enter.

[2] France and Italy refused to attend the conference.

on the invitation of Secretary of State Kellogg and France's premier, Aristide Briand, signed the 1928 Pact of Paris, renouncing war and agreeing to settle disputes solely by peaceful means; and 47 lesser governments followed suit. Washington showed its good faith by pushing a series of bilateral agreements, based on foundations laid by Root and Bryan, for arbitration, and investigation of disputes.

President Hoover pursued the effort further in 1930, cooperating when London became host to the signatories of the "Five Power Treaty." There was phrased a treaty which extended the battleship "holiday" to 1936 and included auxiliary vessels within ratio limitations; but the ratio was raised to 10-10-7, Britain admitted the United States to naval parity with her, the United States admitted Japan to submarine parity with her, and all three sought safety in an "escalator" clause, permitting any signatory to disregard limitations if threatened by the building program of any non-signatory. As the signatories numbered but three [1] and one, Japan, was scarcely quiescent under her subsidiary status, it appeared that the peace conference of 1930 chiefly admitted progress in preparation for war.

[1] France and Italy failed to ratify.

WHAT PRICE PROSPERITY

1918-1933

CHAPTER XXXV

PROSPERITY PURSUED

Apart from foreign affairs, life in the United States went on—but not at the same kind of tension as the war years. War left Americans in a condition of exhaustion of the altruistic emotions. Internationalism had been sold to them on a program of liberal democracy, and the feeling which sloughed off the one was matched by a willingness to abandon the other. As Americans, like Britishers, came to frank admissions of selfish wartime motives, they discounted war idealisms. Many came to sneer at altruism as a mark of simplicity. By the same token, low standards became respectable. Thus to war's material waste was added spiritual loss.

Dominant Characteristics

There was a general reluctance to exercise foresight or to apprehend strange emergencies. Some of the gains which war occupations had brought them, people wished to retain, but it did not seem inconsistent to expect to keep the advantages and privileges, and dispense with the disadvantages and responsibilities, which had come together between 1914 and 1918. It was easy to assume that the clock could be turned back—hard to learn that galloping change had become the dominating characteristic of life. People wanted nothing so much as to return to what seemed, in retrospect, an unhindered concentration upon personal gain. They were eager for selfish ease. Daily living came to be dominated largely by such characteristics as materialism, lawlessness, standardization and intolerance. These qualities and resistance to them were bound to ramify throughout American culture, affecting trends in literature, education, science, the arts and religion.

In her pursuit of prosperity, America appeared highly successful, for it was obvious between the outbreak of the war and 1929 that the total national income was rising; statisticians later estimated that it jumped from 34 to 83 billions. The less encouraging fact that wealth distribution was not improving proportionately, that 60% of the national wealth was accruing to 2% of the population, went little noticed as long as the "average" person knew some rise in standards of living. Egged on by installment selling, by the speculative fervor and the sense of insecurity and change natural to a postwar period, they spent their past, present, and future earnings. They bought an increasing variety of attractive, electric timesavers such as washing machines, mixers and irons; they went in for such amusements as the movies, radios, automobile-riding and touring. They allowed themselves the luxuries of speculation and college courses for their children.[1]

Private expenditures often brought only temporary satisfactions; but public outlays of tax money and private benefactions, for such things as schools, hospitals and social-minded foundations raised the national averages in longevity, health, education, and other indices of well-being, and advantaged the poorest classes. This group felt less poor, although their percentage of improvement lagged behind the others, and contributed but little to the evidence of increased bank accounts and home ownership. Thus, practically all groups were encouraged in an optimistic belief in mounting prosperity.

Rampant money-making would ill brook interference. Losing such sensitivity to social responsibility as distinguished the progressive era, the majority became more indifferent to consequences, cynical and lawless. The law-abiding class by its quiescence cooperated in law breaking. This emboldened public and private criminals to count more on lax enforcement and to tap new sources of gain. The social climate was well fitted to foster Harding scandals in politics, stock-jobbery on Wall Street and wholesale defiance of the prohibition act everywhere.

Prohibition has been loaded with more blame for postwar lawlessness than rightfully belongs to it; but even after due discount its responsibility remains extremely heavy. The constitutional amendment forbidding the "manufacture, sale or transportation" of intoxicating liquors had passed Congress in December 1917, during the uprush of war enthusiasm; and within thirteen months three-fourths of the states had ratified it. Stringent enforcement legislation, mid-West in concept and sponsored by Representative Volstead of Minnesota, obtained the two-thirds vote of Congress essential to override a Wilson veto in October 1919. The 18th Amendment was proclaimed as in force in January 1920, at a time when two-thirds of the nation were living under local prohibition and the other third knew severe war-bred restrictions.

This was the fruition of ten decades of temperance agitation by church and women's organizations assisted by corrupt practices of the liquor interests, by control aspects of the southern race problem, by automobile risks and by the efficient pressure politics of the Anti-Saloon League. But before government enforcement could attain efficiency it had to overcome political influence and decentralization; and many signs emerged pointing toward ultimate failure.

[1] Between 1920 and 1930 automobile ownership grew from 8 to 26.5 million; weekly movie attendance from 30 to 100 million; college and university attendance from 355 to 970 thousand; between 1921, when the first broadcasting station was erected, and 1930, receiving sets multiplied from zero to 10 million.

The illegal industry had much public support, expensive drinking became highly fashionable and humbler home brewers blossomed forth as liberty-loving patriots. The Canadian and Mexican borders and the coast line proved hard to police. Easy profits from re-distillation of industrial alcohol and other devices poured into the capacious pockets of bootleggers, speakeasy operators and corrupt government agents, supporting a new and highly organized kingdom of violence ruled by gangsters, hi-jackers and racketeers. Some teetotalers concluded that prohibition fostered crime. The expense was high and the gain hard to evaluate. However, pauperism diminished greatly, savings and other workingmen's investments rose; such businesses as soft drinks and candy, movies and theatres profited; and total alcoholic consumption fell. With a fall in heavy drinking came lighter, more healthful eating.

Prohibition far outdistanced urban sentiment, especially among beer-drinking Germans and Irish and wine-drinking Latins; law-breaking was spectacular and well-publicized and the bootleggers' arrogance hastened their downfall. Legislators in some urban states removed the local props from under the Volstead Act. The national issue helped to split the Democrats into McAdoo and Smith factions by 1924 and to nominate Smith in 1928, although through that year's convention neither party dared to abandon official endorsement of enforcement. Republicans, fearful of alienating their rural vote, gave the louder lip service to prohibition, until a "Wickersham Commission" appointed by President Hoover officially opposed repeal but showed that enforcement had proved a failure. His party in 1932 reached the point of adopting in substance an Al Smith proposition of 1928 for a revised scheme of state regulation, while the Democrats moved to outright repeal. Following the Democratic landslide, Hoover's last Congress passed a 21st Amendment to repeal the 18th; and in less than a year enough states had ratified it to end the "noble experiment." Each state proceded to handle its local situation with its own compromises.

Premature prohibition had helped to change American mores; it had made drinking in public by women respectable; it had taught youth to drink hard liquor; it had weakened the respect of both sexes and all ages for law. The old saloon had corrupted politics; now gangsters trained in the bootlegging business widened their sphere into kidnapping and corruption of legitimate businesses. They levied toll upon proprietors for "protection," exacted ransoms and boldly destroyed property and life where tribute was withheld. Their exploits, reproduced in moving pictures everywhere, tended to displace the Wild West cowboy in post-war thrillers; and the one, like the other, colored the foreign concept of America. Movies made crime familiar to all classes and taught it to such boys and girls as lived in environments suited to gangster imitation. Ethics and morality were widely affected.

Money-making, law-breaking Americans were less free than they imagined, for they were victims of standardization. In all except the most inaccessible regions, Americans were seeing the same movies, hearing the same radio programs, reading the same news, seeing the same advertisements, month after month. The automobile widened the reach but destroyed peculiarities within it. 50% of the population now lived in cities, crowded together in apartments or in row houses, and assumed a superior sophistication. In reality, however, no American remained more insular than many born and bred New Yorkers, Bostonese, Baltimoreans and Philadelphians; and every smaller town and village in the great Mississippi valley and on the Pacific Coast boasted a Main Street, commercial association, country club and church set-up essentially like all the others.

C. D. Batchelor in Philadelphia *Public Ledger*.

The Old and the New in American Homes

Uniformity fostered intolerance and pseudo-patriotism in a people recently trained by war propaganda to attack independent thought and action. Since the majority readily learned to fear idealists, suspect liberals and hate radicals, they soon were denouncing any bold critic of the status quo as a heretic or a "red." Leaders in national and local governments and in social organizations distinguished themselves as baiters; and dangerous discretionary power was entrusted to ordinary police officials. Federal and state law enforcing agencies, the American Legion, the Ku Klux Klan, church fundamentalists, demagogues and persons with an ax to grind, all burst forth into flagrant violation of formerly revered democratic rights. According to their situation and locale they selected groups to persecute—either socialists, aliens, communists, free thinkers, scientists, Catholics, Negroes or Jews—and they then indiscriminately and erratically denied to them freedom of speech, press or assemblage, sometimes even liberty or life.

Scores of illegal imprisonments and lawless lynchings, some deportations and hundreds of terroristic intimidations and raids were countenanced by the surge of intolerance. Massachusetts executed for murder two anarchists—Sacco and Vanzetti—despite world-wide questioning of their guilt. California held in the penitentiary two labor leaders accused of bomb throwing—Mooney and Billings—although evidence accumulated that their conviction was pre-arranged through perjury.[1] Tennessee, Mississippi and Arkansas made the teaching of evolution illegal. No

[1] Mooney was released in January 1939.

less than twenty-one states between 1917 and 1935 singled out teachers as a class which must take oaths to prove their loyalty—oaths which in reality threatened democracy because they discouraged criticism and adaptation. The United States Congress and the New York legislature debarred legally elected Socialists; and thirty-two states enacted criminal syndicalist laws. Textbooks, novels, plays, movies and works of art were called in question where they irritated current, vocal prejudices and often were wantonly mistreated.

Fortunately, such extreme manifestations of undesirable qualities—such as intolerance, standardization, lawlessness and materialism—could cause healthy curative reactions in a democracy. Further examination of America's postwar culture—her literature, education, science, art and religion—shows a wealth of trends.

Expressions in Culture

American literature, after the war period, reflected a people scornful of their past, resentful of their present and sceptical about their future. Sensitive writers felt the impact of scientific discoveries, Freudian psychology, extreme industrialization, abject poverty and political corruption; all these influences and others no less disturbing seemed to make idealism ridiculous. Democracy itself became a thing for merciless ridicule and traditional village mores were lampooned. A spread in knowledge of foreign cultures—Latin American, British, French, German, Japanese and Russian—helped to depreciate American values. Immigrant races formerly without importance in United States literary output obtained recognition. Confused and disillusioned by the failure of the great crusade, artists devoted their abundant energies to strenuous experiment, questioning and criticizing, clamoring for recognition of pet theories.

Old distinctions between literary forms were blurred by the common urge to try new ones, guided solely by individual canons. This made the period notable for insurrection against tradition in literature. Every possible field was explored by the individualists, who set themselves up as critics in their own and other fields, and in contemporary civilization itself; all of which made for the more activity.

Perhaps the most explored field was poetry, where an unprecedented throng of professionals produced volumes of verse, sponsored journals, submitted thousands of manuscripts in poetry contests and, some of them, achieved sudden success. Leaders among the "new poets" were Amy Lowell, Alfred Kreymborg, Harriet Monroe and Louis Untermyer. Edgar Lee Masters exploited the Middle West; Vachel Lindsay, Negroes and exhorters; Carl Sandburg, workers in steel and corn; Stephen Vincent Benét's *John Brown's Body* illuminated the Civil War.

Extreme innovators were followed by poets of more restraint, like Conrad Aiken, T. S. Eliot and Eleanor Wylie.

Fiction became extraordinarily realistic, as witness the *Arrowsmith, Babbitt* and *Main Street* of the popular Sinclair Lewis; he won in 1930 the Nobel prize in literature. Theodore Dreiser's *American Tragedy* typified the common sense of futility and despair among his type. These, with Maxwell Anderson, Ernest Poole and their associates were presenting no program for reform; they wrote exposure for the relief it gave them. Other realists, like Ellen Glasgow and Willa Cather showed more restraint; and there were escapists, like James Branch Cabell, Joseph Hergesheimer, Robert Nathan and Thornton Wilder. A slight shift of emphasis to allow of more writing craftsmanship became evident in writers like Louis Bromfield, Ernest Hemingway and Elizabeth Madox Roberts. Regionalism brought more than 2000 titles into fiction alone, 1918-1938.

The wide range of public interest, and the willingness of literary and other people to write and criticize work outside their closest fields, made for a definite effort at interesting diction—with salutary effects upon biography, history, science and other subjects. In all of these, "outlines" found ready sale.[1] Biography reacted against super-nationalism; Claude G. Bowers, Rupert Hughes and Edgar Lee Masters set themselves vigorously to "debunking" heroes like Hamilton, Washington and Lincoln; Tyler Dennett, Allan Nevins, Henry S. Pringle and others strove for broad, true portraits; fictionalized and semi-historical biographies added to the variety.

Nationalism encouraged interest in and support for broad studies of American experience, written by historians to interest the general reader, such as the *Chronicles of America* and the fifteen volumes of historical picture books, *The Pageant of America*. A twenty-volume, non-commercial *Dictionary of American Biography,* edited under rigorous standards of accuracy, filled a long-felt need. A *History of American Life*—twelve volumes devoted exclusively to social, economic and cultural trends, was highly significant as taking emphasis from politics. The dry bones of American history were animated by living flesh and blood through the writings of such historians as Charles and Mary Beard, Carl Becker, Henry Steele Commager, Samuel Eliot Morison, James Harvey Robinson and Vernon L. Parrington.

Many citizens gave support to patriotic organizations and the government, to aid in preserving historical shrines. An entire environment was recreated for posterity by Mr. and Mrs. John D. Rockefeller Jr., who restored Williamsburg, Virginia, to its 18th century glory, and made

---

[1] "Book of the Month" and "Literary Guild" clubs made fiction and nonfiction best sellers, by choice of them for their wide clienteles.

available a remarkable collection of early American portraits and paintings.

The per capita average of American book purchases was, however, below that of northern Europe, for the trend in the United States was toward fewer purchases and greater circulation through libraries. Nearly as many pamphlets as books were read.

It was in the circulation of periodicals and newspapers that the United States stood foremost; and the shifting intellectual climate made marked changes. The old "respectables"—like the *Atlantic, Harpers* and *Scribners* had to strive to survive. Weeklies of marked liberal and radical opinion—The *Freeman, New Republic, Nation* and *Masses*—sometimes had to search for a financial backer; through them the stimulating comment of such publicists as Harry E. Barnes, Charles A. Beard, Stuart Chase, Walter Lippmann and Benjamin Stolberg reached a special clientele. H. L. Mencken founded the monthly *American Mercury* to ridicule democracy and village morality. Among keen critics of America past and present were Vernon W. Brooks, Waldo Frank, Lewis Mumford and Edmund Wilson.

For the intelligentsia, current events and important phenomena were described monthly by *Current History, Foreign Affairs* and *Fortune;* for more popular tastes, by the weekly *Literary Digest* and *Time.* The largest following was enjoyed by family weeklies and monthlies such as Cyrus Curtis' *Saturday Evening Post* and *Ladies Home Journal,* usually filled with entertaining success stories. Increases in the advertising, size and subscription lists (until the depression) enabled them either to double their price or meet rising newsprint costs with advertising profits, for they kept at the level of current, middle class, taste and ideals. Below that level were the ten cent "pulps" issued monthly for quantity consumption by astute editors of the type of Bernarr McFadden, to catch every variety of interest, whether *Physical Culture, Romances, True Confessions, Detective, Screen* or *Wild West* magazines. All but the erudite periodicals subordinated everything to financial profits.

The same was true of the newspaper owners, who standardized their news and special features to meet the mental age of their average readers, who in turn supplied the circulation figures on which advertising rates could be based. Mounting costs of newsprint raised the price of dailies from two cents to three and tightened the control exercised by advertisers and public-opinion-makers over editorial policy, augmenting its vague and evasive trend; personal journalism almost disappeared, except for special columnists who obtained considerable latitude in expressing personal opinions on public affairs and personages. As owners expanded their pages, elaborating expensive comic, sport, domestic, financial, literary and columnist specialties, the richest bought-out competitors. New Yorkers saw historic rivals merged, the *Herald-Tribune,* and *World-Telegram*. Millionaire owners like Frank Munsey were interested in controlling the field, not in editing. Hearst accumulated a prosperous chain of yellow journals, Scripps-Howard interests a more liberal chain.

To harvest billions of pennies in the wide field of the least literate readers, the *Chicago Tribune* in 1919 catapulted into New York the *Daily News,* first of the straphanger tabloids, filled chiefly with sensational pictures (not always genuine) and advertising, with a minimum of actual news information. Hearst's *Mirror* and Bernarr McFadden's *Graphic* aped the *News* in New York; and soon every large city had its tabloid. For their crass sensationalism they sometimes atoned by a liberal editorial policy or a crusade for fresh air or free milk for poor children.

The expense of producing newspapers and popular periodicals allegedly was met by the advertisers, but they easily shifted it to readers, because Americans showed low resistance to indirect approach. By stress on success, beauty or prestige, or novelty, efficiency or scientific values, the advertisers simultaneously sold their goods to the gullible and revealed the state of American culture to the discerning. Opinions, even more than goods, were prefabricated. Every important group and most important personages came to have press agents or "public relations counselors" to "release information" and "guide" public opinion; their artificial coloring so thoroughly mixed fiction with truth in the news that few could separate them. Necessarily news largely dependent on such a system must fail to note powerful undercurrents developing among the masses, until their force thrust them through the hard crust of upper and middle class complacence. This was capitally illustrated when in 1936 F. D. Roosevelt was re-elected President to the astonishment of the editors of that middle class barometer of public opinion, the *Literary Digest*.

Only an enlightened educational policy can counteract strains inflicted on democracy by the swift machinery of modern life. Appreciation of this cardinal fact occasionally manifested itself; but in large part the belief in education, which now burned with the intensity of earlier religious fervor, found quantitative rather than qualitative expression. Americans found satisfaction in unprecedented enrollments and expenditures, which seemed to more than compensate for the wartime budgetary lag, but brought very uneven results.[1]

Insofar as the schools became clinics or laboratories of child study, and social centers for neighborhood communities, they sharpened their influence upon child and adult life. There was a multiplication in the

[1] Between 1920 and 1930 kindergarten and elementary enrollment increased less than 13%, while secondary, normal and college enrollments almost doubled.

Pennsylvania Rural Schoolhouse, Built
in 1830 and Still in Use

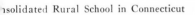

nsolidated Rural School in Connecticut

School and Community House in Kansas

ance to Hollywood's Most Modern High School

ROWTH OF THE MODERN SCHOOL

number of "progressive" institutions which aimed to train future citizens to make their own decisions and to discover and develop their own talents with the directness and strength of natural aptitudes. "Continuation" night schools for ill-educated adults, swimming pools and gymnasiums for regular, free use and auditoriums available for parent-teacher associations and other neighborhood functions became indispensable equipment in even modest urban centers.

Expansion came fastest in secondary schools, formerly organized for "college preparatory" purposes and now forced to meet needs of children thrust back on the schools by child labor laws. They multiplied their outlays for expensive manual training, domestic science and trade instruction, and attempted further efforts at citizen-training through "community civics." The high schools overflowed into the colleges. A few select, private institutions stayed the flood by heightened fees and tightened entrance requirements. The others reflected the period, rushing into a tremendous expansion of plant and curriculum. Presidents apt at business, conciliation and politics, rather than engrossed in educational theories or pure science were in demand to run the standardized "degree factories." Nevertheless, some colleges struggling against standardization essayed bold experiments in science and education; requirements for admission and graduation rose; nor were all students too engaged in campus politics or athletics to do intelligent work in art, journalism, music and the theatre.

The schools were treated as a fair field for propaganda by successive pressure groups, especially those devoted to the status quo; but restrictions on freedom of teaching came indirectly through community prejudices more often than through direct interference of trustees and donors. Freedom was worse restricted by the comparatively low salaries of the majority of teachers and their uncertain tenure, until the depression. Thereafter conditions worsened, because foolish counsel from Chamber of Commerce and other heavy tax-paying sources led to drastic retrenchment. It cut funds and functions off the institution most vital to democracy, especially in hard times. Despite all these unfortunate trends, world leadership in literacy and in breadth of educational functions stayed with America.

In applied science post-war inventors were stimulated by America's eagerness to try new devices and fads for speed, convenience, efficiency and entertainment. Therefore industrialists, governmental units and charitable foundations financed costly laboratories—chemical, physical and medical—to elaborate useful machinery and to keep the human machine going. Practical commercialists perfected such things as automobile self-starters, rayon fabrics, carton products, insecticides, lacquers, radios and sound pictures which revived flagging interest in the movies. Medical science obtained control over epidemics of children's diseases, typhoid, diphtheria and yellow fever; they successfully attacked regional problems like malaria and pellagra and gave tuberculosis, diabetes and social diseases a far less hopeless connotation:—all with such skill that general male life expectancy was raised from fifty-five in 1920 to fifty-nine in 1938. Little advance, however, was made against diseases of old age, cancer, and heart ailments.

In pure science, less in tune with post-war attitudes, America did her best work in astronomy; of the A. B. Nobel prizes awarded in pure science, 1919-1937, Americans won only five.[1] In the "science" of human relations, also, they lagged far behind mechanical advance as homicides, maldistribution and misgovernment proved. A few psychologists, economists and historians like the Beards taught a realistic approach to the study of human behaviour in the modern age. Therapeutic specialists, drug firms and psychologists experimented with serums, glandular substances and psychiatry in an effort to restore the mind and body balance which the machine age was destroying. A few sociologists made suggestions regarding race relations, propaganda, etc. Learned groups cooperated to enlist wealthy backing to set up the "American Council of Learned Societies" and the "Social Science Research Council" as agencies for the study of human relationships; thus far they have not invented devices adequate to restore decent attitudes among crowded, machine-driven humanity.

The Arts and Religion

Patronage proved more successful in the gentler field of the arts, where its aid seems indispensable. In painting, music, drama and literature such sponsors as Mrs. Elizabeth Sprague Coolidge, Mrs. Chester Dale, Mrs. O. H. Havemeyer and Mrs. J. D. Rockefeller Jr., showed that American women had the intelligence and imagination to encourage artistic initiative. Also the middle class had now enough leisure and means to become interested in art appreciation. The combined results were a rise in artists' achievements and development of public taste. Emphasis upon self-expression, new forms[2] and realism, and the use of objects to symbolize emotions brought to artists and public a sense of freedom and the realization that beauty can be found in contemporary and humble things.

Upon painters the influence of France, exerted largely through Matisse, Cezanne and Derain, remained hypnotic through this period;

[1] In physics 1923 to R. A. Millikan, 1927 A. H. Compton, 1936 C. D. Anderson and C. J. Davisson; in chemistry 1932 to I. Langmuir, 1934 H. C. Urey. In physiology and medicine (applied science) 1930 to K. Landsteiner, 1933 T. H. Morgan, 1934 G. H. Minot, W. F. Murphey and G. H. Whipple.

[2] Various varieties of experimentation were known as cubism, impressionism and surrealism.

MODERN COMMERCIAL ARCHITECTURE

Philadelphia Savings Fund Society, 1932

At left, style of 1887; *at right*, of 1910

but a respectable minority showed that the Americans, Ryder and Eakins, of the Brown Decades, had bequeathed to the present something worthwhile of realism and symbolism. Young Philistines showed that promising if not beautiful work could be done when painters stayed home and looked at life honestly instead of going to Europe to look at pictures. Muralists felt the social impulse of the Mexicans, Rivera and Orozco, and emphasized modernity, as did lithographists and portrait painters. Even war memorials improved.[1]

In domestic architecture moderns had a hard struggle; but in skyscraper construction the demand for light and air led to the "set-back" which freed high buildings of tottering decorations and transferred emphasis to mass and line. American skyscraper architecture flowered in the beautiful Nebraska and Louisiana state capitols and in the Empire State and Rockefeller Center buildings in New York. Sculpture did not advance beyond its pre-war attainments.

In musical composition trends conflicted. To the direct educational influence of school instruction was added the continuous, indirect but more powerful stimulus of music in the movies and especially on the radio. Irving Berlin who, it was said, "never learned how to read notes and didn't know unless told in what key he wrote his songs," continued king of Tin Pan America; but he reported that radio brought overproduction and over-distribution of popular songs and shortened their life from a year to one month. Paul Whiteman, ablest exponent of jazz orchestration, declared jazz had become "the folk music of the machine age." At least it had greater possibilities than the later "swing music." A few composers experimented with native Negro and Indian music. Most significant was radio influence in widening musical taste. Musical foundations, choirs, choral societies, symphony orchestras, scholarship schools and opera companies gained in number, patronage and initiative, until the depression. Phonographs were made orthophonic and thus kept a selective clientele against radio competition.

To the theatre also came an unprecedented advance in creativeness and taste. This was partly because of and in spite of the fact that the movies seldom ventured above the twelve-year-old mentality; they had to turn sometimes to theatre-trained playwrights and stars. In New York and several other large centers the Theatre Guild organized their audiences on an annual membership basis, assuring steady, winter, metropolitan patronage in a period of darkening theatres. Off Broadway and in other seasons, young and eager actors cooperated in maintaining modest "little" and "summer" theatres which developed their talents

[1] Thomas Benton's murals on American life development distinguished the New School for Social Research in N. Y.; modern lithographing was done by Mable Dwight, Peggy Bacon and Wanda Gag; John Marin's marines and Georgia O'Keefe's chaste expressions in paint of sex life, passion and womanhood were noteworthy.

and the public's tastes. Thus creative impulses found encouragement for writing and production in the rich mines of American environment and experience.

The best English and Continental playwrights, like Shaw, Galsworthy, Milne and Molnar profited in America; but the record runs went to indigenous light comedy like Anne Nichols' "Abie's Irish Rose," Winchell Smith's and Frank Bacon's "Lightnin'," and to Erskine Caldwell's study of the dregs of character, "Tobacco Road." Preeminent among the playwrights who were making Europe aware of a United States theatre was Eugene O'Neill, who received the Nobel Prize in literature in 1936. He best exemplified the new daring in the use of realism and experimental forms; he and others challenged a people too happily engrossed in worship of prominent business success to become aware of obscure, unhappy situations full of failure.[1]

Failure, being the antithesis of the success which obsessed the nation, scarcely fitted the period. Grim, businesslike competition still dominated even diversions such as sport. Americans better recognized the importance of recreation, but the selling emphasis stressed necessity more than relaxation for the joy of it. To the familiar recreations, which were more than ever commercialized, was added a procession of crazes such as cross word puzzles and mah jong, which followed each other in a rapid succession characteristic of postwar undertakings. Work remained the prime sport of Americans; and at play, in its true sense, they came nearest to failure.

Religion also reacted vigorously to postwar attitudes. The regnant materialism roused in opposition extreme fundamentalism, especially among middle western and southern Protestants with some urban leadership from the East. They insisted that unless one subscribed altogether to the five "fundamentals":—the virgin birth, physical resurrection, inerrancy of the Bible, substitutionary atonement and the "imminent, physical second-coming of Christ," one had no right to be recognized as a Christian. On this platform the Great Commoner, William Jennings Bryan, defeated the greatest free-thinking lawyer, Clarence Darrow, in the conviction of Professor J. T. Scopes on a charge of teaching Darwinism in Tennessee. Faculties of theological seminaries were split by doctrinal and personal controversies; advancing modernism in some was counterbalanced by orthodox Bible Institutes at others. The most liberal theologian, Rev. H. E. Fosdick, and the most fundamental, J. R. Straton, were both "Baptists."

Modern, literate Americans were living in a scientific world which challenged primitive Christianity; but this could not be sensed by Billy

---

[1] Other significant playwrights were Maxwell Anderson, Marc Connelly, Dorothy and Du Bose Heyward, G. S. Kaufman, Elmer Rice, R. E. Sherwood and Laurence Stallings.

Sunday and H. A. Rodeheaver, who kept for revival use the worn hymn, "The Old Time Religion is Good Enough for Me" and then wondered why the line on the mourners' bench shortened. Church membership in fact was increasing faster than the population; and the majority of the middle and upper classes probably remained passively orthodox in belief, although they forgot all about family prayers and quiet Sundays. Lively interest in practical religion (but not in doctrine) was attested by the popularity of eager, unconventional treatises and of such books as Bruce Barton's *The Man Nobody Knows* and *The Book Nobody Knows,* and Lewis Browne's *This Believing World.*

Nevertheless, the Protestants noted a falling off in the number of congregations, in churches in use and in Sunday attendance; and the Jews saw some of their intellectuals stray into the Ethical Culture movement, while their youth abandoned orthodox affiliation. Catholics saw the need for expanded activities.

The interest of the commonalty lay in a direct application of religion to daily living, toward that material achievement with which they were obsessed. To meet this demand a middle group of "institutionalists," neither fundamentalists nor moderns, determined to enhance the social and political influence of the church as a force for reform. They hoped by modern methods to draw attention to spiritual values and they won wide influence. They floated new mortgages to build a business-like wing to the church, to shelter growing Sunday schools, gymnasium classes and divers activities. Religious education became a recognized Protestant profession, with "graded" classes and a wide variety of appeals. Some of the clergy followed the "joining" proclivities of their communities, and went into the Lions, Rotarians and Kiwanis. Also Catholics developed sodality work and aggressive "social action" programs. They staged a tremendously impressive Eucharistic Congress at Chicago in 1926, expanded their systems of schools and charitable institutions and increased their importance in city, state and national politics.

The more liberal of the Protestants struggled to keep the idealistic Interchurch World Movement afloat against the reverse current of postwar attitudes; and some few modest advances were made in the movement toward unification of Protestant denominations. Also, the Y.W.C.A. welded its younger membership into one whole, as the "Girl Reserves," and recognized its "Business and Professional" clubs as a unity; but it had a bitter, prolonged struggle before it opened its doors to electors outside the membership of Protestant Evangelical churches. Christian Scientists also had rancorous disputes, especially over E. F. Dakin's researches into the origins of Mrs. Eddy's doctrines. The most extreme modernists became "new humanists," trusting only to man's innate "Will to goodness" to cope with world evil. Cults sprouted over night, especially those which offered easy recipes for personal happiness and professional success. Spiritualism and occultism increased their following.

The churches no longer held a specialized, monopoly identification with charity, for charity, too, was now highly organized with professional social workers trained to manage city "community chests" and to allot the funds (sometimes $100,000,000 annually and usually collected on a semi-competitive, business basis) among their clients. Large, block charity was dispensed impersonally through officials managing gigantic trust funds established by the Carnegies, Sages, Rockefellers, Rosenwalds and Harknesses for education, hospitals, child welfare and improved well-being generally. By 1929 private philanthropy was spending about $1,000,000,000 annually, most of it in relieving specific ills. There were indications that it sometimes enslaved its beneficiaries; and that it was postponing a wide program of public philanthropy, but not until the great depression was deep under way did the nation come to realize the limits of personal charity and the desperate need for the application of huge public funds to the basic ills of the nation.

The ills could not seem basic as long as prosperity remained the preeminent pursuit of the nation. As this obsession permeated the whole social structure it must show, not only in general culture, but in every other important field of United States activity—in political campaigns, demobilization policy, general legislation, and economic developments.

CHAPTER XXXVI

POLITICS AND DEMOBILIZATION

Between the armistice and the depression political routines brought the normal number of campaigns:—three presidential, six congressional and innumerable local ones. They did not seem to the electorate to be very much more than routine, because pursuit of prosperity seemed more real than politics and largely separate from it. In striking contrast to both the progressive era, and the "New Deal" era to follow, the post-war period showed much more cynicism and indifference than interest in reform. Pressure groups could be relied upon to lobby for their own advantage: for the general welfare, politically speaking, there was little concern. The average politician noted the fact and was grateful. It made many things easy.

Harding "Normalcy"

Harding's election in 1920 showed the negative aspect of the electorate's attitude and its positive effect upon politicians. It registered a desire for change—undefined. The majority voted against what they thought was Wilsonian leadership, rather than for any particular Harding doctrine. The mild progressive and old school liberals nominated by the Democrats, Governor Cox of Ohio and Assistant Secretary of the Navy F. D. Roosevelt, were defeated because big business hated regulation; liberals hated the red-baiting of Burleson and Palmer; some internationalists hated the barter aspects of the Versailles Treaty; and many voters were vaguely nervous over the uncertain economic situation and possible European entanglements. President Harding did not originate the drift back from liberalism to what he labelled "normalcy"; he floated buoyantly on a current set nationally before the end of the Wilson administration. The reversal from liberalism proved unprecedented in violence.

Through the following decade, the Republican party capitalized its backward look—to the days of McKinley and Hanna, to taking government out of business and putting more business in government. However, such business gains, such elimination of competition as twenty years had brought, must be preserved. Let the government abandon supervision and control and hold fast to its higher duty of subsidy. Since four years of war had created more new millionaires than an entire decade of

657

peace, pressure for the doctrines of rugged individualism and laissez faire was amply reinforced.

As the chosen instrument for realization of this philosophy the Republicans kept the presidency through a period of twelve years—eight less than their tenure during the reaction following the war between the states. Their historic sympathy for big business, and usefulness as an instrument for keeping out Democrats, seemed so valuable that the party survived revelations of scandalous corruption, and was even permitted to hound liberals, whose protests they readily smeared with the dangerous colors of the Bolsheviks. They enjoyed an orgy of deportations. Although the wartime censorship of opinion thus was perpetuated for political purposes, over 900,000 Americans dared vote for Debs—still in Atlanta Penitentiary—on the Socialist ticket of 1920 and nearly 5,000,000 for the liberal La Follette ticket of 1924.

Leadership was scarcely exercised by any standard bearer of the successful Republican party. The war had liberated the imaginations of the people without giving them a chart; they floundered about, directionless, in many fields, especially politics. Harding was incapable of leadership, Congress prevented Coolidge from exercising it in the few instances he wished to assume it, and Hoover proved incapable of gathering a following. Republican orators had capitalized the fear of Wilsonian dictatorship, and political leadership to many minds was made a thing suspect. Confused by the world of economic unreality in which they were living, voters split off from both major parties into factions, and congressional leadership was assumed largely by lobbies for special groups.

A farm bloc, harvested from an agricultural depression of 1920, had the help of a Progressive remnant for a year or two in blocking Republican plans for "normalcy." These insurgents lessened the size of ship subsidies and hindered reduction of taxes on opulence while insisting that small incomes get some reductions. Legislation reminiscent of pre-war psychology included prohibition in 1919, industrial rehabilitation in 1920 (to cope with accidents) and women's welfare in 1921 (to reduce childbirth mortality). "Farmer-Labor" and "Non-partisan League" parties of the Middle West reduced Republican Senate and House majorities in 1922. The lobbies profited from insurgency, building up two-thirds votes to offset vetoes on the bonus and farm subsidy. Legislation thus originated and enacted often defeated its own objects, because national prosperity hinges on a breadth of view alien to pressure groups.

Since these administrations aimed to restore to government its historic role as Santa Claus to business, men in responsible positions could the more readily make it a Santa Claus to their private pocketbooks. Behind Harding's nomination had been a convention attended by confused and uncertain partisans, subjected to control by manufacturing and oil interests. The candidate they elevated was an easy-going, reactionary, party-regular, accustomed to obliging Republican friends with florid, meaningless speeches and highly significant politico-economic favors. Friendly and weak, self-indulgent and undisciplined, unintelligent and unassuming, Harding entered the presidency handicapped by the loyal henchman's life-long habit of letting things "ride along" for the taking. The only notables he named to the Cabinet were Secretary of State Charles E. Hughes and Secretary of Commerce Herbert Hoover. The Treasury went to the aluminum-made multimillionaire, A. W. Mellon, whose belief in "trickle" prosperity consistently excused tax evasions and tax reductions for the wealthy.

Harding left a free hand to other intimates whose grafting lifted him and them from obscurity to odious notoriety. His Secretary of the Interior, ex-Senator A. B. Fall, with the passive assent of Secretary of the Navy Denby, assigned control of the government's Elk Hill oil reserve in California to E. L. Doheny and the Teapot Dome reserve in Wyoming to H. F. Sinclair, a liberal contributor to the Republican chest. For this generosity the government received some storage tanks in Hawaii and Fall got at least $100,000 from Doheny and $300,000 from Sinclair. But a Montana Democrat, Senator T. J. Walsh, vigorously led an investigation which forced Denby and Fall to resign. Fall and Sinclair went to prison and the oil leases were cancelled. The extent of the malpractice in oil, of which the United States was the world's greatest consumer was proved to have exceeded the wildest imagination.

A like devotion to his private purse was discovered in Harding's director of the Veteran's Bureau, Col. Charles R. Forbes, in his custodian of alien property, Col. T. W. Miller, and in his Attorney-General, Harry Daugherty, kingpin of the "Ohio Gang." Daugherty, investigated by insurgent Senator Brookhart of Iowa, was tried but never convicted. The courts placed Forbes in the penitentiary for corruption and convicted Miller of criminal conspiracy for selling cheaply some valuable, German, chemical patents. Their Chief, failing in health and repute, for loose personal habits and easy trust, died 2 August 1923. Full exposure of his disreputable entourage came in the next year, but campaign devices conveniently broke the moral force of the revelations.

Coolidge Prosperity

Harding's death elevated to the Presidency a Massachusetts lawyer of provincial mentality, whose cautious policy as a machine politician had made him governor of Massachusetts and Vice-President of the United States. Calvin Coolidge, who took the presidential oath from his father by the light of a kerosene lamp in a Vermont farmhouse, obviously was no alarming agitator. He had kept as silent as Hoover and Hughes during suspicious developments of Harding's administration. But since he was personally abstemious and parsimonious he seemed, to people who did not know the historic idealism of New England, "a sound Yankee." They trusted him to avoid personal scandal and to restore the "good old days" of democratic, confident, practical Americanism. He remained popular with the middle and wealthy classes and with all who did not perceive that America faced problems demanding positive, executive ability—an attribute opposite to Coolidge's negative philosophy. His more significant negatives included opposition to reforms, to taxation of wealth, to subsidy for farmers and to bonuses for veterans.

The question posed by 1924 was whether the Harding scandals, like those in the Grant Administration, would fail to unseat the party in power. The Democrats, split wide on religious, economic and prohibition issues, shared much of the general insensitivity to corruption and lacked leadership capable of uniting them on reform. After an almost even division on the Klan issue, and a bitter McAdoo-Smith fight, they nominated a conservative, J. W. Davis. His career as solicitor-general in Wilson's cabinet, as ambassador to Great Britain and as head of a prosperous New York law firm did not distinguish him markedly from the Republican philosophy. Democratic use of Governor C. W. Bryan of Nebraska, brother of the Great Commoner, as vice presidential candidate did not give weight to an evasive platform.

The Republicans confidently nominated Coolidge, using the wealthy Chicago banker and reparations commissioner, C. G. Dawes, as running mate. Their platform enjoyed normal ambiguity. Coolidge rested comfortably in the belief that Theodore Roosevelt had destroyed special privilege. Senator La Follette, who had conclusively demonstrated that special privilege was more active than heretofore, had organized the "Conference for Progressive Political Action" in 1922 and now ran on a clear reform platform. His running mate was the Democratic chairman of the Senate committee which exposed Teapot Dome, B. K. Wheeler.

The majority of voters was not excited over honesty in government. Lawlessness was flourishing. Homicides were reaching the world's highest total. All classes were speculating on the main chance. La Follette could not divert them from money-making to social problems and he got little more than half as many votes as Davis, who got little more than half as many as Coolidge. Only about 52% of the electorate bothered to vote. But the congressional picture revealed a background of ferment in the hinterland: the Republican Senate majority was cut to twelve and the House majority to sixty.

The Coolidge administration's objective was prosperity—in the narrow sense of the term. It came fortuitously, as proved by its evaporation under Hoover. Since the Republicans did not make their definition broad enough to embrace the unskilled masses, and since they stressed urban at the expense of rural needs, they satisfied neither labor nor agriculture. Those factions fostered a degree of insurgency in Congress which threatened to give their lobbyists the balance of power. This soon forced the Republicans to restore the La Follette faction to party standing and patronage privileges, in the effort to become the actual as well as the titular controlling party. Yet the political balance remained artificial, with economic realities continually breaking party lines. Coolidge often was disregarded by Congress and "normalcy" legislation was mitigated to pacify dissentients.

The Republicans assumed full credit for the unprecedented increase in the national wealth and the phenomenal rise in the standard of living; and they would have nominated in 1928 their curious symbol of lush, vociferous prosperity—the abstemious, frugal and reputedly taciturn Coolidge—if he had not declared "I do not choose to run." This cryptic announcement enabled the ex-mining engineer and current Secretary of Commerce, Herbert Hoover, to capture the Republican convention. His management of relief abroad and at home had endeared him to the humanitarians; his adaptation of departmental machinery to the needs and ambitions of big business had established him in the affections of that class; his financial success and reputed efficiency had earned him the admiring respect of that majority of Americans who shared the ideals of Horatio Alger's heroes. His departmental office had been used as a sounding board.

Secretary Hoover campaigned on pledges of government aid to further prosperity, against the more liberal candidate of the Democracy, Gov. Al Smith, whose progressive leadership in New York indicated a broad understanding of modern governmental and financial problems and who campaigned on honest government. Both the major parties used platitudinous platforms and enjoyed financial endorsement from big business, especially as Smith denied low tariff sympathies and was known by his closest intimates to be untainted with radicalism. Both had ample recourse to the radio.

But Smith's rise from the streets of New York, his Tammany connections, his Roman Catholic faith, his unpolished manners and his frankly wet position alienated voters outside urban areas of the Northeast. This, in spite of equipping him with Senator Robinson of Arkansas as running mate. The revived Ku Klux Klan still had vast political power in the South and West for exploiting the latest post-war reaction against tolerance. It had less excuse than the Klan of the 'seventies and found its greatest satisfactions in attacking persons of Catholic, Jewish and radical beliefs. It had helped to prevent Smith's nomination in 1924. In 1928 it helped to divert attention from serious problems to a "whispering campaign" which increased the number voting by about 23% and gave Hoover 21,000,000 votes and 40 states as against 15,000,000 and 8 states for Smith.[1]

In the last analysis, however, the "stock-market prosperity" of 1928 was little encouragement to a change of labels; the Republican Senate majority rose to 15 and House majority to 101. The significance of the election of independents in such areas as Minnesota, Nebraska, New Mexico, North Dakota, Washington and Wisconsin was briefly over-looked. Hoover set out to advance the prosperity principle with more humanitarianism and less frugality than his popular predecessor, unthink-ing that a panic might wreck his hopes and self-assurance. He subscribed to the conservative Republican doctrine that each American citizen remains pretty well able to look after himself as an individual; but that national welfare occasionally requires government to extend a helping hand to organized industry.

Demobilizing Veterans

Congress also acted on the principle that it need attend to aiding but a few elements in the nation. After the war ended, first and most press-ing attention had had to be given to the elements requiring demobiliza-tion:—to the men, women and transportation units (railroads, steam-ships and airplanes) awaiting release from the gigantic war machine organization and freedom to pursue peacetime vocations.

Other governments had been studying demobilization ever since early in the war in order to cushion the shock of the end of the conflict. But the Wilson administration had been so engrossed in the League objec-tive that the armistice came without due preparation. After some delay, the 4,000,000 soldiers and sailors and the 11,400,000 civilian workers connected with the military machine were turned loose—mostly to fend for themselves.

Similarly, factory production and employments had to wrench them-selves back to peacetime markets with little government aid. Congress hastily repealed war legislation, abolishing emergency powers and boards

---

[1] The religious issue and the radio were two of many factors which brought an extraordinary proportion of voters to the polls:—

Republicans	Democrats	Socialists		% of Electorate Voting
1920 Harding & Coolidge 16,000,000	Cox & Roosevelt 9,000,000	Debs & Stedman 900,000		52.4
1924 Coolidge & Dawes 15,700,000	Davis & Bryan 8,400,000		Progressives LaFollette & Wheeler 4,800,000	50.1
1928 Hoover & Curtis 21,000,000	Smith & Robinson 15,000,000			67.5

without regard to possible usefulness of some of them to post-war America. Most of the guidance government had given industry and labor was summarily withdrawn, notably the United States employment service (in July 1919) just when a tremendous field of usefulness was opening up before it.[1] Contracts for goods were cancelled, manufacturers reimbursed for contract losses, and millions of dollars worth of excess, government-owned materials were sold (largely in France) at mere fractions of cost.

Not as summary was the treatment of the war veterans. A few American officers and men in Paris early in 1919 determined that they should not get off to the slow start of the G.A.R. after the war between the States, and that the current low state of soldier morale should not lead to a radical organization. From a St. Louis convention of the following May, therefore, emerged the American Legion, destined to become a strong force in American politics; other ex-soldiers formed the less aggressive Veterans of Foreign Wars. The early emphasis was placed on compensation for the disabled to whom Congress granted liberal appropriations for pensions, hospitalization and rehabilitation. Next, unmaimed veterans, who came home to find their places in industry taken by other persons (who had received wages of $10 a day while the drafted soldiers were being paid $30 a month) were eagerly organized into a movement for "adjusted" compensation—that is, the bonus. They demanded that the difference in recompense be made up to them, and some 17 state legislatures appropriated modest funds for this purpose. These varied between ten and thirty dollars for each month of service.

The campaign for bigger grants on a national scale secured the passage in 1922 of a law for a $50 grant, which Harding vetoed. Coolidge was no more sympathetic, but in 1924 an endowment insurance measure was enacted over his veto, specifying a bonus of $1.25 a day for overseas service and $1.00 a day for home service. 3,500,000 men thus were made eligible for a gift averaging $1000, payable in 1945. Significantly, the law made no provision for supplying or accumulating the funds to make this payment. Veterans became impatient and demanded the right to cash their policies—in greenbacks; the inflationary aspect of this proposition was apparently the only thing which prevented its enactment in 1929.

After two years of depression, the veterans secured the right to borrow money from the government up to one-half the face value of their policies. As unemployment and distress deepened, they descended upon Washington and Congress early in the summer of 1932, reaching the capital by every known means, including the capture of freight trains.

[1] An "Industrial Board" under W. C. Redfield could not succeed in an atmosphere of complete unsettlement and without congressional cooperation.

This type of efficiency organization did not appeal to President Hoover who sent troops with guns and tear gas bombs down Pennsylvania Avenue to dislodge the "army" and burn the unsightly, unsanitary shack villages which they had set up in the capital to house themselves. A nation which was inclined to question the importunity of the American Legion lobby deplored the President's ineptitude and the bonus agitation thereby was strengthened, although it, too, was left for the next administration to satisfy.

Economic Demobilization

Other problems of post-war immediacy which pressed upon Congress were transportation, tariff, agriculture and industry. Transportation first received minute attention, for the far-flung nation was dependent upon it. First came the railroads, still the main reliance for transporting people and freight, comprising one-tenth the national wealth and with their stocks and bonds still the most important single group of American securities. It was common knowledge that war-time costs, competition from trolleys and government-aided canals, and restrictions imposed by government and labor had cut net profits. Worst was the competition from trucks and buses, for congressional appropriations helped build and maintain heavy-traffic, cross-continental roads, which localities alone could not support.

It was scarcely realized that railroad mileage had reached the saturation point—with more miles abandoned than built, since 1916. Thoughtless persons assumed that return to private control would restore rail prosperity, although permeating and rapid change in conditions dictated drastic reorganization.

The railroad brotherhoods and the A.F. of L. endorsed a "Plum Plan" for government purchase, with lease to a management composed equally of workers, railroad officials and presidential appointees. The operators, fearing government ownership, offered to accept more supervision. President Wilson opposed a peacetime trial of government operation and set 1 March 1920 as the date for return to private ownership. Congress hurried to provide legislation by 28 February.

The terms of the Esch-Cummins law revealed the assumptions held by the three parties at interest in the compromise, with none completely satisfied. The act returned the railroads to private ownership and control, and granted a temporary guarantee of 6% net profits, half the excess to be devoted to a revolving fund for the benefit of weak lines, under a "recapture" clause. It stipulated a Railway Labor Board to arrange agreements, and gave the Interstate Commerce Commission expanded powers over rates, service, traffic, trackage, profits, finance and consolidation.

As applied by the Commission and courts, the new law most favored the operators. The Commission granted increases in rates from 25% to 50% and in wages only to about 22%. The Railway Labor Board failed to prevent a shopmen's strike of 1922, proved ineffective and was replaced in 1926 by arbitration boards, with which the government had very little to do. The capture clause would not work and was repealed. On the question of the basis for estimating net profits, the Commission argued for 1914 reproduction costs; the operators demanded 1920 figures (which would help care for watered stock); the Supreme Court adopted the latter.[1]

Both Commission and courts reversed the trend of the Northern Securities decision, by encouraging, even urging, consolidation of lines and systems—to a point beyond the then desires of the operators themselves. By 1928, 6,000 lines had been reduced to about 800. By 1930, the railroad operators were proposing consolidation of all northeastern lines into four systems:—the Pennsylvania, Baltimore and Ohio, New York Central and Chesapeake and Ohio; but the depression prevented it.

Of almost equal interest was the merchant marine, for the war had shown the nation the need for a permanent merchant fleet auxiliary to the navy, arousing national pride in one. It had taught the farmers their dependence upon merchantmen, moderating their ancient antipathy to subsidies. After bitter dispute, Congress decided to sponsor both public and private ownership and operation. So the Jones Merchant Marine Act of 1920 authorized the Shipping Board to sell government-owned vessels to private corporations controlled by American citizens, to loan money to companies following new trade routes marked out by the Board and to operate unsold ships. Various ancient and dubious devices such as mail-carrying subsidies, preferential tariffs patterned after a 1789 act, and colonial carrying restrictions in imitation of 18th century mercantilism were authorized. The government guaranteed coverage of losses on new routes. Many vessels were sold at $2\frac{1}{2}\%$ of their cost, and the Shipping Board's annual deficit averaged over $142,000,000. Yet in eight years America's percentage of foreign commerce fell from 42.7 to 32.2.

Considerable sentiment arose for a government-owned marine, but Congress fell back again upon the more familiar line of least resistance— lavish subsidy to private capital. Under the Jones-White Act of 1928 the government paid and paid:—for water mail-carrying more than sixty times its estimated actual cost; construction loans—for displacing out-moded vessels with Diesel-driven ships—generous in amount and low in interest; half the salary of naval officers serving in the merchant marine. One-half the crew now could be foreigners, ineligible for the higher wages compulsory under the La Follette Act. The government

[1] St. Louis and O'Fallon Railway Co. v. U.S., 279 US 461 (1929).

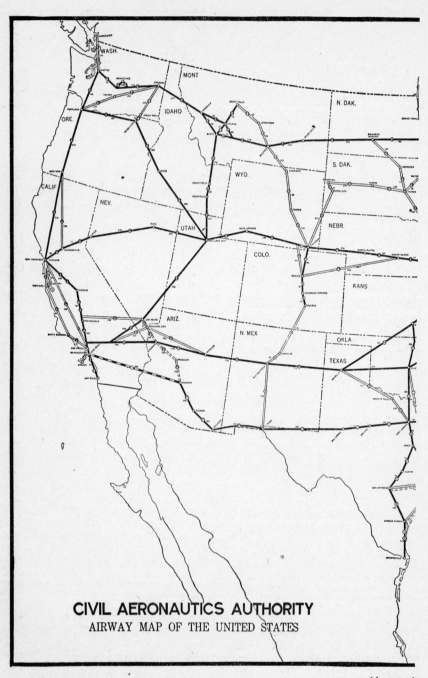

CIVIL AERONAUTICS AUTHORITY
AIRWAY MAP OF THE UNITED STATES

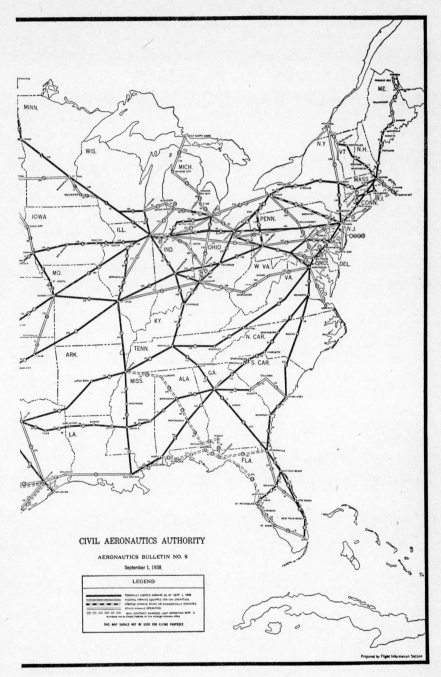

CIVIL AERONAUTICS AUTHORITY

AERONAUTICS BULLETIN NO. 8

September 1, 1938

LEGEND

FEDERALLY LIGHTED AIRWAYS AS OF SEPT. 1, 1938
FEDERAL AIRWAYS EQUIPPED FOR DAY OPERATION
LIGHTED AIRWAYS STATE OR COMMERCIALLY OPERATED
OTHER AIRWAYS OPERATING
MAIL CONTRACT AWARDED (NOT OPERATING SEPT 1)
Numbers not on straight airways are line mileage between cities

THIS MAP SHOULD NOT BE USED FOR FLYING PURPOSES

Prepared by Flight Information Section

September, 1938

engaged to operate unprofitable lines until they paid and then to turn them over to private companies. In spite of all this, marine subsidy was more than offset by a trade-killing tariff policy and proved a pitiable failure.

Subsidy to aviation also became an accepted policy. The war had reminded Americans of the military uses of planes while exposing their deficiencies in construction and personnel. The public imagination was caught by pioneer trans-oceanic flights—the first across the Atlantic in 1919, to the North Pole in 1926 and C. A. Lindbergh's solo flight to Paris in 1927. Municipalities eagerly assumed costs of airport construction. Private capital became interested in the industry as it entered the phase of profitable commercial development, and obtained (in 1925) a law authorizing transfer of air mail to private lines.

The sympathy of the Hoover administration for subsidies and elimination of competition prospered legitimate and illegitimate promoters of aviation, who gratefully contributed to Republican campaigns. Exposure of gross abuses waited until 1934 when a Democratic investigating committee and depression psychology sharpened the public conscience. Then President Roosevelt cancelled exhorbitant private contracts, only to prove that army fliers, ill-equipped and inexperienced as mail carriers, cracked up under bad flying conditions. A special investigation of army aviation intervened, while the mail business was returned to private companies— although under a chastened scale of bidding.

Thus, with aviation as with shipping, railroads and veterans, Congress hastened to rid itself of demobilization problems, without much thought for others to follow. Subsequent legislation had to be piecemeal, because it evolved from compulsory situations. Long range planning again proved itself contrary to the spirit of the post-war period.

CHAPTER XXXVII

THE SAD STATE OF AGRICULTURE AND THE BUDGET

The postwar problems of which Congress never succeeded in ridding itself were the financing of agriculture and government. Agriculture, particularly, went completely out of line with the dominant prosperity trend, taxing the comprehension of presidents, congresses and the farmers themselves.

Agriculture without a Share in Prosperity

Agriculture was descending from its high estate as the occupation of chief importance in America. It had developed food resources for a fast-growing nation, supplied exports to bring in foreign capital, provided half the railroad freight and furnished a growing market for manufactured goods. It had attracted immigrants, produced the nation's leaders and many of its laborers, taken back the unemployed in hard times, and operated with and without profit in good years and bad. Yet that quarter of the nation which depended directly on agriculture had won the least profits from war "prosperity" and got the least benefit from the "prosperity" of the 'twenties.

"Normalcy" escaped them quite. The industry had always known chronic instability, chronic speculation, individualism and waste; now its distress became chronic, notably in the North Central States which had known steady well-being. The 'twenties saw a decrease in the number of farm owners, farms, farm animals, total value of farm lands and acres in cultivation;[1] an increase in the number of non-producing (absentee) land owners and renters, in the size of farms, freight and tax loads, and in outstanding mortgage debts. Readjustments demanded by changing dress and food habits were painful; wool and cotton lost ground to silk and rayon; meat, potatoes and grain to fruit, milk and sugar.

The overhead in interest payments, machinery prices, freights and wages kept up, while crop prices fluctuated (usually downward), swelling the portion of farm return which went to non-farmers, destroying the margin between income and outgo. At the same time the farmers wanted to advance their standard of living in line with that of city dwellers. Debts incurred lightly to "tide over" one bad year could not

---

[1] From 1910 to 1920 the value of farm property rose 90%, then declined over 26% from 1920 to 1930, and by 1933 reached a level under that of 1910.

be discharged under the heavier conditions of the next, even with the aid of special concessions under the Federal Reserve Law. Federal farm loan banks, established under a law of 1916, held only a tiny percentage of the mortgages. Farmers' local banks, state institutions in small towns, went down with them.

To this unhappy situation many powerful factors contributed. Most of them may be grouped under (1) over-emphasis upon productive efficiency and (2) neglect of marketing efficiency.

Mechanization—meaning use of such things as tractors, trucks, automobiles, improved planting machinery, combined harvesters, stationary

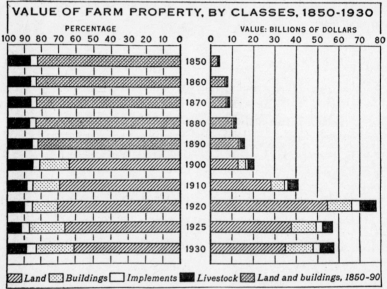

From United States Department of Agriculture.

gas engines and electric power—had encouraged a technical efficiency which defeated its own object, benefiting consumers and middlemen while jeopardizing the producer. The machinery which the farmer found so useful raised competition against him—it released for human food production perhaps 30,000,000 acres formerly needed to feed draft horses and mules; it enticed distant areas into production by bringing them closer to railheads and marketing centers; it encouraged experiments in tilling uncertain regions ill adapted by soil and climate to tillage; it destroyed fertility in a mad rush for immediate profits. Also entire families—fathers, mothers and children—competed enthusiastically in meat, milk and egg production campaigns. The war accentuated their preoccupation with production, removing the last vestiges of caution on raising their capital investment and obligations farther above their normal carrying power.

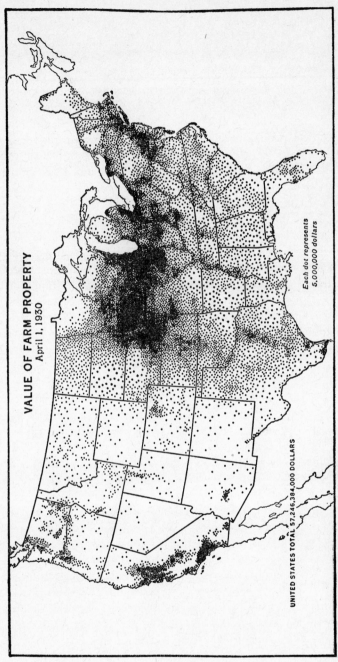

VALUE OF FARM PROPERTY
April 1, 1930

Each dot represents
5,000,000 dollars

UNITED STATES TOTAL 57,246,384,000 DOLLARS

From United States Department of Agriculture.

On the other hand, their marketing inefficiency had not received adequate attention. The Department of Agriculture's Bureau of Markets had continued its spadework; the farmers' cooperatives had grown strong enough to secure exemption from the anti-trust restrictions of the Clayton Act, and permission had been granted farmers (as well as manufacturers) to form export trade associations.[1] But control in agriculture remained absent. The ending of the war opened their eyes. Farmers found their power of production had outstripped peace-time consumption. With machine aid they had increased their crops and reduced farm jobs only to see the demand for American foodstuffs fall and the demand for jobs rise. America in 1870 required two workers out of every four to produce food; in 1920 but one. All governments were entering upon stricter regulation of commerce, thereby reducing world trade. Retaliatory tariffs, manipulated currencies, discriminatory devices and monopolies were giving the 20th century an economic pattern in which control dominated—a pattern into which competitive, individualistic agriculture could not fit. Also national self-sufficiency programs, with their emphasis on managed currency, and the substitution of barter for international trade under the old gold standard, revolutionized world economy. The basic readjustment necessary for agriculture would be hard to make. Sharing prostration, could farmers unite for prosperity? Could they control farming?

Those agriculturists who studied marketing from the narrow angle of domestic prices and who realized that the United States was following the world trend toward economic nationalism, sought control through crop reduction. This principle made headway fastest in the cotton country. There expanding acreage tended to depress prices whenever the boll weevil and bad weather did not intervene; prosperity often eluded the planter, whether the crop yields were good or poor. Slumps were worst when other factors, such as the outbreak of war in 1914 and the postwar deflation in 1920, helped to lower prices. Leadership in the search for relief originated among specialists, local, state and federal, familiar with areas hardest hit. Some suggested reviving compulsory devices of crop reduction used in the Confederacy, but they could not move a large following. The day of a south-wide plan for compulsory acreage reduction was not yet. Even "voluntary" acreage reduction was obtainable only at times and in spots, particularly when credit was withheld for that purpose by bankers and merchants, or when campaigns of education and house-to-house canvasses for pledges were conducted, much after the manner of the Liberty Loan drives.

Such voluntary efforts, when seconded by acute lack of funds for planting and by erratic weather, effected reduced yields. Acreage reductions of approximately 14% and 15% helped improve planter status

[1] Under the Webb-Pomerene Act of 1918.

in 1915 and 1921. It was a Cotton Emergency Committee, appointed by Coolidge, which formulated the Intermediate Credits Act [1] two years later. In 1926 a Southwide conference for reduction was achieved, with fourteen states drawn into varying degrees of cooperation; and other conferences followed. The make-up of state and local committees in the movement became significant. Besides farmers, state agricultural officials and county bureau agents, the committees included bankers, merchants, chamber of commerce leaders and superintendents of education. Fields of cooperative agitation broadened to include such things as diversified feed and money crops, and compulsory school attendance (for children had been producing and gathered 25% of the cotton crop). Patently, cotton difficulties were taking the leaders of the most conservative agricultural section of the United States along radical paths. A marked change was coming in the southern planters' concept of governmental functions.

Farmer Lobby Achievements

Meanwhile, the national government was being asked to practice in the fields of agriculture such skills as it knew for balancing production and consumption. An emergency law of 1920 re-established the War Finance Corporation as an aid to credits and exports. There followed a decade of struggle to make agriculture a united, national force, with lobby influence commensurate to that of industry and labor, potent to devise a program and legislate it into existence.

Expert instruction in the art of high pressure politics soon was offered farmers. The war had stimulated the agricultural colleges and the federal Department of Agriculture to integrate their extension activities through organization of farm bureaus—clubs of farmers united in local groups, for education in improved production. The bureaus could demand public and private contributions in a manner impossible to the older farm groups—the Grange, Equity, and Farmers' Union—for the latter were secret, class and commercial organizations ineligible for tax money and weighted down by accumulated jealousies and personal, sectional and religious connotations.

So the farm bureaus had received help from federal and state funds, under the Smith-Lever Act of 1914, and further appropriations under the Emergency Food Production Act of 1917. In each county the farm bureau agent became a familiar and influential figure and the bureau became the local medium for farmers' social and economic activities. Formation of state federations followed; and finally with a national

---

[1] An intermediate credit bank was established in each federal land bank district to provide credits between the short term (commercial) loans and long term (land mortgage) loans.

organization—the American Farm Bureau Federation founded in 1919—
the educational extension program of the Department of Agriculture
appeared to have come into full power.

Then came the hard times of 1920. Farmers losing foreign purchasers
of their surplus became vitally concerned in debt servicing, distribution,
limitation of production and enlargement of legislative influence. The
Federation, against the wishes of a minority, shifted emphasis from education for efficient production to legislation for restoring profits. It
soon become spokesman for the farmers' economic interests, in dealing
with other groups and with the government. It set up its own permanent

From Sioux City *Tribune*.

Congressional Farm Bloc Takes Aim

secretariat in Washington, where three other farm organizations already
had established lobbies as an outgrowth of the war.[1] The existence of
their Washington offices tended to focalize the work of the executive
committees of the various organizations. They conferred, and formulated
individual and joint programs for congressional action. The Washington
office of the Federation hatched farm blocs in both houses and energized
them with polls of constituent opinion, obtained through the local
bureaus.

County bureaus multiplied rapidly during the 'twenties—under tutelage from the States Relation Service of the Department [2]—and expanded their functions from education into cooperative buying and
selling. Meanwhile at Washington the Department increased its economic usefulness by consolidating (1 July 1922) its marketing, crop
estimating, farm management and farm economics functions into one

[1] A Washington office was established by the National Board of Farm
Organizations in 1917, the left wing Farmers' National Council 1918, the
National Grange 1919.

[2] The States Relations Service circulated *Document 65*, on how to organize
a model farm bureau; most of the states of the East and Middle West and
a few of the Far West established bureaus, under various patterns.

"Bureau of Agricultural Economics." Coordination of Washington efforts, between the Department and the Federation, was increased by the fact that constant lobby watchfulness was essential; the major work of the Department was not carried on under legal authorization of permanent laws, but depended for continuance upon annual appropriations, affecting espécially agricultural experiments, education and investigation.

The ranks of farm lobbyists were strengthened by the energetic county agents trained in the nip and tuck of local farm bureau work, close to the earth and to human nature. They helped to give agricultural influence on Capitol Hill a continuity and force never previously maintained. Thus "organized agriculture" became a reality.

The objectives, strength and mode of operation of the farm lobby of course varied from time to time. The farm bloc first emphasized marketing and credit curatives, employing the filibuster as a weapon. President Harding had to promise far-reaching legislation to Gray Silver—chief Federation representative in Washington—before the Senate farm bloc would permit Congress to adjourn in 1921. The promise materialized as a Packer and Stockyards Act (1921), a Grain Futures Trading Act (1922), an Intermediate Credits Act (1923) and amendments to the federal Farm Loan Law. These laws prohibited unfair and deceptive practices by packers, commission merchants and brokers. The credits acts aimed to stabilize the market by adjusting short term credit facilities to the turnover in crops and to variations in livestock production.[1]

These domestic devices, however, could not bring prosperity to farmers raising surpluses which the world would not buy at American prices; the tariff was useless for that 85% of farm production which raised surpluses. A plow manufacturer, President George N. Peek of the Moline Plow Company, decided that the government must restore the farmer's purchasing power by compensating for export losses. He proposed a government corporation, to buy the most important surpluses and sell them abroad at world prices, the cost to be met by a levy (called an "equalization fee") against the commodities thus marketed. This device was supposed to keep prices up and make the tariff effective.

After wheat sank to new lows in 1923 the Department of Agriculture and wheat growers took up the scheme, which came to be called the McNary-Haugen plan, after the Oregon senator and Iowa representative who introduced in 1924 the first bill embodying Peek's idea. Three similar bills followed in 1926, 1927, 1928, while the corn belt joined the wheat-growers, securing Middle West control of the Federa-

---

[1] The Intermediate Credits Act set up intermediate credit banks supervised by the farm loan system, authorized national agricultural credit corporations, liberalized the agricultural functions of the Federal Reserve System and prolonged the life of the War Finance Corporation.

tion which then actively pushed the plan. Southern opposition was dented and tobacco cooperatives converted.

Five years of hard campaigning made it possible to pass through Congress in 1927 and 1928 the third and fourth McNary-Haugen bills, both of which were opposed by non-farming consumers and vetoed by Coolidge. He also killed a Norris bill for the manufacture of fertilizer at the government-owned, hydro-electric plant of Muscle Shoals, Alabama. Unwilling to give agriculture the outright subsidies granted transportation, he endorsed palliative devices; also he signed a Mississippi Valley Flood Control bill on which agriculture presented a united front, and a Boulder Dam power measure.

Enlistment of the Federation in a project lacking united agricultural support had destroyed farm-bloc solidarity in the sense of 1921-1923 and turned the Federation from a diverse program to a particularized one. Storming of Capitol Hill by the leaders of the McNary-Haugen project had greatly enlarged farm lobby ranks. Both major parties had to do lip service to agricultural surpluses during the campaign of 1928, when the veteran McNary-Haugen lobbyists bolted the Republican party, only to be ostracized by Hoover's victory. The Senate insurgents proceeded to re-name the plan the "export debenture," cut its amount by about 50% and placed the direct cost on the Treasury. Hoover defeated them, saying the government should not buy, sell and fix prices of products.

The reduced-purchasing-power aspect of the farm problem so impressed him, however, that he urged erection of a Federal Farm Board which did these very things. Congress established one, under an Agricultural Marketing Act passed in special session June, 1929, and it bought, sold and fixed prices of grain, cotton, livestock and other things —through cooperatives and stabilization corporations. It strenuously urged voluntary crop reduction while spending hundreds of millions in a contradictory emphasis upon credit and further production. Whatever chance this law might have had for success was offset by the atrocious tariff of 1930, which was first proposed as a measure limited to agricultural relief but ultimately emerged as an effective instrument for destruction of trade. Against it, a new "foreign agricultural service," also part of the 1930 legislation, could make slight headway.

Then followed the 1930 drought, reducing corn, hay and other yields (wheat slightly) but leaving the accumulated surplus still too large for notable price increases. Congress continued at cross purposes, making lavish appropriations the next year for more production and for voluntary crop reduction; and added to these some additional credits under the 1932 Reconstruction Finance Corporation. Still agriculture could not rise and prosper. Organized capital and labor at home kept their power to raise the domestic price of what farmers had to buy; abroad new areas of cultivation and programs for national self-sufficiency further reduced the market and price for what farmers had to sell.

Their reserve resources against the impact of panic and depression had been pretty thoroughly destroyed before the rest of the nation became aware of the impermanence of prosperity. Then between 1929 and 1933 their share of the national income shrank from 15% to 7% and their purchasing power, in terms of their own products, fell nearly 40%. When the F. D. Roosevelt administration came in, it found the farm surplus an acknowledged government obligation; dumped on its doorstep was the terrific problem of balancing farm production with world consumption. With its solution the political fate of the Democrats would be intimately connected.

The Stubborn Budget

Less stubborn than agriculture but no less significant, as a test of how to apply democratic theory and practice in an age of mechanization and monopoly, was the problem of government funds—taxation and the tariff. For even prosperity must be financed.

Somewhere, somehow, the United States had to find new, peacetime, money and credit; else it could not liquidate the expenses of the foreign war, or finance such expanding domestic obligations as subsidies to agriculture, transportation and the veterans. Added to these were new local costs, born of the changing national economy and unloaded upon the federal shoulders because too unwieldy for cities, counties and states to handle. The heaviest tribute went to wars, past and future, covering army, navy, World War debts and veterans; but spending for constructive, social objects also increased. A car-conscious people multiplied their outlays on highways four thousand times between 1916 and 1930. They trebled their educational expenditure over the nation in the two decades following 1916. They inaugurated costly programs of flood control, dams and waterways. Their income never overtook their outgo; per capita debt in America stood at 9.88 in 1914—$228 at the war's close, $134 by 1930. Behind those violent fluctuations is an interesting story.

Long since, John Marshall said that "the power to tax is the power to destroy"; he might well have added "the power to tax is the power to construct." Secretaries of the Treasury, A. W. Mellon (1921-1932) and Ogden Mills (1932-1933) were acutely conscious of the first principle. Mr. Mellon in 1921 found the well-to-do—those paying income and inheritance taxes—supplying about one-half the national revenue; he devoted himself to reducing their taxation, by legislation and refunds, on the theory that as the wealthy prosper they send prosperity trickling down to the masses.

The second principle animated the hopes and ambitions of little citizens and their representatives who hoped to construct a new order for the poor; resistance from them and inexorable world trends retarded full fruition of Mellonism. As the world's postwar emphasis upon national self-sufficiency was making the customs income grossly inadequate and as prohibition destroyed income from liquor, voters with a progressive heritage struggled to shift the burdens and benefits of new taxes. The battle raged over reductions from the wartime levies on wealth and competence; over surtaxes and taxes on excess profits, corporation income, estates, gifts and inheritances; over exemptions on basic income, earned income, income from government securities and salaries; over exemption of income of religious, charitable, scientific, literary, educational, and labor groups and agricultural cooperatives; over taxation of the poor through nuisance and sales taxes; over evasions and publication of tax returns.

The war had furnished a powerful impetus to multiplication of levies; and some old Progressives argued that high income taxes should be retained, because Europe ultimately would default on her indebtedness to the United States and leave Americans to make up the money she owed. But the vast majority of taxpayers cherished the theory that Europe would pay, and forbade Congress to forgive the debt. It amounted to approximately 10.5 billions, over 7 billions loaned the Allies for war purposes after America entered the struggle, and some 3.25 billions loaned for reconstruction purposes after the armistice, to various governments, new and old, including erstwhile enemies.

The victorious debtors undertook to find the money in Germany, levying against her an overwhelming reparations fine of 33 billions—on the curious theories that one power could be solely to blame for the war and that an impoverished and disabled nation could pay a staggering debt. From her they in time collected about three times as much as they repaid to the United States. Badly confused by postwar economic readjustments, all the powers were blindly rushing into extreme, nationalistic devices, rearming and erecting tariff and exchange barriers which strangled the international trade they needed to revive. The debtors felt slight moral obligation to pay America, insisting that "Uncle Shylock" ought to forgive the debts and certainly could expect only fractional payment.

Americans divided. Capitalists who wished to profit by new reconstruction flotation of foreign securities, industrialists and exporters eager for trade, protected industries fearful of payment in competing goods, and some humanitarians and economists conversant with the economic realities of the situation, were among the classes tolerant of cancellation. The citizenry by and large, however, agreed with Coolidge that "they hired the money" and insisted that political platforms and congressional policy should stick to the theory of payment. They felt no responsibility for making payment practically possible:—either by lowering tariff barriers, (for that would have increased unemployment), or by expanding marine use of foreign facilities (instead they further subsidized their own), or by encouraging, instead of practically ending, immigration. American investors did, however, buy lavishly of foreign securities with government encouragement until 1929, so that thus long some payments continued and the assumption persisted that the debts would be paid. Their purchases in German securities (private and public), were greater than the total of reparations Germany paid to all the powers.

There was sufficient recognition of the real situation in the United States for Congress to establish a World War Foreign Debt Commission, which between 1922 and 1930 made agreements with 15 of the 20 debtor nations for payments, over a 62-year period, at interest varying with supposed ability to pay, from .4% to 3.3%. But America admitted no connection between reparations and debts owed her; and after France in 1923 made a futile effort to secure unobtainable reparations by re-occupation of the Ruhr, Europe established two successive bodies under American chairmanship, the Dawes Commission of 1924 and the Owen D. Young Commission of 1928, to amortize payments. Both pared them down, neither plan worked, and the unofficial suggestion of the latter, that reparations be scaled down in relation to reduction of the debt owed America, was politically unacceptable at home.

The depression, however, forced President Hoover to issue in 1931 a one-year moratorium, applied to both debts and reparations, and to call on Europe to devise a new expedient. At Lausanne the next year Belgium, Britain, France, Italy and Japan agreed with Germany to reduce her reparations to 2% of the original sum and to accept that small payment in German bonds. The United States Congress could not follow suit, and therefore, after a few "token" payments, by December of 1933 all governments except Finland were in default. A resentful Congress would respond, as will be explained (p. 741) with the Johnson act embargoing further loans to defaulting nations.

But in the meantime, domestic tax legislation of the twenties was predicated upon the assumption that the foreign debt would be paid. This made it easier to get through Congress laws for reduction of income taxes. Consequently, although incomes rose between 1920 and 1929 to fantastic figures, the federal receipts from income taxes fell from 4 billions to 2.3 billions. Less than 40% of the corporations reporting in 1930 paid taxes. Outstanding federal indebtedness meanwhile was reduced from 24 billions to 17 billions. Such a record might have amazed John Sherman and other Treasury secretaries who together liquidated the Civil War in twenty years; but Secretary Mellon, more than they, had won assurance and optimism from phenomenal success. His rules of safe practice were those acquired in the game of corporation finance as played most successfully early in the twentieth century.

Tax Reduction

Tax legislation and litigation of 1921-1929 proceeded largely upon Mellon's comfortable assumptions. In 1921, although the corporate income tax was increased, the surtax was reduced and excess profits levy repealed. In 1923 the Supreme Court ruled that stock dividends were not taxable; this helped to halve income tax receipts. In 1924 the low-exemption levels were raised, the normal tax and surtax were reduced and earned income partly rebated; the same Congress, however, raised the tax on estates and invented a new levy on money gifts—which last the Supreme Court invalidated.

Full congressional acceptance of the Mellon thesis was indicated two years later, in much wider relief for wealth on surtax and estate levies, in another rise of the exemption level, and in a retroactive repeal of the gift tax. Such policies were further pursued in 1928 and 1929, when taxable wealth was at its highest level in American history. The freed funds poured into the stock market, to contribute to a mad orgy of speculation.

Attempts at sanity on debts and taxation were not wholly lacking. Wilson, Harding and Coolidge regularly discussed injection of business methods into governmental practice. The minor depression of 1921 was reflected in a Budget and Accounting Act, designed to restrict expenditures to funds in hand, with the aid of a Budget Bureau.[1] Lawmakers of 1923 and 1930, struggling for business-like efficiency, established a Personnel Classification Board and made the Director of the Budget chairman of it.

These were but weak weapons for slaying the hydra-headed monster of wastefulness which always lies in wait for democracies. A general indifference to government and law ignored gross laxity in tax administration. Each expansion of function admitted untrained personnel. While the politicians remained distrustful of experts, most of the latter indulged their distaste for political sacrifice. The vast majority of voters, being exempt from direct taxation through low incomes, seldom were sufficiently tax-conscious to protest extravagance. A Congress suspicious of tax evasion in 1924 enacted (against Mellon's wishes) a publicity clause; but gross abuse of it brought prompt repeal. Little was accom-

---

[1] The President was to submit a budget of receipts and expenditures for the previous, the present and ensuing year, annually to Congress; and the Budget Bureau was to receive requests for funds. The provisions were in line with a report from an economy and efficiency commission appointed by Taft.

plished to offset deterioration in the practice and personnel of tax collection and expenditure.

Tax evasion flourished, fostered by the speculation rampant in Wall Street and the over-capitalization in industry. Made ingenius by cupidity, people secured tax exemption by giving land to tax-free religious institutions in exchange for annuities; others invested heavily in tax-free securities, set up foreign or "dummy" corporations, made evasive "joint" returns and "wash sales" to relatives. Secretary Mellon and prominent bankers like C. E. Mitchell, J. P. Morgan and Albert Wiggin were among those who later admitted and defended loop-hole exemption, placing the onus on the law-makers.

Exemption and evasion together ruined the effectiveness of the income tax, drove capital out of productive functions and induced extravagance. But repeal of exemption of government securities met strong opposition; it was argued that interest on them must be kept low and that this would be impossible if they were not tax-exempt. Dispute raged over whether they were owned chiefly by low-income persons and charitable institutions or by chronic tax evaders. Evasion, anyhow, did not seem shameful to the majority of the tax-paying classes.

Depression Taxes

During prosperity, the rich seemed to come off best, in the shifting struggle with the poor over incidence of taxation. The depression violently upset all calculations. Little and big governments proved incapable of cutting outgo as low as income. Although local and state units had continued to depend principally upon property taxes, until real estate values collapsed in 1930, twenty of them had tapped incomes. Some had levied on tobacco, chain stores and sales; all were adopting inheritance and estate levies. The loss of liquor taxes, due to prohibition, had encouraged experimental taxation; and the growing complexity of the problem turned towns, cities and counties to the state for a share of its tax returns. The depression brought all these subsidiary units, as well as private persons and businesses to the federal government for succor.

The national treasury was ill-equipped for the emergency. The same policy which had heightened tariff walls, to keep out goods with which the foreigners might have paid some of their debts, cut the customs income available for national support. Duties had fallen from nearly half the revenue in 1903 to less than 15% of it in 1928. War debt payments collapsed in 1931. The income tax failed miserably as a depression source of funds, although Congress in 1930 and 1932 tightened some of the restrictions it had loosened earlier.[1]

[1] Congress abolished exemption on earned income in 1930; in 1932 raised estate and surtaxes and lowered the figure for normal exemption.

All taxing units turned, as in wartime, to common aspects of everyday life for tax funds. They applied nuisance and sales levies to amusements, bank checks, club dues, furs, gifts and stock sales; to automobiles, lubricating oils and tires; to electricity, matches, refrigerators and toilet articles. But through all these taxes restless America paid less than through the one tax on gasoline, applied at first to maintain roads for a nation on the move, and later diverted to a multiplicity of crying needs. By such means the tax officials reached the poorest citizen, and oftener than Mellon would have dreamed. The proportion of the taxes levied indirectly—on all persons regardless of ability to pay—rose from 27% in 1920 to 58% in 1933. Thus, among the issues challenging the incoming administration was the fundamental question:—should the poor constitute the principal support of the government?

Another outstanding proof of congressional misunderstanding of postwar conditions was the tariff, for the extreme protectionism of recent Republican policy conflicted with America's new status as the great, international creditor. Foreign nationals, lacking gold, asked to pay their obligations in the only coin they had—goods; and Wilson repeatedly told Congress in substance, "If we want to sell, we must be prepared to buy." But American labor and manufacturers naturally took fright at the first signs of European payment in imports. What dire things might not happen to domestic industry if Europe dumped her goods?

Against this alarm, the arguments of the creditor interests, who here broke their long-standing alliance with manufacturers' lobbies, did not carry weight. A congressional majority of protectionists from both parties passed an emergency tariff to dam the flood early in 1921, and Wilson vetoed it. Not so Harding, who promptly sent a special message, "It is our purpose to prosper America first," and signed the controverted measure. It had been repassed with the connivance of the farm lobby; they received agricultural increases which committed them to protection without (as the event proved) enabling them to dispose of their surplus.

The next year they contributed votes for a "permanent" schedule—the Fordney-McCumber Law—built higher than the Payne-Aldrich Law, in the effort to shut out the increasingly clamorous foreigner. It utilized the familiar doctrine of "difference in cost of production" to put through a "flexibility" feature, granting the Tariff Commission and the President a 50% leeway for raising or lowering rates to equalize the differences; this resulted chiefly in increases. The bars were the more firmly fastened, by recodification of the rules for tariff administration.

Additional increases in agricultural duties were granted before the elections of 1924 and 1926; but these, like the extreme protective principle generally, failed "to prosper America first." Foreign debtors de-

faulted and trade diminished in both directions. Surplus food and manufactured goods could not be absorbed at home and foreign governments
retaliated sharply to keep them out. Some manufacturers established
foreign branches to escape the retaliation; but the farmers lacked this
release. Insofar as the rates encouraged monopoly they penalized consumers.

These combined consequences raised doubts among economists, international bankers and some labor leaders, as to the sacrosanct nature of
extreme protection. Yet, in spite of serious losses in the Canadian and
Latin American trade, which was so important to the United States,
Hoover's first Congress put through the even higher Hawley-Smoot
tariff of 1930. The protests of over 1000 economists, against paying
political debts of the Republican party with this shortsighted legislation, failed to secure a presidential veto. The depression was still young;
its lesson had not yet borne home upon the electorate—the lesson that
machinery was imperiously commanding governmental practice to adapt
itself to economic change.

Thus the character of much of the statesmanship of the epoch was
demonstrated. It was one of those periods following the high enthusiasm
and concentrated energy of war-making which find the nation in a
reaction against idealism and wherein low standards dominate with
little check.

CHAPTER XXXVIII

MACHINERY TAKES ALL

Machinery was working a fundamental change in American business following the World War. Economic relationships in nearly all industries were revolutionized and their interdependence sharply revealed; but the revelation went almost unheeded—until the depression.

New Strains in Industry

Americans were living in an age of mass production, with nearly 30% of the workers engaged in industrial occupations and by 1930 over one-third of the national income industrial in origin. A market for goods was the continuing necessity for workers, managers, investors, and for all who sold to any of these. Therefore, anything which stopped factory wheels would jeopardize indirectly the food, clothing and shelter of almost everybody. During the 'twenties forces were at work to undermine that market, to diminish the purchasing power of the farmers and city people who bought most of the goods, and the foreigners who took the remainder.

Trade was being hurt, as already noticed, by speculative psychology, a rich man's tax program and a bad tariff policy. Additional serious strain was put upon industry by several less obvious but no less important factors. Among these was the strain of supporting new classes of unemployables, due to a decline in the increase in the birth rate, a trek from the country to the city and a fall in immigration. Between 1920 and 1930, all but about 2,500,000 of the 17,000,000 increase in population was urban. Ambitious country youth transplanted their energies to city activities. The striding influence of the cities would be realized after a reapportionment law of 1929, which based representation upon the 1930 census.

Urban industry had not had to pay for the rearing of labor or for the maintenance of the aged, for they had been left behind, in Europe and in the farming communities, when workers flocked over to American factories. But in the 'twenties industry had to shoulder more of the cost of supporting unemployables, for reduced immigration lowered the percentage of the population which was in its working prime. Immigration laws of 1921, 1922 and 1924, sponsored by labor and by 100% "Americanism," set quota limits:—first at 3% of each country's nationals resi-

THE AMERICAN PEOPLE—
WHAT THEY DO

Each figure represents 1 *million wage earners*

MANUFACTURING
AND MINING— 15 MILLION PEOPLE

TRADE
AND CLERICAL— 10 MILLION PEOPLE

AGRICULTURE
AND FORESTRY— 11 MILLION PEOPLE

TRANSPORTATION &
COMMUNICATION— 4 MILLION PEOPLE

PROFESSIONAL &
PUBLIC SERVICE— 4 MILLION PEOPLE

 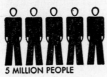

DOMESTIC
AND PERSONAL— 5 MILLION PEOPLE

SOURCE: 1930 CENSUS

Prepared by Pictorial Statistics, Inc., for the Social Security Board.

dent in the United States in 1910; next at 2% of the 1890 number; and from 1929 at a total of 150,000 apportioned by the percentage of each nationality resident in 1920. Since the percentages did not apply on the American continents, the heavy inflow of Mexican adults continued —until executive regulations of 1931 stipulated possession of $1000 as a guarantee against becoming a public charge. Immigration fell from 1901-1910 annual average of about 880,000 to about 411,000 for 1921-1930, and only 35,500 for the depression year of 1932.

Expanding profits, therefore, were required to carry the higher wage

IMMIGRATION SINCE 1820

ORIGIN

Each man represents 30,000 immigrants
From *The United States, A Graphic History,* Hacker, Modley and Taylor, Modern Age Books, Inc.

scales needed to support infants and oldsters. Unfortunately the old, bounding rate of expansion could not be maintained indefinitely; the market ultimately must contract to the slowing down of population increase and to the decline of farmers' purchasing power. These were hard facts, hard to accept.

Furthermore, industry suffered from two drastic kinds of displacement:—displacement of goods and of people.

Displacement of goods destroyed the value of the holdings of all persons engaged in producing those goods. They suffered by increasing substitution of one thing for another and by change of locale. Hay and oats were displaced in part by automotive power; coal in part by oil, water, and gas; cotton by silk and rayon; iron by scrap, etc. Industries migrated within and without the United States. Investments in houses, land, equipment, schools, factories, and churches lost their value when busy industries were silenced and whole towns were abandoned for new sites. Serious displacement in American extractive industries came through foreign competition, particularly noticeable in Russian anthracite and Latin American copper and oil. By 1930 imports of copper reached 98% of exports, of crude oil 70% of exports, with agricultural imports passing exports by $300,000,000.

Displacement of people was even more serious. By 1920 it was clear that in manufactures and minerals machine use had so raised output and reduced jobs that far more was produced than would-be consumers had

OUR AGEING POPULATION

	UNDER 20 YEARS	20-50 YEARS	OVER 50

Each symbol represents 8 per cent of the population

From Hacker, Modley, Taylor, *The United States: A Graphic History,*
Modern Age Books, Inc.

the money to buy. Thus "excess" production, from the sellers' viewpoint, resulted. Machinery raised the productive power of workers and displaced them, particularly in coal, steel, railroading, electric lamp making, clothing and foodstuffs.[1] Some of the victims of this "technological unemployment" found places in mechanized automobile manufacture or in new industries born of the electric stimulus, for electricity spurred invention, investment and a rising standard of living. Use of power was growing three and three-quarters faster than the population.

[1] A steamshovel displaced 199 men out of 200 diggers; a sewing machine, 24 out of 25 clothing makers, a bread-wrapper, 19 out of 20 wrappers, one brickmaker, 725.

But as electricity multiplied the use of machines and the output of individuals, it too displaced workers.

Only a very few leaders appreciated the fact that mass production requires widening of the domestic market if a foreign market fails; nor that a loss in agricultural purchasing power must be compensated for among urban buyers, who are becoming the most important market for American producers. In their study of how to safeguard their profits, the captains of industry had concentrated upon their rivals and their wage bills, to the neglect of their customers; they invented means for keeping prices up and wages down, through elimination of competition and defeat of unions, but gave only superficial study to volume of sales. They were not compelled; national expansion had provided them with a spreading market, postponing a sharp realization that an employee is a consumer. So they poured profits back into plant expansion for more production instead of into wages and lower prices for more consumption.

Stock watering forced production managers who hoped to pay dividends on common either to raise prices or lower wages. War prices largely were retained after income fall set in, until European demand failed in the middle of 1920; by that time public resistance came to a head in buyers' strikes and boycotts, reducing food and clothing prices. With depreciated inventories came wage reductions, countered by an epidemic of strikes. Prices seemed generally adjusted to a lower level by 1924, except in agriculture and a few other directions; but neither capital nor labor could be content with this readjustment or with subsequent, irregular rises. They floundered while a new economic set-up was revolutionizing their status.

Prosperity requires that consumption and production expand simultaneously but between 1919 and 1929 the gap between them widened ominously. While manufacturing output was increasing about 42% real wages in manufacturing were increasing about 15%. The income of the masses was rising less rapidly than that of the rich, until by 1929 the one-tenth percent of American families at the top of the social scale were receiving approximately as much income as the 42% of the families at the bottom of that scale; the latter numbered approximately 12,000,000 families and their annual incomes stood below $1,500. If they could have fulfilled their desires, they would have absorbed an output many times the peak productive output of 1929, for the United States has not yet attained a productive capacity to equal what Americans would like to consume.

Moreover, since approximately 2,000,000 persons and sometimes 4,000,000 remained unemployed during the height of "prosperity," the problem of finding buyers to keep factories operating must become acute. When the unemployed reached 15,000,000, as some estimators counted it in 1932, there would exist a market for perhaps less than half of the potential output of existing establishments. Thus was the process of economic progress retarded by impediments in wealth diffusion. A panic would reveal the desperate need for readjustments between production and consumption; for the direct, material loss, staggering as it was, would prove less than the almost irreparable destruction of human values.

Divisions Among Organized Labor

Organized labor was ill-equipped to see and combat the trend. The aristocratic faction in labor, organized under the A.F. of L., obtained enough wage rises, while prices were going down, to markedly increase

TRADE UNION MEMBERSHIP

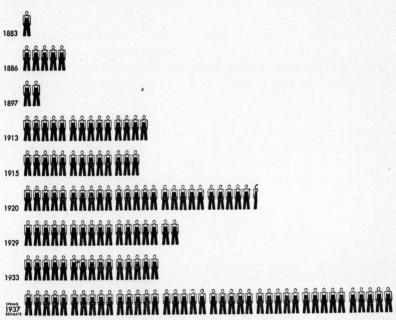

Each man represents 200,000 members — PICTORIAL STATISTICS, INC.

From Hacker, Modley, Taylor, *The United States: A Graphic History,*
Modern Age Books, Inc.

their real wages. They had officially supported the war and otherwise so strengthened their position that their membership grew from 1.6 million in 1910 to about 4 million in 1920, in the midst of an aggressive campaign of strikes. Possessed of property and relatively permanent jobs, their membership as a whole did not care to jeopardize their savings and their influence by close association with the masses of unskilled laborers. Organization of women and children, Negroes and recent immigrants, appeared unprofitable and was long resisted.

Immigration and child labor were in process of reduction, but women workers were increasing until by 1930 over one-fifth of all wage earners were women, with approximately 3% of them estimated as organized. State minimum wage laws helped to raise both the general level of women's wages and the proportion of women getting above minimum wages, but women remained largely employed in low-wage industries under conditions of exploitation where organization was particularly difficult. Negroes—nearly 3 million of them—were moved northward by the postwar agricultural depression and industrial activity. There they acquired the lowest-paid jobs, formerly held by non-voting immigrants, and the ballot. Poor, unlettered, debarred from the A.F. of L. (which might have been unable to organize them if it had tried), they naturally followed radical leadership in labor and politics. They secured the balance of political power in various localities and some became Communists.

While the unskilled massed outside the Federation gates, its leaders clung tenaciously to their narrow craft definition of unionization, a relic from the era of hand labor. Machinery, however, now was making it possible for employers to use an ever increasing proportion of unskilled workers in great industries such as automobiles, oil and steel. Workers there could be organized effectively only as industries—horizontally regardless of particular function—rather than in competing craft groups. Yet hidebound notions continued to control the A.F. of L., which permitted warring crafts to quarrel within industries; they could not see that if they broadened their sympathies they might save their skins.

This aided company executives and radical groups. Capital long since had testified to their fear of expanding unionization; and by now many managers were successfully floating the device of "company unions," especially in the textile and coal industries. The company union gave labor the appearance without the reality of bargaining power. Companies set up unions under employee officers, paid by if not chosen by them; this diverted the natural leaders among employees to managerial functions and sympathies. Isolation was the weapon against solidarity. Just as the feudalistic company town, with its corporation-controlled houses, stores, churches, schools, clubs and (oftentimes) courts kept employees physically isolated from workers in other crafts, so the company unions safeguarded ideological isolation—from fellow-craftsmen under other employers. Spy systems and strict rules against fraternization were maintained to preserve the isolation, which the workers themselves tightened by their suspicion of outside help, especially from northern organizers.

The unskilled barricaded behind the company unions aroused little sympathy from the A.F. of L. but attracted more radical leaders of the unskilled. Ever since the socialists withdrew (in 1895) from the A.F.

of L., leaders like Daniel De Leon, Eugene Debs, St. John, W. E. Trautman and Wm. Z. Foster had been sponsoring various organizations based on the horizontal or industrial union principle. The doctrines of the Socialist Trade and Labor Alliance, the I.W.W., the Western Federation of Miners, the Workers' International Industrial Union, etc., ranged all the long way from Socialism to Anarchism; but frequently they stressed overthrow of the capitalistic system through sympathetic strikes and sabotage spread across all industry.

Gompers' technique was relatively peaceful; it embraced big strike funds and benefits, to finance long, strategic strikes to force employers to make binding agreements for increasing labor's share of the profits. The radicals usually wanted no industrial peace, expensive strikes or binding agreements—but destruction of capitalism itself. Neither was consistent politically; Gompers abandoned his traditional opposition to party affiliation by supporting La Follette in 1924. The Communists, after disrupting the Socialist party in 1919, formed groups of their own, and then determined to bore into the A.F. of L. from within. For this purpose Foster and his following formed the "Trade Union Educational League" to bend the less conservative organized workers in the A.F. of L. toward revolution. Upon the various Communist groups the Communist International forced a united program.

The post war reversion to ultra-conservatism made the 'twenties an anti-labor period, with the government relaxing control and the employers driving for an open shop. Consequently, the continuing fight between the A.F. of L. and the industrial unions was accompanied by the fight of both against capital and unfriendly public sentiment. Among the more important strikes was a Seattle outbreak in February of 1919 when all the city's functions fell into strikers' control and they demonstrated solidarity and capacity for order.

That fall began the third effort of the A.F. of L. to unionize steel; after a titanic struggle at first supported by radical and conservative factions, labor divided, Negro strikebreakers were brought in and charges of communism completed the defeat. Conferences of capital and labor arranged by Wilson failed to reach a solution, and the President went so far in October 1919 as to declare a United Mine Workers strike illegal, on the ground that the United States was still at war. Harding's attorney general, Daugherty, killed a railway shopmen's strike of 1922 with an extraordinarily sweeping injunction. Other big strikes involved the International Typographical Union (1921) and the United Mine Workers (1922).

Defeat and ill repute together reduced Federation membership drastically before Gompers' death, 13 December 1924; and under his successor, William Green, the Federation admitted to membership in 1926 a union organized by communists on an industrial basis—after its out-standing communist leader withdrew.[1] Communists of the Trade Union Educational League, reorganized as the Trade Union Unity League, sponsored between 1925 and 1932 eleven independent unions. The Communists and also the A.F. of L. undertook strikes in various south-ern textile fields. Their desperate struggles at Gastonia, North Carolina, Elizabeth, Tennessee, and Danville, Virginia, at least made southern workers and public aware of the existence of the problem. In the Illinois coal fields during 1931 Communist and Federation factions worked at cross purposes. Mass demonstrations and hunger marches on Washington (more alarming to conservatives than dangerous) marked the Com-munist depression technique.

Defeat seemed the most frequent reward for both craft and industrial union agitation, between the World War and the depression: but there were some gains of note. The effort of the steel workers to get the closed shop moved the Inter-Church World Movement to investigate conditions and their revelations shocked the middle class; an eight-hour day, despite Gary's contention it must ruin steel, came to be successfully substituted for the twelve-hour day. The effort of the coal miners to get a guarantee of permanent employment caused Congress to enlarge the powers of the Interstate Commerce Commission, with the idea of lowering unjust prices and controlling shipments in emergencies; it provided a federal coal director and created an investigating agency which reported that mining was properly regulated by the federal gov-ernment. Broad use of injunctions and contempt-of-court proceedings to break strikes finally brought in 1932 the Norris-LaGuardia Act, which aimed at preferential treatment for labor, to prevent court abuses.

Court opposition undermined state and federal legislation on child labor and minimum wages. Supreme Court majorities twice insisted that a federal child labor law was unconstitutional, whether it regulated through the Interstate Commerce Commission or taxation.[2] So Con-gress in 1924 passed a resolution for a constitutional amendment; but fourteen years have passed without enough state ratifications to validate it. Minimum wage legislation had been enacted by 15 states when the Supreme Court in 1923 declared a District of Columbia law for women and minors unconstitutional.[3] A wave of repeals and adverse decisions ensued, with the minimum wage too often converted into the maximum figure.

As workers found themselves displaced, their earnings sacrificed and their social scale fallen, an increasing proportion of them ceased to

[1] The Communist, Albert Weisbord, had organized the unskilled of the Botany textile mills at Passaic in the first strike under such leadership.

[2] Hammer v. Dagenhart et al., 247 U.S. 251, 1918, and Bailey v. Drexel Furniture Co., 259 U.S. 20, 1922.

[3] Adkins v. Children's Hospital, 261 U.S. 525.

share the middle class conviction that they were their own economic masters. These became aware that classes no longer were fluid; they turned from proletarian individualism toward a mass movement. This change had been retarded by the industrial and agricultural opportunities of a frontier era, which stretched the transition from a mercantile to an industrial economy over most of the nineteenth century. Machinery destroyed all that. It proved that individual proletarianism could no longer work; it established class lines, laying the foundation for a labor movement beyond the imagination of Samuel Gompers.

Monopoly Monopolized

Labor was struggling to adjust itself to the hydro-electric age which the twentieth century had become. As electricity developed into an indispensable servant of modern existence, it also gave the mastery to those who controlled the supply of electricity. American carelessness with water resources, upon which cheap electricity depends, had permitted them to fall into private hands at strategic points, without adequate regulation. Electric power touched closely many social and economic issues, and symbolized the greatest American problem of the twentieth century—the challenge of monopoly.

High prices for power led post-war communities into further experiments in municipal power plants: and made Senators James Couzens and G. W. Norris lead movements for government regulation and operation. The power combine organized the efficient National Electric Light Association to fight the trend; its clever propaganda was fed to governors and legislators, teachers and pupils, clergy and congregations, publishers, writers and readers, speakers and listeners. This helped pull some of the teeth from the legislation of 1920 and 1930 which established first a part-time and then a full-time Federal Power Commission, to license and regulate power companies. Muscle Shoals came to symbolize the contest over public control of natural resources, as private interests repeatedly tried to get control of that plant and defeated legislation for government development of it. Throughout the decade, they waged a hot and usually successful fight against the Norris program.[1]

The power interest, like all the other moving parts of the American economic machine, was geared to mass production for a rapidly expanding market under monopoly management. Monopoly now was monopolized. The interlocking directorates, against which La Follette long had fulminated, had blossomed into holding companies, which in turn were controlled by banker giants who manipulated assets and directorates according to their ideas of profit.

[1] Norris got bills through Congress in 1928 and 1931, but Coolidge and Hoover vetoed them.

One-half the corporate wealth was controlled by 200 corporations, in turn controlled by a handful of men. Their hold upon natural resources and manufacturing processes stretched across land and sea. In addition to hydroelectricity their dominant control over vital parts of mechanized existence included such indispensable modern products as copper, iron, nickel, bauxite (the basis of aluminum), anthracite and oil.

These men who directed the machinery which ran American manufacture, mining, finance, transportation, utilities and trade, had been trained chiefly to safeguard profitable production. Consumption seemed to them, even in the 'twenties, mostly a problem of advertising, because installment selling appeared successful and foreign markets had not yet been too painfully restricted by economic nationalism. Few of the giants in business stopped to reflect seriously upon the possible necessity, for their market, of a broad rise in the actual purchasing power of the lower classes. They could scarcely be expected to show vision in a field which was closed to the minds of presidents of this great nation.

President Coolidge could not ponder the larger aspects of trust control as long as he rested serene in the conviction that the "Big Stick" had destroyed special privilege. President Hoover thought of competition chiefly in terms of its wastefulness. He wished to eliminate what remained of it in important fields. As Secretary of Commerce he had hurried to encourage formation of "trade associations." Over 400 were sponsored; they pooled information and reached profitable agreements—until the Supreme Court found them in violation of the Sherman Anti-Trust Act. That law had been written in a state of fear at the mysterious rapidity of our growth; insofar as it embodied the politico-economic notions swaying Congress in 1887, it could scarcely fit the situation forty years later.

The resourceful secretary thereupon made his Department the clearing house for information; over 200 "codes of fair practice" were drawn up, some of them destined to be copied by the N.R.A. The Federal Trade Commission found next that the Commerce Department had become an instrumentality for open price-fixing; but the Supreme Court declared for the codes. In effect, the courts and the Interstate Commerce Commission suspended efforts to put teeth into the Anti-trust law. Thus, what the tariff and the executives had left undone to encourage monopoly, the courts did.

The Speculative Urge

Americans on the whole felt slight concern over the tightening grip of monopoly or the other little-noticed forces working to grind them between the gears of modern machinery.

The trouble lay in the fact that the attitudes toward wealth, produc-

tion and use did not change as fast as economic processes. Nearly everyone clung to a mental pose which no longer fitted his or her actual
environment. They cherished the war-profiteering spirit, kept the notion
that one can "get something for nothing," anything, in fact, which one
can "get away with." There was confidence that inflation was permanent,
an idea encouraged by the gold influx; and as population shifted
from the country to urban centers people forgot the lesson of the soil—
that one must produce to live—and became infected with stock market
phraseology. Use of modern inventions gave mankind a sense of mastery:
—of miracles they would make no end.

It seemed natural and sensible, during the 'twenties, to buy relatively
less food and clothing—20% less of it—and more "durable" goods,
automobiles, electrical appliances, heaters, radios, lights and refrigerators
—70% more of them. This that they called the higher standard of living was raised by the joint push of mechanization and credit. Credit
had become one of the mightiest instruments of modern capitalism
without people learning how to control instead of abuse it. People
grew contemptuous of self-denial, oblivious to the fact that installment
contracts usually are mortgages, dependent on the maintenance of values.
It seemed that clever mortgages and installment financing could endlessly expand one's comforts and pleasures. Did not the government, in
wartime and peace, issue money on obligations? The more charge
accounts a family carried, the higher seemed its credit status. Therefore
Americans accelerated their growth in indebtedness faster than their
expansion in wealth, raising the debt by 1930 up to one-third the wealth.

More than 21 million Americans had developed familiarity with
paper investments by purchase of Liberty Loan securities; newspaper
headlines had told them of huge profits in stock "war brides." The
number of stock owners, 4 million in 1900, multiplied five times by
1930. Speculation, rather than investment, motivated perhaps 90% of
the purchasers as erstwhile conservative bondholders moved over to
stocks, "unlisted" and "over the counter" paper. Gambling on margin
involved at least 1 million persons in the 'twenties, hoisting brokers' loans
nearly 250% in two years, raising stock prices out of all connection with
dividends, and giving 1929 the unprecedented stock average of 4 million
shares daily. Profits from both speculation and "legitimate" business
were attracted into the market instead of to consumption, at the fatal
juncture that consumption was suffering from the plowing back of business profits into producing plant and surpluses instead of into distribution as salaries and wages.

Wide distribution of stock ownership must ultimately mean wide
sharing of disastrous deflation; but during the period of "benevolent
anarchy" all but the poorest groups were caught by the net. Women,
reputedly the more conservative sex, blindly believed the men's assurances

of a perpetual boom; their rise in economic power gave their faith importance, as percentages of insurance paid to them, estates inherited, and individual wealth held by them, increased greatly. They long had been the chief buyers of goods; now they comprised the majority of stockholders in certain corporations, without directing policy. Like the men, they had become used to colossal figures, were eager to make money for themselves and sceptical of social control.

All classes sought to emulate the example of financiers whose "ability" they worshipped. Financiers, nothing loath, floated new securities— $11.6 billion worth in 1929 alone. Promoters of giant combinations paid themselves in watered common stock, unloaded it upon a gullible public, and set up "investment trusts" to woo the savings of the timid but trustful.[1] The less gullible had their savings quietly misappropriated by trust "fund" managers who displaced bonds and preferred stocks of conservative businesses with common stocks representing no par value and incapable of producing income. The area to be victimized was widened by foreign investors' interest in the American market. Likewise American investors plunged into foreign governmental and private loans, sinking around 12 billions in the same hole where more than 10 billions of American war loans had already disappeared. As long as quotations climbed nearly everybody cheered, for most business indices seemed buoyant and President Hoover breathed supreme confidence.

Unfortunately, these easy assumptions of invincible prosperity assured its end, for leaders stayed blind and deaf to portents of change. In fact the "prosperity" of 1922-1929 was raising storm signals in many areas. At least one-fifth of the banks (more than 6000 of them) were failing and chiefly in farm communities. Vital industries like coal, railroad equipment, textiles, and leather suffered severely from technological changes. Unemployment was seldom less than 2,000,000 and often much more. By 1928 building, automobile and steel trades had begun to lag; the oil market was deluged. Defaults on private debts were increasing, while international repayments continued only because America supplied further loans.

Down into the Depression

During midsummer, 1929, a few well-informed Americans and Europeans cashed in on their stock profits. The two great creditor nations— England and the United States—undertook to withdraw their support from the topheavy structure of foreign and domestic debt. A sag in

[1] The violent disillusionment suffered by purchasers of stock in investment trusts and companies is revealed by the figures:—these concerns rose from about 1.8 billion at the end of 1927, up to 8 billion just before the crash, down to 6.2 billion at the end of 1929 and below 2 billion in mid 1932.

stocks became noticeable 21 October 1929. Complete rout came to Wall Street within the next eight days. Every cog in America's delicate economic machinery was jammed by the collapse of speculation, catching in a vise farmers and factory hands, builders and mortgagors, bankers and tax delinquents. No help was to be had from elsewhere, for the stringency was world-wide. Not counting foreign losses, American speculators had dissipated approximately 25 billions in savings; and thus stripped they entered the depression.

Yet national arrogance died hard. Incredulous businessmen and politicians insisted "Recovery is just around the corner," and "We shall muddle through somehow, as we have before." Thus three painful years dragged by, before realities of the situation came home. Agriculture and industry found their surpluses unexportable. Railroad revenue from freight and passengers fell 50%, with about 16% of mileage practically in receivership. Falling prices indicated "overproduction" of necessities, although "one third of a nation" went ill-fed, ill-clothed, and ill-housed. Wages those three years fell 55%, although dividends and interest fell relatively little. Industries which had been lagging before the collapse by 1930 furnished 90% of the workpeople on strike. Scant impression could strikers make, however, with between twelve and fifteen million unemployed. Organized capital entrenched itself behind court injunctions and price control; and swallowed distressed, independent producers. Some banks saved themselves at the expense of public welfare; more than 5000 fell. Morale was lost with jobs, businesses and deposits.

The United States suffered for lack of a moderate group, both devoted to an intelligent solution and strong enough to force a serious trial of it. The only relief plans which attained much political importance were the "Share Our Wealth" project of the ambitious Louisiana Senator, Huey Long, the $200 monthly-old-age pension plan of the elderly, unprosperous Dr. Francis E. Townsend of California, and an Upton Sinclair "epic" (End Poverty in California) movement. Political endorsement eluded disinterested planners:—such as the Boston businessman-philanthropist E. A. Filene, A. L. Deane of former General Motors connections, Father John A. Ryan of Catholic University who projected a fixed wage to capital, and Howard Scott who figured an economic utopia scheme called Technocracy.

Private charity and local bodies struggled against inadequacy, with at least twenty-two state legislatures trying laws on pensions, yellow-dog contracts, injunctions and shorter hours. The Congress elected in 1930, made more sensitive by a shift of control to a coalition of Democrats and progressive Republicans, essayed the Wagner unemployment law. This, President Hoover vetoed, insisting that relief was a local matter. Federal assumption of relief functions seemed intolerable, to this one who had raised himself from humble surroundings to great wealth and world fame, under a system of restricted government powers. He and his intimate associates took refuge first, in the notion that the depression was a temporary stock market affair, curable by "confidence," second, in the conviction that America's ills lay at Europe's doors.

The idea of the influence of European events was strengthened when

THE UNITED STATES AND THE WORLD

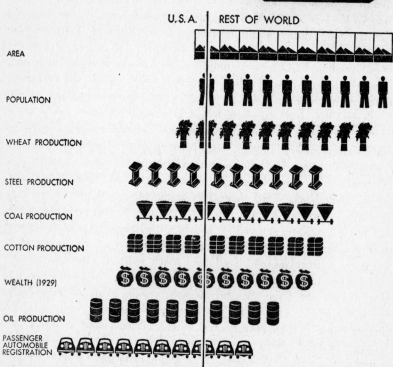

Each symbol represents 10 per cent of the world total in last available year

From Hacker, Modley, Taylor, *The United States: A Graphic History,*
Modern Age Books, Inc.

French politics contributed in May 1931, to banking collapse in Austria and Germany. Thereupon Hoover, 20 June, declared a moratorium on Europe's obligations to the United States. Unfortunately, this proved of permanent help on neither side of the ocean; and Britain had to abandon the gold standard the following September. Gold, indeed, had lost all place as a gauge of international payments and had become the plaything of panic unreason. To American businessmen, however, gold had been sacrosanct since Bryan's defeat and they resented Britain's action. They wanted to believe that this depression like earlier ones could work off through deflation under the gold standard. But the old, swift liquidation was prevented by control of one-half the business wealth by two hundred corporations, each strong enough to prevent and withstand price reductions over a long period. Nor could the water be squeezed out of the railroads; they were now too closely held by insurance and banking corporations whose bankruptcy would wipe out small as well as large savings.

Faced by these problems, by the possibility of direct relief over his veto, and by his own desire for reelection, President Hoover reluctantly signed a "Reconstruction Finance Corporation" law of January 1932, and broad extensions of it in July. Through these the government would loan relief funds, but not to individuals as such:—to bank, railroad, trust, mortgage, insurance, and industrial corporations, and to states, agricultural boards and self-liquidating construction projects. Struggling to end the depression by credit inflation, Congress made appropriations for a Federal Home Loan banking system, and broadened Federal Reserve powers. The Federal Reserve now could use government bonds as collateral for Federal Reserve notes, could lend to individuals and sometimes could omit collateral for member bank loans. A slight rise in the weekly business index occurred. Such measures improved the outlook insofar as they bolstered the sense of security among the relatively conservative groups which received the credit.

This was not as broad a kind of security as the rank and file of voters wanted in 1932. They demanded social security, meaning steady work, paying crops, homes and farms safe from foreclosure, and pensions for old age. In substance they challenged the politicians to preserve these things. The Republicans, loaded down with Hoover as candidate and bourbon traditions and backing, could not promise much more than public works, drought relief, Farm Board aid and local charity. Furthermore, a veterans' "bonus" march on Washington was met by the Administration with tear gas and tanks.

The Democrats, on the other hand, managed to nominate a country gentleman of liberal leanings and record, Governor Franklin D. Roosevelt of New York, and gave him a platform favoring some wide-sweeping financial, industrial and agricultural reforms. Roosevelt, whom none but the power interests then feared as a radical, went to the country with infectious optimism, admitted domestic causes for the depression and gave the platform a personal significance to most of his listeners. He appeared as the chosen instrument for preserving democracy under the capitalistic system.

Following further business recession during October, approximately 23 million citizens went to the polls and cast their votes for a "New Deal." Almost 16 million persons, less affected, voted for Hoover; but only eight Republican governors managed to get reelected, stalwart Republican senators went down, and the Democrats won the House, three to one. Thus did the Democratic leadership receive a mandate, to free Americans from the toils of a world-wide, but little understood, depression. They did not then think of it as more than a passing problem—one calling for but a temporary change in the details of democratic government. They were spared the foreknowledge, that their democracy, like others in Europe, was to be put on trial for its life.

THE NEW DEAL

1933-

CHAPTER XXXIX

STRIVING FOR SECURITY

The mid-depression election of 1932 was an act of faith—faith in the essential soundness of the American economic system, and in the efficacy of a political shift to help lift the depression. Heretofore it had been the habit of Americans (except in dealing with slavery) to modify their institutions haphazardly after persistent pressing from vocal minorities. Thus during the falling price era from 1870 to 1896, greenbackers, populists and Bryanites had made their contributions to the upbuilding and traditions of American democracy. In the more prosperous era of Theodore Roosevelt and Wilson, a majority of the nation had confidently supported liberal legislation for progressive improvements in the American scheme of existence. Next, during the war, citizenry had accepted the rudiments of regimentation as essential to make the world safe for democracy. Even postwar disillusionment, with twelve years of cynical reactions in politics, government and business practice, and mounting evidence that mechanization and large scale organization were attacking democracy at its roots, could not destroy the democratic faith. Through three years of deepening depression fears had been accumulating, but the nation in general remained more stunned by the shock to its optimism than aroused to violent disorder.

Under New Leadership

Intimate, personal experience with struggle, defeat and victory had given superior equipment to the shrewd and able politician to whom 57% of the voters had turned, to lead them out of the depression. The narrow range of his understanding as scion of wealthy New York patricians [1] and student at Groton, Harvard and Columbia Law School had been widened by a successful fight against Tammany in the New York State Senate, by hard, coordinated work as Assistant Secretary of the Navy in Wilson's liberal administration, and by a vigorous vice-presidential campaign and overwhelming defeat with Cox in 1920. An onslaught of infantile paralysis in 1921 had struck him down in his prime (he was 39) apparently cutting short the vigorous activity of body, mind and human association on which he had been well launched.

[1] He belonged to the notable Roosevelt clan, and was a "5th" cousin of Theodore Roosevelt.

A man of athletic and handsome physique thus learned what it meant to be crippled for life. He entered into the endless special exercises necessary to regain in part the power to walk, and by wide reading and correspondence sent his thought and influence ranging over the broad problems of American democracy and the Democratic party. This work of rehabilitation had encouragement from his wife, Eleanor Roosevelt (niece of Theodore), a woman of extraordinarily broad sympathy and courageous honesty, aided by his secretary, Louis M. Howe, and by Governor Alfred E. Smith. There emerged a personality with the imagination, daring and optimism which come to one who wins against a living death and has no more to fear.

The Franklin D. Roosevelt who emerged in 1924 to make an extraordinary comeback with a speech nominating for the presidency the reform governor, Al. Smith, was himself elected governor of New York in 1928, was reelected in 1930, and developed a depression policy of a 100% increase in state income taxes to secure funds for direct relief. Upon his own presidential nomination in 1932, he essayed a nation-wide campaign tour, to demonstrate conquest over paralysis while promising a "new deal" to "the forgotten man." Not only should there be prohibition repeal, lowered tariffs and judiciary reform, but also betterments for consumers, farmers, electricity users, investors, railroads, tax payers and the unemployed. Depression, said he, must yield to a program for the common good.

The men and women with whom Roosevelt mainly consulted, in handling the immediate emergency and projecting a "planned economy" thereafter, were popularly designated and in some quarters derided as "the brain trust." Most of them were of liberal bent, with experience in professional, social, political or business lines which had developed reflection, curiosity and inventiveness. An administration with this slant would rely upon the democratic heritage of the nation to support it in reappraisal and experiment. It would accept leadership with an eager boldness totally foreign to Harding, Coolidge or Hoover, employing the radio, the press and even airplanes to interpret and strengthen that leadership.

Roosevelt underscored his position as party leader by appearing in person before the 1932 (via airplane) and 1936 conventions to "accept" the nomination. To fortify his leadership of the nation he spoke to the people directly, and informally, broadcasting projects and personality in "fireside chats" over the radio. To unite Congress and people behind his program he delivered the opening message to Congress in 1936 over a nation-wide hookup at the best evening hour for listeners-in. To readers he made available books and magazine articles explaining and defending current policies. No daily paper could deny emphasis upon his leadership, for he established press interviews on an oral-question basis, with permissive, direct quotation and free, indirect quotation, except on "off the record" information.

Leadership in Congress, meanwhile, scarcely showed itself. The late winter of 1932-1933 was a nightmare of bank closings and the fear and confusion of the populace found ample expression in Congressmen. Then and thereafter was confirmed in most of them that disinclination toward responsibility which had been fostered by the rapid onslaught of machine age problems. The electorate of the democracy did not look to their local representatives but to the executive for emergency functioning, in the handling of problems which were wider and more intricate than those of any single state and which overflowed the mystic area of no-man's land between federal and state prerogatives. Therefore, without adequate thought as to means for the safe, temporary delegation of emergency powers, Congress participated in a shift of functions from the legislative to the executive.

The principles to be embodied in legislation were formulated by the President and his "brain trust," to be submitted one or two at a time; the phraseology was written by a few expert, executive drafters; authorship was ascribed to the sympathetic senators and congressmen who shepherded the measures through congressional amendment en route to passage; and the resultant statutes usually enhanced the power of the executive at the expense of the legislature.

They expanded the bureaucracy by an unprecedented increase in the numbers and functions of the commissions, with a National Emergency Council as coordinator. They gave bureaucratic orders the effect of laws, for the sake of quick action and coordination in highly specialized fields. Such measures were based on the belief that a democracy could assemble in its bureaus a corps of specialists fitted by training and temperament to discharge impartially the vital, regulatory powers delegated to them. In response an unprecedented number of experts left business, commercial and professional callings from time to time to work with and for the federal government.

Political opponents and representatives of interests resentful of regulation rang the welkin with denunciation of Roosevelt's political ambition and his machine, which latter was run by Postmaster-General James A. Farley with efficient distribution of the loaves and fishes. However, in spite of an approximate increase of 50% in the number of employees in the executive department, 30 June 1933—1 February 1939, the administration calculated that the proportion under civil service then would have fallen only from 80% to 75% if an executive order effective for the latter date had not been upset by Congress.

The vital problem facing Americans during the Roosevelt administrations was whether they could implement their government to protect them and their industrial system from the abuses which were under-

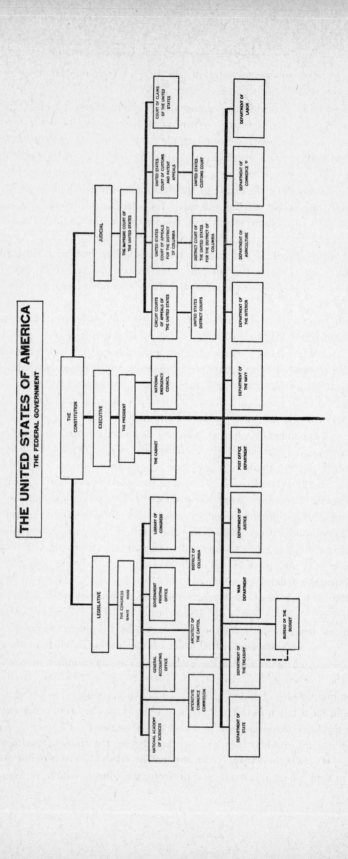

THE UNITED STATES OF AMERICA
THE FEDERAL GOVERNMENT

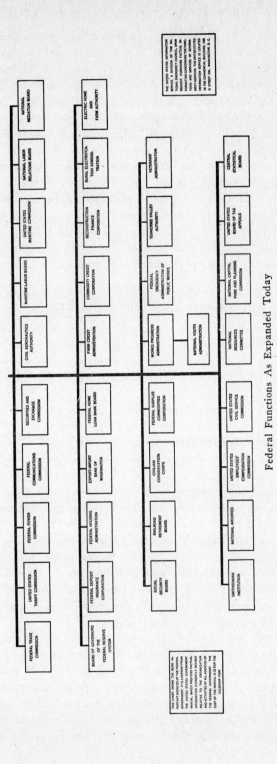

Federal Functions As Expanded Today

mining both. The job had to be tackled in an international atmosphere of unpredictable cross currents. The President and the majority of the people were basically conservative, loyal to historic institutions, feeling their way from day to day. Not design, but the force of circumstances— a stubborn, world-wide depression—was driving both further from laissez faire toward government control. It was not in the American tradition to let millions of people suffer cold and hunger without relief. This depression was forcing America to envisage relief for anyone, anywhere; a share in the cost could not be escaped by the wealthier individuals, classes and sections, fight it though they might. Vast expenditures for relief, recovery and reform could be met only by some redistribution of wealth; outright redistribution conflicted with historic patterns; redistribution through taxation was the solution attempted in this democracy; it involved loss of control by wealthy interests and growing centralization of power in government.

Expanding Money and Credit

Centralization of power in government developed after 4 March 1933 with extreme rapidity, quickened by a succession of intricate measures having the overlapping objectives of relief, recovery, and reform. During the interregnum between Hoover's defeat and Roosevelt's accession, Hoover had tried vainly to commit his successor to a modified form of the old laissez faire pattern for recovery—deflation and economy, wage cutting and bankruptcy. But it had not sufficed to reinforce the weakening money and credit institutions during three years of depression and Roosevelt determined not to bind himself. The RFC instead of following the practice of German and Italian RFC's (also set up in 1932) of taking over banks' bad assets and giving them government bonds to rely upon, had chosen to take the best assets, leaving American banks their weakest securities for use in stress. The United States was the only country suffering a crisis in the first quarter of 1933; the unsound banking system, political hysteria and sudden enthusiasm for moratoria had brought rapid deterioration to the whole business setup. Public apprehension panicked into terror, gold was hoarded and exported and practically all banks and every security and commodity exchange were closed on inauguration day.

Reassurance was the keynote of the Saturday inaugural—"the only thing we have to fear is Fear"; and Monday an executive proclamation placed an embargo on withdrawal and transfer of gold and silver and closed all banks for ninety-six hours. The administration was convinced that the load of public and private debt had been made unsupportable by the fall in prices; and it understood the background of the agrarian, corporate and individual debtors and silver interests who were raising again the historic cry for "more money." Therefore it plunged into efforts to lighten debts, raise prices and increase the volume and circulation of money and credit. It aimed both to save old private institutions and establish new federal agencies.

Congress convened 9 March and passed that day the administration's Emergency Banking and Gold Control law: insolvent banks were to be kept in limited operation by federal "conservators"; solvent ones were to reopen under supervision of the Treasury; the Federal Reserve was to issue more notes to member banks, and lend to persons and corporations on government bond security; the RFC could subscribe to preferred stock of banks and trust companies. The Secretary of the Treasury subsequently called in all gold and gold certificates. Thus the administration attested a midway allegiance to American individualism; instead of nationalizing credit institutions (as some reformers desired) it issued government paper to finance their retention in private hands, under restrictions which the American Bankers Association denounced.

Efforts to reform and strengthen the banking system then and later had the advantage of publicity obtained by Ferdinand Pecora, whose provocative value as counsel for the Senate Subcommittee on Stock Exchange Practice, 1932-1934, proved as high as that of Samuel Untermyer in the Arsene Pujo investigation of 1912. Commercial and investment banking were divorced; a Federal Deposit Insurance Corporation, FDIC, was set up to insure deposits;[1] branch banking was slightly extended and the Federal Reserve System was expanded to embrace Morris Plan and savings bank memberships and to permit loans to non-member banks. Authority of the Federal Reserve Board over the volume and kind of credit was variously enlarged, with power to increase minimum bank reserves developed to discourage violent fluctuations. The RFC became a pipe line of emergency loans. Easier credit was among the objects of a Federal Farm Mortgage Corporation, FFMC,[2] and a Home Owners' Loan Corporation, HOLC.[3] Wide concessions were made for easier bankruptcy of corporations, municipalities and farmers.

Stock market speculation was so intimately associated with the onset of the depression that Congress made security issues subject to approval and registration first with the Federal Trade Commission, and in 1934 with the Federal Securities and Exchange Commission, SEC, which was established to license and regulate stock exchanges.[4]

---

[1] Glass-Steagall Act, 16 June 1933, passed after exposure of the unethical practices of A. H. Wiggin.

[2] Federal Farm Mortgage Corporation Act, 31 Jan. 1934.

[3] Home Owners' Loan Corporation Act, 13 June 1933 and amendments; by 1939 the federal government held more than one-third of the nation's farm mortgages and nearly one-sixth of the urban home mortgages.

[4] Securities Exchange Act, 6 June 1934 and Public Utility Act, 26 Aug. 1935.

To raise prices while expanding the currency and relieving the federal treasury, the administration quickly forbade the hoarding of gold and the use of it to pay indebtedness; everyone was ordered to exchange their gold for paper money, at the old valuation of $20.67 an ounce.[1] The government took over the purchase of all gold which was produced in the United States or might be offered to it from abroad; first, to raise prices and make the American unit a "commodity dollar," fluctuating with trade; this failing, the price was fixed at $35 by the gold reserve act of 31 January 1934. It lowered the "gold content" of the dollar from 25.8 grains to 15 5/21 grains, thus depreciating it to 59.06% of its former gold content. Two billions of the "gain" which the Treasury made by revaluing its stock at $35 was allotted to the Secretary for use as a "Stabilization Fund";[2] this enabled him to practice the secret purchase and sale of exchange, so as to manipulate the international value of the dollar when desired to offset trade balances or speculative and foreign forces.

Government purchases of silver, which remained a metal of low esteem among the most important powers, were reinaugurated through the joint efforts of senators from silver-producing states, of some manufacturers for export and of congressmen with large farm or other debtor constituencies. These allies united, at the depth of the depression, behind a hybrid, contradictory program for fiat currency and bimetallism, aiming at cheap money and dear silver. Seemingly to avoid an intraparty fight on the combination, the administration supported "permissive" legislation along these lines; and it agreed to nationalize silver and to prosecute purchases until either government silver holdings equalled in value one-third of gold holdings or silver reached $1.29 in world markets.[3]

The economic results of this political finesse included: America's first unfavorable balance since 1893; acceptance by the United States of $98,000,000 worth of foreign silver, at fifty cents an ounce, on war debt payments; purchase of varying amounts of world silver stock at prices ranging up to eighty cents an ounce (the average world price in 1932 had been twenty-eight cents) until 9 August 1934; subsequent purchase of all domestic silver in stock at 50.01 cents, newly mined domestic silver at varying prices up to 77.57 cents and foreign production at varying rates, many above the world market; unloading of silver upon the United States; destruction of its monetary position in China; lowering of the silver content of Mexico's currency; purchase,

---

[1] Of the estimated outstanding 125 billions of gold contracts, about 14.5 billions were government bonds; currency policy was pushed by frequent executive orders, under a few "blanket" laws.

[2] 800 millions were used to retire national bank notes.

[3] The principal silver legislation was enacted 12 May 1933 and 19 June 1934.

at a cost over 1 billion dollars, of about 2 billion ounces of silver of which only about 13% was domestically mined; and expansion of American currency through issuance of more than 1.5 billions in silver certificates.

The best effect of the gold and silver purchases was their stimulation of American exports, for there was cutthroat competition for the

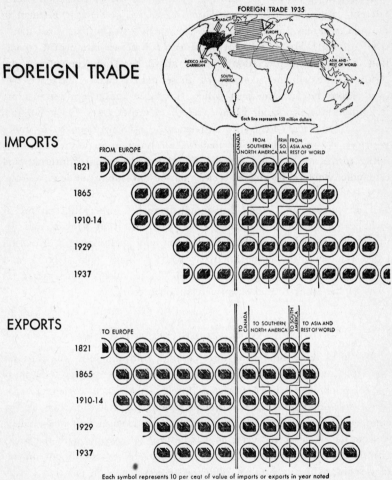

FOREIGN TRADE

FOREIGN TRADE 1935

Each line represents 150 million dollars

IMPORTS

Each symbol represents 10 per cent of value of imports or exports in year noted

From *The United States, A Graphic History,* Hacker, Modley and Taylor, Modern Age Books, Inc.

relatively few remaining world markets. Their worst effect was to concentrate approximately 15 billions of gold—over half the world's known supply—in America, to the detriment of trade and other international relations. They could not achieve the desired rise in the American price level or in the world price of silver. They contributed to a badly unbalanced budget, at the same time as they furnished some metallic backing for the currency which was paid out for the bonus and for the relief-recovery-reform expenditures.

Some of America's trade competitors had fondly hoped that the United States would accept their currency devaluations without retaliation; and an economic conference at London was planned to arrange international economic relations on that basis. Roosevelt astounded the conferees 2 July 1933 by refusing to agree to the perpetuation of the current ratio, although he acceded to a scheme of Senator Pittman of Nevada, whereby the United States shouldered the heaviest load in the silver market. The subsequent entrance of America into world competition in currency depreciation alarmed all of her trade competitors and seriously affected the economy of those nations whose currency was over-valued by the American policy. To make the general uncertainty less intolerable, England, France and the United States (with Belgium acceding) made a "Tripartite Agreement," 25 September 1936, under which each promised not to abandon the current ratio, without due notice to the others. Thus currency control as a weapon of international economic warfare became a secret, day-to-day affair, among "gentlemen."

The banking and credit legislation furnished other illustrations of complicated consequences. RFC loans saved insolvent bankers and ill-managed railroads as well as the solvent and well-managed. Inflation aided some wealthy corporations as well as many poor debtors, and increased prices to consumers as well as for producers. These were all parts of the effort to make captive capitalism work.

Providing Work, Subsistence and a Future

As world trade under the international gold standard was thus set aside for "national self-sufficiency" under "managed currency," the market for goods and labor contracted, forcing America to desperate expedients for finding her own nationals a job and a living. The urgent emergency compelled hasty action, which was taken at first in confident expectation of quick recovery, as was natural to a people with the background and resources of optimistic America. Direct, minimum, monetary relief, as in the English "dole" system was used in part but it was opposed by the majority of the nation, as unproductive and destructive to morale, and on the assumption that Americans would prefer work to idleness.

So the more costly "work relief," in part at "prevailing hourly rates," was stressed. Jobs were created by setting up federal projects and also by part-financing, with federal funds, projects of state and local governments, for which standards of execution were set by federal authorities. Great reliance was placed upon local initiative and supervision of

WPA ACTIVITIES FOR THE COMMON WELFARE

ing Public Water Supply; Building High School Athletic Field; Improving Roads; Mosquito Control and Swamp Drainage (note modern architecture of U. S. Naval Hospital in background)

projects, and the "WPA" adhered consistently to that principle; but at first inexperience and urgent relief necessities hindered the county boards in planning socially-useful undertakings. Other agencies tended to centralize work relief, with the government proposing more of the projects.

President and Congress rapidly established these agencies, variously naming them administrations, authorities, boards, commissions, companies and corporations, and the public designated them by their first letters, so that they were described as "government by alphabet." They usually were independent of existing departments but often worked with and through the latter. Only the most significant aspects of their work can here be noted.

Industry had no jobs to offer the 500,000 youth annually finishing school; and many thousands took to roaming the country aimlessly. A Civilian Conservation Corps,[1] CCC, absorbed first 200,000, then about 300,000 persons—unmarried young men of 17 to 23 and war veterans on relief—placing them in camps to work on reforestation, trails, pest-control, drainage, erosion, floods and fire-fighting. This effort at conservation of human and natural resources illustrated interdepartmental cooperation, with the War, Interior, and Agriculture Departments and the Veterans Administration participating. A few camps to give occupational education to women opened in 1934, and a vast number of work projects—sewing, canning, household aid, nursing and school-lunch activities—subsequently materialized.[2] They were important because women industrial workers had increased tenfold in twenty-five years, until by 1938 nearly one-third of the labor supply was women, with men fighting their advance. A United States Employment Service was set up within the Department of Labor.

An early instrument for supplying federal funds to exhausted state relief agencies was the Federal Emergency Relief Administration,[3] FERA, headed by Harry L. Hopkins. To help the 15,000,000 unemployed through the desperate winter of 1933-1934 a Civil Works Administration,[4] CWA, again under Hopkins, financed work relief on civic projects. Many of the errors and abuses which inevitably entered the first experiments were eliminated in May 1935 by coordinating work relief in a Works Progress Administration,[5] WPA, under the

[1] The Emergency Conservation Work established under act of 31 March 1933 was officially designated the Civilian Conservation Corps by act of 28 June 1937.

[2] The veterans obtained 30,000 places; the women's camps were first under FERA, then WPA.

[3] Act of 12 May 1933; its funds were to be used for both direct and work relief.

[4] The CWA functioned from November 1933 to May 1934, financing projects selected by local and state administrators.

[5] By executive orders beginning 6 May 1935 under emergency relief appropriation laws of 1935-1937.

experienced Hopkins. It made possible construction and rehabilitation of all kinds of public property, and hundreds of kinds of white-collar activity. Direct relief of unemployables was turned back to the localities. To WPA's function of employing manual and clerical adults was added work-finding for needy youth through a National Youth Administration.[1] The NYA subsidiary furnished part-time employment to a small minority of students and out-of-school youths, while training them in job and leisure activities designed to benefit them and their

MORE WOMEN AT WORK

MARRIED | SINGLE, WIDOWED OR DIVORCED

1890

1910

1930

Each symbol represents 1 million women 15 years and over

Bernhard J. Stern, *The Family, Past and Present*, D. Appleton-Century Company, Inc.

communities. Four federal "Arts" projects in painting and sculpture, drama, music and writing, furnished employment and spread culture.

In the meantime a special relief program was devised to rehabilitate the heavy industries vital to both capital and labor. Symptomatic of the sad state of these industries was that of building; between 1928 and 1933, house repair had fallen 90%, residential construction 95% and all construction 73%. Workers in a multitude of interdependent trades, such as steel, iron, copper, lead, wood, brick, plumbing and electrical equipment shared unemployment and loss of purchasing power. Mining, machinery and transportation were depressed together. So a Public

[1] By executive order of 26 June 1935 under appropriation act of 8 April.

Works Administration, PWA, was set up under Secretary of the Interior Harold L. Ickes, to stimulate private employment of machinery and non-relief labor (as distinguished from the WPA emphasis) in heavy construction.[1] Through country, subsistence homesteads and city, low-rental apartments, the government also financed non-profit construction in which private capital could not engage. Suburban housing for city workers was aided by a Resettlement Administration. American public housing, lineal descendant of the social settlement movement, proved costlier than the British because of realtor opposition, high land costs, obstruction through the courts and emphasis upon modern improvements.

The New Deal's relief and recovery program met stiff resistance from vested interests determined to stigmatize it thoroughly. Undeniably waste and error intervened, working evil effects on national morale and economy;[2] but the underlying democratic objective—enhancement of the common good—was achieved in an amazing number of constructive undertakings, which the depression must have denied the nation without government aid.

The program brought new schools and college buildings; libraries, guidebooks, bibliographies and historical, cultural and economic surveys: concerts, plays, art exhibitions and mural decorations: health services, hospitals, playgrounds and slum clearance: sewage, waterworks, grade crossing elimination and road building: reforestation and conservation, federal, state and municipal buildings, airports, irrigation projects, "yardstick" power plants and flood control. Not all of these were needed on the elaborate scales selected nor has a method of finally paying for them been worked out. Yet neither is it possible to estimate the disasters which might have befallen democracy if the administration had acted on the assumption of its severest critics, that the distressed classes would have endured a ruthless, unrelieved deflation.

Raising Agricultural Values

One of the most distressed classes, without whose well-being America never could recover permanent prosperity, was the farmers, crushed in 1933 by surpluses unsaleable at prices below cost of production. Roused out of their native conservatism, they resentfully destroyed milk sup-

[1] Established under the NIRA 16 June 1933 and extended under WPA Act of 29 June 1937. It awards building contracts to private contractors and also gives financial aid to states and localities so that they can award such contracts; labor pressure forced "prevailing hourly rates" upon PWA projects beginning in October 1935.

[2] Charges of inefficiency were aimed particularly at NRA, CCC, TVA (in internal operations) and the Coal Commission.

plies in Iowa, Minnesota and Wisconsin, sponsored some old inflation panaceas and everywhere demanded further government aid to restore their purchasing power. Their congressmen received political support from implement manufacturers and others aware of the penalties of lost farm buying power.

The Roosevelt administration decided to approach the problem from a nationalistic point of view. World markets having disappointed American farmers, salvation must lie in domestic markets. Security might be attained through what later came to be called "an ever-normal granary." This program rested on faith that America could maintain farm prices above the world level (as she had manufacturing prices), could surmount climatic vagaries and could substitute for ingrained, unrestricted, agricultural competition a habit of cooperation in restriction.

So the "Agricultural Adjustment Act," the AAA, of 12 May 1933 and subsequent amendments thereto launched a scheme of reduced crops for higher prices. Prices should be raised to "parity"—to their estimated fair exchange value with other commodities—estimated with due regard to the nation's total purchasing power. To restore the purchasing power of 1909-1914, farmers were to restrict voluntarily production of important staples:—cattle, corn, cotton, dairy products, flax, hogs, peanuts, potatoes, rice, rye, sorghums, sugar beets and cane, tobacco and wheat.[1] The government was to assure them compensation by processing taxes collected at the points of processing, such as meat-packing houses, cotton gins and flour mills; the amount of the tax was to be governed by the difference between "parity" and current farm prices. Recalcitrant farmers exceeding some allotments were to be punished by prohibitive taxes on their excess.[2] Thus far had agricultural philosophy progressed from the old notion that Uncle Sam could remain a Santa Claus without becoming a dictator. These laws, aided by inflationary measures and the severe drought of 1934 (worst in forty years), raised farm purchasing power as of 1934 20% above that of 1932.

At the same time, unfortunately, the AAA program was not unaffected by climatic, economic and political trends in many foreign countries. These trends, combined with the AAA, tended to reduce further our farm export market, to increase an already acute unemployment problem, and to rouse resentment.

By 1935 there was an estimated reduction of 1,000,000 man-hours in farm work. Some southern tenant farmers and sharecroppers, thrust off plantations by crop restrictions, ignored the color line for the first time in forming a "Southern Tenant Farmers' Union" of both races—an

[1] Adjustment programs were not actually effectuated on cattle, dairy products, flax and sorghums.

[2] Applied to cotton, tobacco and potatoes by the Bankhead, Kerr and Potato Acts.

effort greatly limited in scope. Dairymen and poultrymen complained of costlier feed bills, and consumers of dearer milk, butter and eggs. The proletariat felt the pinch most severely in the price of meats, affected by the drought. Some economists declared that the act simply gave temporary relief to agriculture at the expense of consumers, because it did not more drastically reduce the fixed costs (inflated debt load) which cut farm profits to the point of requiring relief; holders of farm mortgages stood in the way.[1]

Other laws and policies aimed to coordinate the agricultural situation with the trade and the national relief problem. A "Federal Surplus Relief Corporation," FSRC,[2] at first received from the AAA donations of products for relief distribution and from 1935 functioned as a commodities corporation to remove surpluses from market channels. Secretary of State Cordell Hull reversed the traditional practice of devoting trade agreements to industrial interests, and under a "Trade Agreement Act"[3] undertook to emphasize reciprocity for agriculture. As the act permitted lowering or raising rates by 50%, without congressional interference, it placed Hull in a strong diplomatic position; by 1939 he achieved (in spite of some farm criticism) nineteen executive agreements, increasing trade in various industrial and agricultural products. A federal Export-Import bank further facilitated trade. The farm credit system was extended until each of the twelve farm credit districts had one each of four kinds of banks:—land banks for mortgage loans, production credit corporations for production loans, intermediate credit banks for intermediate term discounts and banks for loans to cooperatives. Farm bankruptcies decreased.

Some areas stressed the long-term, farm-purchase credit facilities of the "Farm Credit Administration," FCC,[4] and the Frazier-Lemke five-year mortgage moratorium law which the Supreme Court invalidated.[5] The RFC organized a Commodity Credit Corporation to hold crops accepted as security for cash loans. In other areas the trend toward tenantry could be arrested only by revolutionary changes in farming practices:—there the Resettlement Administration classified lands, purchased marginal farms, financed family transplantation and encouraged part-time farming.

In the midst of the struggle for improved farm-purchasing-power suits were brought by processors and on 6 January 1936 the Supreme Court,

---

[1] Total farm mortgage debt was reduced about 21% between early 1930 and 1937 but farm real estate values remained 24% below pre-war levels.

[2] Established in October 1933 to carry out part of the provisions of the AAA.

[3] Of 12 June 1934 extended by act of 1 March 1937.

[4] The Farm Credit Act of 16 June 1933 was but one of at least six acts in this field, 1933-1937.

[5] Congress in August 1935 passed a new measure to cover the objections.

6 to 3, held the processing tax and production control features of the AAA unconstitutional. Undaunted, the administration eliminated the pressure for invalidation by shifting to the federal treasury the direct burden of paying for the farmers' program, with emphasis shifted from production control to "soil conservation" in the "Soil Conservation and Domestic Allotment Act" of 29 February 1936; it stressed state execution under federal direction.[1] Through numerous amendments and amplifications of this measure, culminating (after two years without effective crop control) in a new AAA Act of 1938, they continued to fight surplus crops and low prices. Against drought, flood and insects, the wheat farmers were offered insurance by a Federal Crop Insurance Corporation.[2] Following Canada's lead, export subsidies were provided to facilitate dumping wheat abroad, a practice formerly denounced in America and now made useless by imitation. Benefit payments to growers cooperating in "soil conservation" were widened on some crops to the point where non-cooperating farmers no longer could hold off. Cash farm income increased from approximately $4,330,000,000 in 1932 to $8,600,000,000 in 1937.

Unfortunately the twin spectres of good weather and bad business increased production and decreased consumption, relentlessly defeating "economy of scarcity." The predicament of cotton, which had accounted for about 25% of American exports since 1820, and which ultimately affected national welfare outside of the South as well as in it, became most alarming. World consumption went up, but consumption of United States cotton went down, assisted by the high import tariffs which discouraged exchange for American exports generally. In 1932-1933, the last season of unrestricted cotton output, American growers sold about 60% of world consumption and 45% of consumption outside the United States; in 1936-1937 they sold only 42% and 23% respectively; and in five years American taxpayers footed a direct bill of about $750,000,000 in benefit payments to growers, exclusive of other heavy cotton outlays.[3] Despite reduced acreage 1937 brought an unprecedented American crop of 19,000,000 bales; and an average price of only 8.4¢ per pound. The government shouldered more than one-fourth of it as loan collateral and 1938 acreage was cut 22% lower.

The wheat crop of 1938 was two-thirds planted before the new AAA Act, and record surpluses met an average world price in August 1938, of about 51¢ a bushel compared with a parity price of $1.12, a 1937 price of 96¢ and government loans around 60¢. Dairy products, especially

---

[1] A soil conservation service had been established under an act of 27 April 1935.

[2] Part of the AAA Act of 16 February 1938; it provided for acreage limitation in corn, cotton, rice, tobacco and wheat by a two-thirds vote of the growers of each.

[3] Department of Agriculture Report of 7 July 1938.

butter, potatoes and some fruits struggled with surpluses unsaleable at asked prices. Except for corn, livestock and tobacco generally the outlook was not good. 1938 farm income was approximately 12% below 1937, despite an 11% increase in federal aid. World prices fell to the lowest general level in four years.

Desperately, the administration planned to campaign for new processing taxes to replace those earlier declared unconstitutional. Farmer sen-

Seibel in Richmond *Times-Dispatch.*

The Eternal Question

timent ran toward price-fixing—often proved ineffective; and toward a two-price system, wherein the farmer would produce all he wished, and accept the world price only on exported and relief-use crops, with other prices subsidized by the government. Clearly, mounting American acreage reductions and crop loans were not stopping the world price fall. While supplies stubbornly remained far in excess of demand at current prices, the discerning saw that world political and financial conditions—quite unamenable to control by America—were complicating the agricultural problem beyond immediate solution.

Readjusting Industry and Labor

With equal boldness the administration attacked the equally difficult problem of industrial security, complicated by conflicting interests of capital, labor and consumer. Chaotic conditions revealed and emphasized by the depression inspired a desire for orderliness, which American industry never had known. To a nation with liberal traditions self-government by industry and the recovery of competition appealed as ideals readily attainable, although the long-time, gradual advance largely responsible for Britain's better industrial balance had not been pursued in America. So Congress hurriedly passed the National Industrial Recovery Act of 16 June 1933 as an enabling act, by which industry, under Presidential supervision, could draw up "codes of fair competition" for its own governance.

Big industrial executives interpreted order as meaning suspension of the anti-trust laws by government, in return for concessions to liberalism by industry—on such moot points as minimum pay, shorter hours, better working conditions and abolition of child labor. To this end they transplanted the essential provisions of their trade agreements of Hoover days into the NRA codes, openly inserting price-fixing into more than half of them; and through the advisory group allotted to them—the Industrial Recovery Board—they advised an enforcement of the codes which little regarded the interests of small business, consumers and labor. The codes restricted the opportunities of little local firms to compete against large national corporations. A Consumers' Advisory Board vainly struggled for the knowledge, skill and opportunity to offset monopolistic trends.

The Labor Advisory Board soon was elaborated into a less ineffective National Labor Board, by a separate act of 5 August 1933; but it could not secure enforcement of the evasive Section 7a of the NIRA act, as a guarantee of the right of collective bargaining under unions of labor's own choosing. Although the law eliminated some cut-throat practices, this hastily forged instrument fitted poorly the complex industrial needs of the far-flung nation. Its good [1] and bad features fell together 27 May 1935, when the Supreme Court unanimously decided [2] that it was an unconstitutional delegation of the lawmaking power to the executive and a federal invasion of intra state commerce. The death of the NRA placed heavier duties on the Federal Trade Commission.

Meanwhile, efforts by the National Labor Board and the President to enforce labor's right to bargain sharpened the contest between company, craft and vertical unions over which should be the recognized bargaining

[1] One of these was the ban on child labor under 16 which Secretary of Labor Perkins forced into each code.

[2] The so-called "sick-chicken" case, Schechter Poultry Corp. v. U. S., 295 U. S. 495.

agent in each dispute. Congress decided that the workers involved should choose the agent, by the democratic method of free, secret balloting and provided for a new National Labor Relations Board, NLRB, not subject to presidential review,[1] to apply the principle; in three years it rendered decisions involving about four million workers, with a barrage of criticism from all sides sufficient to indicate that the Board aimed at impartiality. High labor standards were required of all firms receiving government contracts.

The more radical elements turned to the drastic "general strike" at San Francisco, and the sit-down strike in many areas, which devices cost the sympathy of some moderate liberals. Strikes increased in number, scope and violence, with tear-gas a common resort on both sides. 1937 saw more than 1,800,000 workers involved, over twice 1936. Capital, no less intransigeant, frequently smashed the strikes, using injunctions, armed police, militia, vigilantes, spies, intimidation and back-to-work propaganda. A notable exception was an agreement reached peaceably by the United States Steel Corporation and the CIO. It obviated great loss to capital, labor and public.

For the most part, labor and capital continued in defiant challenge, with the National Labor Relations Board struggling to mitigate the discord and with progress out of the depression greatly hindered. A trend into a new labor alignment seemed to emerge. Refusal of the hierarchy of the A.F. of L. to tolerate unrestricted chartering of industrial unions in such large fields as aluminum, automobiles, cement, rubber, utilities and steel in 1935 inspired the industrial faction under John L. Lewis to defy the A.F. of L. with a Committee for Industrial Organization—the CIO—which proceeded to unite ten strong unions, including the powerful United Mine Workers, under the horizontal plan.

One of the strongest groups, the International Ladies Garment Workers' Union, with 250,000 members, three-fourths of them women, trimmed its sails between the CIO and A.F. of L., but technically affiliated with the CIO from its beginning until November 1938. The CIO made their strongest drive between 1935 and 1937 in the vital automobile and steel industries. This rival recruiting had wide effects. Insofar as the CIO adopted the reduced hour and restricted output philosophy of some of the craft unions and the "economy of scarcity" device of some of the New Dealers, it appeared to defeat its own objects; for it forbade technology to bring that increased output at lowered prices on which improvements in consumption and mass income depend.

As 1938 closed, the union membership of 1932 was more than doubled. The A.F. of L. boasted a dues-paying enrollment of about 3,600,000 and the CIO about 3,750,000. Company executives appeared to prefer

[1] Jt. Res. 19 June 1934 and NLR Act 5 July 1935.

the less radical A.F. of L., which took over some company unions. The National Labor Relations Board, while it disclaimed any favoritism, appeared to find the CIO more truly representative of labor's ambitions. Communistic domination of four of the CIO unions weakened it in public opinion, caused revolts among its membership and confused issues. Peace negotiations of October 1937-December 1938 failed. The general public suffered by the costly boycotts by rival unions of goods handled by each other, and the President vainly urged them to compromise a warfare which grew worse. Labor factions and capital had yet to invent a definition of security for industry and labor on which they could unite.

Certain industries received detailed attention, punctuating Congress' retreat from laissez faire. To the ailing railroads were given a federal coordinator to eliminate waste and to direct refinancing; the government aided grade-crossing elimination, electrification and other technological improvements. Congress adjusted railway employees' pension plans to meet Supreme Court objections. The Interstate Commerce Commission put fares and freight rates up and down, passed upon railroad purchase projects and was given responsibility on buses and trucks. Air transport became subject to a Civil Aeronautic Authority.[1] Despite all this effort, 30% of America's rail mileage was in the hands of receivers or trustees, 1 June 1938. For the ailing soft coal industry, legislation was passed and recast to meet Supreme Court objections. A livelier conscience was given the food and drug industry by a new federal food and drugs act which somewhat tightened restrictions on adulteration and deceit and served as a pattern for a model state act pushed by state officials.

The Fair Labor Standards Act of 24 June 1938 set a sliding wage and hour scale, under which certain industries in time should reach a minimum wage rate of not less than 40¢ an hour and a maximum weekly hour base of 40 hours, with time and a half for overtime. Sectional and regional differences made it extremely difficult to overcome southern opposition and amendment is demanded by various factions, but the act as a whole is favored by 71% of the population.

All these efforts, strenuous as they were, failed to solve the subsistence problems of the unfortunate, unemployed and aged poor, for whose provision America had lagged far behind other advanced nations. A few states, such as New York, Ohio and Wisconsin had recognized this kind of responsibility and had emphasized the need for an all-state coordination. Depression-born schemes like the Townsend, Long and Lundeen plans made it impossible for Congress to ignore the rising demand for national social security legislation. After it was realized that America had continuously at least five million unemployed, the Social Security

[1] Civil Aeronautic Authority Act 23 June 1938.

Act of 14 August 1935 was passed. It undertook to coordinate a federal and state program of old age and unemployment insurance, and to aid the states on child and maternity welfare, the blind, public health and vocational rehabilitation; but all farm and domestic laborers were specifically excluded from its benefits.

It was freely predicted that the Supreme Court must invalidate the act, because its theories did not meet earlier court positions. Yet it was a condition—not a theory—which pressed closest upon law makers and law interpreters. During 1935-1936, according to estimates of the National Resources Committee, one-third of America's families and single individuals were netting an annual income averaging only $471; and 30% of the group were on relief part of that year. Practically all the states within two years complied with federal stipulations; and 24 May 1937, a majority of the Supreme Court proved its adaptability by sustaining the pensions clause 7-2, and job-insurance 5-4. The act came to epitomize the social philosophy behind the New Deal, for it admitted the right of everyone—the idle as well as the earning—to the bare essentials of food, clothing and shelter and it suggested their right to health and a modest happiness also.

Within the first three years of the Social Security Act more than 40,000,000 men and women workers made application for old age accounts to assure future income; more than 27,500,000 earned credits in unemployment insurance; more than 1,700,000 old folks, 600,000 dependent children and 40,000 blind received cash assistance. Social security funds pushed the states into active and intelligent disease prevention. Under federal guidance but local control, they expanded the attack in twenty-two important fields, with special emphasis upon trained personnel, public health nursing and education, industrial and dental hygiene, venereal disease, tuberculosis, cancer, malaria, rodent plague and maternal and child care. In innumerable ways the Act instructed the nation in social well-being.[1]

Security through Resources and Taxation

The New Deal viewed permanent security—for all Americans—as requiring a triple effort:—to conserve resources, to recapture control of them from such corporations as used them unfairly, and to impose drastic corporation taxes as a lever in shifting control and paying the costs of

[1] Its long-time application, however, remains problematical. Some statisticians estimate that by 1960 the slowing-down in America's rate of increase will have stabilized the population at 138,000,000 or less, and that then nearly 40% of the people will be over 40—in the age class against which industry discriminates. The indications point to a rising demand for old-age and unemployment pensions, which must impose a mounting charge upon the nation's taxable productions.

the shift. Only a sustained and intelligent public interest, with determined leadership, could make the general welfare an intimate, daily concern of the monopolists who controlled the resources basic to modern American living. Public interest was sustained by a long-lasting depression, droughts, dust-storms, floods, hurricanes and revelations of chicanery; determined leadership came in the person of a President whose experience with the power trusts in New York had educated his understanding and toughened his will. Thus circumstances pushed Americans into a broadened definition of conservation—into the greatest drive in history for the control of national resources. Every agency at work upon relief, recovery, reform or national security became involved.

The traditional notion of conservation had emphasized increased production and future use:—irrigation of submarginal lands and withholding from sale of unappropriated resources. With the depression came a more far-reaching recognition of the need for a planned economy; emphasis shifted to improved use of those privately owned resources which were intimately associated with present, daily living for the millions. This flowered in general acceptance of federal control of public utilities and government oversight of many other businesses vested "with a public interest." This did not mean renunciation of capitalism; probably the majority of Americans shared Roosevelt's announced conviction that their distress was due more to shortsighted, individual capitalists than to the institution of capitalism.

New Deal conservation, therefore, advanced along two lines. The CCC, RA, PWA, WPA and flood control agencies [1] included in their programs the preservation of soils and forests, storing of waters and combating of droughts, floods and forest fires. But they and a host of other agencies engaged in broader experiments in resource control. Most significant of these experiments was conducted by the Tennessee Valley Authority,[2] established to enhance "the general social and economic well-being of the Valley." The TVA proceeded to operate Muscle Shoals and other dams to serve the seven southern states of Alabama, Georgia, Kentucky, Mississippi, North Carolina, Tennessee and Virginia—a region where outside capital had been skimming the cream off southern resources. Its people began to find their daily life revolutionized by the broadest social service agency ever implemented; by flood control, navigation improvement, nitrate manufacture, vocational education, reforestation, subsistence homesteads, scientific agriculture, community life and the generation and cheap sale of electric power. An Electric Farm and Home Authority [3] facilitated purchase

---

[1] Flood control, by reason of its connection with deforestation, overcultivation and erosion inspired almost continuous investigation, legislation and expenditure throughout the Roosevelt administration.

[2] TVA Act 18 May and executive orders 8 June, 1933.

[3] Act of 16 June 1933 and subsequent acts and executive orders.

of appliances, changing kitchens and barns into centers of profitable work. PWA loans and a Rural Electrification Administration [1] enabled municipalities and rural cooperatives to use cheap public current, rather than the more expensive service of privately capitalized companies. Federal funds were sent to Bonneville and Grand Coulee to develop dams for the Columbia River basin. The private power companies neglected no court device to upset this program, but the Supreme Court on 17 February 1936 and 27 January 1939, did not declare the TVA unconstitutional.[2] A series of joint purchases of private utilities by the TVA and public bodies ensued.

Federal intervention ranged up and down the utility field. The powers of the FTC, FPC and SEC were broadened [3] to cover regulation of interstate gas and electric rates and to end the pyramided, holding-company system which was held responsible for the worst utility abuses. The ICC, FCC,[4] Maritime Commission [5] and NLRB also regulated utilities: between them and the congressional investigations American utilities were thoroughly put on the defensive, making heavy outlays of stockholders' funds for legal defense, lowering rates and cleaning house. The Administration and New York Power Authority locked horns with the utilities over the St. Lawrence Waterway treaty.

In other fields also the government moved far beyond the old anti-monopoly objective, of protecting competitors, into the limitless field of protecting consumers. Some non-profit utilities were allowed to merge. Heavy responsibilities were laid on the FTC to regulate advertising,[6] a major American industry. Money was lavished by government and corporations, over investigations and prosecutions of such industrial giants as the aluminum, automobile, oil, telegraph and telephone industries. Although the little businessmen won against the consumers in an anti-chain-store act [7] other laws showed more solicitude for buyers. Most important, the government sharpened the instrument of taxation against the corporations.

Social control more than revenue became the administration's tax motive, for the broad objectives of the New Deal prohibited a balanced budget during a depression. After brief economy pledges in 1933 (involving salary and personnel cuts among congressmen and lesser government employees, reductions in veterans' benefits and a cautious beginning in

[1] Act of 11 May 1935 and subsequent acts and executive orders.

[2] In Ashwander, et al. v. TVA 297 U. S. 288; the Court affirmed, 8-1, a decree of the Court of Appeals on a certain aspect of the TVA; and in Tennessee Electric Power Co. et al. v. TVA, A. E. Morgan, H. A. Morgan, and D. E. Lilienthal the Court ruled, 5-2, that 14 private companies testing the TVA Act had no legal standing in the suit and that utilities are not immune from competition.

[3] Under the Wheeler-Rayburn Utility Act 26 August 1935 and the Robinson-Patman Act 19 June 1936. [4] FCC Act 19 June 1934. [5] Merchant Marine Act 29 June 1936. [6] Wheeler-Lea Act 21 March 1938. [7] Robinson-Patman Act 19 June 1936.

PWA outlays), 1934 saw pay cuts restored and the bonus passed (over executive veto), relief loosened and budget balancing postponed.[1] This was a not unnatural reaction to a continuing world depression wherein powerful governments blandly defaulted on their debts, eminent magnates failed miserably and mortgage foreclosures were nullified by legal and illegal means. So, direct taxation of the masses below the income and estate level was made regressive, and of persons above, progressive, with income and estate taxes dominating all others for the higher groups.

Deficits rose the faster because the masses were insensitive. The net debt of state and local governments, close to them, was declining while federal debt rose. Economists frequently assured them Europeans carried a far heavier load and Americans could carry safely a debt two and one-half times that of 1930, to at least $40,000,000,000 (actually incurred by 1939); sums so large defy imagination and fear.[2] They received no warnings against extravagance from the government bond market, for three strong reasons:—private business outlets for savings were contracted by the depression and regimentation, to a new peak of idle money, while federal control of currency and credit and foreign flight to United States securities assured the Treasury of unprecedented over-subscriptions at nominal rates.

Few reflected that Europe's debt burden made for class rigidity or that indebtedness by the relief method might imperil democracy itself. Most important, all the subsidized businessmen, farmers, laborers, unemployed and veterans acquired a vested interest in extravagant outlays which dictated their continuance. The few politicians who dared to suggest a tax-as-you-go policy, with income levies lowered to reach the masses, were ignored, as Congress from 1931 annually expanded its tax preview.

Since government could proceed by loan, tax policies could include corporation reform levies, regardless of their unproductivity during depression. Transformation of the federal tax system was largely completed during the calendar years 1932-1933:—bringing liquor, gift and nuisance taxes (including 3¢ postage), the first federal automobile and gas taxes, doubled estate rates, AAA processing taxes and income levies second only to 1918. 1934-1936 brought redoubling on estate rates and rises in surtaxes, double taxation of corporation dividends and taxation of corporations' undistributed profits, and a projected levy of 9% on payrolls for social security.

By that time most of the 2600 persons with incomes over $100,000

[1] Of the "extraordinary" budget of $7,500,000,000 projected in June 1933 only about $4,000,000,000 was spent.

[2] The usual civil and military outlays were classified as the "ordinary" budget; relief outlays as "extraordinary"; the administration interpreted the deficit as wholly relief in classification.

were taxed more than half their incomes, but few families apparently were so wealthy that tax rates dissipated their estates. When some found loopholes in personal holding companies, multiple trusts, non-resident-alien ownership, consolidated returns and net income deductions, Congress retaliated with publicity legislation, including an ill-advised "pink slip" return of 1934-1935. Most of the 1937 and some of 1938 tax legislation sought to close loopholes. Constitutional limits of taxation sometimes were exceeded, according to Supreme Court majorities, but the political and economic taxable capacity apparently has not been passed.

By various devices tax receipts of 1933 were almost trebled by 1937;

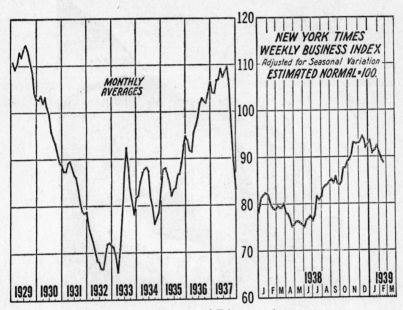

Business Index As of February 26, 1939

but the proportion from "reform" levies—on incomes, profits and estates—sank,[1] overbalanced by new taxes such as those on liquor and by concealed levies such as some fifty taxes hidden in each loaf of bread and quart of milk. Worse, a recession began in mid-1937; between May of 1937 and 1938 industrial production fell from 114[2] (within 11 points of 1929) to 76. Congress, yielding to business pressure, modified the capital gains tax and emasculated the undistributed profits levy; but the President let the bill become law without an approving signature

[1] The reform percentage was lower each year of 1933-1936 than in any since 1917 and in 1937 was still 11% below 1930.
[2] In terms of 1923-1925.

and again urged taxation of government bonds and salaries. Patently, the New Deal had not changed its social philosophy.

The excursions of New Deal agencies into industry—their struggles to handle materials, push processes, deal with contractors and relieve unemployment, educated them upon the trust-controlled character of American business. Federal regulatory bodies struck out against monopoly in directions as various as bakers and buckles, electric machinery and milk. Their efforts were popular with the masses as long as the depression seemed to be lifting.

The serious recession of 1937, however, challenged the democracy's

Fitzpatrick in St. Louis *Post Dispatch*.

Exploring Our Own Land
A cartoon evoked by the O'Mahoney committee

New Deal, in a world trending toward political and economic fascism. Among the important powers, America's industrial production had fallen further than any other (except Germany's) and recovered the least since 1929. Big business blamed the administration and labor, insisting that permanent recovery for capitalism could not be founded upon irresponsible unionism, expanding taxation, close regulation and competition with tax-supported agencies. The administration blamed the recession on industrial sabotage, insisting that prices were made high and profits low by overhead costs of idle machinery kept idle by high prices; that building steel was at $7 a ton above 1929 with payrolls

55% below; and that labor was laid off in the face of accumulated orders.

The issue was joined:—would Americans conclude that big business free of close supervision was necessary for that efficiency and economical mass production on which national prosperity depended? Or did they believe that government pressure was requisite for the price flexibility on which recovery depended?

The administration turned to educate the public—the traditional mode of democracy. The Department of Justice, PWA, FTC and the President trumpeted a clarion call for revision of anti-trust laws. Americans, they argued, had been content with "purely ritualistic" enforcement, craving only the emotional, moral comfort of the competitive ideal, without serious restriction of expanding monopoly.[1] Assistant Attorney-General Arnold argued that unemployment relief was a gigantic subsidy to industries discharging workers; that monopolies taxed the public through high prices in prosperity and through relief outlays in depressions. A special presidential message to Congress, 29 April 1938, indicted monopolies; and investigation by a "Temporary National Economic Committee" was ordered. Its six members of three each from House and Senate and six of one each from the Treasury, Justice, Labor and Commerce Departments, FTC and SEC, commenced with a sober investigation of patent abuse for monopolistic purposes. Senator O'Mahoney of Wyoming, chairman, probably reflected the public's attitude when describing the aim of the committee as "to help develop rules that will set business free to govern itself." It was this question of federal rules for self-governed business which dominated the politics, as well as the economics, of the New Deal era.

Americans expected to solve it. Their superb self-confidence remained with them. For the third time they were proving that a serious depression could not kill their sense of pride in achievement; they supported no less than three costly spectacles:—a "Century of Progress" at Chicago in 1933-1934, and in 1939 a "Golden Gate International Exposition" at San Francisco and a "World of Tomorrow" at New York.

[1] The anti-trust division of the Department of Justice consisted of but five lawyers and four stenographers under T. Roosevelt, had a personnel of but fifteen in 1932, and only fifty-eight attorneys in 1938.

CHAPTER XL

WHICH WAY DEMOCRACY?

The depression made a smashing impact upon the old party organizations. It revealed the Republicans as inadequate in leadership, program, organization and following. It challenged the Democrats to weld together permanently the disparate elements—southern bourbons, northern laborers, western farmers and middle class liberals—whose economic and political resentments in 1932 for the first time had united them behind one candidate. Was the bold innovator, F. D. Roosevelt, in eight years of continuing depression fortifying liberal democracy against political disintegration?

Political Instability

Democracy was on trial for its life, assailed by threat of war, politics and vested interests. Dictatorship supplanted it abroad in areas of worst poverty and fought its continuance elsewhere with such weapons of trade and propaganda as totalitarian states wield. At home some New Deal instruments devised originally to defend democracy against depression were corrupted for political purposes inimical to that ideal. Some devices for investigation of business malpractice, through wire-tapping and seizure of private telegrams, were misused for political purposes. Some emergency powers were grasped at for permanent exercise. Some politicians, Democratic only by label, used relief agencies to bolster reactionary state organizations and to oil personal machines. Public tax funds thus served these Democrats as corporation contributions formerly served certain Republicans. Between 1933 and 1939 nearly one-sixth of the population slipped into the status of acquiring a vested interest in relief, direct and indirect. This ensured its continuance into prosperity and political use of it. Because approximately 6 billions of the 10 billions spent on relief were disbursed through WPA, it remained the great problem, and some of its workers, early unionized as the "Workers' Alliance," persistently agitated for expansion. Into the great new agencies of social welfare it proved difficult to extend civil service, for bipartisan spoilsmen fought it.[1]

The administration was peculiarly vulnerable. The existing bureauc-

[1] With difficulty a 1938 law was passed to carry all 1st, 2nd and 3rd class postmasters into civil service.

racy was none too sympathetic to the New Deal, and in some offices (particularly the Treasury during Secretary Woodin's long and fatal illness) they sabotaged it; could the New Deal hope to succeed if important machinery were manned by unsympathetic employees? Could key agencies such as the TVA obtain ample appropriations if Chairman A. V. Morgan refused generous patronage to members of Congress? Could the rock-ribbed Republican Commonwealth of Pennsylvania have been reclaimed without tolerance for WPA manipulation and special Negro patronage? Did the President extend the merit system over HOLC in September 1936 chiefly for political reasons? Would the issue of clean politics determine voters' allegiance? Much depended upon how long the electorate had faith in the larger objectives of the New Deal.

The elections gave evidence. The Republicans lost in 1934 in spite

POLITICAL RETURNS 1930-1938

Year	Congress	Senate				House of Representatives			
		Rep.	Dem.	Ind.	Vac.	Rep.	Dem.	Ind.	Vac.
1930	72	48	47	1	..	214	219	1	1
1932	73	36	59	1	..	117	313	5	..
1934	74	25	69	2	..	102	322	10	1
1936	75	16	76	4	..	90	328	13	4
1938	76	23	69	4	..	170	262	3	..

of and because of efforts of the DuPonts and wealthy associates to rally property-holders around an "American Liberty League" for protection against the New Deal. Next a threat rose from the left, with Senator Huey Long's "Share the Wealth" party conservatively estimated early in 1935 at more than 3 million voters, with Father Charles E. Coughlin attracting 8 million adherents to the "National Union for Social Justice," and with Dr. F. E. Townsend claiming 6 million members in his "Old Age Revolving Pensions Limited." An assassin eliminated Long, however, and when the three factions attempted to unite behind the presidential candidacy of the radical agriculturist, Representative W. O. Lemke of North Dakota, he obtained less than 900,000 popular, and no electoral votes. The New Deal extended a helpful hand to the eastern flood and western drought areas that summer and fall, and made such inroads upon the various radical tickets that their combined 1936 total was scarcely 3% of the whole.[1]

The Republicans dared not declare against popular subsidies, although they preached a balanced budget and had support from "Jeffersonian (propertied) Democrats," like the Liberty League membership, J. W. Davis (Democratic standard bearer in 1924), W. R. Hearst and Al Smith. Realizing their past blessings in the farm vote, they planned to

[1] Lemke, Union ticket, 882,479; Thomas, Socialist, 187,720; Browder, Communist, 80,159; Colvin, Prohibitionist, 37,847; Aiken, Socialist-Labor, 12,777. Landon received 16,679,583 and Roosevelt 27,476,673.

restore their East-Middle West alliance with a "grabbag" platform and a ticket headed by Alf Landon of Kansas and Frank Knox, respectively the only Republican governor re-elected in 1934 and the editor of the Chicago *Daily News*. They obtained endorsement from most of the important dailies and consistently favorable majorities in polls conducted by the *Literary Digest* and Hearst. But polls by George M. Gallup, who did not omit sampling the masses, revealed a contrary trend.

A last minute attempt of the American Manufacturers Association to turn votes Republican with a payroll-envelope denunciation of social security was poorly adjusted to national psychology. It was easily smashed by a Roosevelt rebuttal over the radio, always skilfully used by him. 1936 has been called a radio election; but the Democratic victory was due more to improving economic conditions, which encouraged a majority to believe that Roosevelt's program—reaffirmed and enlarged in campaign promises—would implement *permanent* prosperity under the American system. A continuing loyalty to that system was demonstrated by refusal to endorse radical tickets. After a campaign no less vitriolic than the quadrennial taste of the nation occasionally demands and enjoys, approximately 45 million men and women participated in one of the most orderly elections ever witnessed. Americans still preferred ballots to bullets for arbitration of differences over the brand of their democracy.

To the farmer and labor endorsement, which had helped to bring Roosevelt in 1932 all but six states, 1936 added the colored vote. The depression had brought north, to relief jobs and suffrage, Negroes who reaudited and closed their emancipation account with the Republican party. This left the Republicans only about 37% of the popular vote, so distributed as to afford but eight electoral votes—Maine's five and Vermont's three; Roosevelt and Garner obtained 60% of the total vote.[1]

The reelected President undertook to use the high tide of his popularity to launch a significant reform in each of the three fields of government—executive, judicial and legislative. He knew that progressive enthusiasms subside; he and his intimates hurried to make American government an instrument for effective, quick and liberal response to the changing needs of the nation. They assumed that with the Republicans eclipsed nationally and locally [2] the President could placate Congress less and command it more. He could insist that Congress go farther to subordinate regional preferences to federal needs, and deprive vested interests of their dominance over economic and political conditions.

[1] They had been renominated by acclamation in a convention which, after a struggle, abolished the 104-year-old two-thirds rule, thus putting at least a temporary end to the southern veto of nominations.

[2] Other than their 16 Senate and 90 House seats the Republicans had only 6 governorships.

Executive Reform

First, in the executive field, it was generally conceded that greater efficiency was badly needed to abolish waste and duplication. Roosevelt called for an administrative reorganization to include:—creation of six assistants to the President to keep him in touch with departmental operations; two new departments—of Social Welfare and of Public Works —with the Interior renamed the Department of Conservation; abolition of the office of Comptroller General and of all congressional authority to "pre-audit" appropriation expenditures. Unfortunately, this proposal of 12 January 1937 was not expertly launched for quick disposal.

The President had had complete authority, during his first two years, to redistribute functions and organize bureaus, including the independent regulatory bureaus, but up until 1936 he had appeared indifferent. Then his own committee, named after the Senate named one, clashed with Senate and House committees and their research experts, over respective fields of inquiry. When the President accepted the report of his committee *in toto* he thereby put critics of it in the unenviable position of attacking himself, who had just been reelected by the greatest popular endorsement since Monroe's of 1820.

This much political advantage for the proposition, which the public in general was receiving favorably, was offset by Roosevelt 5 February when he injected into the situation an unexpected [1] call for Supreme Court reform. Thereupon Congress instead of enacting reorganization before considering court reform, let reorganization hang a year, turning to wage over court reform the bitterest debate since the League of Nations struggle (p. 637).

Meanwhile, the interests which were opposing executive reform revealed themselves as aiming principally against the President and his social and economic program. They weakened his prestige by a hue and cry over constitutionality and dictatorship, although the principle powers granted in the pending administrative bill—to redistribute functions and abolish bureaus—formerly had been possessed by him and two of his predecessors, and although the proposed accounting system was markedly similar to that used before 1921. The opposition developed congressional support with the aid of such events as the recession, the split in the Democratic party and the squabble in the TVA.

All this and a deluge of inspired telegrams could not, however, prevent Senate passage of a compromise measure, after an extended and not unimpressive debate. But at this critical juncture accumulating resentments between the President and the House were capped by an ill-timed presidential reference to purchased votes. Nor would he placate

[1] Apparently without consultation with his party's congressional leaders.

them. Furthermore this matter, unlike pensions and relief, did not lie close to the hearts of humble constituents. So Congress, which had given Roosevelt far vaster power by sanctioning his spending program, on 8 April 1938 put the executive third of his reform program in abeyance. The reorganization law they accepted in March 1939 exempted many important commissions.

Judicial Reform

The judicial third, so suddenly sprung early in 1937, called for:— an increase in Supreme Court justices from 9 to a maximum of 15, if

Russell in Los Angeles *Times*.

The New Deal Struck Out

those reaching 75 declined to retire: a total increase of not more than 50 judges in all classes of federal courts: despatch of appeals on constitutional questions direct from lower courts to the Supreme tribunal: and required hearing of federal attorneys, before any lower court issued an injunction against enforcement of a congressional act.

The main object was to place in a minority that majority of Supreme Court judges who by 5 to 4 decisions had ruled against the government in about half the cases of the 1935-1936 term, effectually blocking the

New Deal approach to social welfare.[1] Holding to the doctrine of laissez faire, they had interpreted the Constitution so as to limit powers of government narrowly while enlarging those of private interests. On such issues as the NRA, AAA and Carter Coal cases, they insisted that agriculture, mining and manufacture were local activities, beyond federal regulation. This flatly contradicted both the intentions of the framers, as expressed in the Constitutional Convention resolutions, and the expositions of Alexander Hamilton in his state papers. Also it perpetuated the wide twilight zone where neither federal nor state governments could intervene to protect public from private interest, erecting judicial barriers to the current trend toward interstate cooperation in executive and legislative functioning. Problems like crime, traffic, relief, liquor, milk, water supply, health, corporation taxes, crops and industrial conditions had crossed state boundaries. Some of the interstate compacts were specifically approved by Congress and certain states joined the national government in defense of federal legislation before federal courts.[2] The need for a "clarifying" amendment to the Constitution had been widely admitted.

Such a gradual method of solution better suited American preconceptions than did the quicker, congressional action demanded by Roosevelt. His plan, a surprise to most all of his closest friends, aroused bitter opposition among special interests, because its end was implementation of the New Deal, and among political conservatives because its means were expansion of executive powers. Fiercely the Senate debated its constitutionality and its threat to independence of the judiciary. Some widely influential Democrats broke sharply with the President, openly acknowledging the schism which long had been cutting deeply beneath the party surface.

Senator Joseph T. Robinson succumbed to heart disease while struggling in hot weather to hold his party in line.[3] This and a complex of other factors combined in mid-summer to defeat judicial reform. But throughout the debate and the year following, Congress, the Court and the Administration did so act that New Deal reversals decreased. Thereby judicial reform was approximated.

Congress passed two compromise laws. One permitted voluntary retirement by Supreme Court judges on full pay at 70—which led conservative Justices VanDevanter and Sutherland to resign and permitted the President to appoint his supporters, Senator Hugo Black and Solicitor General Stanley Reed, to the bench. The other greatly facili-

[1] Taft had named 5 judges, Harding 4, Wilson 3, Hoover 3; 6 of the Court in 1937 were past 70; 5 were not confirmed liberals.

[2] An "American Legislators' Association" grew into the Council of State Governments, which has developed much functional coordination among states.

[3] House Democrats joined senators in revolt 14 July and Robinson died that day.

tated participation by the Department of Justice in cases involving constitutional interpretation.[1]

The Court majority shifted to the liberal side. In 5-4 decisions, it upheld abrogation of gold payments and reversed earlier reasoning against state regulation of women's wages. It unanimously upheld the Frazier-Lemke Farm Mortgage Moratorium Act and significant provisions of the Railway Labor Act. In one case unanimously and in four by 5-4 decisions it upheld the Wagner National Labor Relations Act to such effect as to admit manufacturing to classification as an interstate activity subject to congressional regulation; this suggested ultimate inclusion of mining and agriculture. It approved by 5-4 and 7-2 decisions the unemployment insurance and old age pensions sections of the Social Security Act.[2]

The administration strove to dodge reversals. Framers of the Social Security Act carefully avoided that earmarking (of tax yield from one group for the specific benefit of another) on which the court threw out the AAA. The government restricted its plea in the Wilson dam case to acknowledged functions of national defense and navigation, dodging the two basic TVA activities of public power production and competition with private companies. Altogether, in the 1937-1938 term the government won 92 out of 114 cases argued and decided on the merits, or approximately 80%.

Legislative Reform

Shifts in judicial attitudes could not reunite New Dealers and conservative Democrats, for their political differences sprang from that economic and social cleavage which inspired the President's triple program. Defeat on executive and judicial reform only confirmed his determination to pursue both further, and to press harder for the legislative reform which ultimately would swing the other two. He would purge his party of its "bourbons" to establish it as America's liberal political instrument, in contradistinction to the conservative Republican party. The voters should renominate and elect in 1938 only such Democrats and Republicans as had proved their liberal convictions by consistent support of the New Deal. Democratic opponents of court

[1] Supreme Court Retirement Act, 1 March, Judicial Procedure Reform Act, 25 August; Black's appointment became unpopular for he later was proved to have once belonged to the Ku Klux Klan, a fact said to have been unknown to Roosevelt beforehand.

[2] Gold, 1 March; women's wages, railway act and mortgages, 29 March; Wagner Act, 12 April; Social Security, 24 May 1937; the liberals customarily were Hughes, Brandeis, Stone, Cordozo and Roberts; the Conservatives Sutherland, Van Devanter, McReynolds and Butler. After the Black and Reed appointments, Cardozo died and Brandeis resigned. Felix Frankfurter, a forceful and popular liberal, and W. O. Douglas of the SEC, were appointed to the Court.

reform—particularly Senators Walter F. George of Georgia, Guy M. Gillette of Iowa, Ellison D. Smith of South Carolina, Millard R. Tydings of Maryland and Representative John J. O'Connor of New York—ought to fail of renomination.

Many Democrats, as well as Republicans, were aghast at the proposal for meaningful labels; their earlier conservative alliances, present insecurity and future fears bound them to the familiar. The Democratic majority in Congress became fatigued by the Roosevelt drive, unwieldy and openly resentful of their minor place. Vice-President Garner and many associates in key committee places saw on the horizon no vision of a successful political realignment, based on broad social principles. Behavior reverted. Sectionalism killed an anti-lynching bill and animated objections to lavish expenditures on poor states of relief funds from rich areas; it also caused some states to devise indirect tariffs upon goods from adjacent commonwealths. Bipartisan conservatives joined business interests hating New Deal discipline, in supporting senators marked for the purge and in raising such an outcry about unconstitutionality and dictatorship that they alarmed some mild, middle-class liberals already troubled by the swift pace. A few independents hopeful of a new liberal party freed of New Deal excesses endorsed the launching, by Governor Philip La Follette and Senator Robert M. La Follette, Jr., 28 April 1938, of a National Progressive Party. Such were the second-term defections met by this administration.

Roosevelt's determination to make the 1938 election the vehicle of legislative reform ensured an aggressive campaign. He undertook to improve the economic background by further agricultural subsidies, wage-hour legislation and renewed appropriations for "pump-priming for recovery." The recession was lightened in July by an appreciable gain in industrial production, but farm prices lagged and national income did not regain the level of October 1937 before the 1938 election. Approximately 11 million remained unemployed; many others felt distrustful, vaguely fearing for their own security.

Furthermore, certain peculiar relief expenditures, promises of roads and bridges and political manipulation of WPA, especially in Kentucky, Pennsylvania and Tennessee [1] became notorious. Voters became generally aware of, and expressed considerable opposition to, political use of relief. Thus were the instruments of social reform dulled by political use. The President strove to impress farm and factory with their mutual interdependence, but his hold on these workers was weakened by low farm prices, and the duel between the A.F. of L. and the CIO. The support of the latter hurt the President in some regions where voters took affright at charges, aired before the Dies Committee on "Un-

---

[1] Exposed in detail, January 1939, by the Sheppard Senate Committee on Campaign Practice, consisting of 4 Democrats and 1 Republican.

American Activities," that the New Dealers were cooperating with CIO communists.

The electorate divided on age and class lines. Strongest New Deal support came from the younger voters and from that 36% of the nation on the lower economic level. The 16% on the upper level were violent in opposition. The outcome depended upon the 48% comprising a middle group who held the balance of power. Among these the recession, the purge, the supreme court plan and the sit-down strikes helped to give

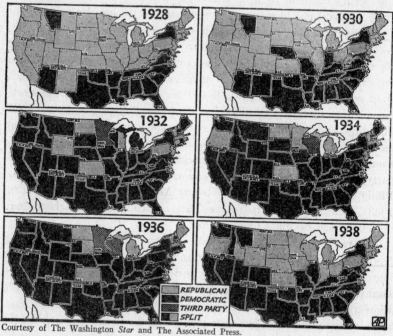

REPUBLICAN
DEMOCRATIC
THIRD PARTY
SPLIT

Courtesy of The Washington *Star* and The Associated Press.

The Political Tides, 1928-1938

the Republicans a gain of 5% and more in a continuous coast to coast line of 27 states. When the shouting was over, as Farley had expected, the electorate had apparently defeated Roosevelt's scheme for legislative reform. The purge had failed, except in the case of O'Connor. The Democratic congressional vote had fallen from the 59% of 1936 to below 53% in 1938. The Republicans had won 80 additional seats in the House, 8 in the Senate and a net gain of 12 governorships, with improved standing in 36 states.

Yet some measure of legislative reform had been won. The incoming Republicans belonged to a "new school." Some of them had out-Townsended Townsend in promises of old-age pensions. All of them knew that the majority of voters had acquired something of Roosevelt's concept of government responsibility; evidently they had small wish to give up the

SEC, CCC, Social Security, federal unemployment relief or trade reciprocity. Even southern planters who had defeated the purge soon were voting, by more than two-thirds, to adopt New Deal marketing restrictions on their cotton crop, and more than half the growers of rice and fine-cured tobacco voted similarly. The swing to the right had not travelled back to the ideas of Coolidge.

Down the "long mile" of Pennsylvania Avenue in Washington a belligerent President and Congress faced each other early in 1939. The election had deprived Roosevelt of many northern and western partisans, while it strengthened the hold of conservative southern Democrats on committee chairmanships and made them, with border state colleagues, preponderant in the reduced Democratic majority. Would the session degenerate into a struggle for control of the party machinery and of the 1940 nomination, as the watchful and unified Republican minority hoped? Or would some miracle spread harmony over the dissident Democrats and permit constructive legislation? Of such there was much need, with various groups clamoring for amendments to laws governing social security, railroad rehabilitation, the NLRB, FCC, WPA, AAA and wages and hours.

Patently the new Congress was revisionist, the electorate rightist, and spending less popular. Within a few weeks the House Appropriations Committee trimmed administration estimates on five measures, and Congress clipped 150 millions off WPA emergency appropriations. The Senate imposed some delay before acceding to the nomination of prominent liberal friends of Roosevelt: Gov. Frank Murphy of Michigan to be Attorney-General, Harry L. Hopkins to be Secretary of Commerce and Prof. Felix Frankfurter to succeed Justice Cardozo on the Supreme Court.

Although the President had insisted that the electoral shift was due to local conditions, the Democratic congressional campaign committee undertook a "realistic analysis" of the voting climate; and the administration apparently concluded that neither Democratic control, nor democracy itself, could long survive in a nation with 10,000,000 or more unemployed. Therefore the New Deal shifted emphasis from reform to recovery, indicating the trend in its treatment of Congress, labor, the utilities, and industry in general. The President announced a shift of some responsibilities to Congress, suggesting that they take more initiative and form their own permanent relief program; they, not his staff, should do the bill-drafting. He intimated in a Jackson Day speech that harmony would advantage them all. Labor was urged, in a carefully prepared plea, to make peace within its own ranks; hope for a reunited labor movement was strengthened by evidence that more than two-thirds of the new units in the A. F. of L. were of the industrial rather than the craft type.

The President told the utilities that federal subsidy of power projects was not to be further expanded; the TVA ended its long feud with the Commonwealth and Southern Corporation by a marked concession in the price paid for Tennessee electrical properties. This encouraged hope for private utility expansion, since the combined federal and private developments could not match the nation's needs. The President assured industry in general that it need have nothing to fear from administration objectives; new or increased taxes were not in prospect. His lead was followed by Secretary of the Treasury Morgenthau, who urged Congressional scrutiny of the tax system to ferret out levies deterrent to business. Secretary of Commerce Hopkins (erstwhile radical of the WPA) issued from a Mid-West platform at Des Moines, Iowa, a message of moderation and conciliation on spending, utilities, labor, agriculture, and taxes. House and Senate were moving to spread the tax load by establishing reciprocal taxation of federal and state salaries.[1] To these various moves people reacted according to their situation, faith and prejudices.

Roosevelt's main preoccupation, as explained in his January message, was no longer with domestic reform but with "adequate defense." He joined spending and relief appropriations with intense naval and military preparations as the immediate, pressing necessities. An accumulated deficit of 44.5 billions by 1940 seemed to him of small moment in the light of the flames of war which he saw flaring up over the world and threatening America. He was pointing to events transpiring across the seas, drawing the eyes of the nation in that direction. Domestic reforms, as in Wilson's day, slipped into the background.

Insecurity in International Relations

The New Deal struggle for political security in the midst of economic insecurity had been continually complicated by international insecurity. Secretary of State Hull had kept reminding the powers that world stability required unhindered trade; but they gave to his "eight point program" along that line only lip service. He pressed an executive project for unconditional, most-favored-nation treaties of reciprocity on two basic assumptions:—that American prosperity required recapture of the foreign markets which formerly absorbed 10% of her production; and that they could be recaptured in face of the managed currency, barter and quota systems widely employed by hostile powers aiming at national self-sufficiency.[2] On the other hand, most of the administration's legislative

---

[1] Similar levies on income from government bonds were strongly resisted.

[2] Bilateral (as distinct from unconditional, most-favored-nation agreements) had resulted, by 1938, in some 380 special arrangements known to exclude the United States. Trade ambitions were the basis for the 1933 resumption, after a 15 year hiatus, of relations with Russia.

program seemed to be predicated on the principle that national self-sufficiency was America's only recourse.

Politically, the nation had remained isolationist. Although Congress accepted affiliation with the International Labor Office (1934) and although officials gave the first United States ratification of an international labor convention (1938), it was only a small group of professional internationalists who kept American ideology, moral support and financial assistance virtually predominant in most of the two hundred and more international associations working in the field of public administration. Isolationism peculiarly attracted a people recently victimized by general defaults on war debts, by munitions grafters, bankers' war profits and upset trade.[1] Their Congress forbade credit and loans to defaulting governments, restricted some exports to cash and carry, denied government protection to American passengers and goods using belligerent merchantmen, and directed the President to place an embargo upon munitions shipments to all countries at war.[2]

A popular referendum before war could be declared, except in case of invasion, was favored by an estimated 75% of voters in 1935 and by 68% in October 1938, even after the administration had defeated such a law by heavy persuasion on congressmen.[3] Thus, determination to avoid war made Congress abandon the traditional insistence upon freedom of the seas, tie strings to diplomatic policy and ignore the possibility that equal treatment of warring powers, as to embargoes on arms, credits and loans, might harm American interests. The Senate stuck to its refusal to enter the World Court—although American reservations were virtually accepted. Articles X and XVI of the League Covenant remained anathema; the Senate would promise neither to guarantee territorial integrity of League members nor to use force—"sanctions"—against nations renouncing their League obligations.

However, as totalitarian governments rising in Italy in 1922, Japan after 1930 [4] and Germany in 1933 (countries which had joined the League), violated League obligations and the territorial integrity of other members of it, American presidents had hinted at joining in sanctions and showed increased sympathy for London and Paris. A Hoover appointee had sat with a League Commission which in 1932 censured Japan for invading Manchuria. President Roosevelt kept an ambassador-at-large, Norman Davis, to test currents between nations. Davis in 1933

---

[1] They were angered by the money-making and propaganda aspects of the World War, as exposed by Senator Gerald P. Nye's munitions investigations of 1934-1936.

[2] By the Johnson Act, Apr. 1934, and successive laws of Aug. 1935, Feb. 1936 and May, 1937.

[3] The Ludlow resolution was killed by only a 21 vote margin and was inspired particularly by disapproval of overt action against Japan.

[4] Japan has not yet travelled the full distance toward totalitarianism.

pledged Geneva that the United States would not hinder "collective security"—only to have Congress repudiate his assumption. After Japan in 1934 served notice that she would not be bound to her subsidiary status beyond 1936, Roosevelt appointees participated with French and British in the futile London conference of 1935; they set naval limitations, supposedly good until 1942, but were careful to make them qualitative, not quantitative. So soon after the close of one disastrous world war, the powers entered another mad armament race.

President Roosevelt became convinced that all policy must take account of that militant fascism in Germany, Italy and Japan which pressed the dictatorships' concentrated power and need for conquest as against the democracies' looser organization and need for peace. He wanted freedom to act as the world's leader in democracy, adjusting policies to contingencies. Straining at the congressional leash, he dodged equal application of the neutrality laws, advocated closer cooperation with Britain and Canada (with whom significant trade pacts were achieved after Nazi victories in 1938) and continually fought isolationism with "educational" propaganda for collective security. He placed experienced career men in four of the most important embassy posts and pushed naval expansion.

The principal foreign wars brought gradations in his policy and in public opinion. When Mussolini seized Ethiopia (1935) Congress refused a Roosevelt request for a change in the neutrality laws to allow cooperation in League sanctions against Italy. After Japan began (August 1937) a relentless invasion of China in an undeclared war of aggression, Roosevelt exhorted the nation (5 October) to help other powers "quarantine" aggressors; but the next week public opinion forced him to deny a Brussels conference, (attended by nineteen powers), that pledge of concrete cooperation and American initiative in support of the Nine Power Pact which Britain had particularly desired. Two months later American newsreels focussed sharply upon Japanese sinking of the American gunboat *Panay,* but the public was content peaceably to accept apologies and indemnities; they had heard that less than 1% of their foreign investments lay in China. Was this a case of British chestnuts? A year later, Japan celebrated further conquests and trade controls in China by defiantly proclaiming the closing of the Open Door. The Administration replied with repeated demands that it remain open, in compliance with the 1922 Nine Power Pact, and hit back by giving renewed gold credits and loans to China.[1] Munitions exports to Japan were discouraged as used for bombing civilian areas.

Japan's campaign for the domination of Asia and subordination of

---

[1] The gold credit had been created by United States purchases of Chinese silver; the Export-Import Bank loan of 25 millions was partly spent for 100 General Motors and Chrysler trucks.

western influence expanded expensively. America's stake in China, never potentially large, became negligible. China latterly has been buying less than 3% of United States exports and selling her only about 3.8% of her imports. The closing, however, has not been to the disadvantage of the United States only. Between her and Japan had sprung up a mutually beneficial trade which in 1937 was so large that Japan was the third largest source of imports to the United States and the third largest foreign buyer of American goods. In 1938 Japanese exports to the United States fell 37% and her imports from the United States fell 30.5%.

Mussolini's and Hitler's support of the fascistic revolt within the

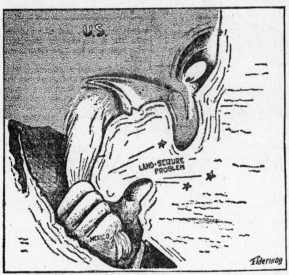

Elderman in Washington *Post*.

Expropriation Hurts!

Spanish democracy moved some Americans to send funds or to enlist on the Insurgent or Loyalist side according to viewpoint; but the isolationist majority secured embargo of munitions shipments and withdrawal of American warships from Spanish waters. By 1939 most volunteers had returned, as the Loyalists were defeated; recognition of the Insurgents approached.

As Hitler's program flowered, German influence upon American attitudes grew. When Wilson and his fellow-peacemakers of 1919 left large German minorities and glorified the principle of self-determination, they bequeathed to Hitler a principle on which he could seize Austria and Czechoslovakia. In seizing them, he imperilled a relatively small commercial stake,—but he violated the democratic sense of fair play. While war threatened Europe over Czechoslovakia, United States interest was fed by a shouting radio until it attained proportions which made this event the outstanding incident of 1938. The masses, as in other countries, rejoiced when war was postponed, although inclined to disapprove of the Munich agreement which prevented war. By urging peace upon all parties then, instead of pledging American support of war measures, Roosevelt raised his declining popularity.

The Nazi persecution of Jews and Catholics (evidently designed to enrich the party) led to considerable American boycott of German and Italian imports,[1] caused lightening of immigration restrictions, cooperation in international refugee work, and helped to bring Ambassador Wilson back home. As Americans cut purchases of Germany, they

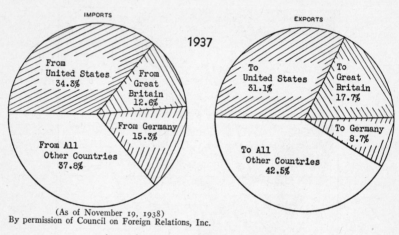

IMPORTS

1937

EXPORTS

From United States 34.3%

From Great Britain 12.6%

From Germany 15.3%

From All Other Countries 37.8%

To United States 31.1%

To Great Britain 17.7%

To Germany 8.7%

To All Other Countries 42.5%

(As of November 19, 1938)
By permission of Council on Foreign Relations, Inc.

Apportionment of Latin American Trade

drained off her precious reserve of foreign exchange to her intense resentment.

Germany further undermined United States isolationism by her Latin American policy. Earnestly seeking richer trade, understanding and political likemindedness, the Roosevelt administration was perfecting Hoover's conciliation program into what it termed the "Good Neighbor" policy. Caribbean imperialism was liquidated by withdrawal of marines; armed intervention was renounced officially at the Seventh Pan American Conference (Montevideo, 1933); an Inter-American Peace Conference was assembled (Buenos Aires, 1936) at Roosevelt's suggestion and he personally attended.[2] Differences with several republics over defaulted bonds and with Mexico over expropriated farm and oil lands

[1] German imports into the United States for the first ten months of 1938 apparently were 21% below the corresponding period of 1932—the last pre-Hitler year.

[2] The Americas signed treaties of non-aggression, binding themselves not to war over boundaries, or recognize war-made boundaries or interfere in each others' internal affairs.

were negotiated with the utmost patience. This most recent expropriation became a most delicate issue, because of the contagion in the Mexican example, because the oil was sold to foreign dictatorships for military purposes, and because the expropriation was financed largely through funds obtained from United States purchases of silver mined in Mexico on property held by Americans!

In the midst of these strenuous overtures from the north, Germany's efforts to strengthen her national banking and credit structure led her into a strenuous campaign to bind Latin America to her own economic system and political ideology. She, and to a lesser extent Italy and Japan, offered a natural market for Latin raw materials; but she paid for them in barter credits, good chiefly for unloading dictatorship manufactures and calculated to reduce southern markets for other competitors. Her bewildering variety of opportunistic trade devices, their ruthless application and their political significance as government-controlled activities, all alarmed competitors. Her purchases were increasingly conditioned upon acceptance of Nazi dogma—as when foreign export houses were required to dismiss Jewish employees and influential places in business were demanded for Nazis.

Although German trade gained chiefly at the expense of other nations, the United States suffered serious reversals in Mexico, was challenged in Brazil, Chile and Uruguay and was the pet target of violent, continuous radio programs of Nazi origin. The figures for Latin American trade as a whole did not justify immediate fear in the north, but contained considerable potential threat. However, German payments in goods could be offset by United States payments in more usable foreign exchange, better liked in the long run. Also, retention of the political influence of the United States was indicated in many countries which sought the privilege of her naval, army and aviation missions.

The Roosevelt administration nevertheless expressed great alarm. It requested of Congress—and was refused—a special 1938 broadcast appropriation. The Departments of State, Agriculture, Commerce and Interior and the Maritime Commission were set to work to weave bonds of unity—particularly through trade encouragement. The most-favored-nation policy should be pushed harder, to increase imports. The Export-Import Bank extended credits for expansion of United States utility systems in the south. Secretary Hull and his associates appealed to the Latin Americans for loyalty to democratic ideals.

Unfortunately for such hopes, the twenty other republics were not committed to representative democracy in the United States sense. Quite accustomed to dictatorships, albeit not the kind that destroyed most personal liberty, many Latin Americans could not excite themselves over the northern cry to arms against totalitarianism. Some of them compared it favorably with the local brand of dictator-republicanism; and many

felt that their economic and cultural ties bound them less closely to the
United States than to Europe. Alarmists claimed, as 1939 approached,
that United States trade was falling, her influence was being nullified,
and the reciprocal trade agreements were being driven to a standstill.
Was the United States about to lose her position as the nation with the
greatest amount of South American trade? Would the Germans, Italians
and Japanese succeed in extending their type of political system to the
western hemisphere and thus violate the Monroe Doctrine?

The issue was defined, behind polite verbiage, at the Eighth Pan
American Conference, which met at Lima 9-27 December 1938. Secretary Hull took down a carefully selected delegation and a cherished
program for political and economic solidarity among the twenty-one
American republics. He conducted himself and his delegation with the
utmost caution, avoiding coercion, protesting that there was no desire
to cut off the western hemisphere from the eastern, and reasserting those
pledges of non-interference, equality of status and cooperation, as between the United States and the other republics, which had been given
at Montevideo and Buenos Aires. Delegate Alf M. Landon assured
the conferees and the world that the Monroe Doctrine was immune
to election vicissitudes—for the Germans were claiming a new administration would abandon it. Pointing to the striking fact of an entire
western hemisphere at peace, Hull preached anew his gospel that economic disarmament is one of the essentials of political stability.

Political stability, however, had no place in vigorous Nazi ambitions.
In the declarations signed at Lima, Brazil and Peru prevented use of
the term "democracy." The Argentine prevented a denunciation of to-
talitarism; nor did the powers bind themselves to political solidarity
against it. The moral, economic and political declarations obtained by
Hull included no sanctions. While they expressed disapproval of racial
and religious persecution and approval of the principle of reciprocal
trade agreements on a most-favored nation basis, they laid down no concrete program for ending the one or rebeginning the other.

The "Declaration of Lima," advancing slightly beyond the Buenos
Aires agreement, reaffirmed loyalty of the Americas to republicanism and
proclaimed their common concern over new dangers. It pledged them to
consult together with a view to solidarity of action in the event of threat
to their peace, security or territorial integrity. But the consultation was
to be on the request of the threatened nation. The Declaration contained
nothing to prevent the adoption of fascism by any country converted to
it. It left the protection of republicanism to be achieved before fascist
influence converts the Americas. Into this can be read almost any meaning occasion may dictate; truly a most supple instrument of diplomacy.
The finance ministers of Argentine, Brazil, Paraguay and Uruguay,
however, heeded Hull's gospel. They announced, 3 February 1939, a

far-reaching program for lowering trade barriers between themselves.

Isolationism was weakened also by domestic factors. Selfish profiteers and honest advocates of collective security busied themselves. There accumulated in the United States, by late 1938, some 9 billions in foreign bank balances, lying convenient for use in war purchases. Much more important in the picture was the composite origin of the population and the national addiction to moral judgments. Every warring faction abroad had its little minority of interventionists in the United States, where the maintenance of democratic institutions left them relatively free to till with propaganda the rich field of a naive nation interested in righteousness. Most important of these minorities were the German-American *Bund* supporting the Hitler regime and the communistic groups infiltrating part of the WPA and the automobile, steel and some other unions of the CIO. Uneasiness over such influences inspired spy hunts under congressional and administration auspices and laws requiring foreign agents to register and barring aliens from the WPA.

More important than aught else, in leading a retreat from isolationism, is the loyalty of the vast majority to what they term "Democracy." The term entered into designs as different as the A.F. of L. boycott of Japanese imports and the unprecedented, peace-time expansion of the navy, merchant marine and army during 1937-39.[1] The people wished for peace but heard continually from the lips of President, cabinet and lesser persons exciting denunciations of the "undemocratic" powers. A carefully arranged visit of Anthony Eden, the British leader conspicuous both for opposition to the Munich agreement and for insistence upon United States support of British and French "Democracy," proved a great popular success in December of 1938. That month preparedness sentiment had risen about 20% above its level at the peak of pacifism; but 70% of the voters still thought American participation in the last great war a mistake and 95% opposed entrance in the next one.

Europe was more confident of United States participation. Shift of emphasis from domestic to foreign affairs was raising the President's popularity. Would he not silence disapproval of a budget of 9 billions and a public debt of 44.5 billions by clanging the alarm bell? He was heard across the ocean, 4 January 1939, assuring Congress, the nation and the world, that spending for recovery had been completely proved, that retrenchment would bring another slump and dangerous dissension to beleagured democracy. The previous six years, said he, had brought

---

[1] Among the measures of April-June 1938 were 2 naval acts, 3 army acts, and a merchant marine law. Motorized infantry, industrial mobilization and lightning aviation expansion were preached. The increasing popularity of rearmament, among voters was estimated thus:—

	Larger Navy		Larger Army		Larger Air Force	
1935	Yes 72%	No 28%	Yes 70%	No 30%	Yes 84%	No 16%
1938	" 86%	" 14%	" 82%	" 18%	" 90%	" 10%

an unprecedented and farflung "internal preparedness"; social and economic reform was as basic to defense as armaments. He asked appropriations of about 1320 millions for national defense and 2266 millions for recovery and relief. He pledged defense of the Western Hemisphere [1] against "new philosophies of force"—"We, no more than other nations, can afford to be surrounded by the enemies of our faith and our humanity." Europe took from the total situation two conclusions: (1) that the outcome of any large continental conflict must be determined by United States war capacity; (2) that the moral force of United States opinion was what was saving the Franco-British, democratic side from being overborne by the authoritarian, Berlin-Rome side in the new world balance of power.

These conclusions were reinforced in February, after an airplane accident revealed that the administration was giving prospective French purchasers special insight into American plane designs, and after Roosevelt was quoted as having told the Senate Military Affairs Committee that the frontier of the United States lay in France. Americans at first objected; would not secret policies entangle them in war? Veterans in both houses of Congress protested against sending their sons to die on foreign soil. Roosevelt quieted the outcry, by denying the quotation and by reasserting opposition to entanglements; he had a good margin of popular support for every possible aid to England and France "short of war." Dislike for the dictatorships went so far that even the World Peace Foundation declared for peace through additional military and naval preparedness. Abroad, American denunciation of totalitarian governments appeared to weaken the Rome-Berlin axis, while American boycott of their goods decidedly hurt their economic position.

A great question, therefore, was posed in the early months of 1939. Was the United States about to be drawn into the maelstrom of another European war, or would careful exercise of the nation's influence avert such conflict? All hoped for the latter, for it is not difficult to foresee the disastrous effects of another world conflict upon the democratic principle. Democracy thrives on hope, not despair, and American democracy has flourished because it has been a thing apart from Europe, developing in its own way, largely unhampered by war.

Made dynamic by abundance and the great confidence arising from seemingly inexhaustible wealth, America's democracy has marched on from achievement to achievement, always with a sense of great power and high purpose. Such a career has stored up a great vitality such as Europe has never possessed and cannot really know, a vitality constantly recharged by migration to America of a multitude of Europe's most enterprising sons and daughters. Under these circumstances a unique

[1] A careful poll indicated that the voters were overwhelmingly opposed to assuming defense of Mexico, Brazil, etc.

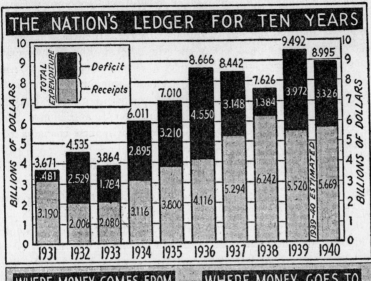

THE NATION'S LEDGER FOR TEN YEARS

Total Expenditure: Deficit / Receipts

Year	Total Expenditure	Deficit	Receipts
1931	3.671	.481	3.190
1932	4.535	2.529	2.006
1933	3.864	1.784	2.080
1934	6.011	2.895	3.116
1935	7.010	3.210	3.800
1936	8.666	4.550	4.116
1937	8.442	3.148	5.294
1938	7.626	1.384	6.242
1939	9.492	3.972	5.520
1940	8.995	3.326	5.669	(1939-40 ESTIMATED)

BILLIONS OF DOLLARS

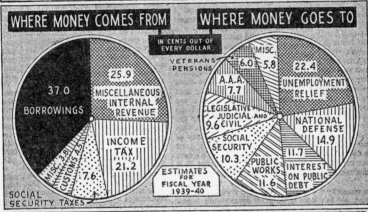

WHERE MONEY COMES FROM

IN CENTS OUT OF EVERY DOLLAR

- 37.0 BORROWINGS
- 25.9 MISCELLANEOUS INTERNAL REVENUE
- 21.2 INCOME TAX
- 7.6 SOCIAL SECURITY TAXES
- 4.3 CUSTOMS
- 3.8 MISC.

WHERE MONEY GOES TO

- VETERANS PENSIONS 6.0
- MISC. 5.8
- A.A.A. 7.7
- 22.4 UNEMPLOYMENT RELIEF
- LEGISLATIVE JUDICIAL AND CIVIL 9.6
- SOCIAL SECURITY 10.3
- NATIONAL DEFENSE 14.9
- PUBLIC WORKS 11.6
- INTEREST ON PUBLIC DEBT 11.7

ESTIMATES FOR FISCAL YEAR 1939-40

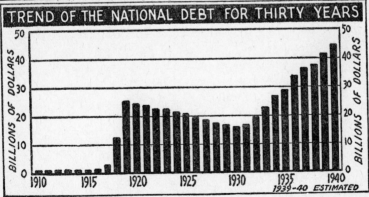

TREND OF THE NATIONAL DEBT FOR THIRTY YEARS

BILLIONS OF DOLLARS

1910 1915 1920 1925 1930 1935 1940

1939-40 ESTIMATED

Courtesy of *The New York Times*.

In the Red

society has been created, based upon an idealistic conception of the maintenance of equality for all.

Some of the fundamental conditions which contributed so largely to the creation of this unique society are being altered. The distance which so long protected the United States from active European interference and entanglement has been sharply reduced—almost annihilated, by invention. The great resources which for so long seemed inexhaustible are now showing signs of approaching limitation. Immigration to these shores has been largely curtailed. What effect will these changing conditions have upon American democracy?

The experiment in equality will be preserved and further advanced if Americans can guard against rivalries between race and class, bred among peoples less blest with abundance; if they can keep themselves free from the heavy load of permanent military establishments which restrict European production of useful goods; if they can successfully avoid the influence of centuries of ancient European rivalries, to escape which so many of their fathers crossed the seas to the new world.

The dynamic American experiment is unique; if it fails it can not be repeated. The rare circumstances which produced it are nowhere to be duplicated. To succeeding generations, the earth offers no untouched continent of opportunity, across some far ocean, for those in search of a new world of hope.

APPENDIX

President and Vice-President	Secretary of State	Secretary of Treasury	Secretary of War
George Washington-John Adams Fed. 1789	T. Jefferson......1789 E. Randolph.....1794 T. Pickering.....1795	Alex. Hamilton.1789 Oliver Wolcott .1795	Henry Knox ...1789 T. Pickering ...1795 Jas. McHenry..1796
John Adams-Thomas Jefferson..1797 Fed.	T. Pickering.....1797 John Marshall....1800	Oliver Wolcott .1797 Samuel Dexter .1801	Jas. McHenry..1797 John Marshall..1800 Sam'l Dexter..1800 R. Griswold....1801
Thomas Jefferson-Aaron Burr..1801 Dem. Rep. George Clinton 1805	James Madison...1801	Samuel Dexter .1801 Albert Gallatin.1801	H. Dearborn...1801
James Madison-George Clinton Dem. Rep. 1809 Elbridge Gerry..1813	Robert Smith....1809 James Monroe ...1811	Albert Gallatin.1809 G. W. Campbell 1814 A. J. Dallas....1814 W. H. Crawford 1816	Wm. Eustis....1809 J. Armstrong...1813 James Monroe..1814 W. H. Crawford 1815
James Monroe-D. D. Tompkins Dem. Rep. 1817	J. Q. Adams.....1817	W. H. Crawford 1817	Isaac Shelby...1817 Geo. Graham ..1817 J. C. Calhoun..1817
John Q. Adams-John C. Calhoun Natl. Rep. 1825	Henry Clay 1825	Richard Rush ..1825	Jas. Barbour...1825 Peter B. Porter.1828
Andrew Jackson-John C. Calhoun Dem. 1829 Martin Van Buren 1833	M. Van Buren...1829 E. Livingston....1831 Louis McLane ...1833 John Forsyth 1834	S. D. Ingham..1829 Louis McLane..1831 W. J. Duane...1833 Roger B. Taney 1833 Levi Woodbury.1834	John H. Eaton.1829 Lewis Cass ....1831 B. F. Butler...1837
Martin Van Buren-R. M. Johnson Dem. 1837	John Forsyth 1837	Levi Woodbury.1837	J. R. Poinsett..1837
Wm. H. Harrison-John Tyler..1841 Whig	Daniel Webster ..1841	Thos. Ewing ...1841	John Bell 1841
John Tyler, Whig............1841	Daniel Webster ..1841 Hugh S. Legaré..1843 Abel P. Upshur..1843 John C. Calhoun.1844	Thos. Ewing ...1841 Walter Forward.1841 J. C. Spencer..1843 Geo. M. Bibb..1844	John Bell .....1841 John McLean ..1841 J. C. Spencer..1841 Jas. M. Porter.1843 Wm. Wilkins...1844
James K. Polk-George M. Dallas Dem. 1845	James Buchanan .1845	R. J. Walker...1845	Wm. L. Marcy.1845
Zachary Taylor-M. Fillmore, Whig 1849	John M. Clayton.1849	W. M. Meredith 1849	G. W. Crawford 1849
Millard Fillmore, Whig.......1850	Daniel Webster ..1850 Edward Everett..1852	Thomas Corwin.1850	C. M. Conrad..1850
Franklin Pierce-Wm. R. King..1853 Dem.	W. L. Marcy....1853	James Guthrie .1853	Jefferson Davis .1853
James Buchanan-J. C. Breckinridge Dem. 1857	Lewis Cass......1857 J. S. Black......1860	Howell Cobb....1857 P. F. Thomas..1860 John A. Dix....1861	John B. Floyd..1857 Joseph Holt....1861
Abraham Lincoln-H. Hamlin Rep. 1861 Andrew Johnson 1865	W. H. Seward....1861	S. P. Chase....1861 W.P.Fessenden 1864 H. McCulloch..,1865	S. Cameron....1861 E. M. Stanton.1862
Andrew Johnson, Rep........1865	W. H. Seward....1865	H. McCulloch..1865	E. M. Stanton.1865 U. S. Grant....1867 L. Thomas ....1868 J. M. Schofield.1868
Ulysses S. Grant-Schuyler Colfax Rep. 1869 Henry Wilson 1873	E. B. Washburne.1869 Hamilton Fish...1869	G. S. Boutwell.1869 W.A.Richardson 1873 B. H. Bristow..1874 Lot M. Morrill.1876	J. A. Rawlins..1869 W. T. Sherman.1869 W. W. Belknap.1869 Alphonso Taft..1876 J. D. Cameron.1876
Rutherford B. Hayes-W. A. Wheeler, Rep. 1877	W. M. Evarts...1877	John Sherman..1877	G. W. McCrary.1877 Alex. Ramsey..1879
Jas. A. Garfield-C. A. Arthur Rep. 1881	James G. Blaine..1881	Wm. Windom..1881	R. T. Lincoln..1881

Secretary of Navy	Secretary of Interior	Postmaster-General	Attorney-General	Recent Depts.
	Established March 3, 1849.	Samuel Osgood. 1789 Tim. Pickering. 1791 Jos. Habersham. 1795	E. Randolph .1789 W. Bradford. .1794 Charles Lee. .1795	Secretary of agriculture. est. 11 Feb., 1889
Benj. Stoddert. .1798		Jos. Habersham. 1797	Charles Lee. .1797	
				N. J. Colman. 1889 J. M. Rusk. . .1889 J. S. Morton. .1893
Benj. Stoddert. .1801 Robert Smith . .1801		Jos. Habersham. 1801 Gideon Granger 1801	Levi Lincoln. 1801 J. Breckinridge.'05 C. A. Rodney 1807	J. Wilson. . . . .1897 D. F. Houston 1913 E. T. Meredith '20 H. C. Wallace.1921
Paul Hamilton. 1809 William Jones. .1813 B. W. Crowninshield 1814		Gideon Granger 1809 R. J. Meigs, Jr. 1814	C. A. Rodney 1809 W. Pinkney. .1811 Richard Rush 1814	H. M. Gore. .1924 W. M. Jardine '25 A. M. Hyde. .1929 H. A. Wallace. 1933
B. W. Crowninshield 1817 S. Thompson. . .1818 S. L. Southard. .1823		R. J. Meigs, Jr. 1817 John McLean. .1823	Richard Rush 1817 William Wirt. 1817	
S. L. Southard. .1825		John McLean. .1825	William Wirt. 1825	
John Branch. . .1829 Levi Woodbury. 1831 M. Dickerson . .1834		Wm. T. Barry. 1829 Amos Kendall. .1835	J. M. Berrien. 1829 R. B. Taney. 1831 B. F. Butler. 1833	
M. Dickerson . .1837 J. K. Paulding. 1838		Amos Kendall. .1837 John M. Niles. .1840	B. F. Butler. 1837 Felix Grundy. 1838 H. D. Gilpin. 1840	Secretary of commerce and labor.
Geo. E. Badger. 1841		Francis Granger 1841	J. J. Crittenden '41	est. 14 Feb., 1903
Geo. E. Badger. 1841 Abel P. Upshur. 1841 David Henshaw. 1843 T. W. Gilmer. .1844 John Y. Mason. 1844		Francis Granger 1841 C. A. Wickliffe. 1841	J. J. Crittenden '41 Hugh S. Legaré '41 John Nelson. .1843	George B. Cortelyou . . . . .1903 Victor H. Metcalf 1904
Geo. Bancroft. .1845 John Y. Mason. 1846		Cave Johnson . .1845	J. Y. Mason. 1845 Nathan Clifford '46 Isaac Toucey. 1848	O. S. Straus. .1907 Chas. Nagel . .1909
W. B. Preston. 1849	Thomas Ewing. 1849	Jacob Collamer. 1849	R. Johnson. . .1849	(Department divided, 1913.)
W. A. Graham. 1850 J. P. Kennedy. 1852	A. H. H. Stuart. 1850	Nathan K. Hall 1850 S. D. Hubbard. 1852	J. J. Crittenden '50	
Jas. C. Dobbin. 1853	R. McClelland . 1853	James Campbell 1853	Caleb Cushing.'53	Secretary of commerce.
Isaac Toucey. . .1857	J. Thompson. . .1857	A. V. Brown. . .1857 Joseph Holt. . . .1859	J. S. Black. .1857 E. M. Stanton 1860	W.C.Redfield 1913
Gideon Welles. .1861	Caleb B. Smith. 1861 John P. Usher. .1863	Horatio King. . .1861 M'gomery Blair 1861 Wm. Dennison.1864	Edward Bates.1861 James Speed. .1864	Joshua W. Alexander . .1919 H. C. Hoover.1921 W. F. Whiting
Gideon Welles. .1865	John P. Usher. .1865 James Harlan . .1865 O. H. Browning. 1866	Wm. Dennison.1865 A. W. Randall. 1866	James Speed. .1865 H. Stanbery. .1866 W. M. Evarts 1868	1928 R. P. Lamont.1929 R. D. Chapin.1932 D. C. Roper. .1933
A. E. Borie. . . .1869 G. M. Robeson. 1869	Jacob D. Cox. .1869 C. Delano . . . . .1870 Zach. Chandler. 1875	J. A. J. Creswell.'69 J. W. Marshall. 1874 Marshall Jewell. 1874 Jas. N. Tyner. .1876	E. R. Hoar. . .1869 A. T. Ackerman '70 G. H. Williams.'71 E. Pierrepont.1875 Alphonso Taft '76	Harry L. Hopkins 1939
R. W. Thompson.'77 Nathan Goff, Jr..'81	Carl Schurz. . . .1877	David M. Key. .1877 Horace Maynard.'80	Chas. Devens.1877	
W. H. Hunt. . .1881	S. J. Kirkwood.1881	T. L. James. . .1881	W. MacVeagh. .'81	

President and Vice-President	Secretary of State	Secretary of Treasury	Secretary of War
Chester A. Arthur, Rep........1881	F. T. Frelinghuysen '81	Chas. J. Folger. 1881 W. Q. Gresham. 1884 Hugh McCulloch '84	R. T. Lincoln..1881
Grover Cleveland-T. A. Hendricks Dem. 1885	Thos. F. Bayard..1885	Dan'l Manning.1885 C. S. Fairchild.1887	W. C. Endicott.1885
Benjamin Harrison-L. P. Morton Rep. · 1889	James G. Blaine..1889 John W. Foster..1892	Wm. Windom..1889 Charles Foster..1891	R. Proctor ....1889 S. B. Elkins...1891
Grover Cleveland-A. E. Stevenson Dem. 1893	W. Q. Gresham..1893 Richard Olney...1895	J. G. Carlisle..1893	D. S. Lamont..1893
Wm. McKinley-Garret A. Hobart Rep. 1897 Theodore Roosevelt 1901	John Sherman ...1897 Wm. R. Day....1898 John Hay 1898	Lyman J. Gage.1897	R. A. Alger....1897 Elihu Root....1899
Theodore Roosevelt, Rep.......1901 Chas. W. Fairbanks 1905	John Hay ....1901 Elihu Root ......1905 Robert Bacon....1909	Lyman J. Gage.1901 Leslie M. Shaw.1902 'G. B. Cortelyou 1907	Elihu Root....1901 Wm. H. Taft..1904 Luke E. Wright 1908
William H. Taft-J. S. Sherman Rep. 1909	P. C. Knox......1909	F. MacVeagh ..1909	J. M. Dickinson 1909 H. L. Stimson..1911
Woodrow Wilson-T. R. Marshall Dem. 1913	Wm. J. Bryan....1913 Robert Lansing ..1915 Bainbridge Colby.1920	W. G. McAdoo.1913 Carter Glass ...1918 D. F. Houston.1920	L. M. Garrison.1913 N. D. Baker...1916
W. G. Harding-Calvin Coolidge Rep. 1921	Chas. E. Hughes.1921	A. W. Mellon..1921	John W. Weeks.1921
Calvin Coolidge, Rep...........1923 Charles G. Dawes 1925	Chas. E. Hughes.1923 Frank B. Kellogg.1925	A. W. Mellon..1923	John W. Weeks.1923 Dwight F. Davis '25
Herbert C. Hoover-Chas. Curtis Rep. 1929	Henry L. Stimson.1929	A. W. Mellon...1929 Ogden L. Mills.1932	James W. Good.1929 Pat. J. Hurley.1929
Franklin D. Roosevelt-J. N. Garner, Dem. 1933	Cordell Hull.....1933	W. H. Woodin.1933 Henry Morgenthau Jr. 1934	Geo. H. Dern..1933 Harry H. Wood- ring 1936

Secretary of Navy	Secretary of Interior	Postmaster-General	Attorney-General	Recent Depts.
Wm. H. Hunt..1881 W. E. Chandler.1882	S. J. Kirkwood.1881 H. M. Teller..1882	T. O. Howe...1881 W. Q. Gresham.1883 Frank Hatton..1884	B. H. Brewster.'81	Secretary of labor. est. 4 Mar., 1913
W. C. Whitney.1885	L. Q. C. Lamar.1885 Wm. F. Vilas..1888	Wm. F. Vilas..1885 D. M. Dickinson.'88	A. H. Garland.'85	W. B. Wilson 1913 J. J. Davis...1921
Benj. F. Tracy.1889	John W. Noble.1889	J. Wanamaker.1889	W. H. H. Miller 1889	Wm. N. Doak 1930 Frances Perkins '33
H. A. Herbert..1893	Hoke Smith....1893 D. R. Francis..1896	W. S. Bissell...1893 W. L. Wilson..1895	R. Olney....1893 J. Harmon...1895	
John D. Long..1897	C. N. Bliss....1897 E. A. Hitchcock.'99	James A. Gary.1897 Chas. E. Smith.1898	J. McKenna..1897 J. W. Griggs.1897 P. C. Knox..1901	
John D. Long..1901 W. H. Moody.1902 Paul Morton...1904 C. J. Bonaparte.1905 V. H. Metcalf..1907 T. H. Newberry 1908	E. A. Hitchcock.'01 J. R. Garfield..1907	Chas. E. Smith.1901 Henry C. Payne.'02 Robt. J. Wynne.'04 G. B. Cortelyou.'05 G. von L. Meyer '07	P. C. Knox...1901 W. H. Moody 1904 C. J. Bonaparte '07	
G. von L. Meyer.'09	R. A. Ballinger.1909 W. L. Fisher...1911	F. H. Hitchcock.'09	G. W. Wickersham 1909	
Josephus Daniels.'13	F. K. Lane....1913 J. B. Payne....1920	A. S. Burleson.1913	J. C. McReynolds 1913 T. W. Gregory '14 A. M. Palmer.'19	
Edwin Denby..1921	Albert B. Fall..1921 Hubert Work ..1923	Will H. Hays..1921 Hubert Work...1922 Harry S. New..1923	H. M. Daugherty 1921	
Edwin Denby..1923 Curtis D. Wilbur.'24	Hubert Work ..1923 Roy O. West...1928	Harry S. New..1923	H. M. Daugherty 1923 H. F. Stone.1924 J. G. Sargent 1925	
Chas. F. Adams.1929	Ray L. Wilbur.1929	Walter F. Brown '29	W. D. Mitchell.'29	
C. A. Swanson.1933	Harold L. Ickes.1933	James A. Farley 1933	H. S. Cummings 1933 Frank Murphy.'39	

SUGGESTIONS FOR FURTHER READING

American history may be considered in its relationship to history in general in Barnes, H. E., *History of Historical Writing,* 1937. The writing of American history itself has had an interesting history detailed in Kraus, M., *History of American History,* 1937, and Bassett, J. S., *Middle Group of American Historians,* 1917, which show how the ideas of the meaning of national growth have changed. Further insight into the development of American history is gained by reading the biographies of the historians which may be found conveniently in Hutchinson, W. T., ed., *Marcus W. Jernegan Essays in American Historiography,* 1937. An effective introduction to the problems of history and their study is Nevins, A., *Gateway to History,* 1938.

The standard general histories of the United States by individuals are Channing, E., *History of the United States* (6 vols. extending to 1865)', 1905-1925, and McMaster, J. B., *History of the People of the United States* (9 vols. covering 1783-1865), 1883-1927. Cooperative series by various scholars are Hart, A. B., ed., *The American Nation: A History* (28 vols. extending to 1917), 1904-1928, and Johnson, A., ed., *Chronicles of America* (50 vols.), 1919-1921. The changing interpretation of American history, illustrating the turn from political to social and economic, is shown in the cooperative work edited by Schlesinger, A. M., and Fox, D. R., *History of American Life* (projected in 12 vols.), 1927-   , in Beard, Charles A., and Mary R., *Rise of American Civilization* (3 vols.), 1927-1939 and Carman, H. J., *Social and Economic History of the United States* (projected in 3 vols.), 1930-   . American history has been effectively illustrated in Gabriel, Ralph H., ed., *Pageant of America,* 1929. The key to American biography is found in Johnson, A. and Malone, D., ed., *Dictionary of American Biography,* 1928-1936.

The richest mine of information on the development of the United States is in the official publications of federal and state governments. They reveal the remarkable expansion in socially-useful functions required of government agencies. The various units publish, in addition to annual reports, a huge number of bulletins, often including excellent statistical graphs, maps and illustrations, and readily obtainable. Federal publications are described in Schmeckebier, L. F., *Government Publications and their Use,* 1936. State publications are ascertainable through the Library of Congress *Monthly Check List* and *Annual Index.* A convenient compilation is Richardson, J. D., comp., *A Compilation of the Messages and Papers of the Presidents*, 1896 (since enlarged).

Convenient works of reference are *Appleton's Annual Encyclopaedia* (before 1876 called *American*); Jameson, J. F., *Dictionary of United States History* (rev. ed.), 1931; Seligman, E. R. A. and Johnson, A., *Encyclopaedia of Social Sciences* (15 vols.), 1934.

The most important periodicals are *American Historical Review*, 1895- ; *Mississippi Valley Historical Review*, 1915- ; *Hispanic American Historical Review*, 1918- ; *New England Quarterly*, 1928- ; *Journal of Southern History*, 1935- ; *Agricultural History*, 1927- ; *Annals of American Academy of Political and Social Sciences*, 1890- ; *Political Science Quarterly*, 1886- ; *Quarterly Journal of Economics*, 1886- ; *American Economic Review*, 1911- ; *American Journal of Sociology*, 1895- ; *Social Forces*, 1922-

The following suggestions for further reading have been divided into two groups. The first includes specialized works which are not confined to any particular period in American history or which cover several. The second group is arranged to correspond with the chronological divisions of the text and contains titles which pertain entirely to the particular period or which are most important for the epoch in question. This method of organization has been adopted to save a frequent repetition of titles.

SPECIALIZED WORKS

The history of the sections is described in Turner, F. J., *Frontier in American History*, 1921; and *Significance of Sections in American History*, 1932; Paxson, F. L., *History of the American Frontier*, 1924; Clark, D. E., *West in American History*, 1937; Brown, W. G., *Lower South in American History*, 1902; Hawk, E. Q., *Economic History of the South*, 1934; Hesseltine, Wm. B., *A History of the South*, 1936. The environment and people of the United States and their relationship may be studied in Bowman, I., *Forest Physiography*, 1911; Brigham, A. P., *Geographic Influences in American History*, 1903; Calhoun, A. W., *Social History of the American Family* (3 vols.), 1917-1919; Hulbert, A. B., *Soil*, 1930; Huntington, E., *Civilization and Climate*, 1915; Semple, E. C., *American History and its Geographic Conditions*, 1933; Stephenson, G. M., *History of American Immigration*, 1926; Wissler, C., *American Indian*, 1922. Much interesting comment upon American society has been made by foreign observers. Illustrations of such comment can be found in Mesick, J. L., *English Traveller in America, 1785-1835*, 1922; Monaghan, Frank, *French Travellers in the U. S., 1765-1932*, 1933; Nevins, A., *American Social Life as Seen by British Travellers*, 1923.

Thought and expression are described in Blair, Walter, *Native American Humor, 1800-1900*, 1937; Blankenship, R., *American Literature as an Expression of the American Mind*, 1931; Bleyer, W. G., *Main Currents in the History of American Journalism*, 1927; Cargill, O., ed., *American Literature: A Period Anthology* (5 vols.), 1933; Hall, T. C., *Religious Background of American Culture*, 1930; Lee, A. M., *Daily Newspaper in America*, 1937; Lee, J. M., *History of American Journalism*, 1923; Mencken, H. L., *American Language*, 1936; Mott, F. L., *A History of American Magazines* (3 vols.), 1930-1938; O'Neill, E. H., *A History of American Biography*, 1935; Parrington, V. L., *Main Currents in American Thought* (3 vols.), 1927-1930; Pattee, F. L., *First Century of American Literature*, 1935; and *History of American Literature Since 1870*, 1915; Quinn, A. H., *A History of the American Drama* (2 vols.), 1923-1927; and *American Fiction*, 1936; Riley, Woodbridge, *American Thought*, 1923; Rowe, H. K., *History of Religion in the United States*, 1924; Sweet, W. W., *Story of Religions in America*, 1930; Taylor, W. F., *History of American Letters*, 1936; Townsend, H. G., *Philosophical Ideas in the United States*, 1934; Trent, W. P. et al., *Cambridge History of American Literature* (4 vols.), 1917-1921; Warfel, H. R., Gabriel, R. H., and Williams, S. T., *The American Mind*, 1937. Histories of individual newspapers are listed under the respective periods in which they were published.

American interest in and contribution to the arts are described in Caffin, C. H., *Story of American Painting*, 1907; Elson, L. C., *History of American Music*, 1904; Howard, J. T., *Our American Music*, 1931; Isham, S., *History of American Painting*, 1903; Kimball, F., *Domestic Architecture of the American Colonies and of the Early Republic*, 1922; La Follette, S., *Art in America*, 1929; Mumford, L., *Sticks and Stones: A Study of American Architecture and Civilization*, 1924; Sonneck, O. G., *Early Opera in America*, 1915; Taft, L., *History of American Sculpture*, 1924; Tallmadge, T. E., *Story of Architecture in America*, 1927.

American interest in science and education are discussed in Cubberly, E. P., *Public Education in the United States*, 1934; Curti, M. E., *Social Ideas of American Educators*, 1935; Dana, E. S., et al., *A Century of Science in America*, 1918; Dexter, E. G., *A History of Education in the United States*, 1904; Packard, F., *History of Medicine in the United States* (2 vols.), 1931; Shryock, R. H., *Development of Modern Medicine*, 1936; Thwing, C. F., *A History of Higher Education in America*, 1906; Woody, T., *A History of Women's Education in the United States* (2 vols.), 1929.

Convenient general histories of American economic enterprise are: Faulkner, H. U., *American Economic History* (4th ed.), 1938; Kirkland, E. C., *History of American Economic Life,* 1932; Shannon, F. A., *Economic History of the People of the United States,* 1934. Various phases of economic activity are described in Beard, Mary R., *Short History of the American Labor Movement,* 1920; Bidwell, P. W., et al., *History of Agriculture in the Northern United States, 1620-1860,* 1925; Clark, V. S., *History of Manufactures* (3 vols.), 1916-1928; Commons, J. R., et al., *History of Labor in the United States* (4 vols.), 1918-1935; Dewey, D. R., *Financial History of the United States,* 1922; Gray, L. C., *History of Agriculture in the Southern States to 1860* (2 vols.), 1933; Gras, N. S. B., *History of Agriculture in Europe and America,* 1925; Johnson, E. R., et al., *History of Domestic and Foreign Commerce of the United States* (2 vols.), 1915; Meyer, B. H., MacGill, C. E., et al., *History of Transportation in the United States before 1860,* 1917; Perlman, S., *History of Trade Unionism in the United States,* 1923; Shultz, W. J. and Caine, M. R., *Financial Development of the United States,* 1937; Taussig, F. W., *Tariff History of the United States* (8th ed.), 1931.

American political and diplomatic history are described in: Bemis, S. F., *Diplomatic History of the United States,* 1936; and *American Secretaries of State* (10 vols.), 1927-1929; Bryce, James, *American Commonwealth,* 1886; Channing, E., *History of the United States* (6 vols.), 1905-1925; Ewing, Cortez A. M., *Judges of the Supreme Court,* 1938; Hart, A. B. ed., *American Nation: A History* (28 vols.), 1904-1928; McLaughlin, A. C., *Constitutional History of the United States,* 1935; Morison, S. E., and Commager, H. S., *Growth of the American Republic* (2 vols.), 1938; Schouler, J., *History of the United States 1783-1877* (7 vols.), 1880-1889; Stanwood, E., *History of the Presidency, 1788-1916* (2 vols.), 1924; Warren, C., *Supreme Court in the United States History,* 1928.

Convenient documentary source collections are: Callendar, G. S., *Selections from the Economic History of the United States,* 1900; Commager, H. S., *Documents of American History,* 1934; Commons, J. R., et al., *Documentary History of American Industrial Society* (10 vols.), 1910-1911; Flügel, F. and Faulkner, H. U., *Readings in the Social and Economic History of the United States,* 1929; Hart, A. B. ed., *American History told by Contemporaries* (5 vols.), 1899-1923; MacDonald, Wm., *Documentary Source Book of American History,* 1916.

Maps are found in: Fox, D. R., ed., *Harper's Atlas of American History,* 1920; Paullin, C. O. and Wright, J. K., *Atlas of Historical Geography of the United States,* 1932.

Guides to further search are Channing, Hart and Turner, *Guide to the Study and Reading of American History,* 1912, to be superseded by *Harvard Guide to American History* (to be published in 1939); Griffin, G. G., *Writings on American History,* 1906-   ; Edwards, E. E.,

Bibliography of the History of Agriculture in the United States, 1930;
Bemis, S. F., and Griffin, G. G., *Guide to the Diplomatic History of the
United States,* 1935; Allison, W. H., et al., *Guide to Historical Litera-
ture,* 1931.

CREATING A SOCIETY
1575-1763

The colonial period has been analyzed by three historians in extensive
works: Andrews, C. M., *Colonial Period of American History* (4 vols.
to date), 1934-   ; Gipson, L. H., *British Empire before the American Revolution* (3 vols.), 1936; Osgood, H. L., *American Colonies in
the Seventeenth Century* (3 vols.), 1904-1907; *American Colonies in
the Eighteenth Century,* 1924. One volume surveys are: Becker, C.,
Beginnings of the American People, 1915; Chitwood, P., *History of
Colonial America,* 1931; Greene, E. B., *Foundations of American Nationality,* 1922; Jernegan, M. W., *American Colonies,* 1929; Nettels,
C. P., *Roots of American Civilization,* 1938.

The period has been covered by volumes in the three series: in the
American Nation Series are Cheyney, E. P., *European Background of
American History;* Tyler, L. G., *English in America;* Andrews, C. M.,
Colonial Self-Government; Greene, E. B., *Provincial America:* in the
Chronicles of America are Wood, W., *Elizabethan Sea-Dogs;* Johnson,
M., *Pioneers of the Old South;* Andrews, C. M., *Fathers of New Eng-
land;* Goodwin, M. W., *Dutch and English on the Hudson;* Fisher,
S. G., *The Quaker Colonies;* Andrews, C. M., *Colonial Folkways:* in
the *History of American Life* are Wertenbaker, T. J., *First Americans;*
Adams, J. T., *Provincial Society.*

The English background is described in: Cheyney, E. P., *A History of
England from the Defeat of the Armada to the Death of Elizabeth,*
1914-1926; Read, Conyers, *Tudors,* 1936; Scott, W. R., *Constitution
and Finance of English, Scottish and Irish Joint Stock Companies to
1720,* 1912.

The planting and organizing of the colonies are detailed in: Adams,
J. T., *Founding of New England,* 1921; and *Revolutionary New Eng-
land, 1691-1776,* 1923; Beer, G. L., *Origins of the British Colonial
System, 1578-1660,* 1922; and *Old Colonial System,* 1912; and *British
Colonial Policy, 1754-1765,* 1907; Brown, A., *The Genesis of the
United States* (2 vols.), 1891; Crane, V. W., *The Southern Frontier,*
1929; Dodd, W. E., *The Old South: Struggles for Democracy,* 1937;
Johnson, A., *Swedish Settlements on the Delaware, 1638-1664,* 1911;
Mereness, N. D., *Maryland as a Proprietary Province,* 1901; Morison,
S. E., *Builders of the Bay Colony,* 1930; Wertenbaker, T. J., *Patrician
and Plebeian in Virginia,* 1910; and *Virginia under the Stuarts, 1607-*

1688, 1914; Wrong, G. M., *Rise and Fall of New France* (2 vols.), 1928; Wuorinen, J. H., *The Finns on the Delaware*, 1938.

Economic conditions are analyzed in: Abernethy, T. P., *Western Lands and the American Revolution*, 1937; Bining, A. C., *Pennsylvania Iron Manufacture in the 18th Century*, 1938; Bruce, P. A., *Economic History of Virginia in the Seventeenth Century*, 1896; Harrington, V. D., *The New York Merchant on the Eve of the Revolution*, 1935; Jernegan, M. W., *Laboring and Dependent Classes in Colonial America*, 1931; McFarland, R., *History of the New England Fisheries*, 1911; Stevens, W. E., *The Northwest Fur Trade*, 1928; Weeden, W. B., *Economic and Social History of New England*, 1890.

Some phases of social development are considered in: Bridenbaugh, C., *Cities in the Wilderness*, 1938; Morison, S. E., *The Puritan Pronaos*, 1936; and *Founding of Harvard College*, 1935; Schneider, H. W., *The Puritan Mind*, 1930; Spruill, J. C., *Women's Life and Work in the Southern Colonies*, 1938; Wertenbaker, T. J., *Founding of American Civilization: the Middle Colonies*, 1938.

Convenient biographies are: Chidsey, D. B., *Sir Humphrey Gilbert*, 1932; Fox, D. R., *Caleb Heathcote*, 1926; Ettinger, A. A., *James Edward Oglethorpe, Imperial Idealist*, 1936; Dobrée, B., *William Penn*, 1932; Waldman, M., *Sir Walter Raleigh*, 1928; Ernst, J. E., *Roger Williams*, 1932.

ESTABLISHING INDEPENDENCE
1763-1819

Two extensive works cover part of this period: McMaster, J. B., *History of the People of the United States, 1783-1865* (9 vols.), 1883-1927; Adams, H., *History of the United States during the Administrations of Jefferson and Madison* (9 vols.), 1890-1891. The volumes in the *American Nation Series* are Howard, G. E., *Preliminaries of the Revolution;* Van Tyne, C. H., *American Revolution;* McLaughlin, A. C., *Confederation and the Constitution;* Bassett, J. S., *Federalist System;* Channing, E., *Jeffersonian System;* Babcock, K. C., *Rise of American Nationality;* in the *Chronicles of America* are Becker, C., *Eve of the Revolution;* Wrong, G. M., *Washington and his Comrades in Arms;* Farrand, M., *Fathers of the Constitution;* Ford, H. J., *Washington and his Colleagues;* Johnson, A., *Jefferson and his Colleagues;* Corwin, E. S., *John Marshall and the Constitution;* Paine, R. D., *Fight for a Free Sea;* Skinner, C. L., *Pioneers of the Old Southwest;* Ogg, F. L., *Old Northwest*.

Accounts of the various phases of the Revolution are contained in: Alvord, C. W., *Mississippi Valley in British Politics*, 1916; Becker, C. L., *Declaration of Independence*, 1922; East, R. A., *Business Enter-*

prise in the American Revolutionary Era, 1938; Faÿ, B., *Revolutionary Spirit in France and America,* 1927; Jameson, J. F., *American Revolution Considered as a Social Movement,* 1920; McIlwain, C. H., *American Revolution,* 1923; Nevins, A., *American States During and After the Revolution,* 1924; Paullin, C. O., *Navy in the American Revolution,* 1906; Schlesinger, A. M., *Colonial Merchants and the American Revolution,* 1918; Trevelyan, Sir G. O., *American Revolution,* 1899-1907; Van Tyne, C. H., *Causes of the War of Independence,* 1922; *War of Independence,* 1929; and *Loyalists in the American Revolution,* 1902.

The formation of the Constitution is described in: Beard, C. A., *An Economic Interpretation of the Constitution of the United States,* 1913; Farrand, M., *Framing of the Constitution of the United States,* 1913; Schuyler, R. L., *Constitution of the United States,* 1923; Warren, C., *Making of the Constitution,* 1928.

Details of the political and diplomatic problems of the new nation are found in: Beard, C. A., *Economic Origins of the Jeffersonian Democracy,* 1915; Bemis, S. F., *Jay's Treaty,* 1923; and *Pinckney's Treaty,* 1926; Bowers, C. G., *Jefferson and Hamilton,* 1925; and *Jefferson in Power,* 1936; Cox, I. J., *West Florida Controversy,* 1918; Fox, D. R., *Decline of Aristocracy in the Politics of New York,* 1918; Lyon, E. W., *Louisiana in French Diplomacy,* 1934; Mahan, A. T., *Sea Power in its Relation to the War of 1812,* 1905; McCaleb, W. F., *Aaron Burr Conspiracy,* 1903; Perkins, D., *Monroe Doctrine, 1823-1826,* 1927; Pratt, J. W., *Expansionists of 1812,* 1925; Sears, L. M., *Jefferson and the Embargo,* 1927; Updike, F. A., *Diplomacy of the War of 1812,* 1915; Whitaker, A. P., *Mississippi Question, 1795-1803,* 1934; and *Spanish-American Frontier, 1783-1795,* 1927.

Social and economic conditions are analyzed in: Bond, B. W., *Civilization of the Old Northwest,* 1934; Curti, M. E., *Social Ideas of American Educators,* 1935; Hinsdale, B. A., *Old Northwest,* 1899; Jones, H. M., *America and French Culture, 1750-1848,* 1927; Mathews, L. K., *Expansion of New England,* 1909; Miller, J. M., *Genesis of Western Culture,* 1938; Morison, S. E., *Maritime History of Massachusetts,* 1922; Roosevelt, T., *Winning of the West* (4 vols.), 1894-1896; Treat, P. J., *National Land System, 1785-1820,* 1910.

Some biographies of importance are: Adams, J. T., *Adams Family,* 1930; Miller, J. C., *Sam Adams,* 1936; Harlow, R. V., *Samuel Adams,* 1923; James, J. A., *Life of George Rogers Clark,* 1928; Van Doren, C., *Benjamin Franklin,* 1938; Faÿ, B., *Franklin, the Apostle of Modern Times,* 1929; Adams, H., *Life of Albert Gallatin,* 1879; Oliver, F. S., *Alexander Hamilton,* 1906; Monaghan, F., *John Jay,* 1935; Chinard, G., *Thomas Jefferson,* 1929; Hirst, F. W., *Life and Letters of Thomas Jefferson,* 1926; Muzzey, D. S., *Jefferson,* 1918; Beveridge, A. J., *Life of John Marshall* (4 vols.), 1916-1919; Morison, S. E., *Life and Letters of H. G. Otis,* 1913; Fitzpatrick, J. C., *George Washington Himself,* 1933; Hughes, R., *George Washington* (3 vols.), 1926-1930; Little, S., *George Washington,* 1929; Sears, L. M., *George Washington,* 1932.

MULTIPLYING AND DIVIDING
1819-1865

Part of this period is covered in the extensive work of J. F. Rhodes, *History of the United States from the Compromise of 1850* (9 vols.), 1893-1922. Volume surveys are: Adams, J. T., *America's Tragedy,* 1934; Randall, J. G., *Civil War and Reconstruction,* 1937; Turner, F. J., *United States, 1830-1850,* 1935. The *American Nation Series* contains Turner, F. J., *Rise of the New West;* Hart, A. B., *Slavery and Abolition;* MacDonald, W., *Jacksonian Democracy;* Garrison, G. P., *Westward Extension;* Smith, T. C., *Parties and Slavery;* Chadwick, F. E., *Causes of the Civil War;* Hosmer, J. K., *Appeal to Arms;* and *Outcome of the Civil War.* The appropriate volumes in the *Chronicles of America* are Ogg, F. A., *Reign of Andrew Jackson;* Hulbert, A. B., *Paths of Inland Commerce;* Skinner, C. L., *Adventurers of Oregon;* White, S. E., *Forty-Niners;* Hough, E., *Passing of the Frontier;* Dodd, W. E., *Cotton Kingdom;* Macy, J., *Anti-Slavery Crusade;* Stephenson, N. W., *Texas and the Mexican War;* and *Abraham Lincoln and the Union;* and *Day of the Confederacy;* Wood, W., *Captains of the Civil War.* In the *History of American Life Series* are Fish, C. R., *Rise of the Common Man;* Cole, A. C., *Irrepressible Conflict.*

Sectionalism and politics are discussed in: Adams, J. T., *New England in the Republic, 1776-1850,* 1926; Barker, E. C., *Mexico and Texas, 1821-1835,* 1928; Barnes, G. H., *Anti-Slavery Impulse,* 1933; Billington, R. A., *Protestant Crusade, 1800-1860,* 1938; Boucher, C. S., *Nullification Controversy in South Carolina,* 1916; Bowers, C. G., *Party Battles of the Jackson Period,* 1922; Carpenter, J. T., *South as a Conscious Minority,* 1930; Cole, A. C., *Whig Party in the South,* 1913; Cotterill, R. S., *Old South,* 1936; Dumond, D. L., *Secession Movement, 1860-1861,* 1931; Goodwin, C., *Trans-Mississippi West,* 1922; Nichols, R. F., *Democratic Machine, 1850-1854,* 1923; Perkins, D., *Monroe Doctrine, 1826-1867,* 1933; Ray, P. O., *Repeal of the Missouri Compromise,* 1909; Russel, R. R., *Economic Aspects of Southern Sectionalism, 1840-1861,* 1924; Schaper, W. A., *Sectionalism and Representation in South Carolina,* 1901; Shryock, R. H., *Georgia and the Union in 1850,* 1926; Smith, J. H., *War with Mexico* (2 vols.), 1919; Van Deusen, J. G., *Economic Bases of Disunion in South Carolina,* 1928.

The economic background of the struggle is described in: Benns, F. L., *American Struggle for the West India Carrying Trade 1815-1830,*

1923; Buck, N. S., *The Development of the Organization of Anglo-American Trade, 1800-1850*, 1925; Carter, C. E., *When Railroads were New*, 1909; Catterall, R. C. H., *Second Bank of the United States*, 1903; Chittenden, H. M., *American Fur Trade in the Far West* (3 vols.), 1902; Clark, A. H., *Clipper Ship Era, 1843-1869*, 1910; Cole, A. H., *American Wool Manufacture* (2 vols.), 1926; Coman, K., *Economic Beginnings of the Far West* (2 vols.), 1912; Craven, A. O., *Soil Exhaustion as a Factor in the Agricultural History of Virginia and Maryland, 1660-1860*, 1925; Cutler, C. C., *Greyhounds of the Sea: The Story of the American Clipper Ship*, 1930; Flanders, R. B., *Plantation Slavery in Georgia*, 1932; Harlow, A. F., *Old Towpaths*, 1926; and *Old Waybills*, 1934; Hungerford, E., *Story of the Baltimore and Ohio Railroad, 1827-1927* (2 vols.), 1928; Kaempffert, W., *History of American Inventions* (2 vols.), 1924; McGrane, R. C., *Foreign Bond-holders and American State Debts*, 1935; and *Panic of 1837*, 1924; Paine, R. D., *The Old Merchant Marine*, 1919; Phillips, U. B., *Life and Labor in the Old South*, 1929; and *American Negro Slavery*, 1918; Quick, H., *Mississippi Steamboatin'*, 1926; Robert, J. C., *Tobacco Kingdom, 1800-1860*, 1938; Shotter, H. W., *Growth and Development of the Pennsylvania Railroad*, 1927; Stephenson, G. M., *Political History of the Public Lands from 1840 to 1862*, 1917; Sydnor, C. S., *Slavery in Mississippi*, 1933; Ware, C. F., *Early New England Cotton Manufacture*, 1931; Ware, N. J., *Industrial Worker, 1840-1860*, 1924; Wellington, R. G., *Political and Sectional Influence of the Public Lands, 1828-1842*, 1914.

Social and cultural phases of the period are analyzed in: Adams, W. F., *Ireland and Irish Immigration to the New World from 1815 to the Famine*, 1932; Blegen, T. C., *Norwegian Migration to America*, 1931; Branch, E. D., *Sentimental Years*, 1934; Brooks, V., *Flowering of New England*, 1936; Faust, A. B., *German Element in the United States* (2 vols.), 1909; Ford, H. J., *Scotch-Irish in America*, 1915; Janson, F. E., *Background of Swedish Immigration, 1840-1930*, 1931; Krout, J. A., *Origins of Prohibition*, 1925; Minnigerode, M., *Fabulous Forties*, 1924; Mumford, L., *Golden Day*, 1926; Pierce, B. L., *A History of Chicago*, 1937; Tewksbury, D. G., *Founding of American Colleges and Universities before the Civil War*, 1932.

The Civil War is treated in: Adams, E. D., *Great Britain and the American Civil War* (2 vols.), 1925; Baxter, J. P., 3rd, *Introduction of the Ironclad Warship*, 1933; Fite, E. D., *Social and Industrial Conditions in the North during the Civil War*, 1910; Lonn, E., *Desertion during the Civil War*, 1928; Owsley, F. L., *King Cotton Diplomacy*, 1931; Randall, J. G., *Constitutional Problems under Lincoln*, 1926; Schwab, J. C., *Confederate States of America: A Financial and Industrial History*, 1901; Simkims, F. B. and Patton, J. W., *Women of the*

Confederacy, 1936; Wesley, C. H., *Collapse of the Confederacy,* 1937; Wiley, B. I., *Southern Negroes, 1861-1865,* 1938.

Biographies of the period are: Clark, B. C., *John Quincy Adams,* 1932; Porter, K. W., *John Jacob Astor, Business Man* (2 vols.), 1931; Smith, W. E., *Francis Preston Blair Family in Politics,* 1933; Meigs, W. M., *John C. Calhoun* (2 vols.), 1917; Mayo, B., *Henry Clay,* 1937; Van Deusen, G. G., *Henry Clay,* 1937; Cutting, E., *Jefferson Davis,* 1930; McElroy, R., *Jefferson Davis,* 1937; Milton, G. F., *Eve of Conflict: Life of Stephen A. Douglas,* 1934; James, M., *Andrew Jackson* (2 vols.), 1933-1937; Bassett, J. S., *Andrew Jackson* (2 vols.), 1911; Freeman, D. S., *R. E. Lee: a Biography* (4 vols.), 1934-1935; Beveridge, A. J., *Abraham Lincoln* (2 vols.), 1928; Stephenson, N. W., *Lincoln,* 1922; Hutchinson, W. T., *Cyrus Hall McCormick* (2 vols.), 1930-1935; Commager, H. S., *Theodore Parker,* 1936; Nichols, R. F., *Franklin Pierce,* 1931; McCormac, E. I., *James K. Polk,* 1922; Bancroft, F., *William H. Seward* (2 vols.), 1900; Pendleton, L., *Alexander H. Stephens,* 1908; Swisher, C. B., *Roger B. Taney,* 1936; Phillips, U. B., *Robert Toombs,* 1913; Fuess, C. M., *Daniel Webster* (2 vols.), 1930; Waterman, W. R., *Frances Wright,* 1924.

THE NEW SECTIONALISM
1865-1878

The most extensive treatment of the period from 1865 to the present is Oberholtzer, E. P., *History of the United States since the Civil War, 1865-1901* (5 vols.), 1917-1936. Convenient one volume presentations are: Beard, C. A., *Contemporary American History,* 1914; Hacker, L. M., and Kendrick, B. B., *United States since 1865* (3rd edition), 1939; Lingley, C. R., and Foley, A. R., *Since the Civil War* (3rd edition), 1935; Mead, N. P., *Development of the United States since 1865,* 1930; Paxson, F. L., *Recent History of the United States* (Revised and enlarged edition), 1938; Stephenson, G. M., *American History since 1865,* 1938.

Surveys of the period 1865-1879 are found in the *American Nation Series,* the *Chronicles of America* and the *History of American Life,* respectively: Dunning, W. A., *Reconstruction, Political and Economic;* Fleming, W. L., *Sequel to Appomattox;* Nevins, A., *Emergence of Modern America.* Reference should also be made to Bowers, C. G., *Tragic Era,* 1929; Fleming, W. L., *Documentary History of Reconstruction* (2 vols.), 1906-1907; Henry, R. S., *Story of Reconstruction,* 1938.

For conditions in the South, special studies are: Caskie, W. M., *Secession and Restoration of Louisiana,* 1938; Coulter, E. M., *Civil War and Readjustment in Kentucky,* 1926; Davis, W. W., *Civil War and Reconstruction in Florida,* 1913; Eckenrode, H. J., *Political His-*

tory of Virginia during Reconstruction, 1904; Fleming, W. L., *Recon-struction in Alabama,* 1905; Garner, J. W., *Reconstruction in Mississippi,* 1901; Hamilton, J. G. de R., *Reconstruction in North Carolina,* 1914; Lonn, E., *Reconstruction in Louisiana after 1868,* 1918; Patton, J. W., *Unionism and Reconstruction in Tennessee,* 1934; Rams-dell, C. W., *Recostruction in Texas,* 1910; Simkins, F. B. and Woody, R. H., *South Carolina during Reconstruction,* 1931; Staples, T. S., *Reconstruction in Arkansas,* 1923; Thompson, C. M., *Reconstruction in Georgia,* 1915; Dunning, W. A., *Essays in Civil War and Reconstruc-tion,* 1910; Beale, H. K., *Critical Year: A Study of Andrew Johnson and Reconstruction,* 1930; Buck, P. M., *Road to Reunion,* 1937; Lewin-son, P., *Race, Class and Party,* 1932; Lester, J. C. and Wilson, D. L., *Ku Klux Klan,* 1905. Significant biographies include Milton, G. F., *Age of Hate* (Andrew Johnson), 1930; Stryker, L. P., *Andrew Johnson, A Study in Courage,* 1929; Winston, R. W., *Andrew Johnson: Plebeian and Patriot,* 1929; Haynes, G. H., *Charles Sumner,* 1909; Woodley, T. F., *Great Leveler: The Life of Thaddeus Stevens,* 1937; Mitchell, S., *Horatio Seymour,* 1938; Coulter, E. M., *William G. Brownlow,* 1937; Pearce, H. J., *Benjamin H. Hill,* 1928; Cate, W. A., *L.Q.C. Lamar,* 1935.

For Eastern dominance, reference should be made to: Seitz, D. C., *Dreadful Decade, 1869-1879,* 1926; Ross, E. D., *Liberal Republican Movement,* 1919; Barclay, T. S., *Liberal Republican Movement in Missouri,* 1926; Barrett, D. C., *Greenbacks and Resumption of Specie Payments, 1862-1879,* 1931; Haworth, P. L., *Hayes-Tilden Disputed Presidential Election of 1876,* 1906; Adams, C. F., Jr., *Chapters of Erie,* 1886; Hungerford, E., *Men and Iron: The History of the New York Central,* 1938; Giddens, P. H., *Birth of the Oil Industry,* 1938; Hesseltine, W. B., *U. S. Grant, Politician,* 1935; Woodward, W. E., *Meet General Grant,* 1928; Nevins, A., *Hamilton Fish and the Grant Administration,* 1936; Eckenrode, H. J., *Rutherford B. Hayes,* 1930; Larson, H., *Jay Cooke,* 1936; Nevins, A., *Abram S. Hewitt: With some Account of Peter Cooper,* 1935; Seitz, D. C., *Horace Greeley: Founder of the New York Tribune,* 1926; Stone, C., *Dana and the Sun,* 1938; Fuller, R. H., *Jubilee Jim: The Life of Colonel James Fisk, Jr.,* 1928; Smith, A. D., *Commodore Vanderbilt,* 1927; White, B., *The Book of Daniel Drew,* 1910; Josephson, M., *Robber Barons,* 1934.

The advance of the West is particularly studied in: Branch, E. D., *Westward, the Romance of the American Frontier,* 1930; Caughey, J. W., *History of the Pacific Coast,* 1933; Foreman, G., *Advancing the Frontier,* 1933; Fuller, G. W., *Inland Empire* (3 vols.), 1928; Rich-ardson, R. N. and Rister, C. C., *Greater Southwest,* 1934; Riegel, R. E., *America Moves West,* 1930, and *Story of the Western Railroads,* 1926; Hedges, J. B., *Henry Villard and the Railways of the Northwest,*

1930; Lewis, O., *Big Four,* 1938; Trottman, N., *History of the Union Pacific,* 1923; Debo, A., *Rise and Fall of the Choctaw Republic,* 1934; Foreman, G., *Five Civilized Tribes,* 1934; Vestal, S., *Sitting Bull,* 1932; Dale, E. E., *Range Cattle Industry,* 1930; Dick, E., *Sod House Frontier,* 1937; Garland, H., *Son of the Middle Border,* 1917; Gates, P. W., *Illinois Central Railroad and Its Colonization Work,* 1934; Henry, S., *Conquering Our Great American Plains,* 1930; Lyman, G. D. *Saga of the Comstock Lode,* 1934; Osgood, E. S., *Day of the Cattleman,* 1929; Pelzer, L., *Cattlemen's Frontier, 1850-1890,* 1936; Rister, C. C., *Southwestern Frontier, 1865-1881,* 1928; and *Southern Plainsmen,* 1938; Webb, W. P., *Great Plains,* 1931, and *Texas Rangers,* 1935; Buck, S. J., *Granger Movement,* 1913; and *Agrarian Crusade,* 1921; Hubbart, H. C., *Older Middle West,* 1936.

THE IMPACT OF LARGE SCALE ORGANIZATION
1878-1900

For general surveys see the appropriate volumes in the three series: in the *American Nation Series* are Sparks, E. E., *National Development;* Dewey, D. R., *National Problems;* Latané, J. H., *America as a World Power.* In the *Chronicles of America* are Thompson, H., *Age of Invention;* Moody, J., *Railroad Builders;* Hendrick, B. J., *Age of Big Business;* Orth, S. P., *Armies of Labor;* and *Boss and the Machine;* Moody, J., *Masters of Capital;* Thompson, H., *New South;* Ford, H. J., *Cleveland Era.* In the *History of American Life* are Schlesinger, A. M., *Rise of the City;* Tarbell, I. M., *Nationalizing of Industry.* Also see Peck, H. T., *Twenty Years of the Republic,* 1905; and Beer, T., *Mauve Decade,* 1926.

For industrial development see: Casson, H., *Romance of Steel,* 1907; and *History of the Telephone,* 1910; Collins, J. H., *Story of Canned Foods,* 1924; Glasscock, C. B., *War of the Copper Kings,* 1935; James, F. C., *Growth of Chicago Banks,* 1938; Jerome, H., *Mechanization in Industry,* 1934; Martin, T. C., and Coles, S. L., *Story of Electricity,* 1919; Moody, J., *Truth About Trusts,* 1904; Rickard, T. A., *History of American Mining,* 1932; Ripley, W. Z., *Railway Problems,* 1913; and *Railroads; Rates and Regulation,* 1913; Shinn, C. H., *Story of the Mine,* 1896; Tarbell, I. M., *History of the Standard Oil* (2 vols.), 1904; Leech, H., and Carroll, J., *Armour and His Times,* 1938; Hendrick, B. J., *Andrew Carnegie* (2 vols.), 1932; Carnegie, A., *Triumphant Democracy,* 1886; Dyer, F. L. and Martin, T. C., *Edison, His Life and Inventions,* 1929; Harvey, G., *Henry Clay Frick: The Man,* 1928; Tarbell, I. M., *Life of Elbert H. Gary,* 1928; O'Connor, H., *Guggenheims,* 1938; Kennan, G., *E. H. Harriman,* 1922; Pyle, J. G., *Life of James J. Hill,* 1917; Corey, L., *House of Morgan,* 1930;

Flynn, J. T., *God's Gold: Life of John D. Rockefeller*, 1931; Nevins, A., *John D. Rockefeller* (soon to appear).

For labor, see: Adamic, L., *Dynamite: The Story of Class Violence in America*, 1931; Childs, H. L., *Labor and Capital*, 1930; David, H., *History of the Haymarket Affair*, 1936; Gompers, S., *Seventy Years of Life and Labor* (2 vols.), 1925; Harris, H., *American Labor*, 1938; Lorwin, L. L., *American Federation of Labor*, 1933; McMurray, D. L., *Coxey's Army*, 1929; Powderly, T. V., *Thirty Years of Labor*, 1889; Ware, N. J., *Labor Movement in the United States, 1860-1895*, 1929; Wolman, L., *Growth of American Trade Unions, 1880-1923*, 1924.

For agrarian conditions, see: Arnett, A. M., *Populist Movement in Georgia*, 1922; Brooks, R. P., *Agrarian Revolution in Georgia, 1865-1912*, 1914; Clark, J. B., *Populism in Alabama*, 1927; Haynes, F. E., *Thiry Party Movements since the Civil War*, 1916; Hicks, J. D., *Populist Revolt: A History of the Farmers' Alliance and the People's Party*, 1931; Kendrick, B. B. and Arnett, A. M., *The South Looks at Its Past*, 1935; Mitchell, B., *Industrial Revolution in the South*, 1930; and *Rise of the Cotton Mills in the South*, 1921; Odum, H., *Southern Pioneers*, 1925; Sheldon, W. D., *Populism in the Old Dominion*, 1935; Simkins, F. B., *Tillman Movement in South Carolina*, 1926; Thompson, H., *From the Cottonfield to the Cotton Mill*, 1906; Woodward, C. V., *Tom Watson, Agrarian Rebel*, 1938.

For social and cultural progress, see: Mumford, L., *Brown Decades, A Study of the Arts in America, 1865-1895*, 1931; Wecter, D., *Saga of American Society*, 1937; Dondore, D. A., *Prairie and the Making of Middle America*, 1926; Hazard, L., *Frontier in American Literature*, 1927; Seldes, G. V., *Stammering Century*, 1928; Cushing, H., *Life of Sir William Osler* (2 vols.), 1925; James, H., *Charles W. Eliot, President of Harvard University, 1869-1909*, 1930; Winkler, W. R., *Hearst, An American Phenomenon*, 1928; Seitz, D. C., *Joseph Pulitzer, His Life and Letters*, 1924; Josephson, M., *Portrait of the Artist as American*, 1930.

For politics, see: Bryan, W. J., *First Battle*, 1896; Fish, C. R., *Civil Service and the Patronage*, 1904; Josephson, M., *Politicos, 1865-1896*, 1938; Laughlin, J. L., *History of Bimetallism in the United States*, 1897; Merriam, C. E., *American Party System*, 1923; and *American Political Ideas, 1867-1917*, 1920; Overacker, L., *Money in Elections*, 1932; Stanwood, E., *American Tariff Controversies in the 19th Century*, 1903; Tarbell, I. M., *Tariff in Our Times*, 1911; Walker, A. H., *History of the Sherman Law*, 1910. Influential figures include Barnard, H., *Eagle Forgotten, The Life of John Peter Altgeld*, 1938; Howe, G. F., *Chester A. Arthur*, 1934; Muzzey, D. S., *James G. Blaine*, 1934; Hibben, P., *Peerless Leader: William Jennings Bryan*, 1929; Barnes, J. A., *John G. Carlisle*, 1931; Nevins, A., *Grover Cleve-*

land, 1932; Chidsey, D. B., *Gentleman from New York: the Life of Roscoe Conkling,* 1935; Smith, T. C., *Life and Letters of James A. Garfield,* 1925; Caldwell, R. G., *James A. Garfield,* 1931; Croly, H., *Marcus Alonzo Hanna,* 1912; Beer, T., *Hanna,* 1929; Dennett, T., *John Hay,* 1933; Olcott, C. S., *William McKinley* (2 vols.), 1916; Gosnell, H. F., *Boss Platt and the New York Machine,* 1924; Trimble, B. R., *Chief Justice Waite,* 1938; Haynes, F. E., *James Baird Weaver,* 1919.

For foreign relations, see: Dennett, T., *Americans in Eastern Asia,* 1922; Millis, W., *Martial Spirit: A Study of our War with Spain,* 1931; Perkins, D., *Monroe Doctrine, 1867-1907,* 1937; Pratt, J. W., *Expansionists of 1898,* 1936; Ryden, G. F., *Foreign Policy of the United States in Relation to Samoa,* 1933; Tansill, C. C., *United States and Santo Domingo, 1798-1873,* 1938; Russell, H. B., *International Monetary Conferences,* 1898.

THE PROGRESSIVE ERA
1900-1917

General treatments of this period are found in Sullivan, Mark, *Our Times* (5 vols.), 1926-1935; Dumond, D. L., *Roosevelt to Roosevelt,* 1937; and Paxson, F. L., *American Democracy and the World War: The Pre-War Years, 1914-1917,* 1936. The appropriate volumes in the three series are: in the *American Nation Series,* Latané, J. H., *America as a World Power;* Ogg, F. A., *National Progress, 1907-1917;* in the *Chronicles of America,* Fish C. R., *Path of Empire;* Howland, H., *Theodore Roosevelt and His Times;* Seymour, C., *Woodrow Wilson and the World War;* in the *History of American Life,* Faulkner, H. U., *Quest for Social Justice.*

For the spirit of reform, see: Addams, J., *Forty Years at Hull House,* 1930; Barton, A. O., *La Follette's Winning of Wisconsin, 1894-1904,* 1922; Bok, E. W., *Americanization of Edward Bok,* 1920; Brooks, V., *America's Coming of Age,* 1915; Chamberlain, J., *Farewell to Reform,* 1933; Croly, Herbert, *Promise of American Life,* 1909; DeWitt, B. P., *Progressive Movement,* 1915; Harriman, Mrs. J. B., *From Pinafores to Politics,* 1923; Haynes, F. E., *Social Politics in the United States,* 1924; Hillquit, M., *History of Socialism in the United States,* 1903; Howe, F. C., *Wisconsin, An Experiment in Democracy,* 1912; Regier, C. C., *Era of the Muckrakers,* 1932; Seager, H. R., and Gulick, C. A., Jr., *Trust and Corporation Problems,* 1929; Steffens, L., *Shame of the Cities,* 1904; Stahl, R. M., *Ballinger-Pinchot Controversy,* 1926; Warburg, P. M., *Federal Reserve System* (2 vols.), 1930; Weyl, W. E., *New Democracy,* 1912; Willis, H. P., *Federal Reserve System,* 1923. Significant biographies are Stephenson, N. W., *Nelson W. Aldrich:*

A Leader in American Politics, 1930; Bowers, C. G., *Beveridge and the Progressive Era,* 1932; Howe, F. C., *Confessions of a Reformer,* 1925; Dennett, T., *John Hay,* 1933; Johnson, T., *My Story,* 1911; La Follette, R. M., *La Follette's Autobiography,* 1913; McClure, S. S., *My Autobiography,* 1914; Coolidge, L. A., *An Old-Fashioned Senator, Orville H. Platt of Connecticut,* 1910; *Selections from the Correspondence of Theodore Roosevelt and Henry Cabot Lodge* (2 vols.), 1925; Pringle, H. F., *Theodore Roosevelt,* 1931; Jessup, P. C., *Elihu Root,* 1938; Steffens, L., *Autobiography of Lincoln Steffens* (2 vols.), 1931; Duffy, H. S., *William Howard Taft,* 1930, and *Taft and Roosevelt: The Intimate Letters of Archie Butt* (2 vols.), 1930; Dorfman, J., *Thorsten Veblen and His America,* 1934; Veblen, T., *Theory of the Leisure Class,* 1899; Nevins, A., *Henry White: Thirty Years of American Diplomacy,* 1930; Whitlock, B., *Forty Years of It,* 1913.

For the responsibilities of world power, see: Chapman, C. C., *History of the Cuban Republic,* 1927; Curti, M., *Peace or War: the American Struggle,* 1936; Dennis, A. L. P., *Adventures in American Diplomacy, 1896-1906,* 1928; Dennett, T., *Theodore Roosevelt and the Russo-Japanese War,* 1925; Diffie, B. W. and J. W., *Porto Rico: A Broken Pledge,* 1931; Forbes, W. C., *Philippine Islands* (2 vols.), 1928; Knight, M. M., *The Americans in Santo Domingo,* 1928; Hill, H. C., *Roosevelt and the Caribbean,* 1927; Jenks, L. H., *Our Cuban Colony: A Study in Sugar,* 1928; Lockmiller, D. A., *Magoon in Cuba,* 1938; Nearing, S., and Freeman, J., *Dollar Diplomacy,* 1925; Nichols, J. P., *Alaska,* 1924; Rippy, F. J., *Capitalists and Colombia,* 1931; and *United States and Mexico* (revised ed.), 1931; Roosevelt, N., *Philippines: A Treasure and a Problem,* 1926; Williams, M. W., *Anglo-American Isthmian Diplomacy, 1815-1915,* 1916.

THE UNITED STATES IN A WORLD AT WAR
1917-1919

Barnes, H. E., *Genesis of the World War,* 1929; and *World Politics and Modern Civilization,* 1930; Bassett, J. S., *Our War with Germany,* 1919; Borchard, E., and Lage, W., *Neutrality for the United States,* 1937; Clarkson, G. B., *Industrial America in the World War,* 1923; Creel, G., *How We Advertised America,* 1920; Crowell, B., and Wilson, R. F., *How America Went to War* (6 vols.), 1921; Dixon, F. H., *Railroads and Government, Their Relations in the United States,* 1922; Fay, S. B., *Origins of the World War* (2 vols.), 1928; Grattan, C. H., *Why We Fought,* 1929; Harbord, J. G., *American Army in France,* 1936; Hendrick, B. J., and Sims, W. S., *Victory at Sea,* 1920; Keynes, J. M., *Economic Consequences of the Peace,* 1919; Lippman, W., *Liberty and the News,* 1920; McMaster, J. B., *United*

States in the World War (2 vols.), 1918-1920; Millis, W., *Road to War,* 1935; Schmitt, B. E., *Coming of the War* (2 vols.), 1930; Seymour, C., *American Diplomacy during the World War,* 1934; and *American Neutrality,* 1935; Slosson, P. W., *Great Crusade—and After,* 1930; Tansill, C. C., *America Goes to War,* 1938; Willoughby, W. F., *Government Organization in War Time and After,* 1919.

Important leaders include Palmer, F., *Newton D. Baker: America at War* (2 vols.), 1931; Bernstorff, J. H., *My Three Years in America,* 1920; Bryan, W. J., *Memoirs,* 1925; Arnett, A. M., *Claude Kitchin and the Wilson War Policies,* 1937; Seymour, C. (ed.), *Intimate Papers of Colonel House* (4 vols.), 1926-1928; Houston, D. F., *Eight Years with Wilson's Cabinet,* 1926; McAdoo, W. G., *Crowded Years,* 1931; Hendrick, B. J., *Life and Letters of W. H. Page* (3 vols.), 1922-1925; Pershing, Gen. J. J., *My Experiences in the World War* (2 vols.), 1931; Baker, R. S., *Life and Letters of Woodrow Wilson* (8 vols.), 1927-1939; Seymour, C., *Woodrow Wilson and the World War,* 1921; Tumulty, J. P., *Woodrow Wilson As I Knew Him,* 1925; Wilson, E. B., *My Memoir,* 1939.

WHAT PRICE PROSPERITY
1919-1933

General accounts are: Allen, F. L., *Only Yesterday,* 1931; Hacker, L. M., *American Problems of Today,* 1938; Malin, J. C., *United States after the World War,* 1930.

For politics, see: Anonymous, *Washington Merry-Go-Round,* 1931; Anonymous, *Mirrors of 1932,* 1933; Feldman, H., *Prohibition, Its Economic and Industrial Aspects,* 1927; Merz, C., *Dry Decade,* 1931; Myers, W. S., and Newton, W. H., *Hoover Administration,* 1936; O'Connor, H., *Mellon's Millions,* 1933; Odegard, P., *Pressure Politics: The Story of the Anti-Saloon League,* 1928; Pringle, H. F., *Alfred E. Smith: A Critical Study,* 1927; White, W. A., *Masks in a Pageant,* 1928, and *A Puritan in Babylon* (*Calvin Coolidge*), 1938.

For foreign relations, see: Bassett, J. S., *League of Nations,* 1928; Buell, R. L., *Washington Conference,* 1922; Clark, J. R. (prepared by U. S. State Dept.), *Memorandum on the Monroe Doctrine,* 1930; Hudson, M. O., *Permanent Court of International Justice and the Question of American Participation,* 1925; Miller, D. H., *Peace Pact of Paris,* 1928.

For the general mad whirl, see: Adams, J. T., *Our Business Civilization,* 1929; Berle, A. A., Jr., and Means, G. C., *Modern Corporation and Private Property,* 1932; Bonbright, J. C., and Means, G. C., *Holding Company,* 1932; Carver, T. N., *Present Economic Revolution in the United States,* 1925; Chase, S., *Men and Machines, The Tragedy of Waste*, 1929; Donald, W. J. A., *Trade Associations*, 1933; Dunn, R. W., *American Foreign Investments*, 1926; Epstein, R. C., *Automobile Industry*, 1928; Gellerman, W., *American Legion as Educator*, 1938; Hamilton, J. G. de R., *Henry Ford*, 1927; Lynd, R. S., and H. M., *Middletown*, 1929; Mumford, L., *Technics and Civilization*, 1934; Ripley, W. Z., *Main Street and Wall Street*, 1927; President's Conference on Unemployment, *Recent Economic Changes* (2 vols.), 1929; President's Research Committee on Social Trends, *Recent Social Trends in the United States* (2 vols.), 1933; Rugg, H., *Culture and Education in America*, 1931; Seldes, G. V., *Years of the Locust: America, 1929-1932*, 1933; Tugwell, R. G., *Industry's Coming of Age*, 1927; Turlington, E., *Mexico and Her Foreign Creditors*, 1930; Warner, A. G. et al., *American Charities and Social Work*, 1930; Winkler, M., *Foreign Bonds, An Autopsy*, 1933; and *Investments of United States Capital in Latin America*, 1929.

For the plight of the farmer and the laborer, see: Black, J. D., *Agricultural Reform in the United States*, 1930; Brissenden, P. F., *History of the I.W.W.*, 1920; Fossum, P. R., *Agricultural Movement in North Dakota*, 1925; Gaston, H. E., *Non-Partisan League*, 1920; Frankfurter, F., and Green, N., *Labor Injunction*, 1930; Gambs, J. S., *Decline of the I.W.W.*, 1932; Nourse, E. G., *American Agriculture and the European Market*, 1924; Ostrolenk, B., *Surplus Farmer*, 1932; Russell, C. E., *Story of the Non-Partisan League*, 1920; True, A. C., *History of Agricultural Extension Work in the United States*, 1928.

THE NEW DEAL
1933-

The political phases of the New Deal are described in: Alsop, J., and Catledge, T., *168 Days*, 1937; Anonymous, *New Dealers*, 1934; Backman, J., *Government Price Fixing*, 1938; Berle, A. A. Jr. and others, *America's Recovery Program*, 1934; Buck, A. E., *Reorganization of State Governments in the United States*, 1938; Chase, S., *Rich Land, Poor Land*, 1936; Christensen, A. M., "Agricultural Pressure and Governmental Response," *Agricultural History*, 11:33-42 (Jan. 1937); Clark, J. P., *Rise of a New Federalism*, 1938; Corwin, E. S., *Twilight of the Supreme Court*, 1934; Douglas, P. H., *Social Security in the United States*, 1936; Epstein, A., *Insecurity: A Challenge to America*, 1933; Farley, J. A., *Behind the Ballots*, 1938; Hansen, A. H., *Full Recovery or Stagnation*, 1938; Holcombe, A. N., *New Party Politics*, 1934; Hoover, H., *Challenge to Liberty*, 1934; Lindley, B. and E. K., *A New Deal for Youth*, 1938; Lindley, E. K., *Roosevelt Revolution, First Phase*, 1933; and *Half Way with Roosevelt*, 1936; Nourse, E. G. and others, *Three Years of the Agricultural Adjustment*

Administration, 1937; Nourse, E. G., *Marketing Agreements under the AAA,* 1935; Ogburn, W. F. (ed.), *Social Change and the New Deal,* 1934; Pearson, D., and Allen, R. S., *Nine Old Men,* 1936; Raushenbush, H. S., *Power Fight,* 1932; Raushenbush, H. S., and Laidler, H. W., *Power Control,* 1928; Rogers, L., "Reorganization: Post-Mortem Notes," *Pol. Sci. Quarterly,* 53:161-172 (June 1938); Social Security Board, *Social Security in America,* 1937; Straus, M. W. and Wegg, T., *Housing Comes of Age,* 1938; Tugwell, R. G., *Battle for Democracy,* 1935; Wallace, H. A., *America Must Choose,* 1934.

Economic conditions during the New Deal may be found described in: Beard, C. A., *The Future Comes,* 1933; *Idea of National Interest,* 1934; and *Open Door at Home,* 1934; Buell, R. L., "Death by Tariff," *Fortune,* Aug., 1938; Burns, A. R., *Decline of Competition,* 1936; Corey, L., *Decline of American Capitalism,* 1934; and *Crisis of the Middle Class,* 1935; Daniels, J., *A Southerner Discovers the South,* 1938; Goodrich, C., et al., *Migration and Economic Opportunity,* 1936; Leven, M. and others, *America's Capacity to Consume,* 1934; Lundberg, F., *America's Sixty Families,* 1937; Melder, F. E., "Economic War Among Our States," *Events,* Aug., 1938; Mills, F. C., *Economic Tendencies in the United States,* 1933; Moulton, H. G., *Financial Organization of Society* (rev. ed.), 1938; Nathan, R. R., *Income in the United States 1929-1937,* 1938; National Resources Committee, *Consumer Income in the United States,* 1938; Nixon, H. C., *Forty Acres and Steel Mules,* 1938; Nourse, E. G. and associates, *America's Capacity to Produce,* 1934; Odum, H. O., *Southern Regions of the United States,* 1936; Rogers, J. H., *Capitalism in Crisis,* 1938; Rose, M. A., "States Get Together," *Current History,* May, 1938; Thomas, D. S., *Migration Differentials,* 1938; Twentieth Century Fund, *Big Business: Its Growth and Place,* 1937; and *How Profitable Is Big Business?,* 1937; Vance, R. B., *Population Redistribution within the United States,* 1938.

For labor conditions, see: Brooks, R. R. R., *When Labor Organizes,* 1937; and *Unions of Their Own Choosing,* 1939; U. S. Dept. of Labor, *Characteristics of Company Unions,* 1935; Levinson, E., *Labor on the March,* 1938; Stolberg, B., *Story of the C.I.O.,* 1938; Vorse, M. H., *Labor's New Millions,* 1938; Walsh, J. R., *C.I.O.: Industrial Unionism in Action,* 1937.

Foreign relations are treated in: Beals, C., *Coming Struggle for Latin America,* 1938; Bisson, T. A., *Japan in China,* 1938; Bruntz, G. G., *Allied Propaganda and the Collapse of the German Empire in 1938,* 1938; Dulles, A. W., and Armstrong, H. F., *Can We Be Neutral?,* 1936; Eliot, M., *Ramparts We Watch,* 1938; Fleming, D. F., *United States and World Organization,* 1938; *The German Reich and Americans of German Origin,* 1939; Griswold, A. W., *The Far Eastern Policy of the United States,* 1938; Gunther, J., *Inside Europe* (rev.

ed.), 1938; Lewis, C., *America's Stake in International Investments,* 1938; Quigley, H. S., and Blakeslee, G., *The Far East,* 1938; Savage, C., *Policy of the United States Toward Maritime Commerce in War,* 1936; Thirteen Correspondents of the *N. Y. Times, We Saw It Happen,* 1938; Young, E. J., *Looking Behind the Censors,* 1938.

Some significant phases of the contemporary scene are described in: Anderson, J., *American Theatre,* 1938; Atkeson, M. M., *The Woman on the Farm,* 1924; Bardèche, M., and Brasillach, R., *History of Motion Pictures,* 1938; Burlingame, R., *March of the Iron Men,* 1938; Flexner, E., *American Playwrights, 1918-1938,* 1938; Grouch, W. S., *Winged Highway,* 1938; Hampton, B. B., *A History of the Movies,* 1931; Harlow, A. F., *Old Wires and New Waves,* 1936; Hicks, G., *The Great Tradition,* 1933; Lynd, H. M., *Middletown in Transition,* 1937; Mumford, L., *Culture of Cities,* 1938; National Resources Committee, *Our Cities: Their Role in the National Economy,* 1937; Pidgeon, M. E., *Women in the Economy of the United States,* 1937.

INDEX

777

(I)